Sweet '60:
The 1960 Pittsburgh Pirates

Edited by Clifton Blue Parker and Bill Nowlin
Associate editors: Ron Antonucci, Clem Comly, and Len Levin

Sweet '60: The 1960 Pittsburgh Pirates

Editors: Clifton Blue Parker and Bill Nowlin

ISBN 978-1-933599-48-9

(Ebook ISBN 978-1-933599-49-6)

Design and Production: Gilly Rosenthol, Rosenthol Design

All photographs are courtesy of the Pittsburgh Pirates except as noted. Cover images depict Bill Mazeroski kissing hit bat after Game Seven. and Vernon Law and Elroy Face (R) celebrating (courtesy National Baseball Hall of Fame and Library). World Series ticket image courtesy of Curt Boster.

The Society for American Baseball Research, Inc.

4455 E. Camelback Road, Ste. D-140

Phoenix, AZ 85018

Phone: (800) 969-7227 or (602) 343-6455

Web: www.sabr.org

Facebook: Society for American Baseball Research

Twitter: @SABR

Table of Contents

SWEET 'SIXTY: HOW IT FELT

By Jan Finkel

Beat 'em, Bucs!

—*It's not Yeats. It's Anonymous.*

The Bucs are goin' all the way,

All the way, all the way!

Oh, the Bucs are goin' all the way,

All the way this year! (For about 14 choruses)

—*No, it's not the Gershwins. It's Benny Benack.*

We had 'em all the way!

—*It's not Lincoln at Gettysburg. It's Bob Prince after a Pirate win.*

BUT IN WESTERN Pennsylvania in 1960 it was all poetry and music. The Pirates win the pennant! The Pirates upset the Yankees!

An upset occurs when a presumably inferior individual or team surprisingly defeats a presumably superior individual or team, upsets them as it were. However, to paraphrase legendary football coach Lou Holtz after one of his Arkansas teams had shredded a top-ranked Texas squad, it's not an upset if the team that always considered itself better wins.

From a vantage point of a half-century or more, what happened in 1960? Was the Pirates' win an upset? Or were the Bucs the better team?

One thing is certain: The Pirates took everyone by surprise, and for good reason. They'd been the National League doormats for the 1950s, usually finishing last by a wide margin. They finished last with Ralph Kiner; they finished last without Ralph Kiner. General manager Branch Rickey, trying to repeat the magic he'd conjured up in St. Louis and Brooklyn, embarked on a youth movement. To call it a youth movement is to be kind. Some of the Pirates of the early '50s didn't look old enough to be youths. The world called them the Rickey Dinks and the Kiddie Korps, and worse. But the Bucs of those early years (including a horror show in 1952 that resulted in a 42-112 mark) had four tough hombres who fought

through the losses and humiliation to forge the nucleus of the 1960 squad: Vernon Law, Bob Friend, Dick Groat, and Elroy Face. Friend and Groat endured the carnage in 1952 while Law was away on his obligatory Mormon mission in 1952 and 1953 and Face didn't join the team until 1953, but they all had tasted the bile of losing. They led the team to a stunning second-place finish behind the Milwaukee Braves in 1958 but fell back a bit in 1959, leaving Pittsburghers to mumble, "Same old Pirates."

When the new decade emerged, no one expected much of the Pirates — no one, that is, except the Bucs. Contrary to conventional wisdom, they began to suspect early on that they were about to do something special.

Lost in all the talk about the Pirates' "upset" are two significant points. First, the Bucs on a one-to-one basis matched up pretty evenly with the Yankees. Second, and even more important, the Pirates had dealt with tougher competition because the National League overall was better than the American League.

"You could look it up," Casey Stengel used to say, so I did. What I found surprised me, having heard all the talk for five decades. Overall won-lost records were remarkably similar, the Pirates at 95-59 (1 tie) and seven games ahead of the Braves; the Yankees 97-57 (1 tie) and eight games up on the surprising Orioles. The Yankees' mark is a touch deceiving in that they finished the season with a 15-game winning streak to get their eight-game margin. There still isn't much to choose between the teams.

Taken as a whole, the pitching staffs were basically even. The Yankees and Orioles led the American League with a 3.52 ERA; the Pirates were a *hair* better at 3.49, a figure good for just third behind the Dodgers and Giants.

Hitting numbers show much the same thing. The Yankees led the AL in power figures (193 home runs and .426 slugging average). The Pirates took a somewhat opposite tack: They topped the NL with 236 doubles, a .276 batting average, and a .335 on-base average — and were a surprising second in slugging at .407 to the Braves' .417.

The cumulative figures tell an interesting story. If a team has to do only two things — score runs and prevent runs, with how they do either their own business—the Pirates get a fair-sized edge. That is, the Yankees scored 746 runs to the Bucs' 734, but they gave up 627 while Pittsburgh surrendered 593. Based on the team pitching and hitting numbers, any assertion that the Yankees would run over the Pirates (maybe even sweep them) was just plain flawed.

The Pirates had an advantage that the Yankees and the American League lacked. Simply put, from top to bottom the National League was better. Mantle, even in a poor season, was arguably the best hitter in the league. Year after year it was Mantle and somebody else. In earlier seasons there was Ted Williams, perhaps the greatest hitter of all time, but he'd played something like two-thirds of the Red Sox' games over the last few years. Al Kaline, Roger Maris, Rocky Colavito, Harvey Kuenn, Minnie Minoso, Pete Runnels, Nellie Fox, Jim Lemon, Harmon Killebrew, Roy Sievers, and Brooks Robinson were fine players, but they weren't in Mantle's class. In contrast, the National League was loaded with talent, almost obscenely so. In 1960 alone, in their primes were Hank Aaron, Ernie Banks, Willie Mays, and Frank Robinson. Roberto Clemente was a year away from joining them. Following closely behind were Willie McCovey, Orlando Cepeda, Billy Williams, Lou Brock, Tony Perez, and Willie Stargell. And they're just the Hall of Famers. Vada Pinson, Richie (Call Me Dick) Allen, Maury Wills, Tommy Davis, and many others were on the horizon.

It wasn't just quantity, either. Jackie Robinson was the first African-American to win the Most Valuable Player Award, in 1949. Over the next 14 years, the National League MVP trophy went to an African-American 10 times and every year from 1953 to 1959. Elston Howard was the first African-American to take home the American League award—in 1963.

Think about the pitchers coming along, not quite as rapidly as the hitters but on their way. Does anyone believe that the American League had a trio to match Bob Gibson, Sandy Koufax, and Juan Marichal?

Integration was the key. The Pirates and the National League had been playing in a brave new world. Victims of tunnel vision and slow to adapt, the Yankees and the American League hadn't.

Both teams were experienced. You don't get into the World Series with a bunch of rookies. Nevertheless, the Pirates had one kind of experience about which the Yankees were ignorant. That is, the Yankees were so in the habit of winning, assuming it as their birthright, that they had little idea how to cope with losing. From 1949 to 1964 they had been out of the American League throne room twice. They'd finished second to the Indians in 1954, but they'd won 103 games, their highest total under Stengel's reign; unfortunately for them, the Tribe won 111. It's hard to work up much sympathy for the Bronx Bombers. The 1959 season was something else entirely, as they were never in contention, coming in third, 15 games behind the White Sox. Their 79-75 record, which would have been Nirvana for the Pirates just a few years before, was cause for real concern. In short, the Yankees were much like the playground bully, accustomed to winning every fight.

Generally speaking, we learn more from losing than from winning. The Pirates, through years of bitter experience and crushed hope, had a collective Ph.D. in losing. The stage was set for one of the strangest World Series ever.

Everybody knows what happened in October 1960. The Yankees broke all the records and lost the Series. They doubled the Pirates in runs, 55-27. They hit .338 as a team. Whitey Ford, on his way to breaking Babe Ruth's record for consecutive scoreless innings pitched in World Series play, threw two shutouts. The Yankees won three games by a combined score of 38-3 (16-3, 10-0, 12-0). The Pirates won four games 6-4, 3-2, 5-2, and 10-9.

The argument for Yankee superiority goes, what about that batting average, those outlandish football-like scores? What about them? Each represents one-fourth of what they had to do to win the Series, and they never got that fourth one. Blowouts are easy to absorb, laugh about, and forget. Close losses keep you awake at night because you can't stop wondering what you could, would, or should have done differently. The Pirates had a resilience that the Yankees lacked because they'd rarely had to have it. The 3-2 and 5-2 games came after the 16-3 and 10-0 wipeouts. The Yankees had to win Game Six to stay alive. They won it big, but they and not the Pirates were the ones under pressure.

Enough has been said about Game Seven, and little needs to be added here. The greatness of the game is that it showed both teams doing what they did best—the Yankees flexing their muscles, the Pirates clawing their way back. Nobody flinched. In jackhammer style it went like this: Pirates smack Yankees in the mouth and jump out to a 4-0 lead, Yankees power their way to take a 7-4 lead, Pirates drop a bomb of their own on Smith's three-run homer and grab a 9-7 lead, Yankees strike back to tie game at 9-9, Mazeroski sends Mantle home in tears (so the story goes) with home run to win Series 10-9.

Were the Pirates lucky? Of course they were. The double-play ball that took a weird hop and hit Tony Kubek in the Adam's apple is a case in point. Just about every team that's won a championship in any sport has had an element of luck. It takes nothing away from the Pirates' achievement. It wasn't an upset. By any measure they were equal to and maybe—just maybe—a little better than the Yankees. Their resilience made a huge difference. They wouldn't quit, and the Yankees couldn't put them away.

The Bucs went all the way in 1960. They didn't become a dynasty, but they remained tough competitors throughout the '60s and enjoyed one of their finest overall decades in the '70s with two World Series titles, several division crowns, and some heartbreaking near-misses. For one moment, though, it all came together. As Jackie Gleason and Bob Prince liked to say, "How sweet it is!"

Introduction

THE IDEA FOR this book has its roots in the faraway time of childhood. My grandfather, George F. Reynolds, often regaled me with tales about the Pittsburgh Pirates when I was young boy in the Steel City suburb of Bethel Park in the late 1960s and 1970s. Spellbinding and brilliant—he was a top executive and inventor for ALCOA—he could tell a story like few people I ever met. Then, with wide eyes and mouth agape, I listened to his rollicking accounts of ancient Pirate greats and the teams they played on—he was a walking encyclopedia of Pittsburgh baseball history. My grandfather especially loved the 1960 Pirates and how they staged one of the most unforgettable and dramatic World Series victories ever against the mighty New York Yankees with the help of Bill Mazeroski's Game Seven clout. It is the classic David-vs.-Goliath tale of the underdog team overcoming all the odds.

Maybe there will be another upstart team that ends a World Series so magically in the final inning. But I truly believe the 1960 Pirates are the rarest of teams in the annals of the national pastime—a team of the ages—and we will not see another one quite like it. It is my humble hope for all readers that this book unveils the historic record of the stunning and surprising world of the 1960 Bucs and all the men who played for this iconic team.

— *Clifton Blue Parker*

WHEN CLIFTON PARKER launched this project, I was particularly pleased because I can still remember how excited I was at age 15 to be watching the final game of the 1960 World Series and the unexpected triumph of the underdog over the Yankees, the team that seemed to win every year. I was a Red Sox fan, so rooting for anyone other than the Yankees came naturally. Unfortunately, I was too young to fully appreciate who the Pirates were. I've come to know them better through this book.

In the middle of 2011, Clifton had to relinquish his position as chief editor of this book due to job responsibilities and family obligations. But he'd gotten it underway, and I was glad to come on in long relief and close out the book.

— *Bill Nowlin*

GENE BAKER

By Charles Faber

Near the end of the 1953 baseball season two young men joined the Chicago Cubs and broke the club's color line. Two shortstops, they became roommates and the first African American keystone combination in major-league history when one of them was converted into a second baseman. The shortstop, Ernie Banks, was purchased from the Kansas City Monarchs, spent his entire Organized Baseball career with the Cubs, earned the nickname Mr. Cub, and was elected to the National Baseball Hall of Fame in his first year of eligibility. The second baseman was called up from the Des Moines Bruins and spent parts of only five years with the Cubs before being traded to the Pittsburgh Pirates. Gene Baker was never a serious candidate for the Hall of Fame, but continued making important breakthroughs after his playing days were over.

Eugene Walker Baker was born in Davenport, Iowa, on June 15, 1925, the eldest son of Mildred and Eugene O. Baker. He spent his childhood in the Quad Cities area, in Davenport and across the Mississippi River in Moline, Illinois, where his father at one time labored in the iron works.

Gene attended Davenport High School, where he starred in track and basketball. As there happened to be no blacks on the high-school baseball team, Gene played sandlot ball. Davenport was a perennial powerhouse in Iowa high-school basketball, which was the most popular sport in the state. Baker was a star on the basketball court. In 1943 the 17-year-old, 6-foot, 142-pound guard was named to the All-State first team by the Iowa Daily Press Association, with the following accolades: "Most improved player on this year's Davenport cage team. Clean type of player, fouling infrequently. So alert

that he caused opposing guards to foul. Best passer in the Mississippi Valley loop. Will be 18 in June and it looks like the army after that."

After the state tournament, in which for the second consecutive year Davenport made the final four, a Waterloo coach wrote in the *Waterloo Sunday Courier:* "In Gene Baker, Davenport's dusky guard, the river city boys had one of the outstanding individuals in the tournament. He was easily the best passer in the meet and his rebounding and scoring set him out as one of the better basketball players seen in this meet recently."

As it turned out, Baker went not into the Army, but the Navy, where he played both baseball and basketball, first for the Ottumwa Naval Air Station and then for the Seahawks of the Iowa Pre-Flight School in Iowa City. In newspaper accounts of the games, Baker's race was frequently mentioned, in keeping with the journalistic practices of the era. The Waterloo paper wrote: "Baker, the shortstop, is one of the greatest and most versatile Negro athletes developed in Iowa. Speedy, a good base runner, he also hits the agate hard." An Associated Press report on the Seahawks basketball team referred to "Gene Baker, brilliant Davenport Negro."

His service obligations fulfilled, Baker returned to Davenport, where he played semipro baseball. His exploits on the diamond caught the attention of the Kansas City Monarchs of the Negro American League. By this time Baker had grown one inch in height and added 28 pounds to his still slender frame. He was the Monarchs' regular shortstop in 1948 and 1949. Early in the 1949 season the *Davenport Democrat and Leader* wrote: "Among the [Kansas City] stars is Gene Baker, Davenport high school graduate who sparkled as a rookie shortstop last season. In his second year Baker is set to make his bid for notice from the major league scouts. He was told last year that he would get attention after one year's service in the Negro American League, and there are those who classed him as the second Jackie Robinson." That may sound like hyperbole from his hometown newspaper, but the scouts were indeed paying attention. After the season Gene returned to Davenport and played recreation-league basketball, but the spring of 1950 found him in Organized Baseball in the Chicago Cubs organization. After a few games with the Springfield Cubs in the International League, he was acquired by the Des Moines Bruins of the Western League, as the team's first black player. At the end of June he moved up to the Los Angeles Angels of the Triple-A Pacific Coast League. California newspapers reported that the 25-year-old shortstop was regarded as one of the most promising players in the Cubs' farm system. Bobby Bragan, manager of the Angels' chief rivals, the Hollywood Stars, said Baker was "as good a shortstop as I've ever seen—and that includes Pee Wee Reese."

Baker lived up to his promise. On September 1, 1953, the Cubs purchased his contract from the Angels. It was reported that Baker was the first Negro player to ever appear on the Cubs' official roster. A week later the Cubs purchased Ernie Banks from the Kansas City Monarchs. Both shortstops reported in Chicago on September 14; Banks became the regular shortstop, and suddenly Baker was a second baseman. He made his major-league debut on September 20, striking out as a pinch-hitter in the eighth inning of a Cubs 11-8 loss in St. Louis.

Although Baker had been hailed as the best shortstop in the Pacific Coast League, he was shunted over to second base because it was believed that as he was older and more experienced than Banks, he might be better able to adjust to a new position. Baker proceeded to give his young teammate tips on playing the shortstop position. "He certainly helped me when I came to this club," Banks told an interviewer with United Press International. "He showed me how to study the batters and how to swing (my position) when the infield shifted. He worked with me on coming across the bag for the double play and showed how to make a short toss for it."

Baker hit .275 in 135 games during his rookie season. Both he and Banks made *The Sporting News* all-rookie team. Soon newspapers ceased mentioning Baber's race whenever his name appeared in print. Gene's best season came in 1955, when he hit .268, led the league with 18 sacrifices, and was named to the National League All-Star team. He pinch-hit for Don Newcombe in the seventh inning and flied out. Baker was a good but sometimes erratic defensive second baseman. Three times he led NL keystone sackers in errors. In 1955 he led his cohorts in putouts, assists, errors, and total chances. On May 27 of that year his 11 putouts tied the National League record for putouts in one game by a second baseman.

On May 1, 1957, Baker was traded along with first baseman Dee Fondy to Pittsburgh for infielder Dale Long and infielder-outfielder Lee Walls. There was no way he could match the play of future Hall of Famer Bill Mazeroski at second base, so Baker played mainly third base for the Pirates. On July 13, 1958, the third sacker fell on his left knee while charging a ground ball and ruptured a ligament that attaches the kneecap to the leg. Baker later said, "We were playing at St. Louis and Curt Flood hit a swinging bunt. I came in fast and must have slipped. Then there was a crack that sounded like a 30-30 rifle." The infielder was carried off the field. The knee required surgery, and Baker was out of action for the remainder of the season. He spent rest of the year back in Davenport on crutches.

The Pirates hoped to have Baker back in 1959, but when spring came he was unable to play. Pittsburgh placed him on the 30-day disabled list in April. In May they restored him to the active list and immediately placed him on waivers for the purpose of giving him his unconditional release. But they did not cast Baker aside. They signed him as an instructional assistant for their minor-league clubs. Baker worked predominantly with minor-league players, but also helped with the analysis of minor-league clubs and scouting programs. Pittsburgh manager Danny Murtaugh said that Baker "knows more about baseball than fellows twice his age. He's one of the smartest I've ever met." During the offseason Baker returned to Davenport, spent time with his wife and two children, sold insurance, played an occasional round of golf, and rooted for his favorite basketball team.

In January 1960 Baker began a series of exercises and tests on his injured left knee at Southern Illinois University's

Physical Education Research Laboratory in Carbondale. Impressed by the work at Carbondale, the Pirates' general manager, Joe L. Brown, hired kinesiologists from the lab to work with Baker and to develop a training program aimed at preventing injuries to other players. "We've had encouraging reports on Baker," Brown told the Associated Press in February. "We hope he can make a comeback. He's a fine utility infielder. If he can play for us he'll be a plus factor. But it is still too early to tell whether Gene can play. Regardless, he will remain in the Pirates organization. He's got loads of talent in the field of scouting and instruction." Throughout his ordeal the Pirates were compassionate, generous, and supportive of Baker—qualities not always evident in major-league clubs.

During 1960 spring training Baker went with the club to Fort Myers, Florida, as a nonroster invitee. By late March he was playing well. He was the talk of the training camp and earned a big-league contract. Manager Danny Murtaugh said he expected Baker to be the club's number one utility infielder during the season. As it turned out there was not much need for Baker's services and he became almost a forgotten man during the Pirates' drive to the 1960 pennant. Second baseman Mazeroski and third baseman Don Hoak each played more than 150 games. When Dick Groat was injured, Dick Schofield capably handled the shortstop position. Rocky Nelson filled in for Dick Stuart at first base. Baker played only one game at second and seven games at third base. Otherwise, he was used mainly as a pinch-hitter and occasionally as a pinch-runner. All told, he appeared in 33 games during the season. In the World Series Baker did not play in the field, but he came up three times as a pinch-hitter and failed to make a hit.

During spring training in 1961 the club decided to keep Baker as a utility infielder and send Dick Gray to the minors. In response to a complaint that the Pirates should have kept the younger man rather than the 36-year-old Baker, general manager Brown said, "I don't care if Gene Baker is 136 years old. We are making our plans entirely on a one-year basis." Although Gray had looked good in spring training, Brown said, the club could not base all of its opinions on a short trial. A sportswriter accused Brown of favoritism and wrote that it proved that spring training was a waste of time and money. Actually neither Gray nor Baker played very well in 1961 or thereafter. Gray

was the regular third baseman for Columbus in 1961 and accepted a utility role in 1962 before retiring from Organized Baseball without ever making it back to the majors. Baker sat on the Pirates' bench almost all spring, getting into three games at third base and occasionally pinch-hitting. He played his last major-league game on June 10, 1961. On June 20 he was released as a player to make room for outfielder Walt Moryn, purchased from the St. Louis Cardinals. The Pirates kept their promise that there would always be room in the organization for Baker. On the same day he was released, he was named player-manager of the Batavia Pirates of the Class D New York-Pennsylvania League. He took over a club that was floundering and led it to a third-place finish. He was the first black manager in Organized Baseball in the United States. (One source stated that Nate Moreland had managed Calexico in the Arizona-Mexico League a few years earlier, but this has not been confirmed.) Baker found Class D pitching to his liking, hitting .387 in 55 games, by far the highest average in his career. *Ebony* magazine, in an article about Baker's experience in Batavia, wrote, "Since occupying his new post, Baker has learned that having to be a coach, ball player, bookkeeper, field manager, and big brother to 18 men is not a bed of roses."

In 1962 Baker was promoted to the Columbus Jets of the Triple-A International League as a player-coach, and became the first black coach in Organized Baseball. The promotion put him once again in competition with Dick Gray for playing time at third base. Neither won the position, which was taken by Bob Bailey, the Pirates' $175,000 bonus baby. Baker found Triple-A pitching difficult to hit and wound up with a woeful .115 batting average in 22 games.

In 1963 Baker was again back in the big leagues as a coach for Pittsburgh—the second African-American to coach in the majors behind Buck O'Neil. Sportswriter Red Smith wrote that "Baker snores like a locomotive coming over Crazy Woman Ridge." Baker was assigned Roberto Clemente as his roommate, much to the outfielder's chagrin. "With this coach I could not sleep at all. I keep asking them to let me sleep alone, but they say no, can't do it. All I could do is warm up and play, warm up and play, always sleepy, no pep. One game in Milwaukee they brushed me back at the plate. To brush back a player … you can wake him up. They brushed me back and I felt good, loose. I hit .320 for the year. And now I sleep alone."

In a game at Los Angeles on September 21, 1963, Baker made baseball history. A rhubarb ensued when a Pirates batter was retired on a close play. Pittsburgh manager Danny Murtaugh and coach Frank Oceak were ejected by an umpire after their long and loud protests of the call. Baker assumed command and became the first African-American to manage in the major leagues. Of course, he acted only briefly as manager, so his accomplishment is not listed in most record books. Another managerial stint soon came his way when he was appointed manager of the Aguilas Cibaenas club, which represented Santiago in the Dominican Republic Winter League. Several Pirates and Columbus Jets players were on the Santiago team. Meanwhile, back in Pittsburgh, Murtaugh decided to reduce his coaching staff from six to four. Baker was dropped as a coach, and it was announced that he would manage Batavia again in 1964. After one more season in upstate New York, he became a scout for the Pirates and stayed in that role for many years. For 23 years he was the Pirates' chief scout in the Midwest.

In 1974 Baker gave a long interview to Loren Tate of the *Mount Vernon* (Illinois) *Register-News*. "Arms and legs … that's what I'm looking for," the scout said. "I see as many as six teams in a day when I'm in an area where night ball is played. I watch perhaps 75 percent high schools and 25 percent colleges. Sure, I see a lot of guys who can never make it, but you have to see them all to find the great one. Guys in my business don't worry about positions. We can't look down the road and visualize what the big club will need three years from now…. For the most part I'm just looking for the best players, regardless of position." Watching a game between the University of Illinois

and the University of Minnesota, Baker analyzed for the scribe the strengths and weaknesses of various players he was scouting.

Throughout his life Baker maintained his home in Davenport. His son, also named Gene, was an outstanding sprinter for Davenport Central High School from 1964 through 1966, He was one of the state's top performers in the 100-yard dash, the quarter-mile, and the 220-yard dash. He anchored the school's 440- and 880-yard relay teams, which were among the best in the nation. Not confining his achievements to one sport, he made the all-state football fourth team as a running back.

Eugene Walter Baker died of a heart attack on December 1, 1999, at the age of 74. He had been hospitalized at Genesis East Medical Center in Davenport for three days. He was survived by his mother, Mildred, and his wife, Janice, both of Davenport, his son, a daughter, a stepdaughter, and 12 grandchildren. He was buried in the Rock Island National Cemetery, just across the Mississippi River from his beloved hometown.

Sources

The Baseball Encyclopedia, Ninth edition. New York: Macmillan, 1993.

Clark, Dick, and Larry Lester. *The Negro Leagues Book*. Cleveland: Society for American Baseball Research, 1994.

New York Times

Palmer, Pete, and Gary Gillette. *The Baseball Encyclopedia*. New York: Barnes & Noble, 2004.

Spatz, Lyle (editor). *The SABR Baseball List & Record Book*. New York: Scribner, 2007.

www.baseball-refereence.com

www.newspaperarchive.com

DICK BARONE

By Joe Schuster

BUT FOR A bit of luck—if he'd been with a different organization, in which he wasn't caught behind an all-star like Dick Groat or if he hadn't suffered two broken bones in the seventh of what would turn out to be 10 minor-league seasons—shortstop Dick Barone might have had a longer stint in the major leagues than he had: three games, six at-bats, with the Pittsburgh Pirates at the end of September 1960.

Richard Anthony ("Dick") Barone was born on October 13, 1932, in San Jose, California. He was the youngest of six children of Gus and Anna Barone, who operated a small grocery, Sunnyside Market.[1] Barone's parents were born in Italy and immigrated to the United States in 1901.[2] Barone's father died at 45 when Dick Barone was 8 years old; his mother lived to the age of 94.

As a boy, Barone was obsessed with baseball: "One of my brothers pitched and was catcher and first baseman for a semipro team [that the family market sponsored] and I was the batboy and mascot," he said. "That was where I got my love for the game. Because of the weather, we could pretty much play it year round. And we did. If there was no one around to play with, I would spend hours throwing a tennis ball against the gutter and working on my fielding."

Barone said that when he was 12 he wanted so much to play on a recreational league team that when he couldn't find one he organized one himself, and was its manager and starting pitcher. "I talked to a gym teacher at the middle school about how to register a team with the league," he said. "Then when we started the season, I made up the lineups. I would hit infield to the team and then go and warm up so I could pitch the game."

At San Jose High School, Barone played both basketball and baseball, and was an all-star in both sports.[3] In 1950, when he was a senior, Barone had tryouts with the Chicago White Sox and the Pacific Coast League's San Francisco Seals. According to Barone, Vince DiMaggio, the manager of the class D Far West League Pittsburg (California) Diamonds, offered him a contract to play the summer after he finished high school but, partly because the pay was so low ($300 a month), he turned it down for an opportunity to attend college. "That idea didn't last long and I decided I would rather play baseball," he said.

The next year, he had another tryout, with the Pittsburgh Pirates:

"I used to spend a lot of time playing ball at [San Jose's] Backesto Park and I often saw [Pirates scout] Bob Fontaine there," Barone said. "I knew he was a scout and I asked him about trying out for the team. The Korean Conflict was going on and he said that because of that a lot of teams would be folding. I told him that I understood that but I still wanted a tryout because I'd always wanted to play professional ball. He arranged for me to go to Anaheim for a tryout and the Pirates signed me to a contract for their [Class C Pioneer League] Great Falls [Montana] team."

While the team didn't give him a bonus to sign his contract, his manager at Great Falls, Buck Elliott, did give him a new pair of baseball spikes because, Barone said, "he thought the ones I had were too big."

Going into his first professional season, 1951, Barone was projected to compete with teammate Don Swanson for the starting third-base job.[4] His manager, Buck

Elliott told a sportswriter that Barone "is a power at the plate, has a strong throwing arm and is a better than average runner."[5]

Barone won the job and, despite his relatively small stature (5-feet-9, 165 pounds), proved his manager correct in at least part of his assessment almost from the start: in his second professional trip to the plate, he hit a grand slam in the third inning of what turned out to be a "lopsided 14-2 victory."[6]

Barone was the starting third baseman until the last few games of the season when, because of his strong arm and good range, Elliott moved him to shortstop.[7] He ended the season hitting .255 with six home runs. At least one sportswriter picked him for the second team on his post-season Pioneer League All-Star team, behind the Pocatello Cardinals' Nick Ananias who hit .318 with 18 HR.[8] In retrospect, Jamie Selko in *Minor League All-star Teams, 1922-1962* suggests that Barone should have been on the first team since Selko noted that Ananias played fewer than half of his games at third base, and said that Richard Barone was the best full-time third baseman in the league.[9]

In 1952, Barone played the full season at shortstop at Billings, Montana, also in the Pioneer League, where one of his teammates was future major-league star Dick Stuart, who led the PL in home runs that year with 31. After the season, Barone was drafted into the Army, where he spent 18 months.[10] He completed his basic training at Fort Ord in California then went to Redstone Arsenal in Alabama, where he was in the military police, before ending up in special services, playing baseball for an Army team that traveled the US playing for the troops.

After Barone was discharged, the Pirates sent him to Williamsport in the Class A Eastern League for 1955, where he played shortstop alongside future Hall of Fame second baseman Bill Mazeroski and hit .264 with 9 HRs. The next year, the Pirates promoted him to New Orleans of the Double A Southern Association. Coming into the season, Barone was tagged as "a flashy 23-year-old shortstop" who had "all of the equipment of star baseball material."[11] An opposing manager from the previous year, Reading's Jo-Jo White, rated him "the best [major-league] prospect [in the league]."[12] White added, "He's a

fine fielder, good base runner, fair hitter, and probably will be playing for Pittsburgh during the coming season."[13]

Barone hit .270 at New Orleans and earned a spot on the major-league roster to take spring training with the Pirates the next season. In February, Pirates manager Bobby Bragan told reporters that Barone was "ticketed for reserve duty."[14]

As it turned out, after spring training the Pirates sent Barone to Columbus of the International League, where he had an injury-plagued season in 1957, breaking bones in his foot and hand. He got into only 95 games and batted .182.[15] Even so, the Pirates added him to the major-league roster in September of that year, with yet another spring training invitation for 1958.[16]

Barone was with Salt Lake City of the Pacific Coast League for both 1958 and 1959, where his hitting was weak but fans appreciated his defensive work. Wrote *Salt Lake Tribune* sports editor John Mooney, "[One] of the great defensive shortstops in baseball is performing right out there in the person of little Dick Barone. Eddie Leishman [a former PCL shortstop who went on to become a minor league and then major league executive] is amazed every time Barone goes in the hole and throws out a speeding runner.. . .he says, 'It's worth the price of admission to see that guy field.' "[17]

Barone's play there earned him yet another shot at making the major-league roster in 1960. Reporting on the Pirates once again acquiring his contract, Mooney took another opportunity to praise Barone, saying, "Bee fans will miss little Dick Barone, the hard-throwing shortstop. . .but they will be glad to see Dick get a chance at the majors, especially after working so hard to succeed in the minors. There are those, among them Glen (Buckshot) Wright [a major-league infielder for 11 seasons], who have contended that Barone was a major-league fielder all the time. His only drawback was a light batting average. . ."[18]

Echoing the writer, Barone's manager at Salt Lake City, Larry Shepard, said, "Dick Barone. . .rates with me as the best defensive shortstop out of the major leagues. . .[He will] be a fine prospect for the majors. Good hands, great arm and speed—he's got them all."[19]

In spring training that season, Barone ended up being the last player cut. "It was between me and Gene Baker for a utility infield spot and they decided to go with him because he had more experience already," Barone said. At that point, Baker had six seasons in the major leagues, including several years as a starter and one season (1955) as an All-Star second baseman with the Chicago Cubs.

The team's decision did not sit well with at least one fan, who wrote a letter to *The Sporting News*, expressing his dissent: "I was disappointed to learn the Pirates sent Dick Barone back to the minors. I protested when Frank Howard was named the top minor leaguer over Barone last year. . .I look for Barone to be recalled soon."[20]

Although he ended up at Columbus in the International League for the season, the Pirates gave Barone a major-league contract, and his $7,200 salary for the year was the highest he ever had in baseball. Despite that, by his own assessment, he "didn't do well there at all," He ended the season hitting .204, the worst average of his career except for the season when he broke two bones. He did, however, win a spot on the midseason All-Star team.[21]

It was ironic, then, that at the end of what turned out to be the worst full season of his professional career, Barone finally got the call to the Pirates that September. The team intended it to be a "paper" move, but when Dick Groat broke his wrist and the team found itself down an infielder as it closed in on its first National League pennant since 1927, Barone finally had his ticket to the major leagues. To activate him, the Pirates needed special permission from the baseball commissioner's office since his International League season was not yet over.[22]

Barone got into his first major-league game on September 22 as a pinch-runner for Mickey Vernon with two on, one out in the bottom of the ninth of a 2-2 game against the Chicago Cubs at Pittsburgh's Forbes Field. "A little earlier," Barone said, "[Pirates Manager Danny] Murtaugh had told me to go down in the runway [beside the dugout] and warm up since I might pinch run. When I took the base, I was just thinking about breaking up a double play." He ended up stranded on first.

The team clinched the pennant three days later. Without having had a single major-league plate appearance, Barone found himself in the middle of a celebration. "I remember being in the clubhouse in Milwaukee where, even though we lost the game, everyone was drenching everyone else with champagne," he said. "As I remember, we got back into Pittsburgh at 2 a.m. and fans were lined up all the way from the airport to downtown." A *New York Times* article about the parade from the airport estimated that 125,000 Pittsburgh natives turned up for "a torch-light parade" to cheer the Pirates players passing by in convertibles; the newspaper said it was the largest crowd in the city since the late President Franklin Roosevelt had visited in 1932.[23]

On the day after the celebration, Barone was in the starting lineup for a game against the Cincinnati Reds, playing shortstop and batting eighth. He wound up going hitless in five at-bats, striking out in his first at bat, against Bob Purkey. His second time up, he hit a fly ball to left that he was certain was going to fall in for his first hit. "I remember, because this was Forbes Field, I came out of the [batter's] box thinking I would go for three but [Frank Robinson] tracked it down."

Barone batted three more times, grounding out each time, but playing flawlessly in the field, handling five chances. He got into one more game, as a late-inning substitution at shortstop; he went 0-for-1 and made an error on a groundball.

That was the end of Barone's brief major-league career. He was not a member of the postseason roster, but the players voted him a small World Series share that he recalls was "a few hundred dollars." The day Bill Mazeroski's walk-off home run won the Series was Barone's 28th birthday. Shortly afterward the team sent him back to Salt Lake City.[24]

Barone played two more years in Triple-A. The Pirates traded him to the White Sox organization and he played shortstop for San Diego in 1961. Then he was traded to the Los Angeles Angels organization and played short for their Hawaii team in 1962. In his last game in Organized Ball (in Salt Lake City where he'd been such a fan favorite) Barone went 3-for-4 and drove in three runs.[25]

When the Angels didn't call him up at the end of the season, Baron decided it was time to leave the game. "That [1962 season] was the last hurrah," he said. "I'd played [10 seasons] and I was just tired of the travel. I decided it was time to move on."

His decision was partly influenced by the fact that he had a family by then. He had married Ruth Talty in 1956 and had two sons at that point. For the first five years after baseball, he drove a milk truck for the Berkeley Farms dairy and then after that became a route salesman for a company called Langendorf Bakery in San Jose, for which he worked for 24 years until he retired at the age of 59. The Barones moved to Hollister, California, south of San Jose, in 1997, where the family began a business, selling Christmas trees and firewood.

Barone's first wife, with whom he had two sons and two daughters, died in the early 1970s and he married Victoria Kangalos in 1976; she had two daughters. As of 2011, he had nine grandchildren and three great grandchildren. His grandson Daniel Barone spent six years in the minor leagues (2004-9), primarily with the Florida Marlins organization, and appeared in 16 games as a pitcher for Florida in 2007, six as a starter. As of 2011, he was planning to undergo Tommy John surgery and attempt a comeback.[26]

Notes

1   Unless otherwise noted, all information about Dick Barone's life before and after baseball, and all direct quotes from Barone, come from an author interview with him, June 4, 2011

2   Year: *1930*; Census Place: *San Jose, Santa Clara, California*; Roll: *218*; Page: *5B*; Enumeration District: *98*; Image: *464.0.*

3   Barone player information card on file in the archives of the A. Bartlett Giamatii Research Center of the National Baseball Hall of Fame and Museum

4   Al Warden, "Great Falls to Start Season with 11 Experienced Men," *Ogden (UT) Standard Examiner* (April 8, 1951): 10A.

5   Joe Stell, "Great Falls Has Talent Aplenty," *Salt Lake Tribune* (April 15, 1951): B11.

6   "G.G. 14, Mustangs 2," (Idaho Falls ID) *Post Register* (April 25, 1951): 12

7   Barone player information card

8   Joe Shepperd, "Spray of the Falls," (Idaho Falls ID) *Post Register* (August 24, 1951): 10; Ananias statistics from Baseball-Reference-dot-com <http://www.baseball-reference.com/minors/player.cgi?id=anania001nic>

9   James Selko, *Minor League All-star Teams, 1922-1962.* (Jefferson NC: McFarland & Company: 2007), 331.

10 Barone player information card

11 Hale Montgomery, "Thirty Uniforms Hang Unclaimed," *Aiken (SC) Standard and Review* (April 5, 1956): 8

12 JoJo White, "Believes Grid Star Will Be Big Leaguer," *The Gettysburg (PA) Times* (March 16, 1956): 5

13 Ibid.

14 "Bragan Still Sure of 4th Place for Pirates," *The* (Huntington and Mount Union PA) *Daily News* (February 28, 1957): 5

15 "Shortstop Test Under Way—Bees Wait Outcome," *Salt Lake Tribune* (March 19, 1958): 21

16 "Four Optioned Pirates Report," *The* (Monessen PA) *Daily Independent* (September 3, 1957): 7

17 John Mooney, "Sports Mirror," *Salt Lake Tribune* (July 28, 1958): 26

18 John Mooney, "Sports Mirror," *Salt Lake Tribune* (October 21, 1959): 27

19 Larry W. Shepard, "Rookie Frank Howard's Power Reaps Raves Despite Tendency to Cut at Bad Pitches," *Joplin* (Missouri) *Globe.* (January 22, 1960): 13A

20 Mike Conway, "Barone Booster's Protest," *The Sporting News* (May 11, 1960): 11

21 "All-Star Team Roster Filled," *The Lima* (OH) *News* (June 21, 1960): 12

22 "Bucs Recall Dick Barone," *The* (Uniontown PA) *Morning Herald (September 10, 1960): 13*

23 "125,000 Cheering Pittsburghers Greet Their Champion Pirates," *The New York Times* (September 26, 1960): 43

24 "Bucs, Farms in Exchanges," *The* (Uniontown PA) *Morning Herald* (October 20, 1960): 21

25 John Mooney, "Buzzers Lose Pair as Season Ends," *Salt Lake Tribune* (September 10, 1962): 27

26 Daniel Barone interview, June 4, 2011

HARRY BRIGHT

By Charles Faber

D URING A PROFESSIONAL baseball career of 20 years the much-traveled Harry Bright played in nearly 2,000 games. None of his exploits on the playing field, not even all of his 1,966 major- and minor-league hits, earned Harry Bright as much notoriety as one time at bat in the 1963 World Series.

It was the opening game of the fall classic between the New York Yankees and the Los Angeles Dodgers. Behind the pitching of Sandy Koufax, the Dodgers had take a 3-2 lead into the ninth inning at Yankee Stadium. At the end of the eighth, a note on the scoreboard said that Koufax had tied the record for the most strikeouts in a World Series game. The first two outs in the ninth were routine putouts. With only one more chance for Koufax to break the record, Bright strode to the plate to pinch-hit for pitcher Steve Hamilton. He ran the count to 2 balls and 2 strikes before swinging and missing. Koufax had his record 15th strikeout, the crowd erupted, the Dodgers won the game, and Harry Bright became a footnote in the record books. "It's a hell of a thing," Bright said. "I wait 17 years to get into a World Series. Then when I finally get up there, and 69,000 people are yelling—yelling for me to strike out."[1]

Harry James Bright was born on September 22, 1929, in Kansas City, Missouri, the third of five children of Frank William Bright, a chauffeur, and Maude Lois (Hayward) Bright. At a very early age the youngster earned a reputation for his baseball prowess on the playgrounds of Kansas City. When he was 16 years old, he was signed as a catching prospect by Yankees scout Bill Essick. The teenager threw and batted right-handed, stood 6 feet tall and weighed 175 pounds. (Later his frame filled out to a sturdy 190 pounds.) The minor leagues were just resum-

ing play after a great scaled-back operation during World War II. Frank Lane, director of the Yankees farm system, said the young catcher had a good arm and was a hitter. He assigned him to the Twin Falls (Idaho) Cowboys of the Class C Pioneer League. One spring day the umpires were late for arriving for a twin bill, so the 16-year-old rookie umpired behind the plate in the opener of the doubleheader. Bright did not hit well in Idaho and was demoted to Fond du Lac in the Class D Wisconsin State League, the first of many moves he was to make during his career. In a 12-year stretch from 1946 through 1957 he played for 14 different minor-league clubs.

As a Yankees farmhand Bright never lived up to his promise. By 1950 he was the property of the Chicago Cubs and was assigned to the Clovis Pioneers of the Class C West Texas-New Mexico League. In the rarified air of that semi-arid area, Harry hit his stride, leading the league with a sensational .413 batting average. He hit 19 home runs in 95 games and compiled a .704 slugging percentage. Two years later he was playing manager for the Janesville Cubs in the Class D Wisconsin State League. At 22 he was the youngest manager in Organized Baseball that season and the youngest ever in the Wisconsin State League. He was no longer strictly a catcher. For Janesville, he managed, caught, played third base and the outfield—and drove the team bus. Such was life in the lower minors. He led the Cubs in hitting with a .325 average and led the league with a club-record 101 runs batted in.

In 1953 Bright was acquired by the Chicago White Sox and assigned to their Memphis affiliate in the Double-A Southern Association, where he had a solid season, playing second base and hitting .295. By this time he had played every position except pitcher. In December the Detroit Tigers secured him in the Rule 5 draft for $7,500. During spring training in 1954, he played well and was given an excellent chance to win the second-base position. However, he lost out to Frank Bolling and it was back to the minors—Little Rock, Buffalo, and Sacramento. Bright had four good years with the Solons, earning him another shot at the majors. In July 1958 the Pittsburgh Pirates purchased his contract. After 12 years in the minors, Bright finally made his major-league debut at the age of 28 on July 25, 1958, coming in as a late-inning defensive replacement for third baseman Frank Thomas. For the remainder of 1958 and all of 1959, Bright was mainly a benchwarmer for the Pirates, pinch-hitting and getting into an occasion game at second base, third base, or the outfield. In the pennant-winning season of 1960, he played no games in the field, and pinch-hit only four times, getting no hits in the entire season. Not surprisingly, he was left off the World Series roster.

In December 1960 Bright was traded with pitcher Bennie Daniels and first baseman R.C. Stevens to the Washington Senators for pitcher Bobby Shantz. Playing mostly third base in 1961 and first base in 1962, Bright had his two best major league years with the Senators. In 192 he appeared in 113 games, batted .273, and hit 17 homers. After the season he was traded to the Cincinnati Reds for first baseman Rogelio Alvarez. After playing only one game for the Reds, he was purchased by the New York Yankees. For the Yanks he got into 60 games as first baseman, third baseman, outfielder, or pinch hitter. In his 17th season in professional ball he finally got in a World Series, famously striking out against Sandy Koufax in his first time at bat and repeating the act against Johnny Podres the next day in his only other World Series appearance.

In 1964 Bright played in only four games for the Yankees, spending most of the season with their Triple-A farm club in Richmond, Virginia. He was released in September before getting a chance at World Series redemption. The Chicago Cubs signed him as a free agent the following spring and he played his last major league game on June 30, 1965, before being sent to Salt Lake City in the Pacific Coast League. In 1966 the Cubs moved their PCL franchise to Tacoma, where Bright played in 83 games. After not breaking into the major leagues until he was 28 years

old, Bright had spent all or part of the next eight years in the majors.

In 1967 the Cubs named Bright manager of their farm club in Quincy of the Class A Midwest League—15 years after he had first held the managerial reins in Janesville. During the next nine years, Bright managed seven clubs in six leagues. It seems he was on the move almost every year—San Antonio, Elmira, Coos Bay, Burlington, Binghamton, Sacramento, and Tucson between 1968 and 1976.

When he managed the Sacramento Solons the club was an affiliate of the Milwaukee Brewers. After the 1975 season the Brewers dropped their agreement with the Solons in order to associate themselves with the new PCL club in Spokane. Bright indicated to the United Press International that he would like to quit the Brewers organization to stay in Sacramento.[2] However, the Texas Rangers, who took over the Solons, did not offer Bright a contract. In December he accepted a position as manager of the Tucson Toros, an affiliate of the Oakland Athletics. The Toros did not play up to the expectations that were held for them, and Bright was fired on July 30, 1976.

"I am now a scout and instructor," Bright told sportswriter Steve Weston. "I am to do advance scouting for the big club and instruct in the spring."[3] However, the A's, under owner Charlie Finley, were an organization in disarray in 1976, and Bright was not with them long. On December 7 United Press International reported that the Montreal Expos had hired him as a scout. Bright remained with the Expos organization the rest of his baseball career. In 1985 he had a final managerial fling with the Carolina Bulls, and Expo affiliate in the Carolina League.

Greg Van Dusen, who was public relations director and a radio announcer for Sacramento when Bright managed the Solons in 1975, said of Bright: "He was a colorful Runyonesque character. He had a passion for the game and for life."[4] As a manager Bright became known for his dislike of umpires. Once during a minor-league game he dropped his trousers and climbed a backstop to show his displeasure with a call. He carried his antipathy toward umpires into retirement. "I remember we were at an old-timers game and Harry saw former umpire Emmett Ashford across the lobby of the Sacramento Inn," Van Dusen said. "The next thing you knew they were bumping midsections, and within 30 seconds they're literally rolling around on the floor. People were laughing, but they weren't kidding. They had to be separated.[5]

For many years Bright made his home in Sacramento with his wife, Agnes, and his daughter, Linda.. (He had established his residence in Sacramento, and maintained a home there even when managing in other cities.) He died of an apparent stroke in California's capital city on March 13, 2000, at the age of 70. He was survived by Agnes, his wife of 50 years; a stepson, Larry Weaver, of Wellington, Kansas; and two grandchildren, Mildred and Heather Tibke of Sacramento. Daughter Linda had died in 1996. There were no funeral services for Harry Bright.

Sources

Time Magazine

www.ancestry.com

www.baseball-reference.com.

www.newspaperarchive.com

Notes

1   Harry Bright, quoted in "K is for Koufax," *Time,* October 11, 1963.

2   *El Paso Herald-Post,* August 22, 1975.

3   *Tucson Daily Citizen,* July 31, 1976.

4   Greg Van Dusen, quoted by Jim Van Vliet, *Sacramento Bee,* March 13, 2000.

5   *Ibid.*

Smoky Burgess

by Andy Sturgill

"Smoky Burgess was fat. Not baseball fat like Mickey Lolich or Early Wynn. But FAT fat. Like the mailman or your Uncle Dwight. Putsy Fat. Slobby Fat. Just Plain Fat. In fact I would venture to say that Smoky Burgess was probably the fattest man ever to play professional baseball."
— *The Great American Baseball Card Flipping, Trading, and Bubble Gum Book.*

"You could wake (Burgess) up at 3 a.m. on Christmas morning, with two inches of snow on the ground, throw him a curveball, and he'd hit a line drive."
—*Joe Garagiola*[1]

SMOKY BURGESS DID not possess the physique of a Greek god, nor even that of the average major leaguer. Standing in at a pudgy 5'8", Burgess was saddled with such unflattering descriptions as "a walking laundry bag"[2] and "barely fit enough to play for the Moose Lodge softball team."[3] Physical conditioning aside, nobody debates that Smoky Burgess could hit at any time, against any pitcher, in any situation.

Forrest Harrill Burgess was born on February 6, 1927 in Caroleen, North Carolina, a town in Rutherford County in the western portion of the state. Burgess was born to Lloyd Luther Burgess and Ocie Lewis Burgess. His father spent his professional life as a weaver in the textile industry, but was also a standout semipro baseball player. Varying sources offer varying explanations as to the origin of the name "Smoky", with credit being given to the Smoky Mountains in the area of Burgess' birth, a nickname his father had, his lack of speed on the basepaths, and the fact that he did not smoke tobacco. Whatever its source, the name stuck and

he was "Smoky" to everyone except his wife Margaret, who always called him Forrest.

Burgess grew up as a fan of the Yankees and especially their catcher Bill Dickey, primarily because Smoky was able to get their games on the radio in North Carolina. He attended Tri High School in Caroleen where he played the infield and led off. His high-school coach Forrest Hunt, who had caught in the minor leagues for the Yankees, gave him a piece of advice that influenced his approach to the game for the rest of his career: You'll never be a hitter unless you swing the bat.[4] In addition to playing for the high-school team, Smoky played for the Shelby and Forest Hills American Legion teams from 1942-44. Smoky signed with the St. Louis Cardinals in 1943 but was determined to be too young by Commissioner Landis, and the deal was voided.[5] A year later he accepted a contract offer from the Chicago Cubs, but Smoky later claimed that this was in large part because the Cubs were interested in signing his brother Grady.[6]

Signing bonus in hand, Burgess purchased a new Mercury to ride around Forest City. He stopped in Roses Dime Store and asked a few of the female employees if they'd like to go for a ride. The girls were told to get back to work by their supervisor, Margaret Head, who Smoky then approached about joining him for a ride in the car. He found out where Margaret lived and waited for her at her house after church the following Sunday. Margaret went for a ride with Smoky - for five hours - and the two were married a year and a half later.[7]

Burgess made his professional baseball debut with a .325 batting average for the Lockport (NY) Cubs of the Pony League as a 17-year-old in 1944. In 1945 he played in only 12 games for the Portsmouth Cubs of the

Piedmont League before he joined the war effort and enlisted in the Army at Fort Bragg at the end of May. He missed the rest of the 1945 season and all but the last game in 1946 while he was away in the service. It was also in the service that two happenings took place that shaped the rest of his baseball career. The first was a single event in 1946. As a jeep driver in Germany the vehicle Burgess was driving ran off the road and rolled over three times, smashing his right, throwing, shoulder in the process. When he returned to the minors his arm was still so damaged that he could barely throw a ball back to the pitcher and he was moved from behind home plate to the outfield. Even after the arm healed enough for him to return to catching, Burgess routinely ranked among the league leaders in stolen bases allowed. The other issue for Smoky from the Army was that he entered as a lean young man and was not nearly as lean when he left. He was given an assignment as a mail clerk, which he described by saying, "I ate too much and didn't get much exercise. I'd just hand the boys out their mail."[8]

When he returned to the minor leagues fulltime, Burgess proceeded to win back-to-back batting titles, capturing the Tri-State League crown with a .387 mark for Fayetteville in 1947 and the Southern Association title with a .386 mark for Nashville in 1948. Smoky made his major-league debut for the Cubs on Opening Day in 1949, pinch hitting and making the final out against Rip Sewell in the North Siders' 1-0 loss to the Pirates. Smoky hit a ball hard to right field, one he thought would leave the yard and tie the game, but the wind at Wrigley knocked the ball down and Dixie Walker made the catch to end the game. Burgess appeared in 46 games for the Cubs in '49, compiling only 60 plate appearances in very limited duty.

He returned to the minors for the entire 1950 season before coming to the majors for good in 1951. He hit .251 in 94 games for the Cubs, and after the season was traded to the Reds in a four-player deal. Two months later, before ever suiting up for Cincinnati, Burgess was traded again, this time to the Philadelphia Phillies in a seven-player swap.

To this point Burgess' career was fairly nondescript, but one man who was happy to see Burgess join the Phils was star pitcher Robin Roberts, who sent Smoky a telegram upon the completion of the trade expressing his pleasure that he would not have to face Burgess any more.[9]

Burgess played three-plus seasons in Philadelphia, and during this time developed into an excellent major-league player. He hit .316 in 327 games for the Phillies and was named an All-Star in 1954 and 1955. He posted a .368 batting average in '54, which would have won the batting title but he did not have enough at-bats to qualify. Smoky led Phillies regulars in hitting all three full seasons he spent with the club, and the team declared him the "unofficial batting champion for 1954."[10]

Any player that hits .368 over the course of a major-league season is obviously a good hitter. Smoky's approach, dating all the way back to high school, was to go up to the plate and be aggressive. He was not particularly concerned with finding a good pitch to hit, explaining, "Any ball I can get a good part of the bat on is a good pitch to hit. Ninety percent of the hitters will get as many hits on balls as they do on strikes."[11] To Burgess, hitting was a simple, straightforward process: the pitcher threw the ball and Smoky tried to hit it. Tom Acker, a 1960s pitcher, said of Smoky, "He doesn't care what you throw up there, just so there's a pitch on the way. I threw to him—too high to be a strike—and he hit it out." The great George Sisler, at the time Burgess' hitting coach, said of Smoky, "I'll admit he isn't very careful. He has an amazing facility for placing the bat on the ball."[12]

Smoky was known primarily as a hitter during his playing career, but his abilities behind the dish were a bit suspect. *Total Baseball* rates his defensive contribution to his teams as -96 fielding runs, and he routinely ranked among the league leaders in passed balls, stolen bases allowed, and errors by a catcher. Despite the numbers, Burgess was a decent fielder, but he was slow with a subpar arm after his accident in the service. Perhaps the most accurate assessment of Burgess' defense came from Smoky himself when he opined, "I'm no Roy Campanella... But I'll tell you one thing. I'm not as bad a catcher as most people think."[13] Whether it helped his defense or not, Burgess was also renowned in the game as a world-class heckler, with Phillies centerfielder Richie Ashburn a favorite target.

Smoky's personality seemed befitting of a pudgy catcher. He was a simple man of simple tastes, who ran a service station back home in North Carolina in the offseason.

He neither smoked nor drank and was a devout Baptist who regularly attended services, at one point inspiring his teammates to make up alternate lyrics to the song "Get Me to the Church On Time" encouraging Smoky to make sure he was OUT of church in time to help his club that day.[14] His easygoing nature allowed him to slough off barbs from teammates, saying, "If they get on me, that means they're leaving somebody else alone."[15]

Seven games into the 1955 season Burgess was traded back to the Reds with two others for Andy Seminick and two other players. Seminick had originally gone to the Reds in the trade that sent Burgess to the Phillies in the first place. He spent the rest of '55 and all of the next three seasons in Cincinnati, hitting .290 in 395 games for the Redlegs, as they were known for a time in that era because of concerns about the connotation of "Reds" in the era of McCarthyism. He generally split catching duties with Ed Bailey, a better defender than Smoky who didn't hit as well. While with Cincinnati, Burgess had a couple of memorable moments. In July of '55 against the Pirates, Smoky had the game of his life, going 4-for-6 with three home runs and nine RBIs in the Redlegs' 16-5 win. He was behind the plate against the Braves on May 26, 1956 when three Reds pitchers combined to hold the Braves hitless for 9 2/3 innings before the Braves won the game in the 11th inning. Burgess' last big moment with the Redlegs came on the last day of the 1956 season. Visiting the Cubs' on the next-to-last day of the season, Cincinnati was one home run shy of a new single-season major-league record for home runs by one team. Sent up to pinch hit in the eighth inning, Smoky was told by manager Birdie Tebbetts, "Home run or nothing."[16] Burgess dutifully complied, hitting Sam Jones' first pitch out to set the new team record.

In January of 1959, Burgess was traded again, this time to the Pirates as part of a seven-player swap. The three pieces that went to Pittsburgh - Burgess, along with Don Hoak and Harvey Haddix - were all key players in the Pirates bringing home the World Series title in the epic seven-game series against the Yankees in 1960. While the deal worked out well for the Pirates as a whole, it also rejuvenated Burgess, who added to his already-stellar set of professional accomplishments. He hit .296 in almost six full seasons for the Buccos, making the All-Star team four times. He twice hit over .300, posting a mark of .328

in 1962. Giving credence to his defense, he also posted the top fielding percentage among NL catchers in both 1960 and '61, joining the fielding percentage title he won in 1953 with the Phillies.

Three years to the day after he caught three Cincinnati pitchers that held the Braves without a hit for more than nine innings in a game his team lost, Smoky took the field behind the dish in support of Harvey Haddix. Haddix had a game for the ages, retiring 36 Braves in a row in 12 perfect innings before an error allowed the first runner to reach base. Milwaukee won the game later in the 13th inning.

The 1960 World Series between the Pirates and Yankees is of course remembered for Bill Mazeroski's series winning home run in the bottom of the ninth of Game Seven. The Series was Smoky's only playoff appearance, and he performed admirably, hitting .333 (6-18) with a double and two runs scored in five games. Interestingly, the Pirates were 4-1 in games Smoky played in the Series, and in the two games that he did not play the Pirates lost, 10-0 and 12-0. Years afterward on the speaking circuit, Burgess liked to say that his single to lead off the seventh inning of Game Seven, not Mazeroski's home run, was the most important hit of the Series. Why? To hear Smoky tell it, "I got a hit off of Bobby Shantz. It was the tying run so (manager Danny) Murtaugh put (Joe) Christopher in to run for me... Hal Smith, who replaced me, hit the home run to tie it (in the eighth)... Now which base hit was the most important in the 1960 World Series? Maz's? No, Maz wouldn't have gotten up if Hal Smith hadn't hit the three-run homer that tied it up. But how did Smith get into the game? If I hadn't gotten the base hit off of Shantz and been a slow runner, I'd still been catching, so which hit was the most important?"[17] Smoky's recollection was a little off, as Smith's home run actually put the Pirates up 9-7, but the spirit of the story he told remains.

Smoky remained a regular with the Pirates until 1964 when he appeared in the field in only 44 games before the White Sox selected him off waivers in September. He spent the next three full seasons with the Pale Hose, but only appeared in the field in seven games. Instead, Smoky embraced his role as a part-time player by becoming the game's premier pinch hitter. His 20 hits in the pinch in 1966 tied the league record set by Ed Coleman in 1936.

Taking to his full-time role in the pinch, Burgess attributed his success to hard work studying pitchers, especially how pitchers worked hitters similar to himself, as well as his aggressive mindset in the batter's box.[18] In contrast to more modern pinch hitters who hit endless balls in a cage or do hours of cardio, Smoky described his pre-at-bat routine by saying, "I didn't do anything."[19]

His role as the pinch ace for the White Sox so clearly defined, he often stayed out in the bullpen to catch pitchers until the seventh or eighth inning, knowing he would never be used earlier. As his career wound down, Smoky's concerns away from the baseball field included his own health (he had issues with ulcers throughout his career), his family's health (his wife had major back issues and his teenage daughter was diabetic), his outside business interests (he owned a Dodge dealership back home in North Carolina), and education (he completed course-work in Business Administration from the International Correspondence School). Outside interests aside, Burgess hit .286 and .313 in his first two full seasons with the White Sox, before slipping badly to a .133 average in 1967. He decided to hang it up after the '67 campaign, by now 40 years old and a grandfather. He knew it was time to move on because he pulled a muscle in his side in May and it took him all season to recover.[20]

Had Smoky come along only a few years later, his career likely would have been extended even further because of the advent of the designated hitter. As it is, when he retired he was the all-time major-league leader in pinch hits with 145, but has since been passed by Manny Mota in 1979, and now sits fourth behind Mota, Lenny Harris, and Mark Sweeney. He passed the former mark of 113 formerly held by Red Lucas, who had played with four teams in the 1920's and '30's. Smoky was a threat not just to get a hit in the pinch, but to knock the ball out of the park. His 16 pinch-hit home runs were good for second place on the all-time list (behind Jerry Lynch's 18) at the time he retired, and as of 2011 he's tied for fifth place with Gates Brown and Willie McCovey, behind Lynch, John Vander Wal, Cliff Johnson, and all-time leader Matt Stairs.

Upon leaving the playing field, Burgess ran a car dealership back home in North Carolina before joining the Atlanta Braves organization. He worked in various capacities for the Braves, serving as a scout, hitting instructor,

and minor-league coach for more than a decade and helping players such as Bruce Benedict, Rafael Ramirez, and Dale Murphy reach the big leagues. He was inducted into numerous Halls of Fame, including Halls for North Carolina Sports, North Carolina American Legion Baseball, and the Cincinnati Reds. He trimmed down and participated in Old Timer's games, saying of a ball he hit against Ryne Duren in an Old Timer's game "I had to wait until I was retired to hit the hardest ball of my life."[21] He returned home to Forest City, keeping his uniform from the 1960 World Series, a bronzed catcher's mitt, and the bat he used to set the pinch-hits record as his most cherished relics from a very good big-league career. He returned to Pittsburgh in 1990 for the 30-year reunion of the World Series championship team, but passed away not long after, on September 15, 1991 back home at Rutherford Hospital, before being laid to rest at Sunset Memorial Park in Spindale, NC. He was survived by his wife, Margaret, son Larry, three brothers, three grandchildren, and two great-grandchildren.

Reflecting on his career some 20 years after it ended, Smoky recalled, "Everything went well, I have no regrets. I don't know a thing I would have changed. If I hadn't played baseball, I would have probably had to work in the cotton mills. That's real hard work. I'm certainly glad I had baseball."[22]

Thanks to David Vincent for his assistance with pinch-hit home run data.

Sources

Other than the sources cited in the notes, the author also consulted Ancestry.com, *Baseball Digest*, Baseball-Reference.com, and *The Sporting News*

Notes

1   Rick Cushing, *1960 Pittsburgh Pirates, Day by Day.* (Pittsburgh, PA: Dorrance Publishing, 2010), 46.

2   *Sports Illustrated,* June 22, 1959

3   Jim, Reisler, *The Best Game Ever; Pirates vs. Yankees, October 13, 1960.* (Cambridge, MA; Da Capo Press, 2007), 4-5.

4   *Baseball Digest,* December 1963

5   Rich Westcott, *Diamond Greats: Profiles and Interviews with 65 of Baseball's History Makers.* (Westport, CT; Meckler Books, 1988), 344

6   *Sports Illustrated*, op. cit.

7   Rutherfordweekly.com. "The Time Has Come To Honor One of Our Own." March 31, 2011.

8   *Sports Illustrated*, op. cit.

9   Bob Cairns, *Pen Men: Baseball's Greatest Bullpen Stories Told by the Men Who Brought the Game Relief* (New York: St. Martin's Press, 1992), 118

10 Rich Westcott and Frank Bilovsky, *The Phillies Encyclopedia, 3rd Edition*. (Philadelphia; Temple University Press, 2004), 343.

11 Paul Votano, *Stand and Deliver: A History of Pinch Hitting*. (Jefferson, NC: McFarland, 2003), 115.

12 *Sports Illustrated*, op. cit.

13 Ibid.

14 Bill James, *The New Bill James Historical Abstract*. (New York: Free Press, 2001) , 393.

15 *Sports Illustrated*, op. cit.

16 Cushing, 47.

17 Cairns, *Pen Men*, 123.

18 James, op. cit.

19 Thomas Boswell, "Smoky's Children." *Why Time Begins on Opening Day*. (New York: Penguin, 1985), 201-6.

20 *The Sporting News*, December 23, 1967

21 Boswell, op. cit.

22 Westcott, 345.

Tom Cheney

By Tim Herlich

"I didn't like how my baseball career ended, particularly because I was so young. I won only 19 games total. But I realized how fortunate I was to have made it to the majors. Not many make it. And how many guys who played for many years didn't get to play in the World Series or win a title? I also cherished the togetherness of players in an era when we didn't make enough money for money to matter. So I got about as much out of the game as a person could ask for."
– Tom Cheney.[1]

TOM CHENEY WAS a proud and humble man, a true Southern gentleman, stubborn, strong-willed, a man's man who loved outdoor life, farming, hunting, and fishing. A country boy to the core, he was far more comfortable in the confines of a duck blind than under the lights of a big city. His teammates good-naturedly called him Skins or Skinhead because of his premature baldness, but family and friends back home knew him by his full first name, Thomas.

The Pittsburgh Pirates obtained Cheney, a minor-league pitcher at the time, from the St. Louis Cardinals on December 21, 1959, along with outfielder Gino Cimoli, in exchange for pitcher Ronnie Kline. After his recall from Columbus in midseason 1960, the Georgia native compiled a 2-2 record in 11 games, starting eight of them, and earned a spot on the World Series roster. Tom pitched three games in relief in the fall classic, posting a 4.50 ERA in four innings while striking out six.

Cheney's stay in Pittsburgh was brief. After just one game with the Pirates in 1961, he was demoted to the minors and later traded to the Washington Senators. The hard-throwing right-hander blossomed into one of the American League's most effective starters in 1962

and 1963, albeit amid the obscurity of pitching for a last-place club.

On September 12, 1962, Cheney stunned the baseball world and established a major-league single-game strike-out record, fanning 21 Baltimore Orioles in a 16-inning complete game in Baltimore's Memorial Stadium. "For that one night," Senators broadcaster Dan Daniels proclaimed years later, "he was as fine a pitcher as I ever have seen."[2]

Cheney opened the 1963 season as the hottest pitcher in baseball. But just as he appeared to be on the verge of stardom and big paychecks, the 28-year-old was dealt a devastating blow. In the sixth inning of a game against the Orioles in July, he threw a pitch that tore up his elbow. He labored through just 63 more major-league innings before calling it quits in 1966. This cruel and sudden twist of fate ended a promising career, and the forgotten record-holder returned to Georgia to a life outside of baseball until his death in 2001.

Thomas Edgar Cheney, III was born on October 14, 1934, near Morgan, Georgia, about 200 miles south of Atlanta. Parents Ed (Thomas Edgar Cheney II) and Perk (maiden name Ollie Geneva Perkins) had inherited a parcel of the vast acreage owned by the first Thomas Edgar Cheney. Their peanut and dairy farm was one of the more prosperous in Calhoun County. Mr. Ed and Miss Perk appreciated the finer things in life, and exuded sophistication uncommon to the area. According to Cheney's close friend Ted Jones, the well-furnished family home featured stained hardwood floors and Persian rugs, an unusual elegance. Mr. Ed drove a sharp automobile, and Miss Perk outfitted Thomas in the most beautiful store-bought shirts, not the plain-sewn homemade clothing worn by most farm kids.[3] Nonetheless, Thomas and his younger brother, Charles, experienced the rigors of farm life growing up. "I remember my Daddy telling me that he would have to get up early in the morning and light the fires and get things going before his parents got up," recalled Terri Cook, Cheney's elder daughter.[4]

Thomas pitched and played shortstop in American Legion and high-school baseball. After graduation, he enrolled in nearby Abraham Baldwin Agricultural College, a two-year institution at that time, with the idea of becoming a veterinarian. He helped lead the Stallions to the state junior-college championship in 1952.[5] Only 18 years old, he stood 5-feet-11 but weighed a scrawny 150 pounds. Still, he was impressive enough to interest major-league scouts. The mound prospect traveled to Atlanta to audition with the Boston Braves before accepting a $1,500 bonus from scout Mercer Harris to join the St. Louis Cardinals' Class D affiliate in Albany, Georgia, close to home.[6]

Moving up to Class C Fresno in 1954, the 19-year-old won 12 games and struck out 207 California League batters in 203 innings. He also met Jackie Bennett, a 16-year-old beautician school student, at a burger drive-in. That summer, a romance flourished, and Jackie was heartbroken when Tom went home to Georgia at the end of the season. Immediately after her 18th birthday on May 29, 1955, the lovestruck young lady drove by herself from California to the Cheney farm near Morgan. Tom was pitching for nearby Class A Columbus at the time. On June 9 the young couple exchanged vows in the family living room.[7]

Cheney matriculated steadily through the abundant St. Louis farm system. The newlywed had a good season at Columbus in 1955, and excelled at Triple-A Omaha in 1956 and 1957, where he was among league leaders in ERA and voted to the American Association All-Star team both years. His stellar performance earned him an invitation to the Cardinals spring-training camp in 1957, and St. Louis skipper Fred Hutchinson named him to the club's Opening Day roster.[8] Cheney hurled four shutout innings in his big-league debut, but wildness overcame him in subsequent games. After walking 15 batters in just nine innings, the rookie was optioned back to Omaha.

"At the time, I could throw hard but my control was off and on, like it would be my entire career," Cheney told author Danny Peary.[9] He threw mostly fastballs, but also had a good curve, and learned how to throw a knuckleball from Cardinals teammate and future Hall of Fame pitcher Hoyt Wilhelm. Later, Cheney added a slider and screwball to his pitching repertoire. "I'll throw a screwball to left-handed hitters, but it's more of a change than a real scroojie," he said.[10] One pitch he tried to learn in Pittsburgh but could not master was Elroy Face's forkball.

Cheney would have returned to the Cardinals as a September call-up, but was drafted into military service. He reported to Fort Jackson, South Carolina, on September 10, 1957, for basic training. From there, Cheney was assigned to Fort McPherson, Georgia, and helped lead the base team to its fourth straight 3rd Army championship in 1958.[11] On April 27, 1959, Jackie gave birth to the couple's first child, daughter Terri Lynn. A month and a half later, the new father was mustered out of the Army. He rejoined the Cardinals on June 16, but struggled to regain his control. In 11 2/3 innings he surrendered 17 hits and 11 bases on balls, and was demoted back to Omaha.

The Cardinals sent Cheney to Havana, Cuba, to play winter ball. "My wife and 8-month-old daughter came with me," he recalled. "We got $350 a month in expenses to go along with my $1,500-a-month salary. It was a life of luxury. We had a nice home, with a maid from the Virgin Islands, and had access to the yacht club and country club. We played just four games a week."[12] It was in Cuba that the young hurler learned he had been traded to the Pirates along with Gino Cimoli for Ronnie Kline.

Pittsburgh faithful scratched their heads, wondering why general manager Joe L. Brown would swap Kline, a durable starter, for Cimoli, a fourth outfielder they seemingly didn't need, and Cheney, a raw and wild hurler totally unimpressive in two abbreviated stints with the Cardinals. As spring training of 1960 unfolded, sportswriter Arthur Daley of the *New York Times* concluded that Devine had shrewdly pilfered the clueless Brown and pulled off an epic heist, proclaiming that "this trade may be the biggest steal since the Brinks robbery."[13] Brown countered at a press luncheon at Forbes Field that "the Pirates can win the pennant—if they want to" and that "Cheney may surprise."[14] As it turned out, both Cimoli and Cheney contributed to Pittsburgh's pennant-winning season while Kline was a major disappointment in St. Louis.

Cheney began 1960 in Triple-A Columbus, Ohio. After two months, his record stood at just 4-8, but he had regained his control and was leading the International League in strikeouts.[15] The Pirates recalled him on June 28. The balding right-hander notched his first major-league win on July 6 at Cincinnati, and his first big-league shutout on July 17, a four-hitter against the Reds at Forbes Field. Cheney stayed with the Pirates the remainder of the season, appearing in 11 games as a spot starter and reliever. He finished with a 2-2 record and 3.98 earned-run average in 52 innings pitched. In the 1960 World Series Cheney saw action in the three blowout victories by the Yankees. In four innings of work he struck out six batters, including Roger Maris and Mickey Mantle. But he also surrendered the triple to Bobby Richardson that broke open Game Six for the Bronx Bombers.

"When I got to Pittsburgh, I discovered I wasn't just on a great team but got to play with a great bunch of guys," Cheney reminisced. "It wasn't cliquish at all. … Any 5 to 10 of us would go out together after games. Stars and non-stars, it didn't matter. I was in only 11 games, 8 as a starter. Yet this team was so tight that I was voted a full World Series share. They accepted me."[16]

Although the 1960 season ended on a promising note for Cheney, 1961 proved to be excruciating painful. He made the Pirates' 28-man Opening Day roster but pitched poorly in his first relief appearance, in Los Angeles on April 16. Failing to record an out, he surrendered five runs on four walks, an error, and a home run by light-hitting catcher Norm Sherry. With the May 10 deadline looming to reduce the major-league roster to 25 players, Tom received a shocking phone call from home—father Ed Cheney had died suddenly of a heart attack at the age of 52.

Tom flew home to Morgan to help his widowed mother and brother, and then called general manager Joe Brown. "It was approaching the cutdown date for rosters, and I knew it was between me and pitcher George Witt to go," he recalled. According to Cheney, Brown gave his word that he would be retained. Upon his return to Pittsburgh, however, Brown informed him that he was being sent down to Columbus. "I cursed him terribly, calling him

everything a man can be called. I could have handled the truth, but don't lie to me. That was the worst thing that ever happened to me in baseball," Cheney fumed. "I never forgave Brown. I told him that 'the best thing you can do for me is to get me out of this whole organization, because I'll never play for you again.'"[17]

"He was very tender and loving," Terri noted, illuminating her father's code of ethics, "but he was also a very firm man. He was the kind of man that you don't need anything in writing, you just do what you say you're going to do. That's pretty much how life was down in South Georgia anyway—you're honorable; you do what you're supposed to do."

Brown granted Cheney his wish on June 29, 1961, swapping him to the expansion Washington Senators for veteran pitcher Tom Sturdivant. The trade reunited Cheney with former Pirates coach Mickey Vernon, now the Senators manager. But misfortune continued to dog the right-hander. A ribcage injury sidelined him for six weeks. Overall in 1961, he walked 30 batters in 29 2/3 innings and surrendered nine home runs, including number 54 to Roger Maris, who broke Babe Ruth's single-season home-run record that year.

Coming into spring training with the Senators in 1962, Cheney's career major-league pitching log was ugly. Of 20 starts, he had failed to pitch past the fourth inning in 14, and he averaged nearly eight walks per nine innings. But manager Vernon had faith that Cheney would come around, and he did. He began the 1962 season in the bullpen, but joined the Nats' starting rotation in mid-May. By the end of the year Cheney had pitched 1731/3 innings, hurled three shutouts, and posted an ERA of 3.17, seventh best in the American League. His control improved and he struck out 147. He was second in the American League in strikeouts per nine innings, and held right-handed batters to a measly .188 batting average.

On September 12, 1962, Cheney hurled a 16-inning complete-game 2-1 victory in which he struck out 21 batters, more than any other major-league pitcher before or since. As a reward for his record-breaking performance, Senators president Pete Quesada gave Cheney a $1,000 bonus. "They had cut my salary a thousand dollars after the 1961 season," Cheney reasoned, "so I didn't consider it a bonus but just getting back what they owed me."[18]

Cheney began the 1963 season on fire. Armed with a nasty repertoire of pitches — a crackling fastball, tumbling curve, slider, screwball, and knuckler — and aided by a rule change that expanded the strike zone, Cheney posted four straight complete-game victories and surrendered only one earned run for a 0.25 ERA.[19] By the All-Star break, he sported an 8-9 record with four shutouts, a 2.88 ERA, and an excellent WHIP (walks and hits per inning pitched) of just 1.04 for a woeful Senators team that was 30-56 and last in the league in batting, pitching, and fielding. "Cheney acquired the last thing he needed to be a sensational pitcher — control," observed rival manager Bill Rigney of the Los Angeles Angels.[20]

Cheney also seemed to have conquered another nemesis — extreme nervousness. "It was a tough life being a ballplayer," confided the moundsman years later. "You were always under pressure even if you weren't in a pennant race. You never forgot that if you didn't do the job, there was someone in the minors who was waiting for you to fail or be injured."[21] Reserve infielder Dick Schofield was a good friend of Cheney's dating back to their days in the Cardinals farm system. "Skinhead had a great arm and threw a great curve," Schofield recalled, "but when he came to Pittsburgh he was still trying to stick in the majors. He was always nervous. He'd light one cigarette right after another."[22] Senators coach Rollie Hemsley felt Cheney was mishandled in 1962. "They should have helped Cheney to forget that he is a nervous pitcher, instead of reminding him of it."[23] Good friend Ted Jones speculated that Tom's rural upbringing contributed to his anxiety. "I think he felt pressure coming from where we all came from and the backgrounds that we had. Thomas was not a big-crowd guy. He was kind of shy. I think that he felt the pressure of the crowd and the fans and the big league players."

Cheney appeared to be ascending to the pitching elite in 1963 when, working on yet another shutout on July 11, he suddenly felt something snap in his elbow. "I threw a pitch and it felt like someone had a knife and ripped me down the forearm," he recalled.[24] Cheney pitched just five more games that year, totaling nine innings. In his final start of the season, on August 26, he faced just five batters before his sore elbow forced him out of the game.[25] The diagnosis was an elbow strain, further defined as epi-condylitis, or "tennis elbow" in layman's terms. The only prescription was rest and physical therapy.

The following spring, given a clean bill of health by the Senators' club physician, Dr. George Resta, Cheney opened the 1964 season in the Nats' starting rotation. Gil Hodges had replaced Vernon as manager the previous midseason, and Cheney didn't get along with his new boss. "I wasn't his favorite person and he wasn't mine," the right-hander conceded.[26] Winless in four starts, Cheney was demoted to the bullpen. "I kept trying to pitch but couldn't take the pain for more than four or five innings. By that time my elbow would start swelling. I could have gone up to three innings without much trouble, but Hodges said that he wanted me to start."[27] Cheney pitched in short relief for nearly a month, but was called upon by Hodges on June 9 to start the second game of a doubleheader against the Kansas City Athletics. The tough hurler battled through pain to earn a 5-1 complete-game win. "He kept me out there much too long," Cheney said decades later. "I stayed out there throwing until tears were coming out of my eyes. Afterward I was sitting in front of my locker. Hodges walked by and said, 'Thataway to go.' I said, 'Yeah, you son of a bitch, that was the last game I'll ever pitch.'"[28] The victory was the 19th and last of Cheney's abbreviated career. He made one more mound appearance, five days later, and then was sent to the Mayo Clinic in Rochester, Minnesota. The injured pitcher was ordered to take nine months to a year off to give his torn elbow muscles time to heal. Cheney missed all of the 1965 season and attempted a comeback in 1966, but after three games was demoted to the minors and ended his career ingloriously in Double-A York of the Eastern League. At about the same time, on July 20, 1966, Cheney's life took on added responsibility; Jackie gave birth to their second daughter, Lacie Ann.

"It was hard to accept," the mothballed pitcher, just 31 years old at the time, said years later. "I had an exceptionally good start in 1963. It's hard to go out and redo your life. It's hard to leave something you really love. There was a big cut in salary for one thing."[29] The premature end to his baseball career proved to be exceedingly difficult for Cheney. "What you have to understand is that his life was taken away from him," daughter Terri reasoned. Her father returned to Morgan to help out on the family farm, but succumbed to the demons of alcohol abuse. To protect their daughters, Jackie filed for divorce in 1969.

She remarried in 1971. Tom also remarried, and divorced, twice during the ensuing two decades.

In 1987, at Terri's wedding, Tom and Jackie reconnected, and two years later, the first Mrs. Cheney also became the fourth. "When they got married a second time, there was such peace between the two of them," said Terri of her parents. "She always told me, from the very first time she met him, her stomach would just flutter and that she still felt that way every time she looked at him, even when they were divorced."

A heavy smoker nearly his whole life, Tom eventually suffered from emphysema. He finally quit smoking, as did Jackie. Over the years, Tom and his brother Charles bought a fertilizer plant, and then got into the propane-gas business. When he sold his share of the company, Tom stayed on as one of their delivery-truck drivers. He finally retired when he couldn't fill out the paperwork anymore. It was the early onset of Alzheimer's disease, which had also afflicted his mother, Miss Perk. The disease finally took the life of Thomas Edgar Cheney, III on November 1, 2001. Ten weeks later, Jackie Cheney died from melanoma cancer.

On the surface, Tom Cheney's career pitching line is mediocre at best. His 19-29 won-loss record is unimpressive. Yet of his 19 wins, eight were shutouts. When Cheney was on his game and healthy, he was dominant. Such was the case on the evening of September 12, 1962, when the determined young right-hander struck out 21 batters in a single major-league game.

Only 4,098 fans showed up at Memorial Stadium in Baltimore that Wednesday night to witness the game between two second-division ballclubs. The 27-year-old Cheney felt good warming up, and was staked to a 1-0 lead early. He recorded his first strikeout in the second inning, and struck out the side in the third and fifth. The Orioles finally broke through, however, to tie the score in the seventh. After nine innings, Cheney had recorded 13 strikeouts, but the futile Senators had managed only four hits and the game stood even at 1-1. Cheney continued to carry the team on his back. After 11 innings he had chalked up 17 strikeouts but the game remained tied.

By the 12th inning, manager Vernon wanted to take Tom out, but he insisted on staying in. "I said I wanted to win or lose it," Cheney recalled. "He never mentioned my coming out again."[30] It was not the first time the determined right-hander had gone deep into extra innings. In an American Association playoff game in 1959, for example, he pitched into the 12th inning against Minneapolis before losing 3-2.[31]

With one out in the bottom of the 14th, Cheney chalked up victim number 18, and over the Memorial Stadium public-address system it was announced that he had tied the modern major-league record, held by Sandy Koufax, Warren Spahn, Bob Feller, and Jack Coombs. "I was surprised. I thought it was more like 13 or 14," Cheney said after the game.[32] Distracted, he threw two pitches high to the next batter, pitching adversary and former outfielder Dick Hall, then regained his composure to fan Hall for his 19th strikeout and a new modern record.

Cheney racked up his 20th strikeout in the 15th inning, breaking the all-time record set by Charlie Sweeney and Hugh Daily in 1884, when rules were much different. But it was getting late. Baltimore's curfew law prohibited any inning from starting after midnight.[33] It became apparent that the 16th inning would be the contest's last—win, lose or tie. Fortunately for the Senators, first baseman Bud Zipfel hit what would become the last home run of his short major-league career. Cheney took the mound in the bottom of the 16th inning with a one-run lead and yielded a one-out single. Incredibly, it was the first Oriole hit Cheney had allowed since the eighth inning! He retired Jackie Brandt on a fly to center, and then faced the dangerous Dick Williams, a .419 pinch-hitter that season. With the game on the line and 11:59 p.m. on the clock, Cheney caught the future Hall of Fame manager looking for his 21st strikeout and a hard-earned 2-1 victory.

Cheney threw 228 pitches that night, fueled by adrenaline and chain-smoking between innings. "That game he must have gone through three packs of cigarettes," recalled teammate Chuck Hinton.[34] "I sat down in the locker room afterward," Cheney reflected, "and in 15 minutes I was exhausted. The tension had worn off. I didn't realize I was that tired."[35] Teammate Don Lock remembered the drive back to Washington after the game, when Cheney began suffering muscle cramps. "Legs, stomach, back, and arms," recalled Lock. "In all honesty, he should have been on a sugar IV drip."[36]

Batterymate Ken Retzer described what it was like catching Cheney that game. "That curveball of his looked like it was falling off the table. Tom was getting a lot of the hitters out with screwballs, too, and he came in with his knuckler now and then and was getting *it* over." Baltimore hitters were duly impressed. "He had great stuff," vouched Russ Snyder, a three-time strikeout victim. "I never saw a better curveball."[37] "He showed me the greatest stuff I've seen from any pitcher," said future Hall of Famer Brooks Robinson.[38] Jackie Brandt felt that Cheney was more formidable than Sandy Koufax, whom he had faced in the left-hander's 18-strikeout game in 1959: "Koufax wasn't that sharp. I don't think Sandy would have struck out 21 in 18 innings. Cheney's curveball was falling out of the sky."[39]

The record-setting masterpiece thrown by Cheney on September 12, 1962, is impressive, but rarely mentioned. The shy, reclusive record-holder returned to Baltimore at the Orioles' invitation in 1992 to mark the game's 30th anniversary, and attended only a few autograph sessions over the years.[40] His last public appearance was at a Washington Senators reunion on February 26, 2000. By that time, Alzheimer's was beginning to take its toll.

Throughout the years, Tom Cheney was always humble about his strikeout record, never one to indulge in self-promotion. He always felt that he was merely doing his job. The fact that it took 16 innings for Cheney to set the record has worked against him, invalidating the achievement in many of baseball's record books.

"Well, I'm very proud of him," exuded Cheney's daughter Terri. "It's a record that hasn't been broken. Other people can say anything they want, but nobody has broken it yet. When I think back on him, I think about his determination. And, yeah, he had some issues and stumbles along the way. But the man he was and the determination he had—to do something like that—I'm very proud of it, proud of him. In my eyes, he's just a great man."

Sources

Interviews with Terri Cook, November 6, 2011, and Ted Jones, January 14, 2012. The author is deeply grateful for their time and recollections.

Baseball Digest, May 1974 and April 1986

Google archives

Peary, Danny, *We Played the Game* (New York: Black Dog and Leventhal Publishers, 2002).

New York Times

Washington Post

The Sporting News, 1956-1966.

www.baseball-reference.com

www.retrosheet.org

Notes

1   Danny Peary, *We Played the Game* (New York: Black Dog and Leventhal Publishers, 2002), 556.

2   Carl Lundquist, "Dapper Dan Labels White Seat Symbol of New Traditions," *The Sporting News*, August 27, 1966, 16

3   Interview with lifelong friend Ted Jones, January 14, 2012. All subsequent quotes from Mr. Jones are taken from this interview.

4   Interview with daughter Terri Lynn Cheney Cook, November 6, 2011. All subsequent quotes from Ms. Cook are taken from this interview.

5   Abraham Baldwin Agricultural College website (www.abac.edu). In 2008 Cheney was named to the college's Athletics Hall of Fame inaugural class.

6   Peary, 181.

7   Bill Turque, "Q: Which Washington Senators pitcher set the all-time record for strikeouts in a single game?", *Washington Post* Magazine, June 22, 2008, 19.

8   Bob Broeg, "Kid Cheney Climbs in Card Hill Ratings as Mizell Tumbles," *The Sporting News*, April 17, 1957, 23.

9   Peary, 356.

10 Bob Addie, "Ex-Bucs Cheney, Leppert Fill Bill in Capital," *The Sporting News*, April 27, 1963, 9.

11 "Cheney, Owens—Stars in Army Title Tourneys," *The Sporting News*, September 24, 1958, 45.

12 Peary, 429.

13 Arthur Daley, "An Unexpected Gift," *New York Times*, March 25, 1960, 32.

14 Les Biederman, "Pirates Can Win by Showing They Want To—Brown," *The Sporting News*, January 20, 1960, 9.

15 *The Sporting News*, July 6, 1960, 37.

16 Peary, 473. It is noted that this contradicts the November 2, 1960, edition of *The Sporting News*, in which it was reported that Cheney had been voted a half-share.

17 Peary, 509.

18 Robert C. Gallagher, "Tom Cheney: He Fanned 21 Batters in a Single Game!," *Baseball Digest*, April 1986, 91.

19 Had it not been for an unearned run surrendered in the second game, Cheney would have thrown 32 ¹/₃ scoreless innings to start the 1963 season, an American League record. The major-league record as of 2012 was 39, set by Brad Ziegler for the 2008 Oakland A's.

20 Shirley Povich, "Nat Fans Flip Over Cheney, Ace Chucker," *The Sporting News*, May 4, 1963, 20.

21 Peary, 577.

22 Peary, 471.

23 Shirley Povich, "Hemsley Tosses Barb at Nats for Mound Strategy," *The Sporting News*, December 1, 1962, 25.

24 Peary, 582.

25 Adding insult to injury, daughter Terri was struck by a foul ball in the stands and required first aid. *The Sporting News*, September 7, 1963, 16.

26 Peary, 582.

27 Peary, 583.

28 Peary, 614.

29 Gallagher, 93. Cheney's highest salary in baseball was approximately $15,000.

30 Peary, 555.

31 *The Sporting News*, September 23, 1959, 44.

32 Emil Rothe, "When Tom Cheney Fanned 21 Batters," *Baseball Digest*, May 1974, 77.

33 Turque, 28.

34 Gallagher, 92.

35 Ibid.

36 Turque, 28.

37 Bob Addie, "Cheney Spins Whiff Magic With Crackling Curve Ball," *The Sporting News*, September 22, 1962, 25.

38 Shirley Povich, "Nats May Offer King Slab Stars for Big Socker, *The Sporting News*, September 29, 1962, 7.

39 Bob Addie, "Tom Cheney's Curve Was 'Falling Off a Table,'" *Washington Post*, September 14, 1963, D7.

40 An impostor would occasionally show up at autograph events and claim to be Cheney. The family learned of this shortly before Cheney's death, but chose not to pursue criminal charges.

Joe Christopher

by Rory Costello

JOE CHRISTOPHER, THE first player from the Virgin Islands to appear in the major leagues, was a backup outfielder for the 1960 Pittsburgh Pirates. Fleet afoot and a top defender, he was often used as a pinch-runner; in the World Series, he appeared in three games and scored twice. Taken by the New York Mets in the expansion draft the next year, Christopher enjoyed his finest season in 1964 when he hit .300 with 16 homers and 78 RBIs.

Fleet of foot and grinning calmly, Hurryin' Joe, as announcer Bob Prince dubbed him, was a champion across the Americas. In addition to his small role with the 1960 Pirates, the outfielder won several more titles in his second home, Puerto Rico, plus two more as a playoff reinforcement in the Dominican Republic and Venezuela. Yet US fans mainly remember him today as one of the original Amazin' Mets.

Joseph O'Neal Christopher was the first player actually born in the US Virgin Islands to make the major leagues. He was born in Frederiksted, St. Croix, on December 13, 1935. This is just a technicality, though—Valmy Thomas, also from St. Croix, was born on Puerto Rican soil only because his mother sought a better hospital. Valmy's major-league debut came in 1957.

Joe's father, Patrick Christopher, was an overseer on a mango and cane plantation in Estate Oxford, part of the "rainforest" section in the northwest corner of St. Croix. His mother, Sarah Richards Christopher, had five other children. There were two brothers, Patrick and Alfred, and two sisters, Elizabeth and Agnes. (Another brother, Augustus, died in infancy.) Joe was the baby of the family, born to Sarah in her 40s.

Baseball was once the most popular sport in the Virgin Islands. Four other major leaguers of the 1960s and '70s also grew up around Frederiksted, which had a population of 2,000 when Christopher was young. Pitcher Julio Navarro, who was born on the nearby Puerto Rican island of Vieques but moved to St. Croix at the age of 5, is just a few weeks younger than Joe. Elmo Plaskett, who used to wake Joe up to play sandlot ball when both were young boys, was born in 1938. Horace Clarke and José Morales came along in 1940 and 1944, respectively.

Christopher played high-school ball at St. Patrick's, a parochial school in Frederiksted. An Irish Catholic priest named Mullin was a driving force behind the program. Joe also became the shortstop for a local team called the Annaly Athletics. This club was sponsored by Frits Lawaetz, a member of one of the old Danish families on St. Croix, which along with St. Thomas and St. John was owned by Denmark until 1917.

Historically, the Catholic Church planted strong roots in the islands under the Danes. In fact, Joe said that his middle name came from a nun called Mother Ermin. "When I was born, she asked to hold me, and she told my

mother that I looked like her brother—except I was black! So I got her family name, O'Neal." He also joked that another priest, Father Caskey, "always told me to tell the truth. And that's gotten me in more trouble during my life than anything else!"

On Sunday mornings the young ballplayers of Frederiksted would go out and do their own groundskeeping, using a handmade roller that weighed at least 200 pounds. They played in the afternoons after resting from their labor and sat around talking baseball past midnight.

At the age of 18 in 1954, Joe was at the crux of Virgin Islands baseball history. A man from St. Thomas named Fernando Corneiro made a connection with the National Baseball Congress (NBC) tournament in Wichita, Kansas. Christopher recalled Corneiro as "one of the most influential men in the islands. He had the ability to get things done, to put things together. If he had never accomplished what he set out to do, I would not be heard of today."

The Christiansted Commandos, with Joe at shortstop, journeyed 3,129 miles to Wichita. The squad also featured Joe's brother Alfred at catcher, Julio Navarro, and 16-year-old Elmo Plaskett. The Commandos lost two games after getting a bye, but Joe Christopher caught the eye of Pirates superscout Howie Haak. After he signed Joe, the Virgin Islands became part of Haak's itinerary. He later signed Plaskett and Al McBean for the Bucs.

As Christopher remembered, though, it wasn't that easy for Haak. "He was offering $150 a month plus a $200 bonus, and I told him I could work in the post office for $600 a month." But Joe did join the Pirates, where he encountered general manager Branch Rickey, "an old man in a Panama hat giving lectures. Everybody was falling asleep—except Joe Christopher." According to Joe, Branch took a liking to the neophyte and passed on thoughts about scouting systems and the process that led to the signing of Jackie Robinson.

In the winter of 1954-55, Joe gained his first pro experience, in the Puerto Rican Winter League. As it did for many of his fellow Virgin Islanders, this league proved to be an invaluable apprenticeship. Christopher's first manager in the US, Jerry Gardner, switched him to the outfield in 1955. With the Mexico City Tigers (a.k.a. the Blues) in 1957, he led that Double-A league in stolen bases, swiping 24 in just 64 games. Joe earned promotion to Triple-A in 1958. He batted .327 with 8 homers, 58 RBIs, and 16 steals for the Salt Lake City Bees. In addition, he led the Puerto Rican Winter League in steals for the first time during the winter of 1958-59, while hitting .318. *The Sporting News* described him as "a flashing Pepper Martin type who steals bases head first and will take an extra sack at the drop of an enemy outfielder's eyelash."[1]

Christopher was ready for the majors. He was a backup outfielder with the Pirates from 1959 through 1961. He was first called up when Roberto Clemente was injured, making his debut in nothing less than Harvey Haddix's masterpiece of 12 perfect innings at Milwaukee's County Stadium on May 26, 1959. Joe Adcock's game-ending hit in the 13th inning went over the wall in right-center. "Christopher, who was playing right field at the time, remembered talk that the taller Clemente would have been able to reach Adcock's shot. He dismissed this, saying, 'It was high over the fence. I don't think even [Clemente] could have gotten that ball.'"[2]

However, Joe appeared in just five games before getting hurt himself. Charging in from the terrace at old Crosley Field in Cincinnati, he turned a somersault as he picked off Wally Post's sinking liner. He was sure he had broken the thumb on his glove hand—and when trainer Doc Jorgensen and manager Danny Murtaugh ran out to tend to their player in pain, they found to their annoyance that Doc's medical bag was filled with ham and cheese sandwiches! The prankster was Pirates coach Jimmy Dykes, still into mischief at age 62.[3]

After later injuring his ankle as he hit first base, Christopher returned to Columbus. Manager Cal Ermer greeted him, "Joe, I hate to see you . . . but I'm glad to see you!" That is, Ermer wished that Christopher could have stayed with the big club, but even so, he was happy to use him on his squad.

Christopher, like fellow Virgin Islanders McBean, Plaskett, and Clarke, met his wife while playing in Puerto Rico. He and Ana Solares were married on December 20, 1959. He then returned to the team with which he would earn his World Series title.

With the 1960 champs, Joe was a role player (61 plate appearances, .232 in 50 games). He came north with the Pirates in April but was barely used over the first several weeks of the season. He was sent down to Salt Lake City to see regular action, but the Pirates recalled him in early June, and he stayed on their roster the rest of the year. On August 7 Joe hit his first big-league homer, a three-run smash off San Francisco's Billy O'Dell at Forbes Field.

During the World Series, he pinch-hit or pinch-ran in three games, scoring two runs. Joe decided not to wear his championship ring. This was a show of solidarity with Clemente, his road roommate and friend from Puerto

Rico. Roberto was upset with his embarrassingly low eighth-place finish in the MVP voting that year.[4]

Joe pointed to the goodness of the late Hall of Famer, especially where sick and underprivileged children were concerned. In a characteristic comment, he said, "I really enjoyed the man and appreciated what he had to deal with. Because deep in his heart he was a very, very sensitive, very caring individual. He was always wanting to give other people respect. Clemente, to me, was one of the nicest people I ever met."[5]

Joe also recalled how he, Roberto, Román Mejías, and Gene Baker—two other Pirates of African descent—hung together during spring training in the segregated Florida of those days. The men endured having to wait on the bus as sandwiches were brought out to them, since they could not join their teammates inside restaurants. They roomed in a private home in Fort Myers, Florida, home of the Bucs' camp. Christopher said that as they watched old movies on TV, Clemente formed the idea of what he would eventually do for the youth of Puerto Rico from the Spencer Tracy film Boys Town.

Joe L. Brown, who succeeded Branch Rickey as the Pirates' general manager in 1955, recalled that Christopher "could run like the dickens, was a good outfielder, and a decent hitter." But the Pirates did not regard him as a regular, giving him just 186 at-bats in 76 games in 1961. So Joe got his chance to start in the majors with Casey Stengel's comical crew. He was the Mets' fifth pick in the expansion draft, costing them $75,000.

Still, it took two more seasons before Christopher emerged as a regular. In 1962 he spent April and most of May at Triple-A Syracuse. The prevalent memory of Joe that year is the oft-told "Yo La Tengo" story: The bilingual Caribbean taught center fielder Richie Ashburn how to say "I got it" in Spanish for the benefit of shortstop Elio Chacón—but Richie was then flattened by left fielder Frank Thomas.

Joe started 69 times in 119 games, playing behind Thomas, Ashburn, and Jim Hickman. He was part of a championship team with the Mayagüez Indios in 1962-63, and won the third of his four stolen-base titles in the Puerto Rican Winter League. But again in 1963, he did not make the Mets out of spring training. He played most of the season

at Triple-A Buffalo, and once he was recalled in July, he put up quiet numbers.

But in 1964, Christopher enjoyed easily his finest season as a major-leaguer—still the best by any batter from the Virgin Islands—hitting .300 with 16 homers and 76 RBIs. He had a career-best day on August 19, with two triples, a double, and a homer in an 8-6 win over the Pirates. The credit went to a little 50-cent pamphlet by Hall of Famer Paul Waner. "I saw the ad for the book in The Sporting News and sent away for it. . . . Waner once talked to me in '61 and helped me a lot."[6]

Christopher did not sustain his hitting form in '65. An injured finger set him back in spring training, and the organization was high on rookie Ron Swoboda. Joe was traded to Boston for Eddie Bressoud after that season, and he played briefly in '66 for the Red Sox, going 1-for-13 in 12 games. He was dealt with pitcher Earl Wilson to Detroit, but his big-league career had come to an end—he never played for the Tigers. His final totals in the majors were 29 homers, 173 RBIs, and a .260 average in 638 games across eight seasons. He stole 29 bases and was caught stealing 19 times. Right field was his main position; he appeared 278 times there and 154 times in left. His 52 games in center field may have been what colored Christopher's reputation as an unsteady fielder.

In 1966 he played for the Syracuse Chiefs, Detroit's affiliate. Joe's marriage to Ana ended in divorce that year, not long after he was sold by Syracuse to the Richmond Braves (for whom it does not appear he played). Their three daughters continued to live in Puerto Rico. Christopher stayed active in the minors through 1968. He returned to the Pirates organization the next year, but after playing briefly with Columbus, he joined the Tulsa Oilers, a Cardinals farm club. St. Louis wanted to send him down to Double-A after the 1967 season, so Christopher asked for his release. Then at the urging of a friend, AP writer Joe Reichler, he wrote to all the major-league clubs, hoping to benefit from forthcoming expansion. Paul "The Pope" Owens of the Phillies extended an offer, albeit also at Double-A Reading.

Joe also continued to play in Puerto Rico through the 1968-69 season. He held out in the 1964-65 season and also sat out 1966-67, but was part of two more champion teams in 1967-68 and 1968-69. Christopher finished his

Puerto Rican Winter League career with 37 home runs, 240 RBIs, a .264 average, and 125 stolen bases in 13 seasons. But he still wasn't quite through as a player. In the spring of 1972, at the age of 36, he made a ten-game comeback in Mexico.

After leaving the field, Joe continued to live in New York for some years. Among other things, he worked for an ad agency named Promotions Colorful, holding a vice presidency. In the early '90s, he was married once again. Joe and Karen Matthews Christopher had a daughter named Kameahle. As of 2011, they lived in the Baltimore area.

A big part of Joe always wanted to be a coach. He used to hold forth like a martial arts sensei, talking about hitting to anyone who will listen. He discussed hitting with the innermost elite—Ted Williams, Rogers Hornsby (a '62 Mets coach), and George Sisler (a special instructor with the Pirates—who first met Joe while serving as US high commissioner at the NBC tournament in 1954).

Yet his consuming passion became art, particularly drawing, in a pre-Columbian style, from which he gained patience and concentration. An individual thinker, he enjoyed debate, and his mental and verbal agility made conversation a test. He developed a broad store of

sometimes baffling esoteric knowledge, ranging from Egyptology to numerology. Joe became a great believer in the significance of birthdates, but his insight into human nature prevents you from dismissing it as bunk. In his mid-60s, he said he could still run the 60-yard dash nearly as fast as ever, and who knows, maybe that was because of his focus on the links between body, mind, and spirit. Said Joe in 1999:

"The whole process of nature, it's there, but the Western world don't want to give heed to anything. You're talking about greed. You talk about the Tao, they spell it today D-O-W."

This biography originally appeared on the website Baseball in the Virgin Islands (http://home.roadrunner.com/~vibaseball), from which it has been adapted. Grateful acknowledgment to Joe Christopher for additional personal memories over the years (most recently by telephone on July 3 and October 19, 2007).

Sources

The National Baseball Congress of America, 1955 Official Baseball Annual

Private database of José A. Crescioni, the late SABR member who compiled statistics for the Puerto Rican Winter League.

Professional Baseball Players Database V6.0

Enciclopedia del Béisbol Mexicano

www.baseball-reference.com

www.retrosheet.org

www.ultimatemets.com

Notes

1   Larry Moffi and Jonathan Kronstadt. *Crossing the Line: Black Major Leaguers 1947-1959* (Iowa City, Iowa: University of Iowa Press, 1994), 203.

2   Brian C. Engelhardt, "Former R-Phil's career was work of art," www.readingphillies.com, April 21, 2006.

3   Mike Shannon, *Tales From the Ballpark* (Lincolnwood, Illinois: Contemporary Books, 1999), 54. Story told by bullpen catcher Bob Enochs.

4   Bruce Markusen, *Roberto Clemente: The Great One* (Champaign, Illinois: Sports Publishing Inc.), 105.

5   Ibid., pp. 67-68, 196.

6   Paul Zimmerman, "Mets' Biggest Hit of '64 Season Is Christopher," *New York World-Telegram*, August 19, 1964.

Gino Cimoli

By Alan Cohen

"They set all the records and we won the game"

THAT WAS GINO Cimoli's comment after Game Seven of the 1960 World Series, won in dramatic fashion by the Pittsburgh Pirates when Bill Mazeroski's home run fell over the ivy in left field, as outfielder Yogi Berra of the New York Yankees could only watch.

Cimoli came to the Pirates in a trade before the 1960 season and, although not a star, played an important role as the team marched to its first pennant since 1927 and its first world championship since 1925.

Gino Anichletto Cimoli was born on December 18, 1929, and grew up in the predominantly Italian-American North Beach section of San Francisco. When he was young, the middle name was changed to Nicholas. He was an only child, and he was the center of his parents' lives. Gino's father, Abramo, was a night supervisor for Pacific Gas & Electric and his mother, Stella, worked for the Chase & Sanborn coffee company. Abramo did a bit of everything. He was also a shrimp and crab fisherman and had a sideline making wine. Young Gino would sometimes show up at school with purple feet.[1]

Gino graduated from Galileo High School in January 1948. Known primarily for his basketball and track exploits in high school, he did not play baseball until his senior year. His baseball success was astounding. In his one year of high-school ball he hit .607. After that he appeared in the Hearst Sandlot Classic at New York's Polo Grounds on August 13, 1947, and played left field for the US All-Stars alongside future major leaguers like Moose Skowron (right field) and Dick Groat (second base). The US team defeated the New York team, 13-2. Cimoli went 1-for-2, steal-

ing a base and scoring a run. On the basketball court, he was named the most valuable player in the California North-South game on February 3, 1948, when he led the North team to a 60-44 victory, scoring 15 points. He was offered a basketball scholarship by the University of San Francisco but passed it up, figuring he was too small at 6-feet-1 to make a career out of basketball. Meanwhile, in the summers of 1947 and 1948, he played baseball for the Portola Merchants team in San Francisco.

Late in 1948 scouts Joe Devine of the Yankees and Howie Haak of the Brooklyn Dodgers sought to sign Cimoli. Devine was speaking with Cimoli's mother, and Haak worked on his father. As Haak recounted it, he spent the better part of four days drinking Ancient Age bourbon with Abramo from 8:00 A.M. to 4:00 P.M. Abramo would then work the late shift for PG&E, until midnight. Usually after he got home there were scouts waiting. Finally Haak went into the Cimoli house at 3:00 A.M. and asked Abramo, "Who wears the pants in this family?" In short order, Abramo woke up Stella and Gino, and Cimoli signed with the Dodgers for $15,000.[2]

Cimoli headed for Nashua in the Class B New England League with his new bride, Irene Zinn, who was expecting their first child. The league started the 1948 season with eight clubs. Nashua was in first place in July when the league was forced to condense to four clubs. On July 3 Cimoli was hitting .370 with six triples. With the league in financial trouble, Dodgers boss Branch Rickey began to reassign his top prospects. Cimoli was sent to Triple-A Montreal. In his sixth game with the Royals, he crashed into a wall, injured his knee, and saw limited action, mostly as a pinch-hitter, in the team's remaining games, batting .231 in 15 games. That fall, he was exposed in the draft of unprotected minor leaguers, but there were no takers. In 1950, playing in 85 games for Montreal, Cimoli hit .275. He spent most of 1951 with the Dodgers' Double-A affiliate in Fort Worth, where he hit .262 and tied for the league lead in triples with 12. (A speedster, Cimoli hit more triples than home runs in both the majors and the minors.) On May 10, 1951, he threw out two baserunners in one inning.

Cimoli began the 1952 season with Montreal, but after playing in six games he was sent to the St. Paul Saints, the Dodgers' other Triple-A team, for whom he hit .319 in 142 games. He was invited to spring training with the big-league club in 1953, but was not deemed ready, and it was back to St. Paul, where his average fell to .262. He began the 1954 season back with St. Paul, then was sent to Montreal in May. Manager Max Macon let the frustrated Cimoli pitch in two games. In the first he pitched three perfect innings, but in his second appearance on the hill, he faced five batters, walking the first three, hitting the fourth, and giving up a triple to the fifth. That put an end to his pitching career. Meanwhile his hitting came around and he hit for a .306 average.

After a good spring in 1955, Gino once again found himself in Montreal, as the Dodgers decided on Sandy Amoros as their left fielder. (Duke Snider and Carl Furillo were locked into center and right.) By that time, Cimoli had gotten the unenviable tag of Lackadaisical Latin.[3]

En route to Montreal from San Francisco, Cimoli's wife and two daughters were in a bad automobile accident in Rawlins, Wyoming, when their car collided with a bus. Gino left Montreal on May 12 to join his family. When Cimoli was able to rejoin the Royals, he came back a changed man. He returned to the lineup on May 20, and delivered a home run and a double in a 6-2 win over Toronto.[4] Dodgers general manager Buzzie Bavasi was full of praise, saying of Cimoli, "He's really hustling, and he can just about cover the whole outfield by himself."[5] Cimoli hit .306 for Montreal in 1955, and hopes were high for 1956. But once again he was fighting for a roster position and playing time with Amoros, who had made a game-saving catch to help secure the Dodgers' World Series win in 1955, and Cimoli could no longer be optioned out by the Dodgers. After a good spring, he

finally made it to the Dodgers along with 19-year-old pitcher Don Drysdale.

Cimoli's season was disappointing. He got into only 73 games, often as a defensive replacement. He had just 36 at-bats, getting four hits and a walk. His major-league debut came in the team's second game, a 5-4 win over the Philadelphia Phillies on April 19. The game was played in Jersey City, and Gino entered the game with one out in the tenth inning as a defensive replacement for Junior Gilliam in left field. He got his first hit on April 23 in a 6-1 win over the Phillies in Philadelphia. He had gone in as a defensive replacement for leftfielder Gilliam. In the ninth inning Cimoli singled off the Phillies' Duane Pillette, driving in Carl Furillo. In May Cimoli played some in right field when Carl Furillo was benched. He had his first extra-base hit, a double, off Warren Hacker in a win over the Cubs on May 8. Once Furillo returned to the lineup, Cimoli was used most often as a defensive replacement. His last hit of the year came on July 4.

In the World Series, against the Yankees, Cimoli had one appearance, going into Game Two as a defensive replacement in the Dodgers' 13-8 victory. He never got to bat.

After the season Cimoli went on the Dodgers' tour of Japan. He had not played much in 1956, and his play on the basepaths and in the field had been erratic. Manager Walter Alston felt it might be the time to give him the chance to play regularly. In one game, he scored from second base on a sacrifice fly. That evening, catcher Roy Campanella took Cimoli aside for a chat and told him he had all the tools, but that his attitude had to change. His words, "Stop popping off, stay out of trouble, and play," were taken to heart by Cimoli, and when spring training came in 1957, Cimoli was ready to turn his career around.[6] Indeed, Jackie Robinson said of Cimoli, "Gino (in 1956) seemed more interested in bridge than in baseball. Last year, Gino seemed to be the last man out on the ballfield. This year he's the first."[7] And sure enough, 1957 was a breakout year. Walter Alston found a place in the outfield for Cimoli. Sandy Amoros started less than 60 games in left field, and Junior Gilliam became the everyday second baseman, opening up left field for Cimoli. If he wasn't stationed in left field, he would spell Duke Snider in center or Carl Furillo in right. He hit his first major-league home run on Opening Day, April 16, in Philadelphia, victimizing future Hall of Famer Robin

Roberts with a game-winning blast in the 12th inning as the Dodgers won 7-6. It was his third hit in six at-bats.

Cimoli's second home run, this time in the 14th inning against the Milwaukee Braves on May 6, gave Sandy Koufax, who was pitching in relief, his first victory of the season. It was Cimoli's best game in a Brooklyn Dodgers uniform. He had five hits and scored three of the five Dodger runs. In the bottom of the 12th he helped prolong the game after the Braves had taken a 4-3 lead in the top of the inning. In the Dodger half of the inning, with two outs, Cimoli doubled and scored on a bad hop base hit by Furillo.

Cimoli's average was .314 after the July 4 doubleheader, and he was named to the National League All-Star team by manager Alston. He pinch-hit in the eighth inning and struck out against Billy Pierce.

The Dodgers began the second half of the season in fifth place. On July 12 they moved into fourth place in the closely-bunched standings. Cimoli drove in two runs with a triple as the Dodgers defeated Cincinnati, 3-1. On the 20th he drove in two runs with a double as the Dodgers defeated Chicago, 7-5. By the end of July, the Dodgers were in third place, with four games separating the top five clubs. Cimoli's average had dipped below .300, but he was still making his presence felt. But in August the Braves created some distance between themselves and the rest of the pack. By mid-September, the Dodgers had been effectively eliminated.

When it came down to the last home game, on September 24, the Dodgers planned to move to Los Angeles, and all that was left were the memories. That night, as if it mattered, the Dodgers beat the Pirates, 2-0. Only 6,702 fans were in attendance. Cimoli scored the final Ebbets Field run after reaching on an infield hit. Cimoli finished tied for third in the league with seven game-winning hits. He had 10 home runs, 57 RBIs, and a career-best .293 batting average.

In 1958, their first season in Los Angeles, the Dodgers played in the Los Angeles Coliseum. The Coliseum was essentially a football stadium and as they set it up for baseball, the left-field fence was only 250 feet from home plate. With their right-handed lineup, the Dodgers figured to do well. After breaking camp in Vero Beach,

Florida, the Dodgers headed west. They played an exhibition against the Cubs in Mesa, Arizona, on April 11. In the first inning, Cimoli slid into third base just ahead of the throw from the right fielder. A photographer had taken a picture and asked the third-base coach, Charlie Dressen, the name of the player. Dressen said "Cimoli." The signal for the squeeze play was for the coach to shout out the player's name. Once again, the photographer asked Dressen the name of the player, and this time Dressen yelled, even more loudly, "Cimoli." On the next pitch, with Gil Hodges at the plate, Gino charged for home and was, of course, tagged out. Oops![8]

On April 15 the Dodgers opened their season against the Giants in San Francisco before 23,448 fans (including a large contingent from North Beach rooting for Gino, the hometown kid). Manager Alston inserted Cimoli into the leadoff spot. When he stepped up to the plate in the first inning against Ruben Gomez, he became the first batter for the Dodgers in California. In that first plate appearance, he fouled off the first pitch and eventually struck out. In his last at-bat, he singled, but the Giants won the game, 8-0.

In the second game of the series Cimoli was beaned by Giants pitcher Paul Giel. The scene was so horrifying that Gino's father rushed onto the field, and helped carry his son to the clubhouse.[9] But Cimoli was determined not to miss any action and he connected for his first West Coast home run in the third game. But the Dodgers, beset by age and injuries, skidded to a seventh-place finish. Cimoli's season was disappointing. Due in part to injury and in part to differences with Alston, he had only played in 109 of his team's 154 games and batted .246. After the season he was traded to the St. Louis Cardinals for outfielder Wally Moon and pitcher Phil Paine. Manager Solly Hemus put Cimoli in center field, and he did not disappoint. He exploded out of the gate and in early May was batting .349 with a team-leading 12 doubles, as well as three home runs and 15 RBIs for the last-place Cardinals. He was fined $100 for his role in a brawl on June 7 that was touched off when he charged the mound after a brushback pitch from the Phillies' Don Cardwell. Through June 21 Cimoli was hitting .322 and had a league-leading 28 doubles. A doubleheader sweep on June 28 moved the Cardinals to within four games of .500. In the second game of the twin bill he drove in five runs with two triples and a double. On July 24 he was leading the league with 35 two-baggers. But he faded and finished the season with a .279 batting average with 40 doubles, fourth in the league, and a career-high 72 RBIs

At the end of the season Cimoli was traded to Pittsburgh with pitcher Tom Cheney for Pitcher Ronnie Kline. The Pirates had rarely been in contention over the prior three decades, reaching an all-time low in 1952 (42 victories, 112 defeats). But they had built themselves a solid core, and manager Danny Murtaugh was confident that his team would improve on the prior year's fourth-place finish. He had quality pitching in Vernon Law, Bob Friend, and Harvey Haddix. His infield was solid with Dick Stuart, Bill Mazeroski, Dick Groat, and Don Hoak.

Outfielders Bob Skinner, Bill Virdon, and Roberto Clemente were back, but the Pirates had no serious power threat in spacious Forbes Field. The acquisition of Cimoli did not address that shortcoming. During the offseason, Kansas City had offered Roger Maris to the Bucs, but Murtaugh was reluctant to give Groat in return.[10]

Cimoli showed enough in spring training that Manager Danny Murtaugh chose to platoon Cimoli and Bill Virdon in center field. Cimoli was the Opening Day center fielder against the Braves in Milwaukee against the great southpaw Warren Spahn. Two days later, in the Bucs' home opener, he went 1-for-4 with a key double that drove in two runs in a six-run fifth inning as the Pirates cruised to a 13-0 win. The team got off to a fast start and won 13 of its first 18 games. The team had a blend of veteran clutch performers, including Cimoli, and a bench that included Rocky Nelson, Hal Smith, Dick Schofield, Hal Smith, and Bob Oldis, enough for them to make a serious run at the pennant. Players like Cimoli and Oldis kept the team loose with their undying sense of humor and flair for pranks.[11]

On May 30 Cimoli singled, doubled, and tripled in a win over the Braves to bring the team's record to 26-14, good enough for a half-game lead over the Giants. On June 15 the Bucs pushed the lead to three games, defeating the Giants 14-6. Cimoli had two hits, including a double, and scored three runs in the win. After defeating Cincinnati on July 7, the Bucs had a four game winning streak and led the league by 5½ games. Cimoli's batting average was at .303. They went into the All-Star break with 49

victories. After the All-Star Game, Cimoli saw less playing time. He was slumping at the plate, and Bill Virdon caught fire. He played in right field for six games in early August after Roberto Clemente hurt himself making a spectacular catch on a ball hit by Willie Mays on the 5th. On the 6th Cimoli broke out of a 6-for-40 slump, getting three hits, including a single that ignited a three-run tenth-inning rally as the Bucs won, 8-7. The next day, after a doubleheader sweep of the Giants, the Pirates' lead was 5½ games. In the sweep, Cimoli tripled in each game.

On a mid-August plane trip to Cincinnati, Cimoli threw a pillow and soon the entire team was involved. Then things calmed down and the card games and storytelling began. The team had won 14 of 18 and led the league by 7½ games. On September 25 the Pirates lost at Milwaukee. Cimoli looked at the somber scene in the clubhouse and said, "Somebody dead?" He knew quite well that the Pittsburgh had clinched the pennant. St. Louis had been eliminated, losing to Chicago. So Cimoli, having been on a pennant winner in 1956 with the Dodgers, was quick to begin the celebration. He created one of the more memorable images when he took the hat of Pittsburgh Press sportswriter Les Biederman, doused it with champagne and wore the hat, inside out, for the bulk of the celebration, even wearing it in the shower. [12]

Playing in 101 games (307 at-bats), Cimoli finished the season with a .267 batting average, but had no home runs and drove in only 28 runs.

In the World Series, Cimoli was slated to play left field against the Yankees' left-handers, with Bob Skinner to face the righties. Virdon would have center field to himself. Cimoli got more playing time than expected after Skinner jammed his thumb sliding in Game One, which the Pirates won, 6-4. In Game Two, with the Pirates trailing 3-0, Cimoli led off the fourth inning with a single and scored on a double by Hoak. But the Yankees won easily, 16-3. Game Three was another Yankees romp, this time 10-0.

The Pirates evened the Series with a 3-2 victory in Game Four. Cimoli went 1-for-4. He singled in the fifth and advanced to second, then scored on a double by Law, tying the game at 1-1. The Pirates took the Series lead in Game Five, beating the Yankees 5-2. Cimoli went hitless but scored a second-inning run after reaching on a force play. Game Six was another blowout for the Yankees, 12-0 behind Whitey Ford. After the game, Dick Groat, noting the three lopsided Yankees wins, said, "The Yankees win them big, but we bounced back after those two earlier losses. We'll bounce back again tomorrow."[13]

Cimoli did not start Game Seven. Skinner's thumb was better and he got the start in left field at Forbes Field against Yankees right-hander Bob Turley. The Pirates jumped to a four-run lead by the end of the second inning, and the Yanks brought in Bobby Shantz to pitch in the third inning. Shantz pitched five brilliant innings, holding the Bucs scoreless, and the Yankees built a 7-4 lead going into the bottom of the eighth. Leading off, Cimoli pinch-hit for pitcher Elroy Face and singled to right. Bill Virdon hit a hard double-play grounder to the Yankees' shortstop, Tony Kubek. But the ball took a bad bounce and struck Kubek in the throat. Both runners were safe. The Pirates went on to score five runs. Cimoli scored on a single by Groat.[14] Clemente singled in a run, then catcher Hal Smith hit a three-run homer, giving Pittsburgh a 9-7 lead going into the ninth inning. In the elation that followed Smith's home run, Abramo Cimoli threw his coat, hat and glasses into the air. All were retrieved.[15]

The Yankees came back with two runs in the top of the ninth inning, and the Pirates came to bat in the bottom of the inning with the score tied. Cimoli, who was no longer in the game, had gone to the clubhouse. When the Yankees tied the game, he was so angry that he picked up the television in the clubhouse and threw it against the wall.[16] His anger was an afterthought when Mazeroski led off the bottom of the ninth and smashed a pitch from Ralph Terry over the left-field wall to give the Pirates the world championship.

Cimoli wasn't with the Pirates much longer. In early May 1961 he injured his rib cage when he was hit by a batted ball during pregame warmups, and missed a few games. At the June 15 trading deadline, he was dealt to Milwaukee for shortstop Johnny Logan. The Bucs saw the versatile Logan as a backup for Groat and Hoak on the left side of the infield. They had, in Joe Christopher a 25-year-old player (Cimoli was 31 at the time) who had distinguished himself during his apprenticeship at Salt Lake City and Columbus, batting .317 with 283 hits in 893 at bats. With Milwaukee, Cimoli contributed one of his team's five home runs in an 8-6 defeat of the Giants on June 22, and

followed that up with three hits in a 13-4 trouncing of the Cubs two days later. Cimoli stayed hot with another two hits as the Braves beat the Cards, 9-6, on June 26. But Cimoli was not able to keep up the momentum. His average had dropped from .296 at the time of the trade to .246 on July 8, and the Braves called up Mack Jones. Gino's playing time dropped sharply, but he had one special game. On August 11 the Braves' Warren Spahn won his 300th game, and Cimoli's his third home run of the season, in the eighth inning, was the deciding blow in the 2-1 victory. With one out in the ninth inning he made a diving catch of a drive hit by the Cubs' Jerry Kendall.

For all his heroics, Cimoli batted only .197 with three home runs and 10 RBIs for the Braves, and it was not surprising that he was put into the pool of players eligible to be selected by the expansion Mets and Colts. He was not taken, and the Braves sent him to Vancouver of the Pacific Coast League. But then in the postseason draft, Cimoli was selected by the Kansas City Athletics, and experienced a revival. On Opening Day, his three-run homer keyed a 4-2 win over the Twins. In a doubleheader sweep against Chicago on April 22, Cimoli had his best day ever, driving in 10 runs with a double, a triple, and two home runs. On April 27 he had five hits as the A's beat the Baltimore Orioles, 14-5. Two doubles and a triple led the Athletics over the Tigers on May 2. As May came to a close, Cimoli was fourth in the league in RBIs, with 31, more than he had hit in either of the previous two seasons.

As the season wore on, the A's fell back and assumed their customary place in the second division (ninth place in the ten-team league). But Cimoli's numbers for the year were his best since 1959. As the A's everyday right fielder, he had career highs in games played and at-bats, and finished with a .275 batting average. His career-best 15 triples were good enough to lead the league. His 10 home runs matched his 1957 output with Brooklyn and his 71 RBIs were one shy of his career best.

In 1963 the A's once again got off to a good start, but after reality set in they finished in eighth place. It was another good season for Cimoli. He hit .263 and was fourth in the league with 11 triples. Cimoli had two of his most productive seasons playing for Kansas City in 1962 and 1963. His 26 triples over the two seasons topped all other major leaguers. But 1964 started out poorly. The A's were going for youth and Tommie Reynolds took over as the everyday right fielder. Appearing in only his fourth game of the season on May 2, Cimoli injured a tendon running to first base. He was released on May 29. At 34, Cimoli was nearing the end of his major-league career. He signed on with Baltimore, but batted only .138, playing in parts of 38 games with eight hits in 58 at-bats. In late July the Orioles assigned Cimoli to their Rochester Triple-A farm club. He played well for Rochester, hitting .315 in 45 games with four homers and 23 RBIs. In 1965, after being released by the Orioles, he signed with the California Angels but played in only four games, going hitless in five at-bats. He was released on May 9 and finished up with Spokane in the Pacific Coast League, where the manager was his old Dodger teammate Duke Snider. He got into 33 games but was hitting just .235 when Spokane released him on June 25.

Cimoli batted .265 in the major leagues with 44 home runs. Few contemporaries, however, could match his achievements in the realm of the three-base hit. He had 48 triples in the majors and, including his minor league numbers, he had 98 triples as a professional.

Toward the end of his career as a player, Cimoli worked part-time for UPS. After his playing days, he worked full-time, delivering to his native North Beach section of San Francisco. In 1989 he retired and was honored for completing his years with the company without an accident. He was known as the "Iron Man" of UPS.

On occasion Cimoli was reunited with old teammates. The Pirates reassembled the 1960 team on July 6, 1985, and the Giants re-enacted the 1958 opening pitch at the beginning of their 40th season in San Francisco on April 1, 1997. On April 15, 2008, he threw out the ceremonial first pitch commemorating the 50th anniversary of the first West Coast game.

On October 17, 1989, Cimoli and a friend, Ed Silva, went for coffee after Gino completed his shift at UPS. Then the rumbling began, as San Francisco experienced one of its more turbulent earthquakes. Cimoli and Silva ran out into the street and the UPS truck became an ambulance. They checked houses along the street. In one house Cimoli rescued a woman who had been trapped on the third floor. He helped out other victims as well, traveling throughout the Marina area.[17]

Cimoli served a term as president of the San Francisco Italian Athletic Club (2001-2002), and in his later years could always be found there at the card table. With his trademark unlit cigar dangling from his mouth, he was always outspoken and friendly with everyone. He often emceed at the annual fund-raiser for the Friends of Marino Pieretti Charitable Organization.

Cimoli died on February 12, 2011, at the age of 81. Two weeks later Duke Snider died. Even on heaven's baseball team, it would seem, Gino Cimoli would be struggling for playing time, or going in as a late-inning replacement. This may have prompted him to say, "Play me or trade me" one last time.

Sources

Books:

Lawrence Baldassaro. *Beyond DiMaggio: Italian-Americans in Baseball.* (Lincoln: University of Nebraska Press, 2011).

Buzzie Bavasi. *Off the Record.* (Chicago, Contemporary Books, 1987).

Jim Brosnan. *The Long Season.* (New York: Harper 1960).

Rick Cushing. *1960 Pittsburgh Pirates: Day by Day, A Special Season, An Extraordinary World Series.* (Pittsburgh: Dorrance Publishing Company, 2010).

Steve Daly, *Dem Little Bums: The Nashua Dodgers.* (Concord, New Hampshire: Plaidswede Publishing Co., 2003).

Brian M. Endsley. *Bums No More The 1959 Los Angeles Dodgers.* (Jefferson, North Carolina: McFarland and Company, 2009).

Carl Erskine. *Tales from the Dodger Dugout.* (Champaign, Illinois: Sports Publishing, Inc., 2000).

Carl Erskine. *Tales from the Dugout: Extra Innings.* (Champaign, Illinois: Sports Publishing, Inc., 2004).

Lew Freedman. *Hard-Luck Harvey Haddix and the Greatest Game Ever Lost.* (Jefferson, North Carolina: McFarland and Company, 2009).

Andrew Goldblatt. *The Giants and the Dodgers: Four Cities, Two Teams, One Rivalry.* (Jefferson, North Carolina: McFarland and Company, 2003).

Roger Kahn. *The Era: 1947-1957: When the Yankees, the Giants, and the Dodgers Ruled the World* (New York, Ticknor and Fields, 1993).

Kevin Kerrane. *Dollar Sign on the Muscle: The World of Baseball Scouting.* (New York:Beaufort Books, 1984).

Neil Lanctot. *Campy, The Two Lives of Roy Campanella.* (New York: Simon and Schuster, 2011).

David Maraniss. *Clemente, The Passion and Grace of Baseball's Last Hero.* (New York: Simon and Schuster, 2006).

Rudy Marzano. *The Last Years of the Brooklyn Dodgers: A History: 1950-1957*. (Jefferson, North Carolina: McFarland and Company, 2008).

Bob Morales. *Farewell to the Last Golden Era: The Yankees, the Pirates, and the 1960 Baseball Season*. (Jefferson, North Carolijna: McFarland and Company, 2011).

Robert E. Murphy. *After Many a Summer: The Passing of the Giants and Dodger and a Golden Age in New York Baseball*. (New York: Union Square Press, 2009).

John R. Nordell. *Brooklyn Dodgers: The Last Great Pennant Drive, 1957*. (Eynon, Pennsylvania: Tribute Books, 2007).

Jim Reisler. *The Best Game Ever: Pirates vs. Yankees, October 13, 1960*. (New York: Carroll and Graf, 2007).

Michael Shapiro. *Bottom of the Ninth: Branch Rickey, Casey Stengel, and the Daring Scheme to Save Baseball From Itself*. (New York: Holt, 2009).

Duke Snider. *The Duke of Flatbush*. (New York: Zebra Books, Kensington Publishing Company, 1988).

Newspapers and magazines:

Bob Broeg. *St. Louis Post Dispatch*, March 30, 1959.

Otto Bruno. Blog under name of The Old Ball Game, on July 21, 2010.

Barbara Cloud. "They're Pennant Fever Veterans—Irene Cimoli Used to Jitters." *Pittsburgh Press*, August 16, 1960.

Arthur Daley. Sports of the Times, "Campy was Right." *New York Times*, September 1, 1957.

John Drebinger. "Dodgers' Travels Prove Rewarding." *New York Times*, June 11, 1957.

Tom Fitzgerald. "Gino Cimoli Can Still Deliver the Goods." *San Francisco Chronicle*, May 7, 1990.

Michael Gaven. "Brooklyn's Best Left Fielder since Medwick." *Baseball Digest*, September 1957.

Sandy Grady. *Philadelphia Evening Bulletin*, June 8, 1959.

John Jeansome. "Black and White and Dodger Blue." *Newsday*, May 5, 2000. Story about Nashua Dodgers, 1946-1949.

Walter Judge. "L.A. Centerfield job for Cimoli." *San Francisco Examiner*, February 10, 1958.

Leonard Koppett. "Pasta e Fagioli and Baseball." *New York Times*, April 12, 1976.

Jack McDonald. "Both Barrels." *San Francisco Call Bulletin*, January 7, 1958.

Neal Russo. "Cimoli first tried baseball to avoid gym workouts." *St. Louis Post Dispatch*, April 28, 1959.

Bob Stevens. "Cimoli Blessed That He's a Cardinal." *San Francisco Chronicle*, December 27, 1958.

David Tobener. Blog under name of GoldenGateGiants, February 15, 2011.

Interviews:

Bob Tobener

Lorraine Vigli

Joe Christopher

Websites:

www.Baseball-Almanac.com

www.baseball-reference.com

www.baseball-fever.com

www.baseballlibrary.com

www.retrosheet.org

Notes

1   Interview with Lorraine Vigli.

2   Kevin Kerrane, *Dollar Sign on the Muscle: The World of Baseball Scouting*. (New York: Beaufort Books, 1984), 81-82

3   *Sports Illustrated*, April 13, 1959. The term was used to describe Cimoli in a preseason preview of the Cardinals.

4   *Montreal Gazette*, May 12, 1955, 21; May 14, 1955, 8; May 17, 1955, 25

5   Dink Carroll, *Montreal Gazette*, May 25, 1955, 22

6   *Sports Illustrated*, March 31, 1958. See also Neil Lanctot. *Campy, The Two Lives of Roy Campanella*. (New York: Simon and Schuster, 2011), 354.

7   Robinson quote is from "Frustration Days Over for Brooklyn's Cimoli." *Milwaukee Journal*, April 19, 1957, 26

8   *New York Times*, April 13, 1958

9   Andrew Goldblatt. *The Giants and the Dodgers: Four Cities, Two Teams, One Rivalry*. (Jefferson, North Carolina: McFarland and Company, 2003), 163

10   Jim Reisler. *The Best Game Ever: Pirates vs. Yankees, October 13, 1960*. (New York: Carroll and Graf, 2007), 57. Clemente and Cimoli had been teammates at Montreal, in the Dodgers organization, in 1954. There is an interesting story in David Maraniss. *Clemente, The Passion and Grace of Baseball's Last Hero*. (New York: Simon and Schuster, 2006), 53-56.

11   Reisler, 117, 118

12   Reisler, xxii

13   "Pirates Praise Ford but Are Still Confident." *Lodi News Sentinel*, October 13, 1960, 17

14   Reisler, 187-188

15   Reisler, 197.

16   The story of Cimoli trashing the television set came from an obituary for Willard G. Bellows that appeared in the *Pittsburgh Post-Gazette* on February 10, 1993.

17   Information came from Tom Fitzgerald. "Gino Cimoli Can Still Deliver the Goods," *San Francisco Chronicle*, May 7, 1990, and interview with Lorraine Vigli.

Roberto Clemente

By Stew Thornley

ROBERTO CLEMENTE'S GREATNESS transcended the diamond. On it, he was electrifying with his penchant for bad-ball hitting, his strong throwing arm from right field, and the way he played with a reckless but controlled abandon. Off it, he was a role model to the people of his homeland and elsewhere. Helping others represented the way Clemente lived. It would also represent the way he died.

Jackie Robinson's breaking of the color barrier opened the way not just for African Americans in organized baseball but to many others whose skin color had excluded them. By the 1960s Clemente had emerged as one of the best of the players from Latin America.

Clemente came from Puerto Rico, which had established its own baseball history extending back to the late 1800s, at about the same time that the island became a possession of the United States.[1] Puerto Rico shares its love of baseball with many of the countries in and along the Caribbean Sea. Professional leagues formed and thrived in the winter in these areas, including Venezuela, Mexico, and the Dominican Republic.

Puerto Rico has produced many great players, such as Pedro "Perucho" Cepeda—because he was black, Perucho never got to play in the major leagues in the United States. His son Orlando did and eventually made the Hall of Fame.

The greatest Puerto Rican player, however, was Roberto Clemente.

Roberto Clemente Walker was born on August 18, 1934, to Melchor Clemente and Luisa Walker de Clemente in Carolina, which is slightly east of the Puerto Rican capital of San Juan. Roberto was the youngest of Luisa's seven children (three of whom were from a previous marriage).[2]

Melchor was a foreman overseeing sugar-cane cutters. He also used his truck to help a construction company deliver sand and gravel to building sites. Luisa was a laundress and worked in different jobs to assist the workers at the sugar-cane plantation. Roberto contributed to the family income by helping his dad load shovels into the construction trucks. He also earned money by doing various jobs for neighbors, such as carrying milk to the country store. Roberto used his money to buy a bike and to purchase rubber balls. He liked to squeeze the balls to strengthen his hands.[3] Many people commented on the size of young man's hands. He had strong hands, and it was clear at an early age that he had athletic ability.

Roberto had not just ability but a deep love of sports, especially baseball. He attended games in the winter and watched the star players from the United States mainland. One of his favorites was Monte Irvin. Irvin played for the Newark Eagles in the Negro National League in the summer and for the San Juan Senadores of the Puerto Rican League in the winter. Irvin remembers kids hanging around the stadium. "We'd give them our bags so they could take them in and get in for free," he said. Irvin didn't know Clemente was among the kids until Clemente told him years later, when both were in the major leagues. Clemente also told Irvin that he was impressed with his throwing arm. "I had the best arm in Puerto Rico," said Irvin. "He loved to see me throw. He found that he would practice and learn how to throw like I did."[4] Roberto began playing baseball himself. He wrote in his journal, "I loved the game so much that even though our playing field was muddy and we had many trees on it, I used to play many hours every day. The fences were about 150 feet away from home plate, and I used to hit many homers. One day I hit ten home runs in a game we started about 11 a.m. and finished about 6:30 p.m."[5]

When he was 14 years old Roberto joined a softball team organized by Roberto Marín, who became very influential in Clemente's life. Marín noticed Roberto's strong throwing arm and began using him at shortstop. He eventually moved him to the outfield. Regardless of the position he played, Roberto was sensational. "His name became known for his long hits to right field, and for his sensational catches," said Marín. "Everyone had their eyes on him."[6]

Roberto also participated in the high jump and javelin throw at Vizcarrondo High School in Carolina.[7] It was thought that he might even be good enough to represent Puerto Rico in the Olympics. Throwing the javelin strengthened his arm and helped him in other ways, according to one of his biographers, Bruce Markusen: "The footwork, release, and general dynamics employed in throwing the javelin coincided with the skills needed to throw a baseball properly. The more that Clemente threw the javelin, the better and stronger his throwing from the outfield became."[8]

Roberto said that throwing the javelin in high school was only part of the reason he developed a strong arm. "My mother has the same kind of an arm, even today at 74," in said in a 1964 interview. "She could throw a ball from second base to home plate with something on it. I got my arm from my mother."[9]

Although he had great all-around athletic ability, Roberto decided to focus on baseball, even though it meant forgoing any dreams of participating in the Olympics. He began playing for a strong amateur team, the Juncos Mules.

In 1952, Clemente took part in a tryout camp in Puerto Rico that was attended by scout Al Campanis of the Brooklyn Dodgers. Clemente impressed Campanis with his different skills, including his speed. The Dodgers did not sign Clemente then, but Campanis kept him in mind.

Also in 1952, Clemente caught the eye of Pedrín Zorrilla, who owned the Santurce Cangrejeros, or Crabbers, of the Puerto Rican League. The Juncos team was to play the

Manatí Athenians in Manatí, where Zorrilla had a house on the beach. Roberto Marín advised Zorrilla to go to the game. Afterward, Zorrilla offered Clemente a contract to play with the Cangrejeros.

Clemente was barely 18 years old when he joined the Cangrejeros. As a young and developing player, he was brought along slowly by the team's manager, Buzz Clarkson. Clarkson had had an outstanding career in the Negro Leagues in the United States and played many winters in Puerto Rico. Like many great black players, Clarkson's best years were behind him by the time he got his chance to play in the majors in 1952 at the age of 37. Two other such players were Willard "Ese Hombre" Brown and Bob Thurman, who were top hitters in the Negro Leagues. Both were outfielders (with Thurman also doing some pitching) on the Santurce team that Clemente joined in the winter of 1952-53.

"Clemente looked up to Bob Thurman," wrote Thomas Van Hyning. "Clemente pinch-hit for Thurman in a key situation and doubled off Caguas's Roberto Vargas to win the game, earning congratulations from Thurman."[10] Despite the big hit, Clemente did not play much his first winter in the Puerto Rican League.

He began playing more in 1953-54 and even played in the league's All-Star Game. (The star of the All-Star Game was Henry Aaron of the Caguas Criollos, who had four hits, including two home runs, and drove in five runs.) By midseason, Clemente's name was appearing along with Aaron's in the list of the Puerto Rican league leaders in batting average. Clemente finished the season with a .288 batting average, sixth best in the league.

The Brooklyn Dodgers had remembered Clemente from the tryout he had had in front of Al Campanis in 1952.[11] Buzzie Bavasi, the Dodgers' vice president, said that during the 1953-54 season a scout in Puerto Rico told him the Dodgers could sign Clemente.[12] Other major-league teams had noticed Clemente, too. One was the New York Giants, the Dodgers' great rivals. Brooklyn outbid the Giants and Clemente agreed to sign. The Milwaukee Braves also made an offer, one that was reportedly much more than the Dodgers', but Clemente stuck with his decision.[13] He knew that New York City had a large Puerto Rican population and looked forward to playing there.

On February 19, 1954, Clemente signed a contract with the Dodgers, who had to make a decision on what to do with him. The Dodgers had signed him for a reported salary of $5,000 as well as a bonus of $10,000.[14] Rules of the time required a team signing a player for a bonus and salary of more than $4,000 to keep him on the major league roster for two years or risk losing him in the offseason draft.[15] Many bonus players of this period were kept at the major-league level, pining on the bench for two years rather than developing in the minors. The Dodgers chose to have Clemente spend the 1954 season with the Montreal Royals in the International League, even though it meant they might lose him at the end of the season.

Buzzie Bavasi had the power to determine Clemente's fate. In 1955, Bavasi told Pittsburgh writer Les Biederman that the Dodgers' only purpose in signing Clemente was to keep him away from the Giants, even though they knew they would eventually lose him to another team.[16] Some writers said an informal quota system was in effect in the early years following the breaking of baseball's color barrier, but this is not supported by the facts.[17] In his biography of Clemente, Kal Wagenheim wrote that the Dodgers would never start all five of their black players in the same game. The box scores prove that is false. (There are other reasons to question the existence of a quota, although it is beyond the realm of this article to fully explore the issue.)[18]

In a 2005 e-mail message to the author, Bavasi wrote that while there was no quota system, race was the factor in the club's decision to have Clemente play in Montreal: "The concern had nothing to do with quotas, but the thought was too many minorities might be a problem with the white players. Not so, I said. Winning was the important thing. I agree with the [Dodgers'] board that we should get a player's opinion and I would be guided by the player's opinion. The board called in Jackie Robinson. Hell, now I felt great. Jackie was told the problem and after thinking about it awhile, he asked me who would be sent out if Clemente took one of the spots. I said George Shuba. Jackie agreed that Shuba would be the one to go. Then he said Shuba was not among the best players on the club, but he was the most popular. With that he shocked me by saying, and I quote: 'If I were the GM, I would not bring Clemente to the club and send Shuba or any other white

player down. If I did this, I would be setting our program back five years.'"[19]

So Clemente went to Montreal to play for manager Max Macon. Most accounts say the Dodgers were trying to "hide" Clemente in Montreal by playing him rarely, hoping that other teams wouldn't notice him and wouldn't draft him at the end of the season.

Several biographers, among them Phil Musick, Kal Wagenheim, and Bruce Markusen, provide examples to back up the contention that Clemente was hidden. However, a game-by-game check of Montreal's 1954 season indicates that many of the examples are incorrect.[20]

Wagenheim and Markusen go so far as to claim that Clemente did not play in the Royals' final 25 games of the season, another claim that is not correct. In fact, by the final part of the season, Clemente was playing regularly against left-handed starting pitchers.[21]

Montreal manager Max Macon, until his death in 1989, denied that he was under any orders to restrict Clemente's playing time. "The only orders I had were to win and draw big crowds," Macon said.[22]

It is true that Clemente, after an initial period when he was being platooned over the first 13 games of the season, played little over the first three months of the season. This was hardly unusual for a 19-year-old in his first season of organized baseball.

Also, for much of the year, the Royals had a full crop of reliable outfielders in Dick Whitman, Gino Cimoli, and Jack Cassini. In addition, the Dodgers sent Sandy Amoros down to Montreal early in the season, and Amoros hit well enough for the Royals that he was recalled by Brooklyn in July. The crowded outfield situation didn't leave a lot of playing time for a newcomer like Clemente. He was often used as a late-inning defensive replacement for Cassini.

When he did play, he struggled. In early July his batting average was barely over .200. Part of that may be attributed to his infrequent playing time; it's hard for a batter to get in a groove and hit well when he doesn't play regularly. On the other hand, it's hard for a player to get regular playing time if he's not hitting well.

Macon said he didn't use Clemente much because he "swung wildly," especially at pitches that were outside of the strike zone: "If you had been in Montreal that year, you wouldn't have believed how ridiculous some pitchers made him look."[23] Clemente got more chances against left-handed pitchers. Macon was known for platooning, and Clemente often split time in the lineup with Whitman, a left-handed hitter.

Through June and July Clemente often went long stretches without seeing any action. Then, on July 25, he entered the first game of a doubleheader against the Havana Sugar Kings in the ninth inning. The game was tied and went into extra innings. With one out in the last of the 10th, Clemente hit a home run to win it for the Royals.

Macon rewarded him by starting him in the second game of the doubleheader, Clemente's first start in nearly three weeks. For the rest of the season Clemente started every game in which the opposition started a left-handed pitcher. He had a few more highlights during this time. Near the end of July, he came to bat in the top of the ninth inning of a scoreless game in Toronto. Clemente doubled and went on to score to put Montreal ahead. The Royals won the game, 2-0.

The next time the Royals were in Toronto, three weeks later, Clemente helped them win in a different way. Montreal had an 8-7 lead over the Maple Leafs in the bottom of the ninth. Toronto had a chance to tie the score, but Clemente threw out a runner at home plate to end the game.

Late in August he had two triples and a single at Richmond, although the Royals still lost the game. A week later he hit a home run to win the game for Montreal and give the Royals a sweep of a doubleheader against Syracuse.

Teammate Jack Cassini said, "You knew he was going to play in the big leagues. He had a great arm and he could run."[24] When Clemente began playing regularly against left-handers, the Royals rose in the standings and finished in second place. Clemente batted .257 in 87 games in his only season in the minors.

By the end of the 1954 season, it had become clear to Bavasi and the rest of the Brooklyn organization that other teams were interested in Clemente. However, Bavasi said he still wasn't ready to give up. The Pirates, by having the worst record in the majors in 1954, had the first pick in the November draft. If Bavasi could get the

Pirates to draft a different player off the Montreal roster, Clemente would remain with the Dodgers organization. Each minor-league team could lose only one player.

Bavasi said he went to Branch Rickey, who had run the Dodgers before going to Pittsburgh. After Bavasi declined Rickey's offer to join him in Pittsburgh, Bavasi said, Rickey told him that, "Should I need help at anytime, all I had to do was pick up the phone." Bavasi said he used this offer to get Rickey to agree draft a different player, pitcher John Rutherford, off the Royals' roster. However, Bavasi was dismayed to learn two days later that the deal was off and that the Pirates were going to draft Clemente. "It seemed that [Dodgers owner] Walter O'Malley and Mr. Rickey got in another argument and it seems Walter called Mr. Rickey every name in the book," explained Bavasi. "Thus, we lost Roberto."[25]

When he was drafted by Pittsburgh, Clemente was in Puerto Rico playing for the Santurce Cangrejeros and on his way to his best-ever winter season. He again played with Bob Thurman, but the Santurce outfield had a new addition in 1954-55. It was Willie Mays, who had just led the New York Giants to the World Series championship and was named the National League's Most Valuable Player. An outfield of Clemente, Mays, and Thurman ranks as one of the best ever in the Puerto Rican League. By mid-season Santurce manager Herman Franks was calling Clemente "the best player in the league, except for Willie Mays."[26]

Clemente and Mays had been providing some real highlights. In late November, the Cangrejeros were behind by a run going into the ninth inning of a game against Caguas-Guyama. Clemente led off the ninth with a single, and Mays then hit a two-run homer to give Santurce a 7-6 win. Not long after that, the pair starred in another 7-6 win. Mays hit two home runs and Clemente one home run in an 11-inning win over Mayaguez.

Both players homered in the league's All-Star Game on December 12, leading their North team to a 7-5 win. By this time, Mays, Clemente, and Thurman were the top three players in the league in batting average, and Santurce moved into first place.[27]

While things were going well on the baseball diamond, there were other problems for Clemente. On New Year's

Eve of 1954, one of his brothers, Luis, died of a brain tumor. Shortly before that, Clemente had been in a car accident that damaged some of his spinal discs. The back injury hampered him for the rest of his baseball career.[28]

Back on the field, Santurce finished first in the Puerto Rican League. The top three teams advanced to the playoffs, so the Cangrejeros had to win another series to capture the league title. They did that, defeating Caguas-Guayama four games to one. Clemente had four hits, including two doubles, and drove in four runs in the first game of the series, which Santurce won. Caguas-Guayama won the next game, but the Cangrejeros then won three in a row to finish the series. As champions of the Puerto Rican League, they advanced to the Caribbean Series.

The Caribbean Series was played in Caracas, Venezuela, in February of 1955. In addition to Santurce, teams from Cuba, Panama, and Venezuela participated. It was a double round-robin tournament. The team with the best record at the end would be the champion.

The Cangrejeros won their first two games and then faced Magallanes of Venezuela. The game went into extra innings. Clemente singled to open the last of the 11th inning, and Mays followed with a home run to win the game, 4-2.

One more win would clinch at least a tie for the title for Santurce. The Cangrejeros' fourth game was a rematch against Almendares of Cuba, a team they had defeated in their first game. Almendares opened up a 5-0 lead, but Santurce battled back to win. Clemente drove in two runs to help in the comeback.

Santurce played Carta Vieja of Panama with a chance for the championship. Clemente had a triple as the Cangrejeros scored three times in the top of the first. In the third, Clemente had another triple as Santurce scored four runs to take a 7-0 lead. Santurce won the game, 11-3, to wrap up the championship.

It was the second Caribbean Series title for Santurce in three years. Clemente had been a part of the team that had won the championship in 1953, but he did not play in the series. This time he was a key member of the team that won. Santurce shortstop Don Zimmer, who was voted the Most Valuable Player of the Caribbean Series, said, "It might have been the best winter club ever assembled."[29]

Soon afterward, Clemente was in training camp with the Pittsburgh Pirates, hoping to earn a spot in the major leagues. The Pirates had been keeping an eye on Clemente over the winter. Rickey said, "He can run, throw, and hit. He needs much polishing, though, because he is a rough diamond."[30]

The Pirates were loaded with outfielders when they began spring training in Florida in March of 1955. Clemente would have plenty of competition for a spot on the team. After the first week of training camp, Clemente earned some good words from Pirates manager Fred Haney. "The boy has the tools, there's no doubt about that. And he takes to instruction readily. Certainly I have been pleased with what I have seen," Haney said. "He has some faults, which were expected, but let's wait and see."[31]

Clemente's chances were helped when Frank Thomas, the Pirates' best outfielder, held out for more money and missed the first part of spring training. Thomas then got sick and missed more time. Clemente took advantage of this opportunity and made the team.[32]

Clemente's original number with the Pirates was 13, but early in the season he switched to 21, a number that became strongly associated with him. It is reported that Clemente chose the number because his full name, Roberto Clemente Walker, has 21 letters.[33]

Clemente didn't play in the first three regular season games. However, he was in the starting lineup, playing right field, for the first game of a doubleheader on Sunday, April 17, 1955, against the Brooklyn Dodgers at Forbes Field in Pittsburgh. Clemente came to the plate with two out in the bottom of the first inning for his first at-bat in the major leagues. He hit a ground ball toward the shortstop, Pee Wee Reese. Reese got his glove on the grounder, but he couldn't field it cleanly. Clemente had his first hit. He followed that by scoring his first run to give Pittsburgh a 1-0 lead. However, Brooklyn came back to win the game.

Clemente started the second game of the doubleheader, this time in center field and batting leadoff. He had a double, but the Pirates were unable to score and trailed the Dodgers, 3-0, going into the last of the eighth. Clemente got another hit, a single, as part of a two-run rally that closed the gap, but the Pirates still lost.

In Pittsburgh's next game, in New York against the Giants, Clemente hit an inside-the-park homer, but the Pirates lost again. At this point, their won-lost record was 0-6. Pittsburgh lost two more games before winning its first of the season. The Pirates went on to finish in last place in the National League for the fourth year in a row. However, Branch Rickey insisted that young players such as Clemente would help turn the team around.

Early in the 1955 season, the new players were leading the Pirates' offense. Clemente was leading the team in batting average over the first three weeks. On the base paths he was even more exciting. "When he starts moving around the bases he draws the 'Ohs' and 'Ahs' of the folks in the ball park," wrote Jack Hernon in *The Sporting News*.

Hernon added, "The fleet Puerto Rican was a stickout on defense."[34] Forbes Field, the home of the Pirates, was a classic ball park that had opened in 1909. The outfield fence was a brick wall. It was only 300 feet from home plate to the wall down the right-field line. But the wall jutted out and changed directions. Clemente learned the angles and how to play balls that caromed off the fence. He could corral long hits quickly and, with his great arm, opposing baserunners were careful on trying to take an extra base.

Less than a third of the way through the season, Clemente already had 10 assists, and he also made some outstanding catches. "The Pittsburgh fans have fallen in love with his spectacular fielding and his deadly right arm," wrote Les Biederman, a reporter who covered the Pirates.[35]

Clemente's rambunctious style in the field could be costly, though. In May, he made a nice catch in St. Louis, but he hurt his finger and ran into the wall. The injury caused him to miss a few games.

Clemente's hitting slumped as the season went along, in part because he still had trouble laying off pitches that were out of the strike zone. However, he became known as a good "bad-ball hitter," able to make good contact on bad pitches. Jack Cassini, who had played in the minors with Clemente the year before, said, "He could hit. He didn't need a strike. The best way to pitch him was right down the middle of the plate."[36]

Clemente played 124 games for the Pirates in 1955 and had a batting average of .255. He walked only 18 times.

Drawing bases on balls would never become a strong point for him. While it wasn't a sensational rookie season, Clemente had earned a spot in the Pirates' outfield. More than that, his exciting style of play made the fans look forward to seeing more of him.

Clemente returned to Puerto Rico in the fall of 1955. It had been reported that he might not play winter ball in his homeland and instead would begin college and study engineering.[37] However, Clemente ended up back on the diamond, playing another season for Santurce.

Back on the mainland in 1956, Clemente had a new boss in Pittsburgh. Bobby Bragan had taken over as manager from Fred Haney. Bragan appeared to be well-liked by the players, although he quickly demonstrated his strictness. In the second game of the season, Clemente missed a signal for a bunt and Bragan fined him.[38] He also fined another player, Dale Long. Biographer Kal Wagenheim wrote, "This harsh action worked like a shot of adrenalin. The club was soon fighting for first place in the league. Dale Long hit eight home runs in as many games. Clemente moved his batting average up to .348, fourth best in the league."[39]

The Pirates were in first place in mid-June, but an eight-game losing streak dropped them to fifth and ended their pennant hopes. Even so, they avoided last place for the first time since 1951 and they were showcasing one of the major league's most exciting players. In the outfield, Clemente had 17 assists, a sign of his strong throwing arm. At the plate, his .311 batting average was third-best in the National League. Two of his biggest hits were game-winning home runs. On Saturday, July 21, the Pirates trailed the Reds, 3-1, in the top of the ninth but had two runners on base as Clemente came to the plate. The Cincinnati pitcher was Brooks Lawrence, who had already won 13 games that season and hadn't yet lost. Clemente changed that, hitting a three-run homer, to give the Pirates a 4-3 win and spoil Lawrence's perfect record.

The following Wednesday, the Pirates were at home, playing the Chicago Cubs. Chicago led, 8-5, but Pittsburgh loaded the bases with no out. With Clemente due up, the Cubs brought in a new pitcher, Jim Brosnan. On Brosnan's first pitch, Clemente hit a long drive to left-center field. Hank Foiles, Bill Virdon, and Dick Cole raced around the bases toward home plate with the runs that would tie the game. Clemente also tore around the diamond. Manager Bobby Bragan was coaching at third base and held up his arms, giving Clemente the signal to stop at third. With no one out and good hitters coming up, Bragan figured they'd still get Clemente home with the winning run and didn't want to take the chance on him being thrown out at the plate. However, Clemente ignored his manager, kept running, and was safe at home. The inside-the-park grand-slam home run won the game for the Pirates.[40]

Bragan, who had fined Clemente earlier in the season for missing a sign, wasn't happy about Clemente deliberately disobeying this one. However, he decided not to fine him.[41]

Clemente's hits were the usual way for him to reach base because he rarely walked. He drew only 13 bases on balls in 1956, and at one point went 50 games without walking.[42] Branch Rickey wasn't concerned: "His value is in not taking bases on balls because he can hit the bad pitches. If I tried to teach him to wait for a good pitch, I'd simply make a bad hitter out of him. The cure would be worse than the disease. He'll cure his own ailments simply by experience."[43]

At the end of the season, Clemente headed home to play another season for Santurce in the Puerto Rican League. However, a couple of significant events took place between Christmas and New Year's Day. First, Santurce owner Pedrín Zorrilla sold the team. A few days later, the new owner of the Cangrejeros traded several players, including Clemente, to Caguas-Rio Piedras. The trade was extremely unpopular and even caused the Santurce manager, Monchile Concepcion, to resign.[44]

Clemente was leading the league in batting average and had gotten at least one hit in 18 consecutive games when he was traded. He continued his hitting streak, which reached 23 to set a new Puerto Rican League record. His streak was snapped when he was held hitless in a game by Luis "Tite" Arroyo, a longtime friend and teammate on the Pirates who was pitching for the San Juan Senadores in the winter.[45] Clemente finished with a batting average of .396.

His batting eye was certainly sharp, but Clemente's back was continuing to bother him, and he reported a day late to spring training in 1957 as a result. Bobby Bragan made

light of the backache because Clemente had always played well even when he had some aches and pains. "The case history of Clemente is the worse he feels, the better he plays," reported *The Sporting News*, which quoted Bragan as saying, "I'd rather have a Clemente with some ailment than a Clemente who says he feels great with no aches or pains."[46]

Clemente's ability to play through pain and perform well may have contributed to charges that he wasn't really hurt. However, this time the back problems forced him to miss the first two games of the season. In all, Clemente played in only 111 games for Pittsburgh in 1957 and his batting average dropped to .253. The back problems lingered into the winter, and Clemente didn't play in the Puerto Rican League until mid-January of 1958.

The Pirates had finished last in 1957, but they made a big jump in 1958 under manager Danny Murtaugh. Clemente, who was feeling better physically, helped them get off to a good start in their opening game. He had three hits, one of which tied the game in the eighth inning against Milwaukee. The Pirates eventually won in 14 innings.

Clemente continued to hit well. He had three hits again in a 4-3 win in Cincinnati on April 25. One was a single in the sixth inning when the Pirates were trailing, 1-0. Clemente eventually scored to tie the game. The next inning he broke the tie with a three-run homer.

Another game-winning home run came in Milwaukee on August 4. Clemente broke a 3-3 tie with two out in the top of the ninth with a home run off fellow Puerto Rican Juan Pizarro, who had also been a winter teammate.

A little over a month later, Clemente had an even more spectacular game, although he didn't hit any homers. He had three triples, tying a National League record, in a 4-1 win over Cincinnati on September 8.

Clemente batted .289 in 1958. From right field, he continued to terrorize opposing baserunners, finishing with 22 assists. Fans loved it when a ball was hit his way with runners on base, rising in anticipation of seeing him uncork a strong throw.

Led by Clemente, the Pirates climbed from last place all the way to second, eight games behind the Milwaukee Braves.

Clemente didn't play winter baseball in Puerto Rico in 1958-59. He wore a different uniform, for the United States Marine Reserves. He fulfilled a six-month military commitment at Parris Island, South Carolina, and Camp LeJeune, North Carolina. The rigorous training program helped Clemente physically. He added strength by gaining ten pounds and said his back troubles had disappeared.[47]

When he reported to the Pirates in the spring of 1959, he complained of a sore right elbow. In May he made it worse when he hit the ground hard while making a diving catch. A few nights later, he had to be taken out of a game because he couldn't throw overhanded. He missed more than a month and continued to feel pain after he returned to the lineup.[48]

Clemente played in only 105 games and batted .296 as Pittsburgh dropped to fourth place. But he and the Pirates were primed for better things in 1960.

For the first time in several winters, Clemente played a full season in the Puerto Rican League in 1959-60. He was on a new team, having been traded to the San Juan Senadores, and he had a batting average of .330. Clemente and the Pirates hoped that he was ready for a big season back in Pittsburgh.

Another encouraging sign was that he was free of injuries. Feeling good and tuned up from his winter play, Clemente got off to a great start in 1960. In the Pirates' second game, at home against the Reds, he went three-for-three and drove in five runs as Pittsburgh won, 13-0. By the end of April, Clemente was batting .386. In 14 games, he had scored 12 runs, driven in 14, and hit three home runs. But he was just warming up. In Cincinnati, he had a home run and four RBIs on the first day of May. The 13-2 win was Pittsburgh's ninth straight and the team was in first place.

The Pirates cooled off a bit, but Clemente stayed hot. In May, he had 25 RBIs in 27 games, raising his season total to 39. He helped Pittsburgh regain the top spot in the National League standings and was named the league's Player of the Month by *The Sporting News*.

The Pirates battled for first with the San Francisco Giants and then the Milwaukee Braves. On the first Friday night in August, the Pirates were locked in a scoreless battle with the Giants at Forbes Field. Vinegar Bend Mizell was pitching for Pittsburgh and getting great help from his outfielders. Bill Virdon made a couple of good catches. Then Willie Mays led off the seventh inning for San Francisco with a long drive to right. Clemente chased the fly, reached out, and caught it, robbing Mays of an extra-base hit as he crashed into the outfield wall. He hurt his knee and also ended up with a gash in the chin that needed five stitches.[49]

Clemente stayed in the game the rest of the inning, but he was replaced by Gino Cimoli to start the eighth. Pittsburgh eventually won, 1-0, starting a four-game sweep of the Giants. Clemente missed the rest of the series as well as another three games.

He was out for a week. The day after he returned, he had a big game against the St. Louis Cardinals. St. Louis had beaten the Pirates the previous two nights and the Cardinals were in second place, only three games behind Pittsburgh. The Cardinals took the lead with a run in the top of the top of the first inning. In the last of the first, Pittsburgh tied the game when Clemente singled home Dick Groat.

With the score still tied, Groat opened the third inning with a double, and Clemente followed with a homer. Clemente had another run-scoring single in the fourth as Pittsburgh won the game, 4-1. Clemente batted in all four of his team's runs.

The Pirates swept a doubleheader from the Cardinals the next day to open up a six-game lead. No one came close to them the rest of the way. Except for one day, the Pirates had been in first place since May 29.

Clemente finished the 1960 season with a .314 batting average and hit 16 home runs, more than doubling his previous high. He also made the National League All-Star team for the first time.

Pittsburgh's first pennant since 1927 put them in the World Series against the New York Yankees. Despite being outscored 46-17, the Pirates split the first six games to force a decisive seventh game.

New York came back from a 4-0 deficit to carry a 7-4 lead into the last of the eighth. The Pirates rallied, helped by a bad hop that turned a probable double-play grounder into a base hit. One run was in and Pittsburgh had runners at second and third with two out when Clemente came to bat against the Yankees' Jim Coates. Clemente swung and topped the ball toward first base. Coates couldn't get to it, and it was left to Moose Skowron to field it. Skowron had no chance of beating Clemente to the base, and Coates's pursuit of the ball left the bag uncovered. Clemente zipped safely across the base, his helmet flying off, while the two Yankees watched helplessly.

Clemente's hit drove in another run and the Pirates took a 9-7 lead when Hal Smith followed with a three-run homer. New York came back in the top of the ninth to tie the game, setting the stage for one of the most dramatic moments in Pittsburgh sports history—a Series-winning home run by Bill Mazeroski leading off the last of the ninth.

Clemente had had a hit in each of the seven games in helping the Pirates win the World Series.

Returning to his homeland following the 1960 season, Clemente skipped the first part of the Puerto Rican League season, but then joined the San Juan Senadores in the second half. Even after he became a star in the major leagues, Clemente continued playing winter ball well past the time that he needed to keep his batting eye sharp. He felt an obligation to the people of his homeland, who otherwise would not have a chance to see him play. Clemente is perhaps the most inspirational figure the island has ever known, and he took that responsibility seriously.

He frequently stood up for himself and his fellow Latin players, speaking out against injustices he saw. He approached this in the same manner in which he played—with a passion, sometimes an anger, which drove him on and off the field.

Much of his anger was justified. Although the game became more open to Latins after the breaking of the color barrier, certain attitudes and prejudices toward these players remained. Latin players were often accused of being lazy or faking an injury if they missed a game because they were hurt or ill. Clemente knew first-hand the feeling of being called a hypochondriac. He suffered through many ailments in his career and he burned when his manager or reporters didn't believe him when he said he was hurt.

One of Clemente's biographers, Kal Wagenheim, wrote, "The legend of his hypochondria became part of baseball's folklore. He claimed so many ills—and performed so well despite them—that his plaints evoked skepticism or laughter." Wagenheim also noted that Clemente had problems in the 1960s with Pirates manager Danny Murtaugh, who "reportedly accused him of feigning an injury and fined him for not playing."[50]

Beyond the injuries and claims of hypochondria, Clemente maintained that Latin players often did not receive the recognition they deserved. Once again, Clemente was an example of this. After helping the Pirates win the National League pennant, and then the World Series championship, Clemente finished eighth in the voting for the league's Most Valuable Player. Clemente thought he should have gotten more votes and finished higher in the balloting.

Each slight, whether at him or a fellow Latin, he took personally. He spoke out often, although some of the claims he made about being mistreated weren't always entirely correct.

Phil Musick, a reporter who covered the Pittsburgh Pirates during the final years of Clemente's career, said, "He was anything but perfect. He was vain, occasionally arrogant, often intolerant, unforgiving, and there were moments when I thought for sure he'd cornered the market on self-pity. Mostly, he acted as if the world had just declared all-out war on Roberto Clemente, when in fact it lavished him with an affection few men ever know."

However, Musick added, "I know that through all of his battles . . . there was about him an undeniable charisma. Perhaps that was his true essence—he won so much of your attention and affection that you demanded of him what no man can give, perfection."[51]

Clemente did eventually receive the respect he sought. Toward the end of his career, fans and reporters recognized his greatness on the field. More than that, they knew of his caring nature for all people.

Clemente said he rarely set goals, but that he did once: "After I failed to win the Most Valuable Player Award in 1960, I made up my mind I'd win the batting title in 1961 for the first time."[52]

Clemente did exactly that, leading the National League with a .351 batting average. He hit 23 home runs, scored

100 runs and drove in 89. He led National League outfielders with 27 assists and won a Gold Glove for his fielding excellence for the first time. Clemente would win a Gold Glove every year for the rest of his career.

In Puerto Rico, Clemente played winter ball less often. He skipped the 1962-63 season altogether. It was the first time he hadn't played in the Puerto Rican League other than the time he was in the Marine Reserves in 1958-59.

However, Clemente was back for a full season with San Juan in 1963-64. The Senadores finished third during the regular season but won the league playoffs and represented Puerto Rico in the International Series, which was played in Managua, Nicaragua. Author Thomas Van Hyning reports, "Clemente was a fan favorite and made a lot of fans in Nicaragua."[53] Clemente developed a fondness for the country and its people and would return again.

The race for the Puerto Rican batting title involved two National League stars—Clemente and Orlando Cepeda—and a young player on the verge of stardom in the American League, Tony Oliva. Back on the mainland in 1964, Oliva and Clemente led their respective leagues in batting average. Oliva, who credited his winter-league experience with helping his development as a hitter, had a .323 average in his first full season in the majors.[54] Clemente's .339 average was good for his second National League batting title.

The winter of 1964-65 was an eventful one for Clemente. He married Vera Cristina Zabala. He also began managing. In December of 1964, Clemente took over as manager of the San Juan Senadores. He still played, although less often. In his first game as manager, Clemente had two doubles off Dennis McLain of Mayaguez. "He drove in two runs with his second double and raced home on a wild throw, but twisted his left ankle slightly and left the game," reported Miguel J. Frau in *The Sporting News*.[55]

Clemente later suffered a more serious injury. He was mowing the lawn at his home when a rock flew out of the mower and hit him in the thigh. He missed some games as a player, but when the league's All-Star Game was played, Clemente felt obligated to make an appearance. He pinch-hit and singled, but he aggravated the injury. "I felt my thigh ligament pop and something like water draining inside my leg," he said. Clemente had partially severed a ligament in his thigh, and he had to have surgery.[56]

The injury, combined with a fever, left Clemente weak, and he got off to a slow start in 1965 with the Pirates. Under new manager Harry Walker, the team also began poorly, losing 24 of their first 33 games. A 12-game winning streak followed, lifting Pittsburgh in the standings. Clemente got hot over this stretch, hitting .458 during the winning streak. The Pirates never overcame their slow start and finished third. Clemente led the league in batting average for the second year in a row and the third time in his career.

No one knew, though, that he was on the verge of his best season ever.

In addition to his other skills, Clemente was increasing his walk total in the mid-1960s. Early in the 1966 season, the Pirates were in Chicago, trailing the Cubs by a run. Clemente came to bat with two out and no one on base in the ninth inning. Cubs reliever Ted Abernathy got two strikes on Clemente. The Pirates were on the verge of losing, but Clemente remained patient. Abernathy's next three pitches were outside the strike zone, and Clemente laid off them. The count was full. Clemente stayed alive by fouling off the next eight pitches. Finally, Abernathy missed again and Clemente was on base with a walk. Willie Stargell followed with a double and Clemente came home with the tying run. Pittsburgh won the game in extra innings.

The win kept the Pirates in first place. They stayed in the pennant race all season, battling the San Francisco Giants and Los Angeles Dodgers. At the end of August the Pirates and Giants were tied for first. On September 2, Clemente hit a three-run homer off Chicago's Ferguson Jenkins that helped Pittsburgh beat the Cubs and take over sole possession of first place. It was the 2,000th hit of his career and his 23rd homer of the year, equaling his previous career high. In addition, it gave him 101 runs batted in, the first time he had ever reached 100 RBIs in a season.

He ended the season with career-highs in home runs (29) and RBIs (119). The Pirates finished third behind the Dodgers and Giants, but Clemente edged out Los Angeles' Sandy Koufax for the Most Valuable Player award.

Clemente had another outstanding season in 1967. He led the league with a .357 batting average for his third batting title in four years and his fourth overall. In addition to 209 hits, Clemente walked or was hit by a pitch more than 40 times, and he reached base at least 40 percent of the time for the first time in his career.

After having taken the previous winter off, Clemente played occasionally in the Puerto Rican League in 1967-68 and had a batting average of .382. Back on the mainland, things did not go well for him in 1968. The Pirates' opener was delayed two days because of the assassination of Martin Luther King. Clemente homered in the first game, but his batting average fell to .222 at the end of May. He said he was having trouble swinging the bat because he had injured his right shoulder in a fall at his home in Puerto Rico in February of 1968. He added that he might retire from baseball if the shoulder didn't get better.[57]

He improved over the last part of the season and finished with a .291 batting average, his lowest since 1958. Clemente didn't play winter ball and rested his body. He felt good when spring training began in 1969, but then he hurt his left shoulder as he tried to make a diving catch and went back to Puerto Rico for treatment. Clemente returned in time for the start of the regular season, but for the second year in a row he got off to a slow start. In the latter half of May, after going hitless in the first game of a series in San Diego, his batting average had fallen to .225.

Clemente claimed something else happened—a strange and scary incident. He did not tell the story in public until a year later, but Clemente said he was kidnapped while in San Diego. According to Clemente, he was walking back to the hotel where the Pirates were staying after going out to eat. He said four men forced him into a car at gunpoint. They took him to an isolated area and took his wallet and his All-Star Game ring. "This is where I figure they are going to shoot me and throw me in the woods," he told Pittsburgh writer Bill Christine more than a year after the incident. "They already had the pistol inside my mouth." Two of the men spoke Spanish, and Clemente talked to one of them in Spanish. After that, the men returned Clemente's money and ring and brought him back to his hotel. They even gave Clemente back the bag of chicken he had purchased at the restaurant. He said he did not report the incident to the police.[58]

Despite the harrowing event, Clemente finished the series in San Diego by getting three hits against the Padres and raised his batting average above .300 by mid-June. For a while it looked like he might lead the league again. He didn't, but Clemente still finished the season with a batting average of .345. The Pirates didn't do as well, finishing third in the new East Division of the National League.

After a slow start in 1970, the Pirates caught fire as they moved from Forbes Field, where they had played since 1909, to Three Rivers Stadium. Pittsburgh and New York fought for first place through July, with Chicago staying close. The Pirates were hanging in without Clemente. He was hit in the wrist with a pitch on July 25 and, except for one pinch-running appearance, was out of the lineup for more than a week. He returned on August 8 and had a double and a home run against the Mets.

Later in August, Clemente had five hits in each of two straight games. The first one came on a Saturday in Los Angeles. Clemente already had four hits as he came to the plate in the top of the 16th inning. He singled, stole second, and later came scored the go-ahead run as the Pirates beat the Dodgers, 2-1. The next day, the Pirates won again, 11-0. Clemente had five of Pittsburgh's 23 hits in the game.

He had raised his average to .363, tops in the National League. However, he played little in September because of a bad back and did not win the batting title. The Pirates still won the National League East Division and advanced to the playoffs. Scoring only three runs in three games, however, they were swept by the Cincinnati Reds.

That winter, Clemente played for the last time in the Puerto Rican League. Although he played in only three games during the regular season, he appeared in one of the playoff series. In addition, he managed the San Juan Senadores in 1970-71. The Senadores' opening game that season was against Santurce, which was managed by Frank Robinson. Both Robinson and Clemente had been mentioned as possibilities to be the first black manager in the major leagues.

After he got off to a slow start with the Pirates in 1971, he said, "My biggest mistake was managing in Puerto Rico that past winter. I had more responsibilities and did not get my rest. The long bus trips out of town, I have to make them because I am the manager. They take something out of me."[59]

Willie Stargell took the lead with Pittsburgh in 1971. He set a major league record by hitting 11 home runs in April and continued his great hitting throughout the year. Stargell finished with 48 home runs and 125 runs batted in.

Although Stargell had emerged as the team's star player, the team leader was still Clemente. He was receiving the recognition he had sought, and he was also showing he could continue playing with the same flair and hustle, even as he approached his 37th birthday. Clemente got off to a bad start, but he got hot in May and went on to finish the season with a .341 batting average. He was still outstanding in the field. In mid-June, Clemente preserved a shutout for Steve Blass, and a victory for the Pirates, on back-to-back plays. Pittsburgh held a 1-0 lead over Houston in the last of the eighth inning. The Astros had a runner on first with one out when Cesar Cedeno hit a soft liner to right field. Clemente hustled in and made a sliding catch of the ball before it could hit the turf. Bob Watson then hit a much harder drive toward the corner in right. Clemente raced toward the ball and made a twisting leap, grabbing the ball and robbing Watson of a two-run homer. Clemente crashed into the wall, bruising his ankle and elbow and cutting his knee. Astros manager Harry Walker, who had managed Clemente in Pittsburgh, said it was the greatest catch he ever made. Because of Clemente's catch, the Pirates maintained their lead and then padded it with two more runs in the ninth. Blass finished with a 3-0 win but said, "That shutout belongs to Clemente."[60]

The win gave the Pirates a 3 ½ game lead over the New York Mets and St. Louis Cardinals. Pittsburgh increased its lead to 9 ½ games at the All-Star break in July. The Pirates had several players in the All-Star game, including two starters—Willie Stargell in left field and Dock Ellis, who pitched. Clemente entered the game as a replacement for Willie Mays in the fourth inning. Later in the game, he hit his first home run in an All-Star Game.

Pittsburgh went on to win the East Division and beat San Francisco in the league playoffs to make it back to the World Series, against the Baltimore Orioles. Clemente turned the event into a showcase for his greatness.

Baltimore took the first two games before the series shifted to Pittsburgh. Clemente drove in the first run of the third game with a fielder's choice. The Pirates added another run, but Baltimore came back on a home run by Frank Robinson to cut the lead to 2-1. Clemente led off the last of the seventh by grounding back to Mike Cuellar, who had briefly pitched for Clemente's San Juan team in the Puerto Rican League the previous winter.[61] However, Clemente hustled down to first so hard that Cuellar hurried his throw and threw wildly. Clemente reached base on the error and, after Stargell walked, Bob Robertson hit a three-run homer. Pittsburgh won, 5-1.

The next game was the first night game in the history of the World Series. The Orioles got off to an early lead with three runs in the top of the first. Pittsburgh came back with two in the bottom of the inning, and the Pirates rallied again in the third. With one out, Richie Hebner singled. Clemente then hit a long drive to right. It cleared the fence and looked like a home run to put the Pirates ahead. However, the ball was ruled foul after the umpires had a long discussion. The ball was foul, and Clemente had to resume his at-bat. He couldn't come up with another long ball, but his single sent Hebner to second. One out later Al Oliver singled, scoring Hebner to tie the game. The score stayed at 3-3 until the Pirates pushed another run across in the seventh inning. Pittsburgh won the game, 4-3, and tied the World Series, 2-2.

The Pirates won again the next day as Nelson Briles held the Orioles to two hits. Clemente had a run-scoring single in the fifth inning to cap Pittsburgh's scoring as the Pirates won, 5-0.

The Series shifted back to Baltimore, but Pittsburgh had the lead. Just as he had done in the 1960 World Series, Clemente had at least one hit in each of the games. In the sixth game, with two out in the top of the first, he tripled off the fence in left-center field. However, Willie Stargell struck out, and Clemente was stranded at third.

By the time Clemente came up again in the third inning, the Pirates had a 1-0 lead. Clemente made the score 2-0 by hitting a home run to right field. The Orioles came back and tied the game in the seventh. In the last of the 10th inning, Brooks Robinson hit a sacrifice fly that scored Frank Robinson, giving Baltimore the win and extending the series to a seventh game.

Cuellar and Pittsburgh's Steve Blass were the starters in Game Seven, and both were sharp. Cuellar retired the first 11 Pittsburgh batters before Clemente came up with two out in the fourth. Cuellar threw him a high curve ball, and Clemente drove it over the left-center field fence. Clemente's second home run of the series gave Pittsburgh a 1-0 lead.

The Pirates got another run in the eighth inning, which they needed. In the bottom of the eighth, Baltimore got the first two runners on base. Blass was able to work out of the jam with only one run scoring, leaving Pittsburgh in the lead. Blass retired the Orioles in order in the last of the ninth. Clemente's homer had given the Pirates a lead they never gave up. Pittsburgh won the game, 2-1, and the Pirates were again champions of the world.

The Pirates had a number of pitchers who stood out, but when the voting was complete for the outstanding player of the World Series, the award went to Clemente. He had 12 hits, including two home runs, for a .414 batting average in the seven games.

There was no doubting his greatness nor his influence on the champion Pirates. Clemente had played in the All-Star Game, the World Series, had won the Most Valuable Player award, and had led the National League in batting average four times. He still had another milestone in his sights. "I would like to get 3,000 hits," he said in 1971.[62]

The Pirates had a rough start in 1972 and were in last place in May. They climbed in the standings and by the last half of June had taken over first place for good. Clemente was also doing well even though he had an intestinal virus that caused him to miss a few games. By the end of June, his batting average was .315, and he was making good progress toward the mark of 3,000 hits. On July 9, he got his 78th hit of the season, leaving him only 40 short. However, the virus returned, and Clemente left the Pirates to go back to Pittsburgh for treatment. He was out of the lineup for two weeks, then came back and got a big hit in a Pirates win on July 23.

Clemente missed another four weeks with strained tendons in both heels. Over a 40-game span between July 9 and August 22, he started only one game. Fortunately, the Pirates were still playing well and opened up a big lead in the National League East Division, but the ill-ness and injuries had slowed Clemente in his drive toward 3,000 hits.

At the end of August he had 30 hits to go. He hit well in September and was within striking distance by the final week of the season. On Thursday night, September 28, he got his 2,999th hit off Steve Carlton of the Phillies. Because the game was in Philadelphia, he was taken out so he could get his 3,000th hit before the home fans.

Even this event would not happen without a bit of controversy as the Pirates opened a series against the New York Mets in Pittsburgh. Facing Tom Seaver in the first inning, Clemente hit a chopper up the middle. Second baseman Ken Boswell bobbled the ball, and Clemente reached first. Official scorer Luke Quay ruled the play an error. Seaver allowed only two hits, neither to Clemente, in winning his 20th game of the season. After the game, Clemente complained about the scoring decision and later made accusations that official scorers through the years had deprived him of two batting titles. Part of the outburst was a result of Clemente thinking (erroneously) that the scorer in the game was Charley Feeney, a local sportswriter who Clemente thought had deprived him of hits on borderline calls in the past.[63]

The next afternoon Clemente struck out in the first inning. The game was scoreless when he came up again, leading off the fourth. He hit a long fly toward left-center field. The ball hit the fence on one bounce, and Clemente cruised into second with a double, the 3,000th hit of his career. The Pittsburgh fans stood and applauded Clemente, who raised his cap to show his appreciation. That hit started a three-run rally, and the Pirates won the game, 5-0. Bill Mazeroski pinch hit for Clemente in the fifth inning.

Clemente played in only one of Pittsburgh's final three games as he rested for the playoffs. The Pirates played Cincinnati and looked like they were on their way back to the World Series. Pittsburgh carried a 3-2 lead into the last of the ninth inning of the decisive fifth game. However, Johnny Bench tied the game with a home run, and the Reds scored the winning run on a wild pitch.

As usual, Clemente went back to Puerto Rico. Although he didn't play baseball, he managed a Puerto Rican team that went to the Amateur Baseball World Series in

Nicaragua. The Puerto Rican team finished third in the tournament.[64]

Clemente was back home a few weeks later when the city of Managua was racked by a massive earthquake on December 23. He had gotten to know people during his visits to Nicaragua. He was concerned about the people there and wanted to help.

Clemente got busy organizing a committee to raise money and get other items, such as medicine and food, that could be sent to Nicaragua. Through Christmas, he worked on the relief efforts. He finally decided he would go on one of the cargo planes that were flying the supplies to the stricken area.

A little after 9 p.m. on New Year's Eve, as others in Puerto Rico were celebrating, the plane took off. Besides Clemente, four other people were on board. Almost immediately, the plane had problems, and the pilot tried to return to the San Juan airport. Before the plane could make it back, however, it crashed into the Atlantic Ocean about a mile from the coast.

The fate of the people on board was not immediately known. But it soon became clear. The five men on the plane, including Roberto Clemente, were dead.[65]

People, not just baseball fans, mourned the loss of Clemente, who left behind his wife, Vera, and three sons, Roberto, Jr., Luis Roberto, and Roberto Enrique.

Normally, a player cannot be inducted into the Baseball Hall of Fame until at least five years after he stopped playing. Because of the circumstances, an exception was made for Clemente. A special election was held, and he received enough votes to be elected. In the summer of 1973, Clemente became the first player from Latin America to be inducted into the Hall of Fame.

There were other honors. An award, established in 1971 to honor a player for his accomplishments on and off the field, was renamed the Roberto Clemente Award.

Clemente had dreamed of establishing a Sports City for young people in Puerto Rico. He had a vision for a place where young people could come and play as well as read and learn other skills they would need in life. Vera Clemente continued her husband's work, and a large sports complex was built. Over the next 30 years, hun-

dreds of thousands of kids took part in its programs. Some became stars in the major leagues, such as Juan Gonzalez, Bernie Williams, and Ivan Rodriguez.[66]

Although he is gone, all sorts of reminders of Clemente still exist. More than anything, Roberto Clemente left behind memories of how he played the game on the field and how he lived his life off it.

Notes

Retrosheet (http://retrosheet.org) provided game-by-game details of Clemente's performance. The information used was obtained free of charge from and is copyrighted by Retrosheet.

1   Peter C. Bjarkman. *Baseball with a Latin Beat: A History of the Latin American Game* (Jefferson: North Carolina: McFarland & Company, Inc., Publishers, 1994), 262.

2   Kal Wagenheim. *Clemente!* (New York: Praeger Publishers, 1973), 15.

3   Bruce Markusen. *Roberto Clemente: The Great One* (Champaign, IL: Sports Publishing, Inc., 1998), 4.

4   Telephone interview with Monte Irvin, June 30, 2005.

5   "Roberto Hit Ten HRs in 'Day-Long' Slugfest," *The Sporting News*, July 6, 1960, 6.

6   Wagenheim, 24.

7   "Starred in Javelin, Jumps Before Turning to Diamond," *The Sporting News*, July 6, 1960, 6.

8   Markusen, 8.

9   Les Biederman, "Pride Pushes Clemente: 'I Can Hit With Best'", *The Sporting News*, March 28, 1964, 11.

10 Thomas E. Van Hyning. *The Santurce Crabbers: Sixty Seasons of Puerto Rican Winter League Baseball* (Jefferson, NC: McFarland & Company, Inc., Publishers, 1999), 39.

11 Frank Graham, Jr. "Spanish-Speaking Al Campanis Lures Latin Talent for Dodgers" *The Sporting News*, January 12, 1955, 21.

12 E-mail correspondence with Buzzie Bavasi, June 2005.

13 Santiago Llorens, *The Sporting News*, January 20, 1954, 23.

14 *The Sporting News*, March 3, 1954, 26.

15 The bonus rule in effect at that time is chronicled in Brent Kelley, *Baseball's Biggest Blunder: The Bonus Rule of 1953-1957* (Lanham, MD: The Scarecrow Press, Inc., 1997).

16 Les Biederman, "Dodgers Signed Clemente Just to Balk Giants", *The Sporting News*, May 25, 1955, 11.

17 Wagenheim, 35; Markusen, 33-34.

18 The claim that the Dodgers would not start five blacks in the same game was made by Wagenheim on page 35 of *Clemente!*

Box scores of Brooklyn Dodgers games in 1954 from *The Sporting News* indicate four instances in which Jim Gilliam, Jackie Robinson, Don Newcombe, Sandy Amoros, and Roy Campanella were all in the starting lineup: July 17, August 24, September 6 (second game), and September 15.

19 E-mail correspondence with Buzzie Bavasi, June 3, 2005.

20 Wagenheim, Markusen, and Phil Musick, *Who Was Roberto? A Biography of Roberto Clemente* (Garden City, NY: Doubleday & Co., 1974).

21 The game-by-game analysis of the 1954 season was done through box scores of Montreal Royals games, published in *The Sporting News* in 1954, and cross-checked by SABR member Neil Raymond from box scores in Montreal newspapers.

22 Musick, 89.

23 Musick, 89.

24 Telephone interview with Jack Cassini, June 20, 2005.

25 E-mail correspondence with Buzzie Bavasi, June 3, 2005.

26 "Jack Hernon, "Backward Buccos Refuse to Go Overboard on Rookie", *The Sporting News*, January 12, 1955, 18.

27 Pito Alvarez de la Vega. "Mays, Gomez & Co. on Top in Puerto Rico: Santurce Takes Over Lead from Caguas; Willie Ups Swatting Average to .423" , *The Sporting News*, December 22, 1954, 24.

28 Wagenheim, 43.

29 Interview with Don Zimmer, July 2, 2005.

30 Jack Hernon. "Clemente a Gem in Need of Polish", *The Sporting News*, February 9, 1955, 4.

31 Jack Hernon. "Haney's Sizeup on Bob Clemente 'Much to Learn'", *The Sporting News*, March 16, 1955, 30.

32 http://www.bioproj.sabr.org/bioproj. cfm?a=v&v=l&bid=1187&pid=14117 Frank Thomas biography by Bob Hurte; Jack Hernon. "Holdouts Thomas and Law Absent as Bucs Start Drills" *The Sporting News*, March 9, 1955, 33.

33 *The Sporting News*, March 16, 1955, 27; "Uniform Numbers Range from 1 to 81," *The Sporting News*, April 13, 1955, 28; Thomas E. Van Hyning. *Puerto Rico's Winter League: A History of Major League Baseball's Launching Pad* (Jefferson, NC: McFarland & Company, Inc., Publishers, 1995), 53.

34 Jack Hernon. "Haney's Young Bucs Shaking off Buck Fever", *The Sporting News*, May 11, 1955, 11.

35 Les Biederman. "Clemente, Early Buc Ace, Says He's Better in Summer", *The Sporting News*, June 29, 1955, 26.

36 Telephone interview with Jack Cassini, June 20, 2005.

37 Les Biederman, "Clemente, Early Buc Ace, Says He's Better in Summer", *The Sporting News*, June 29, 1955, 26.

38 "Bragan Cracks Down Early, Fines Clemente, Long $25," *The Sporting News*, April 25, 1956, 21; Les Biederman, "Bear-Down Bragan Means Business, Buc Fans Learn", *The Sporting News*, May 2, 1956, 7.

39 Wagenheim, 67.

40 Irving Vaughan. "7-Run Cub 8th Isn't Enough! Pirates Win, 9 to 8, on Clemente Homer", *Chicago Tribune*, Thursday, July 26, 1956, part 6, 1.

41 "Clemente Ignored Stop Sign on 'Slam,' But Escaped Fine," *The Sporting News*, August 8, 1956, 18.

42 Les Biederman, "Clemente in 50 Games Without Walk," *The Sporting News*, August 8, 1956, 18.

43 Oscar Ruhl. "Rickey Rates Clemente as Top Draft Dandy", *The Sporting News*, March 20, 1957, 15.

44 Pito Alvarez de la Vega. "New Owner Peddles Trio of Santurce's Stars to Flag Rival" *The Sporting News*, January 9, 1957, 21.

45 Pito Alvarez de la Vega. "Bilko Released in Economy Move; Clemente Sets 23-Game Hit Mark", *The Sporting News*, January 16, 1957, 21.

46 "Clemente, Best When Ailing, Reports Late with Backache," *The Sporting News*, March 13, 1957, 10.

47 "Clemente to Start Six-Month Marine Corps Hitch, Oct. 4," *The Sporting News*, September 24, 1958, 7; "Buc Flyhawk Now Marine Rookie," *The Sporting News*, November 19, 1958, 13; *The Sporting News*, January 21, 1959, 9.

48 "Clemente Put on Disabled List and Baker Released by Bucs," *The Sporting News*, June 3, 1959, 3.

49 Bob Stevens. "Little Things Add Up to Big Plunge for Snoozing Giants", *The Sporting News*, August 17, 1960, 13, 18.

50 Wagenheim, 106.

51 Musick, 14-15.

52 Les Biederman, "Clemente--The Player Who Can Do It All", *The Sporting News*, April 20, 1968, 11.

53 Thomas E. Van Hyning. *Puerto Rico's Winter League: A History of Major League Baseball's Launching Pad* (Jefferson, NC: McFarland & Company, Inc., Publishers, 1995), 66.

54 Interview with Tony Oliva, June 5, 2005.

55 "Puerto Rico: Senators Dip As Clemente Grabs Reins" by Miguel J. Frau, *The Sporting News*, January 9, 1965, 27.

56 "Clemente May Have Trouble As Result of Thigh Injury," *The Sporting News*, February 13, 1965, 25.

57 Les Biederman, "Shoulder Sore; Clemente Says He May Retire", *The Sporting News*, August 24, 1968, 18.

58 "Clemente Reveals Close Call with Kidnapers," *The Sporting News*, August 22, 1970, 24.

59 "Clemente Laments Managing," *The Sporting News*, May 15, 1971, 14.

60 Charley Feeney, "Greatest Catch? This One by Roberto Will Do", *The Sporting News*, July 3, 1971, 7.

61 Phil Jackman, "Orioles Shrug Off Cuellar's Winter Ball Woes", *The Sporting News*, December 26, 1970, 36.

62 Charley Feeney, "Clemente Sets 3,000 Hits As Wish on 37th Birthday", *The Sporting News*, August 28, 1971, 9.

63 Charley Feeney, "Roberto Collects 3000th Hit, Dedicates It to Pirate Fans", *The Sporting News*, October 14, 1972, 15.

64 "Veteran Cuban Team Captures Amateur Title; U. S. Runner-Up," *The Sporting News*, December 30, 1972, 46.

65 "Baseball Mourns Loss of Buc Star Clemente," *The Sporting News*, January 13, 1973, 42.

66 "One more push to realize Clemente's dream of Sports City" by Robert Dvorchak, *Pittsburgh Post-Gazette*, Monday, August 16, 2004 (http://post-gazette.com/pg/04229/362393.stm)

Bennie Daniels

By Greg Erion

THE EXPANSION WASHINGTON Senators had little to cheer about at the end of their inaugural season in 1961. They had lost 100 games and finished in the cellar, tied with the Kansas City A's. Their hitting was dead last in the league. If there were any bright spots to look forward to in 1962, they were centered on a pitching staff that included a tall right-hander named Bennie Daniels who led the staff with a 12-11 record, the only Senator with a winning record. Daniels had started in Organized Baseball 11 years earlier and spent most of his time in the Pittsburgh farm system. After joining the Senators in a trade following the Pirates' championship 1960 season, Daniels seemed to have arrived as a starting pitcher in the major leagues. As it turned out, he did better with the Senators than he had with the Pirates.

Ben J. Daniels was born on June 17, 1932, to Sallie Daniels and her husband, Ben Daniels, Sr., a farmer in Tuscaloosa, Alabama. The 1940 US Census shows the family living in Cherokee, a small town in the northwestern corner of Alabama about 100 miles from Tuscaloosa. Along with Ben's four young siblings, and his parents, the Daniels household included an older sister and her family as well as his aunt and uncle.[1] In 1945 Bennie and his family moved to Compton, California, part of the 1940s migration out of the South. In 1957 Daniels recalled that he had not been expected to survive childhood. "I was sickly all my life until our family moved to California," he said. "As a matter of fact, my mother told me later that I wasn't expected to live. I didn't have any fatal disease; I was just sickly and scrawny. But I began to sprout like a weed after we moved to Compton."[2]

In Compton a climate favorable to health and an interest in sports allowed Daniels to outgrow childhood illnesses. He grew to 6-feet-2 and 190 pounds. He

excelled in baseball, basketball, and track, and was once clocked at 10.4 in the 100-yard dash. Daniels graduated from Compton High School having made All-Coast in baseball and basketball. His performance in high-school and American Legion ball attracted interest leading to his being signed with the Pittsburgh Pirates by longtime major-league scout Rosie Gilhousen in July 1951.[3]

Daniels was assigned to the Great Falls (Montana) Electrics in the Class C Pioneer League. His chances of making the major leagues at that time were daunting. In 1951 there were 50 minor leagues. The Pioneer League was in the lower echelons. In those days fewer than one in 15 players made it to the majors, even if just for a cup of coffee.

His first two years in the minors proved inauspicious. At Great Falls he posted a 2-4 record and at Modesto of the California League the next season, hobbled by a case of ptomaine poisoning, he went 9-14.[4] Then, as with many young men in the early 1950s during the Korean War era, he was drafted into the US Army. Stationed in Germany for most of his hitch, Daniels maintained his athleticism, playing baseball and football for the 1st Infantry Division Artillery team.[5]

Discharged in 1955, Daniels was sent back by the Pirates to the Pioneer League, this time with Billings. He fashioned a solid 10-6 start before being promoted to the Lincoln Chiefs in the Class A Western League. Pitching creditably enough, he returned to Lincoln in 1956 and experienced a breakthrough season, winning his first ten games and finishing 15-3, his .833 winning percentage the best in the league. Daniels showed he could hit too, fashioning a .325 batting average with eight home runs and 38 RBIs and logging some time as a position player. While his hitting was outstanding, especially for a pitcher, Daniels was overshadowed by teammate Dick Stuart, who hit 66 home runs. Daniels was selected to the league's All-Star team. His year ended on a further good note as he married Sue Irving on December 17.[6] They had met at spring training at Huntsville, Texas.[7] The marriage produced two children, son Michael and daughter Vickie.

Daniels' performance earned him a promotion to the Hollywood Stars in the Pacific Coast League for the 1957 season. He picked up right where he left off, winning 17 games. Early in the season manager Clyde King described Daniels' pitching style: "He has one of the best sinking fastballs in the game." Teammate Ben Wade observed, "No other pitcher has shown me as much stuff in the league this year. Bennie's not the fastest, but his ball moves more—real good breaking stuff. When he's in trouble it's because he is wild."[8]

Wade also noted Daniels' continued ability with the bat (Daniels hit .292 with five home runs that season) and his fielding ability. The observation on Daniels' fielding was not an isolated comment. Several times during his career Daniels was described as a "fifth infielder" and occasionally was compared to Bobby Shantz, perhaps the best fielding pitcher of the era. His performance in 1957 earned him selection to the Pacific Coast League's All Star team and promotion to the Pirates in September.

Daniels made his major-league debut on September 24, 1957, against the Brooklyn Dodgers. It was an auspicious occasion, the last major-league game played at Ebbets Field. Starting against the Dodgers, Daniels pitched seven innings before being relieved by Elroy Face. Daniels lost the game to Danny McDevitt but acquitted himself well, giving up just one earned run in his 2-0 loss. Of the game, Daniels later recalled, "It was a dark ballpark. … I was really shocked. I knew I was going to pitch, but I thought I was going to be coming in as a reliever, not as a starter. It was just amazing to be pitching in the big leagues."[9] And it was amazing, particularly because at the end of the previous season, as Daniels recalled years later, "I was going to retire from the game in 1957, but my wife said to hang with it." [10]

The 1957 Pittsburgh Pirates had finished tied for last, a finish the franchise was quite familiar with through the 1950s. The team's fortunes took a decided turn for the better in 1958. Led by players like Bill Mazeroski and the incomparable Roberto Clemente, and a pitching staff anchored by the likes of Bob Friend, Vernon Law, and Elroy Face, the team shot to second place. The Pirates were on the threshold of becoming a bona-fide contender and were looking to augment their starting rotation.

After three solid seasons in the minors, Daniels had a legitimate shot to make the team. He did well, and at one point in spring training, manager Danny Murtaugh said, "Daniels will be one of my five starters."[11] Daniels, described as "the rave" of Pittsburgh's training camp, was voted the "kid with the most potential" by sportswriters on the eve of the season's opening game.[12]

Murtaugh's comments notwithstanding, Daniels began the season with a few relief appearances before making three consecutive ineffective starts. By the end of May, with a 0-2 record, a 9.95 ERA, and 11 walks in 12 innings, Daniels was optioned to the Columbus Jets in the International League. He had not demonstrated the control necessary to be effective.

Once with Columbus, Daniels reverted to the form he had shown at Hollywood, finishing the season with a 14-6 record and a 2.31 ERA, among the league's best. A teammate, catcher Dick Rand, described Daniels' success—and the challenge he faced in getting back to the majors: "When he lets the fastball go, nobody—including Bennie, the catcher, and the hitter—knows just how it is going to move. The ball just moves and it moves different ways at different times. I suppose you could say it is 'wildness' but it's the kind a lot of pitchers wish they had."[13]

Daniels' take was a bit different: "I can't be sure myself just what it's going to do." But while Rand put a positive light on the movement of Daniels' pitches, he in essence captured the main challenge Daniels faced, and never entirely overcame—lack of control. Recalled by the Pirates in September, Daniels did well in two starts, giving up just three earned runs in 15 innings.

As the 1959 season approached, Daniels found himself in almost the identical situation he faced the previous season: that of a well-regarded prospect hoping to make the majors. This time he succeeded in staying with the Pirates. As was the case in 1958, he began the season making a few relief appearances. Then, on May 3, he started against the St. Louis Cardinals.

Cardinals player-manager Solly Hemus provoked a near riot when he threw his bat at Daniels. Pittsburgh sportswriter Les Biederman intimated that Hemus did this to "light a fire" under the listless Cardinals, who had been playing poorly.[14] Biederman said Daniels was so incensed at remarks Hemus made to him that he waited in the runway after the game to confront the manager. Only the intervention of Daniels' teammates prevented a potentially ugly altercation between the 6-foot, 200-pound pitcher and the diminutive playing manager. Both Biederman's article and a subsequent story in The Sporting News treated the incident as a typical baseball confrontation.[15] They missed the mark as to what had occurred.

In his book The Long Season, pitcher Jim Brosnan described Hemus's effort to put a spark into the Cardinals by provoking Daniels earlier in the game. After purposely leaning into and being hit by a pitch, he yelled out to Daniels, "You black bastard." Brosnan wrote, "If that was truly his intention he did it as awkwardly as he could. All he proved to me was that little men — or boys — shouldn't play with sparks, as well as with matches."[16] Brosnan's description of the incident suggests that his teammates felt the same about Hemus as he did.

The incident and its various perspectives were revealing of the insensitivity of things racial in baseball in 1959. Biederman's article wryly compliments Hemus for his maneuvering the incident: "Maybe Solly Hemus knew what he was doing when he engineered the near riot at Forbes Field early in May." In addition, Hemus admitted that he "simply had to do something to light a fire under the Cardinals." Both Biederman and Hemus missed the real significance of what had occurred.

Brosnan was keenly aware of what was at stake when Hemus insulted Daniels. A dangerous and needless confrontation had been narrowly avoided. Ever increasingly, black players were not going to put up with prejudice. Daniels would not take such insults and essentially neither did the Cardinals players.

Years later, in David Halberstam's October 1964, the incident is once again described, with repercussions of what took place more deeply understood. Hemus's comment to Daniels had alienated the Cardinals' black players.[17] Hemus not only misread not only the situation, he misread the temper of the changing times. It was a shortcoming that contributed to the loss of his job two years later. He never managed again.

Daniels' 1959 season with the Pirates proved a disappointment. He finished 7-9 with a 5.45 ERA. Starting 12 games, he completed none. While his control seemed better (he walked only 39 in 100 innings pitched), he too often found himself pitching with a 3-2 count, a tough situation for any pitcher. Despite less than stellar pitching, he showed he still knew how to wield a bat. For the year, Daniels batted .310; on July 28, he hit his first major-league home run, a two-run shot off Larry Sherry of the Los Angeles Dodgers. The Pirates, after finishing second in 1958, disappointed in 1959, sliding back to fourth. Several players had off-years and the team was still looking for a dependable starter to back up Friend, Law, and Harvey Haddix, who had come over from the Reds after the 1958 season. The opportunity was there for Daniels to take.

Murtaugh still felt Daniels held the promise of better things to come. High on him going into the 1960 season, the manager observed, "I think Ben has as much as anyone in the league. He could be a big winner with us. At times last year, he showed it but there were other times he was just so-so. He's big and strong and there were a couple of times when he pitched with just two days' rest."[18]

There were a few flashes of Daniels' potential in 1960. In late May he started against the Dodgers' Sandy Koufax. Koufax was on that day throwing a one-hitter (a single by Daniels) and striking out ten. Daniels gave up only four hits in seven innings, and lost 1-0. Overall, though, he struggled with a 1-3 record and a 7.81 ERA as a combination reliever and starter. Five days after his 1-0 loss, the Pirates traded for Vinegar Bend Mizell from the Cardinals. The Pirates found their fourth starter. A month later Daniels was optioned to Columbus, where he posted an indifferent 4-9 record. Recalled on September 1, Daniels was on hand when the Pirates clinched their first pennant in 33 years. Daniels was voted a $4,208.97 half-share of the World Series receipts.[19]

Daniels had had three seasons to make a mark with Pittsburgh. Now a 29-year-old, with younger prospects on hand, his days in the Pirates organization were numbered. Shortly after the Pirates' World Series victory over the Yankees, Mickey Vernon, a Pirates coach and a 20-year major-league player, was named manager of the expansion Washington Senators. In the expansion draft a few weeks later, the Senators took pitcher Bobby Shantz from the Yankees. Two days later they traded Shantz to Pittsburgh for first baseman R.C. Stevens, infielder Harry Bright, and Daniels. The Pirates said that despite Daniels' "corking fastball, a fine curve and good control," he had failed to develop as fast as they would have liked.[20]

Vernon felt that Daniels still had potential, and had lobbied Murtaugh to make the deal. They were both working in the offseason at a clothing store in Chester, Pennsylvania, and, as Vernon years later recalled, "We discussed and haggled back and forth between sales."[21]

Daniels was coming to a team rushed into existence. After the 1960 World Series it was determined that the two major leagues would expand, the American League in 1961 and the National League in 1962. The hurried nature by which these two teams came to life was reflected in the talent pool they chose from in the expansion draft. Washington's picks were a mixture of rookies not deemed worthy of protection from the draft, players who had failed to make a mark elsewhere, and over-the-hill veter-

ans. That first season was indicative of what lay in store for the Senators. Before the franchise moved to Texas in 1972, the team never moved out of the second division.

For Daniels, however, 1961 represented the peak of his career. He started out slowly, losing his first three decisions before beating Detroit. Five days later he pitched a three-hit, complete-game 2-1 win against the Boston Red Sox. A week later he defeated the other expansion team, the Los Angeles Angels, 6-2 and hit his first American League home run. On July 30 he pitched his first major-league shutout, a 4-0 six-hitter against the Kansas City Athletics. For a 61-100 ninth-place (out of ten) team, Daniels finished 12-11, leading the Senators in victories; his 3.44 ERA was among the league's top 15 qualifiers. After the season Dick Donovan, considered the Senators' ace based on the strength of his league-leading ERA, was traded to the Cleveland Indians, and with Donovan's departure, Daniels became the ace of the staff.

Looking back on Daniels years later, teammate Chuck Hinton recalled, "He was a big gutsy guy, always pitching in pain, getting no support and losing. He was an inspiration to me, a big brother. He made no bones, no excuses when he lost. Just took his lumps. There wasn't a guy in the league that didn't like him. A real athlete." Off the field, Hinton recalled, "He looked real good in clothes … never extravagant, just stylish." Regarding Daniels' hitting ability, Hinton noted that on one occasion he played the outfield for Washington.[22]

Daniels' well-rounded athletic ability was illustrated during this time, when fans seeing number 21 warming up on the sidelines were confused. Knowing Daniels wore number 21, and was right handed, they could not understand why the pitcher was throwing left-handed. It was indeed Daniels. He was ambidextrous.[23]

Years later, looking back on his career, Daniels proudly recalled that one of the highlights of his career was pitching a complete-game five-hit win against the Detroit Tigers on Opening Day in 1962. That day was special to him because it was the only time President John F. Kennedy threw out the season's opening pitch.[24] It was also the first time an African American started on Opening Day for a Washington team.[25] Daniels had been the Senators' starting pitcher in the last game played at Griffith Stadium, in September 1961, and was the starting pitcher for the first game played at D.C. Stadium.[26] (And his first major-league start was in the last game in Ebbets Field.)

With his Opening Day victory in 1962 Daniels reached the apex of his career. He lost his next ten decisions and was relegated to the bullpen. He never again approached the consistency he showed in 1961. Daniels began to experience nagging injuries, most seriously an irritation in his pitching elbow at the beginning of the 1962 season.[27] Chuck Hinton mentioned Daniels pitching with bone chips in his arm, always in pain. His loss of effectiveness worried Daniels to the point that his hair started to fall out. In 1979 he recalled, "I was worried about getting my five years in for the pension."[28] Continuing to alternate between the starting and bullpen roles, Daniels ended the 1962 season 7-16 after his 1-10 start. The Senators finished last. After the season Rollie Hemsley, who had been fired as a coach after the season ended, said, "They pitched (Daniels) 12 times with a sore arm. He never knew whether he was a starter or a reliever. Bennie needed a little help."[29]

Over the next three seasons, Daniels turned in medio-cre records: 5-10, 8-10, and 5-13. He flashed occasional brilliance: a two-hit shutout of Minnesota in 1963, two shutouts of the Chicago White Sox in 1964 that knocked them out of the pennant race. Bob Addie, writing for the *Washington Post*, observed, "Daniels baffled his bosses with his often brilliant and then mediocre performanc-es."[30] By the end of the 1965 season, general manager George Selkirk and manager Gil Hodges had given up on Daniels. Selkirk sold Daniels to the Hawaii Islanders of the Pacific Coast League with the understanding that if Daniels turned his game around he would be brought back.[31] It was not to be. After pitching ineffectively, his arm not getting any better, Daniels decided it was time to hang it up and retired from the game. For Hawaii in 1966, he was 8-15 with a 5.51 ERA.

Leaving the game was a shock. Daniels was among those second-generation African Americans who, once their playing days were over, found there was no place for them in the game. Jules Tygiel in *Baseball's Great Experiment: Jackie Robinson and His Legacy* illustrated this point. In 1964 just before Daniels left the game, only two blacks were full-time coaches in the majors. Chances for employ-ment in the minors were just as rare. [32]

Daniels took on all sorts of jobs to support his family. Over the next few years he worked for the California Department of Motor Vehicles, was an aircraft tool esti-mator, sold insurance, anything to get along. Then two jobs came up. One was with the state giving clinics for youth baseball coaches. He enjoyed teaching the game to people who were working with youngsters. Then fund-ing for the program ended. Daniels next obtained a job at Martin Luther King Jr. Hospital, first as a traffic hazard inspector, community liaison man and finally CETA (Comprehensive Employee Training Act) coordinator for the hospital.[33] He served in that position for nearly ten years when his life took a self-inflicted turn for the worse.

In 1977 Daniels was arrested on charges of misappropriat-ing $107,000 in public funds between 1974 and 1977. He pleaded no contest. According to the prosecution, " For employees who were no longer employed under CETA, Daniels would continue to receive checks in their names. He was forging time cards that were submitted to the county auditor's office, which would process the checks back to him. He was endorsing and receiving the face value of the checks. We presented over 500 warrants — or county checks — he had endorsed."[34] He was sentenced to one the three years in prison.

About six months later Daniels spoke with Thomas Boswell of the *Washington Post* in an interview at the California Institute for Men at Chino, California, where Daniels was serving his sentence. "I did it. I was wrong. But I'm not ashamed," Daniels said.

While Daniels was a counselor for CETA, his function in part was to work with young men to enable them to get jobs. Once a trainee moved on to a job, Daniels kept his time card active, forging the trainee's name, cashing checks, and paying another young person with the cash. Daniels could have claimed his actions were driven by the highest of motives — helping others — but he did not take that route. "That isn't quite right. I did things that were wrong. If you did something that's wrong, like I did, you pay for it. You don't fight the system."[35]

Explanations of what had taken place given, Daniels focused on the future. His wife, Sue, and children visited him at Chino each weekend. Their visits kept up his spir-its. He felt that once he served his time he could rebound with little difficulty. "After what my wife and I have been through, in the minors, then after I quit baseball, we're used to starting over fresh," he said. "This time won't be the worst."[36]

Daniels was right: He rebounded, steering straight. After finishing his term at Chino, he soon obtained a job with a veteran's hospital as a scheduling clerk. He held that position for 15 years before retiring in December 1997.[37] After retiring, he made the rounds of sports card collector shows, signing autographs.

As of December 2012 Daniels, 80, and his wife of 56 years, Sue, lived in Compton. He politely declined to be interviewed for this article. Daniels has led a demanding life. Starting from a sickly childhood as the son of a farmer from the Deep South, he progressed through the minor-league system to the majors when it was hard for blacks to succeed. After baseball ended, new challenges ensued: finding a steady job, time spent at Chino and practically starting all over again as he neared 50.

A life of adversity, some of it self-inflicted, of achievement, but mostly one of perseverance.

Notes

1   http://search.ancestry.com/cgi-bin/sse.dll?db=1940usfedcen&indiv=try&h=65867544.

2   "Daniels follows '56 Script in Fast Start at Hollywood," *The Sporting News*, May 29, 1957.

3   http://www.baseball-reference.com/bullpen/Bennie_Daniels.

4   "Daniels follows…" *The Sporting News*, May 29, 1957, 29.

5   "From Service Front," *The Sporting News*, January 6, 1954, 23.

6   Daniels' file at the Baseball Hall of Fame.

7   "Daniels career blossomed with Senators during 1961," *Sports Collectors Digest*, May 26, 2000, 28.

8   "Daniels follows…" *The Sporting News*, May 29, 1957, 29.

9   "Daniels career…" *Sports Collectors Digest*, May 26, 2000, 28.

10 Ibid.

11 "Bunts and Boots," *The Sporting News*, March 26, 1958, 31.

12 "Six Rookies Rated Spring Surprises," *The Sporting News*, April 16, 1958, 15.

13 "Daniels' Fast One Busts Rival Hitters' Hearts, Catcher's Finger," *The Sporting News*, July 23, 1958, 31

14 Lester J. Biederman, "Cardinals Playing Livelier Ball Since Hemus Affair Here," *Pittsburgh Press*, May 21, 1959.

15 "Hemus Plunked, Lets Bat Sail in Fracas With Bucs," *The Sporting News*, May 13, 1958, 23.

16 Jim Brosnan, *The Long Season: The Classic Chronicle of Life in the Majors* (New York: Harper & Brothers, 1960; reprinted by Penguin Books, 1983), 115-116.

17 David Halberstam, *October 1964* (New York: Villard Books, 1994), 108-109.

18 "Daniels Figures High in Pirates Plans," *Los Angeles Sentinel*, April 7, 1960, B9.

19 "Who Won Series? Tax Collectors Net Top Take, 346 Gs" *The Sporting News*, November 2, 1960, 10.

20 "Buccos Beef Up Bull Pen in Deal for Lefty Shantz," *The Sporting News*, December 28, 1960, 11.

21 Rich Westcott, *Mickey Vernon, The Gentleman First Baseman* (Philadelphia: Camino Books Inc., 2005), 172.

22 "Bennie Daniels Doesn't Regret Going from Rock to Hard Place," *Hartford Courant*, January 26, 1979, 59.

23 "Bob Addie's Atoms…," *The Sporting News*, September 29, 1962, 25.

24 "JFK Goes All the Way With Nats—as Laotian Prince Cools Heels," *The Sporting News*, April 18, 1962, 15.

25 "Twirler Daniels Earns No. 1 Spot on Senator Staff," *The Sporting News*, January 3, 1962, 29-30.

26 "Bennie Daniels Pulled Switch as First Winner in New Park," *The Sporting News*, April 18, 1962, 27.

27 "Flyhawks Feeble Flailing Leaves Vernon Whipped," *The Sporting News*, May 2, 1962, 19, 24.

28 Thomas Boswell, "Daniels in Prison: Nice Guy Gone Wrong," *Washington Post*, January 15, 1979.

29 "Hemsley Tosses Barb at Nats for Mound Strategy," *The Sporting News*, December 1, 1962, 25.

30 Larry Moffi, *Crossing The Line; Black Major Leaguers: 1947-1949* (Iowa City, Iowa: University of Iowa Press, 1994), 164-165.

31 "Old Doc Selkirk To Try Hawaiian Cure on Daniels," *The Sporting News*, January 29, 1966, 18.

32 Jules Tygiel, *Baseball's Great Experiment, Jackie Robinson and His Legacy* (New York: Oxford University Press, 1983), 338-339.

33 "Bennie Daniels Doesn't…" *Hartford Courant*, January 26, 1979, 59.

34 "From Innings Pitched, To Time Served," *Los Angeles Herald Examiner*, July 27, 1978, D-4.

35 Ibid.

36 Ibid.

37 Daniels career …" *Sports Collectors Digest*, May 26, 2000, 28.

Roy Face

By Gary Gillette

BASEBALL IS A game in which one or two numbers can become burned into collective memory, ultimately defining a player's career. In the case of Babe Ruth, the numbers are 60 and 714. In the case of Ty Cobb, they are 4,191 and .367 (even though those numbers were shown to be inaccurate more than 25 years ago). "Joltin' Joe" DiMaggio's career has been forever entwined with 56, while "The Splendid Splinter" Ted Williams has been permanently branded with .406. In the case of Cy Young, the number everyone knows is 511. Bob Gibson's immortal number is 1.12; Orel Hershiser is bonded to 59.

Like many great players, Elroy Leon Face's career in the major leagues was defined by a pair of numbers: 18 and 1. Face's 1959 season, when he won 18 games against a single loss in relief for the Pirates, is certainly a remarkable achievement. At .947, it was the highest single-season winning percentage ever for a pitcher: only three other pitchers have posted a .900 winning percentage in a season since 1901 (minimum, 15 wins). A stalwart member of the Pirates from the mid-1950s through the late 1960s, the slight right-handed relief ace became one of the best-known "faces" of the postwar Pittsburgh franchise.

Standing only 5-feet-8 and listed at between 155 and 160 pounds, Roy Face would seem an unlikely candidate to play a key role in revolutionizing the way the game was played. Since the end of World War II, only seven other pitchers shorter than 5-feet-9 have made their big-league debuts and either started in 50 games or appeared in 100—none since 1976. Only three of those were shorter than Face, who was far from the prototype of the intimidating closer later made famous by practitioners like Goose Gossage, Rollie Fingers, and Bruce Sutter.

Durability is one of the hallmarks of the greatest relief pitchers, and Elroy Face clearly met that test. The right-hander pitched for 16 years, all but two of them exclusively or almost exclusively in relief. In 1956, Face tied the major-league record by appearing in nine consecutive games September 3–13, including five games in four days September 7–10. Even though he shouldered a heavy workload, Face was on the disabled list only once in his career, after knee surgery in 1965.

Consistency is another quality of great relief pitchers. Again, Face made the grade by posting double-digit save totals in all but two seasons from 1957 to 1968. (In that

period, the average NL-leading save figure was less than 23.) He led the league in saves three times and in appearances twice and was a member of the NL All-Star team in 1959, 1960, and 1961.

In the 1950s, the national pastime witnessed many profound changes. Among them was a new philosophy of pitching that coalesced after many teams experimented with true relief pitchers in the 1940s (as opposed to starters coming on in relief in key games between starts). Relievers, heretofore mostly considered to be failed starters, were gaining prominence as many pennant-winning clubs featured a bullpen ace. Nevertheless, most top relievers lacked one or both of the key qualities of consistency and durability.

Joe Black, a Negro League veteran, won the 1952 NL Rookie of the Year Award while going 15-4 with 15 saves for Brooklyn. He never had another season anything like that. Reliever Joe Page of the postwar Yankees had only two really good years. The Phillies' Jim Konstanty was more durable than most, but his MVP-winning 1950 was his only outstanding campaign. Ellis Kinder had several good seasons out of the bullpen for the Red Sox in the 1950s, but he lasted only four years as a full-time reliever. The Dodgers' Clem Labine probably was the most durable and consistent reliever prior to Face, though Labine never achieved Face's level of excellence.

The only relief pitcher of the pre-expansion era whose career was comparable to Face was Hoyt Wilhelm, the ageless knuckleballer who made a brilliant debut at age 29 with the New York Giants in 1952. Wilhelm went 15–3 with 11 saves, leading the NL with 71 appearances, all in relief. However, after two more good seasons, Wilhelm's career stalled. Bouncing from the Giants to the Cardinals to the Indians to the Orioles, he was converted to starting before finally settling in as a relief ace for good in 1961. Wilhelm's career eventually eclipsed Face's, but it was Face who was the pioneer in defining the role of the ace reliever in the 1950s.

Star relievers of the 1960s like Lindy McDaniel (who learned his forkball from Face in the early 1960s), Ron Perranoski, and Stu Miller were, thus, following in Face's footsteps. None of them ever garnered serious support for the Hall of Fame, never climbing above two percent of the vote. Face peaked at 19 percent in Hall balloting in 1987,

showing that he was regarded much more highly than any reliever of his time aside from Wilhelm, inducted into Cooperstown in 1985.

Retroactive save statistics first compiled in 1969 show that Face held the all-time saves lead from 1962 through 1963, being passed by Wilhelm in 1964. Face was the career leader in games finished from 1961 to 1964, again until passed by Wilhelm. From 1956, when he was permanently moved to the bullpen, through 1968, Face led all major-league pitchers in relief games with 717 (87 more than Wilhelm) and in saves with 183 (20 more than Wilhelm).

Considering that he didn't attend college, Face got a late start on his professional career for someone of his level of accomplishment. Born on February 20, 1928, in Stephentown, New York, just over the state line from Pittsfield, Massachusetts, he played baseball at Averill Park High School, a dozen miles east of Albany, before serving in the U.S. Army from February 1946 to July 1947.

Signed by the Phillies at age 20 and assigned to Class D, Face spent two years with Bradford in the Pennsylvania-Ontario-New York (PONY) League. Even though the right-hander pitched well for the PONY League champion Blue Wings in his professional debut (14–2 with a league-leading .875 winning percentage), he was not promoted. The following year, Face was even better, leading the PONY with a 2.58 ERA and compiling an 18–5 record for a fourth-place club. Yet Philadelphia left him exposed to the annual winter draft, allowing Branch Rickey of Brooklyn to snatch Face in December 1950.

Two years later, after successful campaigns with Pueblo in the Class A Western League (three levels above Class D, confirming that the Phillies made a mistake in not promoting him) and Fort Worth in the Double A Texas League, Rickey (now with Pittsburgh) again drafted Face at the 1952 Winter Meetings. The following spring, Face made his major-league debut on April 16. He spent the whole season with the Pirates, making 41 appearances, including 13 starts, but posting a 6.58 ERA.

At that time, the diminutive right-hander was what scouts used to call a "blow-and-go guy": a moundsman who threw as hard as he could for as long as he could, but who was not an experienced pitcher. Despite his small stature, Face threw as hard as, or harder than, Bob Friend and the other Pirates pitchers, according to catcher Hank Foiles, who was with Pittsburgh from late 1956 through 1959. As a rookie, Face's repertoire consisted of a fastball and a curveball. While the young right-hander's success in the minors argued that he might get by with just two arrows in his quiver, big-league hitters argued—successfully—to the contrary in 1953.

As a result of his first-year struggles, Face was sent in 1954 to Pittsburgh's highest-level farm club, New Orleans of the Double A Southern Association. His assignment was to learn an off-speed pitch—a career-changing move that would catapult him to stardom. Contrary to accounts that say Face learned his forkball from veteran relief pitcher Joe Page, Face says he simply got the idea for developing a fork from watching Page as the erstwhile Yankees reliever was trying to make comeback in Pittsburgh's spring camp in 1954. After practicing the new pitch on his own on the sidelines for half the season, Face started using it in ballgames with the Pelicans.

Danny Murtaugh, the Pelicans' skipper who would later manage the Pirates to world championships in 1960 and 1971, converted Face to a full-time reliever. Murtaugh scratched his new charge from his second scheduled start after he took over in the Crescent City, never asking him to start another game. Years later, Murtaugh reaped the benefits of that conversion when he was the man in the Forbes Field dugout during Face's peak years from 1958 to 1962.

After completing his assignment by mastering his new pitch, Face went north with Pittsburgh in the spring of 1955.

"I don't, but neither does the batter."

> —Face, as quoted in *The Cultural Encyclopedia of Baseball*, about whether he knew which way his forkball would break

A forkball is a pitch that is hard to define, hard to throw, hard to control, and very hard to hit. Essentially, it is a change-of-pace offering that gets its sudden drop because the pitcher jams the baseball between his index and middle fingers, allowing the ball to depart his hand with minimal spin. Properly delivered, it should "tumble" toward home plate, dropping out of the strike zone as befuddled batters futilely swing over it. If thrown slowly enough, á la Elroy,

the pitch can also break unpredictably to either side, á la the knuckleball.

The forkball that Roy Face ultimately mastered and which, in turn, allowed him to master NL hitters, is a little-used pitch with a long history. Assuming one accepts that forkballs and split-finger fastballs are different pitches—notwithstanding that many think it a distinction without real meaning—the forkball was invented in 1908 by Bert Hall, a pitcher with Tacoma in the Northwestern League who made his only major-league start for the Phillies in 1911. The next pitcher known to employ the fork was "Bullet Joe" Bush in the 1920s; the only other really prominent pitchers to use it regularly before Face were Ernest "Tiny" Bonham (an All-Star starter for the Yankees during World War II whose career was ended by his premature death while with the Pirates in the late 1940s), and Mort Cooper (who starred for the Cardinals in the 1940s).

Baseball analyst Rob Neyer rated Face as throwing the best forkball of all time (if one separates the fork from the splitter), though Neyer lumped the two pitches together in his top-10 list after devoting several pages to distinguishing them.

Though now identified most closely with his devastating forkball, Face has always maintained that he wasn't dependent on that pitch. When the fork was working, he might throw it 70 percent of the time; when it wasn't working, he might use it only 20 percent of the time. Though he later added a slider, he kept his curve, ultimately providing four pitches in his arsenal to choose from.

Even in his superb 1959 and 1960 seasons, Face mixed his pitch selection according to what was most effective that day.

The epigraph to Chapter III of Christy Mathewson's classic *Pitching in a Pinch* reads: "Many pitchers Are Effective in a Big League Ball Game until that Heart-Breaking Moment Arrives Known as the 'Pinch'—It Is then that the Man in the Box is Put to the Severest Test...Victory or Defeat Hangs on his Work in that Inning."

Armed with his new pitch, Face took off on his excellent career. He split his time between starting and relieving in '55, then led the NL in appearances the next year with 68 (including three starts). In '57, Face registered his first year with double-digit saves; in '58, he led the NL in saves for the first time. His sensational 1959 season marked his first All-Star honors and is now, of course, the stuff of baseball legend.

"When he had that great year in 1959 you had to wonder how he did it, but he did, had that great forkball and I don't think he weighed more than 145 pounds," said Sam Narron, Branch Rickey's first bullpen catcher (as quoted in *Pen Men*).

Face's sole loss in '59 snapped a relief record 17-game winning streak that year as well as a 22-game winning streak over two seasons. Perhaps more remarkable in an era where ace relievers often were called upon with the score tied, it was also his first loss in 99 appearances, dating back to early 1958.

Sally O'Leary, who worked in the Pittsburgh PR department for 32 years and now edits the Pirates alumni newsletter *The Black and Gold*, recalls how Face's record-setting season—which included a healthy dose of good luck, as virtually all great seasons do—has been remembered by retired Bucs pitchers. "[T]he Pirate starters love to tell stories of how they would start a game, pitch really well, and somehow the game would get tied—Elroy

would come in—and get the win! This always provides good copy!"

A key actor in Pittsburgh's 1960 pageantry, Face again topped the NL in appearances while saving 24 and compiling a 2.90 ERA in 114 $^2/_3$ innings. Though bordering on heroic, Face's efforts in the 1960 World Series have been largely forgotten by fans—including many who remember Bill Mazeroski's famous homer. Coming in from the pen to save Games One, Four, and Five, Face narrowly missed becoming the winning pitcher in Game Seven when the Yankees came from behind to knot the score in the top of the ninth. (Face had been removed for a pinch-hitter in the bottom of the eighth at the start of a five-run Pittsburgh rally.)

Face logged 10 $^1/_3$ innings in that Series, more than any other Bucs pitcher—including starters—except Vern Law. Only one year earlier, the Dodgers' Larry Sherry had become the first pitcher ever to save or win every game for a World Series winner.

After an off-year in 1961 (6–12 record, though he again led the league in saves), Face enjoyed his best year in "The Show" in '62. Although Roy's 1962 season isn't as well known as his 1959 or 1960 campaigns, at age 34, Face won his only *Sporting News* Fireman of the Year Award. (*TSN*'s award was first given out in 1960.) The unflappable veteran posted a league-leading, career-high 28 saves to go with a 1.88 ERA (2.09 adjusted for park factor and league offensive level) as well as an NL relief-high 20 Adjusted Pitching Runs (runs allowed compared to the average pitcher).

The durable righty was never as good thereafter, struggling through a mediocre 1963, a rocky 1964, and an injury-shortened 1965. Afterward, with lighter usage, the seasoned stopper rebounded to post three consecutive solid seasons before his Pittsburgh career came to an end.

When he was sold to Detroit, Face held the NL records for games pitched (802), games in relief (775), games finished (547), and relief wins (92). In all of those categories, Face was second to future Hall of Famer Hoyt Wilhelm for the major-league lead. Wilhelm, the first relief pitcher enshrined in Cooperstown, had an advantage in that he had spent most of his career to that point with first-division teams.

According to longtime Pittsburgh sportswriter Lester Biederman in the September 14, 1968, issue of *The Sporting News*, "There was a little dash of cloak and dagger mystery to Roy Face's final turn with the Pirates August 31 before he was sold to the Tigers for a reported $100,000." The deal with Detroit had already been agreed upon, but it hadn't been announced since the Tigers wouldn't have a roster slot open till September 1. (*TSN* also asserted that Face had saved 233 games for the Pirates, apparently using a different definition for the unofficial stat that would finally be codified for the following season.)

Pittsburgh sold Face to Detroit despite his leading the Bucs with 13 saves in only 43 games and posting a 2.60 ERA (Adjusted ERA 13 percent better than the NL norm). His last appearance for the Bucs tied Walter Johnson's record for most appearances with a single team (802); it was arranged as somewhat of a going-away present by Pittsburgh management. Face was invited to start this last game, but declined. Instead, Face relieved Steve Blass after the Pirates' starter had retired the leadoff hitter in the first inning. Blass went to left field temporarily as Face threw a single pitch and recorded a groundout before walking off the mound. While the Pirates had not yet announced Face's sale to Detroit, it seemed that everyone with the club knew what was happening and wanted to bid Roy adieu.

When he pitched his last game in the majors less than a year later, Face stood second with 193 on the all-time saves list to Wilhelm's 210; he was six saves behind Wilhelm when he left Pittsburgh in 1968. That was no mean feat considering that, in Face's 14 years in the Steel City, the Bucs won only one pennant and finished in the first division only three other times. Face remains today atop the Pirates' all-time list in games with 802 and saves with 188.

According to O'Leary, the Pirates' alumni newsletter editor, Face remains extremely popular today, almost four decades after he last pulled off his Pirates uniform. "He is always ready to help the alumni in one way or another—appearances, signing autographs, giving little talks (question and answer things)—and the public enjoys having him at their events," she says.

In one of those fascinating twists of fate, the world champion 1968 Tigers turned to one of the all-time great firemen—the predominant term of that day for what

would today be called closers—late in their season to give them extra insurance for the final month. After only two brief appearances and two more unexpected twists of fate, Face was all but forgotten in Detroit.

In hindsight, the '68 Tigers now seem to have been invulnerable. Yet, after ascending to first place on May 10 and holding leads between 5 1/2 and 8 games for the next three months, they didn't appear to have the American League pennant in the bag in late August. Upon sweeping a doubleheader from the Athletics on August 27, rookie manager Earl Weaver's hard-charging Orioles had blazed to a 35-17 record after Weaver had replaced Hank Bauer at the helm. Worse, the second-place Birds had narrowed the gap to four games when the Tigers dropped a 2-1 decision to the White Sox on the same day. The No. 1 and No. 2 teams were set to clash in a big three-game weekend series starting on August 30 in Motown, then potentially fight it out for the pennant in the last week of the season in Crabtown.

Detroit was only six games ahead of Baltimore at the end of August when Face was purchased from Pittsburgh on August 31. No one knew at that time that Detroit would finish with a flourish, winning 21 of their last 30 games as Baltimore stumbled to the finish line, losing 17 while winning 13 and finishing a distant 12 games back.

Still reeling from the devastation—both physical and psychological—of the 1967 riots, the city of Detroit was going gaga over its Tigers in the summer of 1968. As the long season ground on, however, Detroit's bullpen looked like a potential problem. Such is the luxury of having a great team: worrying about potential problems rather than having to deal with pressing problems. General Manager Jim Campbell, therefore, tried to bolster the club's relief corps by the time-honored tradition of adding several experienced arms.

In that glorious summer of '68, Detroit's bullpen was an amalgam of untested youngsters (rookie righty Daryl Patterson was 24, while rookie lefty Jon Warden was a tender 21) and sophomores with about a year or so of big-league experience (lefty John Hiller, 25, and righties Pat Dobson and Fred Lasher, both 26). Hiller and Dobson filled the swingman roles, making 12 and 10 starts, respectively. The only Detroit pitcher over 27 years old for the first half of the season was veteran starter Earl Wilson (33).

Despite the doubts, the Detroit bullpen as a group was spectacular that year, holding opponents to a .200 batting average (remember, however, that the league batted only .230 in the watershed "Year of the Pitcher") and compiling a 2.26 ERA with a 29–13 record and 29 saves. Their unofficial saves total was tied for sixth in the league. No Detroit pitcher posted more than seven saves, with three relievers each earning at least 17 percent of the team total (Dobson and Patterson with seven each; Lasher with five).

As the season wore on, Campbell strengthened his callow pitching staff by acquiring a handful of old-timers. Don McMahon, who became the Tigers' closer, was 38, though he would soldier on for another six seasons and 244 games, mostly with the Giants. The Tigers also auditioned two other veteran closers, acquiring John Wyatt (only 33 but at the end of his career) from the Yankees in mid-June and Roy Face, age 40. Unlike McMahon, neither veteran thrived in Detroit. Both would finish their careers in 1969, with Wyatt appearing in his final four games for Oakland and Face spending most of the year in Montreal.

On September 2, the day after he reported to Detroit, Face made his AL debut. He was called on in the eighth inning of the second game of a doubleheader, allowing a run-scoring hit and blowing the lead while pitching two-thirds of an inning. Face also appeared the next day, again being nicked for an RBI single and blowing the lead. He never saw game action for Detroit afterward. His stat line for the 1968 Tigers reads: one inning pitched, five batters faced, two hits allowed, one (intentional) walk, and one strikeout.

The Detroit rotation soon made Campbell's insurance policy superfluous by logging complete games in half of its 26 September starts on the way to leading the AL with a total of 59—including a remarkable 12 consecutive complete games from September 6 through September 19. By the time that streak was over, the gap between the Tigers and the Orioles was an insurmountable 12 1/2 games, and Face sat unused for the rest of the season. The veteran closer returned home as Detroit battled St. Louis in what would become one of the greatest fall classics ever.

Face's career came to a close in 1969, the year when the save was officially endorsed as a statistic. The great reliever was released by Detroit late in spring training and was picked up three weeks later by the expansion Expos, for whom he appeared in 44 games before being released in mid-August. Face pitched briefly for Triple A Hawaii in 1970 before hanging up his spikes permanently.

In a November 2, 1968, column by Watson Spoelstra in *The Sporting News*, Tigers pitching coach Johnny Sain was optimistic about the Detroit pitching staff's prospects for the next season. One reason mentioned by Sain was that he thought the club would be helped by the presence of four veteran closers: McMahon, Face, Wyatt, and Dick Radatz (who pitched in the Tigers' organization in Toledo in 1968 after being released by the Cubs).

Sain's prognostication for his veteran quartet would remain mostly unfulfilled, with only Radatz and McMahon pitching for Detroit in 1969. "Four pretty good country relief pitchers" was the way Radatz remembered that group years later in *Pen Men*.

That seems like a fair way to sum up Roy Face's career: A pretty good country relief pitcher who became a pioneer.

Sources

Joe Abramovich and Paul A. Rickart. *Baseball Register* (St. Louis: The Sporting News, 1964)

Bob Cairns. *Pen Men*. (New York: St. Martin's Press, 1993)

Paul Dickson, Paul. *Dickson Baseball Dictionary*. (New York: Facts on File, 1989) and 2nd edition (New York: Avon Books, 1991)

John Duxbury and Cliff Kachline. *Baseball Register*. St. Louis: The Sporting News, 1966 and 1967)

John Duxbury. *Baseball Register*. (St. Louis: The Sporting News, 1968 and 1969)

Eric Enders. *100 Years of the World Series: 1903–2003*. (New York: Barnes & Noble Publishing, 2004)

Bill Felber. *The Book on the Book*. (New York: St. Martin's Press, 2005)

Steve Gietschier. *The Complete Baseball Record and Fact Book*, 2006 ed. (St. Louis: Sporting News Books, 2006)

Gary Gillette and Pete Palmer. *The ESPN Baseball Encyclopedia*, 4th ed. (New York: Sterling Publishing Co., Inc., 2007)

Bill James. *The Bill James Historical Baseball Abstract*. (New York: Villard Books, 1986)

Bill James and Rob Neyer. *The Neyer/James Guide to Pitchers*. (New York: Fireside Books, 2004)

Lloyd Johnson. *Baseball's Dream Teams*. (New York: Crescent Books, 1990)

Cliff Kachline and Chris Roewe. *Official Baseball Guide for 1966*. (St. Louis: The Sporting News, 1966)

----— *Official Baseball Guide for 1967*. (St. Louis: The Sporting News, 1967)

Jonathan Fraser Light. *The Cultural Encyclopedia of Baseball*. (Jefferson, North Carolina: McFarland & Company, Inc., 1997)

Paul MacFarlane Chris Roewe, and Larry Wigge. *Official Baseball Guide for 1970*. (St. Louis: The Sporting News, 1970)

Paul MacFarlane, Chris Roewe, Larry Wigge, and Larry Vickrey. *Official Baseball Guide for 1971*.)St. Louis: The Sporting News, 1971)

----— *Official Baseball Guide for 1972*. (St. Louis: The Sporting News, 1972)

Christopher Mathewson. *Pitching In a Pinch*. (Mattituck: N.Y.: Amereon House reprint of 1912 Knickerbocker Press edition)

Peter Morris. *A Game of Inches: The Game Behind the Scenes*. (Chicago: Ivan R. Dee, 2006)

Peter Morris. *A Game of Inches: The Game On the Field*. (Chicago: Ivan R. Dee, 2006)

David S. Neft, Lee Allen, and Robert Markel. *The Baseball Encyclopedia*, 1st ed., updated. (New York: The Macmillan Company, 1969)

Danny Peary. *We Played the Game*. (New York: Hyperion Books, 1994)

Charles Pickard, Cliff Kachline, and Paul A. Rickart. *Baseball Register*. (St. Louis: The Sporting News, 1965)

David Pietrusza, Matthew Silverman, and Michael Gershman. *Baseball: The Biographical Encyclopedia*. (Kingston, New York: Total/Sports Illustrated, 2000)

Martin Quigley. *The Crooked Pitch*. (Chapel Hill, N.C.: Algonquin Books, 1984)

Joseph L. Reichler. *The Baseball Trade Register*. (New York: Collier Books, 1984)

Chris Roewe and Oscar Kahan. *Official Baseball Guide for 1968*. (St. Louis: The Sporting News, 1968)

Chris Roewe and Paul MacFarlane. *Official Baseball Guide for 1969*. (St. Louis: The Sporting News, 1969)

Lyle Spatz. The SABR *Baseball List & Record Book*. (New York: Scribner, 2007)

J.G. Taylor Spink, Paul A. Rickart, and Joe Abramovich. *Baseball Register*. (St. Louis: The Sporting News, 1955, 1956, 1957, 1958, 1959, 1960, 1961, 1962, 1963)

J.G. Taylor Spink, Paul A. Rickart, and Clifford Kachline. *The Sporting News Baseball Guide and Record Book*. (St. Louis: The Sporting News, 1961, 1962, 1963, 1964, 1965)

Benjamin Barrett Sumner. *Minor League Baseball Standings*. (Jefferson, N.C.: McFarland & Company, Inc., 2000)

John Thorn and John Holway. *The Pitcher*. (New York: Prentice-Hall, 1988)

Jim Trdinich and Dan Hart. *Pittsburgh Pirates 2007 Media Guide*. (Pittsburgh: Pittsburgh Pirates Baseball Club, 2007)

Jim Trdinich, Dan Hart, and Patrick O'Connell. *Pittsburgh Pirates 2004 Media Guide*. (Pittsburgh: Pittsburgh Pirates Baseball Club, 2004)

Les Biederman. "Buc Scribe Gives Bengals An Intimate Look at Face." *The Sporting News*, September 21, 1968

Les Biederman. "Face Leaves Bucs In a Blaze of Glory." *The Sporting News*, September 14, 1968.

Bill Felber. "The Changing Game," in John Thorn and Pete Palmer's *Total Baseball*, 1st ed. (New York: Warner Books, 1989)

Bill Felber and Gary Gillette. "The Changing Game," in John Thorn and Pete Palmer's *Total Baseball*, seventh edition. (Kingston, New York: Total Sports Publishing, 2001)

"National Nuggets," in *The Sporting News*, p. 54, October 5, 1968.

Watson Spoelstra. "It Looks Like Northrup Can Buy Cowboy Boots," in *The Sporting News*, September 21, 1968.

Watson Spoelstra. "Sain, Naragon Give Tigers Early Line on '69," in *The Sporting News*, November 2, 1968.

www.baseballindex.org

www.baseball-reference.com

http://members.SABR.org [SABR encyclopedia, including Home Run Log and Scouting Database]

http://pittsburgh.pirates.mlb.com/

www.retrosheet.org [including Transactions Log]

Gary Gillette. Interviews with Elroy Face, Pete Palmer, Jim Price, and Lenny Yochim.

Rod Nelson. E-mail messages to author.

Sally O'Leary. E-mail message to author.

Pete Palmer. E-mail messages to author.

Notes:

Ages quoted are seasonal ages (i.e., age as of June 30 of each season)

Adjusted ERA stats per Pete Palmer's calculations in *The ESPN Baseball Encyclopedia*. They may differ slightly from similar statistics on baseball-reference.com or those previously published in *Total Baseball*.

Earl Francis

By Gregory H. Wolf

WITH THE MUSCULAR physique of a football player, 6-foot-2, 215-pound rookie pitcher Earl Francis was called up in midseason 1960 by the Pittsburgh Pirates to strengthen their bullpen. The 24-year-old right-hander logged 18 innings in seven appearances and sported a nifty 2.00 earned-run average, but came down with shoulder problems and was sent back to minors when the Bucs signed 11-year veteran Clem Labine in August. Francis was recalled during the team's September pennant drive and was on the Pirates' World Series roster, but did not play. Lauded by manager Danny Murtaugh for his unlimited potential and touted as a future 20-game winner, Francis progressed to the point where he was named the Bucs' Opening Day starter in 1963, but a sore arm led to his demotion to the minors a year later and his retirement from Organized Baseball in 1966 with a 16-23 big-league record.[1]

Earl Coleman Francis was born on July 14, 1935, in the small unincorporated hamlet of Slab Fork, in Raleigh County in southwest West Virginia, about 250 miles south of Pittsburgh. His father, Millard, originally from North Carolina, worked in maintenance at a local coal mine, the main employer in the Appalachian hills. His mother, Cordie, a native of Virginia, found piecemeal work. Together, they nurtured their three children, Earl, his older brother, Millard Jr., and his younger sister, Fredella, in a deeply segregated, rural, and poor society. Stressing an education they themselves were denied as African-Americans, Millard and Cordie sent their children to Stratton High School, an all-black school in Beckley, about 12 miles from home.

A star football player for Stratton, Earl was offered a scholarship to play on the gridiron for West Virginia State College (later

renamed West Virginia State University), a historically black public college in metropolitan Charleston; however, his passion was baseball, and he passed up the chance. Earl remembered accompanying his brother to a tryout for an American Legion baseball team in Raleigh County, West Virginia. "I was only 13 and went along for the ride. … But I didn't think much of the pitchers and asked the manager for a chance to pitch. I made the team before Millard did."[2] Playing four years for Post 70, Earl caught the attention of local bird-dog scout Jimmy Vennari who recommended him to the Pirates' chief scout, Rex Bowen. Bowen signed the 18-year-old Francis in 1954, the same year he signed another prospect born in West Virginia, Bill Mazeroski.

Assigned to one of the Pirates' three Class D teams, the Clinton (Iowa) Pirates in the Mississippi-Ohio Valley League, Francis pitched well and ranked among the top ten in almost all pitching categories, including wins (11), innings (180), starts (23), and ERA (3.10); however, off the diamond, Francis felt alone and far from home. Despite a promising future, he enlisted in the US Air Force. Pitching for base teams during his four years in the service, Francis led Bolling Air Force Base, near Washington, D.C., to the Air Force world title in 1958 by striking out 53 batters in 27 innings in the playoffs, including 14 in the title game. Francis batted .394 with three home runs in the tournament and shared the most-valuable-player honors.

By the time Francis returned to the Pirates organization in the spring of 1959, the team had undergone substantial changes. New general manager Joe L. Brown, building on Branch Rickey's foundations, aggressively signed prospects and in 1958 his team enjoyed its best season since 1944. Brown at first planned to have Francis pitch for the Columbus (Georgia) Pirates in the Class A South Atlantic League, but decided to put him on the fast track to the major leagues and assigned the big right-hander to the Pirates' Salt Lake City affiliate in the Triple-A Pacific Coast League. There Francis fell under the tutelage of skipper Larry Shepard, a longtime minor-league hurler known for developing young pitchers. With a team-high 27 starts for the Bees, Francis won six of 11 decisions and posted a 3.33 ERA, but arm and shoulder tenderness limited him to 154 innings. At the conclusion of the season, during which the Bees won the PCL championship, Francis was added to the Pirates' 40-man roster and sent to play for Ponce in the Puerto Rican Winter League to work on his control after walking a league-high 113 batters. Excited about his future with the Pirates, Francis voiced his frustration with the quality of play in Puerto Rico, where, he said, many players didn't play as hard as they did during the regular season.[3]

Reporting to his first major-league spring training in 1960, Francis competed for a roster spot, but was assigned to the Columbus Jets of the Triple-A International League when the Pirates decided to keep a more experienced right-hander, 29-year-old Jim Umbricht.[4] No doubt the Bucs rued their decision. While Umbricht floundered (5.80 ERA in 15 games through June) with the Pirates, Francis blossomed with the Jets, cutting down on his walks and exhibiting the power pitching the team expected from him. In what was described as a "startling move" by The Sporting News, the Pirates optioned right-handers Bennie Daniels and Umbricht to the Jets and brought up Francis and the hard-throwing Tom Cheney in late June.[5] On June 30 at Forbes Field, Francis made his major-league debut when he replaced reliever Paul Giel to start the fifth inning in mop-up duty against the San Francisco Giants. In his longest outing of the year, Francis pitched five innings, surrendering seven hits and three earned runs in an 11-0 loss.

With six relief appearances in July, Francis seemed to have solved the Pirates' need for a strong right-handed reliever. In 13 innings, he surrendered just seven hits and one earned run (0.69 ERA) while walking just one and striking out eight. In relief of Joe Gibbon on July 16, Francis pitched the last two frames to record his first major-league

victory when Dick Stuart cranked a walk-off solo homer in the bottom of the ninth inning to defeat the Cincinnati Reds, 6-5. In his last outing of the season, on July 27 in St. Louis, Francis "developed shoulder trouble" and was removed after tossing three innings.[6] With Francis unable to pitch, the Pirates signed former Brooklyn Dodgers All-Star reliever Clem Labine in mid-August and returned the ailing Francis to Columbus. Francis was recalled in September but didn't pitch during the last month of the regular season or in the Pirates' exciting and historic World Series victory over the New York Yankees. The players voted him a quarter-share of World Series winnings ($2,104.48, about one-quarter of his annual salary).[7]

After his second spring training with the Pirates, Francis was once again optioned to the Columbus Jets, where he reunited with new Jets skipper Larry Shepard. On a team boasting hard throwers Bob Veale, Tom Cheney, and Al Jackson, Francis stood out. "Earl belongs in the major leagues," said Shepard, who opined that Francis (with a 3-1 record and 1.76 ERA in 41 innings) was the best pitcher in the International League.[8] In early June Francis was recalled by the Pirates to replace the ailing George Witt and shore up the relief corps. After eight appearances, Francis was given a start on June 28 against the Los Angeles Dodgers at Forbes Field. He outdueled Sandy Koufax, striking out a career-high ten batters in eight innings while surrendering three hits and two runs to win his first game as a starter.

Manager Murtaugh was impressed with the 25-year-old, saying, "[Francis] has a major league arm and probably has the best fastball and best curve on our staff."[9] But in his next start, Francis was pulled with arm stiffness after six strong innings against the Reds, missed two starts, and was never able to establish consistency or completely overcome arm problems the rest of the season. He finished with a disappointing 2-8 record and a 4.21 ERA in 102 innings. Privately, the Pirates questioned Francis's dedication and commitment to baseball and challenged him to do better. "He must adjust himself mentally," said Murtaugh.[10] "I have the guts [to play]," said the typically quiet and unassuming Francis, "but I'm lacking in determination. I'll have it next year. I've got to."[11] Throughout their tenure together, Francis and Murtaugh had a strained relationship, no doubt a product of the polar opposite personalities.

In 1960 Bucs outfielder Joe Christopher introduced his roommate, Francis, to Marie "Dee Dee" Stotts, a schoolteacher and Pittsburgh native. With his most important pitch thus far in his career, Francis asked Marie to marry him, and they were wed in December 1961 at St. Benedict the Moor Catholic Church in Pittsburgh. After their marriage they resided in Gary, Indiana, where Marie, a graduate of Cheney University in Philadelphia, was involved in desegregating the school system. In following offseasons, the couple resided in Pittsburgh, where they raised five children, sons Earl, Michael, and Shannon and daughters Lydia and Shawn. Francis was also an avid hunter and enjoyed spending time outside.

Despite an outwardly shy demeanor, Francis was easygoing and a practical joker, and got along with his teammates well. In a 2012 interview Marie Francis recalled how infielder Gene Baker, the most experienced of the Pirates' African-American players and later a team coach, served as a mentor to Francis and helped him find his way in the clubhouse and off the field. She said Earl greatly respected pitcher Vern Law for his professional approach to the game, but also for the way he made Earl feel part of the team. Francis developed a close friendship with Christopher and Baker, and later outfielder Ted Savage. The segregation Francis experienced in West Virginia still permeated major-league clubhouses in the 1960s. Mrs. Francis recalled how they had very little social contact with any of the white players on the team.

After an impressive spring training in 1962, Francis was named to the Pirates' Opening Day roster. They got off to a hot start, setting a team record by winning their first ten games of the season. Francis was an integral contributor with "magnificent relief pitching," tossing 8 1/3 scoreless innings while surrendering just three hits in three appearances.[12] In light of Vern Law's slow start and Joe Gibbon's elbow miseries, Francis was given a spot start on April 28 in Los Angeles against Sandy Koufax. Both pitchers tossed complete games, but Francis was on the losing end after surrendering a two-out walk-off single to Tommie Davis that gave the Dodgers a 2-1 victory. "Thanks to manager Danny Murtaugh for sticking by me when I was going bad," Francis said of his unexpected success to start the season.[13] He also credited fellow pitcher Bob Friend with helping him concentrate and relax on the mound. In June *The Sporting News* ran a feature article on

Francis and described him as the Pirates' "most effective man on the hill."[14] "I have something new I never had before—confidence," Francis said. "I now feel I can do the job and when I go to the mound, I just rear back and throw. I'm not afraid of the batters or not afraid of being sent down to the minors."[15]

Though Francis seemed to have hit his stride as a starter, he struggled to pitch more than six innings (only five times in 17 starts) and was demoted to the bullpen after two bad starts to conclude July. Given a spot start on August 25 in St. Louis, Francis tossed his only major-league shutout by blanking the Cardinals on three hits while striking out five. Unexpectedly, Francis commenced the best five-week stretch in his professional career. His explanation: "I pitched a long time with a 'flat' fastball until I went to [pitching coach] Bill Burwell one day and asked for help. He suggested that I grip the ball across the seams. Now I have more hop to the ball."[16] Francis followed his shutout with three consecutive complete games pitching every sixth or seventh day in Murtaugh's convoluted rotation. After tossing a career-high 10 1/3 innings against the Phillies on August 31 and losing when he surrendered a walk-off triple to Don Demeter, he rebounded to beat the Dodgers in Los Angeles, 10-1, while striking out nine. In San Francisco Francis held the Giants to one unearned run to even his record at 8-8 and also hit his only major-league home run, a three-run shot off Bobby Bolin in the eighth inning. "[His] curveball reminds me of Don Newcombe's," said coach Burwell, impressed with Francis's transformation.[17] Francis also boasted a deceptive changeup and occasionally used a knuckler which he called his "pension pitch" should his fastball ever leave him.[18] In his 23rd and last start of the season, Francis hurled arguably the best game of his career: a complete-game, ten-inning two-hitter to defeat the Cincinnati Reds, 1-0, at Crosley Field. Involved in nine one-run verdicts (he won four of them and lost five), Francis finished with a 9-8 record and a 3.07 ERA in 176 innings, while the Pirates led the NL with a 3.37 team ERA.

After honing his control in the Arizona Instructional League in the offseason and having a subsequent impressive spring training in 1963, Francis was rewarding by being named Opening Day starter in 1963 over longtime veterans Bob Friend and Vern Law. Named the "best young pitcher" on the staff by *The Sporting News*, Francis faced the Reds on April 8 in Cincinnati.[19] The second batter he faced was Pete Rose, making his major-league debut; he drew a walk and scored on Frank Robinson's home run. Francis was lifted for a pinch-hitter after pitching just two innings and was tagged with the loss. Despite the predictions of success, Francis was undone by arm and elbow miseries that accompanied him all season. After pitching 7 1/3 scoreless innings against the Cubs to notch his first victory of the season on April 22, Francis missed two weeks and never fully recovered. Splitting his time between the bullpen and the starting rotation, he managed only four wins in ten decisions and logged just 97 1/3 innings while posting a dismal 4.53 ERA.

Baseball can be a cruel game. Less than a year after becoming the first African-American Opening Day starting pitcher for the Pirates, Francis was back in the minors in 1964, optioned to Columbus at the end of spring training. After leading the Jets with 29 starts and 180 innings while compiling a 10-10 record, Francis was recalled to the Pirates in September. He had two appearances, including his last major-league start in the final game of the season during which he surrendered six runs in five innings in a 6-0 loss to the Braves in Milwaukee.

While playing for Aguilas in the Dominican Winter League, Francis was traded on December 15, 1964, along with outfielder Ted Savage to the St. Louis Cardinals for two utilitymen, Ron Cox and Jack Damaska. After Francis helped lead Aguilas to the league championship, highlighted by his commanding two-hitter with ten strikeouts over Licey in the playoffs, Cardinals general manager Bob Howsam was excited about the 29-year-old's chances of making the 1965 squad and invited him to spring training as a nonroster player.

Francis took a liking to manager Red Schoendienst, whom he respected for his honesty and fairness. However, the reigning World Series champs had a secure staff and highly touted (and handsomely compensated) bonus-baby pitchers waiting in the wings. Consequently, Francis was optioned to the Jacksonville Suns in the International League. Posting an unspectacular 10-11 record and 4.10 ERA in 182 innings, he was again a late-season call-up and made his final two appearances in the major leagues, both in relief.

Francis was a nonroster invitee to the Cardinals' spring training again in 1966, but his contract was sold to the Seattle Angels, the California Angels' affiliate in the Pacific Coast League. Limited to just five games, Francis was sold to the Indianapolis Indians, where he finished his final professional season with the Chicago White Sox' PCL affiliate. Marie Francis said the Cardinals offered Earl a job working with the team's pitching prospects in the Mexican League, but he rejected it in order to spend time with his family in Pittsburgh. After years of chronic arm and back miseries, Francis retired at the conclusion of the season. In his six-season major-league career, Francis posted a 16-23 record with a 3.77 ERA in 405 2/3 innings. In his seven-year minor-league career he won 52 games, logged 942 innings, and posted a 3.55 ERA.

After his playing days, Francis, his wife, and their children settled in suburban Pittsburgh, where he began a long, successful career as a meatcutter for a local grocery chain. Mrs. Francis told the author that her husband felt hurt about the way his career ended and because of the strained relationships with the Pirates' front office. "He was from the coal mines of West Virginia," she said. "He wasn't ready for all of the city slickers taking advantage of him. I was outspoken for him."[20] Francis participated in occa-

sional reunions of the 1960 World Series championship team, but otherwise had limited contact with the Pirates. Suffering from the effects of diabetes, Francis died at the age of 66 on July 3, 2002, at Presbyterian Hospital in Pittsburgh. He was buried in Homewood Cemetery in Pittsburgh. "I remember him as being a man's man," said former teammate Bill Virdon upon learning of Francis's death. "He had a good arm, a strong arm. He was always willing to throw."[21]

The author would like to thank Marie Francis who was interviewed via telephone on December 18, 2012. She provided great insights to her husband's life and career.

Sources

Ancestry.com

BaseballLibrary.com

Baseball-Reference.com

Retrosheet.org

The Sporting News

Notes

1   United Press International, "Stuart May Be Pirates Top Bait in Trade Talks," *Beaver County Times,* Beaver, Pennsylvania, November 14, 1962, 37.

2   United Press International, "Francis Solves 'X' Quantity He Needed," *Raleigh Register*, Beckley, West Virginia, May, 9, 1962, 13.

3   John Flynn, "Earl Francis to Take the First Shot at the Pittsburgh Pitching Staff," *Raleigh Register,* Beckley, West Virginia, February 23, 1960, 9.

4   Tony Constantino, "Postscripts," *Morgantown* (West Virginia) *Post,* June 30, 1960, 15.

5   *The Sporting News,* July 6, 1960, 37.

6   *The Sporting News,* August 3, 1960, 10.

7   *The Sporting News,* November 2, 1960, 10.

8   United Press International, "New Buc Claimed Best in Circuit," *Morgantown* (West Virginia) *Post,* June 3, 1961, 11.

9   *The Sporting News,* December 20, 1961, 30.

10 United Press International, "Murtaugh Sizes Recruits on Pirates Prospect List," *Morgantown* (West Virginia) *Post,* December 8, 1961, 11.

11 George McLaughlin, "Francis Says He'll Do Better in 1962," *Raleigh Register,* Beckley, West Virginia, October 19, 1961, 21.

12 *The Sporting News,* April 25, 1962, 11.

13 United Press International, "Francis Solves 'X' Quantity He Needed," *Raleigh Register*, Beckley, West Virginia, May, 9, 1962, 13.

14 *The Sporting News,* June 23, 1962, 15.

15 Ibid.

16 *The Sporting News,* September 15, 1962, 10.

17 United Press International, "Francis Solves 'X' Quantity He Needed," *Raleigh Register*, Beckley, West Virginia, May, 9, 1962, 13.

18 Ibid.

19 *The Sporting News,* April 20, 1963, 14.

20 Telephone interview with Marie Francis, wife of Earl Francis, December 18, 2012.

21 Rick Shrum, "Obituary: Earl Francis. Pirates Pitcher in the 60s," *Post-Gazette.com.* July 6, 2002. http://old.post-gazette.com/obituaries/20020706francis2.asp

Bob Friend

By Clifton Blue Parker

BOB FRIEND WAS one of baseball's more consistent starting pitchers during his era and a workhorse for the 1960 Pittsburgh Pirates. That year the right-hander led the team in games started and innings pitched while posting an 18-12 record and 3.00 earned-run average in a major comeback from a disappointing 1959 campaign.

Durable at 6-feet and 190 pounds, Friend—nicknamed the "Warrior"[1]—never spent a single day on a disabled list in his 16-year career, in which he pitched mostly for the Pirates. At the beginning of his career, Friend's best pitches were a sinking fastball and a hard curveball—later on he would add a slider to his repertoire. He had unusually good control.

"I had a real good sinker that carried me through most of the prime of my career," Friend said in an interview. "I also had a hard curve and a fair off-speed pitch, but it was the sinker more than anything else."[2]

A winner of 197 major-league games, Friend as of 2012 still held Pirates records for career innings pitched and strikeouts. From 1951 to 1965 he averaged 232 innings pitched and 13 victories for some very lackluster Bucco teams. He pitched more than 200 innings for 11 consecutive seasons (1955 through 1965). As a 24-year-old in 1955, Friend became the first pitcher to lead his league in ERA while pitching for a last-place team. He went on to pace the National League in victories once, innings pitched twice, and games started three times.

Robert Bartmess Friend was born in Lafayette, Indiana, on November 24, 1930. He grew up in nearby West Lafayette, and as a young boy studied piano; his father was an orchestra leader who died when Bob was 16. At West Lafayette High School, Friend was a

sports star—an all-state football halfback and an all-state pitcher, and he also played basketball and golf. It was in high school that Friend earned the "Warrior" nickname.

"That came from high-school football," Friend said. "I was a pretty good tailback, and then later on when I was pitching so many innings, the nickname stuck."[3]

Because his father and many other family members had attended Purdue University, a young Friend dreamed of playing college baseball and football there. But a shoulder injury suffered in high school shifted his interests away from football and to baseball.[4]

He enrolled at Purdue in the fall of 1949, and a year later signed a professional contract with the Pittsburgh Pirates. The scout who inked him to the deal was Stan Feasal, who once worked for Pirates general manager Branch Rickey in Brooklyn. Friend's bonus was $12,500, a decent amount in those days. The 20-year-old was invited to join the Pirates in spring training in 1950, and afterward was given a minor-league assignment.

During his playing career, Friend kept up his pursuit of a college degree, attending Purdue during baseball offseasons for eight straight years. He eventually earned a bachelor's degree in economics in 1957, and was a member of the Sigma Chi fraternity.[5]

After entering Pittsburgh's farm system in 1950, Friend posted a 12-9 record for the Waco Pirates in the Class B Big State League. Bumped up to the Indianapolis Indians of the Triple-A American Association, he finished the year with a 2-4 record. Friend told SABR researcher Gregory Wolf in a published interview that he learned about his promotion from Waco manager Al Lopez, the former major-league catcher.

"He was a big influence on me," said Friend. "In my last game at Waco I pitched a no-hitter and Joe Brown (business manager of the team) called me in and said, 'You're going to Indianapolis.'" [6]

Rickey was intent on developing young talent quickly, especially pitching, so he moved Friend onto the major-league roster at the start of 1951. It came as a surprise to Friend. "I really didn't know that I made the team until Billy Meyer, who was the manager at that time, came up and told me that he liked what he saw and he'd give me a shot," he told Wolf. [7]

Despite the Pirates' losing ways in the early 1950s, Friend admired Meyer, who had to deal with plenty of Pirate misfortunes on the field. "He was one of the good ones. He was losing his patience with the players they were bringing up. I don't think he could go through another losing season, especially like the one in 1952 when we lost 112 games," he said.

Friend's first season was 1951, and the 20-year-old went 6-10, not getting much run support from a dreadful Pirates team that finished seventh in the eight-team league. He posted a 4.27 ERA and switched off as a starter and a reliever in his rookie year, starting 22 games and relieving in 12.

The next few years were more of the same—a young Friend learned the ropes of pitching on lackluster teams. In 1952 he posted a 7-17 record with a 4.18 ERA; in 1953 he went 8-11 with a 4.90 ERA, and then in 1954 he won seven and lost 12 while putting up a 5.07 ERA. All those Pirate teams finished dead last.

At the end of the 1954 season, some of the Pirate coaches worked with Friend to change his pitching windup so he could be more deceptive with the ball. That way he had a better curveball, and the new windup gave batters a more difficult time, Friend said. [8]

It helped greatly—his breakout season came in 1955. Friend's 2.83 ERA was the best in the National League. His 14-9 record was more indicative of the Pirates' last-place finish and league-worst offense. For the first time—of which there would be many—Friend reached

200 innings pitched. He also struck out 98 batters in 44 games (20 starts), as he continued to alternate between starting and the bullpen.

By now Friend had established himself as Pittsburgh's best pitcher (there was not much competition). Teammate Vern Law was the second best hurler on the team at that point. In 1955 no Cy Young Award was given out (it began in 1956), but arguably Friend might have won it.

By this time Branch Rickey's rebuilding effect on the Pirates was well under way. Friend said that Rickey had brought in a lot of his own people—scouts, for example—from the Brooklyn Dodgers, where he had worked before. "His idea was to build an organization like the Brooklyn Dodgers or the St. Louis Cardinals," Friend said. [9]

Friend said the Pirate players both feared and respected Rickey. "They respected him but they were also afraid of him because he was tough on contracts. The way he was sending people in and out of the minors, you didn't know who would be next."

When the Pirates traded left-field slugger Ralph Kiner to the Cubs in 1953, however, that did not sit well with Friend or the players and fans. "Ralph was one of the great guys on the team. That was the only person I thought he mistreated. Ralph Kiner kept bringing people into the ballpark. He was a good influence and really missed," he told Wolf.[10]

Baseball was changing, and on the labor front, Friend soon got active in what would become the players union. Starting in 1953, he served as the Pirates' player representative for ten years and as the National League player representative for five years. While a strong advocate of better pensions and benefits for players, he was not in favor of player strikes.[11]

Friend followed up his 1955 season with another solid one in 1956, where some—not all—of his statistics would improve. Named to the All-Star team for the first time, he went 17-17 with a 3.46 ERA and 166 strikeouts, 68 more than the year before. He pitched an amazing total of 314 innings (league leader) and started 42 games (league leader and the most since Pete Alexander in 1917) in 49 appearances. He had 19 complete games and hurled four shutouts. Meanwhile, the Pirates inched up to a seventh-place finish.

Health problems forced Rickey to retire in 1955, and the Bucs got a new general manager in Joe L. Brown. "Joe was different than Branch Rickey," Friend said. "He wasn't going to copy Rickey. Who can? Joe Brown had his own style. He communicated well with the players. They liked Joe and he was fair in contracts."[12]

The long-suffering Pirate fans were fair, too. According to Friend, they never gave up on the team despite several rough seasons in a row. "They were pretty good, especially considering how much we lost. How can you be happy with that? The Pirates are an old franchise. They were sophisticated baseball fans and they knew what was going on. They kept coming back and they were loyal," he said.[13]

The next season, 1957, Friend, clearly a workhouse on the mound, became a starter exclusively, and he continued to improve. His ERA dipped to 3.38 as he notched a major-league-leading 277 innings. His record was 14-18. The Bucs finished seventh again, tied with the Chicago Cubs.

Finally, in 1958, both Friend and the Pirates put together mutually strong seasons. Pittsburgh slightly ramped up its offense to finish second in the league while Friend won a career-high 22 games (14 losses) with a 3.68 ERA. He won a trip to the All-Star Game, and once again led the league in starts (38) while throwing a hefty 274 innings. His 22 wins were good for a tie for first in the league with Warren Spahn. He made his second All-Star Game and came his closest to winning the Cy Young Award (third place).

Asked what he considered his two biggest career highlights, Friend responded that his 22 wins in 1958 and his durability—perhaps above all—stood out in his mind.

"I was able to pitch every third or fourth day for more than ten years and not miss starts," he said decades later.[14]

Looking ahead, both Friend and the Pirates seemed poised for glory.

However, these things sometimes take time. An out-of-shape Friend battled weight problems in 1959, going 8-19 with a 4.03 ERA. He led the league in losses that year. The Pirates fell back to fourth place, though they showed promise with a 78-76 record.[15]

A determined Friend re-earned his "Warrior" moniker and got into terrific shape that offseason. Though he lost 4-3 on Opening Day (April 12) to the Milwaukee Braves, he rebounded to pitch three complete-game victories in a row. By the end of May, he sported a 2.33 ERA and 5-2 record. In June Friend notched four more victories while keeping his ERA at 2.91. He hurled a complete-game shutout on June 22 against the Cardinals.

Named to the All-Star team for the third time, Friend wobbled a bit in July, going 3-4 en route to a 3.03 ERA and 11-7 record by that point in the season. One big victory came July 25 when he prevailed over St. Louis to put the Pirates in first place for good. He lowered the ERA to 2.95 by the end of August while gaining his 14th victory against 11 losses. He exhibited his best pitching in the all-important September stretch drive, tossing three complete games and winning four of five decisions while the front-running Bucs won his only no-decision start in that span.

Friend elaborated on the 1960 squad in another interview. "The team was a mixture of veterans and young players. We never made too many mistakes and we were a good fielding and pitching team. At the plate, we knew how to spread the ball around."[16]

With the Pirates headed to the World Series, Friend finished 1960 with an 18-12 record and a 3.00 ERA. He was named the UPI's Comeback Player of the Year, and was second in the league in games started (37) and innings pitched (277 2/3, tied), fourth in complete games (16) and fifth in strikeouts with 183, which was a club record. Always an excellent control pitcher, he topped the National League in strikeout-to-walk ratio at 4.07.

In the fall classic the Pirates would be facing a powerful New York Yankee team highlighted by Mickey Mantle, Roger Maris, Whitey Ford, and Yogi Berra. That season they had won 97 games—only two more, however, than the underdog Pirates.

"We respected the Yankees," said Friend. "They were a good team, but we beat some good teams in the National League … and came into the World Series in good shape."[17]

He said, "We weren't intimidated going into it. We knew we had a good team, and we had beaten a lot of good teams—the Braves, Cardinals and Dodgers—during the regular season."[18]

As has been well chronicled, the insurgent Pirates won one of the most dramatic World Series ever with Bill Mazeroski's Game Seven home run—plus a whole lot of other help from different players in that 10-9 victory.

But Friend's performance in the Series was not up to the benchmark he had established during the season. Simply, he got rocked.

He started Game Two and was chased after four innings (though he gave up only two earned runs) as the Yankees pummeled Pittsburgh, 16-3. In his next start, Game Six, Friend caught the brunt of the Yankee attack, surviving only two innings while coughing up five runs in a 12-0 shutout of Pittsburgh. With the Series tied at three apiece, all Bucco hands were on deck for Game Seven; Friend was called in to pitch the ninth inning, but he could not stop the Yankee offense then, either, giving up two runs and not even securing an out.

Overall, Friend went 0-2 with a 13.50 ERA for the World Series—but his team won. Here is how one Associated Press writer summed up manager Danny Murtaugh's choice of Vern Law—and not Friend—to start three games. "He followed up twice with Bob Friend, who simply didn't have it but deserved the slot after winning 18 in the pennant race."[19]

It sounds as if Murtaugh knew that Friend had been taxed with a heavy pitching load in September in which he had given his total effort—he started six games and threw 38 innings on top of an August when he hurled 56 innings. Arguably, there was probably not much left in his arm come October. And the Yanks were just darn good hitters, of course.

Friend understood what had happened. "I had my best season in 1960, I believe, but did not have a good Series."[20]

As he explained to Wolf, "I think I put too much pressure on myself. I expected to have a good Series. I was one of the hottest pitchers coming down the stretch, but didn't perform well in the World Series. We end up winning, though, and that's the big thing."[21]

To Pittsburgh fans, it did not matter—they were champions! The city went wild after the final game at Forbes Field, which gave the Pirates their first World Series title since 1925.

Years later Friend recalled the pandemonium throughout the Iron City: "We heard that a celebration was going on, so some of us went downtown to see what is was all about. It was pretty wild. I didn't stay around long. It was really something. … A couple days later they gave us a ticker-tape parade. They were throwing IBM cards from the buildings."[22]

The Pirates never did reach those heights again while Friend played for them—the best they would do was third place in 1965, his last season with the organization. In the afterglow of that magical World Series win, he compiled a respectable 3.85 ERA in 1961, but led the league in losses with 19 while winning 14. He hurled 236 innings, the seventh consecutive season he had more than 200. The next season, 1962, he led the league with five shutouts while crafting an 18-14 record and a 3.06 ERA.

Friend tallied one of his best seasons in 1963 when he recorded a career-low ERA of 2.34 en route to winning 17 games (he lost 16). In walking just 44 batters, he topped the league in fewest bases on balls per nine innings (1.5).

His season of 1964 was consistent if not spectacular—13-18 with a 3.33 ERA—as was the next one, his final season in a Pirates uniform: 8-12 and 3.24 ERA. He made a salary of $37,500 that year, and for 1966 would make $47,000—the only figures on record for him.[23]

Some might say Friend's low ERAs were a result of his home-field environment in spacious Forbes Field. But Friend, like many Pirates, understood that while the park was a hindrance for home-run hitters, it actually proved quite beneficial for singles and doubles and triples—the Pirates enjoyed a high number of batting champions throughout the years. Forbes Field was not unfriendly to run scoring, though it varied like every park year-by-year. In fact, it was about average league-wise during Friend's tenure, according to Baseball-Reference park factors.[24]

Friend said, "I was never concerned about the long ball like you would in Chicago or Brooklyn. I got to the point that if I kept the ball down and had good control, I'd do well. I liked Forbes Field. A lot of the guys would try not to hit the long ball at Forbes Field and became better hitters. That was our team, too. We didn't hit a lot of home runs, but we knew how to hit. We'd spray the ball around and that'd drive opponents nuts."[25]

But Forbes Field no longer was Friend's home come the winter of 1965-66. The Pirates traded him to the Yankees for reliever Pete Mikkelsen. In his last season in professional baseball, Friend went 6-12 with a 4.55 ERA. During the season, the Mets purchased Friend for cash, and he played his final game with New York's National League team on September 24, 1966. Afterward, the 35-year-old Friend retired from baseball.

"At age 35 and with the Mets rebuilding, Seaver and others were starting to come up. They had a plethora of pitching prospects in their organization. It wasn't a big surprise," Friend recalled.[26]

Bob Friend finished his 16-year career with a 197-230 record, a 3.58 ERA, 1,734 career strikeouts, and 3,611 innings pitched. He pitched 36 shutouts in 163 complete games. In 602 games, he gave up 1,438 earned runs. Friend remains as of 2012 the only pitcher to lose more than 200 while winning fewer than 200, mostly due to playing with five last-place Pirate teams. On the sabermetric front, he had a career Wins-Above-Replacement total of 42.1.

As a batter, Friend hit .121 with two home runs and 60 RBIs, three coming on May 2, 1954, in an 18-10 win over the Chicago Cubs.

Off the field, Friend in 1957 married Patricia Koval, a nurse in the office of the Pirates' team doctor. They had two children—one of them, Bob Jr., turned out to be a highly successful professional golfer on the PGA Tour.

After retiring from baseball, Friend worked as an insurance broker and served as Allegheny County controller from 1967 to 1975. (He ran at the urging of Pirates co-owner Tim Johnson.) He also played a lot of squash and sang in a barbershop quartet. But perhaps his consuming retirement passion was golf—he sported a 6 handicap, and a *Sports Illustrated* article in 2004 described Friend as a "golfaholic" who had played most of the great courses in the game.[27]

On the political front, when he won his first election—it was a tight race—Friend said it was like coming into the ninth inning, "but there was no Elroy Face in the bullpen."

He elaborated: "You don't have as much control over the results of an election as you do a ballgame. Here you go all out and meet the public and they decide the outcome." He believed that simply being a well-known ballplayer was not a big advantage.[28]

"It's one thing to be a ballplayer, but so what?" Friend said, adding that sometimes he spent 20 hours a day campaigning. "I went to 40 mill gates and talked to workers. Politics is a good competitive game now that I'm out of baseball."[29]

He added, "I had a wife who was a good campaigner, and I'm thankful for that."[30]

Re-elected as controller in 1971, Friend went on to serve as a three-time delegate to the Republican National Convention, but did not run for higher office beyond controller. On the philanthropy front, he led a popular annual fundraising drive for Children's Hospital in Pittsburgh in the 1980s.

"Friend wages an annual letter campaign urging friends and business acquaintances to look deep into their hearts and dig deep into their pockets to help patients who otherwise would not have the means to pay for medical care," a writer for the *Pittsburgh Press* remarked.[31]

Friend retired from his post-baseball business and political career in 2005. In 2012, at the age of 81, he lived in O'Hara Township, which is northeast of downtown Pittsburgh. Bob Friend the "Warrior" is considered one of the Pirates' most historically significant pitchers of all time.

Notes

1   Rick Cushing, *1960 Pittsburgh Pirates: Day by Day: A Special Season, An Extraordinary World Series* (Pittsburgh: Dorrance Publishing, 2010), 363.

2   Clifton B. Parker interview of Bob Friend, November 17, 2012.

3   Ibid.

4   Bob Friend Wikipedia entry, http://en.wikipedia.org/wiki/Bob_Friend

5   Ibid.

6   SABR member Gregory Wolf's oral interview of Bob Friend found at hardballtimes.com, April 6, 2012, "A Friend of Pirates History."

7   Ibid.

8   Rick Cushing, 363.

9   Wolf interview.

10   Ibid.

11   Rick Cushing, 364 and Bob Friend Wikipedia entry at http://en.wikipedia.org/wiki/Bob_Friend

12   Wolf interview.

13   Ibid.

14   Parker interview.

15   Baseball-reference.com entry at http://www.baseball-reference.com/bullpen/Bob_Friend.

16   Parker interview.

17   Wolf interview.

18   Parker interview.

19   Associated Press article in the *Miami News*, "Pirate Victory Like Pep K.O. Over Rocky," October 16, 1960.

20   Parker interview.

21   Wolf interview.

22   Rick Cushing, 364.

23   Bob Friend Wikipedia entry.

24   Pittsburgh Pirates Attendance, Stadiums and Park Factors, at http://www.baseball-reference.com/teams/PIT/attend.shtml

25   Wolf interview.

26   Ibid.

27   Bill Syken, "Bob Friend, Pitcher," *Sports Illustrated*, August 9, 2004.

28   Associated Press story in the *Daytona Beach* (Florida) *Morning Journal*, "Bob Friend Elected on the First Try," November 9, 1967.

29   Ibid.

30   Parker interview.

31   "Ex-Pirate Pitcher Proves He's Hospital's Best Friend," *Pittsburgh Press*, November 17, 1981.

Joe Gibbon

By Thomas Van Hyning

JOE GIBBON FULFILLED his dream when he made the Opening Day roster of the 1960 Pittsburgh Pirates, the World Series champion that season. Joe pitched 12 full big-league seasons plus part of a 13th before retiring in 1972. He was talented enough in basketball to be drafted by the NBA champion Boston Celtics in 1957, after finishing second in NCAA scoring his senior season for the 1956-57 University of Mississippi (Ole Miss) Rebels. The 6-foot-4 forward made several collegiate All-America hoop teams. He helped Ole Miss finish third in the 1956 College Baseball World Series in Omaha, their first-ever appearance. Gibbon propelled little Hickory High School to Mississippi's 1953 state high-school basketball tournament title, over bigger schools.

Joseph Charles Gibbon was a 12-pound bundle of joy when he was born at his family's Hickory, Mississippi, home on April 10, 1935.[1] Joe's parents were Eugene Opie Gibbon of Newton County and Elsie Gibbon, from Chunky, Mississippi. Eugene Opie's grandparents had moved to East Central Mississippi from Turberville, South Carolina, near Sumter. Joe's two siblings were Jean, an older sister, and Billy, a brother.

The St. Louis Cardinals were Joe's favorite big-league team, and Stan Musial his favorite player. Joe vividly recalled listening to Game Seven of the 1946 World Series between Boston and St. Louis, when Harry Walker's hit drove in Enos "Country" Slaughter from first base with the winning run. "I played for (Harry Walker) in Pittsburgh (1965) and Houston (1972)," said Joe. "He had a brother named Dixie who was also a good big-league outfielder." (Walker played for five major-league teams, most notably the Brooklyn Dodgers from 1939 through 1947.)

Hickory didn't have a high-school baseball team, so Joe played American Legion baseball in Newton, about three miles away. Joe rode a bicycle (or hitchhiked) to and from the baseball field. Hickory was a basketball hotbed back then and Joe did the rebounding with another tall guard. "Our two forwards were 5-foot-8 when I went to Ole Miss. I told them my scoring average was 5 points per game my senior year. … They couldn't believe that!"

Mississippi basketball fans were aware that Hickory, a Class B school, had won the 1953 state title over larger schools, somewhat reminiscent of the movie Hoosiers. Gibbon: "I didn't play but two years of high-school basketball—the small schools had eight-month schedules back then—and we did have a football team my senior year, where I played fullback in the old single wing, and defensive back, under coach Billy Coleman."

Joe's baseball career formally began when he was a college freshman at Ole Miss in 1954, but he had worked out with the Meridian Millers, in the old Cotton States League, and played semipro ball in Lauderdale County, Mississippi. Joe, a lefty, and Archie White, a right-handed pitcher from Meridian, recalled that the Millers' general manager was Dough Rawlings, a big supporter of Ole Miss athletics, and that he, along with Martin Van Buren Miller, a local lawyer, secured baseball scholarships for Gibbon and White. Gibbon recalled, "Mr. Miller called Ole Miss and said: 'Take this guy (Gibbon). If he doesn't play for you in basketball and baseball his first year, then I'll pay his way.'"

Joe lettered in basketball his freshman year, but not in baseball, since he was winless for the 1954 Rebels. He pitched well, said teammate Robert "Cob" Jarvis, a senior on the team, which won the

Southeastern Conference Western Division title and faced Georgia for the 1954 SEC title. "Joe was an outstanding pitcher as well as a great hitter." Against Mississippi State, Jarvis recalled, "In the ninth, State had the bases loaded and no outs. The first batter hit into a force play at home. Joe then struck out the next two hitters."

Tom Swayze, Gibbon's baseball coach at Ole Miss, recalled that he pitched six superb relief innings against the Meridian Millers in a 1954 exhibition game, giving up no runs and one hit. Swayze said Gibbon's control was excellent, but he developed slight arm trouble and was used sparingly the rest of that season. But he started the second game of the best-of-three SEC title series, in Athens, Georgia, a series won by the Georgia Bulldogs.[2] Gibbon pitched semipro ball in Silver City, Mississippi, the summer of 1954, earning $25 a game but paying his driver $12, since Joe did not own a car.

By the spring of 1956, Ole Miss was a collegiate baseball powerhouse, with pitchers including Archie White, Cecil Burford, Don Goad, and Buddy Wittichen; Gibbon, who could pitch, play first base, or play the outfield; Bernie Schreiber, an All-American second baseman; shortstop Buddy Garrison; Bill Scott, first base; Eagle Day, third base; plus a talented outfield with Eddie Crawford and Billy Kinard (who also caught). Mississippi finished 24-10, including four games in the 1956 College World Series, part of a postseason in which pitchers Goad and White and position players Crawford, Garrison, Schreiber, and Scott could not play.[3]

But Gibbon was able to play, and he stood out. Florida defeated Ole Miss, 8-3 and 5-1, at Gainesville, Florida, in the battle for the SEC championship, but Ole Miss went on to the district playoffs because NCAA sanctions prevented the Gators from qualifying. In the district tourney, in Gastonia, North Carolina, Mississippi swept Tennessee Tech in the first round, then defeated Duke, two games to one, in the finals, and qualified for the College World Series in Omaha, Nebraska. In Omaha, Ole Miss was called the Cinderella team because, as Gibbon put it, "we had so many adversities to overcome." Ole Miss defeated New Hampshire, 13-12, with Gibbon getting the win in relief, then Bradley, 4-0, before losing to Minnesota and Arizona to finish third in baseball's showcase tournament. In nine postseason games—five in Gastonia plus four in Omaha—Gibbon hit .396 (13 hits in 33 at-bats), with

three doubles, one triple, four home runs and 11 runs batted in, and had a .909 slugging percentage. Swayze, Gibbon's coach, later said, "In my 35 years of playing and coaching in all sports, I have never seen Joe Gibbon's peer so far as sheer physical ability is concerned."

This ability became evident on the hardwood in 1956-57, when Gibbon averaged 30 points and 14.1 rebounds per game to earn All-American designation by the Helms Foundation. His 30-point average was second nationally to Grady Wallace of South Carolina and just ahead of Elgin Baylor (29.7) and Wilt Chamberlain (29.6). Gibbon was named the SEC MVP in the *Atlanta Constitution* Players' Poll.[4]

The Boston Celtics notified Gibbon during the 1957 college baseball season that they intended to draft him. Gibbon made it clear to the Celtics that his heart was in pro baseball, not basketball. The Celtics drafted him anyway and true to his word, he didn't report to Boston's training camp.

In 1957, after hitting .425, the third highest single-season average in school history, and being named to the All-SEC team, Gibbon signed with the Pittsburgh Pirates after being scouted by the Pirates' regional scout, Sammy Moses, of Yazoo City, Mississippi.

"The Braves and Phillies—from my high school days—were interested in me," said Gibbon, "but Milwaukee had a (1957) rotation of Spahn, Burdette, and Buhl. ... I was not interested in the Phils; the Pirates were a weaker team[5], in need of left-handed pitching, so I signed with them for a $1,000 bonus, plus $3,000 for my first pro season ... bought my first car: 1957 Chevrolet Sports Coupe for $2,700; got it financed for one year. Atley Donald of the Yankees scouted me in high school. Cecil Burford, Pepper Thomas, and Archie White signed with the Braves."

The Pirates sent Gibbon to their farm team at Lincoln of the Class A Western League, managed by Larry Shepard, who Gibbon said was someone who could "motivate me better than the rest of them; had a different personality; he said, you can do it." Gibbon started out as a pitcher and outfielder for the Chiefs, hurling in 17 games and appearing in 39 games overall. On the mound he impressed Shepard with his poise and three-quarters delivery, and after impressing Shepard with two solid relief appearances, he became a pitcher full time. He finished the season 9-4 with a 1.83 earned-run average in 15 starts and two relief appearances for the league champs. His hitting was less impressive: .220 in 91 at-bats. Shortly after the season, at the request of Pirates general manager Joe L. Brown, Gibbon traveled to Chester, Pennsylvania, the hometown of the Pirates' new manager, Danny Murtaugh. There he was sworn in to the US Army Reserve.

For 1958 Pittsburgh promoted Gibbon to the Triple-A Columbus Red Birds, managed by Clyde King. "I got off to a bad start in Columbus," Gibbon said. "That was a bigger jump, from A ball to Triple-A than Triple-A to the big leagues. My 6-13 record didn't help; at that time, you had to win to be promoted to the majors."

The Pirates sent Joe to Santiago, in the Dominican Republic, for the 1958-59 winter season. "Kenny Hamlin and I were the only Americans without wives or family, and we were going crazy. They checked your mail—if you wrote a letter saying something 'bad' about the country, your family would never get it. ... I lost three or four in a row. They wanted to run me out of the country; then I started winning, ..."

Gibbon returned to the US so he could fulfill his two-week Reserve commitment. He returned to Columbus for 1959 and posted a 16-9 record with a league-leading 152 strikeouts. Columbus made it to the postseason, but was swept in the semifinals by the Havana Sugar Kings. In a game in Havana, Gibbon said, while he was on third base, Columbus manager Cal Ermer's wife, in the stands, overheard Cuban soldiers saying: "If he scores, I'm going to shoot him." Joe said, "I'm glad I didn't know about this."

Gibbon turned 25 and made the Pirates during 1960 spring training. He made his major-league debut—and got his first victory—in the second game of a double-header against Cincinnati at Pittsburgh's Forbes Field on April 17. Gibbon entered the game in the eighth with the Pirates down 5-0. He held the Reds scoreless for two innings and was the winner when the Pirates rallied for six runs in the ninth and won, 6-5, on Bob Skinner's two-run walk-off homer.

The 1960 Pirates finished 95-59 despite having only one superstar, Roberto Clemente. Gibbon called the team "a special club" that won about half its games after the sixth

inning (including 21 in the ninth). General manager Joe L. Brown, who had maintained that "power does not win pennants, balance does," had engineered a major deal with Cincinnati in 1959, acquiring Don Hoak, Smoky Burgess, and Harvey Haddix, for Frank Thomas, Jim Pendleton, Whammy Douglas, and Johnny Powers. Dick Hall and Ken Hamlin were traded to the Kansas City A's for catcher Hal Smith. Vinegar Bend Mizell was acquired from St. Louis for Julian Javier. Brown picked up Rocky Nelson and catcher Bob Oldis via the minor-league draft.

Oldis recalled of catching Gibbon, "He threw easy and hard; had great movement on his fastball— 92-plus miles per hour." Bill Virdon said that Gibbon "had a good arm and threw fairly hard and it takes 25 players doing their job to win it all." Gibbon made nine starts for the 1960 Pirates, winning four games and losing two. Virdon said that Gibbon and outfielder Joe Christopher, "who won several games for us with his legs," were "the types of players it took to help win championships."

Gibbon, a quiet, low-key individual (manager Murtaugh gave him the ironic nickname Gabby), and a team player, just wanted to get the opposing hitter out. Gibbon told the author that Murtaugh did not adhere to a strict curfew in 1960, when the Pirates won it the pennant and the World Series on Bill Mazeroski's seventh-game home run, but that this changed when the Pirates started losing more often, between 1961 and 1964.

Gibbon pitched in two games in the 1960 World Series. In Game Two, a 16-3 blowout loss to the Yankees, he gave up three runs in two relief innings, the three runs coming on a home run by Mickey Mantle. Gibbons had given up back-to-back singles to Tony Kubek and Joe DeMaestri and struck out Roger Maris before giving up the home run to Mantle, which may have been the longest home run ever hit in a World Series game at Forbes Field.[6] Gibbon pitched again in Game Three, another blowout, a 10-0 complete-game shutout by Whitey Ford. Gibbon pitched one scoreless inning, the eighth, walking Elston Howard, before retiring Bobby Richardson on a pop fly to Bill Mazeroski to end the inning.

Virgil Trucks, at 43, pitched batting practice for the Pirates in the Series. He was on the staff as a special "batting practice pitcher, coach/scout," and recalled of Gibbon: "He had good coordination and poise; and control, for a lefty. ... I gave him 'ideas' on how to pitch in certain situations." Trucks, who had been with the Yankees in the 1958 World Series, passed on information to Murtaugh on "how to pitch to certain Yankee hitters."

Gibbon's World Series pay check was $8,400—more than his $7,500 salary that season. After the Series the Pirates sent him to Ponce, Puerto Rico, along with Tom Cheney, Al McBean, Bob Veale, and Donn Clendenon, to get more seasoning under Cal Ermer in the Puerto Rico Winter League. Gibbon left Ponce with a 2-0 record and a minuscule 0.56 ERA.[7]

Gibbon had his best big-league season in 1961, starting in 29 games and going 13-10, with three shutouts and a 3.32 ERA. He might have won a few more if reliever Roy Face's forkball was as effective in 1961 as in 1959 and 1960. Gibbon experienced some arm problems in 1962, and was briefly sent down to Kinston in the Class B Carolina League. For the Pirates he was 3-4 in 19 games. On September 28, just as the season was winding up, he married the former Donna Jean Price, of Parkersburg, West Virginia—a marriage that produced five children. Gibbon was only 5-12 in 1963, rebounded to a 10-7 record in 1964, but 4-9 in 1965. Harry Walker replaced Danny Murtaugh as the Pittsburgh skipper in 1965. Walker was

the opposite of the low-key Murtaugh; he was, Gibbon said, "the best baseball man I ever played for; the kind of guy if you asked what time it was, would tell you how the watch was made."

On December 1, 1965, the Pirates traded Gibbon and infielder Ozzie Virgil to the San Francisco Giants for outfielder Matty Alou. Joe was mainly used in relief by manager Herman Franks from 1966 through 1968. He and Donna adjusted to life in a new city, and their third child was born in California. Gibbon maintained that Willie Mays was the "real manager" of those San Francisco teams—and that Mays, not Herman Franks, called the shots. During spring training with Giants, Joe got to meet actor John Wayne in Casa Grande, Arizona.

On June 10, 1969, Gibbon was traded back to Pittsburgh, for pitcher Ron Kline. There he was reunited with Larry Shepard, his first skipper in pro ball, now managing the Pirates. He finished 5-1 with a 1.93 ERA plus nine saves for the Pirates, after his 1-3, 3.60 ERA and two saves with the Giants. Alex Grammas, the ex-baseball star at Mississippi State, replaced Shepard the last week of the season.

Danny Murtaugh was the manager in 1970, and led the Pirates to the National East title. Gibbon contributed five saves. Gibbon pitched twice against Cincinnati, winner of the West Division, as the Reds swept the Pirates in three games. In Game Three, Gibbon surrendered the hit by Bobby Tolan that drove in the game-winning run. Gibbon was released by Pittsburgh on October 26. The Reds signed him as a free agent on April 1, 1971. Joe enjoyed playing with Pete Rose ("one of the most dedicated players I've been around"); pitching to Johnny Bench ("a real good catcher; had more to him than anybody I ever pitched to"); having Hall of Famer Tony Perez as a teammate; pitching for Sparky Anderson, the future Hall of Fame manager, whom he had pitched against in the International League in 1958.

In that 1971 season, Gibbon was the losing pitcher in the only major-league game documented to have ended on catcher's interference. Manny Mota tried to steal home with two outs in the 11th inning, the bases loaded, and the score tied, 4-4. Johnny Bench came in front of home plate, to wait for a throw and tag Mota. Umpire Harry Wendelstedt called catcher's interference on Bench and a balk on Gibbon, citing Rule 7.07: "If with a runner on third base and trying to score by means of a squeeze play or a steal, the catcher or any other fielder steps on, or in front of home base without possession of the ball, or touches the batter or his bat, the pitcher shall be charged with a balk, the batter shall be awarded first base on the interference and the ball is dead."

The next season, 1972, was Gibbon's last. He began the season with the Reds but was released on May 11. On the 25th he signed with the Houston Astros, managed by Harry Walker, but was released on June 21. He was 37 years old. He had pitched a total of 7 ⅔ innings for the two teams.[8]

Joe, Donna, and their children moved back to East Central Mississippi. He coached the Clarke College baseball team in Newton, Mississippi, for eight seasons, and afterward continued coaching Babe Ruth and other youth baseball teams. He was inducted into the Mississippi Sports Hall of Fame in 1979, and the Ole Miss Athletic Hall of Fame in 1988. On February 21, 2009, he was honored as a member of the Ole Miss Men's All-Century Basketball Team.

Gibbon participated in fantasy baseball camps along with ex-teammate Steve Blass and others. In October 2010 he, Bill Virdon, Joe Christopher, and Bob Oldis took part in ceremonies in Pittsburgh marking the 50th anniversary of the 1960 World Series.

In retirement Joe, a widower, lives on his Jasper County farm, just south of Hickory. His five children—Joseph C. Jr., David Opie, Jennifer Diane, Luke Andrew, and Robert Daniel, and three grandchildren are spread among Mississippi, Minnesota, Texas, and Utah. Joe summarized his Ole Miss athletic career and his pro baseball career as "very special, (especially) playing in a Golden Era of National League baseball between 1960 and 1972."

Sources

Phone conversations with Joe Gibbon between June and October 2010.

Personal interview with Gibbon in Newton, Mississippi, September 25, 2010.

Phone conversations with three of Gibbon's 1960 Pirates teammates: Bob Oldis (September 27, 2010); Joe Christopher (September 28, 2010); Bill Virdon (September 28, 2010). Oldis also furnished written responses.

Phone conversations with 1960 Yankees Jim Coates and Ralph Terry (May 3, 2010); and Bobby Richardson (May 4, 2010)

Phone conversations with Tony Bartirome; Forrest "Spook" Jacobs; Virgil Trucks (October 25, 2010); Cal Ermer (early 1990s); Langston Rogers, Ole Miss senior associate athletic director emeritus; Bailey Howell, ex-Mississippi State and pro hoop star (October 11, 2010).

Mail correspondence with Robert "Cob" Jarvis, an Ole Miss basketball and baseball teammate of Joe Gibbon.

Interviews with three Ole Miss baseball teammates of Gibbon, Cecil W. Burford, Jr. (September 27, 2010); and Pepper Thomas and Archie White (September 28, 2010).

Pat Kelly, Baseball Hall of Fame and Museum, Cooperstown, New York, furnished a Joe Gibbon photo.

Mark Brown, a native of Somerset County, Pennsylvania, furnished insights on Western Pennsylvania. Bill Webb, a native of Newton, Mississippi, shared insights on Game Two of the 1960 World Series.

Baseball-Reference.com.

Big League Stew Sports Blog by Duk. Bing Crosby's wine cellar produces vintage 1960 World Series film, September 24, 2010. http://sports.yahoo.com/mlb/blog/big_league_stew/post/Bing-Crosby-s-wine-cellar-produc...

www.Hickory.Mississippi.com.

www.olemisssports.com.

Chris Blake. *Bill Mazeroski homers to win World Series. Inside Pitch,* October 13, 2010.

Bobo Champion. Letter outlining Joe Gibbon's sports accomplishments, March 3, 1978.

Jim Coates with Douglas Williams. *Always a Yankee.* Infinity Publishing.com, December 2009.

Rafael Costas. *Enciclopedia Beisbol Ponce Leones, 1938-1987.* Editora Corripio, 1989.

Robert W. Creamer. *Stengel: His Life and Times.* (New York: Simon and Schuster, 1984)

Billy Gates. Ole Miss Athletic Department Press Releases on Joe Gibbon, 1955-1957.

Gary Gillette and Pete Palmer, eds. *The ESPN Baseball Encyclopedia.* (New York: Sterling Publishing Co., 2008)

John B. Holway. *Josh and Satch.* (Westport, Connecticut: Meckler Publishing, 1991)

Lloyd Johnson and Miles Wolff, eds. *Encyclopedia of Minor League Baseball,* Third Edition. (Durham, North Carolina: Baseball America, 2007)

Ed Lucas and Paul Post. "Former Yankee Ralph Terry: Right-Hander Revives World Series Memories From 1960 Loss Against the Pirates and 1962 Victory Over the Giants." *Baseball Digest,* October 2005.

David M. Maraniss. *Clemente: The Passion and Grace of Baseball's Last Hero.* (New York: Simon and Schuster, 2006)

Ole Miss Announces Men's Basketball All-Century Team. Ole Miss Athletics Media Relations, February 12, 2009.

Ole Miss Baseball Media Guide 2009, Athletics Media Relations Office.

Ole Miss Rebel Basketball Media Guide 2009-2010, Athletics Media Relations Office.

Richard Peterson, ed. *The Pirates Reader.* (Pittsburgh: University of Pittsburgh Press, 2003)

Bobby Richardson. *The Bobby Richardson Story.* (Grand Rapids, Michigan: Fleming H. Revell Company, 1965)

Tom Swayze. Letter to Dick Smith, sports editor, *Meridian Star,* March 1957.

"Dodgers Arrange Pact with Venezuelan Club," *The Sporting News,* March 7, 1951.

Bob Timmerman. *The World of Catcher's Interference.* Baseball Analysts, August 21, 2008.

Notes

1   Hickory, in Newton County, was and is a tiny town—its population according to the 2000 US Census was only 499. The town was named after Andrew Jackson—nicknamed Old Hickory—who passed through the area on his way to command the American forces in the Battle of New Orleans during the War of 1812, five years before Mississippi became a state.

2   Gibbon's career won-loss record at Ole Miss was 9-7, with a 2.19 earned-run average. His best season was 1956, when he had a 5-2 record and a 1.26 ERA. His .384 career batting average tied him for fourth place, as of 2010, for Ole Miss players with 100 or more at-bats, behind Don Kessinger (1962-64), .400; Charlie Conerly (1947-48), .399; and Jimmy Yawn (1965-67), .390. Gibbon (1954-57) is tied at .384 with Jake Gibbs (1959-1961). In the 1956 NCAA Division III Regional Tournament at Gastonia, North Carolina, Gibbon was named the best hitter and best outfielder after hitting .438 in five games. Like other scholarship athletes at Ole Miss, Gibbon got $15 a month for his laundry expenses.

3   The NCAA at the time barred seniors who had lettered as freshmen from playing in postseason collegiate competition. This did not affect Gibbon in 1956, since he was a junior, but six of his teammates in 1956 had lettered as freshmen in 1953. Archie White, one of the six, told me that he returned for his senior baseball season at Ole Miss because "Coach Swayze was like a father to me."

4   Gibbon earned four varsity letters in basketball at Ole Miss. He was named to the United Press International second team and given an honorable mention by the Associated Press in 1957. After he scored 29 points and had 20 rebounds in a loss to Kentucky on February 8, 1957, Adolph Rupp, the Kentucky coach, said, "That was one of the best performances I've ever seen." Gibbon scored 1,601 career points for the Rebels, seventh all-time as of 2009-2010. He led the SEC in scoring in his senior season with 32.5 points per conference game. His 827 career rebounds rank third all-time at Ole Miss as of 2009-2010. Gibbon's 14.1 rebounds per game in 1956-57 are the school's best per-game for a single season.

5   The Pirates' composite won-lost record for 1950 through 1957 was 454-777. Gibbon was fully aware of this reality when he enrolled at Ole Miss in the fall of 1953. He rejected the opportunity to sign with the Yankees, knowing he would remain buried in their farm system for a fair amount of time.

6   Babe Ruth, with the 1935 Boston Braves, hit his last three major-league home runs in a game at Forbes Field; his last, over the right-field fence, may have been the longest major-league regular-season homer at Forbes Field by a left-handed hitter. Right-handers Ralph Kiner of the Pirates and Frank Howard of the Los Angeles Dodgers each hit 560-foot homers at Forbes Field. Dick Stuart hit a tape-measure blast there, and Josh Gibson of the Homestead Grays may have hit the longest homer in the ballpark's history, a drive reported to have been 600 feet in a 1929 Negro League contest. SABR historian John Holway wrote that Gibson's hit flew over the center-field fence, 457 feet from home plate. No one, Holway wrote, had cleared the spot before, and only three did it after, Mantle, Stuart, and Negro Leaguer Oscar Charleston.

7   Cal Ermer was respected for his ability and tact in handling players in his long managing career. This view was expressed by two former players the author interviewed: Bob Oldis, who caught for Ermer on the 1951 Charlotte Hornets (the only pro baseball team to win 100 regular season games that season), and Joe Christopher, with Ermer's 1960-61 Ponce Lions. Ponce started strong with a bevy of Pirates players and Pittsburgh prospects—Joe Gibbon, Tom Cheney, Al McBean, Al Jackson, Bob Veale, Elmo Plaskett, Donn Clendenon—and were 17-15 in the first half. They faltered to 12-20 in the second half.

8   Gibbon's career totals for Pittsburgh, San Francisco, Cincinnati, and Houston from 1960 through 1972: 419 games, 127 games started, 61-65 won-loss record, 3.52 ERA, 4 shutouts, 32 saves, 743 strikeouts, 414 walks. In his four minor-league seasons: 75 games, 72 games started, 31-26 won-loss record, 2.71 ERA, 5 shutouts, 295 strikeouts, 196 walks.

Paul Giel

By Cary Smith

GREAT ANTICIPATION EXISTED regarding which sport Paul Giel would play after finishing his degree in physical education at the University of Minnesota. As a two-time all-American in both baseball and football, he had his choice of pursuing a career in either sport. In 1954 the Chicago Bears of the National Football League (NFL) drafted him in the ninth round with the 102nd overall pick. The Winnipeg Blue Bombers and the Toronto Argonauts of the Canadian Football League (CFL) both offered Giel contracts to play for them. Instead, Giel decided to test his skills at baseball and signed with the New York Giants as a bonus baby. The amount that he signed for is unclear, but it was somewhere between $50,000 and $80,000 for three years. The Giants figured he would eventually become a star pitcher and that they could survive the early years of his career, which would be rocky. Unfortunately, Giel never got out of the rocky stage and his baseball career was full of potential that never came to fruition. However, once his baseball career was over, he wasn't done with sports.

Mr. Gopher, Paul Robert Giel, may be best known for his impressive college football career at the University of Minnesota, but his life as a sportsman was more than that. He was an all-around sports star from a very young age. He was born on September 29, 1932 in Winona, Minnesota, where he grew up with three siblings, Edward Jr. (born July 21, 1929), Lawrence (May 5, 1931), and Ruth (February 20, 1934), and played football, basketball, and baseball. His father, Edward Sr., born in Indiana, was of German heritage and worked as an engineer for the Chicago & North Western Rail Road Company, and their mother, Marion Flannery, was born in Minnesota and was of Irish heritage.

As early as age 14, Giel was making headlines in the local newspaper for his sports feats. He set the midget-league basketball half-season record with 175 points. After basketball season, he stepped onto the baseball field, and the achievements were non-stop. On Opening Day he pitched a one-hitter with ten strikeouts. A little more than a week later, on June 13, he struck out 21 batters in a seven-inning game. The following month he only got better, when he pitched a no-hitter for the Federal Bread team versus the Merchant Banks team with 19 strikeouts in seven innings. Giel was overpowering his competition with his fastball, and scouts like Angelo "Tony" Giuliani were starting to take notice of his dominance.

In 1948 and 1949, when he was still in high school, Giel played shortstop for the Rollingstone team of the Bi-State League (a Minnesota amateur league). Coming out of high school in 1950, Giel pitched for the Winona Braves of the Class B Hiawatha Valley League, where he threw another no-hitter. After he graduated, six or seven major-league teams interviewed him, including the Chicago Cubs, Brooklyn Dodgers, and New York Giants. He could have signed a contract with any one of them and jumped right into their minor-league system. However, since he wanted to stay close to Minnesota, he decided instead to attend the University of Minnesota to pursue football. He believed that by going to the University he could also improve his baseball skills with four years of training under coach Dick Siebert. His first year at Minnesota (1950) also happened to be the last year for legendary football coach Bernie Bierman. Under Bierman the team had been a powerhouse for many years, winning five national championships. However, in the last few years of his tenure the team had slipped, and the fans had become unhappy. Many fans saw the addition of Giel to the football team as the start of an effort to rebuild and regain its national status. Due to rules at the time, Giel was not allowed to play as a freshman, but he sat on the sidelines for many of the games and learned a great deal from Bierman. He may not have been able to play football or baseball for the college teams his first year, but he was able to play town ball for the Winona Braves, where he had a 5-0 record in 1951.

Giel joined the Gophers football team as a quarterback, but soon new coach Wes Fesler turned him into a passing halfback and punter as part of the team's single-wing offense. Giel started with a bang; in his first five games he had 805 yards, 263 of them running and 542 of them passing, to go along with his 37.5 yard punting average. It was clear that Giel could become a star on the gridiron if that's what he chose.

Getting his first chance to pitch for the Gophers in the spring of 1952, Giel went 5-0 in Big Ten play with 43 strikeouts and a 0.42 ERA. He was elected to the first of three All-Big-Ten teams that he would be selected to. When school ended he once again returned to pitch for his hometown of Winona, but this season it was for the Chiefs of the Class AA Southern Minny League. He was named to the All-Star team and finished the season with a 6-3 won-list record with 85 strikeouts and an ERA of 2.56 in 59 $^2/_3$ innings. His baseball season was shortened due to a severely pulled muscle in his left leg. Gophers fans were worried that it would not only end his baseball but also his football career. The injury would delay his progress in training camp, but he was back to full strength in time for the football season

In 1952 the whole country was taking notice of Giel's football skills. The Gophers were improving, and Giel was carrying them. In the season's final game, versus Wisconsin, Giel had one of the best performances of his football career. He ran for 111 yards on 29 carries and scored a touchdown. He completed nine of 19 passes for 167 yards and two touchdowns, to go with his 252 yards punting for a 42-yard average. Unfortunately the game ended in a 21-21 tie. For all his hard work, he was named All-American on three different teams: Associated Press, Chicago Tribune, and Look. Heisman Trophy voters recognized Giel's great talent when he placed third in the voting, behind winner Billy Vessels (Oklahoma) and Jack Scarbath (Maryland). He was only a junior at the time.

On the baseball field, it was another good season for Giel. In Big Ten games he had a 2-2 record with 58 strikeouts in 41 $^2/_3$ innings to go with a 1.73 ERA. On May 3 he showed his strength by pitching seven innings in the first game of a doubleheader versus Michigan and then pitching a full nine innings in the second game. Less than a month later, in the last inning of the last game of the year, Giel felt a popping in his arm. Again fans' concerns regarding his football and baseball career at Minnesota, as well as with the Winona baseball team, became apparent. He was able to recover but instead of playing for Winona that summer he joined Reserve Officers Training Corps (ROTC). As part of ROTC, he was committed to complete two years of military service, which would later slow his baseball career.

For the 1953 football season Giel was named team captain. His greatest game of the year came against Michigan when he had 57 touches on 73 plays, ran for 112 yards, passed for 169 yards, and led the team in tackles to go with two interceptions, while also doing the punting. The Gophers beat the Wolverines for the first time in 11 seasons, by a score of 22-0. It was an important game for the two teams because it was the 50th anniversary of the battle for the Little Brown Jug. Giel's triple threat of running, passing, and punting could not be ignored. He was named the Big Ten Conference Player of the Year for the second time. For the second year in a row, he finished second for *The Sporting News* outstanding football player of the year, this time behind Johnny Lattner (Notre Dame) by a point total of 232 to 248. Every major football award for the season would be a battle between Lattner and Giel as they were the only two players named to all 10 major All-American teams. The voting for the Heisman Trophy was similar as it came down to Lattner and Giel, with Lattner coming out ahead, 1,850 votes to 1,794, one of the closest votes in Heisman history. In the three years that Giel was on the football team, the Gophers finished with a 10-13-4 record. Giel ended his career at Minnesota with 2,188 rushing yards and 1,922 passing yards. In 1975 he would be inducted into the College Football Hall of Fame.

People were still keeping an eye on Giel on the baseball field to see how he was progressing. Yogi Berra was seen talking to him for the Yankees at Toot Shor's restaurant in

New York. Tigers Muddy Ruel and John McHale brought him to Briggs Stadium in Detroit for a tryout. What they saw from Giel was a 1-3 record in the Big Ten and a conference-leading number of strikeouts. For his three years on the baseball team he finished with a 21-8 overall won-lost record. For the second time Giel was named to the All-American baseball team, but this time he made the first team instead of the second team. He was the first person to be named All-American in both football and baseball in two different seasons. At the end of his Gophers career there was a movement by the students to get his number 10 jersey retired by the school. The problem was that the school had never retired a jersey before, and it was not going to start with Giel because it would be seen as disrespectful to former Gopher greats who did not receive the same honor. Eventually the school would retire both his baseball and football numbers.

After college, there was one more venture into town ball before joining the major leagues. Gophers baseball coach Dick Siebert had convinced Giel to come pitch for him on the Litchfield Optimists team. People were critical of Giel for pitching again and risking an injury just before he was set to sign a big contract. Giel was heavily scouted by professional teams in both baseball and football, but there was some question about how much he was actually going to be able to help a team. Because he was a member of ROTC in school, he was required to serve two years in the military, which would take away from his playing time. Giel had to weigh his options between the Bears of the NFL, Blue Bombers of the CFL, and any number of baseball teams. All Giel knew of Bears owner George Halas was that he was cheap, so he was not likely to sign with them. Moreover, Giel believed that he would have to play exclusively as quarterback in the NFL, and he was not interested. The Blue Bombers had territorial rights for Giel and the open field and high speed of the CFL would fit well with Giel's style of football. However, the team was not offering as much money as he could make playing baseball. Every major-league baseball team had some level of interest in signing Giel except for the Phildelphia Athletics, Baltimore Orioles, and Pittsburgh Pirates. On June 9, 1954 Giel traveled to Milwaukee to meet up with the New York Giants, who were there for a series against the Braves. He signed with the team and right away was placed on the team's major-league roster because he was classified as a bonus baby. Any amateur player who signed a contract for over $4,000 at the time was classified as a bonus baby, which meant he had to stay on the major-league roster for two full calendar years or be subject to be drafted by other teams at the end of the season. This rule was designed to stop the wealthy teams from signing players and hiding them in their minor-league system. Most bonus players sat on the bench for two years, seeing little game action before they were sent down to the minor leagues. Giel was no different in this regard.

Giel got to the Giants training camp in Arizona in 1954 as a highly respected prospect but quickly learned that the fastball that had dominated all the way through college was not going to be enough at the major-league level. When Hall of Famer and Giants farm director Carl Hubbell first saw Giel, he made a statement that would often be repeated during Giel's career: "Giel could win in the big leagues as soon as he learned a third pitch." Pitching coach Frank Shellenback and teammates Sal Maglie, Marv Grissom, and Larry Jansen would all try to teach the young star to throw a change-up. He worked for years on trying to learn a third pitch, but he could never master one.

The first game in which he saw any action was during a Red Cross exhibition game against the Boston Red Sox. Giants manager Leo Durocher watched his young prospect warm up before the game and became worried about how bad his pitches were looking. As it turned out Durocher was right. Giel pitched six innings and had five strikeouts, but he also gave up five walks and a grand slam to Grady Hatton. His real major-league debut started out much better, versus the Pirates on July 10. He faced three batters—George O'Donnell, Gair Allie, and Vic Janowicz—and struck them all out. Much like his first season with the Gophers, Giel sat on the bench watching and learning for most of the year. He only would get into five more games and pitch another 3 1/3 innings. It cannot be found in his major-league record, but August 11 must have been a special game for Giel even if it was only an exhibition game. The Giants were playing their minor-league affiliate, the Minneapolis Millers, at Nicollet Park. Giel had been to Nicollet Park to cheer on the Millers many times in his youth and even got to know some of the players during the days he was being scouted. Giel started the game and went five innings before being replaced.

The Giants would go on to win the 1954 World Series in four games against the Cleveland Indians, but Giel was there only as a spectator. He was eligible to play in the Series, got a ring, and was awarded a full share of the winnings, but he did not pitch in the Series. Giel did not participate in the clubhouse celebration, most likely because he did not feel that he had contributed to the team's victory. Instead he was sitting in a corner trying to learn new pitching grips for the 1955 season. After the season was over, he took his first step into what would be a productive career in broadcasting. He had a weekly Sunday afternoon sports show in Minneapolis with newspaper writer Sid Hartman and sports announcer Jack Horner. Giel also had another show the same day every week that recapped the NFL games.

In spring training of 1955, Giel was trying to make the starting rotation as the fourth starter. Durocher was giving him regular starts and expected big things out of his bonus baby when he said, "Watch Paul Giel in 1955! He's going to do a lot of pitching for us. And he's going to be as great a credit to baseball as he was to football." In a poll taken by the sportswriters during training camp, Giel was voted as the best-looking Giants player, which only added to his Golden Boy image.

When the regular season came along, things had not worked out as well as Giel and Durocher had hoped. Giel made two starts that year, but for most of the season he was working out of the bullpen because he could not crack the rotation of Johnny Antonelli, Jim Hearn, Ruben Gomez, and Sal Maglie. The season started very well for him as he did not give up an earned run in his first four games and, in one of those games, even got out of a bases-loaded, no-out situation in the 11th inning before losing in the 12th inning, the first loss of his major-league career. On June 15, he earned his first big-league win when he entered a game in the seventh inning against the Chicago Cubs and pitched three scoreless innings. He helped himself with the bat that day, leading off the top of the ninth with a double, setting off a five-run rally that broke a 2-2 tie. When asked about the win he reflected back to the previous season by saying, "I am glad I finally have been able to do something for the Giants. I felt embarrassed accepting a World Series ring last fall, because I had done nothing to earn it." When the season was over, Giel had a won-lost record of 4-4 with a 3.39 ERA in

82 $1/3$ innings. The season ended with the Giants in third place, 18 $1/2$ games behind the first-place Brooklyn Dodgers. Everyone said his goodbyes and hoped to see each other the next season, but for Giel it would be two years before he pitched in the major leagues again. Before leaving for his military duty he went back to Minnesota and did some reporting for the local newspaper covering the Gophers football team.

As part of his joining ROTC in college, Giel had committed to serving two years of active duty in the military. On November 11, Giel was shipped to Aberdeen, Maryland, as a second lieutenant for the Army. After leaving Aberdeen, he was stationed at Fort Dix, New Jersey; Vaihingen, Germany; and Stuttgart, Germany, where he would spend the most time. While in Stuttgart he pitched and coached for one of the military baseball teams, which won 12 of 13 games one year and won the Western Conference baseball championship of Germany the following year. He also coached one of the army football teams but was unable to play because of clauses in his baseball contract. However, the biggest event that happened to Giel in Germany was finding and marrying the woman who would be his wife for nearly 50 years. Nancy A. Davis was the daughter of Colonel Thomas Davis, stationed in Vaihingen. Nancy attended George Washington University and the University of Colorado. The couple planned to live in Winona when Giel's active duty was over.

Back in the United States for the 1958 season, Giel would not be returning to the New York Giants but the San Francisco Giants. While he was away the team's owner, Horace Stoneham, had moved the team to California with promises of better attendance and larger profits. Because Giel had signed his original baseball contract in the middle of the season, he still had half a season left to fulfill on the two-year requirement for bonus players to stay on the major-league roster. However, in February the majors rescinded the two-year requirement and dropped the bonus status for all players. The Giants were now free to send Giel to the minor leagues, where he could get more playing time and have a better chance to learn the ever elusive third pitch that he needed. At first Giants manager Bill Rigney wanted to test Giel in spring training to see if he had matured enough in his two years away from the game to make the team. Rigney was also undecided about using Giel either as a starter or a relief pitcher when he said, "I'm going to see how I'm set up on my pitching before deciding whether to use Giel in relief or as a starter, but I think he's fine relieving material. He wants to be a good pitcher and doesn't beat himself. Paul is as strong as an ox and he can stand a lot of work. He can almost work every day, if he pitches only a few innings."

Giel's change-up was looking good in spring training, and he was able to make the club out of camp as a relief pitcher again. He pitched two games with the Giants before he was optioned to the team's Class AAA team in Phoenix on May 5. With Phoenix he was 3-0 with a 2.77 ERA. When he was brought back to the Giants on May 21, he was tried as a starter, but in less than a month he was back to working out of the bullpen. However, in that time as a starter he had one shining moment in which he pitched a complete game, allowing only four hits and one run for a victory against the Pirates. Overall, it was not a good year as he finished up 4-5 with a 4.70 ERA. Rigney summed up Giel's season and was looking toward the next when he repeated what had been said about Giel for his whole career, "Paul needs to develop a change-of-pace pitch, but maybe we can bring him into camp early next spring and have him work on a change-up." Off the field things were going much better with the birth of his first son, Paul Jr., on July 8. During the offseason Giel worked as a sales representative for the Minneapolis office of Investors Diversified Services, Inc.

Giel went to spring training with the Giants in 1959 and was expected to be a part of the team. Soon after training started he ran into problems: He walked the pitcher with the bases loaded in one game and give up five runs in one inning in another. Before the Giants broke camp for San Francisco they had decided to waive Giel. The Pittsburgh Pirates were quick to pick him up on April 13 for the $20,000 waiver price. He lasted four games with the team before he was demoted to the Pirates' Class AAA team in Columbus, Ohio, where he would spend the rest of the season. In that fourth game with the Pirates he gave up six runs in one inning against his former team. Before he was shipped to Columbus, Giel played in an exhibition game at Midway Stadium against the St. Paul Saints. It was a bittersweet game, so close to his home while about to be sent to the minors. He went six innings against the Saints, beating them 6-3 and driving in two of the runs him-

self. With Columbus, Giel would once again become a starter, going eight and nine innings in his first two starts. However, on July 29 he suffered a hairline fracture in his pitching hand when he was struck by a ball from the bat of Buffalo's Bobby Morgan. He was out until mid-August because of the injury. The Columbus Jets finished second in the International League behind the Buffalo Bisons.

Giel was invited to play with the Pirates in their 1960 spring training in Fort Myers, Florida, but he was expected to start the season in Salt Lake City playing for the Bees. However, as spring training went on, Giel was looking better and better because he had added to his pitching repertoire. As described by sportswriter Les Biederman "Giel has added a screwball and a slider and looked fine the first time he tested his new deliveries. There's an outside chance he might crash the roster." He went on to later say, "Giel . . . really has been the No. 1 star in training camp. . . . Few gave him a chance to win a regular job. But Giel was determined to make good or quit baseball and devote full time to the investment business in Minneapolis." Giel said that the biggest boost in his confidence came during a game against the Washington Senators, when he entered with the bases loaded and no outs to face Harmon Killebrew. Killebrew doubled and emptied the bases, but Giel proceeded to retire the next three batters by getting Bob Allison to foul out and striking out both Jim Lemon and Julio Becquer. On May 27, with the season just over a month old, Nancy gave birth to the couple's second child, daughter Gerilyn. On June 7 in a game against the Cubs, Giel suffered a slight muscle pull in his leg that was traced back to a football injury he had received in college. Giel pitched just 33 innings for the Pirates in 16 games, compiling a 2-0 record, all in relief before being sent down to play for the Salt Lake City Bees on July 15. In Salt Lake he was thrown into the starting rotation, getting nine starts in his 13 games with the team, but could only muster a record of 0-3.

In Minnesota, the people were happy about major-league baseball coming to the Twin Cities with the transfer of the Washington Senators for the 1961 season. Minnesota fans had been watching the high-caliber baseball of the Minneapolis Millers and the St. Paul Saints for years and could not be dazzled by ordinary baseball skills. Due to their need for a unique connection to the area, the Twins front office was looking for someone with whom the fans would identify. The easy answer was bring back the home-town golden boy to the area for the fans to come see play. This is exactly what the Twins did when they purchased Giel's contract from the Pirates in February of 1961. Fans from Giel's hometown, Winona, chartered a plane up to the Twin Cities for the home opener to cheer on Giel and the rest of the Twins. Pitching coach Ed Lopat, like every other pitching coach who had worked with Giel, tried to teach him a third pitch. Lopat's pitch of choice was a change-up screwball. Giel only lasted 12 games with the team and had a few bad outings. In one game he gave up seven earned runs in a third of an inning to the Kansas City Athletics. In another game, against Baltimore, he walked in what turned out to be the winning run. The last win of his career came on May 25 against the Tigers. He replaced Jim Kaat in the 11th inning and retired the first three batters that he faced. The Twins pushed across a run in the bottom of the 11th. A week later the hometown hero was traded with Reno Bertoia to the Athletics for Bill Tuttle.

Giel refused to report to the Athletics, instead decid-ing to retire from baseball. The Twins officials talked to Giel and got him to agree to stay in baseball and play for the Athletics. However, one day after the trade Giel pitched his first game for the Athletics and shelled by the Washington Senators for seven runs in 1 2/3 innings. Giel again announced his retirement, and this time it was for good. Athletics owner Charles Finley was upset that he had given up Bill Tuttle for a player who would retire after his first day with the team. He wanted to be compensated for Giel's services by the Twins and took his argument to Commissioner Ford Frick. Finley claimed that Giel had told him that he had previously informed Twins officials that he was going to retire from baseball and that the Twins did not disclose that information to the Athletics before making the trade. Twins owner Calvin Griffith ended up paying the Athletics $20,000 to make up for the loss of Giel's services and to complete the trade.

Giel may have been finished with baseball, but he was far from done with sports. Capitalizing on Giel's Minnesota fame, the newly formed Minnesota Vikings football team hired him in 1961 as an assistant business manager; he would stay for two seasons. In 1963 he traded on his past experience as a broadcaster and became the sports director for WCCO radio and television. For 10 years he coordinated coverage of sports programming. During his tenure with WCCO, his second son, Tom, was born on Christmas of 1967.

Giel had already done a great deal of good for the advancement of sports in the state of Minnesota, but his next venture would be one of his largest contributions. On December 12, 1971 the University of Minnesota announced that Giel would become the director of athletics. He was going back to the place where he had gained most of his fame. However, instead of trying to help a troubled football team as he did in the 1950s, this time he was trying to help the whole struggling sports department. He took on the job knowing that the sports department was $500,000 in debt, but he was able to turn the debt into a surplus during his 16-year tenure. The Gophers won a number of championships during the years that Giel directed the athletic program: two national hockey titles, three Big Ten baseball titles, three men's gymnastics championships, and a men's basketball Big Ten championship. Giel is also credited with the hiring of some important team coaches, such as Lou Holtz (foot-ball) and Clem Haskins (basketball). However, one of the proudest moments for Giel as the Gophers' athletic direc-tor actually had little to do with Gophers sports. It was his connection to the United Sates hockey team's "Miracle on Ice" victory when they beat the Soviet Union at the 1980 Olympics. The head coach for the team, Herb Brooks, and many of the players were from Minnesota. Giel was proud that the sports program at the University was able to make such a large contribution to the historic event.

There were many turbulent times at the University, as well. When basketball coach Bill Musselman left the school for the American Basketball Association, it was later dis-covered that under his tenure the team had more than 100 National Collegiate Athletic Association (NCAA) violations. Giel had to deal with the fallout of NCAA sanctions and the loss of scholarships. In 1986, another incident with the basketball team occurred in Madison, Wisconsin, when three players were accused and arrested for sexually assaulting a young woman. The players were later acquitted, but Giel, who was not involved in the incident, still took a lot of heat from people for letting his players act in such a disturbing manner. In 1988 there was a scandal with the Gophers football team from which Giel was unable to recover and that was partially instrumental in his losing his job. The university's interim director of the office of minority affairs, Luther Darville, was caught giving money to student-athletes and breaking NCCA rules. Darville was convicted of stealing $200,000 of the university's funds, although he claimed that he gave the money to student-athletes at the request of his superiors at the school.

After leaving the University of Minnesota Giel was an executive at the Minneapolis Heart Institute Foundation. By the age of 56, Giel had already received a quadruple bypasses and an angioplasty, so it was a cause that he was able to identify with very closely. On May 22, 2002 Giel passed away at the age of 69 from a heart attack after leaving a Twins game on his way to his grandson's Little League game. Even in his last moments he was a true sports fan and dedicated family man. Giel will always be remembered as one of the greatest sports figures in Minnesota history: from his slashing runs and long passes as a Gophers football player, to his blazing fastball for the Winona Braves and Minnesota Gophers, and for his off-the-field accomplishments of broadcasting sporting events with WCCO and his abilities as a decision-maker while directing the athletic department at the University of Minnesota.

Note: A version of this biography appeared in the book Minnesotans in Baseball, *edited by Stew Thornley (Nodin, 2009).*

Sources

Steve Bitker. *The Original San Francisco Giants: The Giants of '58.* (Champaign, IL: Sports Publishing, 1998)

College Football Hall of Fame. Retrieved July 26, 2008, from National Football Foundation's College Football Hall of Fame Web site: http://www.collegefootball.org/famersearch.php?id=50061.

Genealogy.com - Family Tree Maker Family History Software and Historical Records. Retrieved July 27, 2008, from Genealogy.com Web site: http://www.genealogy.com/index_r.html.

Frank Litsky (May 26, 2002). Paul Giel, 70, All-American in Two Sports and Pro Pitcher. *New York Post.*

Paul Giel. Retrieved July 27, 2008, from Retrosheet web site: http://www.retrosheet.org/boxesetc/G/Pgielp101.htm.

(November/December 1988). Paul Giel: I wanted to go to 59. Twenty Years. *Minnesota*, 36-39.

Armand Peterson and Tom Tomashek. *Townball: The Glory Days of Minnesota Amateur Baseball.* (Minneapolis: University of Minnesota Press, 2006)

Patrick Reusse (May 30, 2002). Baseball did Giel a disservice. *Minneapolis Star Tribune*, 1C.

SABR Minor Leagues Database: Paul Giel. Retrieved July 27, 2008, from SABR Minor League Database Web site: http://minors.sabrwebs.com/cgi-bin/person.php?milbID=giel--001pau.

Chip Scoggins (May 30, 2002). Paul Giel: 1932-2002; Giel is remembered; Services for former Gopher Paul Giel recalled his stature as a man as well as his exploits as an athlete. *Minneapolis Star Tribune*, 10C.

Sports Reference LLC. "Paul Giel" Baseball-Reference.com — Major League Statistics and Information. Retrieved July 26, 2008 from http://www.baseball-reference.com/g/gielpa01.shtml.

Steve Treder (November 1, 2004). Cash in the cradle: The Bonus Babies. The Hardball Times, Retrieved July 26, 2008 from http://www.hardballtimes.com/main/article/cash-in-the-cradle-the-bonus-b....

University of Minnesota Archives (2008) Paul Giel Folder 1.

Minnesota Daily 1953-1954.

The Sporting News 1953-1964.

Winona Republican-Herald 1946.

Fred Green

By Bob Hurte

A T 3:36 P.M. on October 13, 1960, Fred Green watched a ball hit by Bill Mazeroski sail over the left-field wall as Forbes Field erupted into bedlam. The improbable Pirates pulled off their stunning upset over the highly favored New York Yankees!

Years later, Fred's widow, Mona, shared her husband's feeling on the experience: "Fred's biggest thrill was playing in a World Series, although he didn't pitch well. But the fact that the club won the Series delighted him very much!"[1]

Fred Allen Green was born to David and Edna Green in Titusville, New Jersey, on September 14, 1933. Fred had one sibling, his younger brother Robert. David Green was a carpenter and Edna a homemaker. Titusville, a tiny hamlet, is a few miles north of where George Washington and his Continental soldiers crossed the Delaware River on Christmas night of 1776 and surprised the Hessian garrison at Trenton.

The Greens' son grew to be 6-feet-4 and 190 pounds. His athletic agility allowed him to become a star in baseball, basketball, and soccer at Titusville High School. His prowess as a left-handed pitcher brought him the most attention, and the Pirates signed him after he graduated from high school in 1952. His signing was a part of Branch Rickey's youth movement, a group jocularly known as Rickey's Dinks.

Green began with the Brunswick Pirates of the Class D Georgia/Florida League. He finished with a 20-12 record, a 2.54 earned-run average, and a league-leading 265 strikeouts, and was selected to the league All-Star team. For the next four seasons he moved up on the minor-league ladder, to Waco, Williamsport, New Orleans, and finally the Hollywood Stars of the Pacific

Coast League in 1956. There, pitching mostly in relief, Green posted a 5-4 record, then was drafted. He spent his two-year Army stint in the Special Services, which basically meant playing baseball.

Discharged in 1958, Green returned to pitch for the Salt Lake City Bees, who had replaced the Stars as the Pirates' farm in the Pacific Coast League. Manager Larry Shepard welcomed him with open arms; the Bees had only one other lefty. Green compiled a 10-8 record. After the season the Pirates purchased his contract. They invited him to spring training in 1959 to compete with 18 other pitchers for a spot on the roster. Green impressed the Pittsburgh brain trust and went north with the team to start the season.

He made his major-league debut against Cincinnati on April 15, relieving Bennie Daniels in the seventh inning with the Pirates losing 8-5. He walked Jerry Lynch, the first batter he faced, then gave up a homer to Ed Bailey. On the 27th he pitched again, giving up two runs to the Los Angeles Dodgers. It became obvious that he needed more seasoning, and the Pirates sent him to Triple-A Columbus. While his future in the major leagues seemed to be as a left-hander out of the bullpen, he was used as a spot starter at Columbus, and on May 30, soon after he was sent down, Green hurled a two-hit shutout against Richmond.

While he was not spectacular at Columbus, going 3-5 with a 3.46 ERA, neither were the Pirates. Between July 21 and August 2 they lost 12 of 13 games, and Green was recalled.

On August 15 Green proved his worth in the bullpen during a game against the Milwaukee Braves, who were rallying against Elroy Face. It was one of the rare occasions when Face was unable to stomp out a threat. Manager Danny Murtaugh brought in Green to face Frank Torre with the bases loaded. Torre reached on an error after a force play and two runs scored, cutting the Pirates' lead to 10-8. Bobby Avila doubled, but Green struck out Eddie Matthews with the tying run on base, then retired the side in the top of the ninth.

Two days later Green won his first major-league game. He entered a one-run game against the Cubs in the sixth inning and allowed the tying run to score, but got the victory when the Pirates scored a run in the seventh. Green finished 1959 with a 1-2 record and 3.13 ERA in 17 appearances. He made his only major-league start on September 11, against the second-place Dodgers with the Pirates struggling to stay in the pennant race. Green pitched well until Wally Moon hit a three run homer in the fifth, and lost the game, 4-0. After the season Green and a group of other Pirates prospects played for Aguilas Cibaenas in the Dominican Winter League.

In 1960 Green joined Face and others in the Pittsburgh bullpen. On April 21 he came in against the Philadelphia Phillies in a third inning, pitched out of a jam and went 3 $^2/_3$ innings for his first win of the season. In a lefty-righty combination, Green was the first left-handed reliever Murtaugh called upon. On July 27 *The Sporting News* proclaimed Face and Green as the best bullpen combination in the National League. Face finished at 10-8 with 24 saves and Green was 8-4 with three saves as the Pirates won the pennant.

In a Series of contrasts, the victorious Pirates' four victories were by scores of 6-4, 3-2, and 5-2, while the Yankees crushed the Bucs, 16-3, 10-0, and 12-0. Green pitched in all three of the Pirates' losses, and was hit hard. In four innings he yielded ten runs. He gave up two home runs to Mickey Mantle, including a mammoth shot over Forbes Field's right-center-field wall in Game Two. Although he appeared to be throwing batting practice for Yankees hitters during the World Series, Green was named to *The Sporting News'* 1960 All-Star rookie team.

Green developed a palmball after the season and experimented with changing speeds on his pitches. The Pirates had him penciled in for their 1961 bullpen. He ended splitting his time between Pittsburgh and Columbus. His 7-3 record helped Columbus win the International

League pennant. With Pittsburgh he was 0-0 in 13 games and his ERA ballooned to 4.79. He never won another major-league game. The Pirates skidded to sixth place. Just before the end of the season Green was sold on waivers to the expansion Washington Senators.

Green became reacquainted with the Yankees early in the 1962 season. On April 28 he entered a game at D.C. Stadium in the sixth inning with the Yankees leading, 5-1. He gave up an unearned run. Then in the seventh, he gave up home runs to Hector Lopez, Clete Boyer, and Roger Maris. A few days later Green was sent to Jacksonville. He split the rest of the season between Jacksonville and Syracuse, combining for a 4-7 won-lost record and a 5.13 ERA. In May of 1963 the Senators released Green. He signed with the Pirates, who sent him to Columbus to finish the season. He made the Pirates' roster in 1964 but was used sparingly, pitching 7 $^1/_3$ innings in eight games with a 1.23 ERA. On June 14 he made his last major-league appearance, against the Chicago Cubs. Green entered the game in the seventh game and pitched to two future Hall of Famers, Billy Williams and Ron Santo, retiring them both. Shortly afterward Pittsburgh sent Green back to Columbus.

Green finished the season with Columbus and returned in 1965, hoping to work his way back to Pittsburgh. He appeared in 37 games and was 1-4 with a 4.66 ERA. After the season he retired from professional baseball, at the age of 32.

Green went to work for Leaseway Transportation Company and eventually became a manager for the firm. He and Mona had two sons, Gary and Gregg. Gary played shortstop for the San Diego Padres, Texas Rangers, and Cincinnati Reds, and managed Pirates and Tigers farms teams for 11 season. Fred loved being around baseball and occasionally pitched batting practice for the Pirates.

Fred Green died of a heart attack in Titusville on December 22, 1996. He was 62 years old. He was buried in the Harbourton Cemetery in Lambertville, New Jersey.

Nellie King, a former teammate and Pirates broadcaster, put Green's baseball career in perspective: "He was a journeyman … a good, friendly guy who had to work like hell to get where he was, but there are great players who never played on a championship team. He did!" [2]

Sources

In addition to the sources cited, the author also consulted:

Jim O'Brien, *Maz and the '60 Bucs* (Pittsburgh: Jim O'Brien Publishing, 1993), 502-03.

Lloyd Johnson and Miles Wolff, eds. *The Encyclopedia of Minor League Baseball* (Durham, North Carolina: Baseball America, 1997).

The Sporting News, May 1958 — July 1964.

Notes

1   TheDeadballera.com.

2   Letter from Mona Green to the author, October 14, 2011.

Dick Groat

by Joseph Wancho

Before Bo Jackson and Deion Sanders made "two-sport athletes" a vogue term in the 1980s and '90s, there was Dick Groat. Groat lacked the power of Jackson or the speed of Sanders. But what he lacked in physical gifts he more than made up in guile and spirit. His collegiate career at Duke University earned him All-American honors in basketball and election to the College Basketball Hall of Fame. His baseball career saw him rise from the college ranks directly to the major-league level. He did not play an inning of a minor-league game.

At 5-feet-11 with a modest build, Groat may not have looked the part of a professional athlete. But he excelled under the guidance of two giants of their profession. At Duke, Groat was coached briefly by Red Auerbach, who went on to a career as coach and then general manager of the Boston Celtics that earned him election to the Basketball Hall of Fame. Later he was signed by Branch Rickey, a Hall of Famer as a baseball executive, to join the Pittsburgh Pirates. These two larger-than-life personalities helped shape Groat into the athlete and person he became: Auerbach taught Groat how to attain a competitive edge in competition, and Rickey instilled a mental discipline and fortitude in him.

Richard Morrow Groat was born on November 4, 1930, in Wilkinsburg, Pennsylvania, which is adjacent to Pittsburgh. He was the fifth and youngest child (after Martin, Charles, Elsie, and Margaret) of Martin and Gracie Groat. Martin Groat worked in the real-estate investment business.

At Swissvale High School Groat earned letters in basketball, baseball, and volleyball. He attended Duke University on a basketball scholarship. He became a two-time All-American in both basketball and baseball. On the hardwood, Groat was named the

National Player of the Year after his senior season (1951-1952), when he averaged 26 points and 7.6 assists per game. He is the only player in NCAA history to lead the nation in both scoring and assists in a season. On May 1, 1952, he was the first player at Duke to have his uniform number (10) retired.

In baseball Groat played shortstop and helped to lead the Blue Devils to a 31-7 record and their first College World Series appearance in his senior year, 1952. He hit .370 and led the team in doubles, hits, runs batted in, and stolen bases. He was a two-time winner of the McKelvin Award, given to the Athlete of the Year in the Southern Conference.

In the summer of 1951, between Groat's junior and senior years, Branch Rickey, general manager of the Pirates, invited Groat and his father to stop in his office. "We got there in the afternoon and Mr. Rickey pulled out a document and said: 'If you sign this contract, you can play shortstop against the Phillies tonight,'" Groat recalled. After Groat pointed out that he still had another year of college, Rickey suggested that he could complete his education during the offseason. "Mr. Rickey, I'm down at Duke on a basketball scholarship," Groat said. "I feel obligated to play the full four years. But I will tell you this much — if you make the same offer to me next June, I'll sign."[1] (That was in the days before the free-agent draft.)

True to his word, Groat signed with the Pirates the next year, in June 1952, after Duke had been eliminated from the College World Series. His contract included a bonus said to be in the $35,000 to $40,000 range. Bypassing the minor leagues, he joined the Pirates in New York, where they were playing the Giants. His first day in uniform, June 17, Groat observed the action from the visiting team dugout at the Polo Grounds. The next day he made his major-league debut, pinch-hitting and grounding out to Giants hurler Jim Hearn. Groat got his first two hits the next day, stayed in the lineup for the rest of the season and led the team in hitting with a .284 batting average. Only two other regulars ended the season with a batting average above .270, catcher Joe Garagiola (.273) and first baseman-outfielder George Metkovich (.271). Under manager Billy Meyer, Pittsburgh finished the 1952 campaign in last place with a 42-112 record, 54½ games behind first-place Brooklyn.

Groat was helped during his rookie season by Pirate Hall of Famer Paul Waner, who operated some batting cages in nearby Harmarville. Groat would visit the batting cages before heading to Forbes Field each morning for practice. "He was fun to be with, I really liked Paul Waner," Groat said. "He couldn't have been nicer to me in every way. He helped me build confidence. … He was very patient, very understanding, and had a great hitting philosophy. Even at that age (49), he could still hit that machine and hit that ball hard." [2]

After the season Groat returned to Duke to finish his degree. He was drafted by the Fort Wayne Pistons in the first round (third pick overall) of the NBA's college draft. (Groat always favored basketball, feeling that was the sport he excelled at the most.) "I never practiced with them," Groat said of the Pistons. "I was still trying to get those credits from Duke, and the Pistons would fly me from school to games in a private plane. I loved pro basketball. Basketball was always my first love, mainly because I played it best and it came easiest to me." [3] In 26 games with the Pistons, he averaged 11.9 points per game.

His basketball season was cut short when he was drafted again, this time by the US Army. For the next two years he fulfilled his military commitment at Fort Belvoir in Virginia. While serving in the military, he kept in shape playing basketball and baseball on the Belvoir Engineer teams.

Although the Pirates floundered during the Rickey era, the general manager was laying the groundwork for future success. In addition to signing Groat, Rickey also selected Roberto Clemente from Brooklyn via the Rule 5 Draft in 1954 and signed Bill Mazeroski the same year. Clemente

and Mazeroski were key ingredients in bringing two world championships to Pittsburgh, and both are in the Baseball Hall of Fame.

A move Rickey made before Groat got to Pittsburgh benefited the player. He brought George Sisler to Pittsburgh in 1951. Sisler, who had worked for Rickey in Brooklyn, was the Pirates' scouting supervisor and unofficial hitting coach. "Sisler teaches us to be ready for the fastball and adjust our swing for the curve," Groat said at the time. "If you're looking for a curve and get a fastball, you never hit it. But you can cut down on the speed of your swing to hit the curve." [4]

When Groat returned from military duty in 1955, he wanted to play both baseball and basketball. "Basketball was fun to me, and baseball was work," he said. The Pistons offered a higher salary and would allow him to leave the team early for spring training. Groat cited the example of Gene Conley, who pitched for the Milwaukee Braves, and played basketball for the Boston Celtics. "Don't bring up Conley with me," Rickey told Groat. "As a starting pitcher he only works every fourth or fifth day, and he's only a backup center in basketball. You are a regular player in both baseball and basketball. I think you should realize that eventually you won't justify your salary in either sport." [5] Persuaded by Rickey's logic, Groat chose to focus on baseball.

Groat started slowly in 1955, hitting .229 in April and .235 in May. A slow start might have been expected, but Rickey would cut him no slack. Groat recalled talking to himself in the batting cages when he heard Rickey say just loud enough to be heard, "There is no way that the boy can improve. He never was an All-American in baseball and basketball." [6] This may have been Rickey's way of getting him to concentrate more at the plate. Groat ended the year hitting .267 for the last-place Pirates, who finished 38½ games out of first place under manager Fred Haney. He capped off the year by marrying Barbara Womble, once a top New York model, on November 11. They eventually had three daughters, Tracey, Carol Ann, and Allison.

Before the 1956 season, Rickey was replaced as general manager by Joe L. Brown. Brown did not share Rickey's high opinion of Sisler, and dropped him as one of his first moves. He brought in Bobby Bragan to replace Haney.

The change made little difference: The Pirates rose to seventh place but were still a distant 27 games behind pennant-winner Brooklyn. When Bragan began 1957 with a record of 36-67, he was fired and replaced by third-base coach Danny Murtaugh.

Groat began to flourish under Bragan, and then Murtaugh. His batting average leaped from .273 in 1956 to .315 in 1957 and .300 in 1958. The Pirates went from a last-place finish in 1957 to second place in 1958, with a record of 84-70, eight games behind Milwaukee. Both Groat and the Pirates regressed in 1959. He still hit well, batting .275, but he led the league with 29 errors at shortstop as the Pirates ended the season in fourth place. Groat appeared in the 1959 All-Star Game, the first of five appearances in his career.

One knock against Groat was that he could not hit with power. He did not strike out much, fanning more that 60 times in only one season. But as a contact hitter he was adept at hitting the ball through the open hole in the infield. Murtaugh allowed Groat to pick his spots to hit and run, often with Groat flashing a sign to the baserunner. Critics also pointed to his lack of range at shortstop and weak arm. Fellow shortstop Alvin Dark defended him. "They say he doesn't have much range at shortstop. What's range but getting to the ball?" Dark said. "You watch Groat. He's always in front of the ball. He's smart and he knows the hitters and plays position as well as anyone I ever saw. Maybe he doesn't have a great arm, but he makes up for it by getting the ball away quicker than anyone else." [7]

Pittsburgh put it all together in 1960, winning the pennant by seven games over the Milwaukee Braves and then capturing the team's first world championship since 1925 by defeating the New York Yankees on Mazeroski's dramatic walk-off home run. Groat led the league in hitting with a .325 batting average, finished third with 186 hits, and was named the National League's Most Valuable Player by both *The Sporting News* and the Baseball Writers Association of America. He had his best day at the plate on May 13 in Milwaukee when he went 6-for-6 with three doubles. He earned MVP honors (though teammate Roberto Clemente felt he should have won the award) even though he was sidelined for most of September with a broken left wrist after being hit by Milwaukee pitcher Lew Burdette. Returning to the lineup just before the end of the season, Groat hit .214 in the World Series with two doubles and two RBIs.

Over the next two years, the Pirates slipped back to the middle of the pack. In 1962, Groat led the league's shortstops with 38 errors. After the season rumors circulated that Groat, who turned 32 in the offseason, Dick would be traded.

Meanwhile, in St. Louis, August Busch, Jr. had lured Branch Rickey to work as a senior consultant to the Cardinals' front office. Busch was dismayed at the Cardinals' inability to win a championship since 1946. Cardinals general manager Bing Devine and Rickey clashed immediately. Their relationship was rocky at the beginning, and got worse as the months went by. Devine had been working to acquire Groat from the Pirates, but Rickey quashed it. Rickey believed in trading older players, not acquiring them. He looked to dump players a year early, when there was some value, as opposed to a year too late.

Cardinals skipper Johnny Keane also wanted Groat to join the team. "With Groat to assist and guide him, I believe Julian Javier would develop into a truly great second baseman," Keane said. "Our infield also would be improved by the presence of a take-charge guy such as Groat. Our infield as constituted last season was not an aggressive combination." [8] A deal was made on November 19, 1962, and Groat went to St. Louis with relief pitcher Diomedes Olivo in exchange for pitcher Don Cardwell and shortstop Julio Gotay.

After some initial apprehension, Groat was happy to be heading to St. Louis. "I think the Cardinals are a good club that got some tough breaks last season," he said. "I know I am not young, and I'd like to play on a contender a few more years." [9]

The Cardinals started 1963 with a 14-6 record in April. They held a slim 1½-game lead over the Dodgers and Giants at the end of June. The infield quartet of first baseman Bill White, second baseman Julian Javier, third baseman Ken Boyer, and Groat were having very good years at the plate. At midseason White, Boyer, and Groat were hitting .300 or better and Javier was holding steady with a .270 batting average. All four infielders started for the National League in the All-Star Game.

Late in the season the Cardinals went on a torrid pace, winning 19 of 20 games from August 30 to September 15. On September 16 they trailed Los Angeles by one game, with the Dodgers coming to St. Louis for a three-game series. The Dodgers swept the series, including a four-hitter by Sandy Koufax in the second game and a 6-5 Dodgers victory in 13 innings in the finale. The Cardinals went on the road and dropped five games in the final week of the season, putting an end to their pennant hopes.

Groat ended the 1963 season with career highs in hits (201), doubles (43), triples (11), and RBIs (73). His .319 batting average tied for third and his 43 doubles led both leagues. He finished second to Koufax in voting for the MVP.

During the season center fielder Curt Flood said he learned a lot about positioning from the veteran short-stop. "I'll play a hitter a certain way, and then I'll notice that Dick is a bit further to the right than I would have thought. His knowledge of the hitters is so good, I figure he must be right, so I move to the right too," Flood said. [10]

The Cardinals finally broke through in 1964, capturing their first world championship since 1946. Groat hit .292, drove in 70 runs and stroked 35 doubles. In a thrilling race to the finish, St. Louis went 21-8 in September. The Philadelphia Phillies held a 6½-game lead over St. Louis and Cincinnati on September 20, but then closed out the month on a ten-game losing streak. When the Cardinals sewed up the pennant in the final game of the season, against the New York Mets, Groat hit two doubles and scored twice in the Cards 11-5 victor.

After going down two games to one in the World Series against the Yankees, the Cardinals won three out of four and were crowned world champions. Groat had only five hits for a .192 batting average, but also got on base four times with walks.

In Game Four, relief pitcher Roger Craig walked Mickey Mantle and Elston Howard with two outs in the third inning. The next batter was Tom Tresh. Groat knew that Craig had an excellent move to second base, and at times they ran what they called "the daylight play." If Groat got inside the runner at second base and there was daylight between them, they would try for the pickoff. There was no signal to the play; Craig and Groat just did it. Groat

was able to get between Mantle and the base. Craig turned and threw, and they picked Mantle off. Mantle headed back to the dugout, past Craig. "You son of a bitch," Mantle said. "You show me up in front of forty million people." [11]

Manager Johnny Keane surprised everyone by resigning after the World Series and replacing Yogi Berra as manager of the Yankees. Cardinals coach Red Schoendienst took over for Keane. Groat was happy for the switch. "He understands ballplayers," Groat said of Schoendienst. "Everything he does, he does for the good of the players. He's considerate of their feelings at all times. That's why I think he is going to do a tremendous job for us." [12]

Neither Groat nor the Cardinals enjoyed a successful season in 1965. The team slipped to seventh place in the ten-team league and the 34-year-old Groat hit .254. After the season the Cardinals traded Groat with first baseman Bill White and reserve catcher Bob Uecker to Philadelphia for pitcher Art Mahaffey, outfielder Alex Johnson and catcher Pat Corrales. "We got him because I know he can still hit. But, more important, he knows he can still hit," said Phillies manager Gene Mauch. "And a player like Groat always hits better when his ballclub is in the game all the time." [13]

Besides playing shortstop for the Phillies, Groat also played 20 games at third base, a position he disliked but nonetheless was willing to play. The team finished fourth, eight games behind the first-place Dodgers. On May 18, facing the Cardinals, Groat got his 2,000th career hit, a single to center field off Bob Gibson.

Groat was hobbled during the 1967 season by cellulitis, an inflammation of the tissues and veins in his right ankle. The ankle swelled to three times its normal size and Groat's temperature rose to 104 degrees. He was hospitalized for two weeks and missed two months of the season. He played in only ten games for the Phillies before being sold to San Francisco on June 22. After batting a puny .156 for both teams, he retired after the season. Groat ended his playing career with a batting average of .286 in 14 major-league seasons.

For many years Groat had worked during the offseason as a salesman for Jessup Steel in Washington, Pennsylvania. In 1965 he took a new direction. Groat and former

Pirates teammate Jerry Lynch built a public golf course, called Champion Lakes, in Laurel Valley, 50 miles east of Pittsburgh. As of 2011, Groat was still spending half his time living at Champion Lakes and keeping active in the day-to-day operations of the course. He also spent 33 years (as of the 2011-12 basketball season) as a color analyst on radio broadcasts of University of Pittsburgh basketball games. In 1990 Barbara Groat died of lung cancer. She and Dick had been married for 35 years.

In November 2007 Groat was inducted into the National Collegiate Basketball Hall of Fame in Kansas City, Missouri. He has also received the Arnold Palmer Spirit of Hope Award, given annually to people who serve as an inspiration to children all over the world. He remained active with charity events involving the Pittsburgh Pirates Alumni Association.

Sources

List of Web sites used

http://www.retrosheet.org/

http://www.goduke.com/

http://minors.sabrwebs.com/cgi-bin/index.php

http://pittsburghpanthers.cstv.com/sports/m-baskbl/pitt-m-bask-bl-body.html

http://pittsburgh.pirates.mlb.com/index.jsp?c_id=pit

http://www.collegebasketballexperience.com/inductees.aspx?alpha=all

http://www.pittsburghpanthers.com/genrel/111907aad.html

http://www.basketball-reference.com/players/g/groatdi01.html

Notes

1   *The Sporting News*, April 2, 1966, 7

2   Jeremy Anders. Article dated July 22, 2007, located at http://www.baseballhall.org

3   *Boston Herald*, August 13, 1978

4   Rick Huhn. *The Sizzler* (Columbia, Missouri: University of Missouri Press, 2004), 18-27; 270-271

5   Lee Lowenfish, *Branch Rickey—Baseball's Ferocious Gentleman* (Lincoln: University of Nebraska Press, 2007), 529-530

6   Ibid.

7   *Sports Illustrated*, August 8, 1960, 26

8   *The Sporting News*, November 24, 1962, 29

9   *Pittsburgh Press*, November 20, 1962

10 *Sports Illustrated*, July 22, 1963, 34

11 David Halberstam. *October 1964* (New York: Random House, 1994), 334

12 Phil Pepe. Undated article in Groat's player file at the National Baseball Hall of Fame

13 *The Sporting News*, May 21, 1966, 20-21

Don Gross

By Joel Gross

Don Gross HAD a 13-year career in professional baseball as a left-handed pitcher, including a brief spell with the Pittsburgh Pirates at the beginning of the 1960 season. He pitched in 1950-1952 and 1954-1963, with time out in most of 1952 and all of 1953 while in military service). For much of his time he was hampered by arm trouble that might have been alleviated by modern-day advances in sports medicine.

Donald John Gross was born on June 30, 1931, in Weidman, Michigan, a tiny community in the central part of the state. According to the 1940 US Census, his father, Charles Gross, was an Illinois native who worked as a painter, busy with interior painting for houses and painting oil tanks for Pure Oil Co. His mother was Agnes Gross, a native of Michigan. Charles and Agnes had six children as of that census year: Virginia 12, Patricia and Donald, both 8, Marilyn 6, Joan 4, and Robert 3.

Gross wasn't always a left-hander. "I was right-handed as a young boy," he said in 1956. "At the age of 7, I caught my arm in a washing machine and broke my arm. I switched to the left and have been throwing and batting that way ever since."[1]

Gross said in a 2012 interview that his interest in baseball was simple: "I played it in high school and I just wanted to pursue it."[2]

The 5-foot-11, 186-pound Gross was scouted by Frank Nelspaugh, a bird dog from St. Louis, Michigan.[3] He signed with the Cincinnati Reds after his freshman year at Michigan State and was assigned to the Reds' Muncie farm team in the Class D Ohio-Indiana league. There the teenager posted the most wins in his professional career, going 15-7, pitching 187 innings, and winding up with a 3.13 earned-run aver-

age. He capped off his strong year on the mound by hitting .330 in 88 at-bats, a feat he was never able to duplicate.

In 1951 Gross was on the move, playing first for the Welch Miners in the Class D Appalachian League, where he pitched 21 innings and posted a 2-1 won-lost record. The Reds promoted him to Charleston in the Class A Central League, where he fell to 1-3 with a 5.68 ERA. Probably sensing that they had moved Gross up too quickly, the Reds sent him to Ogden in the Class C Pioneer League, where he finished the year with his best career ERA, 1.11, on the way to a 10-4 record in 15 games.

Instead of having a chance to build on the strong finish to his 1951 season, Gross was drafted—"I was a damn foot soldier in the infantry"—and spent the 1952 and 1953 seasons in the Army. Though the war in Korea was on in earnest, Gross spent his time at Fort Riley, Kansas. "I was fortunate enough to play ball in the Army," he said. "Some damn officer was a jock and kept us there. I tended bar in the Officers Club and they had to make me a sergeant to have that job. I should have been a damn private, but it goes with the territory."

Back from the service, Gross spent the 1954 season with Columbia in the Class A South Atlantic League, compiling a 12-9 record with a 3.14 ERA in 189 innings. Season highlights included a 5-0 shutout of the Macon Peaches on June 19 and an appearance on the winning Sally League All-Star team against Jacksonville. At the end of the season he moved up to the Tulsa Oilers, but pitched only eight innings. After the season Gross pitched winter ball for Vanytor in the Colombian League. In one outing, pitching a one-hitter through seven innings, he was hit by a baseball and taken to the hospital. He must not have been injured seriously, since no further mention of the injury was noted in *The Sporting News*.

Gross started the 1955 season with the Reds, although he didn't count against the reserve list due to his military service.[4] Eventually he was sent down to Nashville of the Double-A Southern Association, where he won eight games and lost two with a 3.69 ERA. He was named to the Southern Association All-Star team. In July the Reds called him up and he made his major-league debut on the 21st at Connie Mack Stadium in Philadelphia. He started the game and went five innings, giving up two runs, but was not charged with the Reds' loss. In all, Gross made 11 starts (two complete games) and six relief appearances. His first complete game, on August 17 at home, was a 3-2 loss to the Chicago Cubs, in which he gave up two home runs to Hank Sauer, accounting for all three runs. His second complete game was a four-hit (all singles), 4-0 shutout over St. Louis on August 21. Gross finished 4-5 with an ERA of 4.14.

As hopes soared for Gross in the offseason, catcher Smoky Burgess said that Gross "has a good curve, a good fastball and a whale of a changeup, and it's the last named pitch which makes me think he's going to be a winner. He can get right-handers out with that changeup on the count of 3-2 and that's one reason I like his chances of becoming a top-flight hurler."[5] But in a precursor of things to come, Gross was sent home from Licey of the Dominican League with arm trouble.

After one appearance for the Reds in April, Gross was sent on May 1 to the Havana Sugar Kings of the International League. In 54 innings with Havana, he had a 3-2 won-lost record with a stellar 1.67 ERA. Again the Reds noticed, recalling him at the end of June. In his first appearance, on July 1, he held the Cardinals to seven hits in a 7-1 victory. (Stan Musial's home run was the only blemish.) Overall, he pitched in 20 games (seven starts) and went 3-0 with a spectacular 1.95 ERA.

Gross again played winter ball following the 1956 season, this time joining the Estrellas Orientales of the Dominican League. Echoing a different era in baseball, Gross began to seek different offseason work. A co-worker in an automobile assembly plant in Cincinnati — one with 20 years on the job — had cut off a finger while working. "I need all my fingers for pitching," Gross said.[6]

The 1957 season started off with a lot of promise. Gross was included in *The Sporting News'* list of the "best young pitchers" in the National League. In his first 56 innings pitched, he limited his foes to 11 earned runs and 37 hits, finishing four complete games in five starts for a 4-1 record. His performance fell off, however, and he finished the season with a 7-9 record and a 4.31 ERA. Still, that season gave Gross what was most probably the most memorable moment of his career. On May 28 at Milwaukee County Stadium, he held the powerful Braves lineup hitless through 7 $\frac{2}{3}$ innings, until Joe Torre singled and Bobby Thomson tripled, making the score 1-0. When the Reds failed to score in the top of the ninth, Gross was a 1-0 loser to Warren Spahn.

In his three starts after the Spahn game, Gross was belted freely by the Cubs, Phillies, and Pirates, yielding nine runs and 17 hits in less than eight innings. He didn't win again until September 2, against the Cardinals in ten innings. It was his first win since May 23. He had lost nine games in a row.

During the winter, Gross again pitched for Licey of the Dominican League. He also became engaged and planned a February 1958 wedding.

On December 9, 1957, Gross was traded to the Pirates for Bob Purkey. The trade turned out to be a great one for the Reds, as Purkey blossomed into a three-time National League All-Star, winning 103 games for Cincinnati in seven seasons, including a 23-5 record with a 2.81 ERA in 1962. By 1962, Gross had been plagued with arm problems and had only one more year left in his then minor-league, injury-riddled arm. Pirates general manager Joe L. Brown later called the Gross/Purkey trade the worst of his career.[7]

Gross was considered a disappointment, having gone from 3-0 with a 1.96 ERA in 1956 to a 7-9 record with a 4.32 ERA in '57. He won his first game as a Pirate when he downed the Reds on April 26 in relief. In fact, he pitched ten innings in relief without allowing a run while giving up only four hits. On May 5 he shut the door on a nine-run Giants rally that preserved an 11-10 Pirates victory. On May 13 Gross turned in his seventh consecutive impressive relief job to save a victory over the Reds for Ron Kline. After pitching in relief in 11 games with a 0.78 ERA, Gross failed in his first start, being KO'd by the Cubs in the eighth inning on June 7. (The Bucs won the game in the tenth.) In his first season in Pittsburgh, Gross was 5-7 in 75 innings, but with a serviceable 3.98 ERA. After the season he was awarded a full share of the Pirates' second-place money, $1,507.04.

The 1959 season marked the beginning of the end for Gross. He had arm troubles in spring training, and then a sore shoulder. He was examined by Dr. George Bennett in Baltimore who advised rest. Plagued by arm trouble, Gross pitched only six innings for the Pirates and was sent to the Triple-A Columbus Jets on May 29. The Pirates brought him back in July. In the midst of the disappointing season, on August 26, 1959, Gross became a father for the first time when his wife gave birth to a son, Donald Martin Gross.

Trying to pitch through his arm troubles proved difficult, and Gross had perhaps the worst inning of his career on August 27 in a game against the International League All Stars; he gave up seven hits and nine runs (eight earned) while walking two and striking out no one. He then blew a save on September 26, giving up two runs in the ninth and costing debuting starter Jim Umbricht his first major-league win. This was Gross's last save opportunity. In his career he had 10 saves and three blown saves. Gross was able to pitch only 33 innings for the Pirates that season. His record was 1-1 with a 3.55 ERA.

Arm problems continued into 1960. Though *The Sporting News* said Gross "appeared to be free of injuries and may be the southpaw needed to work in relief," it did not come to fruition.[8] Gross was forced to miss the first two weeks of spring training and didn't do much pitching, but somehow made the Pirates' Opening Day roster. He nursed slight injuries to his right ankle and little finger on his left hand, hurt while bunting against automatic pitching machines. It was to be his final stint in the big leagues and lasted only 37 games into the season. Having pitched only 5 1/3 innings in five games, Gross was released outright to Salt Lake City of the Pacific Coast League on May 28, the same day that the Pirates traded for Vinegar Bend Mizell. Pitching 117 innings for the Bees, Gross won five games and lost six, but had a respectable 3.46 ERA. He received a cash grant of $250 from the Pirates' World Series money.

In 1961 Gross was listed as starting the season with the Columbus Jets, but he was placed on the disabled list on April 18 and allowed to remain with the boy. On May 23 he was sent to the Macon Peaches of the Double-A Southern Association. His career wound down with an 11-4 record in 119 innings and a 3.02 ERA.

In 1962 Gross signed with the Syracuse Chiefs but threw only four innings; he was released on May 16. He began to pitch for a northern Kentucky softball team, but even then had to leave a game with arm trouble. His professional baseball career ended in 1963—again with the Columbus Jets—where he was 1-1 in 17 innings with a 3.71 ERA. He had played 13 years with 12 minor-league and two major-league teams.

As a minor leaguer Gross was 68-39 with a 3.07 ERA. In the major leagues he won 20 and lost 22, with a 3.73 ERA. In 145 major-league games, he started 37, with one shutout and ten saves. He must have had good baseball genes; a nephew, Todd Benzinger had a nine-year big-league career. Gross didn't really have a direct influence on Benzinger. "He's my wife's sister's boy. When he was in high school, I had a sporting-goods business in Cincinnati and I used to go over and see the baseball coach."

After baseball Gross became a partner in a sporting goods business in Cincinnati, selling to schools and colleges in the area. His oldest son, David, signed a letter of intent to play baseball for the University of Missouri, and when he

went off to college, Don moved back home to Michigan. Dave Gross, a right-handed pitcher, played four years at college, then signed with the Minnesota Twins and played one year, 1982, in the minor leagues. "My other son played four years at Michigan State," Don said. "A couple of grandkids might be going on when they get out of high school, too."[9]

Ultimately, Don Gross had a chance to be a very successful major-league hurler, but was limited by injury. One wonders if later advances in medicine could have fixed what ailed him.

Thanks to Nate Schneider of Michigan Newspapers. Thanks also to Don Gross for his February 2013 comments on this article.

Notes

1   *Washington Post*, March 18, 1956.

2   Interview with Don Gross by Bill Nowlin on December 18, 2012.

3   Gross 2012 interview.

4   *New York Times*, October 14, 1954.

5   *The Sporting News*, January 25, 1956.

6   *The Sporting News*, December 26, 1956.

7   See, for instance, the *Pittsburgh Post-Gazette* of May 8, 2003, where Purkey said, "Joe Brown always said trading me [for Don Gross] was the worst deal he ever made."

8   *The Sporting News*, March 9, 1960.

9   The December 2012 interview with Don Gross is the source of the quotations in the last few paragraphs..

Harvey Haddix

By Mark Miller

WHENEVER THE NAME Harvey Haddix is mentioned, there is usually a reference to a 115-pitch game he threw in Milwaukee in 1959. His career in professional baseball, however, was much more—lasting parts of five decades.

Haddix was born on September 18, 1925, the third son of Harvey Haddix, Sr. and Nellie Mae Greider-Haddix. His parents were farmers near Westville, in west central Ohio, but Haddix was born 20 miles away, in Medway, Ohio. "My mother had an aunt who was a midwife who lived there," Haddix explained in a public appearance in 1989.[1]

Life on the farm was typical for the Haddix boys, Harvey, older brothers Ed and Ben, and younger brother Fred. "There on the farm we didn't have any money and there were no kids out there to play ball with, except the neighbor kids, so we played baseball two on a side." His first glove was a first baseman's mitt made from a leather horsecollar.

In 1940, before his freshman year in high school, the family purchased a farm near South Vienna, Ohio. Catawba High School had a successful baseball team loaded with upperclassmen, including brother Ben. Harvey became the team's left-handed shortstop, "I could catch a ground ball," he explained. [2]

Equipment continued to be an issue. Haddix elaborated: "I made the ball team but I didn't have a pair of spikes so I took a pair of my dress shoes and punched holes in the bottom of my dress shoes and riveted cleats on the bottom for my first pair of spikes."[3]

As a senior he began to pitch. "When I became a senior the pitcher had graduated so I took over

the pitching chores and we won the county championship." He had an excellent instructor at home in the person of his father, who was a renowned amateur pitcher.[4] Brother Ben, two years older, was playing minor-league baseball for the local Springfield Cardinals, a Class C Middle Atlantic League club managed by Walter Alston.

In 1943, after Haddix graduated from high school, "I was pitching, semipro, and a scout was there from the Philadelphia Athletics. He comes to me and says, 'I am going to write Connie Mack about you.' I said, 'That would be fine' and I sat around waiting for two weeks and didn't hear anything. One day I picked up the newspaper and there was a little article in the paper that said that there is a Redbird tryout in Columbus.

"I had to go to Columbus, at 9 in the morning until 4 in the afternoon for the tryout camp. They had 350 kids there. … They looked at me and said you will be a pitcher. Pitchers went down to the bullpen, and we sat there until 4. They said: OK warm up and go in and throw nothing but fastballs. They said, 'Can you come back tomorrow?'

"I came back the next day. Now throw what the catcher calls. I probably threw three to four curveballs, and three to four fastballs. As I walked off the mound he says, 'Do you want to sign?' I said no. I am an old country boy, I am thinking about the guy back home that saw me first. I never heard anything more from him and went back over to Columbus and signed with the Cardinals.

"Now (World War II) was going on and I took a two-week trip with the Columbus baseball club. I just turned 18 so I had to leave the trip in Louisville and return to Springfield to register for the draft."[5]

Haddix's next road trip would have to wait three years. As a farmer he received a three-year deferment from military service, which meant his only employment could be the farm.

In 1947, after the war ended, Haddix started his professional baseball career, in Triple-A. "I took off for Columbus for spring training. Now I know I can't play with them, I sat there about two weeks and I finally had enough and went up to the office and said, 'Where am I going to go play ball?' He said you are going to Pocatello, Idaho. I looked at him and said, 'No I'm not. That is too far from home. You got something closer to home than that.'"

A couple of days later Haddix was sent to Winston-Salem of the Class C Carolina League and met the team in Lynchburg, Virginia. "I got there and was setting on the steps waiting for someone to come and here comes a little old school bus with Winston-Salem Cardinals on the side of it. There was one guy on the team that knew me who introduced me to the manager (Zip Payne)." Haddix was 5-feet-6, 175 pounds, and Payne's first impression was not positive. Haddix said he was told the manager said, "Do they expect me to win a pennant sending me something like that down here?" [6]

Haddix's first two appearances were in relief. He did not allow a run in a win and a loss. From then on he was a starter and changed the manager's opinion by winning 19 and losing 5, with 275 strikeouts while also hitting over .300 (including a pinch-hit homer). On August 11 he pitched a seven-inning no-hitter, later threw a nine-inning one-hitter, and had a 19-strikeout game. He was selected a league all-star, the left-handed pitcher of the year, the rookie of the year, and the most valuable player. His 1.90 ERA easily beat out the second-best (3.18).

"The next year I jumped to Triple-A ball. I pitched there for three years, '48, '49, and '50. Now I thought I was good enough to go to spring training with (the Cardinals) but the Cardinals didn't want to see me. They had five good left-handed pitchers (Harry "The Cat" Brecheen, Max Lanier, Howie Pollet, Al Brazle, and Ken Johnson.)" [7]

In Columbus Haddix got the nickname "Kitten." General manager George Sisler, Jr. called him "a second Brecheen," adding, "Won't that be something when he joins the Cards and teams up with Brecheen to pitch a doubleheader? 'The Cat and the Kitten.'" [8]

As Haddix matured he had grown a little and was generously listed at 5-feet-9. In 1948 at Columbus he had 11 wins and a .337 batting average. For a second straight year he was an all-star. Cardinals catcher Joe Garagiola said, "I don't know how far Haddix is away from the majors, but I do know he will be there one of these days." [9]

The 1949 season was more of the same. Haddix won 13 games for the Red Birds and was again selected an all-star. In 1950 he had 18 wins and another all-star selection, as he added a change-up to his repertoire of pitches, which included a fastball and slider. On August 16 for Columbus he retired 28 Milwaukee Brewers batters in a row during an 11-inning game. Retiring more than 27 Milwaukee batters in a row in an extra-inning game might come up again in his future. [10]

On September 9 the playoff-bound Red Birds had Harvey Haddix Day. It was also announced that his contract had been sold to the Cardinals. But a trip to St. Louis would have to wait as he was drafted into the Army and sent to Fort Dix, New Jersey. He got leave to travel to Baltimore to pitch for Columbus in a Junior World Series game. The Orioles were not accommodating, taking the game 8-1.

Haddix served as a Fort Dix athletic director in 1951 and 1952, and managed and pitched for the camp baseball team. In 1952 he led the team to the state semipro championship. In August, his Army service complete, he joined the Cardinals and made his major-league debut on the 20th in St Louis against the Boston Braves, winning a complete-game five-hitter, 9-2. He finished the season with three complete games, a 2-2 record and a 2.79 ERA. He singled in his first big-league at-bat.

To make up for lost time, Haddix headed to winter ball in San Juan, Puerto Rico. He threw shutouts his first two starts and when the Cardinals shut him down December, he was 6-2. He was so popular that the team threw a banquet in his honor.

Haddix entered spring training in 1953 as the Cardinals' top prospect, coming to camp in great shape and having a great spring. He even won a box of cigars for winning three pitcher's batting awards: collecting the most hits, scoring the most runs, and stealing the most bases.

Haddix opened his rookie season in the starting rotation and shut out the Chicago Cubs on a four-hitter in the Cardinals' home opener. By June 27 Haddix had won ten games and led the team with 79 strikeouts. He earned a spot on the National League All-Star team, but didn't pitch in the All-Star Game. Returning to action after the game, Haddix threw five straight complete games from July 19 through August 6. The August 6 game was a two-hitter against the Phillies, both Phillies hits coming in the ninth inning. Richie Ashburn, who got the first hit, created controversy by trying to bunt his way on. Haddix's only comment was, "He was only trying to win, that's all."[11] Haddix finished with 20 wins, 19 complete games, six shutouts (leading the league), and a 3.06 ERA, while batting .289. He was second to the Dodgers' Jim Gilliam for Rookie of the Year. Gilliam said he was surprised to have won.[12]

Cardinals manager Eddie Stanky was happy with his southpaw. "What can I say about the guy? He can run, hit, and field better than most pitchers. … What more can you expect?"[13] Haddix won three new suits from Stanky, who had challenged his pitchers to pitch complete games with no walks.

Haddix again ranked among the elite National League pitchers in 1954. Again selected a National League All-Star, he had to be replaced on the team due after being struck below the right kneecap by a line drive off the bat of someone who would play a significant role in his future, Milwaukee first baseman Joe Adcock. Haddix said the injury bothered him the rest of his life and affected his pitching. "I was never the same after that," said Haddix. "I didn't have the same spring off the mound."[14]

Haddix had won 12 games at the time of the injury. He won only six games the rest of the season but ended on a high note, pitching nine shutout innings against Milwaukee in a no-decision and winning his 18th on September 19 with one inning of relief.

In February Haddix said his injury had healed and was giving him no trouble during the hunting season, but added, "After the leg was hurt I couldn't run well and my conditioning suffered. A pitcher is still only as strong as his legs."[15] And Haddix and the Cardinals got off to rocky starts.

The team began 9-12 start in a rainy spring. Haddix and Brooks Lawrence made 15 appearances as starters or relievers in the first 21, games winning only two. Haddix's ERA was 5.91.

The Cardinals' slow start got manager Stanky fired and replaced by Harry Walker. Haddix's record stood at 2-8, so he spent hours throwing pitches against the outfield wall trying to harness his curveball. Giants coach Frank Shellenback gave him a tip about gripping his curveball. This, plus the fact that he learned he was tipping his pitches helped him turn around his season to some extent.

Despite his poor record (6-9 and a 5.43 ERA), Haddix was selected to the National League All-Star team and for the first time pitched in the game. It would be his sixth and final time as an All-Star. He ended a disappointing season with a 12-16 record and a 4.46 ERA, still good enough for new general manager Frank Lane to call him a Cards untouchable. He would also enter the 1956 season with his new wife, Marcia Williamson. After a honeymoon and a winter of hunting at his South Vienna farm, he entered 1956 spring training ready to go. But on May 11 the "untouchable" was traded to the Philadelphia Phillies with pitchers Stu Miller and Ben Flowers for pitchers Herm Wehmeier and Murry Dickson.

"I didn't want to go to the Phillies," Haddix said in 1989. "But good things come out of bad things. I had a house free of rent there, and with the money I saved the two years in Philadelphia, I bought my first farm."[16]

After pitching coach Whit Wyatt noticed some mechanical flaws in his motion, he regained his form. He had a 12-8 record, and could have been 16-4 if the Phillies bullpen had not blown four leads. Phils manager Mayo Smith listed the acquisition of Haddix as the year's most pleasant surprise.[17]

Haddix was inconsistent in 1957. At times he was the staff ace, but later he was sent to the bullpen. In July he pitched an 11-inning shutout against the Cubs, but in his next game he was knocked out by the Braves in the third inning. He ended the season with a 10-13 record and a 4.06 ERA, and he suffered with a stiff arm for the first time in his career. In the offseason the Phillies, needing hitting, traded Haddix to Cincinnati for slugger Wally Post. "I figured at the end of last season that I would be traded," Haddix said. "I thought I would go to one of any four clubs, but going to the Reds is the best that could have happened....The Reds have always been my team, even when I was a kid."[18]

For Haddix, 1958 was another season with flashes of greatness and mediocrity. He went to a no-windup delivery to try to stop the recurring problem of tipping his pitches. "I cut down the windup so I could hide the ball from the third base coach," he said.[19] For the season he was 8-7 with a 3.52 ERA and gave up 191 hits in 184 innings, including 28 home runs. On the brighter side, he received his first Gold Glove Award. Then in January he was traded with catcher Smokey Burgess and third baseman Don Hoak to the Pirates for Frank Thomas, Whammy Douglas, Jim Pendleton, and Johnny Powers.

The Pirates were poised to contend. Haddix got off to a hard-luck, start, with poor run support. On May 26 his record was 4-2 with a 2.67 ERA. On that day he was scheduled to pitch against the Milwaukee Braves in Milwaukee. He had the flu, spent most of the chilly, windy, and rainy day in bed and if he hadn't been pitching would not have gone to the ballpark.

In their pregame meeting to go over hitters Don Hoak said, "Harve, if you pitch the way you say you will, you'll have a no-hitter."[20] Matched against the Braves Lew Burdette, he did just that. After 12 innings he hadn't allowed a baserunner. But the run support, lacking all spring, was still lacking this night, and going into the bottom of the 13th inning, the game was still scoreless. The end came quickly for Harvey. In that fateful inning, the Braves' leadoff hitter, Felix Mantilla, reached on a wild throw by Hoak. Eddie Mathews bunted Mantilla to second and Henry Aaron was given an intentional walk, bringing Joe Adcock to the plate, the same Adcock who had smashed a line drive off Haddix's knee in 1954. On a one-ball, no-strike pitch, Adcock hit Haddix's 115th pitch of the night into the right-center-field bleachers. On a base-running blunder, Adcock was called out and credited with a double when Aaron left the basepath and was passed. The final score was 1-0.

Haddix was amazed to find out he had broken the record for consecutive perfect innings to start a game. "Who, me? All I know is we lost. What is so historic about that?"[21] He turned down an opportunity to appear on the televi-

sion shows *To Tell the Truth* and *The Ed Sullivan Show* feeling it more important to stay with the team. But accolades came from all over the country. National League President Warren Giles presented him with an inscribed silver tea service with 13 cups. Few days would pass the rest of his life when Haddix wasn't asked about the game.

Meanwhile, as the season wore on, Haddix's pitching faltered. He continued to receive little run support and ended the season 12-12 but with a 3.13 ERA. For the second consecutive year, he was recognized for his fielding with the Gold Glove Award. "Haddix really never pitched a bad game for us all year," said manager Danny Murtaugh. "I figured on him for 12 victories but he was consistently good. We just didn't score many runs for him." [22]

The 1960 season began with high expectations for the Pirates, especially if the talented outfielder Roberto Clemente could stay in the lineup. The Pirates were a tight-knit cast of characters. After every win Roy Face would strum his guitar while Fred Green, Bill Mazeroski, Bill Virdon, Jim Umbricht, Gino Cimoli, and Haddix harmonized. To a man, they would all say it was the best group of players they ever played with. Vern Law said, "Harve was a fun guy—well liked by everyone." [23]

The only question on Haddix's performance was a lack of stamina. His answer: "I've been a seven-inning pitcher at times because I'm a little man and have to work harder out there than some other fellows. I can't afford to coast."[24] Haddix made 28 starts but had only four complete games and finished with an 11-10 record and a 3.97 ERA. Supplemented by midseason acquisition Vinegar Bend Mizell, the Pirates clinched the pennant on September 25.

Going into the World Series against the Yankees, New York first baseman Dale Long, a former Pirate, asked about the Pirates' pitchers: "The one Pittsburgh pitcher who would be likely to make trouble for our team is left-hander Harvey Haddix."[25] Haddix made Long sound like a prophet. He started and won Game Five, pitching into the seventh inning giving up two runs as the Pirates won, 5-2. The victory gave the Pirates a 3-2 lead in the Series. The Yankees won Game Six, and for the seventh game Haddix found himself in the bullpen. In the top of the ninth, with the Pirates leading 9-7, Haddix relieved Bob Friend after the first two Yankees batters got hits. "That was the only time in my life I was really nervous," Haddix said. "The hair stood up on the back of my neck." [26]

Roger Maris was the first batter he faced. "Maris is in there squeezing the sawdust out of the bat and he can't wait to get to me," Haddix recalled. "They were so anxious to hit. I'm talking to myself: 'This is something you have waited for your whole life and now you are going to blow it because of nerves.'" [27]

Haddix got Maris to pop out to the catcher. Then Mickey Mantle singled in a run, and his savvy baserunning on a grounder by Yogi Berra allowed the tying run to score. Haddix retired the side, and when Bill Mazeroski homered in the ninth, Haddix got the victory. He called it his career highlight. Offseason highlights included an $8,400 World Series check and birth of his second child.

The Pirates were favored to win again in 1961, and though Haddix won 10 games and a third Gold Glove, some wondered whether the 34-year-old, nine-year veteran was on the downside of his career. Haddix's innings pitched had dropped to 172 1/3 in 1960 and 156 in '61. The team fell to sixth place, a disappointing four games under .500. In September Haddix was moved to the bullpen as manager Murtaugh wanted to see how he reacted to late-inning relief. He was paired with Roy Face to finish games. "I don't find it so bad," he said after the season. "I think I can do the job if that is what they want of me." [28]

In 1962 the plan was for Haddix to stay in the bullpen but an injury to Vern Law changed the plan and Haddix started 20 times in 29 appearances totaling 141 innings, winning nine games and losing six. Although the Pirates won 93 games (in the National League's first 162-game season), they finished in fourth place, behind the Giants, Dodgers, and Reds. Haddix's mother, Nellie, died on June 22. Whether coincidence or not, he struggled for the remainder of the season, which he attributed to losing control of his curveball.

In 1963, the 37-year-old Haddix was the oldest player on the team, and was in the bullpen full time, except for one start. In August teammate Vern Law retired and it appeared the Pirates were preparing to jettison other veterans as they started to rebuild. Haddix pitched 70 innings and ended with three wins, one save, and a 3.34 ERA. The Pirates finished eighth. His relief stint on

September 21 turned out to be his last game with the Pirates. On December 14 he was traded conditionally to the Baltimore Orioles for minor-league shortstop Dick Yencha and cash. Although he would always consider himself a Pirate ("A part of me belongs in Pittsburgh"[29]), he said, "It's all right. Wherever there is money I'll go, although this will be my first appearance in the American League." [30]

Haddix's fastball was back in spring training. The Orioles plan was for him to be the left-handed complement to Dick Hall in the bullpen. His career was rejuvenated. For the third-place Orioles in 1964 he pitched 89 2/3 innings, all in relief, and had five wins, ten saves, and a 2.31 ERA. He was the runner-up for the Gold Glove Award. (Haddix's offseason highlights included shooting a 900-pound buffalo owned by a neighbor when it ran wild and attacked their cows.)

After such a strong comeback, few might have imagined that 1965 would be Haddix's last as a pitcher and would end with a trade to the team that had broken his heart six years earlier. Haddix hurt his arm in spring training. "It never got well," he said. "Sometimes it was the shoulder, sometimes the elbow hurt. I didn't pitch much but I used it all the time, hoping work would help, but it didn't." [31]

On August 30, Haddix was sold to the Milwaukee Braves, who were fighting for the pennant. Out of sheer honesty, he refused to report and retired instead. "I'd have finished the season if I could have, but there wasn't much sense in changing when I knew I couldn't help a new club the way my arm was feeling," he said at the time. "I wouldn't mind trying again next spring. Or I'd love to catch on with a team looking for a pitching coach."[32] His last big-league appearance was on August 28, 1965.

In November Haddix hired on as the pitching coach of the Vancouver Mounties, the Oakland Athletics' Triple-A team. But on December 29 he resigned and signed as pitching coach of the New York Mets. He would be the first big-league pitching coach for Tug McGraw, Nolan Ryan, Tom Seaver, and Jerry Koosman. In 2009 Ryan said, "Harvey could not have been, from my perspective, more of the right person at the right time for me."[33]

After two ninth-place (out of ten) finishes, Mets manager Wes Westrum was fired near the end of the 1967 season and new manager Gil Hodges replaced the entire coaching staff. Haddix went back to the Pirates' organization in 1968 and coached the Columbus Jets and the Gulf Coast League Pirates. In 1969, he became the Cincinnati Reds' pitching coach. When Reds manager Dave Bristol was fired at the end of the season, it meant back to the minors with Pittsburgh for Haddix. The Boston Red Sox hired him as pitching coach in 1971, but at season's end his wife, Marcia, persuaded him to retire. But when Frank Robinson asked Haddix to join him for his historic managerial tenure in Cleveland, Haddix unretired. From 1975 to 1978, he was the Indians' pitching coach. In 1979 Haddix joined Chuck Tanner and his beloved "Family"—the Pirates—for the next six seasons, getting his second World Series ring in 1979.

A heavy chain-smoker, who described cigarettes as his best friend, Haddix developed emphysema. This hastened the end of his baseball career and eventually his life. Even though his 1984 Pirates pitchers led the league in ERA, he was fired because thrifty general manager Syd Thrift wanted coaches who could also throw batting practice. Haddix no longer was able. His health continued to deteriorate but he never stopped smoking. He died on January 8, 1994, in Springfield, Ohio. "I loved cigarettes, but they finally got to me," he said a year or so before his death.[34]

In 1999 fans voted Harvey Haddix the left-handed pitcher on the Pirates' All-Century Team to celebrate a career that consisted of much more than the 115 pitches thrown on a rainy night in Milwaukee.

Sources

Book:

Jim O'Brien, *Maz and the '60 Bucs* (Pittsburgh: James P. O'Brien Publishing Co., 1993).

Newspapers or Magazines:

Dayton (Ohio) *Daily News*, September 9, 1965

Springfield (Ohio) *Daily News*, 1947-1979.

Springfield (Ohio) *Sun*, 1947-1979.

The Sporting News, 1947-1994.

Urbana (Ohio) *Daily Citizen*. May 27, 1992.

Online Sources

DVD, *Wright State University Major League Baseball Panel Discussion, April 17, 1989*, produced by Professor Allen Hye, 2009 (Cited as WSU Panel Discussion).

www.baseball-reference.com.

Letters:

Letter from Nolan Ryan to Springfield/Clark County Baseball Hall of Fame. May 4, 2009.

Letter from Vern and VaNita Law to Springfield/Clark County Baseball Hall of Fame. January 8, 2009.

Other:

Several discussions between the author and Harvey Haddix on numerous occasions in various settings. These were undocumented as both were acquaintances from the same community.

Notes

1 WSU Panel Discussion.

2 WSU Panel Discussion.

3 WSU Panel Discussion.

4 WSU Panel Discussion.

5 WSU Panel Discussion.

6 WSU Panel Discussion.

7 WSU Panel Discussion.

8 *The Sporting News*, July 21, 1948, 11

9 *The Sporting News*, September 8, 1948, 21

10 *The Sporting News*, August 30, 1950, 22

11 *The Sporting News*, August 18, 1953, 7

12 *The Sporting News*, January 6, 1954, 8

13 *The Sporting News*, September 9, 1953, 12

14 Jim O'Brien, *Maz and the '60 Bucs*, 465

15 *The Sporting News*, February 16, 1955, 19

16 WSU Panel Discussion

17 *The Sporting News*, September 19, 1956

18 *Springfield Daily News,* December 7, 1957, 2

19 *The Sporting News*, June 4 , 1958, 4

20 WSU Panel Discussion

21 O'Brien. *Maz and the '60 Bucs*, 463

22 *The Sporting News*, November 11, 1959, 16

23 Vance Law letter

24 *The Sporting News*, August 31, 1960, 18

25 *The Sporting News*, September 28, 1960, 10

26 Quoted in O'Brien, *Maz and the '60 Bucs*, 462

27 Ibid.

28 *The Sporting News,* January 10, 1962, 23

29 O'Brien, *Maz and the '60 Bucs*, 468

30 *The Sporting News*, December 15, 1963, 15

31 *Dayton Daily News*, September 9, 1965, 22

32 Ibid.

33 Nolan Ryan letter

34 O'Brien. *Maz and the '60 Bucs*, 458

Don Hoak

By Jack V. Morris

To his contemporaries, he was a hard-nosed player, a throwback to earlier days, when players like Ty Cobb played the game as if their lives depended on it. Opponents labeled him "hard-headed" and "red-nosed." Latinos had their own title for him: El Divino Loco or the Divine Madman. But it was Pittsburgh Pirates broadcaster Bob Prince who coined the nickname for Don Hoak that stuck, "Tiger," because of his ferociousness on the field. Tiger often played the game as if he had a chip on his shoulder. One writer went as far to say that he was "cruel and vulgar and aflame with hate."[1]

On the other hand, by many accounts, Hoak was the exact opposite off the field: mannerly and charming. The hometown fans loved him because he was so friendly; the press loved him because he was so quotable.

Don Hoak, a 6-foot-1, 170-pound right-hander, played 11 seasons in the majors. He was the starting third baseman in two World Series' seventh games, and was on the winning side both times. He was named to the National League All-Star team in one season, 1957, and finished second to teammate Dick Groat, for National League MVP in 1960. He set a record for one-game futility that still stands today, and single-handedly caused a midseason rule change. Toward the end of his life he was a minor celebrity and was mentioned in newspaper entertainment pages as frequently as the sports pages.

Donald Albert Hoak was born on February 5, 1928, in tiny Roulette Township, Pennsylvania, population 1,000, about 170 miles northeast of Pittsburgh, near the Pennsylvania-New York state line. He was the second of three children born to Andy and Orissa (Leitch) Hoak. Andy Hoak was a laborer for a road-construction company when Don was born, and later worked for the North Penn Gas Company.

Hoak preferred not to talk much about his childhood. In 1961, he said, "There's no point in discussing (my childhood). It would just hurt a lot of people." What is known is that he attended Roulette High School, where he played football and baseball, and played the trumpet in the band.[2]

While still in high school, Hoak enlisted in the US Navy during World War II, on February 27, 1945, in the waning days of World War II, 22 days after turning 17. On February 21, 1946, while Don was stationed at Pensacola, Florida, a tractor his father was attempting to drive onto a truck tipped over, killing him and leaving Don's mother a widow at home with his 3-year-old brother, Denny. Less than six months later, Don was discharged from the Navy.[3]

It has been written about Hoak that he served in the Marines during World War II, that he went to bat against Fidel Castro when he played in Cuba, and that he was a professional prizefighter, but none of these things have been corroborated. Perhaps Hoak was not above promoting a good story. Subsequent research has debunked the Fidel Castro story. This author has not been able to verify the Marine or professional boxing claims.[4]

During Hoak's military service, he realized that he was a good baseball player. After his discharge he sought out Spencer Harris, the business manager of the nearby Olean (New York) Oilers of the Pennsylvania-Ontario-New York League. According to Hoak, the New York Yankees were interested in signing him, but after finding out that the

Oilers trained in Pensacola in the spring, he set out to talk to Harris.[5]

Since the Oilers were a Class D Brooklyn Dodgers affiliate, Hoak signed with the Dodgers. Instead of Pensacola, he was sent to a minor-league camp in High Point, North Carolina, at his own expense. The Dodgers liked what they saw and sent him to play for the Valdosta Dodgers of the Class D Georgia-Florida League for the 1947 season. It was the lowest rung of baseball but it was a start.[6]

Hoak had a very good season with Valdosta, playing third base and batting .295. In 134 games he scored 71 runs and had 68 RBIs. He struck out 100 times but also managed 87 walks. The next season the Dodgers jumped him two classifications to the Nashua Dodgers of the Class B New England League.

Hoak moved up the Dodgers ladder for the next few years, one rung at a time. After hitting .283 for Nashua, he hit only .231 the following year for the Greenville Spinners of the Class A South Atlantic League. Still, he was promoted to the Fort Worth Cats of the Double-A Texas League.

He had gained a reputation not only as a tough, hustling ballplayer but as a smooth fielder and a fleet runner. The combination of guts, grace, and speed stayed with him throughout his career even when his hitting sometimes did not.

In Fort Worth Hoak found his hitting stroke, batting .280 while playing third base. On August 14, 1950, he wed his hometown girlfriend, Phyllis Warner, in an unusual ceremony at home plate that received national attention. Four teammates and their brides were wed by four ministers of different faiths at the same time before 9,800 fans at Fort Worth's LaGrave Field.[7]

Hoak went back to high school and earned his diploma. In 1951 the Dodgers invited him to their major-league spring-training camp in Vero Beach, Florida. Hoak was now the property of the Montreal Royals, one of their two Triple-A teams.[8] He made the Royals out of spring training and in his first game homered against the International League Baltimore Orioles. The next day, after his second game, he was sent to St. Paul because the Royals had signed someone else to play third base. Hoak responded by tearing up the American Association that

first month, batting over .400.[9] He cooled down, to finish with a .257 average. The Dodgers were still happy with his progress. Their farm director, Fresco Thompson, was said to "rave about him."[10]

Hoak found himself in a tough spot, though, playing for an organization that was deep in talent at all levels, especially at the major-league level. To make matters worse, the Dodgers had Billy Cox, considered by many to be the finest-fielding third baseman in all of baseball.

In 1952 Hoak batted .293 and led the International League in triples (15) to help the Royals win the regular-season crown. He finished second in the International League Rookie of the Year voting, and was named to *Look Magazine's* All-International League team.[11]

Hoak signed a $1,300-a-month contract with Cienfuegos of the Cuban Winter League to play there. But the Dodgers purchased Hoak's contract from the Royals, and offered $6,500 for him not to play in Cuba. They wanted him to be fresh in 1953 spring training to battle for the starting third-base job. The Associated Press's Joe Reichler speculated that the "glowing reports on Don Hoak, a kid third baseman brought up from Montreal for next season, make Cox dispensable."[12]

Dodgers manager Chuck Dressen had four players vying for the third-base position when spring training opened, but Cox emerged victorious and Hoak was sent back to the Montreal for the second year and his third straight season in Triple-A.[13]

Back in Montreal, Hoak was hampered with a thumb injury and had an offyear. The Royals didn't win the regular-season pennant but won the postseason playoff, which put them into the Little World Series against the Kansas City Blues. The Royals beat the Blues four games to one. Hoak batted .263 in the Series and connected for three doubles.[14]

After the 1953 season Hoak played in the Cuban Winter League for Cienfuegos and had a very good season.[15] He was determined not to be sent down again in 1954, and he made it known that if the Dodgers didn't have plans for him on their major-league roster, he wanted to be traded. He battled Cox again for the third-base job and it appeared at first, that the results would be the same.[16]

However, one component was different. The Brooklyn Dodgers had a new manager, Walt Alston, Hoak's former manager in Montreal and an unabashed Hoak fan. Alston liked the way he "got the job done." To Alston, Hoak was "a fine team player with plenty of determination."[17]

Hoak made the Opening Day roster as Cox's backup.[18] He played in 88 games that season, starting at third base more often than Cox, who was injured that summer. Hoak's first major-league hit came on April 25, 1954, when he doubled and scored against the Pittsburgh Pirates' Paul LaPalme in a 4-2 win. He hit his first home run May 27 against the Philadelphia Phillies' Curt Simmons in an 11-5 loss. He recorded his first grand slam on August 8 when he took the Cincinnati Redlegs' Frank Smith deep in a 13-run eighth inning of a 20-4 blowout.

In 1955 Hoak's competition wasn't Cox, who had been traded to the Baltimore Orioles, but Jackie Robinson, who was moved to third base after dividing his time between third base and left field in 1954. Again the Dodgers were filled with talented players and looking for places to play them.

Hoak had become a father for the first time in February to daughter Kimberly. Alston gave Hoak every chance to win the starting job in spring training, which frustrated Robinson. "I'm fit and should be playing—and Alston knows it," Robinson told the press. Eventually, Robinson won the starting job. Hoak, however, was the first player off the bench.[19]

While he got into six more games than in 1954, his production numbers fell. He didn't start a game at third base until July 2, when Robinson hurt his knee. In all, he appeared in 94 games and batted .240. [20]

The Dodgers, however, had a storied season, winning the National League pennant and facing the Yankees for the fifth time in nine seasons. Alston chose to start Robinson over Hoak for his experience and power-hitting ability. Hoak came into Game One as a pinch-runner and to Game Two as a pinch-hitter. (He walked.) In Game Seven Hoak started in place of Robinson, who had a sore Achilles tendon. He acquitted himself well by going 1-for-3 with a walk, and handled two chances cleanly in the field.[21]

The Dodgers won Game Seven, 2-0, to win their only world championship in Brooklyn. Readers of newspapers the next day saw Hoak pictured prominently in the iconic photo jubilantly running in to join an embracing Johnny Podres and Roy Campanella.

That winter Hoak played for Escogido of the Dominican Winter League. Before he left, he told his hometown newspaper, "I hope I'm still (with the Dodgers) but you never know in this business."[22]

Unbeknownst to most, Hoak had irritated Alston by demanding to be traded if he didn't play in the World Series. In December Hoak was traded with outfielder Walt Moryn and pitcher Russ Meyer to the Chicago Cubs for power-hitting third baseman Randy Jackson, and minor-league pitcher Don Elston.[23]

It came as a shock to Hoak but later in his career he considered it one of his luckiest breaks, saying, "(It was) the best thing that ever happened to me. I didn't have a chance in Brooklyn." He felt that he was destined for the minor leagues in 1956 if he stayed in the organization.[24]

Hoak was handed the starting job in Chicago but instead of thriving, he performed poorly. He tried to be a power hitter and starting swinging for the fences. He struggled to hit over .200. Perhaps the lowest point came on May 2, when he set a National League record and tied a major-league record by striking out six times in a 17-inning game against the New York Giants.

As the season closed, Hoak had started 108 games, batting .215 with 51 runs scored and 37 RBIs. He finished last in the major leagues in batting average for players who qualified for the batting title—hardly the breakout season he and the Cubs had hoped for.[25]

Shortly after Hoak finished up barnstorming with Frank "Spec" Shea's baseball tour through New York and New England, he was traded again. This time, he was a throw-in in a trade between the Cubs and the Cincinnati Redlegs. Hoak, pitcher Warren Hacker, and outfielder Pete Whisenant were sent to the Reds for third baseman Ray Jablonski and pitcher Elmer Singleton. Hacker and Jablonski were the main parts of the trade. *The Sporting News* said the Redlegs "did not obtain any outstanding players" in the trade.[26]

After the trade was announced, Hoak called Reds general manager Gabe Paul and told him he wasn't reporting unless he was on the major-league roster. Paul promised Hoak that he would be given every chance to win the third-base job.[27]

Two events during the offseason likely turned Hoak's career around. The first was surgery for a deviated septum that had caused him violent headaches that deprived him of sleep.[28] The second was a change in his batting stance ordered by Birdie Tebbetts, his manager, who told him to stop trying to hit home runs on every pitch. "He changed my whole way of thinking," said Hoak.[29] Previously, Hoak had crouched low at the plate causing *New York Daily News* sportswriter Dick Young to write, "He looked like the Holland Tunnel with a bat in its hands."[30]

Hoak easily won the starting third-base job by hitting .416 in spring training.[31] On April 21, playing against Milwaukee, Hoak was on second base with a runner on first base and one out in the first inning. Wally Post hit a chopper toward Braves shortstop Johnny Logan. Hoak, running toward third, grabbed the ball as it hopped along, then flipped it to Logan, effectively preventing a sure double play. Five days later, a new rule was enacted making both the player hit by the batted ball and the batter out if the runner purposely let himself be hit by the ball.[32]

Hoak continued his torrid hitting through the early 1957 season. On May 8 he was hitting .415 with 21 RBIs. He also was becoming widely popular because of his success at bat and his fiery demeanor on the field. On June 30 he was commissioned as a Kentucky Colonel by Kentucky Governor A.B. "Happy" Chandler, the former commissioner of baseball, and given the key to the city of Lexington, where he planned to reside during the offseason. By the middle of July Hoak was "unquestionably the best third baseman in the majors."[33]

While Hoak had a reputation as a hothead, and was involved in numerous dust-ups, he got into only a few actual fistfights on the field. One occurred on July 11, 1957, against the Dodgers' Charley Neal. Both teams were in a pennant race and tensions were high. In the seventh inning there was a fracas between Redlegs pitcher Raul Sanchez and the Dodgers' Junior Gilliam over an inside pitch. Then the Dodgers' Charlie Neal got involved and landed a punch that decked Hoak. When Hoak recov-

ered, he was livid and had to be restrained from going after Neal in the Dodgers' dugout as the players went back to their benches.[34]

After the game, Hoak did not cool down. He threatened Neal, and when National League President Warren Giles heard the remarks, after fining the four players $100 each, he issued a stern warning to Hoak about retaliation. Hoak later said, "Charlie is all right. I'd just as soon forget the whole thing." [35]

Within a year, stories began appearing in the press that Hoak had boxed professionally before his baseball career. It may have been Hoak's way of backing players off him. In fact, players around the league were aware that Hoak was not really a fighter.[36]

The Neal fight was but a blip in what was Hoak's best season to date. He was voted onto the National League All-Star Team along with six of his Reds teammates due to ballot stuffing encouraged by the Cincinnati newspapers. Commissioner Ford Frick removed Gus Bell and Wally Post and replaced them with Willie Mays and Hank Aaron in the starting lineup. However he allowed Hoak to be the starting third baseman. It was his only All-Star Game appearance.

Hoak finished the 1957 season batting .293 with 78 runs scored and led the National League with 39 doubles. His 89 RBIs and 19 home runs set Redlegs records for third basemen and were career highs. He was voted the Redlegs' MVP by the Cincinnati Baseball Writers Association and finished second to the Giants' Hank Sauer in the voting for the NL Comeback Player of the Year. *The Sporting News* said the trade that brought Hoak to Cincinnati was "one of the finest ever made" in Reds' history.[37]

While 1957 was a coming-out party for Hoak, 1958 was a step backward. Plagued by injuries most of the year, he saw action in only 114 games, batting .261. A rib injury ended his season in mid-September.[38]

In November Hoak's wife, Phyllis, gave birth to a son, Donald Jeffrey, in Coudersport, Pennsylvania, and the couple started building a house in Don's old hometown of Roulette, Pennsylvania, that they moved into in 1959.[39]

By early December, there were rumors that Hoak was to be traded. The Redlegs needed a right-handed power hitter and Pirates' third baseman Frank Thomas fit the bill. On January 30, 1959, Hoak was traded to Pittsburgh with catcher Smokey Burgess and pitcher Harvey Haddix for Thomas, outfielder John Powers, outfielder Jim Pendleton, and pitcher Whammy Douglas. Twenty-four years later, Paul called call it the worst trade he ever made.[40]

Hoak responded with a great season at bat for the Pirates. Playing in all 155 games for the Pirates, he hit .294 with 60 runs scored and 65 RBIs, and led the league's third basemen in putouts, assists, and total chances. He even garnered some votes for Most Valuable Player. It was during this season that Pirates broadcaster Bob Prince coined Hoak's nickname of "Tiger."[41]

It wouldn't be a typical Hoak season without the Tiger being in the middle of something strange. On May 26, 1959, Pirates pitcher Harvey Haddix had a perfect game going through 12 innings in Milwaukee against the Braves in what would be remembered as one of the greatest pitching performances in major-league history. But in the bottom of the 13th, Hoak committed a throwing error on a Felix Mantilla grounder that ended the perfect game. Three batters later, Joe Adcock registered the first Braves hit of the game, a double, which drove home Mantilla with the winning run. (Adcock actually hit the ball out of the park, but was ruled out for passing Hank Aaron on the basepaths and his "homer" was reduced to a double.)

The Pirates were injury-riddled that year and limped home to a fourth-place finish. But in 1960 it was a different story. Pittsburgh, led by Dick Groat (who was voted the league's Most Valuable Player) and Hoak, and with fine pitching from Vernon Law and Elroy Face, won the pennant and the World Series. Hoak had another fine year, again playing every game for the Pirates. He batted .282 with 97 runs scored and 79 RBIs. Beyond his bat, his leadership seemed to propel the Pirates to their first World Series championship since 1925.

"I'd say Don Hoak was the difference," said Law. "He was the backbone. He had the fighting spirit that rubbed off on everyone. He just wouldn't let us lose."[42]

Hoak played much of the season in pain. On August 13 he cut his foot severely at a pool party. He had his foot stitched up by a doctor whom he had sworn to secrecy, and played a doubleheader the next day. The injury both-

ered him for much of the season but wasn't revealed until midway through the World Series, when Hoak had a painful groin injury as well. If that wasn't bad enough, he had a temperature of 103 degrees during Game One. All the injuries prompted broadcaster Joe Garagiola to quip during the Series, "He's the first ballplayer in World Series history to be sponsored by Blue Cross."[43]

Hoak's Series wasn't sensational; he batted just .217 and drove in three runs, but the Pirates still were able to beat the Yankees in seven games propelled by Bill Mazeroski's dramatic Game Seven walk-off home run. After the season, Hoak finished second in the MVP voting to teammate Dick Groat.[44]

With the team's first World Series championship in 35 years, Pittsburgh was crazy for its Pirates. The Pirates were "feted endlessly" throughout the offseason. While Hoak made his share of banquet appearances, he didn't become complacent. He went to Puerto Rico as an instructor in a series of clinics for youths of the island. Then when February rolled around, he was the first everyday player in camp.[45]

While many of his teammates had subpar seasons in 1961, Hoak responded with career highs in batting average (.298) and on-base percentage (.388). The team didn't fare as well, finishing a disappointing sixth.

Hoak found himself in the news after the 1961 season as much as during the season. In a whirlwind few months, Hoak divorced and remarried. At the same time, he managed a team in the Dominican Winter League.

In 1960 he had separated from his wife and become smitten with singer and actress Jill Corey, who was introduced to him at Forbes Field during a pregame publicity appearance. Corey, born Norma Jean Speranzo, also hailed from a small town in Pennsylvania.[46]

Though Hoak was smitten from the outset, Corey rebuffed his advances because she was dating a Brazilian diplomat. Eventually she agreed to a date, and by late October 1960 the two became a regular item in the entertainment gossip columns.[47]

He filed for divorce in September 1961, then left for the Dominican Republic to manage Santiago in the Winter League there. The season ended abruptly, however, when the country devolved to chaos months after the nation's dictator, Rafael Trujillo, was assassinated.[48] When he came home he was a single man, and a few months later married Corey in Pittsburgh.[49]

Hoak came roaring out of the box to start the 1962 season. Typically, he began a season hitting well early and then limped home by the end of the season. He played hard during the season, and wore himself down. So this spring training, he told reporters that he was not going to hustle to conserve energy for the end of the season. It didn't work.[50] Hoak played in only 121 games, his lowest total since his injury-plagued year of 1958. Nagging injuries sidelined him for more than 30 games. His batting average dropped to .241, his lowest since 1956. However, he did get his 1,000th hit, off the Cubs' Dick Ellsworth on June 14.

The Pirates finished fourth, though only eight games back of pennant-winning San Francisco Giants, and rumors soon started that Hoak would be traded. The Pirates had decided to rebuild, and on November 28 he was sent to the Philadelphia Phillies for first baseman Pancho Herrera and outfielder Ted Savage.

The Phillies moved one of their best players, Don Demeter, from third base back to the outfield to accommodate Hoak. But Hoak fizzled. By late May, hitting only .197, he was benched. Age and injuries had taken a toll. Allen Lewis, a Phillies beat reporter, wrote in *The Sporting News*, "It has become evident that he had slowed down noticeably in running speed."[51]

Hoak also encountered a problem he never had before: The Philadelphia press came down on him hard. He was back into the lineup in July and was the starting third baseman for the rest of the year, but batted only .231, fueling rumors that after the season the Phillies would make him available in the expansion draft for the New York Mets and Houston Colt .45s.[52]

Hoak considered retirement but when 1964 spring training rolled around, he was still part of the Phillies. Instead of being handed the job however, he would have to beat out a much-heralded rookie by the name of Dick Allen.[53]

Allen tore up spring training pitching while Hoak brooded. Hoak took to standing behind Allen during infield practice with his arms crossed and staring at Allen's

back. Allen, when asked about their relationship late in spring training, simply said, "We haven't spoken to one another."[54]

Hoak made the Phillies' Opening Day roster but didn't last long. He pinch-hit in six games, went 0-for-4 with 2 sacrifices, and was released on May 18. The Phillies kept him on the payroll as a special-assignment scout. Toward the end of the season, when it looked as if the Phillies might make the World Series, he scouted their possible American League opponents.[55]

After the season Hoak was rumored to be in line to manage the Pirates after Danny Murtaugh's departure. But in December it was announced that he would replace Claude Haring as the Pirates' color commentator, working with Bob Prince.[56]

For two seasons Hoak was in the Pirates broadcast booth. During the first year, his wife gave birth to a daughter, Clare Michelle.

It was long rumored that Hoak was vying for a managerial or coaching position, and in December 1966 he accepted the third-base coaching job for the Phillies. However, Hoak lasted only one season with the Phils. He was arrested during the season when he knocked down a security guard in a Cincinnati hotel bar. The charges were later dropped when both attorneys claimed it was a misunderstanding. But Hoak was fired by the Phillies in October. The Phillies claimed they were going with only three coaches rather than the traditional four coaches on the bench. Whatever the reason, Hoak was out of a job.[57]

The Pirates quickly hired Hoak to guide their Class A team in the Carolina League, the Salem Rebels. Hoak won the Carolina League's West Division with that club and was promoted in 1969 to the Pirates Triple-A team, the Columbus Jets.

After the 1969 season the Pirates fired manager Larry Shepard. Hoak was one of the three candidates mentioned for the job, along with Alex Grammas and Bill Virdon. On October 8, in typical Hoak fashion, he announced on television that "I'm the man for the job."[58]

But unbeknownst to anyone, Pirates general manager Joe L. Brown had a fourth candidate—one who was eminently qualified: Danny Murtaugh. Murtaugh's suspect health had forced him to quit the Bucs years before. Once Murtaugh decided that he was healthy enough to manage once again, Brown hired him on the spot.[59]

After being told he wasn't the next Pirates manager, Hoak was downtrodden. He was planning to resign from the Pirates and possibly take a job with Gene Mauch in the Montreal Expos organization.[60]

On October 9, the day that Murtaugh was announced as the Pirates new manager for 1970, Hoak and Jill were sitting in an apartment when Hoak noticed that his brother-in-law's car was being stolen. He ran down to his car and pursued the thief. He never caught him and was soon found slumped over the wheel of his car and was pronounced dead upon arrival at Pittsburgh's Shadyside Hospital.[61]

The cause of death was officially "acute coronary occlusion" with "strong clinical evidence" of prior heart problems. Two hours after Murtaugh was announced as Pirates manager, Hoak was dead.[62]

In addition to his wife, Jill, and ex-wife, Phyllis, he was survived by three children, Kimberly, Donald, and Clare. Clare became a model, and an actress like her mother, Jill.

More than 600 people paid their respects the night before Hoak's funeral. He was laid to rest in his old hometown of Roulette at Fishing Creek Cemetery. He was only 41 years old.[63]

Sources

Donn Clendenon, *Miracle in New York. The Story of the 1969 New York Mets Through the Eyes of Donn Clendenon* (Sioux Falls, South Dakota: Pine Hill Press, 1999).

Rick Cushing, *1960 Pittsburgh Pirates: Day by Day: A Special Season, An Extraordinary World Series* (Pittsburgh: Dorrance Publishing, 2010).

Robert Gordon, *Legends of the Philadelphia Phillies* (Champaign, Illinois: Sports Publishing, 2005).

Jeff Guinn, *When Panthers Roared: Fort Wayne Cats and Minor League Baseball* (Fort Worth, Texas: TCU Press, 1999).

Colleen Hronich, *The Whistling Irishman: Danny Murtagh Remembered* (Philadelphia: Sports Challenge Network, 2010).

Robert R. Lyman, *History Of Roulet, Pa. and the Life of Burrel Lyman (The Founder)* Coudersport, Pennsylvania: Potter County Historical Society, 1967).

Jim Reisler, *The Best Game Ever* (New York: Carroll & Graf Publishers, 2007).

Jim Brosnan, "Two Inside Slants on the Big Series: A Pitcher-Author Writes his 'Book' On Pirate Lineup," *Life*, October 10, 1960.

Everardo J. Santamarina, "The Hoak Hoax," *The National Pastime* (Cleveland: Society for American Baseball Research, 1994).

Baseball Digest.

Sports Illustrated.

The Sporting News.

Baseball-reference.com

jillcorey.net/DonHoakPage.html.

Retrosheet-org.

Notes

1 Walter Bingham, "A Gung Ho Marine At The Hot Corner" *Sports Illustrated*, July 3, 1961, 40.

2 Walter Bingham, "A Gung Ho Marine."

3 *McKean County* (Pennsylvania) *Democrat*, February 28, 1946; Pennsylvania Veterans Burial Cards, 1777-1999 database (Ancestry.com).

4 Everardo J. Santamarina, "The Hoak Hoax," *The National Pastime*, 1994, 29-30.

5 Robert R. Lyman, *History of Roulet, Pa., and the Life of Burrel Lyman (The Founder)*, 198; *Syracuse Herald-American*, April 26, 1953.

6 Robert R. Lyman, *History of Roulet, Pa.*

7 *Chester* (Pennsylvania) *Times*, August 22, 1950; *Bradford* (Pennsylvania) *Era*, August 19, 1950; *The Sporting News*, August 30, 1950.

8 Robert R. Lyman, *History of Roulet, Pa.; McKean County* (Pennsylvania) *Democrat*, November 11, 1954; *New York Times*, March 1, 1951.

9 *Syracuse Herald-Journal*, April 17, 1951; *Portland* (Maine) *Telegram*, May 6, 1951.

10 *Kingsport* (Tennesse) *News*, June 9, 1951.

11 *Hagerstown* (Maryland) *Daily Mail*, October 11, 1952; *San Mateo* (California) *Times*, September 15, 1952; *Syracuse Herald-American*, April 26, 1953.

12 *The Sporting News*, October 15, 1952; *Idaho Falls* (Idaho) *Post-Register*, December 2, 1952.

13 *The Sporting News*, February 25, 1953; *Williamsport* (Pennsylvania) *Gazette & Bulletin*, March 26, 1953.

14 *Nashua* (New Hampshire) *Telegraph*, January 14, 1954

15 *Charleston* (West Virginia) *Daily Mail*, January 12, 1954; Everardo Santamarina, , "The Hoak Hoax."

16 *The Sporting News*, February 24 and March 21, 1954.

17 *Racine* (Wisconsin) *Journal-Times*, November 25, 1953; *Nashua* (New Hampshire) *Telegraph*, January 14, 1954.

18 *Springfield* (Massachusetts) *Union*, March 12, 1954; *Trenton* (New Jersey) *Times*, April 11, 1954.

19 *Bradford* (Pennsylvania) *Era*, February 14, 1955; *The Sporting News*, March 7, 1955; *Springfield* (Massachusetts) *Union*, April 6, 1955.

20 *The Sporting News*, July 20, 1955.

21 *Burlington* (Iowa) *Hawk-Eye Gazette*, November 21, 1955.

22 Robert Boyle, "The Latins Storm Las Grandes Ligas" *Sports Illustrated*, August 9, 1965, 24-28; *Bradford* (Pennsylvania) *Era*, November 26, 1955.

23 *Dallas Morning News*, December 7, 1955; *New York Times*, December 8, 1955.

24 *Cumberland* (Maryland) *Evening Times*, June 24, 1961; *Pacific Stars and Stripes*, March 14, 1956.

25 Roy Terrell, "Don Hoak—Then and Now," *Sports Illustrated*, May 27, 1957, 41-44.

26 *Berkshire Eagle*, Northampton, Massachusetts, October 6, 1956; *Springfield* (Massachusetts) *Union*, November 17, 1956; *The Sporting News*, November 21, 1956.

27 *The Sporting News*, May 15, 1957; *Springfield* (Massachusetts) *Union*, November 17, 1956.

28 *Cleveland Plain Dealer*, March 8, 1958.

29 *The Sporting News*, March 20, 1957; *High Point* (North Carolina) *Enterprise*, March 22, 1961.

30 Roy Terrell, "Don Hoak—Then and Now."

31 *Delta Democrat-Times*, Greenville, Mississippi, March 8, 1957; *The Sporting News*, April 3, 1957; Ray Robinson, ed. *Baseball Stars of 1958*. (New York: Pyramid Books, 1958), 141.

32 *Cleveland Plain Dealer*, April 22, 1957; *Dallas Morning News*, April 26, 1957.

33 *The Sporting News*, May 15 and July 10, 1957; *New York Times*, April 3, 1958.

34 *New York Times*, July 13, 1957; *Binghamton* (New York) *Press*, July 12, 1957; Carl Erskine, *Carl Erskine's Tales From the Dodgers Dugout: Extra Innings* (Champaign, Illinois: Sports Publishing, 2004), 139.

35 *Binghamton* (New York) *Press*, July 12, 1957; *The Sporting News*, July 24, 1957.

36 Richie Ashburn, "The Day Seminick Wiped Out the Giants Infield," *Baseball Digest*, August 1974, 76-78.; Jeff Guinn, *When Panthers Roared: Fort Wayne Cats and Minor League Baseball* (Fort Worth, Texas: TCU Press, 1999), 68; Jocko Conlon, Jocko, *Jocko* (Lincoln, Nebraska: University of Nebraska Press),122.

37 *Mansfield* (Ohio) *News-Journal*, January 8, 1958; *The Sporting News*, July 10 and September 25, 1957.

38 *The Sporting News*, January 28, 1959; *Uniontown* (Pennsylvania) *Evening Standard*, August 11, 1958.

39 *Lock Haven* (Pennsylvania) *Express*, December 1, 1958; *McKean County* (Pennsylvania) *Democrat*, December 4, 1958.

40 *Uniontown* (Pennsylvania) *Evening Standard*, December 3, 1958; *New York Times*, April 2, 1982.

41 *Uniontown* (Pennsylvania) *Evening Standard*, March 1, 1960.

42 Rick Cushing, *1960 Pittsburgh Pirates: Day by Day: A Special Season, An Extraordinary World Series* (Pittsburgh: Dorrance Publishing, 2010), 351.

43 Reisler, Jim, *The Best Game Ever* (New York: Carroll & Graf Publishers, 2007), 102; *Cleveland Plain Dealer*, October 6, 1960; *Springfield* (Massachusetts) *Union*, October 8, 1960; *Kingston* (New York) *Daily Freeman*, October 14, 1960.

44 *Binghamton* (New York) *Press*, November 17, 1960.

45 *New York Times*, March 19, 1961; *Titusville* (Pennsylvania) *Herald*, February 6, 1961; *Augusta* (Georgia) *Chronicle*, February 26, 1961.

46 *Uniontown* (Pennsylvania) *Morning Herald*, November 21, 1961.

47 *Doylestown* (Pennsylvania) *Daily Intelligencer*, August 7, 1961.

48 Donn Clendenon, *Miracle in New York* (Sioux Falls, South Dakota: Pine Hill Press, 1999), 74-75.

49 *Titusville* (Pennsylvania) *Herald*, December 22, 1961; *Valley Independent*, December 28, 1961.

50 *Aberdeen* (South Dakota) *American-News*, April 14, 1962.

51 *Oakland Tribune*, May 21, 1963; *The Sporting News*, June 1, 1963.

52 *The Sporting News*, July 20, 1963; *Ogden* (Utah) *Standard-Examiner*, October 10, 1963.

53 *Kingston* (New York) *Daily Freeman*, March 19, 1964.

54 Robert Gordon, *Legends of the Philadelphia Phillies* (Champaign, Illinois: Sports Publishing, 2005), 12; *Titusville* (Pennsylvania) *Herald*, April 9, 1964.

55 *Hope* (Arkansas) *Star*, May 14, 1964; *Salisbury* (Maryland) *Times*, August 31, 1964.

56 *Augusta* (Georgia) *Chronicle*, October 17, 1964; *Springfield* (Massachusetts) *Union*, December 9, 1964; *The Sporting News*, December 26, 1964.

57 *The Oregonian*, Portland, Oregon, July 18, 1967, August 30, 1967; *Dallas Morning News*, October 19, 1967.

58 *Cleveland Plain Dealer*, September 27, 1969; *Chillicothe* (Ohio) *Constitution-Tribune*, October 10, 1969.

59 Colleen Hronich, *The Whistling Irishman: Danny Murtaugh Remembere.* (Philadelphia: Sports Challenge Network, 2010) 166-67.

60 *Altoona* (Pennsylvania) *Mirror*, October 10, 1969.

61 *Lowell* (Massachusetts) *Sun*, December 19, 1972; *Altoona* (Pennsylvania) *Mirror*, October 10, 1969; *Dominion News*, Morgantown, West Virginia, October 10, 1969.

62 *Altoona* (Pennsylvania) *Mirror*, October 10, 1969

63 Miss Jill Corey: Husband Don Hoak, www.jillcorey.net/DonHoakPage.html.

Danny Kravitz

By James Forr

OF THE TENS of thousands of people who took in the thrilling 1960 World Series at Forbes Field, Danny Kravitz might have been the only one who wasn't completely happy to be there.

His gut was a cauldron of clashing emotions—excitement, pride, envy, resentment. He had been up and down a lot of roads with those men in black and gold—with Bob Skinner in Waco, with Roy Face in New Orleans, with Bill Mazeroski in Hollywood. Not to mention five seasons playing alongside all of them in Pittsburgh. Now there they were, soaking up the spotlight while he sat and watched from afar, just another anonymous fan. They were his friends and he was happy for them, but it hurt.

Taking the long view, though, even without a World Series ring, Kravitz was living the American Dream. He had traveled a long way from meager beginnings. His parents, John Kravitz and Eva Hubiak, each immigrated to the United States from Europe and met in the bustling little town of Lopez, Pennsylvania, one of the many small industrial communities that dot the state's heavily wooded, sparsely populated northern tier. John, a native of Russia, was a strong-backed, hard-drinking coal miner who spent three decades underground, where the toxic air clotted his lungs and turned him into an old man at a young age. His wife, an Austrian of Russian descent, was dignified and traditional, with waistlength hair wrapped into a bun and covered with a babushka. Russian was the lingua franca in their home. The smattering of English they knew they picked up from their kids, who brought it home from school.

Daniel, born December 21, 1930, was the baby of the family. Each night he and his eight siblings—all boys except for one—wedged themselves

into three upstairs bedrooms, the boys two to a bed, while their parents slept downstairs in the living room. There was poor, and then there were the Kravitzes. John brought in the money; Eva stretched it to its limits and beyond. "We lived the old-fashioned way," Danny remembered. "We used to eat dried apples; that was our candy. We raised our own vegetables, potatoes, cabbage, everything."[1] Meat came courtesy of the pigs and chickens they kept out back, while an old heifer supplied Eva with milk for homemade butter and cheese.

The kids were expected to do their share, too. They labored under a grinding regimen of chores, work, and school, which left Danny little time for baseball. But he followed the sport closely and grew especially fond of young Stan Musial, who, as it happened, was another Pennsylvania kid with Slavic roots. Years later he enjoyed greeting Musial from behind the plate in Polish. *"Jak sie masz?"* he would ask. ("How are you?"), to which Musial would turn and nod, *"Dobre."* ("Good.")

Kravitz participated more actively in sports as a teenager and became a standout high-school basketball player. "I was a rough guy," he chortled mischievously. "I weighed 195 pounds and was just 6 feet but I was pretty mean on that floor." He took up baseball at 16, pitched for his high-school team, and played all over the field on an adult team sponsored by the Weldon Pajama Factory. Even against much older players he excelled. More than once he sent a long drive splashing down into the creek that ran beyond the outfield fence.

Then after graduation, out of nowhere, the Pittsburgh Pirates called. Kravitz claimed to have no idea how the Bucs heard about him, but the next spring, in 1949, he was aboard a bus headed to a tryout camp in Greenville, Alabama, where they pinned a number to his back and put him through his paces alongside hundreds of other prospects. At first the Pirates tried Kravitz on the mound but, as he tells it, he was so nervous he could hardly throw a strike. Still, his raw talent was plain to see. "I could throw a ball through a wall, that's how hard I could throw. And I always hit good." The Pirates signed him for $175 a month and assigned him to their Class D affiliate in Greenville (where his teammates included a smallish, light-hitting catcher named Jack McKeon).

To John Kravitz, the whole thing made no sense at all. "Play ball?" he said to his son skeptically. "You've got to work!"

His son just shrugged. "They call that work, too, you know."

Kravitz played the outfield during his first three minor-league seasons and seized the attention of the Pirate brass by hitting for both average and power, including 17 home runs and 102 RBIs in just 112 games at Class D Mayfield in 1950. But then Uncle Sam put things on hold as Kravitz spent the 1952 and '53 seasons as a lifeguard in the Marines.

Then while on leave in 1952, he married 18-year-old Mary Jane Cole, his sweetheart from back home. When she died, they were just nine days short of their 51st wedding anniversary. Over the years she and their three children moved more than 30 times as they followed the meandering path of Danny's itinerant career. "I took her all over the country, Puerto Rico, the Dominican. She knew baseball better than me," he joked.

He and Jane made a fun couple in the same way that the Kramdens or the Flintstones made fun couples. Danny was genuinely good-hearted, but in private he often turned impatient and blustery, with a thundering voice that could set the walls trembling. Jane had a little more finesse, but she refused to sit quietly for his nonsense. As a result, they were always bickering about one little thing or another. It wasn't that they were particularly angry most of the time; it's just how they communicated. If they weren't picking at each other, that's when you knew something was really wrong.

After being mustered out of the service, the young husband returned to Pirate camp in the spring of 1954, whereupon Pirates general manager Branch Rickey summoned him into his office.

"Son," Rickey bellowed. "How would you like to become a catcher?"

Kravitz knew the right answer. "I'll play anywhere, any position. Just let me play."

The organization was thin on left-handed-hitting catchers—or, for that matter, catchers who could hit at all. Kravitz filled that void, and with the position switch found himself with a clear path to the major leagues. A defensive wizard he was not, but he got the job done. He was adequate at throwing out baserunners and matured into a competent game-caller. He had just one peculiar flaw—according to play-by-play summaries he committed at least ten errors on dropped pop flies in just 171 major-league games behind the plate. A fan observed a tad ungraciously, "Danny Kravitz … couldn't catch a foul popup behind home plate without a catcher's mitt glued to the top of his head."[2]

At any rate, the Pirates probably never expected a Gold Glove out of Kravitz. They just wanted him to hit, and in the minors he did plenty of that, earning a place on the Southern Association All-Star team after a stellar 1955 season in which he batted .298 with 19 home runs. Then he kept it up in camp the following spring. "I hit everything they threw at me," he crowed. "I made those pitchers look silly." On April 17, 1956, Kravitz started behind the plate in the Polo Grounds as the Pirates opened the season against the New York Giants. (It was a nightmare debut, though. His two errors led to two unearned runs and handed the Giants a 4-3 win.)

Kravitz popped in and out of the lineup during the first 2½ months of the 1956 season, showing only occasional glimpses of his offensive prowess. On May 11 he blasted his first major-league home run, an upper-deck grand slam in the bottom of the ninth to beat Jack Meyer and the Phillies. As of 2012, he was one just 27 players in major-league history to record a walk-off grand slam. Kravitz's teammates mobbed him at home plate, while an apoplectic Meyer stormed back to the Philadelphia dugout, snatched a bat out of the rack, and pounded a porcelain drinking fountain into shards.

The grand slam aside, Kravitz was scuffling. It seemed as though his fortunes had turned in late June, when he started three straight games, went 5-for-8 with a home run, and hiked his average from .220 to .269, but all that got him was a trip back to the minor leagues, where he remained the rest of that year and most of the 1957 season.

Things like that just seemed to happen to Kravitz. "He wasn't the luckiest ballplayer in the world," offered long-time teammate Bob Skinner. "He was a dangerous hitter but he never really got a chance to play every day for a period of time where he could really show his stuff."[3] Kravitz found it hard to figure. Catcher had been a revolving door for the Pirates for ten years; he was the only viable long-term solution at hand. Publicly, anyway, the Pirates brass insisted they were counting on him. Manager Bobby Bragan went so far as compare him to a young Yogi Berra, and predicted in December 1956, "If Kravitz comes through as expected and we land an additional power hitter, we'll be a much-improved outfit next year."[4]

Nonetheless, over the next few seasons Kravitz appeared only sporadically, and always on a short leash. A teammate, quoted anonymously, told the *Pittsburgh Press*, "He [has] a tendency to be all tightened up instead of relaxed but that's easy to understand. You can't expect a man to come off the bench as a sub and not be afraid that one mistake could run him back to the bench for a long spell. He's so eager to make good he fights himself."[5] On June 21, 1959, Kravitz rapped out five hits in a game, boosting his average to .356. Five hits surely were enough to earn another start, he assumed. The following day he bounded into the clubhouse eager for a look at the lineup card—only to learn that he was back on the bench. He glowered in the dugout all afternoon, doing a slow, bitter burn. "We lost that game. Not that I was wishing we lost but it kind of tickled me to see it happen." In July he started 12 games in a row due to an injury to starter Smoky Burgess. He batted .311 over that stretch, but inevitably returned to his backup role when Burgess got healthy again.

Kravitz was an enormously confident, fiercely proud man who took the lack of playing time almost as a personal insult. He had never really known failure on the baseball field, and in his mind he wasn't failing in Pittsburgh either, he just wasn't being allowed to succeed. In some ways his grievances sound like sour grapes; on the other hand, it is difficult not to empathize. All of us have walked in those shoes at one time or another, feeling we are doing everything that is asked, everything that is demanded, but there we remain, trapped in the cage. "I did the best I could [but] what they were doing to me, gee! Smoky Burgess came over. He was a good hitter but he couldn't throw. He couldn't run. They'd work me against the hard throwers because Smoky couldn't hit the good fastball. Hank Foiles couldn't hit me, but he was a good receiver." Kravitz waited and waited but new faces kept appearing and it was always someone else's turn.

He also longed for financial security. Toiling as a young backup catcher was not a lucrative business. "I try to save a few dollars each year on my salary but it isn't much," he told a reporter in 1960. "I haven't even been able to buy my own home and I live in a small town of only 700 people."[6] In the winters he resorted to fur trapping, which proved a surprisingly profitable avocation. A mink or beaver pelt got him $25.

Socially and economically, Kravitz wasn't far removed from the average Pirates fan. He was busting his hump to make ends meet the way many of them were. He grew up in a large, working-class, immigrant family as many of them did. So people identified with him and embraced him as almost a minor folk hero. A big, affable bear of a guy in public, completely without pretense, Kravitz moved easily among fans and genuinely enjoyed their attention. He wore his Russian Orthodox heritage proudly and became a frequent guest of the city's many ethnic organizations. "The people liked me [in Pittsburgh]," he declared. "They were all Polish, Russian, Italians, and I fit right in with them."

But by 1960 Kravitz clearly did not fit in with the Pirates' plans. Recently acquired veterans Burgess and Hal Smith split all the work, reducing Kravitz to a seldom-used pinch-hitter. The inevitable came on May 31, when the Pirates traded him to the Kansas City Athletics. General manager Joe L. Brown talked as if he were doing Kravitz a favor, sending him to the American League rather than back to the minors. "Danny is a nice kid. I wanted to make sure of placing him with another major league club."[7]

Kravitz saw it much differently. He was devastated, and still sounded crestfallen more than a half-century later. "I got a little shafted there," he lamented. The deal probably shouldn't have surprised him, but it did. "I never thought I'd be traded out of Pittsburgh. I never did. The fans hated to see me leave, but that's baseball, I guess."

The other thing about the trade to Kansas City—it was Kansas City. "It was just a lousy club. They were in last place all the time. It wasn't easy for me to go over there because I was used to playing on a winner." The Athletics finally gave him a chance to play regularly, but he didn't make much of the opportunity, batting just .234 in 59 games. And while his new team was pushing 100 losses, Pittsburgh was winning the World Series. "It really shook me up. I was so close to getting one of those nice rings, but I got nothing." His buddies on the Pirates did award him $250 out of their Series winnings, but that did little to salve the wound. "I was happy they won, but it sure shocked me what [management] did to me."

Over the next three years Kravitz bounced from organization to organization but never made it back to the big leagues. He retired after the 1963 season and returned to Dushore, Pennsylvania, just a few miles down the road from his hometown. As time went on, Jane, at least, began to feel cramped and wondered whether they had made the right decision. "There was some talk that he shouldn't have come back home, that he should have stayed in Pittsburgh. He could have gotten a job with the organization," according to Kravitz's daughter, Pam. "I think they got so tired of moving that home was a welcome sight, but then that got old, too. I think she regretted that they came back to that little mining community."[8]

But theirs was a good life in many ways. Danny and Jane purchased ten acres and built a lovely house with an outsized pond in the back yard, which their friend Joan Skinner thought was as peaceful as a place could be. "My favorite thing was to sit on the dock and listen to the bull-frogs," she said wistfully.[9] He spent 23 years as an inspector for the electronics firm Sylvania while Jane operated a hair salon out of their basement. Together, they usually scraped together enough money for an annual vacation to the Jersey Shore. Danny drove to Pittsburgh for reunions of the 1960 Pirates team and got together often with former teammates Bob Skinner and Bill Mazeroski.

In the early 2000s Kravitz endured a crushing series of personal tragedies. In a nine-month span he lost two brothers, his 42-year-old son Danny, who collapsed and died of a heart attack right in front of his dad, and then his beloved Jane, who seemed to lose her will to live after her son's death. And then the years finally began to catch up to him as he entered his 80s. His legs and hands gave him trouble and his heart became an ongoing concern. But as of 2012 he still managed to keep pace with his teenage grandsons, cheering (sometimes a little too loudly) at their baseball games and taking them into the woods to hunt and fish. He was the kind of grandfather the typical teenage boy would love—a colorful, charmingly gruff old goat with a fondness for sports and guns. In return, his grandkids helped keep him young. "They come here and ride my four-wheeler to hell and back. We have a lot of fun together."

Even though Kravitz is merely a footnote in Pirates history, he remained prominent in Sullivan County, Pennsylvania. A half-century after he walked away from baseball, people still asked him to speak at banquets and sign autographs. "Everybody likes me around here. They know me when they see me and they respect me." To people in town, Danny Kravitz was not the poor guy who got robbed of a World Series ring or the frustrated slugger who never got a real shot. Instead, he was someone to look up to, someone who made it.

Sources

Richard Peterson, *The Pirates Reader* (Pittsburgh: University of Pittsburgh Press), 2003.

Baseball Digest, October 1978.

Pittsburgh Post-Gazette and Sun-Telegraph; June 3, 1960.

Pittsburgh Press, April 4, 1956; March 10, 1960.

The Sporting News, May 2, 1956; December 19, 1956; November 2, 1960.

Sullivan (Pennsylvania) *Review;* July 27, 2006; November 10, 2010.

Retrosheet.org.

National Baseball Hall of Fame player file, undated articles.

1920 United States Census.

Danny Kravitz, telephone interview with author, October 4, 2011.

Pamela Kravitz-Arthur, telephone interview with author, October 9, 2011.

Bob Skinner, telephone interview with author, October 17, 2011.

Joan Skinner, telephone interview with author, October 17, 2011.

Lenny Yochim, telephone interview with author, October 11, 2011.

Notes

1   All quotations are from an October 4, 2011, interview with Danny Kravitz, except as noted.

2   Richard Peterson, *The Pirates Reader* (Pittsburgh: University of Pittsburgh Press, 2003), 6.

3   Bob Skinner, telephone interview with author, October 17, 2011.

4   *The Sporting News*, December 19, 1956.

5   *Pittsburgh Press*, March 10, 1960.

6   Ibid.

7   *Pittsburgh Post-Gazette and Sun-Telegraph*, June 3, 1960.

8   Pamela Kravitz-Arthur, telephone interview with author, October 9, 2011.

9   Joan Skinner, telephone interview with author, October 17, 2011.

Clem Labine

By Alfonso L. Tusa C.

ONE OF THE most important games hurled by Clement Walter Labine took place at Ebbets Field in Brooklyn on October 9, 1956. The day before, Don Larsen had pitched a perfect game for the New York Yankees to beat the Brooklyn Dodgers, 2-0, in the fifth game of the World Series.

Dodgers manager Walter Alston gave the ball to the right-handed Labine, who was usually a reliever, because he knew about Clem's courageous and smart demeanor once he got on the mound. With the Yankees up three games to two, manager Casey Stengel sent starter Bob Turley to try to win the Series. Labine and Turley battled in a scoreless game until the bottom of the tenth, when Jackie Robinson's single drove in Jim Gilliam to tie the Series at three games apiece and break a streak of 18 scoreless innings for the Dodgers.

Labine played in five World Series—four with the Dodgers (1953, 1955, 1956, 1959) and one with the Pirates (1960). Three of his teams were winners: the 1955 Brooklyn Dodgers, the 1959 Los Angeles Dodgers, and the 1960 Pittsburgh Pirates.

Clement Walter Labine was born on August 6, 1926, in Lincoln, Rhode Island, and grew up in nearby Woonsocket, where he played football, hockey, and baseball. His parents were French-Canadian. The father was a weaver and the mother was in charge of the family.

At Woonsocket High School right-hander Labine was said to have had a curve like a left-hander. That was his pitch. As a youngster he had broken his right index finger. He thought his baseball dreams as a player were over, but his coach told him that some things that appear to be disasters turn

out to be blessings in disguise. That became the greatest advice Labine got, because it shaped his attitude to the game and life. Clem met the most important person in his life; he met the power inside of him that would destine him for greatness.

In 1944, after high school, Labine was signed by Branch Rickey and Chuck Dressen of the Dodgers. Labine had a tryout scheduled with the Boston Braves, but it fell through, and he was still available when Rickey and Dressen met him. Still only 17 years old, he was assigned to the Newport News Dodgers of the Piedmont League (Class B) and appeared in 12 games (2-4, in 56 innings of work with a 4.18 earned-run average). World War II was on and soon after Labine turned 18 in August, he volunteered for the paratroopers. He was out of baseball all of 1945 and, after his discharge from the Army, returned to Newport News late in the 1946 season. His only decision was a win, and he allowed four earned runs in 14 innings for a 2.57 ERA in his brief time with the team.

In 1947 Labine, now 20 years old, pitched for three teams, Newport News, the Asheville Tourists (Class B Tri-State League), and the Greenville Spinners, of the Class A South Atlantic League. He pitched exceptionally well for Asheville (6-0, 2.07 ERA), but poorly for the other two teams (one victory, four defeats). He spent the following year, 1948, entirely in Class A, playing in Colorado for the Western League's Pueblo Dodgers (13-10, 4.32 ERA).

Labine's last full year in the minors was 1949 with the Triple-A St. Paul Saints. He was 12-6 with a 3.50 ERA, and he made the Brooklyn Dodgers out of spring training in 1950, debuting on April 18 and pitching the final two innings of a 9-1 loss to the

Philadelphia Phillies allowing one run. That was his first, albeit brief, taste of the majors. He was then sent back to St. Paul, where he won 11 and lost 7, with a less successful 4.99 ERA.

After the 1950 season Labine went to play winter ball in the Venezuelan League, for the Magallanes Navigators. In 24 games he was 13-4 with 93 strikeouts and an ERA of 1.95, beating rival Cerveceria Caracas eight times. Caracas fans called him "La Vaina," a derogatory term (which means he was considered annoying, like Bugs Bunny) that sounded like Labine, because of how difficult it was for their team to defeat him. Labine was a key player for that championship Magallanes team.

Labine tried hurling spitters in Caracas once. Someone explained to him how to throw the spitball, which was illegal in Venezuelan baseball, and which pitchers threw at risk of being fined or suspended if they were caught. But the first time he threw it he hit the catcher in the throat and he stopped using the pitch because he couldn't control it. Labine also developed a sinkerball and threw an unorthodox curveball, called a "cunny thumb" curve. It's thrown by holding the thumb parallel to the index and middle fingers, as opposed to the common method of placing the thumb on the opposite side of the ball. To remind himself to turn his non-pitching hand over his pitching hand to better hide the ball from the batter, Labine printed the letters "T-U-R-N" on the four fingers of his glove.

In 1951, after going 9-6 for the Saints, with a 2.62 ERA, Labine was called up to Brooklyn and racked up five wins against just one loss, with two shutouts (the only regular-season shutouts of his major-league career). He then found himself thrust into the middle of the best-of-three National League pennant playoff between the Dodgers and the New York Giants. After the Giants won the opener, Brooklyn had no regular starter available for Game Two. Labine got the assignment by default and threw a six-hit shutout to keep the Dodgers alive in the series. The Dodgers won 10-0. In the third inning, when it was a 2-0 game, the Giants' Bobby Thomson came to bat with the bases loaded. Thomson had doubled in his previous at-bat. With a 3-and-2 count, Labine threw his curve. It broke a foot wide of the strike zone, but Thomson swung and Labine got a strikeout. The next day Thomson's ninth-inning home run won the pennant for

the Giants. Labine was in the bullpen with Carl Erskine and Ralph Branca. When the ball went out of the park, Labine and Erskine both bit the wooden bench where they sat. Labine later said: "I broke down a little, but I learned a lot about losing."

The 1952 season was up and down for Labine. He was briefly with St. Paul (0-1). With the Dodgers he was 8-4 with an earned-run average of 5.14. As a reliever he was 6-1, with a 3.54 ERA. He gave up 47 walks in 77 innings. In 1953 he turned it around and he became the Dodgers' bullpen ace thanks to the mastery of the sinkerball he had developed in Venezuela.

Labine's sinker forced batters to pound the ball into the ground. "They go to swing at it, and it drops on you, and you get the top of the ball," he told Peter Golenbock in *Bums*, an oral history of the Brooklyn Dodgers. "So you're not gonna hit a lot of line drives off of me, just a lot of groundballs. And don't forget who we had scooping them up: Gilly (Gil Hodges), (Jackie) Robinson, (Pee Wee) Reese, and (Billy) Cox." [1]

In 1953 Labine pitched in 37 games, with 11 wins and six losses, a 2.77 ERA, and seven saves in 110 $\frac{1}{3}$ innings of work. In the World Series, against the Yankees, he lost two games in relief and saved one. Labine lost the first game, 9-5, giving up a tiebreaking home run to first baseman Joe Collins. He saved the fourth game for Billy Loes, coming in with the bases loaded and nobody out in the ninth inning. He got two quick outs, then gave up a hit to Mickey Mantle, allowing Gene Woodling to score. But Billy Martin was out trying to score behind Woodling with the Yankees still down by four, and the game was over. Labine lost the deciding Game Six in relief. He entered the game in the seventh inning with the Dodgers down 3-1 and held the Yankees scoreless in the seventh and eighth. After his teammates tied the game with two runs in the top of the ninth, Labine walked Hank Bauer, then gave up a single to Mantle and a solid grounder up the middle by Billy Martin that won the Series for the Yankees. In three games and five innings of work, Labine was 0-2, with a 3.60 ERA but he had protected the only lead he was given.

In 1954 Labine was 7-6, 4.15 ERA and five saves. In 1955, as the Dodgers won the pennant and the World Series, he appeared in a league-leading 60 games, eight of them starts, and compiled a 13-5 record, with 11 saves, and a 3.24 ERA in 144 1/3 innings.

Clem was never much of a batter. In his 13 major-league seasons he had only 17 hits and a batting average of .075. In 1955 he had three hits and a .097 batting average. But all three hits were home runs—and they were the only three he ever hit in the major leagues. (He hit three in the minors.)

Labine appeared in four games in the 1955 World Series, winning one and saving one with 2.89 ERA. On back-to-back days, in Games Four and Five, he got a win and a save. In Game Four he pitched 4 1/3 innings, retiring 11 of the final 12 batters, and got the victory as the Dodgers came from behind to top the Yankees, 8-5, and tie the Series at two victories apiece. In Game Five Labine pitched three innings in relief of Roger Craig, allowing a homer by Yogi Berra but inducing two double plays to preserve the 4-3 Dodgers win. The Dodgers won the Series in Game Seven on Johnny Podres' shutout.

Although save totals were not kept in that era, retroactively Labine was credited with leading the National League with 19 saves in 1956 and 17 in 1957. He led the league in games finished (47) in 1956 and rolled up a 10-6 record. In 1957 he was 5-7. He also was fourth (1956) and third (1957) in games pitched.

"Clem Labine was one of the main reasons the Dodgers won it all in 1955," said Dodgers announcer Vin Scully. "He had the heart of a lion and the intelligence of a wily fox … and he was a nice guy, too."

In 1958 the Dodgers moved to Los Angeles. There Labine posted a 6-6 record with a 4.15 ERA and 14 saves in 104 innings. The next season, though he finished 5-10 with nine saves, he broke Brickyard Kennedy's franchise record of 382 games pitched from the turn of the century. That season the Dodgers reached the World Series after defeating the Milwaukee Braves in a postseason playoff. They defeated the Chicago White Sox in six games in the World Series, with Labine's only appearance a one-inning stint in one of the Dodgers' two defeats.

Over the years Labine started 38 games all but one for the Dodgers. Fellow Dodgers pitcher Carl Erskine said he thought the reliever "would have had a great career" as a starter. But Erskine said Labine told him, 'I didn't want

to start. I liked the pressure of coming into the game with everything on the line.'" [3]

In 1960, after he had pitched just 17 innings in the first two months of the season, probably because manager Walt Alston had lost confidence in him after two mediocre seasons, Labine was traded to the Detroit Tigers for right-handed pitcher Ray Semproch and cash. Labine later said he missed the camaraderie and friendship he had with his Dodgers teammates. For the first few weeks, he said, he felt like an orphan in a different country. Then the Tigers released him on August 15. The next day Labine signed with Pittsburgh, won three games, saved three, and went to the World Series with the Pirates. He pitched in three games in relief against the Yankees and was hit hard, giving up 13 hits and 11 runs (6 earned) in four innings. (That was the Series in which the Yankees outscored the Pirates 55 runs to 27, but lost the Series in Game Seven on Bill Mazeroski's walk-off home run.)

In the 1961 season Labine returned to the Pirates, pitched in 56 games, and went 4-1, with a 3.69 ERA, and eight saves. He was released by the Pirates after the season and caught on with the brand-new New York Mets. He pitched in only three games for the Mets (0-0, 11.25 ERA) and was released on May 1, after which he retired as a player.

Labine settled again in the Woonsocket area, where he became a designer of men's athletic wear, serving as general manager for the sporting goods division of the Jacob Finklestein's & Sons manufacturing company.

In 1966 Labine's Dodger career records of 425 games pitched and 83 saves were broken by Don Drysdale and Ron Perranoski respectively but he will remain holding the Brooklyn records.

Labine had some heartbreak off the mound. While interviewing him for his book *The Boys of Summer*, Roger Kahn noticed that Clem drank several martinis. "You heard about Jay?" Labine said. "Who's Jay?" "My son Clement Walter Labine Junior. He stepped on a mine in Vietnam and blew his leg off. The Marines sent a car to our house. Barbara was away. I was out playing golf. My brother-in-law saw this Marine car and went over and said, 'Is this about Jay, Clem Labine, Jr.?' The Marine officer was very polite. He asked who was he talking to and my brother-in-law said he was Jay's uncle and the Marine said that under the rules he couldn't say anything. Next of kin only. So when they came and got me off the golf course, the first thing they said was, 'Jay's been hurt, but he's alive'. He wrote me a letter from the hospital. It was so calm and matter-of-fact." Kahn wrote that this was the second time since the 1953 World Series that he had seen Labine's eyes full of tears. "If I hadn't been a ballplayer, I wouldn't have been away all the time. But the traveling cost me all of it, Jay growing up. If I hadn't been a ballplayer, I could have developed a real relationship with my son. The years, the headlines, the victories, they're not worth what they cost us. Jay's leg."

But on the field, Labine was a master. "If you had a lead, there was this thing where about the seventh or eighth inning, where he'd get up, sort of a ritual, and walk down to the bullpen," the former Dodgers pitcher Roger Craig told Bob Cairns in *Pen Men*, an oral history of relief pitching. "Clem was kind of a cocky, arrogant type, which was good. I liked it. He'd fold his glove up and put it in his pocket. I can see him now, strutting down to the bullpen and the fans cheering."

Labine had, in the words of his former Brooklyn Dodgers teammate Ralph Branca, "the right equipment to be a reliever." His sinker induced many a double play, and he possessed a sharp overhand curve that he could throw to righties and lefties. But that's not what made Labine one of the game's first great closers. "He also had courage," says Branca of Labine. "He really welcomed the challenge of being a reliever. He was a tough bird who loved to be in a crucial spot." [4]

Labine died on March 2, 2007, in Vero Beach, Florida, after suffering two strokes while hospitalized with pneumonia and subsequent brain surgery.

Sources

Bob Cairns. *Pen Men*. (New York: St. Martin's Press, 1993).

Peter Golenbock. *Bums: An Oral History of the Brooklyn Dodgers*. (New York: McGraw-Hill/Contemporary, 2000).

Daniel Gutierrez and Efraim Álvarez. *La Enciclopedia del Béisbol en Venezuela*. Tomo II. (Caracas: Fondo Editorial Cárdenas Lares, 1997).

Roger Kahn. *The Boys of Summer*. (New York: Harper & Row, 1971).

Robert Creamer. "They even sing songs in praise of the ruler of the Dodger bullpen." SportsIllustrated.CNN.com, Volume 6. Issue 22, June 3, 1957.

"Clem Labine, All-Star Reliever for Brooklyn Dodgers, Is Dead at 80," *New York Times*, March 2, 2007.

Ken Gurnick. "Dodgers pitcher Labine dies at 80. Righty was integral member of Brooklyn's first Series win" MLB.com, March 3, 2007.

"Dodgers' Labine dead at 80; relief pitcher loved pressure." Thefreelibrary.com

Notes

1   "Clem Labine, All-Star Reliever for Brooklyn Dodgers, Is Dead at 80.".*New York Times*, March 2, 2007.

2   MLB.com, accessed on March 21, 2008

3   MLB.com, op. cit.

4   *Sports Illustrated*, op.cit.

Vernon Law

By C. Paul Rogers III

THE 1960 PIRATES had their fair share of heroes and players who had career years, but when all is said and done, without Vernon Law they might well have been just another team that came close to glory. Heading into 1960, Law had just turned 30 and was an eight-year veteran of the Pirates, having missed two years of baseball because of military service. His major-league won-lost record heading into the season was an unremarkable 82-86, tempered by pitching for mediocre or worse Pirate teams. Before 1959, his career record was 64-77, but he had shown promise in 1959 of what was to come when he won 18 games while losing only 9 for the fourth-place Bucs. His 20 complete games were tied for second best in the league and his 2.98 earned-run average was fifth best.

Thus, Law's Cy Young year in 1960 did not exactly come out of nowhere. For the record, he won 20 games for the only time in his career, lost only 9, and with 18 complete games he tied Warren Spahn and Lew Burdette for the league lead. Although hampered by a sprained ankle, he won Games One and Four in the World Series and started the historic seventh game on three days' rest. Although the Yankees batted .338 for the Series and the Pirates' earned-run average was a collective 7.11, Law managed a credible 3.44 ERA against the Bronx Bombers in 18 ⅓ innings of work. The Pirates certainly would not have won that crazy, lopsided Series without him.

Vernon Law's path to World Series hero began in Meridian, Idaho, where he was born on March 12, 1930. His father, Jesse Law, was a mechanic who had seven children with his first wife, Audrey, who then died of consumption. Jesse then married Melva Christina Sanders and the two had three more children, of whom Vernon was the second.[1] He was raised in a strict Mormon household on

a farm outside Meridian. By the age of 12, Vernon was a deacon in the church and by 19 an elder. He attended a country school and, with his brother Evan, began playing hardball in the playground in the fifth grade.

During World War II Vernon's father moved to Mare Island, California, near Santa Rosa, to work at a submarine base. When school was out for the year, the rest of the family followed and Vernon and his brothers were able to play more baseball in California.[2] After the war the family returned to Meridian, where Law's father worked as an auto and truck repair mechanic.[3] By Vernon's freshman year in high school, he had reached his full 6-foot-3 height and weighed 175 pounds, so he was recruited to the football team. He quickly became a star, in part because he could run the 100-yard dash in close to 10 seconds and could throw and kick a football long distances.

Law excelled at basketball and baseball in high school as well, despite having to get up at 5 a.m. for part-time jobs that provided the family with much-needed income. During his third year of high school, Meridian won the state championship in football, allowing opponents only six points all season, and in baseball. Vernon was the star pitcher and brother Evan his catcher and the cleanup hitter.[4]

After his junior year, Vernon spent the summer in Boise playing American Legion baseball because Meridian did not have enough players to field a team. Behind Law, the team won their district, state, and regional Legion championships, advancing to the sectional tournament in Billings, Montana, as one of the top 12 Legion teams in the nation. There he met and obtained an autographed ball from Babe Ruth, who was the banquet speaker.[5] Meeting Ruth cemented Law's desire to make a career for himself in baseball.[6] He also began attracting professional scouts, spurred on by a 25-strike-out performance in a tournament game.

During his senior year, Law pitched a game against rival Payette that was 0-0 going into the ninth inning. Desperate to get someone on base, the Payette coach sent a 3½-foot-tall midget to bat as a pinch-hitter. With a number of scouts in the stands, Law struck him out on three pitches.[7]

One of the people in the stands that day was a Payette attorney named Herman Welker, who would later become a U.S. senator from Idaho. Welker had attended Gonzaga University with Bing Crosby, who had a minor ownership stake in the Pittsburgh Pirates, so Welker called Crosby to tell him about Law.[8] The Pirates quickly dispatched scout Babe Herman to check on young Vernon but found they had stiff competition.[9] Law had earned 12 letters in high school and had attracted scholarship offers from a number of colleges, as well as the attention of a number of major-league baseball teams.[10]

The Pirates offered a modest $2,000 bonus[11] but the deciding factor may have come when, during a visit from Herman, the Laws' phone rang. Vernon's mother answered it and found herself talking to none other than Bing Crosby himself. He promised that Vernon would receive the best treatment with the Pirates[12] and also promised an expense-paid trip to the World Series if Vernon and the Pirates ever made it that far. Thirteen years later, the Pirates made good on that promise.[13] It probably did not hurt that the Pirates also signed Vernon's brother Evan to a minor-league contract.

Three days after his high-school graduation in 1948, Vernon and Evan reported to the Santa Rosa Pirates in the Class D Far West League. The boys were back in the area where they had spent parts of two years growing up during World War II. Although Law was a work in progress, he showed promise, winning eight and losing five in 21 games. Although his earned-run average was 4.66, he struck out 126 batters in 110 innings, while walking 96. His club finished fourth in the eight-team league, but won the four-team playoffs, defeating the Klamath Falls Gems in seven games in the final.[14]

Law's performance with Santa Rosa earned him a promotion to the Davenport Pirates of the Class B Three-I League for 1949. There he won only five games against 11 defeats but posted an impressive 2.94 earned-run average and allowed only 112 hits in 144 innings. His team again finished fourth in an eight-team league but won the league championship in the playoffs, sweeping the Evansville Braves in three games in the final round. Brother Evan played for the Greenville, Alabama, Pirates in the Class D Alabama State League, but was released after batting only .125.

Before leaving for spring training in 1950, Law married VaNita McGuire on March 3 in Logan, Utah.[15] The couple had been dating since high school and would have five sons, Varlin, Vaughn, future major leaguer Vance, Veryl, and Veldon, and a daughter VaLynda.

Once the 1950 season began Law found himself promoted all the way to the New Orleans Pelicans of the Double-A Southern Association. He got off to a strong start, winning six of his first ten decisions with a stingy 2.67 earned-run average. On June 6 he was in Nashville preparing to start a game against the Nashville Vols when he learned of his call-up to the Pittsburgh Pirates.[16] He was barely 20 years old.

Law's big-league debut and first start came in Forbes Field on June 11 in the first game of a doubleheader against the Philadelphia Phillies and their young ace Robin Roberts. Those Phillies, better known as the Whiz Kids, would win their first National League pennant in 35 years that season, largely through winning an inordinate amount of one-run games.[17] Law's debut was no exception as he led 4-2 before the Phillies scored five runs in eighth and held on for a 7-6 win. A three-run double by Jimmy Bloodworth with the score tied 4-4 was the big blow. Still, Law pitched a complete game.

His second start was a no-decision five days later against the Boston Braves in Boston in a game the Pirates lost in the bottom of the ninth. Four days later Law again squared off against the Phillies, this time in Philadelphia's Connie Mack Stadium. He lost 7-3 to Russ Meyer as the Phillies, aided by misplays in the outfield, scored all their runs in the sixth and seventh innings.[18] Law continued to pitch in bad luck for a woeful Pirates team that would finish in the cellar, 33½ games out of first place. He did win six of his last 11 decisions to finish with a 7-9 record in 27 games, 17 of which were starts. He completed five of those starts and ended his debut year with a 4.92 earned-run average.

Law's 1951 season was very similar, as he won six and lost nine as the Bucs improved slightly to seventh place. He started 14 of the 28 games he appeared in as manager Billy Meyer continued to use him as a spot starter and in long relief, improving his ERA to 4.50. For both the 1950 and 1951 seasons Law's earned-run average was above 5 as a starter and almost 1½ runs lower in games in which he relieved.

The Korean War was in full swing and Law knew that he would likely be drafted. Instead, after the season, he enlisted in the Army at Fort Eustis, Virginia, which had an active baseball program. He mostly played first base rather than pitch for the base team while missing the 1952 and 1953 major-league baseball seasons. While in the service, he played with or against Willie Mays, Johnny Antonelli, and Don Newcombe, as well as teammate Dick Groat.[19] Law was mustered out of the service in December 1953, in plenty of time to get ready for the Pirates' 1954 spring training.[20]

Branch Rickey had become the Pirates' general manager in 1950 and his evaluation of Law suggested that he might be switched to an everyday player:

"Law…has a chance for the outfield. He is highly intelligent, a good athlete, a good runner, and very adventurous. Could easily be the best base runner in the Pittsburgh organization. He has never had an opportunity of hitting very much for he has always been a pitcher."[21]

Law did, however, remain a pitcher. The Pirates team that he returned to had finished last in both 1952 and 1953 and was destined for the basement in 1954 and 1955 as well. Manager Fred Haney gave him plenty of work in 1954 both as a starter and reliever. He was only 5-13 as a starter but won four games in relief to finish 9-13 for the year. His earned-run average was an unsightly 5.51 and he gave up 201 hits in 161 innings. The two years of military service certainly had not advanced his baseball career but he did show promise. According to Wayne Terwilliger, Law threw a shutout against the New York Giants during a game in which the Giants were stealing signs and knew every pitch that was coming.[22]

Law improved to 10-10 in 1955 and, with 24 starts, he pitched 200 innings for the first time in his career. His earned-run average dropped to a respectable 3.81. On July 19 of that year, Mel Queen, who was slated to be the starting pitcher, came down with a stomach bug and Law was asked to pitch on three days' rest and little notice against Lew Burdette of the Milwaukee Braves. Both teams scored early before both hurlers shut the door. The game went into extra innings tied at 2-2 and after nine more innings the score was still 2-2 and Law was still on the mound. After manager Haney finally pinch-hit for Law in the 18th, Bob Friend came in and gave up a run to put the Pirates behind heading into the bottom of the 19th inning. But the Pirates roared back to score two runs for a 4-3 win, with Friend the winning pitcher. In 18 innings of work, Law had thrown approximately 220 pitches, given up nine hits, struck out 12, and walked only two, all for a no-decision.[23]

Afterward Haney reported that in every inning from the 12th on he asked Law if he was getting tired. The answer was always the same, "No I'm fine." When he finally pinch-hit for Law after 18 innings, he did so because he was afraid he would be run out of town if Law hurt his arm.[24]

Five days later Law took his regular turn and pitched a ten-inning, complete-game 3-2 victory over Chicago, giving up just four hits.[25]

The 1956 season was another long one for the Pirates and Law, even with the boundless energy and enthusiasm of new manager Bobby Bragan. The club did manage to climb out of the basement to seventh place, but Law struggled to an 8-16 won-lost record, going 7-13 as a starter. After five full seasons in the big leagues, his record stood at a cumulative 40 wins and 57 losses, with an earned-run average of 4.55.

The Bucs returned to the cellar in 1957 and in early August, GM Joe Brown replaced Bragan with Danny Murtaugh, who guided the team to a promising 26-25 finish. This was the year that Law finally started fulfilling his potential, putting together ten wins in 18 decisions with a sparkling 2.87 ERA, fifth best in the National

League. However, Ruben Gomez of the New York Giants ended Law's season prematurely by hitting him in the left ear with a pitch, rupturing his eardrum.[26]

During the 1957 season Law was thrown out of a game for the only time in his career and it was a game in which he was just sitting on the bench. The Pirates thought home-plate umpire Stan Landes was missing a lot of pitches and were complaining loudly and profanely. Finally Landes looked over to the dugout, pointed to Law, and to Law's surprise, ejected him. Later in his report to the league, Landes said that he had thrown Law out because there was a lot of abusive language coming from the bench and he didn't think Law, with his religious beliefs, should have to hear it.[27]

About the strongest language ever to come out of Law's mouth was "Judas Priest," when he was called out on a pitch he thought was not a strike.[28] He did pitch on Sundays, generally only a day of worship for Mormons, believing that the church would want him to fulfill his contractual obligations.[29]

Law was generally reluctant to throw at hitters. In 1958, however, he precipitated a bench clearing brawl after throwing at San Francisco Giants pitcher Ruben Gomez. (That was the season the Giants had moved from New York.) Gomez was known as a head-hunter and had beaned Law the previous year. In this game, with the score 1-1 in the fourth inning, Gomez hit Bill Mazeroski after Maz had missed a home run on a long drive that was just foul.[30] Manager Murtaugh instructed Law to knock down the first batter in the next inning. Law said, "Skip, it is against my religion. After all, the Bible says, 'Turn the other cheek.'"

Murtaugh replied, "Well, it will cost you $100 if you don't knock him down."

Law paused for a second and said, "The Bible also says 'those who live by the sword, die by the sword.'"[31]

Gomez happened to be the first batter and Law whizzed the first pitch right under his chin, sending him sprawling. Umpire Frank Dascoli started out to the mound to warn Law and Murtaugh raced out of the dugout to protect his pitcher. About that time Gomez made an obscene gesture at Murtaugh, who started for Gomez, precipitating an old-fashioned free-for-all.[32]

Teammate Roberto Clemente was the target of a lot of beanballs early in his career. On one occasion Clemente was laid flat in Philadelphia by a pitch right at his head. After grounding out weakly, he came back to the dugout just livid, cursing and yelling. Law told him, "Calm down. I'll take care of this." He proceeded to deck the first Phillies hitter, Richie Ashburn, prompting the umpire to warn both teams that the next pitch close to anyone's head would cost $500 plus a five-day suspension.[33]

Law once hit Hank Aaron a glancing blow to the helmet after getting him out three times on balls away. After the game, however, Aaron said it was just as much his fault because he was leaning over the plate, looking for another pitch outside.[34]

Law's teammates came to call him Deacon, since Law was an elder in the Mormon Church.[35] Law did not proselytize his teammates, however, and he had their respect. They viewed him as a leader by example. Often his teammates would watch their language when around him, knowing that he did not swear. The opposition would sometimes try to rile Law by calling him names such as "dirty Deacon," but he was unflappable and just went about his pitching business.[36]

In 1958 the Pirates shot up to second place, finishing eight games behind the Milwaukee Braves. Law struggled the first half of the season and at one juncture had a 9-11 record with an earned-run average of almost 5.00. But he won five of his last six decisions to finish with 14 wins against 12 losses, and in the process reduced his earned-run average to 3.96. He gave up 235 hits in 202 innings and some in the Pirates' front office wanted to trade him. General manager Joe Brown refused but did want Law to stop relying on his curveball so much.[37] It was a good decision because while the 1959 Pirates slipped to fourth place, Law at long last became the ace of the staff, winning 18 games and losing only 9. His earned-run average dipped to 2.98 and his 20 complete games were tied for second most in the league.

Thus, the stage was set for 1960 as Law and the Pirates would reach the pinnacle of success individually and collectively. Law trained hard in the offseason in Idaho, running as many as six miles a day and throwing to his brother Evan. It paid off as he won his first four starts before losing to the Giants on May 6.[38] He was a clutch performer all season, for example ending an early-season four-game slide by beating the Dodgers 3-2 in LA and pitching the Pirates back into first place on May 29 with a win over the Phillies to bring his record to 7-1.[39] In fact, the Pirates had only two four-game losing streaks in 1960 and each time Law ended the streak with a victory in Los Angeles.[40]

Thus, it was no surprise when Law, with an 11-4 record at the break, was named to his first National League All-Star team, joining seven other Pirate teammates.[41] That was the second year of a four-year experiment of hosting two All-Star Games. The two 1960 games were played on July 11 in Kansas City and on July 13 in Yankee Stadium in New York. The National League won the first game, 5-3, in 100-degree heat as teammate Bob Friend got the win with three scoreless innings to start the game, while Law recorded a save by getting Brooks Robinson to fly out to Vada Pinson in center field and Harvey Kuenn to line out to Clemente in right for the last two outs of the game, both with two men on. Law then started and was the winning pitcher for the second game, pitching three scoreless innings to beat Whitey Ford as the National League blanked the American League, 6-0, on the day that John F. Kennedy won the Democratic nomination for president across the country in Los Angeles.[42]

Law continued to pitch well after the All-Star break as the Pirates finally broke away from the Braves and Cardinals. On August 29 he won his 19th game, but it would take him four attempts to get number 20. He finally secured his first and only 20-win season by defeating the Cincinnati Reds 5-3 in a complete-game performance at Crosley Field.[43] For the regular season Law finished with 20 wins against 9 losses and a 3.08 earned-run average. He walked only 40 batters in 271 innings and pitched 18 complete games in 35 starts to tie Warren Spahn and Lew Burdette for the league lead. It was the only season in Law's career in which he did not make a relief appearance.

The Pirates clinched the pennant on September 25 while losing to the Braves in Milwaukee. Afterward the Pirates celebrated with champagne in the clubhouse and on the team bus. In the midst of the hubbub aboard the bus, several of Law's teammates restrained him while catcher Bob Oldis playfully yanked a shoe off his foot, spraining Law's

left ankle in the process.[44] Although Law soldiered on in the World Series, starting Games One, Four, and Seven, he injured his arm while favoring his bad ankle and thereafter struggled for several years to regain his 1960 form.

In Game One, in Forbes Field, Law faced Art Ditmar, who had led the Yankees with 15 wins. In the first inning he got a slider too high to Roger Maris, who deposited it in the upper deck in right field. But the Bucs quickly got to Ditmar for three runs in the bottom of the inning and Stengel pulled the Yankee ace in favor of Jim Coates. In the fourth, Bill Virdon in center field made a fine catch of a 407-foot drive by Yogi Berra with two on and no outs. Moose Skowron then singled to knock in a run before Law retired the last two hitters, stranding two runners. Pittsburgh had stretched the lead to 6-2 by the top of the eighth when Law gave up singles to Hector Lopez and Roger Maris to start the inning. Manager Murtaugh brought in ace reliever Roy Face, who promptly struck out Mickey Mantle, got Berra to fly out, and then struck out Moose Skowron to safeguard the four-run lead. A two-run pinch-hit home run by Elston Howard in the ninth made the final score 6-4.[45]

By the time Law's start in Game Four, in Yankee Stadium, came around, the Pirates were down two games to one after losing two Yankees slugfests, 16-3 and 10-0. In the first inning, Law escaped a second-and-third jam with no one out by getting Maris to pop up and Berra, after an intentional walk to Mantle, to hit into a double play. Skowron hit a home run in the fourth to make it 1-0 but in the fifth inning Vernon helped his own cause by doubling in the tying run off Yankees starter Ralph Terry. Virdon's Texas Leaguer drove in two more runs and gave the Pirates a 3-1 lead. In the seventh the Yankees scored their second run on a double and two singles before Face came in to shut the door. He retired all eight batters he faced to close out the 3-2 win.[46]

The teams split the next two games, the Bucs winning Game Five 5-2 behind Harvey Haddix and Face before the Yankee sluggers again broke loose for a 12-0 win behind Whitey Ford in Game Six. That set the stage for Game Seven.

Law was still nursing his injured ankle but started the deciding game, looking for his third win in the Series. Manager Murtaugh was hoping for five or six innings

from his starter before turning the game over to Face. The game certainly started out as planned with Law holding the Yankees scoreless in the first two innings as the Pirates raced to a 4-0 lead off Bob Turley and Bill Stafford. In the top of the fifth Law got ahead of the first hitter, Moose Skowron, 0-2. He tried wasting a fastball outside, but left it over the corner of the plate and Skowron drove a line drive into the lower deck in right field for a home run. Law settled down to retire the next three batters, leaving the score 4-1.[47]

The Pirates failed to score in their half, so Law trudged out to start the sixth on his throbbing ankle. Bobby Richardson led off with a hard single to center, which got the bullpen going. Tony Kubek was next and drew a full-count walk, Law's first of the game. Murtaugh bolted to the mound from the dugout and asked Law about his ankle. Law responded that his ankle was fine, admitting later that it was "a little white lie." It didn't convince Murtaugh, who told Law he didn't want another Dizzy Dean on his hands, injuring his arm because of a bad ankle, and he called in Roy Face from the bullpen.[48]

Face promptly gave up a line single up the middle to Mickey Mantle and a three-run homer into the upper deck of the right-field bleachers to Yogi Berra. Berra's drive was fair by inches; when the dust settled, the Yankees surged into the lead, 5-4, Law had a no-decision, and the stage was set for perhaps the most exciting World Series finish in history.[49] The Yankees' lead grew to 7-4 before the Pirates, aided immeasurably by Hal Smith's three-run home run, scored five runs in the bottom of the eighth to regain the advantage, 9-7. The Yankees clawed back with two runs in the top of the ninth to tie and set the stage for Bill Mazeroski's Series-winning home run off Ralph Terry to lead off the bottom of the last inning of the last game.

For the Series, Law finished with two wins and a 3.44 earned-run average in 18 innings of work. Only one other Pirates pitcher logged more than ten innings and that was the workhorse reliever, Face.[50] Although the Cy Young Award is based on the regular season, Law certainly put an exclamation point on the award for his performance in the World Series, all on an injured ankle. Certainly the Pirates could not have come close to winning the Series without him. For the record, he tallied more than twice as many Cy Young Award votes as the runner-up, Warren

Spahn.[51] He also finished sixth in the Most Valuable Player voting, won by teammate Dick Groat.

As Law drove home to Utah after the Series, he felt weakness in his pitching arm, but was not overly concerned since he had the entire winter to rest. But it was still not right when he began his pre-spring-training workouts. It turned out that he had torn muscles in the back of his shoulder during the Series while favoring his bad ankle. It would take him three full years to recover.[52]

Law appeared in only 11 games in 1961, starting ten and struggling to a 3-4 record in late June before going on the disabled list in July for the remainder of the season as the world champion Pirates fell all the way to sixth place.[53] The 1962 season saw some improvement as Law won 10 and lost 7 in 23 games and 20 starts. He pitched seven complete games and even threw two shutouts, but was still hampered by arm miseries as the Pirates improved to fourth, winning 93 games.

Although Law insisted in 1963 that he was throwing pain-free for the first time in three years, by August his record was only four wins and five losses while his earned-run average hovered just below 5.00. Manager Murtaugh suggested that Law voluntarily retire and Law reluctantly agreed, since it was clear that the Pirates had no plans to use him.[54]

In a 2006 interview, Law said that he didn't have enough sense to quit. During the offseason, he said, he was given a blessing by a Mormon High Priest during a youth conference in Salt Lake City. According to Law, the Mormon Church believes in miracles and when he went from the conference and picked up a baseball, his arm was totally without pain.[55] A couple of other teams showed interest that winter, but Law elected to attempt his comeback with the Pirates.[56] He worked his way back into the rotation and finished 1964 with a 12-13 record, starting 29 games and completing seven, with five shutouts and a 3.61 era.

Law began 1965 with five straight losses, but the Pirates scored only five runs in those games, so manager Harry Walker never considered pulling him from the rotation. Law repaid the confidence by reeling off eight wins in a row as the Pirates surged into pennant contention.[57] He finished the season for the third-place Pirates with 17 wins against 9 losses, and his 2.15 earned-run average

trailed only those of Sandy Koufax and Juan Marichal. For his efforts, Law was named the National League's Comeback Player of the Year, an award he was reluctant to receive "considering the implications."[58]

Law went 12-8 in 1966, but he was losing his effectiveness. His earned-run average slipped to 4.08 and he gave up 203 hits in 177 innings. He struggled even more in 1967. He had won only two of eight decisions by August when he suffered a groin injury. On August 29 he retired again, this time for good. Law was 37 years old. He finished his career with 162 wins and 147 losses in a 16-year career, all with the Pirates. In 364 career starts, he recorded 119 complete games and 28 shutouts.

Although often overlooked, Law was a good hitting pitcher, batting .216 overall and smacking 11 career home runs. Three times he hit over .300 for the season, topped by a .344 average in 1951, and 12 times in his career he was used as a pinch-hitter. He even started one game in right field in 1954, and in August 1956 manager Bobby Bragan batted Law seventh in the lineup for four consecutive mound starts, ahead of future Hall of Famer Bill Mazeroski. Law was also considered an excellent baserunner and was used as a pinch-runner 23 times.

Law stayed close to the game after the end of his playing career, serving as the Pirates' pitching coach in the late 1960s before becoming an assistant baseball coach at Brigham Young University in Provo, Utah. He served in that capacity for 11 years, and tutored Jack Morris, among others,[59] before accepting a position as pitching coach for the Seibu Lions in Japan's Pacific League. After spending the 1979 and 1980 seasons in Japan,[60] Law returned to professional baseball in the US as the pitching coach for the Portland Beavers of the Pacific Coast League. In 1982-83 he was the pitching coach for the Denver Bears in the American Association for the White Sox organization[61] before becoming the manager of the team in 1984. Although the Bears were in second place in early June, a midseason slump led to his dismissal in early July.[62]

Afterward Law scouted for the White Sox in the Utah area and spent a number of years in corporate sales. In 1987, when the Pirates celebrated their 100th anniversary, he was named the team's all-time best right-handed pitcher.[63] His son Vance, a 39th-round draft pick, was a major-league third baseman for 12 years for the Pittsburgh

Pirates, Chicago White Sox, Montreal Expos, Chicago Cubs, and Oakland Athletics. In 2000 Vance became the head baseball coach at Brigham Young University, with his father as a volunteer coach. Vernon regularly pitched batting practice for the Cougars well into his 70s."[64] He continued to live in retirement in Provo, Utah, with VaNita, his wife of more than 62 years, surrounded by his six children, 31 grandchildren, and 13 great-grandchildren.

Sources

Baseball—The Biographical Encyclopedia (Kingston, New York: Total/Sports Illustrated, 2000).

The Baseball Encyclopedia (New York: MacMillan Company, 1969).

Les Biederman, "A Long Road Back—But Law Made It," *The Sporting News*, September 4, 1965.

John T. Bird, *Twin Killing: The Bill Mazeroski Story* (Birmingham: Esmerelda Press, 1995).

Jim Brosnan, *The Long Season* (New York: Harper & Row, 1960).

Dan Coughlin, "For Law, Order is a Way of Life," *Cleveland Plain Dealer*, February 2, 1976.

Rick Cushing, *1960 Pittsburgh Pirates—Day by Day: A Special Season, An Extraordinary World Series* (Pittsburgh: Dorrance Publishing Co., Inc., 2010).

Richard Deitsch, "Catching Up With … Vernon Law, Pirates Ace, October 10, 1960, *Sports Ilustrated*, May 28, 2000.

Lew Freedman, *Hard Luck Harvey Haddix and the Greatest Game Ever Lost*, (Jefferson, North Carolina: McFarland & Co., Inc., 2009).

Bill Furlong, "Law's Spirit Matches Arm," *Baseball Digest*, July 1960.

Dick Groat and Bill Surface, *The World Champion Pittsburgh Pirates* (New York: Coward-McCann, Inc., 1961).

Jack Heyde, *Pop Flies and Line Drives—Visits With Players From Baseball's Golden Era* (Victoria, British Columbia: Trafford Publishing, 2004).

James S. Hirsch, *Willie Mays—The Life, the Legend* (New York: Scribner, 2010).

Colleen Hroncich, *The Whistling Irishman—Danny Murtaugh Remembered* (Philadelphia: Sports Challenge Network Publishing, 2010).

Lloyd Johnson and Miles Wolff, *The Encyclopedia of Minor League Baseball, 2nd ed.* (Durham, North Carolina: Baseball America, Inc., 1997).

Gene Karst and Martin L. Jones, Jr., *Who's Who in Professional Baseball* (New Rochelle, New York: Arlington House, 1973).

Kerry Keene, *1960—The Last Pure Season* (Champaign, Illinois.: Sports Publishing Inc., 2000).

Nelson "Nellie" King, *Happiness Is Like a Cur Dog—the Thirty-Year Journey of a Major League Player and Broadcaster* (Bloomington, Indiana: AuthorHouse, 2009).

Richard H. Letarte, *That One Glorious Season—Baseball Players With One Spectacular Year* (Portsmouth, New Hampshire: Peter E. Randall Publisher LLC, 2006).

Lee Lowenfish, *Branch Rickey—Baseball's Ferocious Gentleman* (Lincoln, Nebraska: University of Nebraska Press, 2007).

Major League Baseball Productions, *Baseball's Greatest Games—1960 World Series Game 7* (DVD 2010).

David Maraniss, *Clemente—the Passion and Grace of Baseball's Last Hero* (New York: Simon & Schuster, 2006).

Rich Marazzi and Len Fiorito, *Baseball Players of the 1950s* (Jefferson, North Carolina: McFarland & Co., Inc., 2004).

Bruce Markusen, *Roberto Clemente: The Great One* (Champaign, Illinois: Sports Publishing Inc., 1998).

John McCollister, *Tales from the Pirates Dugout* (Champaign, Illinois: Sports Publishing, LLC, 2003).

John McCollister, *The Bucs! The Story of the Pittsburgh Pirates* (Lenexa, Kansas: Addax Publishing Group, 1998).

Hub Miller, "The Law of the Pirates," *Baseball Magazine*, June 1951.

Larry Moffi, *This Side of Cooperstown—An Oral History of Major League Baseball in the 1950s* (Iowa City, Iowa: University of Iowa Press, 1996).

John Moody, *Kiss It Good-Bye—The Mystery, the Mormon, and the Moral of the 1960 Pittsburgh Pirates* (Shadow Mountain Press, 2010).

Bill Morales, *Farewell to the Golden Era—The Yankees, the Pirates and the 1960 Baseball Season* (Jefferson, North Carolina: McFarland & Co., Inc. 2011).

Jim O'Brien, *Maz and the '60 Bucs* (Pittsburgh: James P. O'Brien, 1993).

Andrew O. O'Toole, *Branch Rickey in Pittsburgh* (Jefferson, North Carolina: McFarland & Co., Inc., 2000).

Danny Peary, ed., *We Played the Game*—65 Players Remember Baseball's Greatest Era—1947-1964 (New York: Hyperion, 1994).

Richard Peterson, *Growing Up With Clemente* (Kent, Ohio: Kent State University Press, 2009).

Richard Peterson, ed., *The Pirates Reader* (Pittsburgh: University of Pittsburgh Press, 2003).

David L. Porter, ed., *Biographical Dictionary of American Sports: Baseball, Revised and Expanded Edition* (Westport, Connecticut.: Greenwood Press, 2000).

Joseph Reichler, *Baseball's Great Moments* (New York: Bonanza Books, 1983).

Jim Reisler, *The Best Game Ever—Pirates vs. Yankees, October 13, 1960* (New York: Carroll & Graf Publishers, 2007).

Ed Richter, *The Making of a Big-League Pitcher* (Philadelphia: Chilton Books, 1963).

Robin Roberts and C. Paul Rogers, III, *The Whiz Kids and the 1950 Pennant* (Philadelphia: Temple University Press, 1996).

Michael Shapiro, *Bottom of the Ninth — Branch Rickey, Casey Stengel, and the Daring Scheme to Save Baseball from Itself* (New York: Times Books, 2009).

Wayne Terwilliger with Nancy Peterson and Peter Boehm, *Terwilliger Bunts One* (Guilford, Connecticut: Globe Pequot Press, 2006).

Frank Thomas with Ronnie Joyner and Bill Bozman, *Kiss It Goodbye — the Frank Thomas Story* (Dunkirk, Maryland.: Pepperpot Productions, Inc., 2005).

David Vincent, Lyle Spatz, and David W. Smith, *The Midsummer Classic — The Complete History of Baseball's All-Star Game* (Lincoln, Nebraska.: University of Nebraska Press, 2001).

Chase Walker, "Inner Control Also Means Outer Control for Vernon Law, a … Shy Guy," *Guideposts*, May 1956.

Warren N. Wilbert, *The Greatest World Series Games* (Jefferson, North Carolina: McFarland & Company, Inc., 2005).

www.retrosheet.org.

www.byucougars.com/home/m-baseball.

Notes

1 John Moody, *Kiss It Goodbye — the Mystery, the Mormon, and the Moral of the 1960 Pittsburgh Pirates*, 19.

2 John T. Bird, *Twin Killing: The Bill Mazeroski Story*, 82.

3 Larry Moffi, *This Side of Cooperstown — An Oral History of Major League Baseball in the 1950s*, 187.

4 Moody, 45.

5 Bird, 82.

6 Jim O'Brien, *Maz and the '60 Bucs*, 384.

7 Dick Groat and Bill Surface, *The World Champion Pittsburgh Pirates*, 133.

8 Moffi, 186.

9 Moody, 47-48, 65-66.

10 Welker and Herman apparently advised scouts from other teams to offer cigars to Law's father as a way of currying favor. Of course, as practicing Mormons, Mr. and Mrs. Law abhorred tobacco. John McCollister, *Tales from the Pirates Dugout*, 88; Moody, 75-76; Moffi, 186. One source has Herman passing out stogies to competing scouts before they entered the Law's house. See Richard Deitsch, "Catching Up With … Vernon Law, Pirates Ace, October 10, 1960," *Sports Illustrated*, May 22, 2000.

11 Richard Peterson, ed., *The Pirates Reader*, 180.

12 Hub Miller, "The Law of the Pirates," *Baseball Magazine*, June 1951, 228.

13 Moody, 76-77.

14 Miller, 228

15 Moody, 71-75; Chase Walker, "Inner Control Also Means Outer Control for Vernon Law, a … Shy Guy," *Guideposts*, May 1956, 7-8.

16 Moody, 115-16.

17 Robin Roberts and C. Paul Rogers, III, *The Whiz Kids and the 1950 Pennant*, 365-67.

18 Several sources have Law pitching his first two games against Robin Roberts and losing both because of fielder misplays. Bird, 83-84; Moffi, 192; Moody, 122.

19 James S. Hirsch, *Willie Mays — The Life, the Legend*, 154.

20 Moody, 124-27.

21 Andrew O'Toole, *Branch Rickey in Pittsburgh*, 47.

22 Wayne Terwilliger with Nancy Peterson and Peter Boehm, *Terwilliger Bunts One*, 117. It actually may have been a complete game 4-3 win over the Giants on May 31, 1954, since according to Retrosheet, Law did not have a shutout against the Giants in the applicable years, 1950, 1951, and 1952. Terwilliger was with the Giants in 1955 and so the game would have been before Terwilliger was a Giant, since he describes the game as one occurring before he joined the team.

23 Bird, 84-85; Moffi, 181; Moody, 141-44; O'Brien, 383.

24 Groat and Surface, 134; Moffi, 182.

25 Several sources incorrectly have Law pitching 13 innings with three days' rest. Bird, 85; Moffi, 182; Moody, 145.

26 Hirsch, 287.

27 Jim Reisler, *The Best Game Ever — Pirates vs. Yankees, October 13, 1960*, 112; Groat and Surface, 134; Moody, 149-51.

28 Moody, 150-51.

29 Bill Furlong, "Law's Spirit Matches Arm," *Baseball Digest*, July 1960, 51; Moffi, 187.

30 Retrosheet. Moffi, 183, has a slightly different version.

31 Correspondence with Vernon Law on file with the author. See also John McCollister, *The Bucs! The Story of the Pittsburgh Pirates*, 160; David Maraniss, *Clemente — The Passion and Grace of Baseball's Last Hero*, 111; Danny Peary, ed., *We Played the Game*, 471-72; Reisler, 111-12; McCollister, *Tales from the Pirates Dugout*, 90; Dan Coughlin, "For Law, Order Is a Way of Life," *Cleveland Plain Dealer*, February 2, 1976 (clipping located in Law's player file at the Baseball Hall of Fame Library).

32 Moffi, 184.

33 Moffi, 182-83; Moody, 152-53.

34 Lew Freedman, *Hard-Luck Harvey Haddix and the Greatest Game Ever Lost*, 24.

35 Moffi, 181.

36 Peavy, 294, 471.

37 Richard Peterson, ed., *The Pirates Reader*, 181.

38 Furlong, 51; Moody, 177-79.

39 Reisler, 118; Richard H. Letarte, *That One Glorious Season—Baseball Players With One Spectacular Year*, 289.

40 Kerry Keene, *1960—The Last Pure Season*, 105; Reisler, 117.

41 Letarte, 291; Bill Morales, *Farewell to the Last Golden Era—The Yankees, the Pirates and the 1960 Baseball Season*, 119-21.

42 David Vincent, Lyle Spatz, and David W. Smith, *The Midsummer Classic—A Complete History of Baseball's All-Star Game*, 176-89; Morales, 121.

43 Groat and Surface, 99; Keene, 105; Reisler, 124; Letarte, 294.

44 Moody, 204-06; Rich Marazzi and Len Fiorito, *Baseball Players of the 1950s*, 210. Another source has the culprit as Don Hoak. See Michael Shapiro, *Bottom of the Ninth—Branch Rickey, Casey Stengel, and the Daring Scheme to Save Baseball From Itself*, 223. Yet others list the "raucous" Gino Cimoli as the bad guy. *Baseball—the Biographical Encyclopedia*, 650; Law has always refused to identify the player involved except to say it was not a starting player, which would eliminate Hoak. Morales, 356.

45 Groat and Surface, 21-23.

46 Groat and Surface, 26-27.

47 Reisler, 125-26.

48 Reisler, 152-53. Of course, Dizzy Dean was injured coming back too soon from an injured toe, but the comparison was still apt.

49 Reisler, 159-61; Warren N. Wilbert, *The Greatest World Series Games*, 152-60; Richard Peterson, ed., *The Pirates Reader*, 187-198; Groat & Surface, 17-34; Joseph Reichler, *Baseball's Great Moments*, 100-103.

50 *The Baseball Encyclopedia*, 2301.

51 *Baseball—the Biographical Encyclopedia*, 650.

52 Moody, 313.

53 Colleen Hroncich, *The Whistling Irishman—Danny Murtaugh Remembered*, 131.

54 Les Biederman, "A Long Road Back—But Law Made It," *The Sporting News*, September 4, 1965, 3; Cushing, 356; Moody, 313-14.

55 Cushing, 356-57.

56 Biederman, 3.

57 Ibid.

58 Moody, 314-15.

59 Rich Marazzi and Len Fiorito, *Baseball Players of the 1950s*, 210.

60 Wayne Graczyk, ed., *1989 Japan Pro Baseball Handbook and Media Guide*, 100.

61 David L. Porter, ed., *Biographical Dictionary of American Sports—Baseball—Revised and Expanded Edition*, 863.

62 "Law Fired—Denver Skipper Axed at Mid-Season, *Baseball America*, August 1, 1984, 11.

63 Cushing, 358.

64 Brigham Young University baseball website, www.byucougars.com/home/m-baseball.

Vern Law and Roy Face combined for wins and saves in both Game One and Game Four of the 1960 World Series.

Courtesy of the National Baseball Hall of Fame and Library.

Bill Mazeroski

By Bob Hurte, Jr.

ALMOST EVERY KID who has ever played baseball fantasizes coming up in the bottom of the ninth inning during the seventh game of the World Series and hitting a home run to win it.

As of the 2012 World Series, only one person has ever accomplished this. It occurred on October 13, 1960, at 3:36 p.m. That was when the Pittsburgh Pirates' second baseman, Bill Mazeroski, deposited New York Yankees pitcher Ralph Terry's slider over the brick wall at Forbes Field to bring a World Series championship to Pittsburgh for the first time in 35 years. It was perhaps the most notable moment of a career that led to the Baseball Hall of Fame—although, ironically, more for his fielding than his hitting.

The hero of this tale was, with a little stretch of the imagination, a hometown boy. William Stanley Mazeroski was born on September 5, 1936, in Wheeling, West Virginia, 60 miles from Pittsburgh. His parents, Louis and Mayme Mazeroski, lived in Witch Hazel, Ohio, a town nestled in the hills between Steubenville, Ohio, and Wheeling. Louis was a coal miner. The Mazeroski family—the parents, Bill, and a sister, Mary—lived in a one-room dwelling with no electricity or indoor plumbing. According to Bill's childhood friend Bill Del Vecchio, the house was slightly bigger than a chicken coop.[1]

Bill grew up loving to play sports—any sport. But the family rarely had the extra money for things such as a baseball glove. Family legend has it that young Bill bought his first glove with the money he earned digging his uncle Og's outhouse. He purchased a three-finger model that was slightly bigger than his hand.[2] (During his professional career Mazeroski preferred to play with a smaller glove, so the ball would not get "lost" in the webbing. He spent a lot of time breaking in his glove, and used it for five or six years, unlike teammate Bill Virdon, who broke in a new one each season.)

Bill's childhood nickname was Catfish. During his youth, he fished every day—out of necessity, to provide food for the family table.

Bill's father, Louis, was a promising player as a youth, and had a tryout with the Cleveland Indians, but his baseball dreams were extinguished when his foot was crushed by falling coal in a mine. Mazeroski said his father steered him away from working in the coal mines. The closest he got to the mines was playing baseball in the coal mine leagues with adults at the age of 13.

Louis and Bill played catch often in their backyard. Louis also threw an endless amount of tennis balls against a brick wall, forcing his son to use both hands and sharpen his reflexes for bad hops. Those sessions proved helpful years later, when Bill began playing on the rock-hard infield of Forbes Field. Louis was able to see his son play in the major leagues before he died on February 1, 1959, at the age of 59.[3]

Baseball was young Mazeroski's favorite sport, but his high-school classmates remembered how he could punt a ball 60 yards. Of course, Louis never allowed him to play on the football team. Bill also excelled in basketball as a 5-foot-11 center. During his senior year at Warren Consolidated High School in Tiltonville, Ohio, he averaged 27 points a game. He was named to the All-Ohio State basketball team, and was offered scholarships by Ohio State, Duquesne, and West Virginia Universities.

Still, it was on the diamond where Mazeroski stood out. When Al Burazio, his high-school coach, saw him play as a freshman, he promised Bill, "I'm going to make a big leaguer out of you."[4] Mazeroski played several positions, mostly pitcher and shortstop, and was named team captain in his junior year. He led his team to the Ohio state championship tournament in 1953. The team from the small rural school—his graduating class had only 60 students—was a ragtag group, with mismatched uniforms. But playing schools from Akron and Cincinnati, the team went to the finals, only to lose 2-1. Mazeroski pitched and won a game in the morning but lost in the afternoon, despite Bill's two-hitter. Both runs scored when a ball went through the center fielder's legs.

When Mazeroski was 16, Coach Burazio took him to a Pirates tryout at Forbes Field. The experience left a positive effect on the youngster, because he returned the following year. After he finished high school, he was courted by the Cleveland Indians, Philadelphia Phillies, Boston Red Sox, Chicago White Sox, and the Pirates. All but the Pirates wanted to start him in Class D. While Mazeroski was a big Indians fan—he grew up listening to Jimmy Dudley and Jack Graney announce their games—he chose to sign with Pittsburgh, which gave him a $4,000 bonus and promised to start him at Class A Williamsport (Eastern League).

There was a glut of shortstops in the Pirates' system, so Mazeroski was asked to take some groundballs at second base. After the Pirates' general manager, Branch Rickey, saw him make the pivot a couple of times, he informed the rookie that he was now a second baseman.

Maz batted just .235 his first year at Williamsport, but it was his glove and not his bat that kept him in the lineup. He showed enough to receive a promotion to the Triple-A Hollywood Stars his second season, but when his batting average sank to .170 after 21 games, he returned to Williamsport, where he finished strong, batting .293 with 11 home runs. Back in Hollywood in 1956, he was batting .306 at midseason when the Pirates brought him up. He was 19 years old.

Mazeroski made his major-league debut on July 7, starting at second base against the New York Giants at the Polo Grounds in New York. He collected his first hit, off John Antonelli, and was the middleman in the first of the 1,706 double plays he would take part in during his 17-year major-league career. His fielding drew praise, but the teenager needed work at the plate. After 17 games his batting average was an anemic .188, but he finished the season at.243 in 81 games for the seventh-place Pirates.

Mazeroski won the second-base job in spring training in 1957. His amazing glove won him the job over Johnny O'Brien, and it didn't hurt that he hit an impressive .442 in 18 exhibition games. Hall of Famer George Sisler, then a Pirates coach and hitting guru, took Mazeroski under his wing, teaching him to go with the pitch and not try to pull everything. Mazeroski rewarded his teacher with a .283 average, eight homers, and 54 runs batted in.

While the 1957 season was impressive, 1958 was a breakout one for Mazeroski. He was selected to the National League team for the All-Star Game for the first time. In recent years he recalled that the game was the site of his biggest embarrassment. It was not because he went 0-fort-4 and struck out once. After two seasons in the major leagues he had earned a reputation for turning the double play, so the American League players came out to watch the National Leaguers take fielding practice. Mazeroski told friend and former teammate Nellie King that he bumbled and stumbled, even forgot which foot to touch the base with, how to catch or throw to first.[5] But in the game he turned two double plays.

Mazeroski won the first of eight Gold Glove Awards in 1958, and his fellow players chose him for *The Sporting News* All-Star Fielding Team, edging out Johnny Temple of Cincinnati. Mazeroski appeared in 152 games and handled 857 chances, including 496 assists, while turning 118 double plays.[6] At the plate he hit .275, with 19 home runs. After the season he and Milene Nicholson, secretary to Rex Bowen, the head of the Pirates scouting department, were married. Manager Danny Murtaugh had "ordered" the shy second baseman to ask her out. A teammate, pitcher Bob Purkey, was his best man.

As much as 1958 was a breakout, the following season could be considered a disappointment. Mazeroski pulled a leg muscle early in the season and put on excessive weight. He admitted to "loafing" and not exercising during the offseason. He did not join his teammates until June 17, but still made the All-Star team, probably more on reputation than playing. He finished the season with a .241 batting average.

After a second-place finish in 1958 the Pirates slid to a fourth-place finish in 1959. The Pirates' management decided to make players' weight a contract issue for the following season. Murtaugh blamed poor seasons by Mazeroski, pitcher Bob Friend (8-19), Bob Skinner, and Bill Virdon as the culprits in the team's poor performance. The manager felt that the extra pounds held back Friend and Mazeroski.[7] Bill took the hint and responded by changing his diet, exercising regularly, and reporting each week to the Pirates office to have his weight checked. He quickly returned to his normal playing weight.

Optimism ran rampant in Pittsburgh before the 1960 season. Some baseball insiders liked the Pirates' chances of winning the pennant. The season did not start out promising. The Pirates opened the season by losing 4-3 to the Braves in Milwaukee. They rebounded by winning their next game, the home opener, pounding the Reds 13-0. Bob Friend was the winner and Mazeroski had a home run and four RBIs. But it was their performance on April 17 that defined the team. They defeated Cincinnati 6-5 on a walk-off home run by Bob Skinner. It was the first of 28 Pirates victories in games in which they were losing or tied after the sixth inning. In the process, the Pirates became known as the "Battlin' Bucs." They saved their most dramatic performance for the end — Game Seven of the World Series.

The Series was tied at three wins apiece. Each victory by the Yankees was a blowout; in the three games they outscored Pittsburgh 38-3. The Pirates' three victories were by 6-4, 3-2, and 5-2. Game Seven was a seesaw battle. The Pirates struck first with a two-run homer by Rocky Nelson in the first inning. They added two more on a single by Virdon single in the second. Vernon Law, the starting pitcher, cruised into the sixth inning leading 4-1. Battling fatigue and pain, he left without retiring a batter, leaving runners on first and second.[8] Manager Murtaugh brought in Elroy Face, who gave up a run-scoring single to Mickey Mantle, then a three-run homer by Yogi Berra that put the Yankees ahead, 5-4. New York increased its lead with two more runs in the top of the eighth. Undaunted, the Pirates began to bounce back. Gino Cimoli led off the bottom of the inning with a

single. Virdon hit a "tailor-made" double-play ball, which took a wicked hop and struck shortstop Tony Kubek in the throat. After Kubek left the game, Dick Groat singled to drive in a run. Manager Casey Stengel removed pitcher Bobby Shantz in favor of Jim Coates. Bob Skinner sacrificed the runners along. Roberto Clemente beat out a grounder to first baseman Moose Skowron when Coates was late covering the base, and Virdon scored. With a count of 2 and 2, Hal Smith hit a three-run homer, and the Pirates were back in the lead.

Thirty years later Mazeroski recalled, "After Smith got us ahead, I just raced onto the field. I just couldn't wait to get those last three outs. Of course, we didn't get those three outs, we didn't get them before they scored two runs."[9]

Bob Friend came in to pitch the ninth. He quickly gave up singles to Bobby Richardson and pinch-hitter Dale Long. Murtaugh yanked Friend in favor of Harvey Haddix. Roger Maris fouled out to the catcher but Mantle drove in Richardson with a single as pinch-runner Gil McDougald advanced to third. Yogi Berra grounded to first baseman Nelson, who stepped on the bag then looked to throw to second but Mantle alertly slid back to first. This allowed McDougald to score, tying the game. Skowron grounded out to end the inning.

As the bottom of the ninth began, radio announcer Chuck Thompson noted, "Cletus Boyer moves over to play shortstop and Ralph Terry, of course, on the mound will be facing Bill Mazeroski."[10] Mazeroski had forgotten that he was leading off until Pirates coach Lenny Levy reminded him to get a bat. William Stanley Mazeroski selected one of his 125 Pro-model Louisville Sluggers and walked out to the plate to meet destiny. Yankee catcher Johnny Blanchard reminded Terry to keep the ball down because Maz was a notorious highball hitter.

Thompson again: "…Here's a swing and high fly ball going deep to left. … It may do It! Back to the wall goes Berra; it is over the fence! Home run! The Pirates win! 3:36 pm October 13, 1960."[11]

Fifty years later, a 12-foot-tall statue depicting Mazeroski rounding second, batting helmet raised high in his right hand, was unveiled on September 5, 2010, on Mazeroski's 74th birthday. Mazeroski's comment: "How could anyone ever dream of something like this?"[12]

It is ironic that the man, who arguably hit the most dramatic postseason game-winning home run took more pride in his defense. Mazeroski is most identified with the double play, or as Branch Rickey referred to it, the pitcher's savior.[13] Baseball expert Bill James called his defensive statistics the most impressive of any player at any position.

Former teammate Dave Giusti recalled seeing Mazeroski for the first time while playing for the Houston Colt 45s. It was the last inning of a game in Pittsburgh; the Pirates were leading by one run. Houston had the bases loaded with one out. Ronnie Brandt, a catcher who ran well, hit a ball deep in the hole between short and third. Gene Alley backhanded it, spun and threw to second. Giusti did not see the ball being caught at second. The next thing he knew Brandt was out at first and the game was over. Giusti remembered thinking, "Who the hell is that?"[14]

When Mazeroski joined the Pirates, he partnered with Dick Groat. Their pairing resulted in four appearances in the All-Star Game and three Gold Gloves for the second baseman. The partnership ended on November 19, 1962, when Groat was traded to St. Louis. The next season Mazeroski replaced his friend as the team captain. Groat went to another World Series in 1964 with St. Louis; his keystone partner was Julian Javier, the young second baseman traded away by the Pirates because they already had Mazeroski.

Dick Schofield followed Groat as starting shortstop, a position he held for the 1963 and '64 seasons. Mazeroski won his fourth and fifth Gold Gloves. Although they formed a successful combination, it was temporary as another shortstop was being groomed at Columbus, Gene Alley. Years later Alley confessed that he was intimidated seeing Mazeroski take groundballs during spring training. He thought, "If you had to be that good in the majors, I'll never make it!"[15]

Together Alley and Mazeroski formed the most successful double-play combination in the major leagues from 1965 to 1972. They turned 113 double plays in 1965, their first season together. It was the sixth time Mazeroski had led in the category. That achievement was especially remarkable because Mazeroski did not begin his season until May because he had broken his foot at the end of spring training. (The injury occurred on a single by Alley,

Mazeroski rounded third and when he attempted to stop in the soft dirt he broke his fifth metatarsal.)

The duo's high-water mark together was arguably 1966. The Pirates' 215 double plays broke the National League record held by the Brooklyn Dodgers, though it fell short of the Philadelphia Athletics' major-league record. Mazeroski won his seventh Gold Glove and Alley picked up his first. It was Mazeroski's finest defensive season. He played in every game, committing only eight errors for a fielding average of .992. He led the National League in chances, putouts, and assists. The season seemed to establish Mazeroski as one of the best fielders ever, yet he did it without much fanfare. As Jim Murray noted in a column, "A half-century ago, a second base combination made something like nine double plays in a season and a poet (Franklin P. Adams) immortalized them with a poem, 'Tinker to Evers to Chance.' ... Maz makes 161 and they abbreviate his name in the box score."[16]

Mazeroski appeared in his last All-Star Game in 1967 and also won his final Gold Glove. He had pulled muscles in both legs, yet played in 163 games, starting 160 of them, and turned 131 double plays.

The 1968 season was decent; the 107 double plays marked the last time Mazeroski reached the century mark. Indications that he was winding down became noticeable. He was still a valuable commodity but in a different way. He quietly assumed a new position on the team. He became a mentor, the elder statesman to a new crop of young players. The 1969 alignment featured Richie Hebner (21 years old) at third, Freddie Patek (24) played short, and Bob Robertson (22) was at first. There was no communication gap among them; their willing ears devoured Mazeroski's wisdom and information on how to play hitters.

Mazeroski passed Frankie Frisch's career total for assists with his 6,027th at Wrigley Field in Chicago on April 14, 1969. Statistically, however, 1969 was a subpar season for him both defensively and offensively. He played in only 67 games. While several people figured on a reduced role for him during the 1970s, neither Mazeroski nor manager Murtaugh was ready for the veteran to relinquish his incumbency at second. His faithful manager still expected big things from him. Mazeroski worked hard during the offseason, running in the morning and swimming in the afternoon. The season proved to be full of eventful moments. It was also the last in which he played in more than 100 games.

The Pirates played their last game at the fabled Forbes Field on June 28, 1970. They won both games of a doubleheader with the Cubs, winning the finale by a score of 4-1. Mazeroski recorded the last defensive out of the game and got the last hit. It was not a sad parting between the second baseman and the field. He felt that it possessed the worst infield in the league. He admitted that eventually he became used to it and almost liked it.

A week later on August 5, during a 4-0 win over the Phillies, Mazeroski passed Billy Herman on the all-time list for putouts with 4,781. He had four putouts and three assists and turned a double play during the game.

Bill was known for his quick feet around the bag but was also nicknamed "Tree Stump" because sliding baserunners usually were unable to take him out. Dave Giusti recalled the time a young Ron Stone of the Phillies went into second with intentions of taking Mazeroski out. As Giusti described it, Stone went in and upon contact, slowly melted into a clump and was rewarded with three broken ribs.

Mazeroski's playing time diminished greatly in 1971. He played in only 70 games, 46 of them at second, as Dave Cash took over at the keystone. Still, Mazeroski was able to reach another milestone, this time for hitting. He lined a double off Wade Blasingame of Houston on August 17 for his 2,000th hit. He also played in his second World Series that year. The Pirates defeated the Baltimore Orioles in seven games. Mazeroski's only appearance came when he pinch-hit in Game One, flying out to center field. This experience was the polar opposite of 1960. When reporters asked him which championship team was better of the two, he surprised them by saying that no question, the 1971 version was.

Mazeroski turned 35 in 1972 and he was eager to head south for spring training. His old friend and new manager, Bill Virdon, envisioned him as a super utilityman. Not only could he fill in at second but he could also play some third, as well as serve as a valuable instructor and mentor. He was asked to supply similar instruction for Rennie Stennett as he did for Dave Cash the year

before. As Joe Morgan, the hall of Fame second baseman, noted, Maz was the "gold standard" for second basemen. He also passed along some advice on how to act like a major leaguer, much as Dale Long did for him during his rookie season.

Willie Stargell, who served the same role later in his own career, said, "Maz taught me the value of patience and consistency."[17]

Mazeroski retired after 1972. He pinch-hit for Nellie Briles in his last regular-season at-bat, on October 4. His last appearance for the postseason was to pinch-hit for Dock Ellis on October 10. Roberto Clemente tried to persuade him to spend a winter getting in shape with him in Puerto Rico so he could play longer, but Mazeroski declined, saying he was done fighting his weight issues. Instead he became the Pirates' third-base coach in 1973. Later he filled the same job description for the Seattle Mariners during the 1979 and 1980 seasons. While coaching did not suit him, he continued to return to the Pirates' spring training each year as an instructor, teaching players the nuances of playing second base.

As of 2011 Bill and Milene Mazeroski resided in Greensburg, Pennsylvania, about 30 miles east of Pittsburgh, and spent January through May at their second home in Panama City, Florida. Much of his retirement was spent fishing and playing golf. They have two sons and, as of 2011, three grandchildren.

After Mazeroski was inducted into the Hall of Fame a street outside the Pirates PNC Park was renamed for him. The team retired his number in 1987, and in 2010 the statue of him was placed outside the ballpark.

Mazeroski was elected to the Baseball Hall of Fame by the Veterans Committee in 2001. Some critics scoffed at his election, saying his offense (career batting average .260) did not live up to that of others already residing at Cooperstown. Others replied that the caliber of pitchers he faced had to be considered, among them Hall of Fame pitchers like Warren Spahn, Don Drysdale, Sandy Koufax, Bob Gibson, Juan Marichal, Gaylord Perry, Tom Seaver, Steve Carlton, and Ferguson Jenkins. Also, they said, his sterling defensive play had to be considered.

During his short induction speech, Mazeroski summed it up: "I think defense belongs in the Hall of Fame. Defense deserves as much credit as pitching and I'm proud to be going in as a defensive player. I want to thank the Veterans Committee for getting me here. I thought when the Pirates retired my number that would be the greatest thing ever to happen to me." He choked. "I don't think I'm gonna make it, I want to thank everyone who made the trip up here to listen to all this crap. …Thank you to everybody!"[18]

Sources

Magazines:

Flowers, Kevin, "Bill Mazeroski Merits Spot in Hall of Fame for his Defense." *Baseball Digest,* August 1998, 64.

Meyer, Paul, "Bill Mazeroski Awaits His Induction to the Hall of Fame," *Pittsburgh Post-Gazette,* June 2001.

Vass, George, "Kings of the D.P.s.," *Baseball Digest,* August 1966

Bouchette, Ed, "Maz Recalls That Glorious Moment in '60 World Series," *Baseball Digest,* October 1990.

Williams, Edgar, "Real Quick-Like a Pickpocket," *Baseball Digest,* July 1958.

Newspapers:

The Sporting News, July 25, 1956 — June 23, 1973

Pittsburgh Post-Gazette, July 29, 2001 (Robert Dvorchak)

Books:

Bird, John T. *Twin Killing: Bill Mazeroski Story.* (Esmeralda Press, 1995).

Cicotello, David and Angelo J. Louisa. *Forbes Field: Essays & Memories of the Pirates Historic Ballpark, 1909-1971.* (Jefferson, North Carolina: McFarland & Co. Inc., 2007).

Finoli, David and Bill Rainier. *The Pittsburgh Pirates Encyclopedia.* (Champaign, Illinois: Sports Publishing LLC, 2003).

Freedman, Lew. *Hard-Luck Harvey Haddix and the Greatest Game Ever Lost.* (Jefferson, North Carolina: McFarland, 2009).

King, Nellie. *Happiness Is Like a Cur Dog: The Thirty Year Journey of a Major League Pitcher and Broadcaster.* (Bloomington, Indiana: Authorhouse, 2009).

Maraniss, David. *Clemente: The Passion and Grace of Baseball's Hero.* (New York: Simon & Schuster, 2006).

Markusen, Bruce. *Roberto Clemente: The Great One.* (Champaign, Illinois: Sports Publishing LLC, 2001).

Markusen, Bruce. *The Team That Changed Baseball.* (Yardley, Pennsylvania: Westholme Publishing, 2006).

Moody, John. *Kiss It Good-Bye: The Mystery, the Mormon and the Moral of the Pittsburgh Pirates.* (Golden, Colorado: Shadow Mountain Press, 2010).

O'Brien, Jim. *Maz and the '60 Pirates: When Pittsburgh and Its Pirates Went All the Way.* (Pittsburgh: O'Brien Publishing, 1993).

O'Brien, Jim. *We Had 'em All the Way.* (Pittsburgh: James P. O'Brien Publishing, 1998).

Peterson, Richard. *The Pirates Reader.* (Pittsburgh: University of Pittsburgh Press, 2003).

Reisler, Jim. *Best Game Ever: Pirates vs. Yankees Oct 13, 1960.* (New York: Graf Publishing, 2007).

Shannon, Mike. *More Tales from the Dugout: More of the Greatest True Baseball Stories.* (New York: McGraw Hill, 2004).

Stargell, Willie and Tom Bird. *Willie Stargell: An Autobiography.* (New York: Harper and Row, 1984).

Thomas, Frank with Ronnie Joyner and Bill Bozman. *Kiss it Goodbye! The Frank Thomas Story.* (Dunkirk, Maryland: Pepperpot Productions, 2005).

Interviews:

Sally O'Leary, January 8, 2011

Dave Giusti, January 9, 2011

Bob Friend, January 26, 2011

Tom Walker, February 22, 2011

Bill Mazeroski, March 2, 2011

Audio replays:

October 13, 1960, Game Seven, World Series, Pirates vs. Yankees. (The Miley Collection, 1997).

June 28, 1970, Last game played at Forbes Field, Pirates vs. Cubs. (The Miley Collection, 1997).

Video replays:

1960 World Series, Pittsburgh Pirates vs. New York Yankees (MLB Home Video, 1991).

You Tube video, "Unveiling of Mazeroski's statue at PNC Park, September 5, 2010, filmed by Pirates' Report.

Notes

1 Robert Dvorchak. *Pittsburgh Post-Gazette,* July 29, 2001.

2 Jim O'Brien, "Maz and the '60 Pirates: When Pittsburgh and Its Pirates Went All the Way." James P. O'Brien Publishing, 1993, 92.

3 *The Sporting News,* February 11, 1959, 26.

4 "Mazeroski Dazzles 'Em; Bucco Glove Wizard," *The Sporting News,* July 30, 1958, 10.

5 Nellie King. *Happiness Is Like a Cur Dog: The Thirty Year Journey of a Major League Pitcher and Broadcaster.* (Bloomfield, Indiana: Author House Publishing, 2009).

6 "The Players Pick N.L. All-Star Fielding team of 1958: McMillan leads Voting as Repeat Choice at Shortstop." *The Sporting News,* November 5, 1958, 17.

7   "Bucs counting on Friend and Maz, Calorie Counts," *The Sporting News,* November 11, 1959, 16.

8   John Moody. *Kiss It Good-Bye: The Mystery, the Mormon and the Moral of the Pittsburgh Pirates* (Golden, Colorado: Shadow Mountain Press, 2010), 271.

9   Ed Bouchette, "Maz Recalls That Glorious Moment in '60 World Series," *Baseball Digest, October* 1990, 26.

10   Audio replay, Game Seven, World Series, Pirates vs. Yankees, October 5, 1960. Announcers: Chuck Thompson and Jack Quinlan. MLB, the Miley Collection, Inc., 1997.

11   Ibid.

12   You Tube video, "Unveiling of Mazeroski's statue, September 5, 2010, at PNC Park, Pittsburgh, Pa., filmed by Pirates' Report.

13   Interview with Bill Mazeroski, March 2, 2011.

14   Interview with Dave Giusti, January 9, 2011.

15   John T. Bird. *Twin Killing: Bill Mazeroski Story* (Esmeralda Press, 1995)

16   "The Best of Murray: Mazeroski long on Skill, Short on Talk." *The Sporting News,* June 17, 1967.

17   Willie Stargell and Tom Bird. *Willie Stargell: An Autobiography.* (New York: Harper and Row Publishers, 1984), 101.

18   John McCollister. *Tales from the Pirates' Dugout.* (Champaign, Illinois: Sports Publishing LLC, 2003), 99.

Courtesy of the National Baseball Hall of Fame and Library.

Román Mejías

By Ron Briley, Rory Costello, and Bill Nowlin

OUTFIELDER ROMÁN MEJÍAS played in 627 big-league games from 1955 to 1964. Alas, just three of those came with the 1960 Pirates, his one US team that won a pennant. He was not on the roster when Pittsburgh won the World Series that year. Mejías was "an affable, good-natured player … whose demeanor, humility and enthusiasm reminded some people of Ernie Banks."[1] He stood an even 6 feet tall, weighed 175 pounds, and was right-handed. He had the tools: He could hit for power and average, and he ran, threw, and fielded well. His primary position was right field, though—so that meant he was stuck behind his good friend Roberto Clemente during his time in Pittsburgh. Though Mejías could play anywhere in the outfield, the Pirates also had fine-fielding Bill Virdon in center and solid pro Bob Skinner in left. And when Pittsburgh obtained Gino Cimoli in December 1959, Mejías lost his backup position.

Mejías had played only two full years in the majors when he finally got a chance to be a regular in 1962. At the age of 31, he had a breakout year with an expansion club, the Houston Colt .45s—he slugged 24 of his 54 major-league home runs during his season in the sun. He did not sustain that success, though, after an ill-considered trade to the Boston Red Sox that winter. The Houston franchise long failed to capitalize on the strongly Hispanic demographics of the Southwest by developing and marketing Latino ballplayers. The Afro-Cuban Mejías was the first example of this lack of sensitivity and appreciation.

Román Mejías Gómez was born to Manuel Mejías and Felipa Gómez on August 9, 1930. Accounts during his playing days (including his baseball cards) typically gave his year of birth as 1932, but Mejías himself later declared

that it was 1930.[2] Mejías also clarified his place of birth. US references have shown the city of Abreus, but it was actually Central Manuelita.[3] This sugar mill complex was in the vicinity of Abreus in the former province of Las Villas. The closest major city is Cienfuegos.[4]

Young Román completed three years of high school in Cuba, and played baseball at that level, but from the age of 15 he worked alongside his father in a shoe factory.[5] On June 13, 1948, at the age of 17, he married Nicolasa Montero. (This date too is two years earlier than American sources showed during his career.[6]) The couple had two children, Rafaela and José.

Mejías began to climb the baseball ladder—and gain broader attention—by playing in the Pedro Betancourt Amateur Baseball League.[7] This league was based in Matanzas province in western Cuba, far from his home. It was composed of young men from around the country who sought to advance their game.

In 1953 Mejías was working as an assistant engineer on a train in Central Manuelita, loading sugarcane.[8] He joined pro baseball because the Pirates had been invited to spring training in Havana that year. Branch Rickey (then their general manager) decided to hold a tryout camp to search for prospects from the Cuban countryside. A Cuban lawyer named Julio "Monchy" de Arcos—who was also part-owner and general manager of the Almendares Alacranes, a team in Cuba's professional league—paid for Mejías' trip to Havana to attend the camp.

Hall of Famer George Sisler, who was then a scout for the Pirates, noticed the outfielder and signed him after a 100-mile ride with de Arcos to Mejías's home. "If you've never traveled by car into the interior of Cuba, you can imagine what kind of ride we had," said Sisler. The whole mill town (population 300) turned out en masse to witness the signing.[9] The modest bonus was later reported to be $500.[10]

Mejías had much early success in the Pirates' minor-league chain, beginning with Batavia in the Pennsylvania-Ontario-New York League (Class D). In 117 games in 1953, he batted .322, which was second on the club, but he was team leader in slugging (.475), doubles (30), and triples (10). His 42 stolen bases led the league. He did not play in Cuba's professional league that winter, though; it's likely that he was not yet deemed ready for the high-level circuit.

Promoted to Class B in 1954, the Cuban hit in 55 straight games, finishing with a batting average of .354 (and 15 homers) for the Waco Pirates in the Big State League. The *New York Times* story about his hitting streak said that Mejías "can't speak English, but his blistering bat knows the language of base hits."[11] "What a ballplayer!" said Branch Rickey that year. "Mejias is sure to go all the way. He defends well, runs well, has a good arm and good power."[12]

The gifted young athlete faced racial and cultural obstacles. Southern segregation forced dark-skinned Latino players to live apart from the rest of the team, and Mejías—classified as a "Cuban Negro"—arrived in the United States unable to speak a word of English. He had to endure the taunts black ballplayers still faced then in minor-league ballparks of the American Southwest and South.[13] As Peter C. Bjarkman noted in his 1994 history, *Baseball With a Latin Beat*, "Dark-skinned Caribbean ballplayers were noteworthy when … Román Mejías first came upon the scene. … They have been truly commonplace only over the past decade."[14]

Mejías later recalled, "I never expec' to be so lonely in the U.S. I couldn't eat. … I thought I would have to go back to Cuba for food. Finally, we learn to go into eating place and we go back in kitchen and point with fingers—thees, thees, these. [*sic*] After while, somebody teach me to say ham and eggs and fried chicken, and I eat that for a long time."[15] Mejías's fears that he would not be able to eat in the United States correspond well with Samuel O. Regalado's characterization of Latino major leaguers as having "a special hunger."[16]

Mejías made his Cuban debut with Almendares in the winter of 1954-55. The Scorpions won the league championship and appeared in the Caribbean Series in Caracas, Venezuela. Branch Rickey had been watching Mejías in Havana, and the outfielder then made the big club in Pittsburgh coming out of spring training.[17] In fact, he was the starting right fielder on Opening Day, ahead of his fellow rookie and roommate, Roberto Clemente.[18] In his debut, on April 13, Mejías singled and walked in four plate appearances. The next day, he hit a two-run homer in the bottom of the first inning.

Clemente soon became the regular in right, however; for the year, Mejías appeared in 71 games and hit only .216. Even though his age was rather advanced for a prospect, one could argue that the Pirates rushed him without sufficient seasoning. Indeed, after another winter with Almendares, Mejías went back to the minors again in 1956, playing for the Hollywood Stars in the Pacific Coast League. He hit .274 during the long PCL season, appearing in 166 games, with another 15 home runs. Before the 1956-57 winter season, Almendares sent him and three other players to the Havana Rojos for Edmundo "Sandy" Amorós.

In 1957 Mejías spent much of the year in Pittsburgh, appearing in 58 games and batting .275. During most of August and the beginning of September, he played for the Columbus Jets in the International League. He led the league in RBIs for Havana with 43 during the 1957-58 winter season and won "Player of the Year" honors, even though he missed several games after an auto accident.[19] The softhearted man had swerved to avoid hitting a cat.[20]

Before the 1958 season *The Sporting News* wrote of Mejías, "Potentially, he has always rated highly and it was just a question of time when he'd start to blossom out." Bobby Bragan, who'd managed Pittsburgh in 1956 and part of 1957, had also been the skipper of Almendares for several seasons. He'd seen Mejías firsthand for years and told Pirates general manager Joe Brown that Mejías was the best player in Cuba.[21]

Mejías spent all of the next two summers with the big-league club, and his games played rose from 58 in 1957 to 76 in 1958 and 96 in 1959. His batting average declined each year, but he drove in and scored more runs, a function of more playing time. He started 72 games in 1959, playing left field when Bob Skinner was injured in April, and right field in May and June when Clemente was on the disabled list. A personal highlight came in the first game of the May 4, 1958, doubleheader at Seals Stadium in San Francisco—Mejías clubbed three home runs. He hit two in a game on four other occasions, twice with Houston and twice with Boston.

About a third of the way through the 1959-60 Cuban season, Mejías went to a new team, the Cienfuegos Elefantes. After shortstop Leo Cárdenas made three errors in a game, Havana sent Cárdenas packing along with Mejías for Chico Fernández, Panchón Herrera, and Pedro Cardenal (older brother of José).[22] The Elefantes had been in a dreadful slump but turned their season around with the help of Mejías, who led the league in hits with 79. Cienfuegos won the championship that winter and then swept the Caribbean Series.

In 1960, however, Mejías was stuck on Pittsburgh's bench in the season's early weeks while the roster numbered 28. His only three games with the Pirates that year came within a week, on May 5, 8, and 11. He pinch-ran twice and struck out in his only at-bat, as a pinch hitter. The deadline to get down to 25 men came on May 12, and Mejías was sent to Columbus. With the Jets, he hit .278 and drove in 71 runs with a new high in homers, 16.

Meanwhile, the Pirates recalled Joe Christopher in June to be the spare outfielder. Though Mejías, too, was recalled near the end of the season, he broke his wrist in a game the weekend before he was to arrive. After the Pirates won the World Series, Mejías was one of seven players awarded a $250 payment in recognition of their short-term contributions.

Cienfuegos repeated as Cuban champion in the winter of 1960-61, but the Caribbean Series was not held because Cuba had withdrawn (the tournament remained on hiatus until 1970). Indeed, Cuba's professional winter league ceased to exist after that season. Mejías finished his career there with 31 homers, 181 RBIs, and a .276 average in 408 games. He was inducted into the Cuban Baseball Hall of Fame (in exile) in 1997.

When Mejías returned to Pittsburgh, his 1961 season played out more or less the same as 1960 had—three April games and one on May 2. Again he got just one at-bat; again it was a strikeout. Once more he spent the rest of the year with Columbus after he was optioned out on May 8. For the Jets, he lifted his annual high in homers to 21.

On October 10, 1961, Mejías got a good break: The Houston Colt .45s plucked him from the Pirates in the 1962 expansion draft. The Pirates were banking on young Donn Clendenon to fill the extra outfielder slot. They chose to leave Mejías (as well as Joe Christopher) unprotected in the draft. Each expansion club—the Mets and the Colts—selected four "premium" players for whom they paid $125,000 apiece. Mejías was one of the "first-round" selections, players whose contracts were sold for $75,000 apiece.

Not long after the expansion draft, Mejías went to play winter ball in Puerto Rico for the Ponce Leones. He left his wife and family behind in Havana—not to see them again for well over a year. The diplomatic and economic pressures of the evolving Cold War confrontation between the United States and Fidel Castro caused many such separations for Cuban ballplayers.

Houston needed Mejías, and used him, and he had the best year of his big-league career in 1962. When the fledgling club drafted the Cuban and awarded him the starting right-field position, he was determined to cash in on his opportunity. During spring training, Mejías's five home runs and 17 RBIs carried the Colt .45s to the championship of the Arizona Cactus League. The Colts did have another Cuban at spring training, but when they broke camp, pitcher Manuel Montejo was returned to the minor leagues, leaving Mejías as the only Latino on the major-league roster.[23]

Mejías continued his onslaught against big-league pitching by hitting two three-run homers on Opening Day as the Colts won, 11-2. The *Houston Chronicle* described the Mejías home runs as a "double-barreled salute" to the introduction of major-league baseball "in the land of the Alamo." Any irony that this shot was fired by a Latino ballplayer was lost upon *Chronicle* sports editor Dick Peebles, who focused upon pitcher Bobby Shantz's complete-game performance. Nevertheless, Peebles did not entirely ignore Mejías, commenting that if the outfielder kept up the pace of Opening Day, he would hit 324 home runs. The editor, in a rather stereotypical fashion, noted that Mejías' response to the ridiculous prediction was a "toothy grin."[24]

Mejías continued to wreak havoc upon National League pitchers early in 1962. He started the season with an eight-game hitting streak, and by May 7 he had homered seven times. The press touted him as Houston's answer to proven sluggers like the San Francisco Giants' Willie Mays and Orlando Cepeda. Mejías entered June with 11 home runs and was leading the team in assorted offensive categories. He hit seven of those homers in cavernous Colt Stadium (360 feet down the foul lines, 420 feet in center, and 395 feet in the left and right power alleys).

After having hit only 17 home runs in six part-time seasons with the Pirates, Mejías found it difficult to account for his newly discovered power. He told the *Chronicle*, "I am more surprised than anyone else that I hit the long ball. In spring, I worked hard just to be patient and wait for the ball. I hit with my wrists and arms only. Before I was a line drive hitter. Not a home run hitter. The fences were a thousand miles away. Today, none of the fences are too far away. I think of the home run more because I know I can hit the ball far." In addition to his work ethic, Mejías attributed his success to clean living. Claiming that his only vice was an occasional Cuban cigar, the athlete main-

tained, "Even if you are strong, sometimes you cannot do your work on the baseball field. So how can you hope to do it if you drink too much and don't sleep enough?"[25]

A sense of modesty, along with his prolific hitting—especially at home—made Mejías a fan favorite in Houston. Media perceptions of Mejías were still framed through the lens of ethnicity, however—and his annual salary was just $12,500. The team's Most Valuable Player was far from being the highest-paid Colt .45. The *Chronicle* also observed that Mejías was succeeding despite his concerns about his wife and two young children, who remained in Cuba. Mejías exclaimed, "There is not much food there, and I worry if they are eating properly."[26]

Yet Mejías refused to complain publicly about his problems, and he continued to make the most of his opportunity to play every day in Houston. Even so, he did not make the National League All-Star team, despite standing third in the league in homers with 19. He also had 48 RBIs and was hitting .311. The players voted for the All-Stars in those days, not the fans, and they chose Mays and Clemente, along with Tommy Davis, who was also having his best year in the majors. NL manager Fred Hutchinson picked Anglo pitcher Dick "Turk" Farrell as Houston's representative. Despite his more than respectable marks for an expansion club, Farrell expressed dismay that he was picked over Mejías. On the other hand, Mejías refused to raise issues of racial discrimination in the selection process. Though disappointed by the player balloting and Hutchinson's choice of Richie Ashburn and Johnny Callison as reserve outfielders, he stated, "How do you like dot [*sic*]? Well, nothing to do but jus' keep swinging."[27]

But Mejías did not keep swinging as effectively during the second half of the 1962 season. Talk of the Colts finishing in the first division and Mejías attaining 30 to 40 home runs faded in the hot Texas sun of August and September. Slowed by nagging injuries and adjustments by opposing pitchers, his power numbers declined. Meanwhile, the hard-throwing and hard-partying Farrell became the darling of the Colts fans and media. The slumping Latino, Mejías, received generally respectful but certainly reduced attention.[28]

Nonetheless, Mejías ended the season with respectable numbers. He led the Colts in home runs (24), RBIs (76), and batting average (.286). He was really the only slugger on the team—the team's runner-up in homers, Carl Warwick, had just 16. Yet when Dick Peebles compiled a review of Colts highlights for the inaugural campaign, the contributions of Román Mejías were conspicuously missing.[29]

This was still a club that needed to build, and it was not a total surprise when Mejías was traded after the 1962 season—manager Harry Craft had said that any player was expendable. But the transaction was hardly part of a youth movement by Houston management. On November 26 Mejías was dealt to the Boston Red Sox for American League batting champion Pete Runnels. Mejías was either 30 or 32, depending upon which birthday one chose to count—but there was no doubt as to Runnels' rather advanced baseball age of 34. Also, Runnels had little speed or power (just 10 homers and 60 RBIs during 1962).

So why did Houston make the trade? Marketing was a factor. While Houston executives apparently saw little potential in the Hispanic market of Texas, they were very interested in acquiring Runnels, a native of Lufkin, Texas, who resided in the Houston suburb of Pasadena. According to Houston sportswriter Clark Nealon in *The Sporting News*, the Colts had been trying for two years to land Runnels, a three-sport star at Lufkin High who had also attended Houston's Rice University before turning pro in baseball. [30]

In his 1999 history of the Colt .45s, Robert Reed illustrated the role played by ethnic stereotypes in the controversial trade, arguing that Houston general manager Paul Richards was convinced that the "affable Cuban" was 39 years old rather than the "official" 30. But the transaction was risky because Mejías had "become somewhat of a fan favorite for his happy-go-lucky nature and occasionally unintentionally humorous turn of a phrase." Reed, whose training was in journalism, seemed to have no problem with perpetuating the outdated image of the smiling, but somewhat lackadaisical, Latin ballplayer.[31]

As for Mejías, he was wished the best of luck by his former manager, Craft, who insisted, "He is a fine competitor. He carried us for the first two months of the season. … There were two reasons for his slump. He had played winter ball and started to run out of gas. Then he got hurt, missed a

couple of weeks and when he got back into the lineup he couldn't generate the steam he had before."[32] However, Craft failed to mention Mejías's growing concerns regarding his family in Cuba. Though the separation from his wife and two children was weighing upon his performance, Houston management showed little concern.

On the other hand, after acquiring Mejías, Red Sox owner Tom Yawkey instructed his front office to spare no expense in reuniting the ballplayer with his family. Red Sox management worked with the State Department and the Red Cross to, in the overwrought Cold War rhetoric of reporter Hy Hurwitz, "ransom the outfielder's brood from the clutches of Castroism."[33] Accordingly, on the evening of March 16, 1963, Román Mejías's spring training in Phoenix was interrupted with the arrival of Nicolasa, 12-year-old Rafaela, 10-year-old José, and the athlete's two younger sisters, Esperosa and Santa. He hadn't seen them for 15 months. Señora Mejías had only been permitted to bring three dresses and one pair of shoes. The children were allowed only to bring the clothes they wore.[34] Following this joyous reunion, Mejías expressed his appreciation for the Red Sox organization, exclaiming, "Now, I don't have to worry any more, and I can't thank the Red Sox enough. I want to do everything possible for the Red Sox, and I hope very soon I'll be helping them win the pennant."[35]

The Red Sox had added slugger Dick Stuart the week before they'd added Mejías. They were looking forward to a real one-two punch. However, baseball reality failed to mirror the happiness of the Mejías family reunion. He had some good moments, certainly, such as the two-run double he hit in the bottom of the 15th inning on April 20 to cap a 4-3 Red Sox victory. On June 16 he hit three homers in a doubleheader, helping the Red Sox sweep Baltimore. It was "Maine Day" at Fenway Park, and Mejías received a toboggan as prize. The gift convinced him to spend the winter with his family in Boston.[36]

But Mejías first climbed above .200 only by June 22 and never got above .228 all year long. He finished the season at .227, with just 11 homers and 39 RBIs. He may have placed too much pressure on himself to show his appreciation for the Red Sox—but columnist George Vecsey argued that Mejías was another righty power hitter who pressed too hard while taking aim at Fenway Park's inviting Green Monster in left field.[37]

After the season ended, Mejías took part in the one and only Latin All-Star game at the Polo Grounds on October 12. The charity game, which benefited the Hispanic-American Baseball Federation, was the last time baseball was ever played at the ballpark before it was demolished.

Mejías's output declined even more during his second season in Boston, with a batting average of .238, two homers, and four RBIs in just 101 at-bats—his last in the majors. However, Pete Runnels' return to his home state was even less productive and shorter-lived. In 1963 the Texan hit only.253-2-23. After going 10-for-51 (.196) to start 1964, Runnels retired in the middle of May.

Mejías played winter ball in 1964-65, going back to Puerto Rico after a couple of seasons away. He then served as a player-coach for Boston's Triple-A team, the Toronto Maple Leafs, in 1965. He hit .269 in 99 games with nine homers and 46 RBIs. The Boston organization sought to assign the veteran to Double-A Pittsfield in 1966, but he refused to report, and the team released him so that he could accept an offer in Japan.[38] Mejías played 30 games for the Sankei Atoms in the Central League (.288-0-4).

That was Mejías's final season playing professional baseball. As late as 1985, however, he was still playing ball—softball, for the Orlando Cepeda All-Pro Stars. This squad—which also featured Wes Parker, Don Buford, and Dick Simpson, among other major leaguers—paid a visit to another of New York's since-demolished ballparks, Shea Stadium. The team competed in the Los Angeles Advertising Softball League.[39] Mejías had moved to LA, where he invested some of his baseball earnings in an apartment building.

In 1999 author Jack Heyde met with Mejías as part of his series of visits with players from baseball's "Golden Era." Mejías talked about how Bill Mazeroski was a good friend to him with the Pirates, making him learn one new word in English each day—although the theft of his car wheels on a snowy winter day colored his feelings towards the city of Pittsburgh. Heyde concluded, "I feel very happy to have met and visited with Román. He is a man of unique pride, as evidenced by the meticulous care that he takes in maintaining his home, his property, and his flowers. … He is a genuinely friendly and appreciative person, the type one wishes the best for."[40]

Sources

This biography was adapted by Rory Costello and Bill Nowlin from Ron Briley's work on Román Mejías, which has a much deeper focus on his year in Houston.

"Roman Mejias: Houston's First Major League Latin Star and the Troubled Legacy of Race Relations in the Lone Star State," *Nine*, Volume 10, No. 1 (Fall 2001), 73–88.

Chapter 16 of *Class at Bat, Gender on Deck and Race in the Hole* (Jefferson, North Carolina: McFarland & Co., 2003).

Books (thanks to SABR member José Ramírez for research from the Cuban sources):

Jorge S. Figueredo, *Who's Who in Cuban Baseball, 1878-1961* (Jefferson, North Carolina: McFarland & Company, 2003).

Roberto González Echevarría, *The Pride of Havana* (New York: Oxford University Press, 1999).

Ángel Torres, *La Leyenda del Béisbol Cubano, 1878-1997* (Montebello, California: Self-published, 1997).

Robert Reed, *Colt .45s: A Six-Gun Salute* (Boulder, Colorado: Taylor Trade Publishing, 1999).

Newspaper and magazine articles:

Román Mejías File, Baseball Hall of Fame Museum and Library, Cooperstown, New York.

Internet resources

Bill Thompson's biographical web page on Román Mejías (http://thompsonian.info/roman-mejias.html). On this page, one may find a scanned copy of *Here Come the Colts — Roman Mejias*, by Joe Reichler of the Associated Press. This eight-page booklet was published in 1962 by the Houston Sports Association/Prentice-Hall, Inc.

www.baseball-reference.com

www.retrosheet.org

www.japanbaseballdaily.com (Japanese statistics)

Notes

1   Clay Coppedge, *Texas Baseball* (Charleston, South Carolina: The History Press, 2012), 77.

2   Player questionnaire that Mejías completed and returned to the National Baseball Hall of Fame.

3   Ángel Torres, *La Leyenda del Béisbol Cubano, 1878-1997* (Montebello, California: Self-published, 1997), 185. Translated passage: "The outfielder Román Mejías was born in the Manuelita Sugar Mill in the Las Villas Province on the 9th of August, 1930—not in Abreus, as it reads in the *Macmillan Baseball Encyclopedia*, or in Río Damují, as stated in the *Official Baseball Encyclopedia* by Hy Turkin and S.C. Thompson. According to *Who's Who in Baseball*, he was simply born in Las Villas in 1932. In the old records of the Cuban League, his birthplace was shown to be in Central Manuelita, Matanzas instead of Las Villas. All

this left me very confused and I had to find Mejías where he resides in Los Angeles so he would clarify this."

4 In 1976 Cuba's original six provinces were subdivided. This area is today in the province of Cienfuegos.

5 Joe Reichler, *Here Come the Colts — Roman Mejías.*

6 Mejías player questionnaire, National Baseball Hall of Fame.

7 Torres, *La Leyenda del Béisbol Cubano, 1878-1997.*

8 *New York Times,* August 1, 1954.

9 Les Biederman, "Bucs Found Mejias Loading Cane in Interior of Cuba," *The Sporting News,* April 20, 1955, 11. This article misspelled Mejías' first name as "Ramon" and de Arcos' name as "Munchy D'Arcos." SABR's Scouts Committee gives the credit, as was often the case with international signings, to several men: Corito Varona, regional superscout Howie Haak, and Sisler.

10 *Boston Globe,* November 26, 1962.

11 *New York Times,* August 1, 1954. The *Times* story ran after the streak had reached 53 games. The *Los Angeles Times* of March 1, 1986, is one of the publications listing the 55-game streak.

12 Oscar Larnce, "Mejias of Waco Batting .345 for Pirate Farm Club," *The Sporting News,* August 11, 1954, 35.

13 For issues of segregation in minor league baseball, see Bruce Adelson, *Brushing Back Jim Crow: The Integration of Minor-League Baseball in the American South* (Charlottesville, Virginia: University of Virginia Press, 1999).

14 Peter C. Bjarkman, *Baseball With a Latin Beat: A History of the Latin American Game* (Jefferson, North Carolina: McFarland & Co., 1994), 6.

15 Mickey Herskowitz, ".45s Charge Puny Attack with Missile Man Mejias," *The Sporting News,* June 2, 1962.

16 Samuel O. Regalado, *Viva Baseball: Latin Major Leaguers and Their Special Hunger* (Urbana: University of Illinois Press, 1998), xiv.

17 Roberto González Echevarría, *The Pride of Havana* (New York: Oxford University Press, 1999), 323.

18 Bruce Markusen, *Roberto Clemente: The Great One* (Champaign, Illinois: Sports Publishing, LLC, 2001), 41.

19 Ruben Rodriguez, "Shaw Shapes Up to Follow Jim Bunning," *The Sporting News,* January 22, 1958, 24.

20 Ruben Rodriguez, "Reds Smash Way Into Hot Pennant Fight," *The Sporting News,* January 15, 1958, 20.

21 Les Biederman, "Pirates Tab Three to Back Virdon as Middle Gardeners," *The Sporting News,* January 22, 1958, 18.

22 Ruben Rodriguez, "Marianao, Almendares Set Up Two-Club Race," *The Sporting News,* December 3, 1958, 29.

23 Jim Pendleton was the team's only African-American until J.C. Hartman was called up at midseason.

24 *The Sporting News,* April 18, 1962, and *Houston Chronicle,* April 11, 1962.

25 Zarko Franks, "Mejias' Season of Milk, Honey?" *Houston Chronicle,* May 30, 1962.

26 Franks, "Mejias' Season of Milk, Honey?"

27 *Houston Chronicle,* June 30, 1962; *The Sporting News,* July 14, 1962; Reed, *Colt.45s: A Six-Gun Salute,* 112-13.

28 *Houston Chronicle,* July 21, 1962.

29 *Houston Chronicle,* August 28 and September 24, 1962.

30 For the Mejías-Runnels trade, see *New York Times,* November 26, 1962, and *The Sporting News,* December 8, 1962.

31 Reed, *Colt.45s: A Six-Gun Salute,* 140.

32 *The Sporting News,* March 3, 1963.

33 Hy Hurwitz, "Red Sox Worked to Rescue Mejias' Family from Cuba," *The Sporting News,* March 30, 1963.

34 *Chicago Tribune,* March 17, 1963.

35 Hy Hurwitz, "Red Sox Worked to Rescue Mejias' Family from Cuba," *The Sporting News,* March 30, 1963.

36 Bryant Rollins, "Toboggan Sways Him — Mejias to Winter Here," *Boston Globe,* June 23, 1963.

37 George Vecsey, "Boston's 'Dream' Wall Is Really a Nightmare," July 13, 1963, clipping from Román Mejías File, Baseball Hall of Fame Museum and Library, Cooperstown, New York.

38 *The Sporting News,* July 2, 1966, 52.

39 Jim Coleman, "Shades of Shea: Ghosts of Pennant Races Past Haven't Changed, but Their Playing Field Has," *Los Angeles Times,* July 18, 1985.

40 Jack Heyde, *Pop Flies and Line Drives: Visits with Players from Baseball's "Golden Era"* (Victoria, British Columbia: Trafford Publishing, 2004), 72-73.

Wilmer "Vinegar Bend" Mizell

By Michael H. Jaffe

THE SMALL COMMUNITY of Vinegar Bend, Alabama, provided an unusual nickname to major-league pitcher and U S Congressman Wilmer "Vinegar Bend" Mizell. Contrary to the belief that he was born in Vinegar Bend, Wilmer was born in neighboring Leakesville, Mississippi, and graduated from high school there in 1949, but the little town of fewer than 200 people on the other side of the state line offered a better moniker.[1] The town of Vinegar Bend got its name when a train passing through the area careened off the tracks and spilled its load of vinegar there. Mizell was born on August 13, 1930, to Walter David and Addie Turner Mizell, and routinely received his mail in the Washington County, Alabama, town his nickname made famous.

Walter Mizell died when Wilmer was only 2 years old and his mother became sick shortly thereafter, so he was raised by his grandmother and uncle. Young Wilmer's throwing motion was so wild that his older brother couldn't play catch with him. He improved his control by throwing at a knothole in the side of the family's smokehouse until he knocked the door down. He further refined his skills throwing rocks while hunting squirrels. The family earned their living as subsistence farmers raising cattle and hogs as well as growing fruits and vegetables. Wilmer also earned money tapping pine trees for turpentine, logging, and hauling hardwood from the swamps along the Escatawpa and Chickasawhay Rivers.

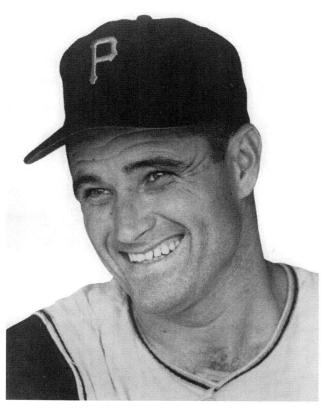

Mizell started playing baseball when he was 16 years old and pitched in Sunday leagues around Vinegar Bend, which became his adopted home. In 1948, when he was 17, he attended a St. Louis Cardinals tryout camp in Biloxi, Mississippi, and the left-hander struck out the only three batters he faced before the camp shut down due to a rainstorm. Buddy Lewis, a Cardinals scout, took note of the youngster and made a point to watch him pitch again the following spring. When Lewis returned on Mizell's high-school graduation day to watch him pitch, Vinegar Bend showed up barefoot, having just returned from a swimming hole. He pitched for the scout barefoot and his fastball had such great movement that Lewis offered to sign him after graduation for $500. Later that evening, Mizell received his high-school diploma, signed his contract, and left on a train for Georgia after the graduation without even returning home from the ceremony.

Mizell was first assigned to Albany, Georgia, of the class D Georgia-Florida League. Having never been more than 50 miles from home, he became homesick and did not unpack his suitcase for a month after arriving. His debut was inauspicious, with his first professional pitch landing 20 feet above the backstop. After his nerves settled, he went on to go 12-3 with a 1.98 ERA, striking out 175 batters in 141 innings as Albany won the league pennant.

In 1950 Mizell pitched Winston-Salem to the championship of the Class B Carolina League, where he compiled a 17-7 record and a team-leading 2.48 ERA despite a 1-6 start. He struck out 227 and walked 81 in 207 innings. In the final game of the season, against Burlington, Mizell hit the only home run of his professional career in a 3-2 victory. The crowd passed the hat and he collected $220. He later commented, "I would have liked for my homer to win the game 1-0, and referred to the home run as his "$220 homer."[2]

Moved up to the Houston Buffaloes in 1951, Mizell led the Texas League with 257 strikeouts in 238 innings (18 in a game against Dallas tying the league record), and was 16-14 with a 1.96 ERA. For one game the ballclub sponsored a Vinegar Bend Mizell Night and brought in more than 30 members of his family and friends from Vinegar Bend (a good percentage of the town's population) by bus. Mizell responded by striking out 15 Shreveport batters but taking a 3-1 loss. During the Cardinals spring training in 1952, sportswriter Red Smith described Mizell as a "left-handed Dizzy Dean," comparing his delivery to Dean's "loose, easy motion" with "a singing fastball."[3]

On February 14, 1952, Mizell's local draft board ordered him to report for induction into the Army. He applied for and was granted a deferment because he was supporting his ailing mother and grandmother. With that out of the way, Mizell stuck with the Cardinals in 1952, and made his major-league debut on April 22, in Cincinnati. He gave up two runs on three walks and a triple by Joe Adcock in the first inning, then held the Reds scoreless for the rest of the 2-1 loss. Before the game Mizell had complained of a toothache and the team doctor found that he had a wisdom tooth cutting through the gum line.

Mizell also lost his second start, 6-3, to the Cubs on April 27. His first major-league victory came in his next start, on May 2, as the Cardinals defeated the Phillies, 3-2, a complete-game four-hitter for Vinegar Bend. (After the win he celebrated by happily parading around the Cardinals' humid locker room and steamy shower-room until a fellow Redbird reminded him that he still had his red windbreaker on.)

Mizell finished the 1952 season with a 10-8 record and a 3.65 ERA, giving up 171 hits, striking out 146 batters, and allowing a league-leading 103 walks in 190 innings (he led the league in strikeouts per nine innings pitched). After the season, on November 16, he married Nancy Ruth McAlpine.

Wildness (114 walks in 224 innings) continued to be a problem for the 6-foot-3 Mizell in 1953, as he won 13 games and lost 11 with a 3.49 ERA. The highlight of his season was a two-hit shutout against the Pittsburgh Pirates on May 4, and his 6.9 strikeouts per nine innings pitched led the league again. A week after the end of the season, after two deferments, he was inducted into the Army. Stationed at Fort McPherson, Georgia, he continued to pitch. In two seasons of service ball he compiled a

record of 36-2 (22-0 in 1955 with four no-hitters and 16 shutouts in all). He pitched his team into the All-Army championship in Fort Belvoir, Virginia, in 1955. Working on his curveball and slider, he struck out 324 strikeouts and walked only 48 (mostly against GIs who had never played professionally). He was discharged as a sergeant on October 5, 1955.

After his discharge Mizell played winter ball in the Cuban League, and showed that he had lost very little in his two years away from the professional game. In Havana he struck out 206 batters, a league record, and fanned 15 strikeouts in a game, also a record. He finished second in the league's MVP voting with a 12-9 record and a 2.16 ERA. In February 1956, while he was still in Cuba, Nancy gave birth to their first child, Wilmer Jr. When he heard the news of his new son, legend has it, he was so preoccupied that he stepped to the plate with his glove instead of a bat.

Mizell returned to the Cardinals for the 1956 season. St. Louis was about a .500 club (76-78), and so was Mizell, at 14-14, with a 3.62 ERA. His 14 victories were his major-league high. (He won 14 again in 1960.)

In 1956 Mizell seemed to have lost something off his blazing fastball, and that continued in early 1957; it seemed even flatter, and his control was not sharp. He was also giving up more home runs than before he went in the service (20 in 1956 and 18 in 1957). There were concerns over Mizell's weight and his exaggerated windup motion. After 97 starts for the Cardinals, he was sent to the bullpen for the first time in his career. Pitching out of the bullpen, making an occasional start, and watching films of his delivery (a new concept at the time), Mizell finally regained his control in midseason and finished with an 8-10 record. His strikeouts were down, but so were his walks. At one point the Cardinals tried to option Mizell to Houston in hopes that he could work out his control problems there, but they couldn't get waivers on him

Mizell spent the offseason before the 1958 season working out with a steel ball to keep his arm strong, and doing other exercises. When he signed a $17,000 contract for the 1958 season (the same as his 1957 contract) he proclaimed that he was 12 pounds lighter than his spring reporting weight in 1957. He showed up to spring training early, determined to improve his performance. Pitching primarily as a starter (only one relief appearance) Mizell finished the season with a 10-14 record and a 3.42 ERA (the eighth lowest in the league). His walk ratio increased again, to 4.3 per nine innings, and his strikeout ratio dropped to 3.8. His high point may have been a duel with Joe Nuxhall of the Reds on Labor Day. Mizell won, 1-0, but walked nine batters, setting a National League record for the most walks allowed in a shutout. At the end of the season, the Cardinals embarked on a goodwill tour to Japan; Mizell pitched well in those games.

Mizell continued to stay in shape during the offseason, working out at a YMCA across from Busch Stadium. He was a holdout but eventually signed another $17,000 contract. Vinegar Bend looked good as the season started and seemed to have his fastball back to his pre-Army velocity. He finished with a 13-10 record for the seventh-place Cardinals. His walk ratio was down and his strikeout ratio was up, but his earned-run average rose to 4.20. Mizell was named to the National League All-Star team for the only time in his career, but had back troubles and was replaced on the All-Star roster by Don Elston. The first half of the season Mizell was 9-3 with a 3.05 ERA. After the All-Star Game his fortunes changed, with a 4-7 record and a 5.94 ERA in the second half of the season.

Mizell's career with the Cardinals ended in 1960. On May 28 he was traded with infielder Dick Gray to the Pittsburgh Pirates for infielder Julian Javier and right-handed pitching prospect Ed Bauta. The Cardinals were in need of a second baseman and the 23-year-old Javier was blocked at that position in Pittsburgh by Bill Mazeroski. The Cardinals felt that Mizell had never lived up to his potential. Javier remained a fixture in the St. Louis lineup for the rest of the season, starting in every game after the trade. Mizell was 1-3 for the Cardinals and had been hit hard in his nine starts, allowing 10.4 hits per nine innings despite an impressive strikeout rate of 6.8 that nearly matched his pre-military days. But his acquisition was critical to Pittsburgh's pennant run, as he started 23 games for the Pirates, going 13-5 with a 3.12 ERA. He had one impressive stretch of 30 consecutive scoreless innings, the longest such stretch in his career, and cut his walk rate nearly in half. The trade benefited the Pirates in other ways; they no longer had to face Mizell, who owned a 14-6 record against the Bucs to that point. Mizell's high point of the season came on July 29 when he tossed a two-hit shutout in defeating the Cubs 4-0. He also threw a three-hit shutout against the Reds in a 1-0 victory on September 18.

In the World Series—Mizell's only trip to the postseason—the Pirates faced the New York Yankees in the World Series that year and Mizell pitched in two games. He started Game Three in New York and didn't last long, lasting just a third of an inning and allowing four runs on three hits and a walk. Mizell took the loss as the Yankees won, 10-0. In Game Six, a 12-0 laugher for the Yankees, Mizell came on in relief in the fourth inning. He pitched two scoreless innings, allowing one hit and a walk and striking out Roger Maris. (Roger was the only batter Mizell had retired in his Game Three loss.) Vinegar Bend's pitching line for the Series was an 0-1 record, 2 1/3 innings pitched, four hits, four runs (all earned), a 15.43 ERA, two walks and one strikeout. The Pirates won the Series on a dramatic walkoff home run by Bill Mazeroski in Game Seven.

Mizell remained a Pirate in 1961. He started 17 games and relieved in eight. His 7-10 record and 5.04 ERA were career worsts for him, highlighted perhaps by his 4-3 vistory over his former Cardinals teammates on May 17. Mizell had twice lost to the Cardinals since his trade. (For his career, Mizell did best against his own Pirates, with his 14-7 record against them before he was traded to the Bucs. At one point Mizell was 14-3 against the Chicago Cubs, but the Cubs rebounded, against him winning 12 of the next 16 decisions.)

In 1962 Mizell reported to spring camp three days late because of the birth of his second son, James Daniel Mizell, in St. Louis. In his first start of the season he shut down the brand-new New York Mets, allowing one unearned run in seven innings. After going 1-1 in three starts and four relief appearances, Mizell was traded to the Mets for first baseman Jim Marshall on May 7. The trade was not well received among Pirates fans, who appreciated Mizell's efforts in the run to the 1960 championship, and by his teammates, among whom he was popular because of his good nature and strong religious beliefs.

The 31-year-old Mizell pitched in 17 games for the lowly Mets (two starts) and was 0-2 with a 7.34 ERA. The Mets released him on August 4. The defeat of the Mets early in the season turned out to be Mizell's 90th and final major-league victory. Mizell accepted an offer to pitch for the Columbus Jets, the Triple-A affiliate of the Pirates. Until roster room could be cleared for him, he agreed to serve as an instructor. Mizell pitched in four games for the Jets, starting three. He compiled a 2-1 record with a 3.27 ERA.

After the season Mizell worked out in the Arizona Instructional League in hopes of re-gaining his form. But no team offered him a job for the 1963 season, and at 32 he retired as a player. In May he became a broadcaster for Winston-Salem, one of his old minor-league teams. That same year he took a job with the Pepsi-Cola Co. as a sales manager and public relations executive. In the fall he was elected to the board of county commissioners for Davidson County, North Carolina. In 1966 he was the board's chairman. Mizell left Pepsi-Cola in 1967, and in 1968 he was elected to the US House of Representatives from North Carolina. A Republican, he spent three terms in the House and was defeated in 1974, an election in the aftermath of the Watergate scandal in which many Republican lawmakers were unseated.

In 1975 President Gerald Ford named Mizell the assistant secretary of commerce for economic development. In 1976 Mizell made another run for Congress but was defeated. In 1981 he was appointed assistant secretary of agriculture for governmental and public affairs in the Reagan administration. In the administration of George Bush the elder, he was deputy assistant secretary for intergovernmental affairs in the Department of Veterans Affairs. He also served as executive director of the President's Council on Physical Fitness and Sports.

Nancy Mizell died on November 30, 1990. In 1991 Vinegar Bend married Ruth Cox, whom he had met in Washington at a prayer breakfast. They worked through the ensuing years promoting prayer study.

Mizell died of a heart attack on February 21, 1999, at the age of 68, while visiting family in Kerrville, Texas. He was buried in Faith Missionary Alliance Church Cemetery, Winston-Salem. He was survived by Ruth, his two sons, and four grandchildren.

Mizell was best known in baseball for his Southern drawl and country-boy wit. His laid-back walk and style were a hit with fans and teammates as he was often compared to the comic strip character Li'l Abner. He was once asked why he never swore. Vinegar Bend's simple reply was, "Son, I decided a long time ago swearin' was a waste of words. You cain't get a man out by cussin' him out."[4] Never at a loss for a good story, Mizell once recalled, "The worst thing that happened to us back home in Vinegar Bend was the time we had the fire. It started in the bathroom. Fortunately, we were able to put it out before it reached the house."[5]

Mizell's pitching motion was a bit unorthodox; he was known for hiding the ball well before he delivered his pitch. Teammate Ken Boyer once commented that "the guy shows you his glove, his rear, and somebody tells you it's a strike."[6] Mizell never reached his potential, as many believed that he would someday be a 20-game winner. His two-year service in the military at the peak of his career hurt his statistics. Despite this, he was remembered by teammates as a great clubhouse presence who always had a smile on his face. His abilities on the mound in his prime were noted by players widely for his dominance at times.

Sources

Newspaper and Magazines

Mercer Bailey, "Mizell Will Get To Finish Season," *Tuscaloosa* (Alabama) *News*, September 10, 1953.

Bob Broeg, "'Vinegar Bend' Strikeout Star of the Texas League," *The Sporting News*, April 23, 1952.

Bob Broeg, "Mizell Cuts a Molar, Loses in Debut by Skin of Teeth," *The Sporting News*, April 30, 1952.

Bob Broeg, "Vinegar Visions Win Bulge With Trimmed Torso," *The Sporting News*, January 15, 1958.

Richard Goldstein, "Vinegar Bend Mizell, Pitcher, Is Dead at 68," *New York Times*, February 23, 1999.

Harry Grayson, "Vinegar Bend Acting Like Anything But A Dizzy Dean," *Gastonia* (North Carolina) *Gazette*, March 15, 1956.

Milton Gross, "Want Color? Here Comes Mizell," *Baseball Digest*, November 1951.

John Malmo, "Mizell Prepares to 'Sharpen Up' in Winter Ball," *The Sporting News*, October 12, 1955.

Red Marston, "Cards Count on Vinegar to Catch Fans," *The Sporting News*, March 28, 1956.

Red Smith, "Views of Sport," *Youngstown* (Ohio) *Vindicator*, March 21, 1951.

"Board Defers Cards' Vinegar Bend Mizell," *St. Petersburg* (Florida) *Times*, March 16, 1952.

"Cardinals Sign Wilmer Mizell In Youth Move," *Tuscaloosa* (Alabama) *News*, January 1, 1952.

"Chiefs-Asheville Tangle at Stadium," *Rock Hill* (South Carolina) *Herald*, September 8, 1951.

"From Cracker Barrel to Top Comes Vinegar Bend Mizell," *Lawrence* (Kansas) *Journal World*, March 6, 1951.

"Mizell Receives Orders To Don Army Khakis," *St. Petersburg* (Florida) *Times*, February 1, 1952.

"Mizell Will be Released by Mets," *Bonham* (Texas) *Daily Favorite*, August 1, 1962.

"Mizell Yields Spot to Elston," *Kingsport* (Tennessee) *Times*, July 5, 1959.

"'Vinegar Bend' Inks Cardinal Contract," *Telegraph-Herald* (Dubuque, Iowa), January 1, 1952.

"'Vinegar Bend' Mizell Running For Congress," *Times-News* (Hendersonville, North Carolina), February 6, 1968.

"Vinegar Bend to Pittsburgh," *Leader Post*, Regina, Saskatchewan, May 28, 1960.

Bill McCurdy, "Wilmer David Mizell: The Buff from Vinegar Bend!," http://bill37mccurdy.wordpress.com/2009/09/02/wilmer-david-mizell-the-buff-from-vinegar-bend/, accessed January 30, 2011.

Notes

1   Richard Goldstein, "Vinegar Bend Mizell, Pitcher, Is Dead at 68," *New York Times*, February 23, 1999.

2   Milton Gross, "Want Color? Here Comes Mizell," *Baseball Digest*, November 1951.

3   Red Smith, "Views of Sport," *Youngstown Vindicator*, March 21, 1951.

4   Red Marston, "Cards Count on Vinegar to Catch Fans," *The Sporting News*, March 28, 1956.

5   Bill McCurdy, "Wilmer David Mizell: The Buff from Vinegar Bend!," http://bill37mccurdy.wordpress.com/2009/09/02/wilmer-david-mizell-the-buff-from-vinegar-bend/, accessed January 30, 2011.

6   Red Marston, "Cards Count on Vinegar to Catch Fans," *The Sporting News*, March 28, 1956.

Rocky Nelson

By David L. Fleitz

ROCKY NELSON CAME to Cleveland in the spring of 1954 with an impressive pedigree. He had won the Most Valuable Player award in the International League in 1953 and followed it up with a fine performance in the Cuban Winter League, where he won the batting championship. The Indians expected Nelson to win the starting position at first base, but the minor-league sensation struggled mightily in spring training and, though he made the Opening Day roster, he appeared in only four games for the Indians. He failed to hit safely in four times at bat, and in mid-May Cleveland sent Nelson back to the minor leagues, from which he eventually emerged to play backup roles with the Brooklyn Dodgers, St. Louis Cardinals and Pittsburgh Pirates.

Born in Portsmouth, Ohio, on November 18, 1924, Glenn Richard Nelson, called Spike as a child, was the second and last child of Marshall and Esta (Sunday) Nelson. Marshall worked as a catcher in a steel mill when Glenn and his brother, Alfred, two years older, were young. But by 1940 he held a job as a processing clerk in a WPA program. (The Works Progress Administration was a New Deal creation that put unemployed Americans to work on public projects.) As a youth Glenn was a batboy for the Portsmouth Red Birds, a St. Louis Cardinals farm club in the Mid-Atlantic League. A left-handed pitcher who stood 5-feet-10, he starred on the baseball team at Portsmouth High School and was signed by the Cardinals in 1942. Nelson earned his nickname in a Cardinals training camp when teammate Whitey Kurowski bounced a ball off his head during a pepper game. Nelson was unhurt, and Kurowski tagged him with the name Rocky, which he carried for the rest of his life.

Cardinals general manager Branch Rickey, enamored of Nelson's hitting skill, shifted the youngster to first base and sent him to Johnson City in the Appalachian League. The 17-year-old batted .253 that season, then enlisted in the US Army on February 20, 1943, and served three years, including time in the Pacific theater during World War II. Returning to the Cardinals organization in 1946, Nelson won the Piedmont League batting title for Lynchburg in 1947. On August 20 of that year, he married Alberta Burns of Portsmouth in a pregame ceremony at home plate.

Nelson wore out minor-league pitching and, after hitting .303 for Rochester in 1948, earned a shot in the big leagues with the Cardinals in 1949. He shared the first-base job with Nippy Jones, but batted only .221 with four homers in 82 games, driving in 32 runs. The Cardinals, hampered by weak offensive production at the first-base position, lost the pennant to the Brooklyn Dodgers that year by one game. Sent down to Columbus in 1950, Nelson battered American Association pitching for a .418 average in 48 games, but hit poorly after his recall to St. Louis. He was quickly earning a reputation as a minor-league superstar who could not, for whatever reason, break through at the major-league level.

The Cardinals gave up on Rocky after another slow start at the plate in 1951 and traded him to the Pittsburgh Pirates in May. He hit better for the Pirates, posting a .267 average, but his lack of power (one homer in 71 games) led the club to put him on waivers in September. The White Sox picked Nelson up, then sent the 27-year-old player to the Brooklyn Dodgers, where he spent the 1952 season recovering from a broken leg and backing up Gil Hodges at first base. He played little, batting only 46 times and going hitless in four World Series plate appearances, and found himself back in the minor leagues with Brooklyn's top farm team, the Montreal Royals, in 1953.

Despite his troubles, Rocky was popular with fans and teammates. He was a colorful individual and clubhouse prankster with one of the most unusual batting stances in the game; as Jim Murray of the *Los Angeles Times* described it, his stance was "right out of a lithograph from the archives of baseball—right foot at right angles to the left foot, knees bent. It was so archaic that a magazine once devoted a whole, fascinated story to it on the notion it was obscene to have this kind of a stance without a handlebar mustache to go with it." Murray also wrote that Rocky "was a marathon talker who chain-smoked evil-smelling Cuban rope cigars. He even smoked them in bed, and roomie Gino Cimoli once told me he got tired of answering excited calls from hotel switchboards who thought the room was on fire."[1]

In Montreal Nelson suddenly found his power stroke. On a team managed by Walter Alston and filled with future major leaguers including Tommy Lasorda, Don Hoak, and Dick Williams, Nelson led the International League with 34 home runs and 136 runs batted in, earning Most Valuable Player honors. This performance established Nelson as a hot prospect once again, but because Gil Hodges owned the first-base job in Brooklyn, Rocky would have to play elsewhere to establish himself in the majors. In October 1953 the Dodgers sent Rocky to the Cleveland Indians for pitcher Bill Abernathie and a reported $15,000.

The Indians had finished second to the pennant-winning Yankees in 1953 despite a glaring weakness at first base. Luke Easter, the veteran first sacker, was 37 years old and could no longer play the field, while Bill Glynn, a slick glove man who had led the league in fielding percentage, was a mediocre hitter best suited to a role as a late-inning defensive replacement. Manager Al Lopez hoped that Nelson, the minor-league slugging sensation, could fill the first-base hole and provide more power for the Cleveland offense. Walter Alston gave Nelson a strong recommendation. "I don't see how he can miss if he plays the kind of first base for Cleveland that he did for me all year," Alston told *The Sporting News*.[2]

Rocky welcomed the opportunity. "In my opinion," he said in February of 1954, "I've never had a chance in the big leagues to stay in the lineup long enough at one time to show what I could do."[3] But he got off to a bad start in spring training, hitting poorly and fielding worse. In a game against the New York Giants in Tulsa, Oklahoma, Rocky failed to catch two popups and misplayed a line drive into a three-base error. Lopez nonetheless remained hopeful. "I'm going to keep him on first, especially after an exhibition like that," said the Cleveland manager. "If I jerked him out of there now, I would really ruin his morale."[4] In mid-March Lopez offered encouragement. "I'm sure he can do better than he has shown so far," he told the press. "I know he's a good glove man, but he hasn't even been impressive in the field. That's what makes me think he's pressing, trying too hard."[5]

As Rocky's spring average fell to the .150 level, another newcomer, infielder Rudy Regalado, impressed the Cleveland management with his strong hitting and fielding. Regalado quickly became the darling of the local sportswriters, while Lopez and general manager Hank Greenberg considered a plan to move star third baseman Al Rosen to first base, with Regalado on third. Nelson earned a spot on the Cleveland roster, but watched from the bench on Opening Day as Bill Glynn, who hit well in

spring training, played first. Nelson entered the game in the eighth inning as a defensive replacement, but did not bat as the Indians pounded the Chicago White Sox, 8-2.

The presence of Regalado, and an unexpected season-opening hot streak by Glynn, spelled the end for Nelson in Cleveland. He played in four games as a pinch-hitter and late-inning replacement, with no hits in four times at bat, then spent the next few weeks on the bench. In late April, after Glynn's bat cooled down, the Indians moved Rosen to first base and inserted Regalado into the lineup at third. Nelson was the odd man out. He had failed his fifth major-league trial, and on May 11 the Indians returned Rocky to his previous club, the Montreal Royals. "Well, if I must play in the minors," said a disappointed Nelson, "I'd rather play with Montreal than with any other team."[6]

A few years later Nelson expressed his dissatisfaction with Cleveland management. "They gave me the position in the spring, sure, but they didn't spend all that money just to find out if I could hit in the spring," he told *Sports Illustrated* in 1958. "They bought me because of the great season I had in Montreal in '53. I've never been a good hitter in the spring. I need to get to know the pitchers. Even in the minors, what little hitting I do in the spring, I do against pitchers I've seen before. I never hit the new ones right at first. And that's the way it was up there. Just about the time I was learning what they could throw, I was on the bench. And then I was back at Montreal."[7]

Cleveland coach Red Kress had a different perspective. "You should have seen him that spring," said Kress. "He was tighter than a drum. Just plain nervous. He looked terrible; he couldn't even catch the ball. And at the plate, it wasn't some particular pitch that he couldn't hit. He couldn't hit strikes." Al Lopez agreed. "Rocky talked a lot," said Lopez, "and he gave the appearance of being nonchalant. But I think part of this was just a coverup. Inside he must have been burning."[8]

Predictably, Rocky turned into a slugger again upon his return to the minor leagues. Though he missed the first few weeks of the 1954 International League season, he led the circuit in home runs that year, and in 1955 he won the Triple Crown and another Most Valuable Player award. A .394 average in 1956 earned him another call-up to Brooklyn (where he was reunited with his old Montreal skipper, Walter Alston), but Nelson failed once again to

stick with the club. "It was a complex of some kind," said Fresco Thompson of the Dodgers. "Rocky looked just as bad for us as he looked good down in the minors."[9] Nelson developed an unfortunate knack for hitting long, arching fly balls over the right-field fence just barely foul. "If they had just moved the foul pole over about ten feet," one writer quipped, "Rocky would have broken Ruth's record in a breeze."[10] The Dodgers sent Nelson on waivers to the Cardinals, and at season's end St. Louis sold his contract to Toronto of the International League.

In Toronto Nelson won his second Triple Crown and third MVP award in 1958. This performance earned him another shot with Pittsburgh, a club that already owned two established first basemen in right-handed batter Dick Stuart and lefty slugger Ted Kluszewski. Rocky performed so well in spring training, however, that manager Danny Murtaugh kept all three first sackers on the roster as the 1959 season began.

Nelson started slowly, as usual, and served exclusively as a pinch-hitter in April and early May while Kluszewski went on a tear. Eventually, however, Rocky's bat came around, while Kluszewski went cold, batting .188 in June and .095 in July. Nelson claimed the backup first base job, cementing his hold on the position with two homers against the league-leading San Francisco Giants on August 24, leading the Pirates to a 6-0 win. The next day Pittsburgh management traded Kluszewski to the Chicago White Sox. Rocky batted .291 for the Pirates in 1959 with six homers, a performance that assured him a spot on the roster to start the 1960 season.

Solidly entrenched as Dick Stuart's backup, the 35-year-old Nelson enjoyed his finest major-league campaign in 1960. One memorable performance came on July 5, when he led off the ninth inning against the Braves in Milwaukee with the Pirates down 2-0. Nelson belted a homer off Carlton Willey, igniting a rally that put Pittsburgh ahead, 3-2. The Braves tied the score in the ninth, but in the tenth Rocky belted his second round-tripper of the day, a two-run shot off Joey Jay that proved the winning margin in a 5-4 Pirates win. In all, he played in 93 games for the Pirates in 1960 with 50 starts at first base, all against right-handed pitchers. He batted .300 with seven home runs, providing important support as the Pirates won their first pennant in 34 years and earned a World Series berth against the New York Yankees.

Though the Yankees named right-hander Art Ditmar as their starting pitcher for Game One of the Series, manager Murtaugh gave Dick Stuart the starting assignment at first base. Nelson started the second game, collecting two singles in five at-bats against right-hander Bob Turley as the Pirates fell by a 16-3 score. He appeared as a defensive replacement in Game Five and struck out as a pinch-hitter in Game Six, but with Turley on the mound in the deciding seventh game, Murtaugh put Nelson in the lineup in the cleanup spot. In the first inning Rocky smacked the biggest hit of his career, a two-run homer that gave the Pirates an early lead.

Nelson almost emerged as the goat of the Series. With one out in the top of the ninth inning and the Pirates leading 9-8, the Yankees had Gil McDougald at third and Mickey Mantle at first when Yogi Berra hit a sharp grounder to Rocky at first base. A 3-6-3 double play would have ended the game and given the Pirates the world championship, but instead of throwing to second, Nelson stepped on first to retire Berra, then turned his attention to Mantle, who was caught only a few feet away from him. Mantle somehow eluded Rocky's tag, twisting his way around the Pirates' first sacker and diving safely back to first as McDougald scored to tie the game. Fortunately for Nelson, all was forgotten when Bill Mazeroski led off the bottom of the inning with his Series-winning walk-off homer.

Nelson's hitting fell off sharply in 1961, and the Pirates released the 37-year-old at season's end. He played one more year in the minors, then retired from the game and opened a painting business in his hometown of Portsmouth, Ohio. He and his wife, Alberta, who had adopted a son in 1958, lived in Portsmouth until his death at the age of 81 on October 31, 2006.

Sources

Steve Treder, "Rocky Nelson," *The Hardball Times* (http://www.thehardballtimes.com), April 5, 2006.

Ed McAuley, "The Eternal Door-Knocker," *Baseball Digest*, March 1959.

Roy Terrell, "The Man With a Million and One Alibis," *Sports Illustrated*, August 18, 1958.

The Sporting News, November 18, 1953; February 3, 1954; April 14, 1954; May 19, 1954.

Youngstown Vindicator, February 25, March 15, and March 29, 1954.

Los Angeles Times, July 25, 1963.

Notes

1   *Los Angeles Times*, July 25, 1963.

2   *The Sporting News*, November 18, 1953

3   *Youngstown Vindicator*, February 25, 1954.

4   *Youngstown Vindicator*, March 29, 1954.

5   *Youngstown Vindicator*, March 15, 1954.

6   *The Sporting News*, May 19, 1954.

7   Roy Terrell, "The Man With a Million and One Alibis," *Sports Illustrated*, August 18, 1958.

8   Ibid.

9   Ibid.

10 Ibid.

Bob Oldis

By Dan Even

Bob "Bucky" Oldis wasn't an All-Star, or even a journeyman major leaguer, but he had much more than just a "cup of coffee." He was a true lover of the game who liked to have fun. Along the way, he played in 135 games, hit a major-league home run, got three hits in one game, and played in a World Series. If someone wanted to depict the consummate baseball man, Oldis would be a good candidate; in his lifetime, he played, managed, coached, and scouted, and was still going strong in his seventh decade of Organized Baseball.

"I just wanted to play," Oldis told a biographer. "It sure beat working. It's always been a fun game, and I'm a fun kind of a guy. I knew I would have to work hard to play, and play smart. But I was fortunate, lucky. I played for, or with, some of the best minds in baseball in the minors, and the majors. And I had a lot of fun."

While Oldis was never a "can't miss" prospect, he could thank his father, Edward, for turning him in the right direction. Oldis was born Robert Carl Oldis in Preston, Iowa, a small farming community in the foothills of the Mississippi River Valley, on January 5, 1928. His father was the town postmaster. The family moved to Iowa City when he was a young man, and his high school, Iowa City High, didn't have a baseball program until his junior year. He didn't play as a senior because he graduated at the semester break. His involvement in the game consisted of fast-pitch softball and American Legion Junior Baseball.

"I'd tag along with my brother Eddie, who had a hardball team, and I got to play," Oldis recalled. "A year after high school, I played a lot of fast-pitch softball. Those were the golden years of fast-pitch, the Peoria Caterpillars and teams

like that traveled around the Midwest playing the locals. We had some great fast-pitch teams here in Iowa; the Iowa City Cardinals were among the best. And Legion ball was big, really big." It was in Legion play that he first caught, moving from third base. His opportunity came when the team's all-star catcher moved on. "Dad told the Legion coach, 'Hey, put Bob back there, he'll stop the ball,' but I had a hell of a time starting out," Oldis remembered. "The day I was to catch my first game, I told him and his only reply was, 'I'm not going to miss that show.' I was on my way." But there were no scouts watching, so Dad came up with another plan in January of 1949.

"Dad had played semipro ball, so he knew the game. He came to me one day and told me he was sending me to a baseball camp in Cocoa, Florida. "It was a five week-camp that cost $25 a week. It was run by Jack Rossiter, a scout, and had Cecil Travis, Andy Seminick, and Pete Appleton as instructors."

After the third week Oldis was one of nine, out of about 200, who were offered professional contracts. He received no signing bonus. Oldis called home to break the news to the family, and his father told him to stay there for the final two weeks so he could report directly to his first pro club, the Emporia Blue Jackets, a Washington Senators affiliate in the Class D Virginia League.

Oldis started the season as backup to a heralded prospect named Orlando Echevarria. One hot July afternoon, Echevarria got sick, and the manager put Oldis, then a 21-year-old rookie, in. It was his career break.

"It was a doubleheader on a sweltering July day, and I batted eighth. I hit two home runs, and in the fourth inning Echevarria came and told the skipper that he felt better, but I caught all of both games. After that I caught a lot more games."

Oldis batted .285, hit five home runs, and led the league's catchers in fielding percentage; and Emporia made the playoffs. In 1950 Oldis returned as the everyday catcher. He hit .289 and earned a promotion to Charlotte of the Class B Tri-State League. Another good season at the plate (.285 and 69 RBIs) helped the Hornets win the regular-season pennant with a 100-40 record.

In 1952 there was another step up to the Senators' top farm team, Chattanooga of the Southern Association. Instead, Oldis made the Senators' varsity in 1952 but never got in a game, and was sent back to Chattanooga.

The demotion caused a problem because over the winter Oldis had married Rose Mary White, a University of Iowa student, and she was with him in spring training. The Senators flew her home to Iowa with a promise that she would be with Bob in Washington when the season started eight days later. But shortly into the season, Oldis was sent down, and was told he would be back in the majors in a couple of weeks.

When that did not happen, Oldis told his manager at Chattanooga, Cal Ermer, that he was "PO'ed and was going home." Fifty years later he admitted it was a ploy to get the $800 he felt he had lost by being sent down, and having to pay rent in two cities, while his wife remained in Washington.

"I wanted it out with Joe Engel, the owner of the Chattanooga club, and Mr. Griffith (Cal, the Senators' owner)," he said. "Both catchers on the club were hurt. I said we'd win the pennant if I stayed. And we went on a seven-game winning streak."

The Lookouts won the Southern Association pennant in the eight-team league, by five games. Oldis was the number one catcher, hit .277, and was one of the top defensive receivers in a league loaded with future major leaguers. Ermer and Oldis built a strong rapport. Oldis was picked for the midseason all-star game but skipped it to drive his wife from Washington to Chattanooga. And he got his $800.

Oldis labeled himself as "kind of clown in those days," and a bit hotheaded. Once, he was called into the league president's office for trying to pound a ball into the ground with his bat after fouling off a pitch; on July 27, 1952, he was ejected and fined after being thrown out in a close play at the plate, after which a melee ensued. He believed he was ejected 19 times that season, at a cost of $25 per violation.

"I told Charley Hurth, the league president, that the umpiring was *ridiculous*, and he should come out that night and see for himself. He did, but the only thing that happened was he told me the next time I got chased it would cost me *fifty* dollars!"

Oldis made his major-league playing debut on April 28, 1953, as a late-inning substitute catcher after the Senators pinch-hit for Mickey Grasso. His first start came in the second game of a doubleheader on May 10 against the Philadelphia Athletics, in which he went 1-for-4 with a single, and caught all nine innings in a 6-2 complete-game victory by Chuck Stobbs. On June 25 Oldis was 3-for-3 facing Harry "The Cat" Brecheen, in a 3-1 loss to the St. Louis Browns. After playing in seven games, he was shuffled back to Chattanooga again. So he wound up 4-for-16 in his rookie season, with three RBIs. The Lookouts had a good season, but didn't win the pennant. Oldis was in a mix of four catchers there, and played in only 28 games hitting .266.

Out of spring training in 1954, Oldis went north with the Senators as the number three catcher behind Ed Fitz Gerald and Joe Tipton. He played in 11 games, eight behind the plate, two at third base, and one as a pinch-hitter. He hit .333 in 24 at-bats.

In 1955 Oldis again made the Senators varsity as the backup to Fitz Gerald and Bruce Edwards. After seeing action in four of the first five games, he was sent down. Recalled in May, he started a pair of games in late May and early June, but after the club obtained Clint Courtney, Oldis was farmed out to Chattanooga and Charlotte. He was 0-for-6 for the season, and even though he went back to the Washington minor-league system, his days as a Washington Senator were over.

After a season in which he hit .286 with Chattanooga, Oldis's contract was sold to the New York Yankees in the fall of 1956. Three seasons at the Triple-A level, with Denver, Richmond, and Denver again, set the stage for his return to the majors, and his most rewarding years. The minor-league years helped Oldis gain the baseball acumen for his long nonplaying career that followed.

"Going to the Yankees system was a great break for me; (the organization) was loaded with talent, great baseball brains. I got to play for the Major (Ralph Houk), Eddie Lopat, and Stan Hack. I was on a team that won the Little World Series (1957), and above all, I learned a lot about the game," he said.

After two seasons of hitting .294 in each of his two stops at Denver, and .268 at Richmond, the Pirates spent $25,000 to select Oldis in the Rule 5 draft in November 1959. It was fortuitous for Oldis that Bucs manager Danny Murtaugh liked to carry three, sometimes four, catchers

"Going into spring training, the Pirates had Smoky Burgess, Hal Smith, Danny Kravitz, and me," he remembered. "I figured Burgess and Smith would do most of the catching, but I had a chance to be in the mix." Kravitz caught in only one game, and on June 1 was traded to the Kansas City Athletics. The number three slot became Oldis's alone.

Murtaugh employed a platoon system at catcher that worked great: left-handed hitting Smoky Burgess, 33 years old, did the bulk of the work. He started 86 games and 29-year-old Hal Smith started 66. Oldis, 32 years old, started three games. Burgess hit .294, with 39 RBIs; Smith, .295 with 44 RBIs; and Oldis, .200 (4-for-20) with one RBI. "My job was to just show up, pitch some batting practice. … I was the number three catcher, so any time we got a lead late and Smoky (Burgess) or Hal (Smith) got on base, Joe Christopher would come in to run for them and I would take over as a defensive replacement."

As a key role-player, Oldis appeared in 22 games, all behind the plate. He handled 44 chances without an error. Nothing spectacular, but he contributed.

"That was a talented and deep club. They didn't need my meager talents to win that year. They had Maz (Hall of Famer Bill Mazeroski), Vern Law, Roy Face, Harvey Haddix, Clem Labine, Stuart (Dick), Groat (Dick), and, of course, that great outfield of Clemente (Roberto), Virdon (Bill), and Skinner (Bob). And we had a lot of role (players) that made great contributions," he recalled. "We won a lot of come-from behind games, a lot of one-run games." Oldis remembered the 1960 team as a spirited club that got along well and "was a great comeback team."—26-22 in one-run games, and a remarkable 15 victories in their last at-bat—and 12 of those came with two outs.

The club finished 95-59, seven games ahead of the Milwaukee Braves for their first pennant since 1927—ending a 33-year drought. They had a winning record in every month, at home (52-25), and on the road (43-34).

The Pirates' prize for winning the pennant was a meeting with a 97-57 New York Yankees team that had captured their tenth pennant in 12 seasons, and were heavily favored to win the World Series.

This was the pinnacle of Oldis' major-league career. "Nothing else was close. I got into two games—both in Yankee Stadium and (we) won both of them. We made a fabulous comeback and won it all thanks to Maz," he recalled. "It was a Series no one who played in it, watched it, or listened to it can forget. Surely the city hasn't forgot."

In one of the zaniest of fall classics, the Yankees outscored the Bucs 55-27, but came up one run short when they needed it most, in the seventh game, and lost, 10-9. The Pirates won their first world championship since 1925. One statistic stands out in bold and shouts of an opportunistic team; the Pirates left only one runner on base in the seventh game.

Oldis saw action in Games Four and Five as a ninth-inning defensive replacement. Both times it was three up and three down for the Yankees. He never even came to bat. But he was a world champion nonetheless, and the winner's share of the Series changed things for him in a big way back in Iowa City.

"Our share was about $8,400 a man. After taxes, I was left $6,400—enough to buy the lot for (our) house and start building. We raised our family here, (and) never lived anywhere else."

"The 1960 Series team is still a big thing in Pittsburgh. In the last two years, I've been back for five reunion events. You can't believe how they love that team." One of those events was a theater showing of a film shot from the screen of his television (a kinescope) that part-owner Bing Crosby had made of the seventh game.

Oldis returned to the Pirates in 1961 and he was 0-for-5 in four games. He spent most of the year with the Columbus Jets of the International League, the Pirates' top Triple-A club. They won the regular-season championship by four games. Oldis hit .224 with two home runs and 21 RBIs. Soon his days as a Pirate were over. On October 13 the club sold his contract to the Phillies, managed by Gene Mauch, who Oldis believes was "the brightest mind" he ever came in contact with. "We had played against each other in the minors. And one day Mauch said he hoped someday I could play for him. So going to Philly was another great opportunity for me. I picked up a lot about the game from Mauch.

"One day sitting next to him in the dugout in St. Louis, we were discussing the Cardinals' batting order. (Stan) Musial was due up in the seventh and Mauch cautioned it would be wise to make sure no one got on, saying, 'We don't want him up in (the) ninth in a crucial situation.' He was thinking three innings ahead. That's the kind of manager he was."

While Clay Dalrymple started at catcher against right-handers, Oldis and 10-year vet Sammy White split the other half of the platoon. Oldis started 23 games and played in a then career-high 38 games with a .263 batting average. He hit his only major-league home run, and had 10 RBIs in 80 at-bats. The Phillies started fast but faded, and finished seventh.

In 1962 Maury Wills stole a modern record 104 bases, and was caught stealing only 13 times during the season. He was caught stealing twice in only one game; on June 4 in Philadelphia, by the all-Iowa battery of Jack Hamilton, born in Burlington, and Oldis, born in Preston. Oldis threw Wills out trying to steal second base in the second inning for the final out of the inning, and third base in the seventh inning. Wills had stolen second base in the first inning off starting pitcher Art Mahaffey. Hamilton had replaced Mahaffey with two outs in the second inning.

On July 20 Oldis came into the game as a pinch-hitter for Dalrymple and was 2-for-2 with two singles off left-hander Jack Curtis in a 7-5 loss to the Milwaukee Braves. Oldis had three hits, all of them singles, and two RBIs against the New York Mets in an 11-9 victory at the Polo Grounds on August 1, 1962. The Phillies starter was Jack Hamilton, though he lasted only 1 1/3 innings. Two of the hits were off lefty Alvin Jackson, and the third off righty Bob G. Miller. Oldis collected a career single-season high 21 hits. On August 9, 1962, he had two hits in an 8-3 loss to the Dodgers, a single, and a home run hit off rookie Pete Richert to lead off the sixth inning that had given the Phillies a brief 2-0 lead.

Oldis returned to the Phillies in 1963 and both his and the club's fortunes improved. The team shared first place temporarily for a couple of days in early April, but eventually finished fourth, 12 games behind the pennant-winning Dodgers. Oldis saw action in 47 games. He was the senior partner in the right-handed part of the platoon to Earl Averill, but Mauch was gaining confidence in Dalrymple as an everyday player. Oldis hit .224, with eight RBIs.

In 1964 the Phillies acquired veteran power-hitting catcher Gus Triandos along with Jim Bunning from the Detroit Tigers. Triandos batted right-handed, making Oldis and Averill superfluous. The Phillies hired Oldis as a coach, while Averill caught in the Boston Red Sox system. In those days most teams carried three coaches—two base coaches and a pitching coach. "You were on your own when it came to hitting in those days." Mauch added Oldis as a fourth coach, for the bullpen. It was quite a baptism, and quite a year. Fans could taste a third pennant, and a chance for a first-ever World Series championship.

Oldis kept his catching skills sharp by playing in Phillies' exhibition games. When rosters expanded in September, he was released as a coach and signed as a player but did not see action in a major-league game. The final two weeks were wild. St. Louis went on a 9-2 final run, coupled with the Phillies' epic collapse. On September 20 the Phillies were 90-60 after a 3-2 victory in Los Angeles. With 12 games left—the next seven at home—they held a 6½-game lead, but they lost 10 straight games.

The bleeding didn't stop until game number 161, with a 4-3 victory in Cincinnati. Down 1½ with just game left, the best the Phillies could salvage would be a play-off. Behind Jim Bunning, they beat the Reds 10-0, tying Cincinnati. But the Cardinals, behind Bob Gibson's relief work, rallied to beat the Mets 11-5. The Reds and Phillies finished tied for second, a game back. The Cardinals won the World Series four games to three, over the Yankees.

Many saw the collapse as a disaster, and blamed Mauch for starting Bunning and Chris Short with only two days' rest. Oldis's assessment was a bit different: "In a way that was an over-achieving team. Aside from (Dick) Allen, (Johnny) Callison, Bunning, and Short—who were great players who had great seasons—the club didn't have a lot of stars. There were a lot of good players but not like some of the other clubs in the league that season. We just couldn't get that key game or two in the final 12."

Oldis spent two more years on Mauch's staff at Philadelphia, then coached with the Minnesota Twins in 1968, and scouted for the Phillies a year. He rejoined Mauch as a coach in Montreal in 1969. In the 1970s Oldis moved to scouting full-time with Montreal, but in 1971 he managed Watertown (South Dakota) in the Class A Northern League. The Expos hired their closest scout, Oldis, after the manager they signed quit upon first seeing the field.[1] His club was 30-40-1 in the league's final season.

Stephen Fuller, a scout for the Chicago Cubs, recalled playing for Oldis the manager: "He was a good baseball man, fun to be around, taught us a lot, but didn't take it too seriously. We had a lot of fun with him, played a lot of pranks, and it was the first time a lot of us kids experienced some of the shenanigans that could come from a big leaguer's mind. Maybe he spent too much time sitting in the bullpen or on the bench—too much time to think to pull some of that stuff."[2]

Bob wanted to spend more time at home with a family that had expanded to include three sons and a daughter. Scouting players in the Midwest was ideal, and it was a career he was good at. His colleagues voted him the "major-league scout of the year" in 2002. He got a ring—"the size of a small apartment"—that he jokingly said he didn't usually wear but kept to help him "recall the year."

To supplement his meager baseball income, Oldis worked in the offseason at various jobs. His favorite "nonbaseball job" was as a referee with longtime friend Don "Bones" Farnsworth. They worked hundreds of prep football and basketball games together for more than 40 years. Oldis remained a bench official at the Iowa Boys' Basketball Tournament until 2010. He also worked 25 years at the Girls' Tournament, mostly in the days when it was a six-girl, half-court game. Oldis worked 14 years for the Iowa State Highway Commission, Not a desk job, but outside in the harsh Iowa winters putting up snow fences, running a snowplow, and repairing potholes.

In the fall of 2010 Oldis worked his final game as a member of the "chain gang" at University of Iowa football games. Over 55 years, "I had a job, not really, call it a *free seat* that everyone would love to have." Oldis was on the sidelines during years that the Hawkeyes won five Big Ten titles, and went to 24 bowl games.

He had but one regret: "I only wish my dad could have lived to see me play in the majors." Edward Oldis' dad died of cancer at the age of 59 when Oldis was a minor leaguer.

Over his career Oldis collected two World Series rings, one from the Pirates and the other from the Florida Marlins in 2003. He believed he was responsible for "19 or 20 guys" making the major leagues, including Shane Rawley, Bill Gullickson, Jeff Huson, Casey Candaele, David Herndon, and Brad Hand.

Seldom did a night go by that Oldis wasn't at his younger brother Phil's house next door, watching the Marlins. He scouted Iowa, Nebraska, Minnesota, and the Dakotas for high-school and college talent. After the June draft, he evaluated Class A players in the 16-team Midwest League during home games of Cedar Rapids and Quad Cities.

Not a bad way for a true lover of the game to spend his retirement.

Sources

Books:

Baseball media guides: Minnesota Twins, Montreal Expos, Pittsburgh Pirates, and Philadelphia Phillies, various years.

Lloyd Johnson and Miles Wolf, eds. *The Encyclopedia of Minor League Baseball* (Durham, North Carolina: Baseball America, 2003).

Sporting News Official Baseball Guides, 1950 through 1965.

Jim Ecker. "Back on the Chain Gang," *Cedar Rapids Gazette*, September 9, 2008.

Iowa City Press-Citizen, December 2007.

Pittsburgh Post-Gazette, June 19, 2010, November 13, 2010.

www.baseballbytheletters.com, Bob Oldis: "8 Decades in Pro Baseball," April 23, 2010.

BaseballAlmanac.com

Baseball-Reference.com

Personal interviews with Bob Oldis, May-June, 2011.

Note: Additional information on the Pittsburgh Pirates' 1960 season, and Oldis's best games as a player, was added by Mel Marmer.

Notes

1   Andy Hamilton. "For the Love of the Game," *Iowa City Press-Citizen* (http.seniorliving.press-citizen media.com/ december2007).

2   Ibid.

Diomedes Olivo

By Rory Costello

IN HOMER'S *ILIAD*, Diomedes was one of the strongest Greek warriors. He was also the youngest—unlike his namesake, Dominican pitcher Diómedes Olivo. Olivo made his big-league debut with the 1960 Pirates at the age of 41. As of 2011, he was still the second-oldest "rookie" in major-league history, behind only Satchel Paige. Like Paige, Olivo had already been a durable star pitcher for many years. And as both Roberto Clemente and Danny Murtaugh are said to have remarked, the man may have been in his 40s, but his arm was 20.

"Guayubín" (as Olivo was called, for his hometown) earned elite status among his nation's hurlers during the 1950s. He didn't even turn pro until his late 20s, but after he did, he pitched in at least six other nations: Puerto Rico, Mexico, Cuba, Venezuela, Nicaragua, and Colombia. His pro career—both summer and winter—spanned from 1947 to 1964.

In the majors the lefty's lifetime record was just 5-6, with a 3.10 ERA in 85 games (1960; 1962-63). During the 1962 season, at the age of 43, Olivo was a revelation to Stateside fans. His fastball was still lively, and "the way that guy throws a curve is murder," said one unnamed player.[1] Although Pittsburgh called Olivo up too late for him to be eligible for the 1960 World Series, he joined Virgil Trucks in throwing batting practice for the team during the Series.[2]

Diómedes Antonio Olivo Maldonado was born on January 22, 1919 (but rumors persisted that he was actually older). His parents were Arcadio Emilio Olivo Báez and Juana Ramona Maldonado Mejía. "Mamá Juana," as she was known, died in 1983 at the remarkable age of 103. She had five other children besides

Diómedes: sons Arcadio, César Blas, and Federico; daughters Zena and Lucrecia. Federico—known as Chichí (or Chi-Chi in the US)—was also a star pitcher at home who had a short major-league career (1961; 1964-66).

Guayubín (full name San Lorenzo de Guayubín) is the second largest city in Monte Cristi Province, in the northwestern corner of the Dominican Republic. For this reason, Olivo earned another nickname, La Montaña Noroestana: The Northwestern Mountain. Emilio "Cuqui" Córdova, the dean of Dominican baseball writers, made that the subtitle of his short book about Olivo, which became the definitive biography in 2006.

Arcadio Olivo was a cattle rancher. During spring training in 1960, Diómedes recalled through interpreter Román Mejías, "When I put the cows away, I go into town to play. I start when I am 5 or 10 with pickup teams at home in Guayubín."[3] Olivo never picked up more than a smattering of English, relying on teammates such as Mejías, Clemente, Julián Javier, and Al McBean to get his message across. What didn't need translation, though, was his lively, cheery personality.

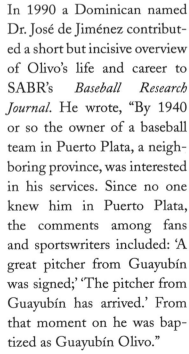

In 1990 a Dominican named Dr. José de Jiménez contributed a short but incisive overview of Olivo's life and career to SABR's *Baseball Research Journal*. He wrote, "By 1940 or so the owner of a baseball team in Puerto Plata, a neighboring province, was interested in his services. Since no one knew him in Puerto Plata, the comments among fans and sportswriters included: 'A great pitcher from Guayubín was signed;' 'The pitcher from Guayubín has arrived.' From that moment on he was baptized as Guayubín Olivo."

In 2010 Dominican sportswriter Rafael Peña chronicled

Olivo's early years in Dominican ball, noting that he first played in the nation's capital, Santo Domingo, in 1944.[4] That year Guayubín was named to the Dominican national team that went to Caracas, Venezuela, for the seventh Amateur World Series. Two years later the Dominicans went to Barranquilla, Colombia, for the Central American and Caribbean Games. Olivo's standout performance included a 13-inning win over Colombia, in which he allowed just one run on four hits.[5]

Professional baseball had been on hiatus in the Dominican Republic since 1937, and it did not resume until the summer of 1951—yet there was still an active club scene. On September 28, 1947, Olivo pitched a no-hitter for Escogido against archrival Licey, the team for which he would later play 11 seasons. That winter Guayubín joined Aguadilla of the Puerto Rican Winter League, serving as both pitcher and outfielder. He was a robust man (6-feet-1, 195 pounds) who always took great pride in his hitting.

Olivo said in 1960 that he turned down an opportunity to join the Chicago White Sox in 1948 "because I do not speak English and because I do not want to come to the United States and play in minor leagues."[6] Pittsburgh sportswriter and broadcaster Myron Cope expanded on this theme in a feature for *Sports Illustrated* in the summer of 1962. "Back home in Guayubín . . . Olivo owns 500 acres of pasture, 50 cows and 200 acres on which he plans to build a small housing development. He labored hard over the decades, milking cows and pitching baseballs, and though he received occasional feelers from big-league clubs, he turned them down. For one thing, he had no taste for working his way up through the minors; then, too, he feared being shipped to a segregated southern town and felt his ignorance of English would make life doubly hard."[7] Olivo was a coffee-colored man who was termed a "Negro" by US standards.

Instead, Guayubín's travels took him to Colombia during the summer of 1948, when pro baseball began in that nation. He joined Tejedores (Weavers) de Filtta, an industrial team sponsored by a woolen mill in Barranquilla. In his debut, on June 27, he took a perfect game into the ninth but finished with a two-hitter.[8] Colombian baseball historian Raúl Porto said Olivo went back to Filtta in both 1949 and 1950. He was a league all-star in both '48 and '49, leading the circuit in strikeouts both years. In 1949, the Tejedores were league champion.

Olivo also played ball in Venezuela during this period. One glimpse comes from May 1950, when the lefty was with Gavilanes, one of three teams in La Liga Occidental, in the western state of Zulia. The Sparrowhawks had a rivalry with Pastora, another team based in the oil city of Maracaibo.[9] Negro Leaguers like Max Manning and Terris McDuffie (the latter Olivo's teammate) were also in the league.[10] Sandalio "Sandy" Consuegra, then a Washington Senators farmhand, had also signed with Gavilanes the previous winter. The Cuban spent his $3,000 signing bonus, though, and when he asked Senators owner Clark Griffith to refund it in the spring, Griffith sent Consuegra back to Havana, delaying his big-league debut.[11]

Olivo remained in Puerto Rico for six more winters. In the 1950-51 season, Aguadilla sold him to San Juan after he suffered seven straight defeats.[12] This was a good break because the Senadores were a winning ballclub and the Tiburones (Sharks) were not—in fact, San Juan absorbed Aguadilla for the 1951-52 season. That team won the Puerto Rican championship and went to the Caribbean Series as a result. The tournament was held in Panama City (it is not certain whether Olivo ever played in the Panamanian winter league). The Dominican relieved in two games for Puerto Rico, which went winless, and became the first man from his country to pitch in the Caribbean Series.[13]

Guayubín was among the league leaders in wins (9) and ERA (2.07) for San Juan in 1952-53. That season he conceived a child with a Puerto Rican woman named Crucita Rondón. The boy, Gilberto Rondón, was born on November 18, 1953, in the Bronx, New York. Gil inherited a bit of his father's talent, as he pitched 19 games for the Astros in 1976 and four for the White Sox in 1979. In later years he became a pitching coach, and one of his stops was with the Nicaraguan national team. He told Nicaraguan baseball historian Tito Rondón (they jokingly called each other "cousin"), "My mom had a thing for ballplayers, and one day she saw Guayubín Olivo, and decided she had to have him, and I was born!" However, Olivo married his wife, Olga Chávez Gómez, in 1953.[14] They had three children: Pedro, Olga (known as Titi), and Guillermo.

When pro ball returned to the Dominican Republic in the summer of 1951, Guayubín came back home and joined the Licey Tigres. He won the Triple Crown of pitching that year, going 10-5 (in a 54-game schedule), striking out 65, and posting a 1.90 ERA in 128 innings. The 1951 season was tarnished, however, by an out-of-character incident on July 22. Olivo, after arguing a ball-and-strike call with umpire Willis Thompson, threw a ball at the ump's head, knocking him cold. He was ejected from the stadium and went to jail overnight. Originally, the star pitcher was going to be suspended for the season, but after Licey lobbied intensely, and Guayubín himself wrote a public letter of apology in the magazine *La Nación*, the punishment was reduced to just six games.[15]

Olivo led the Dominican league in ERA again in both 1952 and 1954. Highlights of the 1954 season included breaking up Negro Leaguer Johnny Wright's no-hit bid on May 22. His ninth-inning pinch single made a winner of Ewell Blackwell, who was still hanging on (The Whip's major-league career ended in 1955). One week later Guayubín threw a no-hitter of his own over Escogido, which had Hall of Famer Ray Dandridge and another powerful Negro Leaguer, Bob Thurman (who joined the Cincinnati Reds the next year).

After the 1954-55 season ended in Puerto Rico, Olivo came back home to face Japan's leading team, the Yomiuri Giants, as part of the Giants' Caribbean tour. The Dominicans took four of five games, losing only the opener as Olivo allowed the two tying runs in the ninth inning and five more in the tenth.[16]

Shortly thereafter, Guayubín played in the US minors for the first time. The absence of Dominican summer ball was clearly a factor. Havana of the International League signed him, as owner Bobby Maduro stocked his team with players who had performed all around the Caribbean.[17] However, Olivo pitched just 13 innings in seven games for the Sugar Kings before going to the Mexican League. "My finger is smashed in a car door one day," he recalled in 1960. "It grow big, but they pitch me. Then they sell me to Mexico City."[18]

Olivo spent 1955 through 1958 with the Mexico City Diablos Rojos, with an aggregate record of 34-21. His 15-8, 2.65 performance helped the Red Devils win the league championship in 1956. However, Diómedes pitched just five games in Mexico in 1957. The Nicaraguan League (which played in the summers in 1956 and 1957) lured him and Cuban teammate Vicente López away.[19]

Tito Rondón and his fellow local historian Carlos Mena recalled how Guayubín was part of a group called The Lost Squadron that was supposed to reinforce the Bóer club but took weeks to arrive. When they finally did, it inspired Nicaraguan poet Oscar Pérez Valdivia to write verses in their honor. Olivo pitched very well for the Indios, going 8-5, 2.16 in 23 games (16 starts). It was too late for Bóer, though, which lost the championship to León (there were no playoffs). López and Olivo then went back to Mexico.[20]

Guayubín continued to pitch at home after the Dominican season switched to the winter. Myron Cope's *Sports Illustrated* story opened with a recollection from a teammate. "In 1959 Dick Stuart, the Pittsburgh Pirates' nonconformist first baseman, returned from the Dominican Republic Winter League and described to Pirate brass an elderly left-handed pitcher he had seen there. 'I told them I'd been hitting against this guy for three years down there and I got two hits off him,' says Stuart. 'I told them, 'Sign this guy!' But you know how it is with me. Anything Stuart says around here, they say forget it.'"[21]

Olivo joined the Poza Rica Petroleros in Mexico for the summer of 1959, which was one of his best as a pro. He was 21-8 with a 3.02 ERA, helping the Petroleros become the league's champion by leading the league in victories and in strikeouts, with 233 in 247 innings. He set a league record by striking out 16 in a seven-inning game (the opener of a doubleheader).[22] He followed up with a typically capable winter for the Tigres (7-6, 2.33).

Howie Haak, the trailblazing scout who opened up all of Latin America, "prevailed upon General Manager Joe L. Brown to take the gamble" in signing Olivo.[23] Myron Cope wrote, "Even after the Pirates persuaded Diomedes to sign a contract . . . he failed to report to spring training. The Pirates finally sent a wire: REPORT TO TRAINING CAMP AT ONCE. The other day Diomedes explained through an interpreter that it was the wire that convinced him he was wanted in the U.S."[24]

Olivo was impressive in camp, surprising many with his hard stuff and "no trick deliveries."[25] Yet at the beginning of the 1960 season, Pittsburgh decided to keep righty Paul Giel instead. They returned Guayubín to Poza Rica, which in turn sold his contract to the Pirates' top farm club, Columbus in the International League. He pitched well (7-9, 2.88 in 42 games, including 12 starts), and so Pittsburgh called the 41-year-old vet up that September. He made his big-league debut on September 5—becoming the sixth player (and third pitcher) from the Dominican Republic in The Show.

Olivo pitched in four games for the Pirates that month, with three of those appearances being mop-up duty. His most significant outing came on September 27 at Forbes Field, in a 16-inning win over Cincinnati. Diómedes pitched the 10th through the 13th innings, striking out six of the 19 men the Bucs' pitchers fanned that night.

Although Guayubín's visa was due to expire on October 1, it was extended so he could be on hand for the 1960 World Series.[26] After the Pirates defeated the Yankees, the team awarded him a very modest $250 in cash for his September and postseason batting-practice services (Virgil Trucks, who joined the team in August, got $500). That winter Olivo again won the Triple Crown of pitching for Licey. He had 10 victories (against six losses), struck out 160 men—a league record that still stood as of 2011—in 142 innings, and posted a 1.58 ERA.

Despite this performance, Olivo found himself back at Columbus in 1961. The Pirates had traded for another veteran lefty, Bobby Shantz, the previous December; Guayubín was one of the last three men manager Murtaugh cut in spring training. He pitched very well in Triple-A, though, going 11-7 with a 2.01 ERA and 20 saves in 66 games. The Jets won the regular-season pennant (though they were knocked out in the playoffs) and manager Larry Shepard was still talking about the veteran's importance to the club nearly four years later.[27] The IL Writers' Association voted Olivo as the league's most valuable pitcher.

Dominican dictator Rafael Trujillo was assassinated on May 30, 1961, and the atmosphere in the country remained extremely tense. A nationwide strike and street fighting crippled attendance, and the Dominican League halted the 1961-62 season after the games of December 3.[28] Olivo then spent another short stretch in Puerto Rico with San Juan.

Before the 1962 season *Baseball Digest* issued this scouting report on Guayubín: "Superb relief pitcher—perhaps the best in International League. Baffling prospect: Some say he's as old as 45—but still pitches with great effectiveness." Danny Murtaugh kept Olivo with the Pirates that year, and he got his first big-league win at Wrigley Field on April 16. He thrived on frequent work, appearing 62 times, and formed an effective lefty-righty tandem with Elroy Face. He went 5-1 with a 2.77 ERA, also picking up seven saves. Murtaugh frequently used Olivo in a way that would become much more common in the future: as a lefty specialist to get one or two outs. Yet he could also pitch in long relief and got one start, in the season finale.

Dominican League play remained suspended altogether in 1962-63, but exhibition games were still taking place, and Guayubín participated.[29] He also tended to his farm, although that December cattle rustlers made off with seven of his steers![30] Meanwhile, on November 19 the Pirates traded him to the St. Louis Cardinals along with Dick Groat for pitcher Don Cardwell and infielder Julio Gotay. Olivo started the 1963 season with St. Louis, but things did not go well, as he went 0-5 with a 5.40 ERA in 19 appearances. Manager Johnny Keane also used the vet in a specialist role, giving him just 13 1/3 innings total. One of those outings came against the New York Mets at the Polo Grounds on June 7. Ron Taylor had weakened in the ninth inning, putting two runners on. Duke Snider was coming to the plate, and another lefty, Ed Kranepool, was on deck. The Mets won, 3-2, as the Duke hit a three-run homer to end the game.

Keane gave Olivo just two more chances to pitch before the Cardinals sent the 44-year-old down to Triple-A Atlanta in early July. There he enjoyed a late-career highlight, throwing a seven-inning no-hitter on July 22 in the opener of a doubleheader against Toronto. It could have been a perfect game except that he walked Bubba Morton on four pitches with two out in the seventh. Not only that, Guayubín singled and scored the game's only run in the third inning.

Olivo wrapped up his pro career with one final season in Dominican winter ball. He was 9-3, 2.37 in 18 games for Licey. In 2006 his son Guillermo said, "The saddest day of my father's life was when he played his last game with Licey in 1964. He always felt most comfortable when they called on him to pitch with this team."[31] Olivo's totals with Licey from 1951 through 1964 were 86-46, 2.11 in 198 games and 1,166 1/3 innings pitched. That

ERA is second only to Juan Marichal's 1.87 in league history, but Guayubín pitched nearly twice as many innings. The Dominican League named its equivalent of the Cy Young Award for him.

After retiring as a player, Olivo spent seven years scouting for the Cardinals and then one more with the Mets in 1971. He signed at least one major leaguer, Pedro Borbón, Sr.[32] He most likely also signed his nephew, Milcíades "Mike" Olivo, who played pro ball from 1964 through 1975, getting as high as Triple-A for a few years. Mike and Chichí Olivo were both part of the Licey team that won the 1971 Caribbean Series for the Dominican Republic, led by player-manager Manny Mota. Forty years later, Mota and Diómedes Olivo remained Licey's two leading idols.

As of 1977, Guayubín was undersecretary of state for sports in the Dominican Republic.[33] In an odd coincidence, he and his brother Chichí died less than two weeks apart. José de Jiménez wrote, "On February 15, 1977, at 57 [sic] years of age, [Diómedes] Olivo looked young and strong. That afternoon he went to play softball and early in the evening, reading some comments about the death of his brother Chi-Chi . . . Olivo suffered a sudden heart attack, dying a few minutes later.

"His death was a national catastrophe, the whole country was mourning, there was no music anywhere, the sky was cloudy. . . . The president of the Dominican Republic, Dr. Joaquín Balaguer, sent a telegram of condolence to his widow. To be frank: we all cried."

In the spring of 1960 Julián Javier (then a Pirates farmhand) discussed Olivo's stature in the Dominican Republic. Javier said, "His name means something down there like Mays and Mantle mean in the United States. If we had Hall of Fame in Dominican, Olivo would be in it."[34] The Dominican Sporting Hall of Fame was established in 1967, and in 1973 it inducted Guayubín Olivo. Judging by the number of stories that are still written about him, his legend at home has not lost any luster since.

Special thanks to Eddy Olivo Cruz for providing the family tree compiled by his second cousin, Emilio Olivo (nephew of Diómedes Olivo). Continued thanks to Raúl Porto (Colombian information) and to SABR member Tito Rondón.

Sources

Córdova, Cuqui. *Guayubín Olivo: La Montaña Noroestana*. Issue 5 of *Historia del Béisbol Dominicano*. Santo Domingo: Revista Historia del Béisbol, 2006.

De Jiménez, José. "The Great Dominican, Diómedes Olivo." *Baseball Research Journal*, Volume 20. Society for American Baseball Research: 1990: 91-92.

Crescioni Benítez, José A. *El Béisbol Profesional Boricua*. San Juan, Puerto Rico: Aurora Comunicación Integral, Inc., 1997).

Bjarkman, Peter C. *Baseball with a Latin Beat*. Jefferson, North Carolina: McFarland & Co.: 1994.

Bjarkman, Peter C. *Diamonds Around the Globe: The Encyclopedia of International Baseball*. Westport, Connecticut: Greenwood Press, 2005.

www.baseball-reference.com

www.retrosheet.org

http://www.pabellondelafamadeportedom.com

Notes

1   "Bucs' Olivo Thriving On Relief." United Press International, August 29, 1962.

2   Lester J. Biederman. "Olivo, Trucks New York-Bound, Too." *Pittsburgh Press*, October 6, 1960.

3   "Buccos Pick Up Diomedes For Insurance." Associated Press, April 1, 1960.

4   Rafael V. Peña. "Guayubín Olivo." Blog of Asociación de Cronistas Deportivas de Santo Domingo — Filial Nueva York, May 14, 2010. (http://acdny.blogspot.com/2010/05/guayubin-olivo.html)

5   Cuqui Córdova. "La crónica de los martes." *Listín Diario* (Santo Domingo, Dominican Republic), December 9, 2008.

6   "Buccos Pick Up Diomedes For Insurance"

7   Myron Cope. "An Elderly Diomedes In The Big Show." *Sports Illustrated*, July 16, 1962.

8   Córdova, op. cit.

9   Alexis Salas H. Los Eternos Rivales: 1908-1988. Caracas, Venezuela: Seguros Caracas, 1988: 112.

10   "Sulia [sic] State League Opens." *The Sporting News*, April 19, 1950: 48.

11   *The Sporting News*, April 19, 1950: 52. Hand, Jack. "Cuban Talent Pays Off For Senators." Associated Press, June 22, 1950.

12   Santiago Llorens. "Yankee Rookie Tops Star Poll in Puerto Rico." *The Sporting News*, January 3, 1951: 25.

13   Bienvenido Rojas. "Serie del Caribe: Olivo, primer criollo en lanzar." *Diario Libre* (Santo Domingo, Dominican Republic), January 26, 2007.

14   Bob Broeg. "He Comes on Strong." *Baseball Digest*, July 1963: 32.

15   Rafael Baldayac. "José Offerman revive caso Guayubín Olivo." *La Información* (Santiago, Dominican Republic), January 28, 2010.

16   Robert K. Fitts. *Wally Yonamine*. (Lincoln, Nebraska: University of Nebraska Press, 2008), 183.

17   Pedro Galiana. "Cubans Rolling on Warm-Up in Winter Loops." *The Sporting News*, May 4, 1955: 29.

18   "Buccos Pick Up Diomedes For Insurance"

19   Miguel A. Calzadilla. "Trautman Probes Reports of Raids." *The Sporting News*, May 1, 1957: 36.

20   Miguel A. Calzadilla. "Sultans Renew Cincy Pact." *The Sporting News*, August 21, 1957: 46.

21   Cope, op. cit.

22   "Ramon Lopez in Whiff Show." The Sporting News, June 6, 1964: 35.

23   Harry Keck. "How Old Is Olivo? 'About 42,' He Says." *The Sporting News*, May 23, 1962: 17.

24   Cope, op. cit.

25   Les Biederman. "Olivo, Pirates' 40-Year-Old Rookie, Dominican Hill Ace." *The Sporting News*, March 23, 1960: 15.

26   "Spanish Rolls, Pirate Olivo To See Series." *Pittsburgh Press*, September 6, 1960.

27   "Sam Jones to Lead Pennant Push by Jets, Shepard Says." *The Sporting News*, May 1, 1965: 35.

28   "Political Turmoil Forces Dominican League to Fold." *The Sporting News*, December 13, 1961: 34.

29   "Alou Fined for Winter Activities." Associated Press, February 5, 1963.

30   "Cardinals Pitcher Victim of Thieves." Associated Press, December 18, 1962.

31   Nathaneal Pérez Neró. "El Licey bautiza 'dogout' con el nombre de Guayubín Olivo." *Diario Libre* (Santo Domingo, Dominican Republic), December 12, 2006.

32   Questionnaire received by Rod Nelson of SABR's Scouts Committee. Caveat: in retrospect, Nelson has not been able to confirm the other two names listed on the questionnaire, Larry Dick and Monchín Pichardo, as being Cardinals scouts. However, Pichardo became president and general manager of Licey in 1963-64, and Borbón Sr. spent his entire Dominican career with Licey.

33   "Obituaries." *The Sporting News*, March 5, 1977: 54.

34   Biederman, "Olivo, Pirates' 40-Year-Old Rookie, Dominican Hill Ace"

Dick Schofield

By Rodney Johnson

DICK SCHOFIELD SPENT 19 years in the big leagues working for seven teams as a versatile utility player. Born on January 7, 1935, in Springfield, Illinois, to John and Florence Schofield, John Richard "Dick" Schofield was the second in a succession of four generations of professional baseball players. His father, John "Ducky" Schofield, played ten minor-league seasons, also with seven different teams. He finished up in 1938 with Springfield of the Three-I League. A shortstop like his son, the diminutive elder Schofield batted .234 in a career in which he was noted more for his glove work than his bat.

In Springfield the Schofield family took up farming. "Everyone here were farmers," said Dick. "We weren't very good ones I suppose, but that's what everyone in Springfield did."[1] Growing up as an only child, Dick benefited by the coaching and constant practice sessions provided by his father. By the time he was going to Springfield High School, he was the best player in the region. "One night after a game, a couple of Dodgers scouts asked me if I was intending to sign after what they thought was my senior year," said Schofield. "I informed them that I was just a freshman. I thought I was kind of hot stuff."[2] In his junior year, 1952, Schofield led Springfield to the Illinois Junior American Legion Championship. After he graduated he had the choice of going to Northwestern University on a basketball scholarship or signing with 14 of the 16 major-league teams.

A lifelong Red Sox fan, Schofield preferred to sign with Boston but the club had just signed some other expensive players, including shortstop Don Buddin. The best offer, as it turned out, came from the St. Louis Cardinals. Scouts Joe Monahan and Walter Shannon made the 18-year-old shortstop the Cardinals'

first bonus baby when they signed him to a $40,000 bonus contract in June 1953. Fourteen players signed that year for bonuses of more than $6,000.[3] Under the rules of the day, such bonus players were required to spend two years on the major-league roster.

Just weeks out of high school, Schofield reported to the Cardinals. When teammates learned his father's nickname, Ducky, they started calling the youngster by the same name. (His father had gotten the nickname when he was growing up in Linwood, Pennsylvania, near Philadelphia, where seeing flocks of the birds was common. The nickname stuck with Schofield throughout his career although it was just as common for teammates to call him Schoy (pronounced Sko-ee).) "I pretty much kept to myself and didn't socialize with the other players," remembered Schofield the younger. "It was a veteran team and there were those that resented me taking up someone's spot on the roster." Although he didn't get into a game for a few weeks, Ducky did see action of a different kind. On June 25 the Cardinals took on the Giants in St. Louis. In the second inning, Cardinals manager Eddie Stanky came out of the dugout to argue with umpire Augie Donatelli. First one towel and then another came flying out of the Cardinals dugout. As Stanky made his way down the dugout steps, Donatelli warned that if another towel came out, an ejection would follow. "I'm just sitting there quietly watching and Stanky comes back and says, 'Schofield, throw a towel.' Of course he knew I wasn't going to play anyway so it didn't matter to him if I got tossed," recalled Schofield. "So I threw the towel and Donatelli came over and said, 'Who threw that towel?' "Stanky pointed to me and said, 'Schofield!' "I was ejected before I had ever gotten into a box score." It was the only ejection of his career.

On July 3 in Chicago, Schofield finally got into his first big-league game when he pinch-ran for Del Rice in the seventh inning of a 10-3 loss to the Cubs. Playing time was tough to come by and, although he was in the big leagues, Schofield would have rather been playing every day in the minors. Stanky did the best he could to make the season a learning experience for the rookie. "He always would come around and ask me questions during the game and point things out," said Schofield. He was probably the smartest manager I ever had." On July 17, Ducky got his chance to bat in the first game of a doubleheader in Brooklyn. After coming in defensively in the bottom of the fifth inning of a Dodgers blowout, Schofield led off the sixth with a line single to left field off southpaw Johnny Podres. Nearly a month later, on August 16 in Cincinnati, Schofield hit his first home run when he connected against Frank Smith. On the 26th the rookie circled the bases again, this time off the Giants' Jim Hearn at the Polo Grounds. Schofield wouldn't homer again until 1958. In September he batted only once and his final seven appearances of the season were as a pinch runner. In all, he appeared in 33 games and gathered 41 plate appearances. In 1954 the bonus baby saw even less action. Despite being with the club all season, Schofield played in only 43 games and came to the plate just seven times. Often used as a pinch runner, he scored 17 runs. During the offseasons he attended Springfield Junior College.

Freed of the bonus-baby restriction that required him to spend his first two years on the Cardinals' bench, Schofield spent the next two seasons as the starting short-stop for Omaha of the American Association, St. Louis's top farm club. Each year he earned a September call-up to the Cardinals. Playing for manager Johnny Keane at Omaha, Ducky responded with batting averages of .273 and .295 while continuing to play exceptional defense. In 1956 he hit 11 home runs and had 57 RBIs, both career highs. His most memorable highlight of the 1956 season came on June 16, when he wed Donna Jean Dabney.

Schofield thought he was going to be the Cardinals starting shortstop in 1957, but his plans were derailed when newly acquired veteran Al Dark refused to move to third base. "Dark got there in June of '56 and the plan was for Boyer to move to center, Dark to play third and me to play short the next year," recalled Schofield. "Dark didn't want to play third so he stayed at short and rookie Eddie Kasko

was handed the third base job." It became apparent that Schofield's future in St. Louis was limited. He spent the entire season with the Cardinals but was used mostly as a pinch runner and defensive replacement; he played in 65 games and had only 56 at-bats.

Early in the 1958 season Dark was traded away, Boyer went back to third base, Curt Flood became the center fielder, Kasko moved to shortstop and Schofield was obviously expendable. On May 13 he got a parting gift from the Cardinals when he had a bird's-eye view from the on-deck circle of Stan Musial's 3,000th hit. At the June 15 trading deadline, Schofield was shipped to the Pittsburgh Pirates with cash for infielders Gene Freese and Johnny O'Brien. The prospects of becoming an everyday player weren't any better in Pittsburgh; Schofield found himself behind Dick Groat, who was entrenched as the club's regular shortstop.

On May 26, 1959, Schofield was in the starting lineup and leading off for the Pirates against the Braves in Milwaukee. Harvey Haddix was pitching for Pittsburgh. Schofield had become friends with Haddix when they were team-mates with the Cardinals. The Pirates left-hander pitched 12 perfect innings but lost when the Braves scored the only run of the game in the bottom of the 13th. Schofield had a game-high three hits as the Pirates rapped out a dozen singles but still couldn't score. His third-inning single would have driven in a run if Roman Mejias had not been thrown out trying to advance from first to third on an infield hit by Haddix. Schofield's hit sent Haddix to third but there were two outs instead of one; Bill Virdon flied out and Pittsburgh didn't score. Schofield had also contributed with his glove, making a long throw from the hole in the sixth inning to just nip Johnny Logan at first. "That was a bizarre, pressure-packed game," Schofield lamented. "It was just a shame that we couldn't score for him."[4]

In September 1960, Schofield enjoyed the greatest month of his career. The Pirates were locked in a pennant race when on September 6 Groat's wrist was broken when he was struck by a pitch from Braves pitcher Lew Burdette. He was lost for the rest of the season. Groat was the team captain and, despite the injury, won the National League batting title and was named the Most Valuable Player. Little Dick Schofield filled the big shoes and then some. After the injury to Groat that day, he came into the game in an 0-for-18 slump and without a hit since May 31. He proceeded to collect three hits to lead the Pirates to a 5-3 win. He played the rest of the season, batting .403 (27-for-67) and getting at least two hits in a game eight times. During their final 22 games, the Pirates had a stretch of three straight doubleheaders (September 18, 20, and 22). Schofield played every inning of all six contests as the Pirates swept all three twin bills to effectively wrap up the pennant. He went 10-for-19 in those games. It was the Pirates' first pennant since 1927. The World Series against the New York Yankees was bittersweet for Schofield. Although the Pirates won in dramatic fashion, he was barely a part of the effort. Before the start of the Series, Groat proclaimed himself healed and ready to play. He later admitted that he had to catch nearly everything barehanded but hid that fact because he didn't want to miss the Series. He batted .214. Schofield was disappointed but said he understood the decision. "I thought I deserved to play, but I understand why (Pirates manager Danny) Murtaugh played Groat," he said. "We really both deserved to play." The only action seen by Schofield was three meaningless pinch-hitting appearances in Yankee blowouts. He had a single in Game Two, a 16-3 loss, and made outs in Game Three's 10-0 loss and Game Six, a 12-0 shutout. After pinch hitting, Schofield stayed in the game to spell Groat defensively in Games Two and Six.

His September success in 1960 didn't earn Schofield any additional playing time. He remained a utility player and filled in at second, third, and short as well as seeing some action in the outfield. In 1961 he appeared in 60 games and the next season in 54.

After waiting ten seasons to become a big-league starter, Schofield finally got his chance in 1963. An offseason trade sent Groat to St. Louis and Ducky was named the starting shortstop and leadoff hitter. He was in the Pirates' Opening Day lineup for each of the next three seasons. In 1963 he set career highs in nearly every offensive category. He played in 138 games and had more than 600 plate appearances. His .246 batting average was fourth among National League starting shortstops. He drew 69 walks to help justify his batting in the leadoff spot. On April 17, 1964, Schofield became the first batter to come to the plate at Shea Stadium in New York. He popped out to second baseman Larry Burright to inaugurate the Mets' new ballpark as the Pirates won. 4-3. Schofield dupli-

cated his .246 average that season but played in 17 fewer games. The most memorable of his three openers was in 1965 when Bob Bailey hit a tenth-inning homer off Juan Marichal to give Bob Veale and the Pirates a 1-0 win in Pittsburgh. Less than two months later, Schofield would be Marichal's teammate. On May 22 the Pirates traded him to the Giants for infielder Jose Pagan. The already offensively loaded Giants upgraded their defense and the Pirates opened up the shortstop job for Gene Alley. Schofield provided the defense the Giants were looking for as he led the league in fielding percentage. However, he batted just .203 after coming to San Francisco and .209 for the season. This was Schofield's best chance to be the starter on a World Series team. The Giants held a four-game lead over the Dodgers on September 20 with 12 games to play. They had won 17 of their last 18 games and appeared poised to take the pennant. But the Giants went 5-7 the rest of the way and the Dodgers went 11-1 to win the pennant title by two games. "We should have won," agonized Schofield. "All we had to do was win a couple of more games and we couldn't do it. That was a terrific team."

Tito Fuentes was called up in August and played well for the Giants, so when the 1966 season started, Schofield was relegated to a utility role. In May his contract was purchased by the New York Yankees. "Houk brought me in to play short," said Schofield of Yankees skipper Ralph Houk, "But I just couldn't get healthy. I'm not sure what it was, but my arm just swelled up and I couldn't throw." By the time Schofield was ready to play, Horace Clarke was playing shortstop for New York. On September 10 Schofield was traded to the Dodgers for pitcher Thad Tillotson and cash. It was his third team of the 1966 season. When he arrived in Los Angeles as the club's fifth switch-hitter, manager Walter Alston told him he would be the Dodgers' third baseman. Schofield hadn't played third since 1963. John Kennedy and Junior Gilliam had shared the Dodgers' third-base chores all season but both were banged up. "I played every day at third down the stretch and we ended up winning the pennant," recalled Schofield. "The tough part was that I got there after the trade deadline so I wasn't eligible to play in the series." The Dodgers were swept by the Orioles in the World Series. In 1967 the Dodgers were a shell of the club that had won two straight National League pennants. Sandy Koufax retired and Maury Wills had been traded to

Pittsburgh. Schofield shared the shortstop job with Gene Michael but hit just .216. Michael hit .202 on a Dodgers club that was last in the National League in batting. Los Angeles tumbled all the way to eighth place with a 73-89 mark. In December the Dodgers released Schofield.

The World Series champion Cardinals invited Ducky to spring training in 1968 and he signed with the club on April 1. In his second tour of duty with St. Louis, Schofield settled into a utility role. He started 13 games at shortstop and 17 at second base while appearing in a total of 69 games for the pennant-winning Cardinals. He appeared in two World Series games but did not get to the plate as the Cardinals bowed to the Tigers in seven games. In December Schofield was on the move again; the Cardinals sent him to the Boston Red Sox for pitcher Gary Waslewski.

Schofield never felt more comfortable in a utility role than he did with the Red Sox in 1969. Playing mostly second base, he also filled in at shortstop and third base and even ended up in left field and right field a few times. He started 44 times but appeared in a total of 94, his most since 1965. "Dick Williams was a good manager," Schofield said. "Every day when I came to the park, I knew I would probably play. I was the first pinch-hitter off of the bench after the seventh. Williams liked it that I was a switch-hitter and he could use me in double switches because I played several positions." Schofield responded by hitting .333 (11-for-33) in a pinch-hitting role. His average was third best in the American League among players with at least 30 pinch at-bats, and his nine pinch RBIs were fourth best in the league. With nine games left in the season, Dick Williams was fired as manager. Eddie Kasko became the manager in 1970 and everything changed for Schofield. "I didn't get to play in the field much under Kasko and I never knew when I was going to pinch-hit," he recalled. "I could be in the game to hit in the fourth or fifth inning at a meaningless time. I never really could get into any kind of rhythm." He hit only .163 (7-for-43) in 1970 as a pinch batter. Only two American League hitters with at least 30 at-bats were worse. In October the Red Sox traded him back to the Cardinals for first baseman Jim Campbell.

Now 36 years old, Schofield started the 1971 season with the Cardinals and on May 11, he hit the last of his career 21 homers. It came off Carl Morton in Montreal. He later accepted an assignment to Triple-A Tulsa, which lasted just 18 games. On July 29 Schofield was traded again, this time to the Milwaukee Brewers along with outfielder Jose Cardenal and pitcher Bob Reynolds for minor league pitcher Charlie Loseth and infielder Ted Kubiak. His final game in the big leagues came on September 30, 1971, as the Brewers lost to the White Sox 2-1 in Chicago.

After the season the Brewers gave Schofield the choice of managing San Antonio in the Texas League or playing another season with Milwaukee. He chose playing in the big leagues but became a victim of baseball's labor wars. With a strike looming during spring training, teams were releasing veterans and not keeping unsigned players. "One day in Tempe our manager Dave Bristol comes up and tells me 'Dick, I think you're in trouble,' " said Schofield. "Sure enough, a couple of days later I was released." Players went on strike on the last day of spring training and the first ten days of the season were wiped out. The 37-year-old Schofield's 19-year career was over. He had entered the game in 1953 as one of baseball's youngest players. When he left baseball in the spring of 1972, he was one of the oldest. In a testament to his versatility, he was used as a pinch-runner 190 times and as a pinch-hitter in 283 games.

Through the years he had opportunities to return to the game as a coach but instead decided to go home to Springfield. "I had been away from my home and family for so long, it just felt right that I should be with them," Schofield said. So he went home to his wife, Donna, and their three children, Dick, Kim, and Tammy. Son Richard "Dick" Craig Schofield went on to a 14-year major-league career. His father's choice of returning to Springfield played a large role in young Dick's ability to make it in baseball. "I did the same thing my dad did," beamed the elder Schofield. "I threw him a million baseballs, live batting practice. His sisters would shag balls."[5] "In all of my years in baseball, my greatest day was when I watched Dick take the field in the big leagues for the first time."[6] The girls were also fine athletes. Kim was a track star at the University of Florida and competed in the 1976 Olympic trials. Tammy excelled on the links as an excellent golfer. Kim's son and Dick's grandson is Jayson Werth, who was also born in Springfield. He is the fourth generation of professional ballplayers in the family. Werth, an outfielder, was with the Washington Nationals in 2012, his tenth big-league season. He is the stepson of former major-league first baseman/catcher Dennis Werth.

In 1975 Schofield began a 23-year career as a salesman for Jostens, which makes class rings, yearbooks and awards such as championship rings. From 1983 to 2003 Schofield served on the board of the Springfield Metropolitan Exposition Authority, which runs the local convention center. He resigned from the board to spend more time at home with his wife, Donna, who was diagnosed with Alzheimer's disease.

Notes

1 Dick Schofield, telephone interview with author, May 10, 2011. Unless otherwise indicated, all of Schofield's quotes are from this interview.

2 Danny Peary, *We Played the Game* (New York: Hyperion, 1994), 216.

3 Jonathan Fraser Light, *The Cultural Encyclopedia of Baseball* (Jefferson, North Carolina: McFarland, 1997), 99.

4 Peary, 435.

5 Paul Povse, St. Louis Beacon, http://www.stlbeacon.org/issues-politics/112-region/12691, accessed February 12, 2012.

Bob Skinner

By Joseph Wancho

AFTER STAGNATING AT the bottom of the National League for much of the 1950s, the Pittsburgh Pirates showed some life toward the end of the decade, finishing in second place in 1958 and in fourth place in 1959.

They began the 1960 season with an Opening Day loss at Milwaukee. They began the home portion of their schedule with a four-game series against Cincinnati starting on April 14. After splitting the first two games, the teams closed out the set with a doubleheader on the 17th, Easter Sunday. Bob Friend pitched a four-hit shutout in the opener as Pittsburgh won, 5-0. In the nightcap, Reds pitchers Don Newcombe and Raul Sanchez pitched their team to a 5-0 lead heading into the ninth inning. But the Pirates battled back in the bottom of the frame. They scratched for a run and after Hal Smith's pinch-hit three-run homer, the deficit was just one run. Then shortstop Dick Groat singled to center field and left fielder Bob Skinner homered to right off Reds reliever Ted Wieand, giving the Pirates a most improbable victory. Besides providing the winning margin in the second game, Skinner enjoyed a wonderful day at the plate, going 4-for-9 with two runs scored and two runs batted in. Those Pirates fans who remained among the announced Easter Sunday attendance of 16,196 left Forbes Field happy after witnessing a different type of resurrection before their very eyes.

For many baseball fans the arrival of spring brings the promise of warm weather and hopes for a pennant in the autumn for their heroes. But even the most astute Pirates fan could not have imagined how Skinner's game-winning blast would foreshadow how the Bucs' season would end in October.

Robert Ralph Skinner was born to Ralph and Lula Skinner

on October 3, 1931, in La Jolla, California. At La Jolla High School he earned two varsity letters in baseball and was named to two all-star teams. Ralph, his father, was a Spanish teacher at the school and coached track and field. After high school, Bob enrolled at San Diego Junior College, where he played basketball as well as baseball.

Pittsburgh scouts Tom Downey and Art Billings signed Skinner to a contract with the Pirates in 1951. Sent to Mayfield, Kentucky, of the Class D Kitty League, the 19-year-old Skinner played in 29 games and smacked 50 hits in 106 at-bats for an amazing .472 batting average. Moved up to Waco of the Class B Big State League, he cooled off, batting .283 in 98 games. His combined average was .326 with 87 runs batted in, 107 runs scored, 15 home runs, and 31 doubles. The 6-foot-4, 190-pound left-handed hitting first baseman showed patience at the plate, accumulating 86 walks against 52 strikeouts.

The US was fighting in the Korean War and Skinner was drafted into the Marines. He spent two years at the San Diego Recruiting Depot, where he played for the base team. Toward the end of the 1953 major-league season Pirates general manager Branch Rickey told manager Fred Haney to check Skinner out when he got back home to the West Coast.[1] Haney's report on Skinner prompted Rickey to invite the young player, who was about to be discharged, to the big-league camp the following spring.

On January 4, 1954, Skinner and Joan Phillips were married. The next month he reported to spring training at Jaycee Park in Fort Pierce, Florida. In 1953 the Pirates had finished in last place, 55 games behind pennant-winning Brooklyn. (In '52 they had also finished in last place, 54½ games out.) Whatever the team's goals were, Skinner, in his first spring training camp, hoped to make the Pirates' top farm team. "I hoped to do well enough to be assigned to New Orleans," he said.[2]

The Pirates were high on Skinner's ability. Rickey called him "absolutely the best natural hitter I've seen in many years. . . . who gets an awful lot of power into his swings. He does not seem to go for too many bad balls. Rickey predicted: "The boy has a tremendous future."[3]

Manager Fred Haney concurred with his boss. "He's destined to be one of the great hitters in baseball," he said. "He has a wonderful attitude too. He doesn't try to be fancy. I asked him the other day how he got so much power in that swing and he said, 'I dunno, I just go up there and swing.'"[4]

Though all he had hoped for in his first big-league camp was to be assigned to Triple-A, Skinner performed well enough to make the Pirates roster. On the team's way north he received a call informing him that Joan had been in a head-on car accident in Oklahoma. Bob went to Oklahoma to be with her, and was relieved to find out that. It turned out that she had not been badly injured, and he was able to rejoin the team the day before the season opened.

Skinner started 116 games at first base in his rookie year, hitting .249 with eight home runs and 46 RBIs. Just over a week into the season, on April 22, he got four hits in a 7-4 victory over the New York Giants, the first of several four-hit games in his 12-year major-league career. At season's end the Pirates found themselves in last place for the third season in a row, 44 games off the pace.

In 1955 the Pirates decided Skinner needed more seasoning and sent hin to the New Orleans Pelicans of the Double-A Southern Association. After 86 games he was leading the league with a .346 batting average but his season ended when he broke his left wrist. When he reported to spring training in 1956, Bobby Bragan was the manager; he had replaced Haney after another last-place showing by the Bucs in 1955.

Skinner made the team in 1956 but was supplanted at first base by Dale Long. He played only 24 games at first, 36 games in the outfield, bouncing between left field and right field, and even played two innings at third base.

Skinner, who had never played in the outfield before, spent the season learning the nuances of being an outfielder. Because of that defensive focus, and as is common with many part-time players, he was unable to establish a smooth flow to his offensive game. He hit .202 for the season as the Pirates left the cellar and moved up to seventh place.

Left fielder Lee Walls was traded to the Chicago Cubs at the beginning of the 1957 season, and Skinner replaced him against right-handed starters. Although the Pirates were still struggling in the standings, they were forming a good nucleus of ballplayers. Bill Mazeroski and Dick Groat were becoming a terrific keystone combination, Bill Virdon was solid in center field, and Bob Friend and Vern Law were leading a young pitching staff. But the player who brought it all together for the Pirates was Roberto Clemente. He could run, throw, and hit for power and average; the complete player. The Pirates were on the cusp of being a pennant contender.

The 1957 Pirates were 36-67 when Bragan was fired on August 4 and replaced by third-base coach Danny Murtaugh, who would enjoy a long managerial career in Pittsburgh. The new manager informed Skinner, "You're playing left field until you play your way out of it."[5] And 1957 became Skinner's breakout year. Showing he was the hitter Rickey and Haney predicted he would be, Skinner batted .305 and hit 13 home runs. Almost half of his 118 hits came after the patient Murtaugh took the reins of the club.

The Pirates had slipped back to the cellar in 1957 but finished the 1958 season in second place, eight games behind Milwaukee. Skinner led the team in batting average (.321), on-base percentage (.387), and walks (58), and was second to Groat in doubles (33, to Groat's 36). He shined in his left-field position at Forbes Field, leading the league with 17 outfield assists. Skinner was the starter in left field for the National League in the All-Star Game, in Baltimore. He went 1-for-3 with an RBI in a 4-3 loss to the American League.

Skinner was earning respect from his teammates for his hitting. He was being compared to St. Louis Cardinals great Stan Musial as the best left-handed hitter in the league. Teammate Dick Groat rated him the best left-handed hitter in the league after Musial. "And I'm not so sure he isn't about up with Stan," said the Pirates shortstop.[6]

Skinner said his approach at the plate was simple: "My objective is to meet the ball in a level swing. Then it has a chance to go some place whether you hit it in the air or on the ground."[7] Murtaugh, true to his word, penciled Skinner in the lineup and left him there. It didn't matter to Murtaugh which arm the opposing pitcher used to pitch. "He's a hard-working kid," said the manager. "He took up handball to help him get the angle of playing balls hit off the wall and that big scoreboard in left field in Pittsburgh."[8]

The Pirates finished the 1959 campaign in fourth place, nine games behind pennant-winner Los Angeles. Skinner's average dipped some, but he still batted a respectable .280, smacking 13 homers and driving in 61 runs. Both figures were good enough for second on the team behind first baseman Dick Stuart (27 HRs, 78 RBIs). Skinner led the team with 78 runs scored. In a four-game series in Cincinnati in late May he was 7-for-16, with five home runs and 11 RBIs, including a grand slam in the finale. The Pirates stayed in the hunt throughout the season, and as the calendar turned to September they were only five games out of the top spot. An 8-14 record that month, however, sealed their fate, and they finished in fourth place, nine games out of first.

The Pirates brought it all together in 1960, clinching the pennant when the second-place Cardinals lost to the Cubs on September 24. They finished the year with a 95-59-1 record. (The tie was a 7-7 duel with San Francisco on June 28 that was never completed.) Skinner hit for an average of .273, with 15 home runs and 86 RBIs, a career high. He was chosen to start in left field for the National League in both of that year's All-Star Games.

Skinner missed five games of the epic seven-game World Series against the New York Yankees. He went 1-for-3 with an RBI and a run scored in Game One, but jammed his thumb when he slid head-first into third base in the fifth inning, then was hit by a pitch in the seventh. After that he was replaced by Gino Cimoli, and didn't return to the Pirates' lineup until the epic seventh game, in Pittsburgh. Down 7-4 to the Yankees in the eighth inning, the Pirates scored five runs to take a 9-7 lead. During the rally, Virdon was on second and Groat on first when

Skinner laid down a perfect sacrifice bunt along the third-base line to move the runners up. After the Yankees tied the game with two runs in the top of the ninth inning, Bill Mazeroski won the Series with a dramatic home run off Ralph Terry that gave Pittsburgh its first world championship since 1925.

Success did not last for long. In 1961 the Pirates dropped to sixth place, 18½ games off the pace. They were in third place at the All-Star break, but started the second half with a 3-14 record. For the third straight year, Skinner's average dropped, this time to .268. Virdon and Groat also turned in poor years and no starter won more than 14 games.

In 1962 the National League expanded by two teams, adding Houston and New York. That season Skinner rebounded at the plate with a .302 batting average. He led the team in home runs (20) and walks (76), and ranked second in doubles (29) and RBIs (75). The Pirates improved as well, finishing fourth with a record of 93-68. But in 1963 the team was dismal, finishing ahead of only the two expansion teams. Skinner was not there at the finish, as he became the fourth regular from the 1960 World Series winners to be shipped out of Pittsburgh. Groat, Stuart, and Hoak had all left before the trade that sent Skinner to Cincinnati for pinch-hitter extraordinaire Jerry Lynch on May 23. The *Dayton Daily News* summarized the trade with the following headline: "Reds Get Regular for Lynch the Pinch." "I've got to like this deal," said Reds Manager Fred Hutchinson. "Skinner can play more for us—he can do more things. Jerry has done a great job for us, but I'd rather have a guy who can play every day. It's nice to have a good bench, but not at the expense of the regular lineup."[9] Skinner had a similar take on the swap: "You always have a soft spot for the first team, but I'm real glad to come to this team. I'd been playing regular, but the last few days Willie Stargell and Ted Savage had been in the lineup for me and Clemente. So I kind of had an inkling that something might be going to happen."[10]

Skinner played regularly at first, but as the season wore on he was sitting on Hutchinson's bench. He was in the starting lineup for only 10 games from July 11 to the end of the season. Skinner hit .253 for the Reds, to end up at .259 for the season. People started to think that perhaps the Pirates were following the adage of trading a player a year too early instead of a year too late. Skinner dismissed these criticisms, instead putting the onus on himself to work hard that winter, and report to spring training in top shape.

Now 32 years old, Skinner was a part-time starter for the Reds as the 1964 opened. Hitting just .220 in 59 at-bats, he was dealt to the Cardinals on June 13, 1964 for a career minor-league catcher, Jim Saul. At first the move proved to be a bit of a rebirth for Skinner. He was inserted into the starting lineup by Cardinals manager Johnny Keane. He was also reunited with Groat, who had come to the Cardinals a year earlier. But on June 15 St. Louis pulled off a blockbuster trade, acquiring Lou Brock from the Cubs in a six-player deal, and by mid-July Brock was getting most of the starts in left field. Skinner was once again relegated to the bench, starting only on occasion for the rest of the season.

The Cardinals won the pennant with a remarkable late-season rush, aided by the Phillies' collapse. In the World Series their opponent was again the New York Yankees, whom Skinner and Groat had faced when they were on the Pirates four years earlier. This Series also went seven games, with the Cardinals winning. Skinner didn't play in the field; in four pinch-hitting appearances he went 2-for-3 with a walk, a double, and an RBI.

In 1965 Skinner was used primarily in a reserve role by new St. Louis skipper Red Schoendienst. He spelled either Brock in left field or Mike Shannon in right. "Bob's still a good hitter—and good hitters are hard to find," Schoendienst said. "He can jump off the bench after a long layoff and do a real good job with the bat. And he's still dangerous as a long-ball threat."[11] In 152 at-bats Skinner hit .309, showing his professionalism by being ready when called on. He also started in 28 games in the outfield. In 1966, though, Skinner was used strictly as a pinch-hitter, 48 times, and not once seeing the field in a defensive position.

Skinner was released by the Cardinals after the season. He managed the San Diego Padres of the Pacific Coast League, the Philadelphia Phillies' Triple-A affiliate, in 1967 and 1968. He led the Padres to the PCL championship in his first season and was named Minor League Manager of the Year by *The Sporting News*. (Skinner was inducted into the San Diego Hall of Fame in 1976.)

When Gene Mauch, manager of the Phillies, was fired in mid-June of 1968, Skinner was promoted from San Diego to replace him. When Mauch was fired the Phillies were in fifth place, but only 5½ games out of first place. It was believed that difficulties with Richie Allen, the Phillies' star outfielder and a consistent discipline problem, led to Mauch's sacking. Nevertheless, Skinner was pleased with the promotion: "The organization has been great to me and it's a real thrill and pleasure to be able to manage the team," he said.[12]

The Phillies posted a 48-59 record under Skinner's watch in 1968, finishing 21 games out of first place. The 1969 season was a frustrating one for Bob and the Phillies. Although Skinner said all the right things about being positive and about the team having the proper attitude, it did not take long for the inevitable clash between the manager and the star. Allen skipped a doubleheader in New York on June 24. He was suspended for 26 games and did not play until July 24 in Houston. In addition to the suspension, it was reported that Allen was fined $450 each game he did not play, for a total of $11,700. On August 5, Allen informed Skinner that he had an agreement with Phillies owner Bob Carpenter and that he refused to accompany the team to Reading for an exhibition game against the Phillies' Double-A affiliate. Skinner resigned a few days later.

"Now I know what Gene Mauch went through," said Skinner. "You can fine Allen and he just laughs at you. He negotiates with the front office, makes his own private agreement and it's like handing the money right back to him. I don't want to go on managing this club under the circumstances."[13] The Phillies were 44-64 when Skinner resigned. Bob Carpenter said that Skinner really resigned because the Phillies wouldn't extend his contract past the 1969 season. Carpenter's But his assertion largely fell on deaf ears. An article by New York columnist Jimmy Cannon was headlined, "The Richie Allen Mess — Skinner: Class Guy." Cannon wrote of Skinner: "He isn't working, but he goes voluntarily for matters of pride. He went down with style because he refused to maim his dignity as a man. There aren't many men in baseball who would make this choice. The world is short of them. And that is why there is so much trouble."[14]

Skinner spent the next 30 years in a variety of posts. He coached for the Padres, Angels, Pirates, and Braves from

1970 through 1988. In 1979, he was the hitting coach for the Pirates, who won the World Series that year. One of Skinner's projects in 1979 was Tim Foli, the Pirates' light-hitting shortstop. By getting Foli to hold the bat parallel to the ground and choke up, Skinner helped him raise his batting average that season by 40 points over his career average. Foli proved valuable in the second position of the batting order behind speedster Omar Moreno.

Skinner managed the Tucson Toros, Houston's Triple-A affiliate, in 1989 and 1990. After that he stayed in the Houston organization as a special assignment scout until 2009.

As of 2011 Skinner and his wife, Joan, resided in the San Diego area. They had four sons, Robert, Craig, Andrew, and Joel. In 2002 Bob and Joel became only the second father-and-son combination (George and Dick Sisler were the first) to be major-league managers, when Joel became the Cleveland Indians manager.

Sources

Bill Ranier and David Finoli. *When the Pirates Won It All*. (Jefferson, North Carolina: McFarland and Company, Inc. 2005).

Peterson, Richard. *The Pirates Reader*. (Pittsburgh: University of Pittsburgh Press. 2003).

The Pittsburgh Pirate Encyclopedia. (Champaign, Illinois: Sports Publishing LLC. 2003).

The Sporting News

1930 United States Census.

http://www.sabr.org/

http://minors.sabrwebs.com/cgi-bin/index.php

http://www.baseballlibrary.com/homepage/

http://www.retrosheet.org/

http://www.sdhoc.com/

Notes

1   *Pittsburgh Press*, June 1, 1958.

2   *New York Times*, April 19, 1959.

3   National Baseball Hall of Fame Archives.

4   Ibid.

5   *New York Times*, April 19, 1959.

6   *Baseball Digest*, June 1959.

7   Ibid.

8   Ibid.

9   *Dayton Daily News*, May 24, 1963.

10 Ibid.

11 National Baseball Hall of Fame Archives.

12 Ibid.

13 National Baseball Hall of Fame Archives.

14 Ibid.

Hal Smith

By Dick Rosen

ANDY WARHOL ONCE suggested that "In the future everyone will be world-famous for 15 minutes." Hal Smith was no exception, even though he had only about 13 minutes of fame, or even less.

Smith could have been the hero of the 1960 World Series were it not for several events that occurred shortly after his heroics in Game Seven. The catcher had entered the game in the top half of the eighth inning after Smoky Burgess had been removed for a pinch-runner in the seventh. Smith donned the hero's mantle—for Pittsburgh Pirates fans, at least—when he hit a three-run home run in the bottom of the eighth that gave the Pirates the lead over the New York Yankees, 9-7.

But Smith's heroics were overshadowed by one of the most remarkable World Series endings ever. Thanks to an inspired bit of baserunning by Mickey Mantle, the Yankees proceeded to tie the game in the top of the ninth inning. Then, as the leadoff batter in the bottom of the ninth, Bill Mazeroski lived out the fantasy of nearly every American kid who has baseball in his or her blood. Perhaps there weren't two out and maybe the count wasn't 3-2 as we all had fantasized, but it was Game Seven of the World Series and the score was tied in the bottom of the ninth. With one swing of the bat, Mazeroski's new reputation was launched, and Hal Smith, the hero for a moment, had to make room for him in the limelight.

The eighth inning had been remarkable as well. The Pirates scored five runs in the inning, which featured some of the most memorable plays in World Series history. With the Pirates trailing 7-4, Gino Cimoli led off with a single, and left-handed-hitting Bill Virdon sent what appeared to be a routine grounder toward

Yankee shortstop Tony Kubek. It was tailor-made to produce a shortstop-to-second-to-first double play, but not that day. On the Forbes Field infield, which was often called the Pirates' "secret weapon" because of its flinty surface,[1] the ball took a crazy bounce, hit Kubek in the throat, and caused him to gag and almost lose his breath. Kubek had to be removed from the game. *New York Times* sports columnist Arthur Daley said of this ground ball that it was "spitefully steered by Dame Fortune."[2] The Pirates now had men on first and second with nobody out.

Shortstop Dick Groat singled, sending Cimoli home. Bob Skinner was out on a sacrifice that sent Groat to second and Virdon to third. After Rocky Nelson flied to right, Roberto Clemente hit a ground ball to first base. The removal of pitcher Bobby Shantz after Groat's hit was felt on this play because his replacement, Jim Coates, did not cover first base as Shantz, an eight-time Gold Glover, might have done. Clemente was safe; Virdon scored; and Groat went to third. The stage was set for Hal Smith. With the score 7-6 in favor of the Yankees and two runners on base, Smith was looking for something that would enable him to drive in the run that was only 90 feet away. Smith knew the Yanks pitching staff well; he had handled most of them coming up through the Yankees' farm system and catching for the Kansas City Athletics. "They didn't scare me," he said.[3]

Smith fell behind in the count, 0-and-2, on two fastballs from Jim Coates. (The second strike was a swing and miss.) On the third pitch, he checked his swing to stay alive. Then Coates threw another fastball that Smith did not miss. He met the pitch and drove it deep into the left-field stands as his former teammate Yogi Berra, playing left field that day, watched it sail into the seats.[4] As Smith rounded the bases, he recalled feeling little emotion ("just another home run") until he came around second and could see fans along the third-base line standing on the dugout, cheering, screaming, jumping. Only then did he realize the import of that hit. Dick Groat called it "the most forgotten home run in baseball history."[5] Perhaps not so forgotten as just put on the back burners of people's memories. Joe L. Brown, the Pirates general manager, called this shot "the single most memorable play of my life." And play-by-play announcer Chuck Thompson, who was calling the game on the radio, said of the homer, "We have seen and shared in one of baseball's greatest moments."[6]

But the Yankees were not finished. Bob Friend was sent into the game to close out the game but he could not; he put two Yankees on base in the ninth and Harvey Haddix allowed them to score the tying runs. That set the stage for Mazeroski's Series-winning blast. But if not for Hal Smith's three-run bomb in the eighth inning, who knows what might have happened?

Harold Wayne Smith was born on December 7, 1930, in West Frankfort, Illinois, to Earl and Ruth Smith.[7] His father, who wanted to get out of the Southern Illinois coal mines, moved the family to Detroit when he was 11, and became a house painter. Harold played football and baseball in high school. His father insisted that he concentrate on baseball, and Harold became a competent sandlot third baseman. He signed with the Yankees out of high school, and began his professional career in 1949 at Ventura of the Class C California league (ten games) and then Twin Falls (seven games) in the Class C Pioneer league. The following year, still a teenager, he found himself at Newark in the Class D Ohio-Indiana league.

From this point on, Smith made steady progress toward the major leagues. After hitting .363 at Newark he moved up to Quincy of the Class B Three-I League. He progressed through the Yankee system to Beaumont of the Texas League, and Birmingham of the Southern Association, where he hit a healthy .311 in 1953. By this time, Smith was just behind Yogi Berra in the Yankees' table of organization. His mentor was Bill Dickey, soon to be elected to the Hall of Fame, who had been a mentor to Berra as well. After spring training in 1954, manager Casey Stengel chose Smith to catch the final exhibition game against the Brooklyn Dodgers at Ebbets Field. But

Smith didn't play in the game, and in fact never played a single inning for the Bronx Bombers. He contracted infectious mononucleosis (often referred to as glandular fever), had a fever as high as 107 degrees, and was hospitalized for ten days. He lost 13 pounds. When he left the hospital he had to do spring training all over again.[8] The Yankees optioned him to Columbus, a St. Louis Cardinals farm team in the Triple-A American Association. There he made a remarkable recovery, winning the league batting crown with a .350 average.

Still blocked by Berra, Smith was involved in a 17-player deal between the Yankees and the Baltimore Orioles after the 1954 season.[9] The next year, 1955, he was with Baltimore and remained in the majors for ten years. (One of the Baltimore players in the massive deal was Don Larsen who had led the American League with 21 losses in 1954 but two years later pitched a perfect game in the 1956 World Series.

Smith played in 135 games as the Orioles' regular catcher in 1955 and batted .271. Then in August of 1956 he was traded to the Kansas City Athletics for catcher Joe Ginsberg. In 1957 Smith batted .303 with 26 doubles and 13 home runs, both career highs (good enough to get him a $2,500 raise after a holdout). He was with the Athletics through 1959, even spending a half-season at his sandlot position, third base, and spending some time at first base. In later years he said he felt the Athletics fostered a losing mentality, always trading away their good players. "In spring training the manager would say, "Let's look good losing this year. Let's do things right."[10]

After the 1959 season Smith was traded to the Pittsburgh Pirates for three players, catcher Hank Foiles and two farmhands, pitcher Dick Hall and shortstop Ken Hamlin. The A's had tried to convert Smith into a third baseman, but the Pirates were looking for a catcher to platoon with left-handed batting Smoky Burgess and beef up the hitting of the catcher corps. Smith succeeded, catching in about half the team's games in 1960 and batting .295. The team of Smith and Burgess (who batted .294) made the Pirates' catching a serious one-two punch. Smith often seemed to provide the final punch in many victories that year. He was especially lethal against the Dodgers, hitting several of his own "Moon shots" (named for the Dodgers' Wally Moon) at the Coliseum. In Los Angeles he hit more home runs in 1960 that he had hit the entire previous year with Kansas City. In two consecutive games in Los Angeles in July, he hit four home runs.

Smith slumped in 1961, batting only .223 in 67 games. When the National League expanded from eight to ten teams after the season, Smith was made available in the expansion draft, and was picked up by the Houston Colt .45s. He was Houston's starting catcher when the 1962 season began, and hit a double and a home run in the team's first game. But by season's end Smith had caught in only 92 games and batted a weak .235 with 12 home runs.

In 1963 Smith broke a finger in spring training and wound up spending half the season at Triple-A Oklahoma City. Recalled at the end of July, he backed up 23-year-old catcher John Bateman. At the end of the season he was released by the Colt .45s. "But I wasn't out of a job long," he said.[11] Within about two months he had joined the Cincinnati Reds, who were looking for an experienced catcher to play a backup role and help the team's young pitchers develop. Smith had a good reputation for handling pitchers. (He said a former Kansas City teammate, pitcher Ned Garver, had tutored him well. Still, his tenure with the Reds was short-lived and he was released at the end of July. In his last major-league at-bat, on July 22, he faced Mets left-hander Willard Hunter and popped out

to the second baseman. He stayed on for a few weeks as a batting practice catcher, but in September was sent to the Reds' Triple-A team at San Diego, played in a few games, and retired as a player at the end of the season.

Smith returned to Houston, where he became a salesman for Jessop Steel, a Pittsburgh company for whom he worked in Houston during much of his post-baseball career.

Outside of baseball and steel sales, Smith was a man of many talents, and being a World Series hero had opened several doors. After the 1960 World Series he sang on the *Ed Sullivan Show* with teammate Roy Face. (Casey Stengel grunted in the background.)[12] He once made $2,500 a month for four months playing the guitar and singing in nightclubs, in a routine with Roy Face.[13] When he was with the Reds in 1964, he was a part of a trio including Johnny Temple (guitar) and coach Dick Sisler (harmonica), and sometimes his wife, Ann. Smith's wife was a welcome addition to the group when she consented to sing with them. Ms. Smith had "a professional voice," according to Temple.[14] They were married on February 4, 1960, and had three children, daughter Debby and sons Danny and Mike. They were later divorced and Hal married the former Ann Shannon in 1979.

An amateur cook, Smith owned a Houston eatery, K-Bobs. Running a restaurant turned out to be a great chore, and that venture ended after about seven years.

In 2012 Smith lived with his second wife in Columbus, Texas, and enjoyed golfing and fishing. In 2010 he had heart bypass surgery, which forced him to miss the 50th-anniversary reunion of the 1960 Pirates.

Speaking of his career, he called his era a "great time for baseball," and said, "I got to play against some of the greatest that ever played … like Ted Williams, Stan Musial, Yogi Berra, Whitey Ford, Hank Aaron, Mickey Mantle, and Bob Gibson."[15] Smith's nephew, Tim Flannery, a former San Diego Padres infielder and as of 2012 the third-base coach for the San Francisco Giants, told him that if he had "played in my era, you'd have been a multimillionaire."[16] Smith expressed no resentment at the thought that he may have been overshadowed by other players during his career. He said he and Mazeroski have become better friends over the 50-plus years since those two famous home runs. Every time "we see each other, Maz thanks me," Smith said. Other baseball experts also appreciated him. Paul Richards, who managed Smith at Baltimore, called him "a blood-and-guts ballplayer; he goes all out to win and delivers the winning hit."[17]

After the 1960 World Series, Smith's father, Earl, brimming with pride, said something that Hal said he still carried with him: "I saw my son play in the major leagues, and I saw him help win a World Series. If I bowl a 300 game now, my life will be complete."[18] We can only hope that Mr. Smith "hit for his cycle," but even if he never bowled his perfect game, 2-for-3 is great in baseball.

Notes

1   Joe Williams, "Adam's Apple Is Achilles Heel in Yankee Tragedy," *New York World Telegram and Sun,* October 14, 1960.

2   Jim O'Brien, *Maz and the '60 Bucs: When Pittsburgh and Its Pirates Went All the Way* (Pittsburgh: James P. O'Brien Publishing, 1993), 280.

3   [3]Jennifer Langosch, "Smith Reflects on 1960 World Series," MLB.com, June 14, 2008.

4   Chris Hottensen, "Hal Smith: History's Footnote," *The Southern Illinoisan,* Carbondale, Illinois, July 5, 2011.

5   Jim O'Brien, op. cit.

6   Jim O'Brien, op. cit.

7   It should be noted that there were two catchers named Hal Smith playing in the major leagues at roughly the same time. The subject of this biography is Harold *Wayne* Smith. Harold *Raymond* Smith, born six months earlier than Harold Wayne Smith, played from 1956 to 1961 with the St. Louis Cardinals, and played briefly with the Pirates in 1964. He was born in Barling, Arizona, and was sometimes known as the Barling Darling.

8   Neal Russo, "Smith Yankee in 1953, Laid Low by Illness," *St Louis Post-Dispatch,* October 14, 1960.

9   Traded by the Yankees: Hal Smith, Harry Byrd, Jim McDonald, Willy Miranda, Gus Triandos, Bill Miller, Kal Segrist, Don Leppert, Ted Del Guercio, and Gene Woodling. Traded by the Orioles: Billy Hunter, Don Larsen, Bob Turley, Mike Blyzka, Darrell Johnson, Jim Fridley, and Dick Kryhoski. (Some of the players were unidentified at the time of trade, and were named on December 1.

10 Norman Macht, "Hal Smith Was a World Series Hero — for 15 Minutes," Rogers Hornsby SABR Chapter website, posted September 14, 2009.

11 Lou Smith, "Hal Smith Wants a Job," *Cincinnati Enquirer,* March 3, 1964.

12 Oscar Fraley, "Song and Chatter by Casey," October 27, 1960, United Press International article in Hal Smith file at the Baseball Hall of Fame.

13 Pat Harmon, "Newest Red Gets Around," *Cincinnati Post and Times Star,* December 12, 1963.

14 Earl Lawson, "Hutch's Hootenanny Makes Lips Quiver, Hearts Ache, Tears Flow," *Cincinnati Post,* March 21, 1964.

15 Hottensen, op. cit.

16 Hottensen, op. cit.

17 Pat Harmon, op. cit.

18 Jim O'Brien, op. cit., 283.

R C Stevens

By Alan Cohen

R C STEVENS, said one of his minor-league managers, was "capable of breaking up a game anytime he took his bat in hand." He hit 191 home runs in 12 minor-league seasons, but didn't meet the test in the major leagues, and played only briefly in four seasons, three of them (including 1960) with the Pirates.

Stevens did have one distinction—he was among the very few players who threw left-handed and batted right-handed. Originally he batted from the left side with a cross-handed grip, but on the advice of one of his high school teammates, rather than change his grip he switched to the right side of the plate.[1]

The only son of I.H. Crapps, Jr. and Minnie Stephens, R C Stevens (he had no first name, just the initials; "Seaboat" was his boyhood nickname, a reference to his size) was born in Moultrie, Georgia, on July 22, 1934.[2] Shortly after he was born, his parents married other people. His mother married Solomon Griffin, and they reared R C. I. H. Crapps married Rachel Wiley and had eight more children. He was a farmer who later went on to work for Swift foods. The Crapps and Griffin families both lived in Moultrie and R C had frequent contact with his eight half-sisters and half-brothers

R C played baseball, basketball, and football at the Moultrie High School for Negro Youth. After graduating in 1951, he worked in construction. Branch Rickey, who had left the Brooklyn Dodgers to take over as general manager of the Pirates, was on the lookout for talented young black ballplayers. Rickey wrote to baseball coaches at black high schools throughout the South. Stevens' high-school coach, A.F. "Papa" Shaw, encouraged the 6-foot-5-inch first baseman to try out for the Pirates. He went to the

Pirates' minor-league facility in Deland, Florida, and, after a tryout, was signed by Pirates scout George Pratt.[3]

Stevens made his way from Class D to Triple-A over the next six seasons before making his big-league debut with the Pirates in 1958. He broke in with the Batavia (New York) Clippers of the Pennsylvania-Ontario-New York League, under shortstop-manager George Genovese, who had spotted Stevens at Deland and took a keen interest in the big 17-year-old. He hit well from the start. A home run on June 3 earned him a bonus. Genovese had promised to reimburse him $19.50 for the cost of his new glove if he hit four home runs in two weeks, and the June 3 homer was number four. Four home runs in the next two weeks would get R C a new set of spikes.[4] He wouldn't need the home runs. When word got out about R C needing spikes, a fan took up a collection and $20.04 later, Stevens had his spikes.[5] It was a good thing, because he didn't hit the four home runs. Stevens got into 102 games and batted .246 (six home runs in all), earning himself a promotion in 1953 to the St. Jean (Quebec) Canadians of the Class C Provincial League, again managed by Genovese. He hit .313 with St. Jean, and increased his home run output to 12. After the season Stevens married his high-school sweetheart, Carrie Bell Moss.

After St. Jean, the next stop on the Pirates' minor-league ladder was less hospitable: the Burlington-Graham Pirates in the Class B Carolina League. Stevens was the only black on the team. In his first game, an opposing fan brought a black cat to the game and taunted Stevens with racial epithets. He was denied accommodations with his white teammates and stayed in either black hotels or with families in the area. Despite this, he had a good season, batting .293 with

31 doubles, 25 home runs, and 115 RBIs.[6] July 28 was a highlight, with a grand slam and a two-run homer against Reidsville. The team finished the regular season in second place. The Pirates won the semifinal round of the playoffs but lost to Fayetteville in the next round. Stevens had three home runs in the ten playoff games.

The 20-year-old Stevens was initially scheduled to play in Double-A New Orleans in 1955, but instead was sent to Hollywood, the Pirates affiliate in the "open" classification Pacific Coast League. At his first batting practice, Stevens discovered that the catcher, Bill Hall, was from Moultrie. (Hall and Stevens were later teammates on the 1958 Pirates.) On June 5 Stevens had two home runs and three RBIs in a 5-1 win at Portland. Stevens injured his knee on July 3 and was used sparingly for the balance of the season. He got into only 18 games during July and August, mostly as a pinch-hitter or defensive replacement. His batting average dropped to .241 for the season. After the season Stevens played for the Jalapa Chileros in the Mexican winter league. In a game in November, Stevens hit a grand slam in a win over the Mexico City Aztecas (Mexico was one of six countries in which he hit home runs). He batted.306 at Jalapa with 47 RBIs.

Stevens returned to Hollywood for 1956. He was leading the Stars with five home runs and 14 RBIs when he was hit by a Jerry Casale fastball in a game against San Francisco on May 2, and broke his hand. He missed a month of play.[7] After he returned he went on a tear as the Stars won 15 of 16 games and climbed to third place. In July he hit seven home runs in his first 12 games. For the month, he had nine homers and 25 RBIs. But Stevens and the Stars slumped in late August and early September. He wound up with a .262 batting average, was third in the league with 27 home runs, and had a team-leading 72 RBIs, while cutting down his strikeouts. After the season he played winter ball for Aguilas Cibaenas in the Dominican League.

Stevens trained with the Pirates in Fort Myers in 1957, but began the season with Hollywood. After an early-season slump, his bat came alive, and he had several key hits as the Stars gained first place. Over a 24-game span from April 23 through May 17, he had six home runs and 20 RBIs, and the team went 18-6. But despite his productivity, his batting average was mired in the low .200s. Manager Clyde King suggested he choke up on the bat

and Stevens went 11-for-28 as the Stars took five of seven games at Vancouver in mid-June.[8] But it was all downhill from there. Stevens went into a prolonged slump, going 1-for-27 against Portland, and sprained his back at the end of June. His average had slipped to .221, and he was reassigned to the Columbus Jets of the International League on July 9. In his first weeks with the Jets, both he and the team did poorly. But between August 5 and 31, Stevens batted .327 with six home runs and 22 RBIs, capping the month on the 29th when he doubled and homered off Satchel Paige, then pitching for the Miami Marlins. Stevens batted .341 in his last 19 games and finished with a .294 batting average at Columbus, with eight home runs and 36 RBIs.

Stevens reached the major leagues in 1958. Before spring training in Fort Myers, he wrote to general manager Joe L. Brown: "I see you have a lot of first basemen. There are Ted Kluszewski, Frank Thomas, Dick Stuart, and me. I just want to let you know I'm going to make trouble for all of them."[9] In Fort Myers Kluszewski had back problems due to a slipped disc and Stuart came down with the flu. Stevens hit well, with a triple and two home runs in a short span while keeping his strikeouts down, and went north with the Bucs.[10] He made his debut on Opening Day, April 15, replacing Kluszewski at first base in the bottom of the ninth with the Pirates leading Milwaukee by a run. The Braves tied the game. Stevens singled off Gene Conley in the 12th inning, then drove in the winning runs in the 14th with another hit off Conley. Four days later he hit a pinch-hit two-run homer off Harvey Haddix of the Cincinnati Reds in a 9-6 loss. The next day he hit a ninth-inning walk-off homer against Willard Schmidt of the Reds. After three game appearances he was 4-for-4 with two home runs, and had driven in the decisive run in each of the Bucs' first two wins.[11] He commented, "Man, I'm still up in those clouds. ..."[12]

Stevens continued to come in as a defensive replacement, then had a few starts in May. On the 5th at San Francisco, batting cleanup, he hit a three-run home run. It was Stevens' fourth home run of the year, and he gained the distinction of having hit home runs in the same ballpark (Seals Stadium) as both a major leaguer and a minor leaguer.

But Stevens did not start many games, only 19, as he sat while Kluszewski started against right-handed pitchers.

He continued to have a knack for getting game-winning hits. On May 11, after striking out in his first three at-bats against Philadelphia's Curt Simmons, he broke up a scoreless game, singling in the bottom of the 11th inning to give the Bucs a 1-0 win. Still, he went back to the minors in July, when the Pirates brought up Dick Stuart from Salt Lake City. Despite his clutch hits, Stevens had been striking out far too much—25 K's in 85 at-bats. His average had dropped to .259, as he went only 7-for-36, striking out 11 times, after June 1. Meanwhile, in 79 games at Salt Lake City, Stuart had hit 31 homers and his average stood at .314.

After batting .276 with 12 home runs at Salt Lake City (the Bees had replaced the Hollywood Stars after the Brooklyn Dodgers moved to Los Angeles) Stevens was called up to the Pirates at the beginning of September, but saw little late-season action. For the season with the Pirates he batted .267 with seven home runs and 18 RBIs in 90 at-bats. His .556 slugging percentage was tops on the team, but the Bucs, who finished second in the standings with an 84-70 record, made the decision that Stuart was to be their first baseman. As a left-handed thrower, Stevens' opportunities in the field were limited. The Pirates were set in the outfield with Bob Skinner, Bill Virdon, and Roberto Clemente, and Stuart was placed at first base despite his fielding inadequacies. Stevens would never again see meaningful playing time in Pittsburgh, where his teammates had given him the nickname Real Cool, a reference to his initials, and his demeanor. After the 1958 season, with the military draft still in effect, the 24-year-old Stevens enlisted in the US Army Reserve. He was on active duty until May 1959, after which he rejoined the Pirates. He pinch-hit once, then was sent to the minors. After a brief stint at Columbus, he was sent to Salt Lake City on June 4. After a strong start, his average plummeted to .243. Things turned around when he homered in each game of a doubleheader sweep of Portland on August 2. On the 21st the Bees reached first place, then kept winning, with Stevens delivering some clutch hits. By the end of the season, his average stood at .287 with a team-leading 19 home runs and 75 RBIs. The Bees won the PCL championship. Exclaimed manager Larry Shepard asked, "Where would we have finished without big R C Stevens, who was capable of breaking up a game anytime he took his bat in hand?"[13] Before Pittsburgh's

season ended, Stevens was called up and went 2-for-6 in two games.

Stevens spent most of 1960 with Salt Lake City. He hit a league-leading 37 home runs and finished second in the league to teammate Harry Bright with 109 RBIs. Both were personal bests. The Pirates called him up on September 12. He got into only nine games, mostly as a defensive replacement. He had only three at-bats and went hitless. He was not on the roster for the World Series.

After the 1960 season Stevens was dealt to the expansion Washington Senators along with infielder Bright and pitcher Bennie Daniels for pitcher Bobby Shantz. For a time at the beginning of the season, Stevens was platooned with Dale Long at first base, but Long was one of the few recognizable names in the Washington lineup and the platoon was short-lived. Long started most of the games at first base. Stevens only had eight hits in 62 at-bats with Washington, and in June he was sold to the Toronto Maple Leafs of the International League. In his last major-league game, on June 10, he struck out as a pinch-hitter. Stevens's major-league statistics were disappointing, but he had been part of "The Show" and took away memories to last a lifetime. He appeared in 104 games and batted .210 with eight home runs and 19 RBIs. He was strong on defense, with only two errors in 426 chances at first base.

After Washington, Stevens played three seasons in the minors before hanging up his spikes. In a holiday doubleheader at Buffalo on July 4, 1961, he had the best day in his career. In the first game he went 3-for-3, all solo home runs, in the seven-inning opener, won by Toronto 6-0. In the nightcap, he went 2-for-3 with a double and two runs scored as Toronto completed the sweep. Three weeks later, he hit homes runs in three consecutive games. He broke his thumb on August 1 and missed 35 games. Despite his power outburst, for the season, he batted .243 with 12 homers.

Just after the end of the season, during the height of the Berlin Crisis, Stevens was activated by the Army and spent most of the 1962 season stationed at Fort Lewis in Washington. While there, he played on the Fort Lewis Rangers team along with Tony Kubek, Deron Johnson and other major leaguers. He didn't join the Maple Leafs until August 3, and saw limited action in his team's remaining 43 games, batting only .224. Released by Toronto early in the 1963 season, he signed with the Quad Cities Angels of the Class A Midwest League, who played in his adopted hometown of Davenport, Iowa. He batted .245 in 57 games, and ended his 12-season run in Organized Baseball.

During his time with the Pirates, Stevens had become friends with infielder Gene Baker, and their friendship extended beyond their playing days. Baker persuaded R C and his wife, Carrie, to move from Moultrie to Baker's hometown of Davenport after the 1960 season, and they were next-door neighbors for almost 40 years. R C and Carrie did not have children. Carrie Stevens died in 1995, and Baker died in 1999.

Another lasting friendship from Stevens's years in baseball was with pitcher Dean Stone. They played a season of winter ball in Venezuela in 1959-60 for the Elders of Vargas in the Valencia Industrial League. Stone lived in Silvis, Illinois, not far from Davenport, and after their baseball careers ended, they were frequent companions on the golf course.

Ensconced in Davenport, R C first worked for Ametek in nearby East Moline before going to work for International Harvester, where he rose to the rank of department manager. He was laid off in 1985 when the company sold off its agricultural division, and he became a Davenport city bus driver for 12 years.

Stevens was among the first inductees into the Colquitt County (Georgia) Sports Hall of Fame in 2000. Among the others in that first class of honorees were one of his opponents from his minor-league days, John Glenn, and their high-school coach, A.F. Shaw. Former Pirates teammate Bill Hall was inducted in 2003. On April 25, 2003, Stevens joined with Buck O'Neill, Monte Irvin, and Art Pennington as Augustana College in Rock Island, Illinois, near Davenport, paid tribute to Negro League baseball.[14]

Stevens died on November 30, 2010, at the age of 76, in Davenport.

Sources

Books:

Richard E. Beverage, *The Hollywood Stars: Baseball in Movieland—1926-1957* (Placentia, California:, Deacon Press, 1984).

Wayne Grandy, *Heroes of the Games: The Colquitt County Sports Hall of Fame 2000-2004* (Moultrie, Georgia: *Moultrie Observer*, 2004).

Newspapers and magazines:

Bob Addie, "Just Call him R C or Steve: Nats Stevens southpaw oddity, Bats right, has no first name", *The Washington Post*, March 12, 1961, C1

Ned Cronin, "Cronin's Corner," *Los Angeles Times*, September 6, 1956, A3.

Don Doxsie, "Ex-major leaguer, Q-C resident Stevens dies," *Quad City Times,* Davenport, Iowa, December 3, 2010.

Les Goates, "Bees in Basement on June 7, Cop Flag in Honey of Finish," *The Sporting News*, September 3, 1959, 39.

Wayne Grandy, *Moultrie* (Georgia) *Observer*, December 3, 2010.

Wayne Grandy, *Moultrie* (Georgia) *Observer*, October, 2000.

Jerry Johnson. "Derks—A Field You Don't Forget," *Deseret News* (Salt Lake City, Utah), April 21, 1993, C-2.

Earl Lawson, "R. C. Stevens Toast of Pittsburgh; Rookie's Hits Net Bucs Two Wins," *Cincinnati Times*, April 21, 1958.

John Naughton, "Des Moines Sunday Register's Sports Hall of Fame: Gene Baker," *Des Moines Register*, July 18, 2009.

Eric Page, "Davenport's Stevens made big splash in majors 50 years ago this week," *Quad Cities Times* (Davenport, Iowa), April 12, 2008.

Edward "Abie" Robinson, "Abie's Corner," *California Eagle*, Los Angeles, April 10, 1958.

Chester L. Smith, "Buc Rookie Saves All His Hustling for Playing Field," *Pittsburgh Press*, March 27, 1958.

"For Place on Cloud 100: Rookie Wins Second Game for Pirates," *Simpson's Leader-Times*, Kittanning, Pennsylvania, April 21, 1958.

"Young R.C. Stevens Shows Some Strong Power at Plate," *Tonawanda* (New York) *News*, April 4, 1958, 7.

Batavia (New York) *Daily News,* June 4, 1952, June 10, 1952.

Website:

Baseball-Reference.com

Interviews

Joe Christopher, January 3, February 7, February 8, 2012.

Wayne Grandy, February 13, 2012.

Bob Oldis, October 12, 2011.

Everlene Register, November 4, 2011, February 12, 2012, February 23, 2012,

Dean Stone, October 10, 2011.

Research assistance was provided by John Sollito, author of *Building the Pirates for the Future: Race, Mr. Rickey, and R.C. Stevens, 1952-55.*

Notes

1   Bob Addie, *Washington Post*, March 12, 1961

2   Although his mother spelled her surname as Stephens, R C's was always rendered as Stevens.

3   Wayne Grandy, *Moultrie Observer,* December 3, 2010.

4   *Batavia Daily News*, June 4, 1952.

5   *Batavia Daily News*, June 10, 1952.

6   Eric Page, "Davenport's Stevens made big splash in majors 50 years ago this week," *Quad-City Times* (Davenport, Iowa), April 12, 2008.

7   Edward "Abie" Robinson, "Abie's Corner," *California Eagle*, Los Angeles, April 10, 1958.

8   *The Sporting News*, June 26, 1957

9   Chester L. Smith, "Buc Rookie Saves All His Hustling for Playing Field," *Pittsburgh Press*, March 27, 1958.

10 "Young R.C. Stevens Shows Some Strong Power at Plate," *Tonawanda* (New York) *News*, April 4, 1958, 7.

11 Earl Lawson, "R. C. Stevens Toast of Pittsburgh; Rookie's Hits Net Bucs Two Wins," *Cincinnati Times*, April 21, 1958.

12 "For Place on Cloud 100: Rookie Wins Second Game for Pirates," *Simpson's Leader-Times*, Kittanning, Pennsylvania, April 21, 1958

13 Les Goates, "Bees in Basement on June 7, Cop Flag in Honey of Finish," *The Sporting News*, September 3, 1959, 39.

14 *Quad Cities Times*, April 26, 2003.

Dick Stuart

By Jan Finkel

DICK STUART WAS fun—as long as you didn't have to be on the field with him.

He ran the bases, head down and looking anywhere except at the third-base coach or the outfield or a teammate who might be able to tell him something, often sending his team out of the inning. As a fielder, suffice it to say that his nickname was "Dr. Strangeglove" and no less an authority than Hank Aaron called him "Stonefingers." A group of fans with a literary bent and a special fondness for Alexandre Dumas christened him "The Man With the Iron Glove." As a first baseman Stuart led his league in errors seven straight years, usually by a wide margin. Playing in only 64 games his rookie year (1958), he managed to commit 16 miscues. Given that he played with one of the great keystone combinations of all time in Dick Groat and Bill Mazeroski, one can only wonder how many double plays they might have turned with any other first baseman. Stuart led the American League in 1963 with 29 errors, a number made uglier by the fact that the runner-up committed only 12. (For the record, future Hall of Famer Orlando Cepeda led the National League with 21, still far behind Stuart.) Stuart once received a standing ovation for catching a hot dog wrapper on the fly. In fairness, he did one thing well with a ball in his hands. He had a terrific kind of halfway behind-the-back toss to the mound to end the inning, delivered in quasi-contemptuous fashion and proving that he could master a skill if he put his mind to it. Life was never dull with Stuart, on the bases or in the field.

A person this annoying—not to mention this destructive—has to do something well to stick around, and Stuart did. Playing among contemporaries like Hank Aaron, Willie Mays, Ernie Banks, Frank Robinson,

Willie McCovey, Orlando Cepeda, and Eddie Mathews, he could hit a baseball farther than just about anybody. True, he didn't connect as frequently or for as long as they did, but for distance he had few equals and no superiors.

And he did it all, the good and the bad, with a wink and a twinkle in his eye—but not without a hint of sadness, perhaps the sadness of someone who sees the joke. An anecdote, possibly apocryphal, illustrates the point. The scene could play out in several ways, but it shows that Stuart was more quick-witted than people assumed. Pirates manager Danny Murtaugh summoned him to his office to discuss a misplay of the day before. Stuart sauntered in, calling Murtaugh by his first name. Exploding at Stuart's familiarity, Murtaugh said that players were to call him Manager or Skip or Mr. Murtaugh, finishing his lecture with "You're nothing! Remember that! I'm mister and you're nothing!" Waiting for his point to sink in, Murtaugh said, "Who am I?" Stuart answered, "I guess that you're the manager of nothing."[1]

The quintessential nonconformist in an era that demanded conformity, Stuart often had a hard time of it with teammates, opponents, and many fans who didn't think he took the game or anything else seriously enough. To get a glimpse of Stuart's penchant for individuality one had only to walk down Grant Street in Pittsburgh to the Carlton House Hotel, where the Pirates gathered to take the bus to the airport. Bunched together around their Samsonite luggage would be the Bucs—Groat, Mazeroski, Skinner, Virdon, Law, Friend, Face, Hoak, even Clemente—a few smoking, all chatting among themselves, wearing dark suits or sport coats with starched white (or the occasional blue or striped) shirts and dark solid or conservatively patterned ties. Off a fair bit to the side would be Stuart, pure Hollywood, in a white suit with a black shirt open at least three buttons down, shades, maybe combing his hair, a cigar or cigarette at the ready. Alone, that's how the scene struck an outsider.

The future slugger was born Richard Lee Stuart on November 7, 1932, in San Francisco of Scots-Irish descent to Roy Tresmour Stuart, an electrical engineer for Pacific Utility, and the former Phyllis Dickerson, who worked in a grocery store.[2] He graduated from Sequoia High School, where he played basketball and baseball, in Redwood City in 1951. Soon after graduation, Bob Fontaine of the Pittsburgh Pirates signed him as an amateur free agent.

Stuart's start with Modesto in the Class C California League wasn't auspicious—a .229 average with 4 home runs and 31 RBIs in 66 games. His work in the outfield was even less impressive, nine errors against 91 putouts and seven assists. He matured enough over the offseason to tear up the Pioneer League (Class C) at Billings, Montana in 1952, hitting .313 and leading the league in homers (31), RBIs (121), runs (115), hits in a four-way tie (161), and total bases (292). Not so impressively, he struck out 99 times.

Shortly after the season ended and just five days before his 20th birthday Stuart married Diane Mellen. They had a daughter, Debbie Lea, but the marriage ended in divorce a few years later.

Just when the right-handed Stuart seemed to be hitting his stride, and his full growth of 6-feet-4 and 210 pounds, Uncle Sam came calling, and he spent the 1953 and 1954 seasons in the peacetime Army—at Fort Lewis, Washington (26 home runs), and Fort Ord, California (24 homers). Coming out of the service in 1955, he might have been a bit rusty or overmatched; short stints in New Orleans (Double-A Southern Association) and Mexico City (Double-A Mexican League) yielded a combined 10 hits in 57 at-bats, a home run, 7 RBIs, and 18 strikeouts, garnering Stuart a demotion back to Billings, where in just 101 games he hit .309, led the league with 32 round-trippers and in slugging at .650, drove in 104 runs, and fanned 109 times. The pattern for Stuart was clear: home

run or strikeout, all or nothing, and he was perfectly happy even if no one else was.

Stuart's work in Billings got him a promotion to Class A Lincoln in the Western League. It was a blessing or a curse, depending on who was looking at it.

For the third time in his career Stuart spent what amounted to a full season in one place. Each year he led his league in home runs, but he was astounding in 1956. Batting .298, he sent 66 balls out of the park, a league record that was never broken. He topped the league in slugging at .736 while accumulating 385 total bases and 158 runs driven in. He also set another league record that's never been broken, striking out 171 times, a number that becomes particularly ugly when set against his 156 hits. In addition, playing the outfield and first base (where he was moved for the first time in his professional career because he was such a liability as an outfielder), he committed 30 errors for an abysmal .936 fielding percentage. To make matters worse, Stuart's homers failed to earn him a call-up to the majors. Stuart maintained that the home runs worked against him, that the number didn't look real and that he'd have been better off with 30 to 40 bombs. It seems more likely that his terrible fielding, his all-or-nothing approach to hitting, and his attitude kept him down.[3] Whatever the reason, Stuart knew what put his name out front: For the rest of his life he signed all autographs "Dick Stuart 66."

The Pirates tried moving Stuart up in 1957, to Hollywood in the open-class Pacific Coast League and Atlanta (presumably on loan to the Milwaukee Braves) of the Southern Association, but it didn't work out, as he evenly split 46 games in the two cities with a combined 14 homers and 38 RBIs for a .222 average to go with 63 strikeouts. Back to Lincoln went Stuart, where he played 97 games, hitting .264 with 117 strikeouts to go with 31 homers and 84 RBIs. Stuart did one thing to help himself. He played for Frank Oceak's Santiago team in the Dominican Republic Winter League, where he came under the wise tutelage of George Sisler, who helped him reduce his strikeouts and improve his fielding.

His marriage to Diane having dissolved and now a bachelor, Stuart moved to Salt Lake City in the newly classed Triple-A Pacific Coast League for the 1958 season. Sisler's instruction began to pay off as Stuart struck out just 76 times in 80 games. He didn't lose his hitting stroke, going .311 with 98 hits, 31 homers, and 82 RBIs. Playing exclusively at first base, he even brought his fielding percentage up to .986. He also found time to marry Lois Morano on May 31; they would have two sons, Richard Lee Jr. and Robert Lance.

The Pirates, seeing his numbers and perhaps thinking marriage might have matured him, brought Stuart to the majors in July. Their plan was to make him the regular first baseman, replacing the platoon of Ted Kluszewski and R C Stevens. He made his debut on July 10 against left-hander Taylor Phillips and got his first hit, a home run, a three-run shot off reliever Don Elston in the ninth inning of an 8-7 loss to the Cubs in Chicago. He got his second hit the next day, a grand slam off Moe Drabowsky in the fifth, as the Pirates beat the Cubs 7-2. After a month Stuart became Kluszewski's platoon partner at first but earned some starts against right-handers. The year was a mixed bag, as Stuart hit .268 while homering 16 times and driving in 48 runs in just 64 games, occasionally being lifted for a pinch-runner or to allow Stevens to finish at first base. On the flip side, he tied Rookie of the Year Orlando Cepeda (who needed 147 games) with 16 errors to lead the league.

Stuart had nothing like a sophomore slump in 1959; in just 397 at-bats he hit .297 with 27 home runs and 78 RBIs. He was in the majors to stay, albeit as part of a platoon, getting all of the starts against southpaws and splitting starts against right-handers with lefty swingers Kluszewski and winter waiver pickup Rocky Nelson until Big Klu was traded to the White Sox for their pennant run. In addition, he got something of a promotion. Murtaugh had batted Stuart third in 1958 but moved him to the cleanup spot in 1959, where he stayed for the rest of his tenure in Pittsburgh. The Pirates, for their part, slipped from their second-place finish of 1958, falling to 78-76 and fourth place.

Nobody needs to be reminded about 1960, that magic year. The Pirates win the pennant! The Pirates win the World Series—over the aristocratic, mighty New York Yankees! Stuart contributed with a pair of huge games in June: 5-for-6 in game one of a doubleheader on the 12th in St. Louis with two homers and five RBIs in a 15-3 romp; 4-for-5 against the Giants in the nightcap of a doubleheader on the 30th with three homers and seven

RBIs, helping the Pirates win 11-6. Nevertheless, it was something of a down year for Stuart. His average fell to .260, his home runs to 23, with just 48 runs scored. He drove in 83 runs, but the number has a hollow ring to it. The Series wasn't much for Stuart, either, with three singles in 20 trips in five games with Nelson playing first base when Yankees right-hander Bob Turley started Games Two and Seven. However, Stuart was in the on-deck circle waiting to pinch-hit for Harvey Haddix when Bill Mazeroski supposedly made Mickey Mantle cry and became Pittsburgh's greatest hero since the French and Indian Wars. Stuart was dreaming of being the hero but wound up jumping up and down with everybody else.

Stuart had his first breakout year in 1961, with career-high batting and slugging averages of .301 and .581 to go with 35 homers and 117 RBIs. He made the All-Star team, playing in both games that year and contributing a double in the first. Unfortunately for the Pirates, only Stuart and Roberto Clemente, who hit .351 to earn his first batting title, improved on their performances of 1960. Fresh off their supposed upset of the Yankees, the rest of the Pirates fell flat and finished sixth with a mark of 75-79; it was little comfort that they outscored their opponents. Although Stuart led the league with 121 strikeouts, life looked good, so good that he decided to tweak the noses of the boobirds by having bumper stickers printed saying "Don't boo Stu in '62." How could he not feel good about himself? After all, several people noted seriously that he seemed better in the field. Not believing everything said about him, Stuart observed, "Your fielding improves when you hit 35 home runs." He also knew the significance of his fine season. Asked if he thought he could hit 61 homers, as had Roger Maris in 1961, Stuart answered, "You have to understand that Maris has that short right field in Yankee Stadium, whereas it's a cab ride to the scoreboard in Forbes Field."

Optimism and bumper stickers aside, the 1962 season was an unmitigated disaster for Stuart, made more obvious as the Pirates improved to 93-68 as nearly everybody emerged from the slump of 1961. Stuart reached career lows, for a full season, in almost every offensive category: 114 games (only 100 started at first base), 90 hits, 11 doubles, 16 homers, 64 RBIs, .228 average, .286 on-base percentage, and .398 slugging percentage. And all of this came about in an expansion season, diluted pitching and all, engendered by the birth of the Houston Colt .45s (now the Astros) and the New York Mets (losers of 120 games). It got so bad that Stuart had another set of bumper stickers printed: "Don't boo Stu. He's due." It never happened. By August Murtaugh was playing the young Donn Clendenon at first. The move was little help defensively, as Clendenon went on to lead National League first basemen in errors in three different seasons. At season's end, Stuart and the Pirates had come to the end of the road, and Stuart had still another set of bumper stickers printed: "Free in '63!" That last one came true. On November 20 the Pirates traded Stuart and pitcher Jack Lamabe to the Red Sox for catcher Jim Pagliaroni and pitcher Don Schwall.

Going to Boston was good for both Stuart and the Red Sox, as he had the second outstanding offensive season of his career, leading the American League in RBIs (118) while slugging 42 home runs (second behind Harmon Killebrew's 45). Apart from the homers and RBIs, he led the league in grounding into double plays (24).

It was in the field, however, that the big guy really left his mark. According to Retrosheet, among American League first basemen he ranked first in games (155), games started (155), complete games (143), innings (1376 ¹/₃), putouts (1207), and assists (134). He missed the top only in double plays with a mere 100. It looks like a terrific year, maybe even worthy of a Gold Glove, until one sees 29 errors and a .979 fielding percentage. The errors are the most by any first baseman since the shortened 1919 season, when Harry Heilmann booted 31. The fielding percentage was the lowest by an American League first baseman since Red Kress managed a mere .978 in 1933. (It wasn't Stuart's worst, though; his fielding percentage with the Pirates in 1959 was .976, the NL's lowest since Fred Luderus's .975 performance in 1914.) Particularly interesting about the number of errors is that Stuart was error-free for the first 26 games of the season (from April 9 against the Angels until the first game of a doubleheader against the Angels on May 15). Proving the error in the first game was no fluke, he committed his second one in the nightcap.

Stuart did well in 1964, too, with 33 homers and 114 RBIs to go with his .279 average. He also cut his errors to 24 but still led the American League. For his efforts

he was named the first baseman on *The Sporting News'* American League All-Star Team.

But Stuart was wearing out his welcome in Boston, primarily because of his fielding and his constitutional inability to get along with manager Johnny Pesky. As to his fielding, all one needs to know is that Red Sox reliever Dick "The Monster" Radatz suggested that Stuart's license plate should be E-3. Stuart actually took Radatz's suggestion to heart and got a vanity plate. Stuart seemed to have been put on Earth to bedevil Pesky, a fine ballplayer and hitter, a baseball lifer, a good man, and a universally respected and even loved institution in Boston. Radatz told one particularly good story about the two strong-willed individuals: "When John told us one day there were going to be fines for violating curfew—500 bucks for first offense, 1,000 for a second—Stuart sat in the back of the clubhouse, and when Pesky asked if there were any questions, Stuart said, 'John, is this tax-deductible?' "[4]

To the surprise of no one, the Red Sox traded Stuart to the Phillies for pitcher Dennis Bennett on November 29. Life in Philadelphia was hardly pleasant. Stuart contributed 28 home runs and drove in 95 runs, but those feats were negated by a .234 average and .287 on-base percentage. In addition, Phillies manager Gene Mauch, who had started eight different players at first the year before, had hoped Stuart would solidify the position. That didn't happen although for the first time in eight seasons he didn't lead the league in errors. After the season the Phillies worked out a trade with the Cardinals to get first baseman Bill White.

On February 22, 1966, the Phillies traded Stuart to the Mets for Jimmie Schaffer, Bobby Klaus, and Wayne Graham. Only weak-hitting catcher Schaffer played in the majors after the trade. In 31 games for the Mets Stuart hit a miserable .218 with 4 homers, 13 RBIs, and 26 strikeouts. The Mets twice moved Ed Kranepool into a left-field platoon with Ron Swoboda so Stuart could play first every day, but the scheme didn't work out. The Mets released Stuart on June 15, and he signed on with the Dodgers on July 5. Manager Walter Alston gave him a shot as his full-time first baseman, but Stuart didn't hit enough to keep Wes Parker on the bench. He batted .264 for the Dodgers, hit three out of the park, drove in nine, and got into two games as Alston's first pinch-hitter against southpaw Dave McNally in the World

Series (0-for-2), which the Baltimore Orioles won in a humiliating four-game sweep that included shutouts in the last three games. The Dodgers released Stuart on November 21.

With nobody showing interest in him, Stuart moved on to Japan, signing with the Taiyo Whales. He was adequate in 1967, hitting .280 with 33 homers and 79 RBIs while leading the league with 100 strikeouts. The next season was a flameout with a .217 average, 16 home runs, and 40 RBIs in 83 games.

Back in the United States, Stuart had one last fling, spending spring training in 1969 with the California Angels on a minor-league contract, signing with them on April 7 and starting on Opening Day on the 8th. Playing in a strict platoon with Roger Repoz, he could muster only a .157 average, four RBIs, and his last home run, a solo shot off Tommy John of the White Sox on April 14. The homer was Stuart's first hit of the season, which seemed fitting since his first major-league hit in 1958 was a home run. The Angels released Stuart on June 3, a week after manager Bill Rigney was fired.

Finished as a major leaguer, Stuart caught on with the Giants' Triple-A club in Phoenix of the Pacific Coast League. Appearing in 74 games, he hit .244 with 12 homers and 42 RBIs, showing he still had some power, but one must guess that 22 errors and a .966 fielding percentage were intolerable.

For his ten-year career Dick Stuart hit a respectable .264, belted 228 home runs, drove in 743 runs, and had a solid .489 slugging percentage. He hurt himself with 957 strikeouts against only 301 walks and a meager .316 on-base percentage. His fielding became the stuff of legend. Given the nicknames he earned, it's safe to conclude that much of the legend is based in fact.

Life after baseball went on for Stuart. He and Lois were divorced in Stamford, Connecticut, on June 30, 1971.[5] On the other hand, he had considerable success in finance, but felt compelled to joke about it at an affair in his honor in 1981: "I'm in the finance business in New York City. I can't tell you its name; I'm trying to duck my ex-wife."[6] Presumably, not everybody laughed.

Dick Stuart died of cancer in Redwood City on December 15, 2002, survived by his daughter, Debbie, sons Richard Jr. and Robert, and a brother, Daryl. His remains were cremated.

The life and career of Dick Stuart strike one as a "What If?" story. What if he hadn't been obsessed with the home run? What if he had learned bat control and plate discipline? What if he had taken the time to develop the skills required of a complete player? What if he had taken better care of himself? Golf and water skiing are fine, but they don't offset late nights. What if he hadn't taken himself so seriously? What if he had taken himself and life more seriously? The last two questions aren't necessarily contradictory. What if others besides Arnold Hano had been perceptive enough to see the real Dick Stuart? "You listen to this Dick Stuart [who had been comparing himself—and not favorably—to Mickey Mantle, Harmon Killebrew, and Frank Howard], and you wonder why nobody has ever suggested he is an introspective person, for all his popping off, a man with the usual self-doubts."[7] Dick Stuart won't have the infamous asterisk beside his name and numbers in any record books, but a question mark might not be out of place.

Special thanks to Clem Comly, Leonard Levin, and Bill Nowlin, for their fact-checking, close reading, and editing. They all made this piece better.

Sources

Some details are personal recollections of the author.

The following list is a sampling of available materials and is in no way complete. For an exhaustive list see The Baseball Index (TBI) (baseballindex.org), easily accessible at the Society for American Baseball Research (SABR) website (sabr.org). Also well worth a visit is Paper of Record (paperofrecord.hypernet.ca) with its complete collection of *The Sporting News.* Helpful, too, is Newspaper Archive (newspaperarchive.com).

Statistics are from Baseball-Reference, Retrosheet, *Daguerreotypes,* and *The All-Time Japanese Baseball Register.*

Various articles and clippings from Stuart's file at the National Baseball Hall of Fame and Museum in Cooperstown, New York.

Carlos Bauer, *The All-Time Japanese Baseball Register: The Complete Statistical Record of All the Great Japanese & American Players* (San Diego and San Marino: Baseball Press Books, 2000).

Jimmy Breslin, "Dick Stuart: Pittsburgh's Problem and Baseball's Dilemma." *True.* September 1959: 40-43, 68, 72-75.

Myron Cope, "Irrepressible Egotist." *Saturday Evening Post.* April 28, 1962: 65-66, 68.

Rick Cushing, *1960 Pittsburgh Pirates Day by Day: A Special Season, An Extraordinary World Series* (Pittsburgh: Dorrance Publishing Co., Inc., 2010).

Ernest J. Green, "Minor League Big Guns." *Baseball Research Journal.* 24 (1995): 53-57.

Dick Groat, *The World Champion Pittsburgh Pirates* (New York: Coward-McCann, 1961).

Arnold Hano, "Dick Stuart: Man and Showman." *Sport.* June 1964. 56-63.

Mark Harris, "The Man Who Hits Too Many Home Runs." *Life.* September 2, 1957: 85-86, 89-90, 92, 97.

Lloyd Johnson and Miles Wolff, eds. *The Encyclopedia of Minor League Baseball.* 3rd ed. (Durham, North Carolina: Baseball America, Inc., 2007).

Kerry Keene, *1960: The Last Pure Season* (Champaign, Illinois: Sports Publishing, 2000).

Anne Madarasz, "Beat 'Em Bucs: The Story of the 1960 Pirates." *Western Pennsylvania History.* Fall 2010. 20-26.

David Maraniss, *Clemente: The Pride and Passion of Baseball's Last Hero* (New York: Simon & Schuster, 2006).

John Moody, *Kiss It Good-Bye: The Mystery, the Mormon, and the Moral of the 1960 Pittsburgh Pirates.* (Salt Lake City: Shadow Mountain, 2010).

Stan Musial, with Bob Broeg, "Stan Musial Rates the Big-Leaguers." *Sport.* June 1964. 20-23, 86-88.

Jim O'Brien, *Fantasy Camp: Living the Dream with Maz and the '60 Bucs* (Pittsburgh: James P. O'Brien, Pub., 2000).

_____. *Maz and the '60 Bucs: When Pittsburgh and its Pirates Went All the Way* (Pittsburgh: James P. O'Brien, 1993).

_____. *We Had 'Em All the Way: Bob Prince and his Pittsburgh Pirates.* (Pittsburgh: James P. O'Brien-Pub., 1998).

Jim Reisler, *The Best Game Ever: Pirates vs. Yankees October 13, 1960* (Philadelphia: Da Capo Press, 2007).

George R. Skornickel, *Beat 'Em Bucs: The 1960 Pittsburgh Pirates* (Baltimore: Publish America, 2010).

Luther W. Spoehr, "Stuart, Richard Lee, 'Dick,' 'Stu,' 'Dr. Strangeglove.'" In David L. Porter, ed., *Biographical Dictionary of American Sports: Baseball.* Revised and expanded edition. Vol. 3 (Q-Z) (Westport, Connecticut, and London: Greenwood Press, 2000): 1497-1499.

Notes

1   Fred Katz, "The Nothing Manager," *Sport* (May 1968), 14.

2   1930 United States Federal Census. Cf. Arnold Hano, "Dick Stuart: Man and Showman," *Sport* (June 1964), 60: "He was born Richard Lee Stuart in tiny San Carlos, California, 20 miles below San Francisco, the son of a dry cleaner." All other sources say he was born in San Francisco. The 1930 Census clearly identifies his father as Roy Tresmour Stuart; it's possible that he lost his job as an electrical engineer during the Great Depression and was a dry cleaner in 1932.

3   For discussion see Mark Harris, "The Man Who Hits Too Many Home Runs," *Life* (September 2, 1957): 85-86, 89-90, 92, 97; and Jimmy Breslin, "Dick Stuart: Pittsburgh Problem and Baseball's Dilemma," *True* (September 1959): 40-43, 68, 72-75.

4   Michael J. Bailey, "Dick Stuart, at 70; Sox Slugger dubbed 'Dr. Strangeglove,'" *Boston Globe*, December 20, 2002.

5   John Gearan, "If He'd Had a Glove on, They'd Have Known Him Instantly." *Worcester* (Massachusetts) *Telegram*, January 23, 1981. Stuart told Gearan that he and Lois had divorced in 1967, remarried in 1970, and divorced "'last year [1980] . . . just before Christmas.'" The date of June 30, 1971, is from the Connecticut Divorce Index at Ancestry.com.

6   Ibid.

7   Hano, 63.

Jim Umbricht

By Thomas Ayers

DETERMINED TO MAKE the major leagues since he was a young boy, Jim Umbricht paid his way to a minor-league tryout camp and, after making the team, was converted from shortstop to pitcher. After he returned from serving two years in the military, Umbricht worked his way up to the majors and then spent three seasons playing sporadically for the Pirates. After the Houston Colt .45s selected him in the expansion draft, Umbricht turned into one of his hometown club's most trusted late-inning relievers in 1962. Umbricht was diagnosed with cancer in spring training of 1963, but was back pitching in the majors within two months and had another fine season in the bullpen. Tragically, the cancer returned and Umbricht died before the 1964 season began, robbing major-league baseball of a fine relief pitcher, and more importantly, of a courageous, optimistic, and considerate man.

James "Jim" Umbricht was born in Chicago on September 17, 1930, to Mr. and Mrs. Eduard Umbricht. Eduard's parents were from Illinois and he was born and raised in the state. Jantina Frank, Eduard's wife, was born in Holland to a Dutch mother and German father. She was a native German speaker. The couple married on April 24, 1920, and had three children by the time of the 1930 US Census. William was eight years older than James and Eduard Jr. was a year older. Eduard Sr. worked as a banker and the family appeared to be relatively well-off, as they had a servant.

Jim wanted to be a baseball player from his early childhood and Eduard Jr. recalled that Jim would be outside every day during the summer playing pickup baseball until dusk.[1] During Jim's childhood, Eduard Sr.'s job required that the family to move to Decatur, Georgia. Jim attended Decatur

High School and won all-state honors in basketball and baseball in 1948, his senior year.[2]

Umbricht was awarded a scholarship to the University of Georgia, where he played basketball and baseball for the Bulldogs and was awarded letters three times in each sport. The tall right-hander was also asked to play football, but declined for fear that an injury would derail his aspirations in baseball. In 1951 he was named the shortstop for the All-Southeast Conference team.[3] Umbricht was the captain of both the basketball and baseball teams in his senior year.[4]

Although his first love was always baseball, Umbricht was a talented basketball player, as well. Louisiana State University star Bob Pettit, Jr., who later played in the NBA, won the league MVP award twice, was named to 11 NBA All-Star teams and was inducted into the Naismith Memorial Basketball Hall of Fame, said of Umbricht, "He scored 50 points against us. We used three men on him and it didn't mean a thing."[5]

After graduating with a degree in education, Umbricht paid his way to a tryout camp in 1953 for the Waycross Bears of the Class D Georgia-Florida League, a team that did not have a major-league affiliation. He impressed the scouts, who were intrigued by the right-hander's 6-foot-4, 215-pound frame, and was signed to the team. Although he played a fair amount of shortstop, managers Alvin Aucoin and Morton Smith also used Umbricht as a pitcher. He hit .246 in 179 at-bats over 54 games, but made perhaps a more noticeable contribution on the mound. Pitching 69 innings, Umbricht posted a 2.87 ERA, the second-lowest mark on the team. As one might expect from a new pitcher still learning his craft, Umbricht struggled with his control, walking 41 batters.

With the military draft still in effect, Umbricht spent 1954 and 1955 in the Army. He began to focus more extensively on pitching when he got the opportunity to play baseball with other service members. While stationed in Fort Carson, Colorado, he struck out 18 in an Army tournament game in 1955.[6]

Umbricht returned to Organized Baseball the following season with the Baton Rouge Rebels of the Class C Evangeline League, another team with no major-league affiliation. He continued to split his time between the mound and shortstop, throwing a team-high 235 innings and playing in 45 games as a position player and pinch-hitter. Again he was more successful on the mound. Umbricht's 3.37 ERA was the lowest of the team's starters, and he showed signs of development by cutting his walk rate noticeably. Because of his willingness to contribute to the team in any way possible, Umbricht was presented with a trophy as the "hardest working Rebel of 1956."[7] After the season his contract was sold to the Milwaukee Braves.

The Braves assigned Umbricht to the Topeka Hawks of the Class A Western League in 1957. He went 13-8 and again led the starters in ERA with a 3.24 mark over 178 innings. He saw some duty as a pinch-hitter, but it was evident that his future in professional baseball was as a pitcher.

After the season, Umbricht played winter ball for the Carta Vieja Yankees, who won their third consecutive Panama League pennant. Finishing with a 6-2 record, he threw a four-hitter for the Yankees in the pennant-clinching game.[8]

The following season, 1958, marked a change for "Big Jim," as he was occasionally known; he was used primarily as a reliever for the first time in his career. Of his team-high 54 appearances for the Atlanta Crackers of the Double-A Southern Association, only 12 were starts. He was used as a multi-inning reliever, as his 173 innings pitched were the third highest on the club. That winter, Umbricht returned to play winter ball for the Carta Vieja Yankees.[9]

Before the 1959 season, the Braves traded Umbricht to the Pittsburgh Pirates for minor-league outfielder Emil

Panko. Pirates scout Howie Haak had always liked Umbricht because "he was young, strong and could throw hard." Haak recalled that the team had given up on Panko by that point and the teams were able to work out a deal fairly easily.[10]

The Pirates assigned Umbricht to the Salt Lake City Bees of the Triple-A Pacific Coast League for 1959. Umbricht made 42 relief appearances and five starts. He finished second on the team with 14 wins, and had the seventh-lowest ERA in the league at 2.78. Umbricht walked only 43 batters, his lowest walk rate in any minor-league season.

This was perhaps Umbricht's best minor-league season and he was rewarded with a September call-up. He reported to the Pirates on September 13 and four days later Umbricht celebrated his 29th birthday in the major leagues. Within a couple of weeks he made his big-league debut when he was given the starting assignment against the Cincinnati Reds on September 26, 1959. Umbricht had a particularly memorable first inning, but not in a positive way, as leadoff hitter Johnny Temple, Frank Thomas, and Buddy Gilbert all took him deep for home runs. Umbricht stayed in the game and left in the seventh inning with a 6-5 lead, but the Reds won the contest with two runs in the bottom of the ninth. That was his only appearance for the Pirates that year, but he played winter ball again, this time for Aguilas Cibaenas in the Dominican Republic.[11]

Umbricht turned some heads in spring training in 1960 when he combined with Bennie Daniels to no-hit the Tigers in Fort Myers, Florida. He broke camp with the club and started the third game of the season. After struggling in two starts, Umbricht was sent to the bullpen. He earned his first major-league win on May 28 by pitching scoreless 12th and 13th innings against the Philadelphia Phillies before Don Hoak hit a walk-off home run. On June 28 the Pirates sent him to Columbus of the International League, where he returned to the rotation and won eight games with a 2.50 ERA and two shutouts. Recalled in September, he went back to the bullpen, pitched twice, and finished the season with a 1-2 record and a 5.09 ERA. He did not pitch in the World Series.

Although he began the 1961 season in the majors, Umbricht didn't pitch until May 5, when he appeared in a blowout loss. Three days later he was sent down to

Columbus, where he again spent most of the season in the rotation. Umbricht posted a 9-6 record with a 2.35 ERA, which was the lowest of any pitcher on the club with at least 10 starts. His standout performance was a one-hitter against Richmond on August 25 with nine strikeouts, where the only blemish was an eighth-inning single to second base. He showed further signs of improved control, bringing his walk rate down to below a batter every three innings.

Despite his continued minor-league success, the Pirates chose not to protect Umbricht for the expansion draft, and he was selected by the Houston Colt .45s.[12] This was a nice surprise for Umbricht, as his parents had moved to Houston and he also lived in the city in the offseason.

Umbricht made his mark as a major-league pitcher with the Colt .45s. He began the 1962 season in the bullpen and didn't allow an earned run in his first six appearances. However he was sent to the minors on May 9 after allowing two runs to the Dodgers in a loss. It was reported that Houston didn't want to send Umbricht down, but he was the only pitcher who could be optioned to the minors without being exposed to waivers.[13] After spending the previous few years going back and forth between Triple-A and the National League, Umbricht was disappointed in the demotion, even if he understood that options necessitated the move in the club's view.[14]

He continued to serve primarily as a reliever for Houston's Triple-A affiliate, posting a 3-4 record and a 3.39 ERA for the Oklahoma City 89ers. Umbricht still felt he hadn't merited the demotion and that it wasn't beneficial to him, later stating, "I didn't change anything or pick up anything new at Oklahoma City."[15]

On July 16, Umbricht was recalled and he pitched in both games of a doubleheader the day after his arrival. With his fine overhand curveball, Umbricht settled into the role of late-inning reliever and had a solid season. He struck out the side against Cincinnati on August 26 for his second major-league save. Umbricht won four games in September, pitching 4 1/3 one-hit innings against the Pirates for his first victory of the season. In September, he pitched in three straight games against the pennant-winning Giants, striking out Felipe Alou and Orlando Cepeda in the first game, picking up the win in the second and striking out Willie Mays and Alou consecutively in

the third. Umbricht posted a 2.01 ERA in 67 innings and finished 4-0. He didn't struggle with his command as he had in his previous exposure to the majors, striking out 55 batters and walking 17. He attributed his success partly to getting regular work, as opposed to his infrequent deployment by the Pirates.[16]

Umbricht said the demotion by the Colt 45's had motivated him. "It was disappointing to be sent back so many times, but it made me keep trying," he reflected. "If I had had family responsibilities, I may have quit and looked for more security. But baseball is my life. They'll have to tear this uniform off me. I'm 32, but I'm a young 32 because I didn't actually get to pitch until I was 25."[17]

During spring training in 1963, Umbricht was golfing with Houston general manager Paul Richards when he mentioned a mole he had noticed on the back of his right leg. He recalled, "I just felt this lump. No soreness, no pain, no nothing."[18] Richards suggested that Umbricht have the lump examined.[19] The team physician referred Umbricht to the M.D. Anderson Cancer Clinic in Houston, and after two days of examinations, he was diagnosed with a malignant cancer that had already spread. The next day, March 7, Umbricht underwent a six-hour operation to remove the growth. Cancer was removed from his groin, thigh, and leg.[20] He later recalled, "Everything happened so fast I didn't have time to think about or worry about cancer."[21]

Umbricht was not prepared to let the cancer diagnosis end his baseball career. He told a sportswriter, "I told them that they wouldn't be able to keep me in here on Opening Day."[22] Nevertheless, Umbricht made the most of his time in the hospital, spreading positivity and optimism among other patients. Houston trainer Jim Ewell said, "He served as an inspiration for other patients and believe me, he cheered up many of the patients."[23]

Umbricht left the hospital on March 25 and began running at Colt Stadium on April 2.[24] A month after his operation, he was in uniform on Opening Day.[25] "The last 30 days have been an eternity. And the next 30 will be twice as long," he said.[26]

Umbricht spent a month on the disabled list but began pitching batting practice on April 22 and, with 100 stitches in his leg, he was back in Houston's bullpen on May 9.

"No one has to feel sorry for me," he said. "…It's all a little embarrassing. I don't mean to sound ungrateful, though. I'm glad people are so interested in one respect, because it helps publicize cancer. Early detection of cancer is a big thing, and maybe if people read about how I was cured it might help them."[27] On his first day back in the bullpen he pitched an inning of relief against the Reds. Three days later, he picked up a win when Bob Aspromonte hit a walk-off home run against Chicago after Umbricht pitched two scoreless innings.

Umbricht made three starts during the season, two of them defeats. In one game, he faced off against Warren Spahn and the great southpaw threw a complete game shutout. However, Umbricht nearly matched him with seven innings of four-hit, one-run ball and eight strikeouts. It was Umbricht's best major-league start.

Umbricht finished his major-league career with 9 2/3 scoreless innings over four appearances, allowing only four hits and a walk and striking out nine. Umbricht picked up a win in relief in what turned out to be his last major-league appearance, against the New York Mets on September 29. In 35 games he finished with a 4-3 record and a 2.61 ERA in 76 innings. He struck out 48 and walked 21. Umbricht posted a 2.33 ERA in his final 143 major-league innings (encompassing 1962 and 1963) and settled into a role as a dependable late-inning reliever for the Colt .45s. He was the only pitcher to record a winning record in both of the team's first two seasons. GM Richards deemed Umbricht so valuable to the club that he named him as one of the players he would trade only for "first-line major league talent."[28]

It has been reported that Umbricht was informed in November that his cancer was incurable.[29] He didn't let that news deter him in his efforts to beat the disease and underwent treatment three times a week during the offseason in Houston. With special permission of the National League, the Colts released Umbricht on December 16 and then signed him to a scout's contract without having to place him on waivers. It was understood that the team would return Umbricht to the player roster once he was healthy again.[30]

Early in 1964, the Philadelphia Sportswriters Association honored Umbricht at a dinner as the most courageous athlete of 1963.[31] In accepting the award, Umbricht displayed his positive attitude, remarking that the illness was "sort of a blessing" in that "six weeks in a hospital bed gives you time to think—and come out a better human being. I'm sure everything will come out all right."[32]

Umbricht spoke during the offseason about trying to stay busy playing cards and golf. Golf was one of Umbricht's strengths and he was known, along with catcher Jim Campbell, as the best golfer on the Houston club.[33] He hinted at the psychological impact of the illness when he said, "I don't like to go to bed early. I just lay there and think too much."[34]

On the first day of the Colts pre-spring-training workouts, Umbricht tried to work out and found it too draining, telling Whitey Diskin, the Houston clubhouse attendant, "Whitey, I just can't make it."[35] He was too sick to attend spring training and he was hospitalized again on March 16.[36] It soon became apparent that no amount of courage or willpower would defeat the disease.

Umbricht appeared to recognize this and, although he hoped to see

Opening Day of the 1964 season, he began to put his affairs in order. He wrote to Houston sportswriter Clark Nealon, "I want to thank you for the many nice things you've written about me in the past year."[37] After he was hospitalized again, the Colt .45s hosted a postgame radio show after a spring-training game so that Umbricht could hear his teammates' voices again. Sportswriter Mickey Herskowitz wrote that the purpose of the call was unstated but evident. "They were saying goodbye to Umbricht, dying in his hospital room in Houston, and they knew it. So did Umbricht." Some of Umbricht's teammates were too choked up to appear on the show and those who did often talked about two of Umbricht's favorite topics, golf and cards.[38]

On April 8, 1964, five days before the Colt .45s played their season opener, 33-year-old Jim Umbricht died of melanoma. He was survived by his parents and his brother, Ed.

The Colts canceled their last spring-training game, which was on the day of his funeral. Russ Kemmerer, an old teammate and friend who was playing for Houston's Oklahoma City farm club, gave the eulogy. Colts front-office personnel, manager Harry Craft, coach Luman Harris, and teammates Bob Lillis, Dick Farrell, and Ken Johnson, who was one of Umbricht's closest friends and his roommate on road trips, all attended the service. Umbricht's ashes were spread at the construction site for the Houston Astrodome.

The tributes to Umbricht poured in from all sources. Richards called Umbricht "one of the finest competitors I've ever known on or off the field." He added, "He was a great inspiration for our club. We will not forget Jim Umbricht. And we will miss him more than we know."[39] His physician said, "He never accepted the possibility of his baseball career being ended. He was a great inspiration to other patients and all who came in contact with him."[40]

In his memory, the Colts wore black armbands during the 1964 season.[41] On Opening Day Ken Johnson pitched 8 2/3 innings in a 6-3 victory. After the game, he said, "I had an extra special reason for wanting to win this one. My ex-roommate."[42]

Although Umbricht had been embarrassed by the attention given to him, he had been optimistic that the publicity may lead to in earlier cancer detection in others. He achieved this goal at least once, as Jack Pardee, a 28-year-old linebacker for the National Football League's Los Angeles Rams, who had recently noticed a mole on his arm, realized that it sounded identical to the mole that had signaled Umbricht's melanoma.[43] Pardee stated, "The way the papers described it, it sounded exactly like what I had. I made an appointment to see the doctor the next morning."[44] Pardee was diagnosed with malignant melanoma and underwent surgery to remove the growth. He missed the 1965 NFL season while recovering, but returned to play several more seasons before becoming a head coach in the NFL, college, and the Canadian Football League. At the time, Pardee reflected, "I don't know how long I might have put it off if I hadn't read that story. I felt fine and … when you're feeling good you hate to see a doctor."[45]

Houston retired Umbricht's number 32—the first retired number in franchise history—on April 12, 1965, and hung his jersey in Minute Maid Park, the home of the Houston Astros. As a tribute to Umbricht's courage and positivity, the franchise renamed its team MVP award the Jim Umbricht Memorial Award.[46]

Notes

1   Loran Smith, "Big League Ball Was Always Umbricht's Goal," *Athens* (Georgia) *Banner-Herald*, February 21, 2003.

2   Ray Kelly, "Colts .45 Hurler Overcame Cancer," *Philadelphia Evening Bulletin*, January 28, 1964.

3   "Jim Umbricht Dead; Pitcher on Colts, 33," *New York Times*, April 8, 1964.

4   Loran Smith, "Big League Ball Was Always Umbricht's Goal," *Athens Banner-Herald*, February 21, 2003.

5   Baseball Hall of Fame Library, player file for Jim Umbricht.

6   Baseball Hall of Fame Library.

7   *The Sporting News*, September 5, 1956, 37.

8   *The Sporting News*, February 12, 1958, 25.

9   *The Sporting News*, November 5, 1958, 24

10 Lester J. Biederman, "Scout's Memory Enabled Pirates to Land Umbricht," *Pittsburgh Press*, March 24, 1960.

11 *The Sporting News*, October 7, 1959, 33.

12 "Jim Umbricht Dead; Pitcher on Colts, 33," *New York Times*, April 8, 1964.

13 Clark Nealon, "Umbricht Made It Big as Colt After Years on Major Pogo Stick," *Houston Post,* February 24, 1963.

14 Ibid.

15 Ibid.

16 Ibid.

17 Ibid.

18 Ray Kelly, "Colts .45 Hurler Overcame Cancer," *Philadelphia Evening Bulletin,* January 28, 1964.

19 Loran Smith, "Big League Ball Was Always Umbricht's Goal," *Athens Banner-Herald,* February 21, 2003.

20 Mickey Herskowitz, "Umbricht Now One of the Boys; Long Wait Is Over," *Houston Post,* May 9, 1963.

21 Lester J. Biederman, "Colts' Jim Umbricht Recovering From Cancer Operation," *Pittsburgh Press,* May 1, 1963. Most sources report the diagnosis as being made on March 6 and the operation occurring on March 7. At least one source reports the diagnosis as being made on March 7 and the operation occurring on March 8 (Mickey Herskowitz, "Jim Umbricht," *The Sporting News,* May 25, 1963, 21).

22 Clark Nealon, "Colts' Jim Umbricht Showing 'Most Satisfactory' Progress," *Houston Post,* March 27, 1963.

23 Lester J. Biederman, "Colts' Jim Umbricht Recovering From Cancer Operation," *Pittsburgh Press,* May 1, 1963.

24 Mickey Herskowitz, "Jim Umbricht," *The Sporting News,* May 25, 1963, 21.

25 "Jim Umbricht Dead; Pitcher on Colts, 33," *New York Times,* April 8, 1964.

26 Mickey Herskowitz, "Umbricht Now One of the Boys; Long Wait Is Over," *Houston Post,* May 9, 1963.

27 Ibid.

28 Clark Nealon, "Ten First-Year Phenoms Land on .45 Roster," *The Sporting News,* October 26, 1963, 19

29 Clark Nealon, "Umbricht Carried Battle Against Dread Cancer Into Extra Innings," *Houston Post,* April 9, 1964.

30 "Jim Umbricht, Colt Pitcher, Dies of Cancer," *The Morning Record,* April 9, 1964.

31 Ray Kelly, "Colts .45 Hurler Overcame Cancer," *Philadelphia Evening Bulletin,* January 28, 1964.

32 Ibid.

33 Mickey Herskowitz, "Umbricht Fidgets While .45s Pitchers 'Duel in the Sun,'" *Houston Post,* March 6, 1963.

34 Ray Kelly, "Colts .45 Hurler Overcame Cancer," *Philadelphia Evening Bulletin,* January 28, 1964.

35 Clark Nealon, "Umbricht Carried Battle Against Dread Cancer Into Extra Innings," *Houston Post,* April 9, 1964.

36 "Colts to Wear Black Arm Bands for Jim Umbricht," *The Day,* New London, Connecticut, April 9, 1964.

37 Clark Nealon, "Umbricht Carried Battle Against Dread Cancer Into Extra Innings," *Houston Post,* April 9, 1964.

38 Mickey Herskowitz, "Strength, Courage and Humor—A Legacy Umbricht Left Behind," *The Sporting News,* April 25, 1964, 25

39 Clark Nealon, "Umbricht Carried Battle Against Dread Cancer Into Extra Innings," *Houston Post,* April 9, 1964.

40 "Colts Umbricht Loses Fight for Life; Cancer Victim," *The Sporting News,* April 18, 1964, 44.

41 "Colts to Wear Black Arm Bands for Jim Umbricht," *The Day,* April 9, 1964.

42 Earl Lawson, "Local Boy Jim Wynn Makes Cincinnati Suffer," *The Sporting News,* April 25, 1964, 22.

43 "Umbricht Death May Have Saved Pardee," *Tuscaloosa* (Alabama) *News,* May 7, 1964, 8.

44 Ibid.

45 Ibid.

46 Loran Smith, "Big League Ball Was Always Umbricht's Goal," *Athens Banner-Herald,* February 21, 2003.

Bill Virdon

by Gregory H. Wolf

FROM 1955 TO 1965 Bill Virdon established his reputation as one of the finest and fastest center fielders of his generation, and was known for his accurate throws from the deep center-field power alleys in spacious Forbes Field in Pittsburgh. Ironically, one of his throws that inadvertently hit his manager may have led to his biggest break in baseball.

Having toiled in the New York Yankees farm system since 1950, Virdon was at his first Yankees spring training in 1954, but his prospects seemed dim. "I could see that I was going to have a problem breaking in on the Yankees," Virdon said. "They had the best outfield in baseball."[1] Indeed, the Yankees, coming off five consecutive World Series championships, had Hank Bauer and Gene Woodling in right and left respectively and Mickey Mantle in center. Like Mantle, Virdon was 23 years old; however, Virdon was fighting for his professional career. Near the end of camp he was in the outfield with Bauer, Woodling, and Mantle practicing. "I fielded a fly ball and fired away," Virdon remembered. "Somehow Mr. Stengel got between me and the relay man and I proceeded to hit him in the back with my strongest throw and knocked him down. The other outfielders were laughing and pointing to me: 'He did it.' Mr. Stengel got up, shook himself and hollered, 'If you guys throw like that in a game, you might throw someone out.' " With a chuckle, Virdon added, "Two weeks later I was traded." The trade sent him to the St. Louis Cardinals and the next year he was named the National League Rookie of the Year for 1955. "The trade came somewhat as a surprise," Virdon said, "but at that point it was probably the biggest break I got in baseball."

William Charles Virdon was born on June 9, 1931, in Hazel

Park, Michigan, to Charles and Bertha Virdon, who had migrated from southern Missouri during the Depression to find work in the automobile factories around Detroit. When Virdon was 12 his family returned to Missouri and settled in West Plains, near Springfield. An avid softball player, his father ran a country store and his mother was a homemaker. Quick and agile, Bill was an excellent athlete at West Plains High School, where he excelled in track, basketball, and football; the school did not field a baseball team. Although he played in informal leagues, his first opportunity to play organized baseball came in the summer of 1948, after his junior year. Persuaded by his friend Gene Richmond to travel almost 300 miles to Clay City, Kansas, to try out for the local AABC (American Amateur Baseball Congress) team, Virdon made the team as a shortstop and was then moved to center field because of his athleticism. Though Virdon was far from home for the 50-game season, his parents were supportive. "I went to a tryout camp for the Yankees in Branson, Missouri, following my senior year," Virdon remembered. "And after that I went back out to play ball in Kansas." When the season ended Virdon returned to Branson and Yankees scout Tom Greenwade, who had signed Mantle a year earlier, signed Virdon for a $1,800 bonus.

Virdon began his professional career with the Independence (Kansas) Yankees of the Class D Kansas-Oklahoma-Missouri (KOM) League in 1950, where he was managed by Malcolm "Bunny" Mick. Virdon called Mick "one of the big influences in my career," adding, "He was an outfielder and knew all about playing. He pushed me." Still learning to play center field, Virdon was promoted after the season to the Yankees' Triple A team, the Kansas City Blues in the American Association, and hit .341 in 14 games. "The reason

I was promoted was Bunny Mick," he said. "He got fired in Independence at the end of the year and ended up going to Kansas City to play. He told them about me and they brought me up."

Despite Virdon's light hitting and lack of power in 1951 with the Norfolk Tars in the Class B Piedmont League and in 1952 with the Binghamton Triplets of the Class A Eastern League (.286 and .261 respectively), the Yankees were impressed enough by his fielding to invite him to the Yankees' pre-camp in Arizona in 1953, where he had the chance to work with the team's top prospects, and then promoted him again to the Kansas City Blues in 1953. This team was loaded with future major-league talent, including Bob Cerv, Elston Howard, Vic Power, and Bill Skowron, all of whom played or could play the outfield. Though Virdon excelled in the field, he struggled at the plate, hitting just .233, and was demoted to the Birmingham Barons of the Double-A Southern Association. "I was disappointed about the demotion but that is part of the business," Virdon said. "I went down and I actually finished the season with a pretty good record." Indeed he did. Rooming with future Pirate Hal Smith, Virdon batted .317 in 42 games. His success at the plate may have been due to a different approach. "He started improving his hitting," Smith said, "because he wasn't trying to hit a home run and learned how to hit line drives to all fields."[2]

After being dispatched to the Cardinals with two other players in a trade for All-Star Enos Slaughter in the spring of 1954, Virdon was sent to St. Louis's Triple-A team, the Rochester Red Wings of the International League. He got off to a torrid start and in mid-June *The Sporting News* wrote that "Virdon now appears to be the best bargain since Manhattan Island."[3] He finished with 22 home runs and a league-leading .333 batting average and was second in the International League's MVP voting behind former minor-league teammate Elston Howard. "That was the best year I ever had," Virdon said. He was considered the second-best prospect in all of minor-league baseball behind Howard.[4] Throughout his career, one of Virdon's defining characteristics was his round, wire-rimmed eyeglasses, which he credited for his improved hitting in 1953 and 1954.

After the 1954 season Virdon continued his hot hitting for the Havana Lions in the Cuban League, the only time he ever played winter ball. Lions manager Dolf Luque was impressed with his hitting and Cardinals Cuban League scout Gus Mancuso declared, "This kid Virdon does amazing things in center field";[5] and by January 1955 Cardinals manager Eddie Stanky already had ideas to move Stan Musial from the outfield to first base in order to make room for Virdon in the starting lineup.[6] Finishing the season with a .340 batting average and as a Cuban League all-star, Virdon commented, "I felt like playing in Cuba was one of the best things I ever did in baseball. It was just a time to develop. I got to face excellent pitching and it was the easiest league I ever played in because you did not travel."

Given Country Slaughter's number 9, Virdon followed a poor spring with a hot start to the season. Stanky rearranged his outfield by moving Wally Moon, the 1954 NL Rookie of the Year, from center to right and Virdon was given center field. Musial was moved from right field to first base. Longtime Cardinals beat reporter Bob Broeg wrote "[Virdon] is a solid ballplayer with no apparent weakness." Though the Cardinals floundered and finished seventh, ahead of only the Pirates, Virdon was named Rookie of the Year for his all-around performance: He hit well (.281) and fielded exceptionally. Club President August Busch, Jr. called the trade for Virdon "one of the best deals we ever made."[7]

Busch wanted immediate success and brought in Frank "Trader" Lane as the new general manager at the end of the 1955 season. Lane had made his reputation with the Chicago White Sox over the previous decade and was known for his propensity to trade players. Even after another slow spring, in which he batted below .200, Virdon was undeterred, saying, "A year up here gives you confidence and I believe in myself."[8] However, his slump continued into the season, and that was all Lane needed. Claiming he had too many left-hand hitters and "Bill wasn't hitting the ball that hard,"[9] Lane traded Virdon to the Pirates on May 17 for light-hitting center fielder Bobby Del Grecco and journeyman pitcher Dick Littlefield. "I was a Missouri and Cardinals guy," Virdon said, "and hated to go." Two months later it was clear that the trade was a phenomenal success for the Pirates.

The trade for Virdon was the first deal for the new Pirates general manager Joe L. Brown, who had joined the Bucs' front office in November 1955 and succeeded Branch

Rickey when he stepped down as general manager. The Pirates had long coveted Virdon and in 1954 Rickey had offered the Yankees pitchers Vern Law and Max Surkont in exchange for him, but was rebuffed.[10]

In 1956 Virdon arrived on a team defined by a culture of failure. The Bucs had not had a winning record since 1948 and had finished in last place four consecutive years and five of the last six. "It wasn't the brightest thing in the world," Virdon said of his trade. "Pittsburgh had been losing for years." But he noticed more than just losing: "I could see that Pittsburgh had some talent." The Pirates were a young team: shortstop Dick Groat was 25; rookie second baseman Bill Mazeroski was 19, and in the outfield Roberto Clemente just 21 and Virdon 25. On June 16 the Corsairs won their 30th game (against 21 defeats), the earliest they had reached 30 wins since 1945.[11] *The Sporting News* ran the headline "The Bucs Turn Pittsburgh Into Boom Town"[12] as fans flocked to Forbes Field. Though the Bucs ultimately finished in seventh place, the hot start revealed the team's potential. After his trade, Virdon hit at a .334 clip and battled Hank Aaron for the batting title, finishing second with a .319 average, the only time in his career that he batted over .300. Because of Virdon's many soft infield bloop hits, Pirates radio announcer Bob Prince tabbed him "Quail," a nickname that stayed with him his entire playing career. Virdon exceeded expectations and was lauded as the "brightest star" and "best all-around player of the team,"[13] while the outfield trio of Virdon, Clemente, and Lee Walls was judged the best in baseball.[14]

With the team floundering with a 36-67 record in 1957, general manager Joe L. Brown made a move that profoundly impacted the Pirates' and Virdon's future: he hired as manager Danny Murtaugh, who then skippered the Bucs to a 26-25 record to close out the season. "Murtaugh knew when to talk, when to correct, and when to discipline," Virdon recalled. "He just seemed to know the right thing to do for a winning ballclub." Murtaugh changed the culture in Pittsburgh and stressed fundamentals. "He pushed me," Virdon said, "and made sure that I got all of the instruction that I should get." Virdon had an inclination to teach baseball (he operated his first baseball school in the 1956 off-season[15]) and Murtaugh encouraged him to follow his coaching passion. Virdon first coached in the Arizona Instructional League after the 1962 season and in the Florida Instructional League in 1964, at which

time he was already being touted by *The Sporting News* as "the best managerial talent" on the Pirates.[16]

Patrolling center field in Forbes Field for ten seasons (1956-1965), Virdon was durable, never suffered a debilitating injury, and was never placed on the disabled list. After hitting .319 in 1956, his second year in the major leagues, Virdon remained a consistent .260s-hitter the rest of his career. Forbes Field no doubt affected his power; after hitting 17 home runs as a rookie, he tallied just 74 more in his career. In the late 1950s, the left-handed-hitting Virdon was considered with Mickey Mantle and Bill White one of the fastest players from home to first base while batting (3.5 seconds) or bunting (3.4 seconds).[17] Batting leadoff for much of his career, Virdon used his speed and the dimensions of Forbes Field to rack up triples, leading the league once. When Murtaugh was asked if he was concerned about Virdon's career-low .243 batting average in 1964, he answered emphatically, "I count the hits he takes away from others as part of his batting average."[18] His cerebral approach to baseball meant that Virdon's value to the Pirates could not be reduced to batting statistics.

"He's an underrated player," Roberto Clemente said of Virdon. "He doesn't get the headlines because he makes everything look easy. He's kept a few of our pitchers in the majors with his glove and hitting."[19] Virdon had a quiet and reserved demeanor, didn't seek headlines, and was overshadowed playing center field in a league that featured perhaps the greatest center fielder of all time in Willie Mays and playing next to perhaps the best right fielder of all time in Clemente. "Virdon wasn't as flashy as Willie Mays," said teammate Bob Friend. "Forbes Field was a big ballpark and Virdon could play short and cover everything. There wasn't a better center fielder in my era."[20] He was regularly among the league leaders in putouts and assists, leading the league in 1959 with 16. Bill James's "range factor," a metric used to evaluate the quality of defensive play, underscores that Virdon was easily one of the best outfielders of his generation; he led the league twice (1959 and 1961) in the statistic. At the age of 31 Virdon won his first and only Gold Glove award in 1962 a year after voting was revamped to award the top three outfielders instead of a position-specific format (RF, CF, LF). "Bill has made amazing fielding plays so common in Forbes Field," Dick Groat wrote, "that Pirate fans are inclined to be disappointed if he doesn't catch everything hit to the outfield."[21] Virdon studied hitters' habits and tendencies and used his speed to neutralize the enormous power alleys at Forbes Field. "Virdon got such great jumps on the ball," teammate Hal Smith said. "He knew exactly where the ball was going."

"It was the biggest in baseball," Virdon said about Forbes Field. "I didn't have to worry about running into the fences." With its irregular shape, Forbes Field was 435 feet to the center-field wall, 457 to left-center, and 419 to right-center, which played to Virdon's strengths: speed and arm strength.[22] The field was so big that "the batting cage was in left-center field," Virdon remembered. "There was a big light pole that sat inside the ballpark and it had a fence around it. The batting cage was next to this fence. It wasn't really that obvious. The ballpark was so big that I played in it for ten years and I don't think the batting cage came into play more than three or four times."

The 1960 season was a magical one for the Pirates, but it began with concern and lingering doubts. After Murtaugh guided the team to 84 wins and a surprising second-place finish in 1958, the Bucs slipped to fourth in 1959. The team sold Forbes Field to the University of Pittsburgh in 1959 and team president John Galbreath had to squash

rumors that the franchise would relocate as the Brooklyn Dodgers and New York Giants had done two years earlier. To add to the core players such as Clemente, Groat, Mazeroski, Virdon, Bob Skinner, Dick Stuart, and pitchers ElRoy Face, Vern Law, and Bob Friend, Brown made wise trades for Smokey Burgess, Harvey Haddix, Don Hoak, and Rocky Nelson in 1959 and for Gino Cimoli, Vinegar Bend Mizell, and Hal Smith in 1960. But one trade Brown attempted failed: He offered the Kansas City Athletics Virdon, Groat, and Ronnie Kline for slugger Roger Maris.[23] "We all played for a pennant," Virdon said of the 1960 season, "and we thought we had a chance to do it." Virdon's optimism was tempered by the public perception of the Pirates; in national polls, sportswriters and players picked the Pirates to come in no better than fourth, behind the Braves, Dodgers, and Giants.[24]

"The 1960 season was unbelievable," Virdon said. "It seemed like every time we needed a run in a crucial situation, we got it." The team was known for manufacturing runs and playing "small ball" in an era of home runs. The Pirates led the league in hitting, runs, and OPS (on-base average plus slugging average), and ranked second in slugging while hitting only 120 home runs (sixth in the NL). "We were scramblers" said Virdon, who was platooned with Cimoli. In 1960 Murtaugh rested Virdon against left-handed pitchers; thus he started only 98 games in center field.

The 1960 World Series will forever be defined by Bill Mazeroski's Series-winning home run, but Bill Virdon's inspired fielding, his speed, and his uncanny knack for timely hitting were keys to the Pirates' victory. "Virdon was the guy who really hurt the Yankees," Friend said, and it started in the bottom of the first inning of Game One. Virdon and his roommate, Groat, who were considered among the best at the hit-and-run, had a chance to execute their specialty when Virdon walked to lead off the game. "When I got to first base I looked to Groat for the hit-and-run" Virdon said, "and he put it on. Dick didn't realize that he had put the hit-and-run on by mistake and tried to take it off, but I didn't bother to look at him again." Virdon took off and Groat took Ditmar's pitch. "Yogi saw that I was running" Virdon recollected, "and threw the ball to second, but nobody was covering. So I moved on to third." The Pirates went on to score three runs and ultimately won, but more importantly that first inning set the tone for the Series.

Virdon's fielding, hailed as "brilliant,"[25] choked Yankee rallies throughout the series. With Law struggling in Game One, Berra hit a deep shot to right-center field with two on in the fourth inning. Virdon chased down the ball and made a tremendous catch at the 407-foot marker while colliding with Clemente and saved two runs. The fielding highlight of the Series may have been Virdon's acrobatic catch of Bob Cerv's deep fly ball in the seventh inning of Game Four with two men on and the momentum shifting in favor of the Yankees. "I thought I was closer to the fence than I really was," Virdon said. "I wanted to make sure I caught the ball before I hit the fence so I jumped." Dan Daniel wrote afterward, "He [Virdon] won the opener with his fielding and hitting, and he did it again in the fourth game."[26]

In the bottom of the eighth inning of Game Seven, Virdon was involved in one of the most famous "what if?" plays in professional sports. With the Pirates trailing 7-4 and Gino Cimoli on first, Virdon hit what appeared to be a routine double-play ball to shortstop Tony Kubek. Forbes Field had a notoriously hard infield (Bucs announcer Bob Prince called it the "House of Thrills" because of the odd hops). "When I hit the ball," Virdon said, "I knew it was a double play all the way. The ball took a bad hop and hit Tony in the throat." Kubek was taken to the hospital. Instead of two outs and the bases empty, there were two on with no outs and the Bucs rallied with five runs, culminating with Hal Smith's three-run homer. The Yankees tied it in the ninth and the rest is history. Despite going only 7-for-30 in the Series, Virdon was one of the heroes of the Pirates' unlikely championship.

Though the Pirates played sub-.500 ball in three of the next four years, Virdon remained an excellent fielder and an integral part of the team. But after the 1964 season, he said, "I could feel myself slipping a little. . . . As you get older, playing every day is a mental problem."[27] His reaction probably referred to a few uncharacteristic lapses in concentration in the field but also pointed to his intention to start coaching. "I planned on quitting in 1965," he said, "and told the Pirates it would be my last year." Virdon, who always held himself to the highest standards, put the Pirates' concern before his own, and with little fanfare he retired after the 1965 season. "I could probably hang on

for a few years," he said. "But I don't want to be a hanger-on."[28] The "Quail" finished with 1,596 hits, 735 runs, and a .267 batting average in 1,583 games, but also as one of the most underrated players of his generation.

Virdon's managerial career began just weeks after his unconditional release and retirement on November 22, 1965, but not the way he had envisioned. "I was encouraged by Murtaugh to go into coaching," he said. "I decided to stay in baseball and I had an opportunity to manage in the Pirate organization. But at that point the pay for managing in the minor leagues was not too good. So I shopped around and found a job in the Mets organization." After managing for two years in the Mets organization, Virdon returned to the Pirates under new manager Larry Shepard. While a coach for the Bucs in 1968, he was placed on the active roster due to the military service of many players. He played in six games and his only hit was a two-run home run, the last hit of his career.

When Shepard was fired with five games left in the 1969 season, many assumed Virdon would get his first shot to manage, but he was bypassed in favor of Alex Grammas and then passed over again to start the 1970 season when Murtaugh came back for his third stint with the Bucs. Though he thought he was ready to be a major-league manager, Virdon refused to criticize general manager Joe Brown or the Pirates organization for any perceived slight. After the Pirates won the World Series in 1971 and Murtaugh retired for the third time, Virdon finally got his chance to manage.

After managing the San Juan Senators in the Puerto Rican league following the 1971 season, Virdon guided the Pirates to a first-place finish in 1972 only to lose a heartbreaking Game Five to Cincinnati in the National League Championship Series when Bob Moose threw a wild pitch that allowed George Foster to score the winning run in the bottom of the ninth. Virdon was fired with 26 games to play the next season even though the Pirates were just three games out of first place (though they had a losing record). Under bizarre circumstances, Virdon was hired by George Steinbrenner to manage the Yankees in 1974 just two months before the season began after A's owner Charlie Finley refused to allow Dick Williams out of his contract to manage the Yankees. Virdon kept the light-hitting Bronx Bombers in the fight for the American League East crown all season and they finished just two games behind Baltimore. Having led the Yankees to their closest pennant race since 1964, Virdon won his first of two *Sporting News* Manager of the Year awards. Despite his self-effacing personality and calm demeanor, Virdon was a competitive, no-nonsense manager who stressed fundamentals and demanded that his players put the team above individual reward. This led to high-profile confrontations with Dock Ellis, Richie Hebner, and Bobby Murcer. "I just tried to be honest and fair and made sure that everyone played hard," Virdon said of his coaching philosophy. "I did not put up with too much. [I was a disciplinarian] to some extent but without being offensive." In 1975 the Yankees failed to match their success of the previous year and Virdon was fired with a 53-51 record. Weeks later the Houston Astros hired him.

Virdon managed in Houston until 1982 and won his second Manager of the Year award after leading the Astros to their first postseason berth and to the brink of the World Series in 1980, only to lose another gut-wrenching Game Five of the NLCS, this time in extra innings. His managerial career concluded in 1984 after a two-year stint with the Montreal Expos. Despite his winning record (995-921) and rumors of being the next manager for a number of teams, he never skippered a team again. From 1985 until his retirement after the 2001 season, Virdon was a coach for the Pirates under Jim Leyland and Lloyd McClendon, as well as a minor-league instructor. He also coached for the Astros and in the Cardinals minor-league system.

With Shirley, his wife of almost 60 years, Virdon still resided in southern Missouri as of 2012. A baseball lifer, Virdon remained active with the Pittsburgh Pirates. "The best part of my career," he said before departing for the Pirates' spring-training camp in 2012, "is that I have not missed a spring training in 62 years!"

Sources

Statistics are from Baseball-Reference and Retrosheet.

David Cicotello and Angelo J. Louisa, eds., *Forbes Field. Essays and Memories of the Pirates Historic Ballpark, 1909-1971* (Jefferson, North Carolina: McFarland and Co., 2007).

Rick Cushing, *1960 Pittsburgh Pirates Day by Day: A Special Season, An Extraordinary World Series.* (Pittsburgh: Dorrance Publishing Co., Inc., 2010).

David Finoli and Bill Ranier, eds. *The Pittsburgh Pirates Encyclopedia* (Champaign, Illinois: Sports Publishing, 2003).

Dick Groat, *The World Champion Pittsburgh Pirates* (New York: Coward-McCann, 1961).

David Maraniss, *Clemente: The Pride and Passion of Baseball's Last Hero* (New York: Simon & Schuster, 2006).

Richard Peterson, ed., *The Pirates Reader* (Pittsburgh: University of Pittsburgh Press, 2003).

Jim Reisler, *The Best Game Ever: Pirates vs. Yankees October 13, 1960* (Philadelphia: Da Capo Press, 2007).

Notes

1   The author would like to express his gratitude to Bill Virdon, who was interviewed for this biography on January 12, 2012. Unless otherwise noted, all quotations from Virdon are from the author's recorded interview.

2   The author would like to express his gratitude to Hal Smith, who was interviewed for this biography on February 7, 2012. Unless otherwise noted, all quotations from Smith are from the author's recorded interview.

3   *The Sporting News*, June 16, 1954, 16.

4   *The Sporting News*, November 3, 1954, 13.

5   *The Sporting News*, December 29, 1954, 25.

6   *The Sporting News*, January 19, 1955, 11.

7   *The Sporting News*, October 12, 1955, 2.

8   *The Sporting News*, March 28, 1955, 26

9   *The Sporting News*, May 23, 1956, 6.

10 *The Sporting News*, December 15, 1954, 16.

11 All game statistics have been verified by Retrosheet (www.retrosheet.com).

12 *The Sporting News*, June 13, 1956, 5.

13 *The Sporting News*, August 1, 1956, 1; and September 5, 1956, 15.

14 *The Sporting News*, August 1, 1956, 9, 14.

15 *The Sporting News*, September 5, 1956, 15.

16 *The Sporting News*, April 25, 1964, 12.

17 *The Sporting News,* November 28, 1956, 3.

18 *The Sporting News*, November 7, 1964, 11.

19 *The Sporting News,* June 29, 1963, 14.

20 The author would like to express his gratitude to Bob Friend, who was interviewed for this biography on March 6, 2012. Unless otherwise noted, all quotations from Friend are from the author's recorded interview.

21 Dick Groat, *The World Champion Pittsburgh Pirates* (New York: Coward-McCann, 1961), 154.

22 Ronald M. Selter, "Inside the Park: Dimensions and Configurations of Forbes Field," in David Cicotello and Angelo J. Louisa, eds., *Forbes Field. Essays and Memories of the Pirates Historic Ballpark, 1909-197.* (Jefferson, North Carolina: McFarland and Co, 2007), 132.

23 *The Sporting News*, December 21, 1960, 26.

24 Groat, 93.

25 *The Sporting News*, October 19, 1960, 10.

26 Ibid.

27 *The Sporting News*, December 25, 1964, 25.

28 *The Sporting News*, December 6, 1965, 24.

Red Witt

By Peter Bauck

"Do what you love. Know your own bone; gnaw at it, bury it, unearth it, and gnaw it still."
    —Thoreau

GEORGE ADRIAN WITT was not born, as most sources will cite, on November 9, 1933. In a bit of historical foreshadowing, the big (6-feet-3, 200-pound) right-hander known as Red (for his red hair) opted to lie about his age "a long time ago" to gain some sort of advantage by presenting himself as two years younger than he actually was.[1] He also doesn't care to relive his baseball career. Sure, he's attended old-timer's games back in Pittsburgh on occasion and appeared at the odd trading-card show, but he was much more enamored with track or basketball. Baseball was only, as he put it, something he "could do well enough to make a living."[2] For a guy who didn't care so much for baseball, though, he was pretty good at it. He earned varsity letters in it as a position player in high school. (He also earned letters in basketball.) On a day when future bonus baby Paul Pettit struck out 27 batters for his Narbonne High School (Los Angeles) squad, Witt managed two hits off Pettit , including a home run. He was also good enough to receive a professional contract in the Brooklyn Dodgers farm system.

A true Southern Californian, Witt was born in Long Beach, the son of an Irish oil-worker father, George B. Witt, from Tennessee, and a Dutch immigrant mother, Jacalline Vangerdinge Witt. He had a sister, Jacqueline, born August 22, 1930, and was educated in nearby Wilmington at Banning High School. He continued his education first at Harbor Junior College (now Los Angeles Harbor College) and then Long Beach State College (now California State University, Long Beach). Even after he was drafted into the

US Marine Corps in 1950, during his first year in the Dodgers' organization, he stayed in the area, playing service ball while stationed at the Marine Recruiting Depot in San Diego. He made his offseason home in Laguna Beach, in Orange County south of Los Angeles. where, as of the end of 2012, he still resided.

Of course, even being good at baseball wasn't always a given. Witt initially preferred playing the outfield, but by his own admission he didn't hit well enough to stick at the position. In his first four seasons as a professional pitcher he advanced only as far as Pueblo of the Class A Western League (where he'd also had stops during the two seasons prior). He had three two-hitters and a 2.87 ERA to his name in 1953, but that season was preceded by a mediocre 1952 and followed by an injury-shortened 1954 (caused by elbow issues that would plague him throughout his career). He was becoming a little bitter and had reported not getting along with a number of his minor-league managers. He seemed ready to quit and use his double major in biology and physical education to become a teacher. In September 1954 he married his first wife, Mildred Powell. His prospects for ever making it to the majors seemed dimmer than ever.

Witt revived his athletic career after that 1954 season, though. At the end of November the Pittsburgh Pirates—acting on the advice of Howie Haak, the former Brooklyn scout who signed Witt in 1950 and who was by then working for the Bucs—instructed their Pacific Coast League affiliate, the Hollywood Stars, to draft Red away from Pueblo and the Dodgers system. Just like that, Red Witt made the jump from Class A all the way to being a heartbeat away from the major leagues. Later, Witt said of his attitude following the draft, "I decided to make a fresh start."[3]

Of course, Witt was still a long way from making an impact at the major-league level. A midseason demotion from Hollywood in 1955 put him back in the Class A Western League again, this time in Lincoln. Witt later recalled his time with the Lincoln Chiefs as instrumental in his development, crediting manager Bill Burwell with teaching him, "about the art of pitching … and he helped instill confidence in me" despite a miserable 2-10 record.[4]

In 1956 Witt was assigned to Double-A New Orleans and, over the course of the entire season, had managed an even .500 record. Going 8-8 with an ERA of 3.62 doesn't necessarily sound terribly impressive unless one considers the condition of Witt's arm and his in-season progress. By midseason he was 2-6 and his heavy reliance on the fastball made him very hittable. The sore arm that had bothered him throughout his pro career had become so bad that Witt was reported to be unable to even raise his right arm high enough to comb his own hair. Red worked through the aches, made a change in his delivery style, going "no-windup" in a manner comparable to that of Don Larsen, and started mixing in his curveball a lot more. He ended the 1956 season by throwing two straight one-hitters. Pittsburgh rewarded Witt's perseverance by purchasing his contract from New Orleans and adding him to the major-league club's 40-man roster.

Out of spring training in 1957, Witt was optioned to Hollywood again, where he had first landed in the Pirates' system two years earlier. This time, however, Red was ready for the Pacific Coast League. Dominant for most of the season, he posted a career high in innings pitched (184 2/3) and a career low in ERA (2.24), hurled six shutouts in 27 starts, displayed excellent control (58 walks compared with 114 strikeouts), and set a league record by throwing 58 1/3 consecutive innings without allowing an earned run. He was 18-7, had earned a shot in the big leagues, and was called up in September.

Witt's major-league debut, a start at Forbes Field against a mediocre New York Giants team on September 21 after a long layoff, was not a rousing success. He lasted only 1 1/3 innings and allowed six runs (all earned) on four hits while walking five. It was his only appearance for the Pirates that season. Still, his manager back in Hollywood, Clyde King, predicted a bright future, calling Witt "the No. 1 prospect in the league," and citing his "supreme self-confidence."[5]

As widely speculated throughout the offseason, Witt found himself on Pittsburgh's Opening Day 1958 roster despite limited action during the spring. Work remained sporadic in the early part of the season, and he was optioned to Pittsburgh's Triple-A club in Columbus on May 9 after making only three relief appearances. While in Columbus, though, Witt got the consistent repetition he needed in his seven starts for the Jets before his June 16 recall. In his first big-league start of the year, he made Pirates fans forget all about his disastrous debut the year before and his forgettable appearances earlier in the season by pitching up a complete game, besting Sandy Koufax and the Los Angeles Dodgers, 2-1. Witt allowed not a hit until Dodgers first baseman Norm Larker lined a single to left field in the fifth inning. That start proved to be the start of something special for Witt. He stayed in the rotation the rest of the season and proved to be up to the task of facing big-league hitters. He finished with the best ERA in the National League (1.61, though he didn't pitch enough innings to qualify for the official title) and a 9-2 record, doing his best to keep the Pirates in contention for the pennant throughout, highlighted by a pair of complete-game shutouts of the eventual National League champion, the Milwaukee Braves. The Pittsburgh chapter of the Baseball Writers Association of American named Witt the year's outstanding Pirate rookie.

Unfortunately for Witt, he never quite lived up to the promise of that rookie season. During his final spring training start in 1959, his elbow began to ache again. He was treated and cleared to play by the team's doctor, but after four subpar starts he was placed on the disabled list and, shortly after being reinstated, lost his position in the rotation. He failed to record a win all that year, and was bothered by his elbow all season. He was 0-7 with a 6.93 ERA. Witt failed to record another major-league win until an August 4, 1960, start against the Dodgers (which followed an extended but unimpressive run with the Salt Lake City Bees back in the Pacific Coast League).

During the 1960 World Series Witt played an unspectacular role, appearing exclusively in Pittsburgh's three losses to the Yankees. In Game Two he relieved ineffective reliever Clem Labine in the sixth inning with the Pirates down by nine runs and promptly allowed a pair of inherited runners to score on back-to-back singles before retiring the side on a fly out. Game Three brought about another nonpressure relief appearance, with Witt taking the mound from Fred Green with two outs in the fourth inning and the Pirates down 8-0, and two Yankees on base, and again allowing the runners to score. A wild pitch and an intentional walk later, he finally ended the frame on a groundout, which was followed by a messy but scoreless fifth inning. In Game Six, he was asked to start the ninth. The Pirates were losing 12-0. He retired all three batters he faced.

In one last flash of the great potential he had shown a few years before, Witt took the mound in his final start for Pittsburgh on May 7, 1961, facing Sandy Koufax (against whom Red had recorded his first-ever major-league win). He carried a no-hitter into the sixth inning until light-hitting second baseman Charlie Neal recorded the first hit, a solo home run to tie the score. In the following inning, Norm Larker and Frank Howard finished Witt off with back-to-back home runs. A few unremarkable relief appearances later, he was sent outright to Class A Asheville, where he finished the season, save for four innings in four games in July, still bothered by lingering elbow issues.

Witt received a couple of other chances later: In 1962 the second-year Los Angeles Angels gave him a five-game tryout in April. When the Angels returned Witt to the Pirates' Asheville club after an unimpressive showing (his ERA was 8.10), he was sold to the expansion Houston Colt .45s for another trial, lasting eight appearances. Witt wound up pitching well for Houston's Triple-A affiliate in Oklahoma City in 1962, but could manage only 19 innings in 1963 for Oklahoma City and Denver before hanging up his spikes for good.

Witt quickly found work after professional baseball. He started at Tustin High School in Orange County by coaching baseball and tennis, including tenure as the school's athletic director. However, he remarked in a 1987 interview that such work was "like a sailor retiring getting a rowboat."[6] In 1969 he moved into the school's science department, teaching biology and enjoying it immensely: "I haven't had a morning yet when I've gotten up and haven't loved the thought of going to work."[7] All the while, Witt did well financially by also becoming a small-time homebuilder.

Despite his diminished interest in baseball, Witt didn't totally withdraw from physical competition. While in his

50s, he reported being "in better shape than when [he] played baseball," and was working out several hours a day, teaching aerobics, and running competitively.[8]

George Witt passed away on January 30, 2013 following a battle with cancer. He and his second wife, Ellen, lived in a house he built that looks out over the ocean in Laguna Beach, California.

Sources

"1940 Census » California » Los Angeles County » Long Beach, Enumeration District 59-44." n.d. National Archives. <http://1940census.archives.gov/>.

Lester J. Biederman, "Hurler Back From Minors Beats Dodgers," *Pittsburgh Press* June 21, 1958.

—, "Ups And Downs End, George Witt Looks To Bright Future," *Pittsburgh Press*, March 29, 1959.

—, "Witt Aims To Make Good With Pirates," *Pittsburgh Press*, March 12, 1958.

—, "Witt Almost Pitched No-Hitter In Fight For Baseball Life," *Pittsburgh Post*, May 8, 1961.

"Colts Add Witt on Tryout Basis," *Houston Post*, May 15, 1962.

Ron Cook, "To Witt, baseball was unhappy time," *Pittsburgh Press*, May 11, 1987, D2.

Frank Finch, "Witt Shuts Door on Rivals, Opens Gate Into Majors," *Los Angeles Times*, August 14, 1957.

Chester L. Smith, "Buc Scout's Faith May Provide Team With Needed Hurler," *Pittsburgh Press*, March 6, 1958.

Henry David Thoreau, "Letter to Harrison G.O. Blake," Concord, Massachusetts, March 27, 1848.

Special thanks to Freddy Berowski, reference librarian, National Baseball Hall of Fame & Museum, A. Bartlett Giamatti Research Library, Cooperstown, New York.

Notes

1 Ron Cook, "To Witt, baseball was unhappy time," *Pittsburgh Press*, May 11, 1987, D2.

2 Ibid.

3 Lester J. Biederman, "Ups And Downs End, George Witt Looks To Bright Future," *Pittsburgh Press*, March 29, 1959.

4 Lester J. Biederman, "Witt Aims To Make Good With Pirates," *Pittsburgh Press*, March 12, 1958.

5 Frank Finch, "Witt Shuts Door on Rivals, Opens Gate Into Majors," *Los Angeles Times*, August 14, 1957.

6 Ron Cook, "To Witt …"

7 Ibid.

8 Ibid.

John W. Galbreath

By Warren Corbett

"He's a little guy. Thinks he can do anything. Damn near can." That description of John W. Galbreath came from the longtime manager of his Darby Dan Farm, Olin Gentry.

Galbreath built his Kentucky farm into a world-renowned thoroughbred racing stable. He owned the controlling interest in the Pittsburgh Pirates for 35 years and celebrated three World Series championships. In his business career he reshaped the skylines of cities from his hometown, Columbus, Ohio, to Hong Kong while amassing real estate holdings estimated at $550 million. At his funeral the famed pastor Norman Vincent Peale summed up his life as an "old, traditional American success story."[1]

John Wilmer Galbreath was born in Derby, Ohio, on August 10, 1897, to Francis Galbreath and the former Mary Mitchell, who was called Belle. He grew up on a farm in Mount Sterling as one of six children, and was a 5-foot-6-inch shortstop on his high-school team. He launched his first entrepreneurial venture when he was 10 years old, selling not horses but horseradish. Needing money for college, he worked for a year peddling high-school graduation invitations and pins before he entered Ohio University. He waited tables, repaired bicycles, and played saxophone in a dance band. He set up a darkroom in his dorm room, took photos of his classmates, and sold them to the students' parents.[2] World War I interrupted his education; he served as a lieutenant in the field artillery before returning to graduate in 1920.

Soon afterward he went into the real-estate business with a college fraternity brother, founding John W. Galbreath and Co. in Columbus. His

marriage to Helen Mauck produced two children, son Daniel and daughter Joan.

When Galbreath took up polo, he bought a stallion named Tommy Boy and several mares, with the idea of breeding polo ponies. But one of his fillies, Martha Long, won a $400 race at Beulah Park in Columbus in 1935, and that hooked him on racing.[3] He bought a farm near Columbus in Galloway, Ohio, and named it Darby Dan Farm after his son and the Big Darby Creek, which ran across the land.

Galbreath turned the hardship of the Great Depression into an opportunity that laid the foundation for his fortune. He assembled investor groups to buy defaulted real-estate mortgages for as little as 40 cents on the dollar and resell when the market recovered. By one account they bought and sold $7 million worth of property, with Galbreath collecting a 5 percent commission on every transaction. As his prominence grew, he served as president of the local and state real-estate boards.

In 1944 Galbreath was elected president of the National Association of Real Estate Boards. The association credited him with creating a strong nationwide organization by persuading real-estate boards in all 48 states to join what is now the National Association of Realtors. He represented the industry in lobbying for the disposal of surplus government property after World War II and in pushing for government-sponsored low-interest home loans for veterans, a key feature of the G.I. Bill of Rights that enabled millions of American families to become homeowners and transformed vast swaths of the landscape into suburbs.

One of Galbreath's Columbus friends and fellow Ohio State

University football boosters was George Trautman, a baseball executive who would become president of the minor leagues' governing body. When Galbreath expressed interest in getting into the game, Trautman tipped him that the Cleveland Indians were for sale. Galbreath decided not to make a bid and Bill Veeck bought the team.

Frank McKinney, a cigar-puffing Indianapolis banker who owned the city's Triple-A team, was seeking investors to buy the Pittsburgh Pirates. On Trautman's recommendation, Galbreath joined McKinney's syndicate as a minority shareholder, along with singer Bing Crosby and Pittsburgh attorney Thomas Johnson. They closed the deal in August 1946. Despite Organized Baseball's horror at any connection with gambling, new Commissioner Happy Chandler, a former governor and senator from Kentucky, did not share the late Judge Kenesaw M. Landis's distaste for horse racing. Chandler made no effort to block Galbreath and Crosby, who was also involved with racing. Galbreath was named vice president and treasurer of the ballclub.

The Pirates had won six National League pennants early in the century, but none since 1927. The club was in last place on the day the new owners took over and rose only one spot, to seventh, by the end of the 1946 season. In December McKinney made his first big move to upgrade the team by acquiring slugger Hank Greenberg from Detroit. The deal fired up Pittsburgh fans, who rushed to buy season tickets. Just one problem: Greenberg announced his retirement.

Greenberg, a proud man, was disgusted at his treatment by the Tigers, after 16 years with the club (four of them in military service). Detroit had to put him on waivers and all other American League teams had to pass before he could be sent to the National League. The Tigers sold the former MVP to Pittsburgh getting no players in return. Greenberg heard about the sale on the radio, then received only a terse telegram from the Tigers. In his memoirs he wrote that it left "a very harsh, bitter taste in my mouth."[4]

To entice Greenberg to Pittsburgh—and assuage those disappointed ticket buyers—McKinney called on his closer. Galbreath met Greenberg in New York and asked what it would take to bring his bat to the Pirates. Greenberg complained that he was sick of long train trips; Galbreath said he could fly between cities. Greenberg was tired of hotel rooms and roommates; Galbreath guaranteed him a suite to himself. Forbes Field, the Pirates' spacious ballpark, was a graveyard for home runs; Galbreath promised to shorten the fences. He also offered Greenberg's wife, an equestrian, one of Darby Dan's thoroughbreds, but she declined.

At 36, Greenberg didn't have much left. His greatest service to the team was as mentor to the young Ralph Kiner, who hit 51 home runs in 1947 and led the league in homers for seven straight years. But the Pirates still finished seventh. They climbed to fourth in 1948, then fell back to sixth.

As attendance dropped along with the team's place in the standings, McKinney and Galbreath squabbled over the direction of the franchise. Partner Tom Johnson described them as "two prima donnas" who couldn't get along.[5] On July 19, 1950, Galbreath and Johnson bought out McKinney, and Galbreath became president of the Pirates. Although he still lived in Columbus, he had put down some roots in Pittsburgh; his company was building a 35-story tower for U.S. Steel and Mellon Bank, and he had opened an office in the city.

Galbreath knew whom he wanted to run his team. Branch Rickey had turned the nearly bankrupt St. Louis Cardinals into the National League's powerhouse, and then moved on to build another powerhouse in Brooklyn. Twice he had created a baseball revolution, by developing the farm system and by signing Jackie Robinson. In racing terms, Rickey's past performance was unparalleled. Besides, Rickey was another small-town Ohio boy who had to work his way through college and was even a member of Galbreath's fraternity, Delta Tau Delta. In his lust for Rickey, Galbreath—widely respected for his integrity—engaged in some chicanery to get his man.

Walter O'Malley, who controlled 50 percent of the Dodgers' stock, wanted to rid himself of Rickey and gain complete control of the franchise. O'Malley was out to make money; Rickey liked to spend it. Under an agreement among the team's stockholders, if any of them found a buyer for his shares, the others had the right to match the offered price. Galbreath conjured up a buyer for Rickey's 25 percent: William Zeckendorf, a fellow real-estate deal-maker and Delta Tau Delta brother, offered $1 million—three times what Rickey had paid for his stock.

O'Malley smelled a rat. Why would a canny businessman like Zeckendorf, who was not particularly interested in baseball, want to be a powerless minority partner? But that was the price for O'Malley to be free of Rickey. When the time came to write the check, O'Malley learned that Zeckendorf had included a twist of the knife: He was due an additional $50,000 as payment for tying up his money while his offer was pending. Zeckendorf endorsed that check over to Rickey, adding to the Mahatma's retirement fund and to O'Malley's anger.[6]

When Rickey signed on as the Pirates general manager in November 1950, he was nearly 69 years old. Still, Galbreath gave him a five-year contract for $100,000 a year, plus an additional five years as a consultant at $50,000. Rickey's tenure would be spectacularly unsuccessful in the standings, but he fulfilled his mission. By signing hundreds of young players—applying his dictum, "Out of quantity comes quality"—he built the foundation for Galbreath's first championship. But the victories did not come fast enough, to the frustration of the Pirates' fans and owners. The ever-blabby Tom Johnson later said Galbreath "thought Rickey was the greatest thing since sliced cheese, and the old phony showed up here."[7]

Rickey began his stewardship by paying baseball's first $100,000 bonus to a high-school pitcher, Paul Pettit, who would win only one major-league game. Rickey spent another $400,000 on bonuses to untried amateurs in his first year. He tripled the size of the scouting staff and expanded the farm system. The major-league Pirates might have been able to win in one of those minor leagues, but not in the National. From 1951 through 1955 they lost at least 90 games every year and finished last in four out of five seasons, bottoming out with 112 defeats in 1952. Events conspired against Rickey's youth movement; several of the best prospects, including Dick Groat and Vernon Law, were drafted for two years of military service.

The dreary team was driving away fans and Rickey was feeling pressure. He wanted to get rid of Ralph Kiner, by far the highest-paid Pirate, but Galbreath refused to sell a player to cover his financial losses. Galbreath personally negotiated Kiner's contracts; when the star's salary reached $90,000, the owner was said to be paying a big chunk of it out of his own pocket rather than the Pirates' treasury. Exasperated, Rickey wrote Galbreath a confidential letter before the 1952 season disparaging Kiner:

He couldn't run, couldn't throw, and demanded special privileges. After Kiner slumped to a .244 average in 1952, while leading the league in homers, Galbreath stepped aside and assigned Rickey to negotiate a pay cut. When Kiner objected, Rickey told him, "We finished last with you and we can finish last without you."[8] In June 1953 Kiner was swapped to the Chicago Cubs in a four-for-six-player deal (four from the Pirates, six from the Cubs), with the Pirates receiving a reported $100,000.

At the same time he tried to build up the Pirates, Galbreath decided to move into the big leagues of thoroughbred racing. He had acquired a second farm, also renamed Darby Dan, in Lexington, Kentucky. He embarked on a buying spree of unprecedented cost and scope. Thoroughbreds were far more expensive than ballplayers. To strengthen his stable of stallions, he paid a record $2 million for Swaps, a former Horse of the Year. He bought another Horse of the Year, Sword Dancer. In 1959 Galbreath paid a stunning record $1.35 million to lease the stud services of the undefeated "wonder horse of Italy," Ribot. One of the Italian stallion's sons, Graustark, was the leading Kentucky Derby contender in 1966 until he broke down. Although some estimated Galbreath had spent more than $5 million on horses, he demurred: "Frankly, I never thought about the total investment, and what with all the many transactions going on all the time I wouldn't know where to begin."[9] The acquisitions secured Darby Dan's position as one of racing's elite stables.

Galbreath married even more thoroughbreds: His wife, Helen, had died in 1946, and in 1955 he wed Dorothy Firestone, a widow. Her horse Summer Tan ran third in the 1955 Kentucky Derby. Galbreath told *The Sporting News* his goal was to win the Derby and the World Series. He was an enthusiastic fan of both his sports teams; he would often drive his convertible around the farm until he found a spot where he could pick up the Pirates broadcasts from Pittsburgh. In 1956 he sat through a nine-hour doubleheader at Forbes Field.[10] He would never say whether he loved baseball or thoroughbreds more; it would have been like a father choosing one child as his favorite.

The baseball franchise was hemorrhaging money, saddled with Rickey's free spending and dwindling attendance. Losses totaled $2.2 million during Rickey's five years. Galbreath said, "I have my hands in several businesses, most of them much bigger than baseball, but none has ever given me the worry and headaches I get from baseball."[11]

With Rickey's contract as general manager coming to an end in 1955, he made noises about staying. Instead, Galbreath nudged him into a graceful retirement. Galbreath said, "We're not too far away from a contending team and it would be nice if Branch gets some of the credit when we do get going." He told reporters he had turned down four offers to buy the club and insisted he would never give up: "When you have a plan you stick with it. You don't quit until the plan has had a chance to work out."[12]

Rickey left a legacy that would vindicate his plan. As their prospects matured, the Pirates clung to first place early in the 1956 season and attendance doubled, even though the team fell back to finish seventh. In 1958 they climbed to second with the core of the 1960 championship team in place. When the Pirates clinched second place, their owner was on a hunting safari in Africa, but was able to hear the game on Armed Forces Radio. During the trip he survived a charging leopard and water buffalo, killing both along with a rhino and several zebras.

As the Pirates closed in on the long-awaited pennant in September 1960, Galbreath joined the team on a road trip for ten days, waiting to witness the clinching game. The backhanded clincher came in Milwaukee on Sunday, September 25; the game with the Braves was in the seventh inning when the scoreboard flashed news that the Cardinals had lost, assuring Pittsburgh its first pennant in 33 years. Galbreath left his box seat and went under the stands to shed tears in private. Drenched with Champagne in the clubhouse, he hugged manager Danny Murtaugh and called it "the biggest thrill of my life—a dream come true after 14 years of striving and hoping. Nothing can match it."[13]

Three weeks later, in another raucous clubhouse celebration after Bill Mazeroski's dramatic homer gave the Pirates an unbelievable World Series victory, he shouted, "Have we paid our debt to the city of Pittsburgh now? We have. We have. Thank heaven, we certainly have." In a calmer moment he reflected, "There will never be a thrill to match this."[14] But he had not yet won the Kentucky Derby.

Galbreath had little time to savor the triumph. That fall, as a member of the National League's expansion committee, he stepped in as mediator when the two leagues butted heads over expansion plans. He herded the contentious owners to an agreement at a meeting that lasted until 2 a.m.

Characteristically, Galbreath became a leader in baseball circles. In 1951 he negotiated the resignation of Commissioner Chandler. He supported the man who had paved his way into the game, but was overruled by other owners who wanted Chandler out. He served on the pension committee for many years. In 1965 he and Detroit owner John Fetzer headed the search committee to find a successor to retiring Commissioner Ford Frick. The committee approached General Curtis LeMay, chief of staff of the US Air Force, but LeMay, who was overseeing the bombing of North Vietnam, would not leave his post in wartime. He recommended his logistics specialist, retired Lieutenant General William Eckert. When the unknown Eckert was elected commissioner, a juicy though unconfirmed story circulated that the owners had confused his name with that of the former Air Force Secretary Eugene Zuckert.

Racing and baseball made Galbreath famous; he and his family appeared on CBS newsman Edward R. Murrow's interview show, *Person to Person*, in 1955. But it was his real estate deals that made him rich. He managed his three careers by traveling in a private plane, sometimes touching down in four cities in a single day. "He never rested," his grandson, John Phillips, recalled. "He was always on the move. He enjoyed life."[15] Sportswriter Whitney Tower called him a "walking dynamo."[16]

Galbreath operated on a grand scale. He put together syndicates of investors that bought several entire towns— company towns unwanted by their corporate owners—and renovated the houses for resale. He built a planned community, Bramalea, outside Toronto. His office towers and industrial complexes became landmarks in more than two dozen American cities. His most ambitious undertaking was Mei Foo Sun Chuen in Hong Kong, said to be the largest housing project ever built with private funds. When completed after 13 years, it encompassed 100 apartment buildings with 13,000 units and 80,000 residents, on land reclaimed from the sea.[17]

In the tycoon-eat-tycoon world of big-time real estate, where a wheeler-dealer could stand atop his skyscraper one day and descend to bankruptcy court the next, Galbreath was a conservative businessman. He took no ownership stake in many of his most famous projects, limiting his risk while he profited by collecting large management fees. He would not break ground until he had lined up an anchor tenant, a large corporation that pre-leased much of the space.[18] *The Wall Street Journal* described him as "ironfisted."[19]

Galbreath didn't smoke or drink, but there was showmanship in his soul; he loved to recite poetry and once signed his name on $100 bills and passed them out to employees to celebrate his birthday. He chartered buses to bring 900 residents of his childhood hometown, Mount Sterling, to see a Pirates game. Women from Mount Sterling catered parties at his Ohio farm in return for a donation to their church.[20] Guests at Darby Dan in Kentucky included President Gerald Ford and Britain's Queen Elizabeth II, who boarded some of her racehorses there.

While entertaining royalty and millionaires, Galbreath regularly attended local Rotary Club meetings in Columbus. As a leading booster of the Ohio State

Buckeyes, he recruited Heisman Trophy winner Vic Janowicz (who later signed with the Pirates) and basketball All-American Jerry Lucas. He remained true to his rural roots; he enjoyed talking to other farmers about crop yields and the price of corn.

Galbreath achieved his second sporting goal when his horse Chateaugay, a son of Swaps, carried Darby Dan's fawn-and-brown silks to victory in the 1963 Kentucky Derby. A 30-to-1 longshot, Proud Clarion, gave Galbreath a second Derby victory four years later. Darby Dan's Little Current won the other two legs of racing's Triple Crown, the Preakness and the Belmont Stakes, in 1974. Galbreath became the first owner to win the premier races on both sides of the Atlantic when Roberto (yes, named for Clemente) edged Rheingold by a head in Britain's Epsom Derby in 1972. "You haven't lived until you've crossed over the track to the infield to get a plate or a trophy," Galbreath said. "There isn't any sport like it."[21]

Galbreath served as chairman of the board of Churchill Downs, the storied Louisville track that is home to the Kentucky Derby. While chairman of the Greater New York Association, he supervised construction of the new Aqueduct race track and the rebuilding of Belmont Park in the 1950s.

When the Pirates claimed their next World Series championship, in 1971, Galbreath chartered two planes and took more than 200 club employees and their spouses—including office personnel, scouts, minor-league managers, and batboys—to the games in Baltimore. In the 1970s he turned day-to-day management of the club and his real-estate company over to his son, Dan. But when Pete Rose crisscrossed North America auctioning his talent to the highest bidder after the 1978 season, John Galbreath invited the free agent to his farm and promised him two mares with good bloodlines, plus the services of Darby Dan's stallions to breed them. Rose preferred the cash offered by the Philadelphia Phillies, but the Pirates won the 1979 World Series without him. After the Series, baseball owners presented the 82-year-old Galbreath with an award for meritorious service to the game.

Just two years after the '79 championship, Pittsburgh's attendance fell to the lowest in the league. By 1984 the Pirates had sunk to last place in the National League East while losing $6 million. Allegations surfaced of cocaine use in the clubhouse, with the team's mascot serving as the players' drug courier. At an emotional press conference in November 1984, Dan Galbreath said the club was for sale, but no buyers emerged. Rumors swirled that the team would leave town until a group of Pittsburgh business and civic leaders stepped up to buy it in October 1985.

John Galbreath's life of striving and succeeding ended on July 20, 1988, three weeks short of his 91st birthday. Within a few years a severe real-estate downturn brought the Galbreath Company, and Dan Galbreath, close to bankruptcy. In 1998 Lizanne Galbreath, the third-generation CEO of the family business, merged the company with Jones Lang LaSalle. The founder's legacy lives on at Darby Dan Farm, now operated by his grandson, John Phillips.

Notes

1   Edward L. Bowen, *Legacies of the Turf: A Century of Great Thoroughbred Breeders*, Vol. 2 (Lexington, Kentucky: Eclipse Press, 2004), 49, 51.

2   *The Sporting News*, December 7, 1960, 7.

3   Bowen, *Legacies of the Turf*, 50.

4   Hank Greenberg, with Ira Berkow, ed., *The Story of My Life* (New York: Times Books, 1989), 177.

5   Andrew O'Toole, *Branch Rickey in Pittsburgh* (Jefferson, North Carolina: McFarland & Company, Inc., 2000), 12.

6   Lee Lowenfish, *Branch Rickey, Baseball's Ferocious Gentleman* (Lincoln: University of Nebraska Press, 2007), 488-492, 495-496.

7   O'Toole, *Branch Rickey in Pittsburgh*, 14.

8   Lowenfish, *Branch Rickey*, 519.

9   Whitney Tower, "The Man, the Horse and the Deal that Made History," *Sports Illustrated*, June 1, 1959, online archive.

10 Rick Cushing, *1960 Pittsburgh Pirates: Day by Day* (Philadelphia: Dorrance Press, 2010), 85; *The Sporting News*, November 30, 1955, 13.

11 O'Toole, *Branch Rickey in Pittsburgh*, 112.

12 *The Sporting News*, November 30, 1955, 13; and June 27, 1956, 2.

13 *The Sporting News*, October 5, 1960, 8.

14 *The Sporting News*, December 21, 1960, 7.

15 John Phillips interview, September 30, 2011. Information about Galbreath's personality and family life comes from this interview.

16 Whitney Tower, "The Derby Victory Prance," *Sports Illustrated*, May 13, 1963, online archive.

17 National Association of Realtors, "Presidents of the National Association of Realtors: 1944—John W. Galbreath," http://www.tourthenewrealtor.com/library/virtual_library/president1944?tourthenewrealtor. Accessed August 14, 2011; "Dan Galbreath 1928-1995," *National Real Estate Investor*, October 1, 1995, online archive.

18 *Wall Street Journal*, February 19, 1991, B1.

19 *Wall Street Journal*, February 19, 1991, B3.

20 *The Sporting News*, July 31, 1957, 20.

21 Associated Press, *New York Times*, "John Galbreath, 90, a Sportsman and Real Estate Developer, Dies," July 21, 1988.

Joe L. Brown

By Rob Edelman

THE CHILDREN OF the elite often will have difficulty establishing their own identities and achieving success, particularly if their interests parallel those of a parent. Such was not the case with Joe L. Brown, whose father was Joe E. Brown, the popular comic actor, film star, and baseball aficionado who (unlike practically all celebrated sports fans) also was a skilled ballplayer. While Joe L. had no inclination to appear before the cameras, he nonetheless carved out for himself an estimable career in major-league baseball.

For two decades beginning in 1955, Brown was the general manager of the Pittsburgh Pirates. He was an astute baseball man with a sharp eye for talent and he transformed the Bucs from perennial cellar-dwellers to world champions in 1960, with a second title following in 1971; additionally, he helped lay the foundation for a third championship in 1979. As *Pittsburgh Tribune-Review* writer Bob Cohn observed on Brown's passing, "His father was a famous entertainer, and he succeeded a baseball legend (Branch Rickey). But Joe L. Brown ended up making his own name, putting his stamp on three Pittsburgh Pirates world championship teams during a span of 20 years."

Joe Leroy Brown was born on September 1, 1918, in New York City. His parents were the aforementioned Joe E. Brown and the former Kathryn Frances McGraw, and he had three siblings: Don, an older brother, and Kathryn Frances and Mary Elizabeth, two adopted sisters. At Joe L.'s birth, his father was performing in vaudeville. Joe E. spent the 1920s headlining on Broadway before moving himself and his family to Hollywood and the movies at decade's end. But in baseball circles, Joe E. primarily was recognized for his athleticism

and love of the sport. In his youth, he played semipro ball—in 1911, at age 19, he even was offered a Boston Red Sox contract—and his fame allowed him to befriend big league luminaries, work out with major-league teams, and organize Hollywood studio ball clubs. Three of his Warner Bros. features—*Fireman, Save My Child* (1932), *Elmer the Great* (1933), and *Alibi Ike* (1935)—were baseball-oriented, and he was responsible for getting his baseball buddies roles in movies. Between 1932 and 1935, he was part-owner of the American Association Kansas City Blues, and he delighted in his ever-expanding baseball memorabilia collection.

It was in this baseball-rich atmosphere that Joe L. came of age. Given his father's contacts, the youngster was privy to the company of baseball's top brass. And so, in 1935, at age 16, he met the man who significantly impacted his career: Branch Rickey. The two became pals, with the legendary Mahatma serving as his mentor. The youngster also befriended ballplayers and their families, and Honus Wagner invited him to work out at the Pittsburgh Pirates training camp. Joe L.'s first priority was a career as a big-league ballplayer. But unfortunately, while trying to impress Wagner with a strong throw from the infield, he broke all the bones in his right elbow—thus ending his dream of a pro playing career. Still, according to his father, the boy's love of the sport "developed into something near an obsession. No one ever had to ask him what he wanted to be when he grew up. It was pretty obvious that he wanted to make baseball a career."

The younger Brown graduated from Beverly Hills High School in 1935 and enrolled at UCLA, where he played varsity football. He entered pro baseball four years later, when

Danny Murtaugh with Joe L. Brown

he became assistant business manager of the Lubbock Hubbers of the Class D West Texas-New Mexico League. Then he was named president of the Waterloo, Iowa club in the Class B Three I League. Meanwhile, the "Milestones" section in the October 7, 1940 issue of *Time* announced the marriage of "pretty, blonde Virginia Lee Newport, 19, of Beverly Hills, Calif.; and Joe Leroy Brown, 21, handsome son of gulf-mouthed cineclown Joe E. Brown." The Browns eventually had two children: a daughter, Cynthia, and a son, Don.

Just over a year later, at the advent of World War II, Brown enlisted in the United States Army Air Force; he entered as a private and was mustered out a captain. After the war, he continued his baseball education working in the front offices of the Pacific Coast League Hollywood Stars and the Cleveland Indians' Zanesville, Ohio, farm team. His Hollywood connection allowed him to secure a gig spinning publicity for *The Babe Ruth Story* (1948), the notoriously awful biopic.

Brown first worked in the Pittsburgh organization in 1950, when he became business manager of the Waco Pirates in the Class B Big State League, and he eventually became president of the New Orleans Pelicans in the Class AA Southern Association. He made it to the big club's front office in 1955 and, at season's end, signed a one-year contract as the Bucs' general manager. The date was November 1; he replaced 73-year-old Rickey, who became the team's board chairman.

At the time, the Bucs were a strictly second-division ball club. During the previous six seasons, they were entrenched in last place with won-lost marks of 57-96 (in 1950); 42-112 (1952); 50-104 (1953); 53-101 (1954); and 60-94 (1955). In 1951, their 64-90 mark was good for seventh place, two games ahead of the Chicago Cubs. (It was for good reason that, in *On the Waterfront*, the 1954 Best Picture Academy Award winner, a dockworker quips that his beat-up windbreaker is "more full of holes than the Pittsburgh infield.") Team president John Galbreath announced that Brown "will have complete charge of the club" and, upon being hired, he pledged to get the Bucs "back in the race and into the World Series." Brown added, "The job, of course, is a great challenge to me, but I think it is a challenge that can be met." At 37, he was one of the youngest big league general managers.

Brown's first priority was to hire a skipper to replace Fred Haney, who had been let go after the team's eighth-place finish. His choice was Bobby Bragan, who led the team to an equally dismal seventh place mark in 1956; however, their 66-88 record was an improvement over their finish during recent campaigns. On November 21, Brown's rehiring for the 1957 campaign was announced. At the time, Galbreath prophetically noted, "I hope Joe will be associated with the Pirates for many years to come."

Midway through the following season, with the Bucs again mired in seventh place with a 36-67 record, Brown replaced Bragan with 39-year-old Danny Murtaugh, an ex-big league infielder and current Pirates third-base coach who also had managed the New Orleans Pelicans when Brown was affiliated with that team. Brown initially offered the post to Clyde Sukeforth, another Bucs coach, but was turned down. Murtaugh, meanwhile, was hired on an interim basis. The general manager told the press that Bragan had been replaced "for the good of the team, now, and in the future."

The 1957 campaign was beyond salvaging, with the Pirates ending up in seventh place at 62-92. But Brown was pleased with Murtaugh's managerial instincts. He rehired the skipper for 1958 and the team broke through into the first division with an 84-70 record, good enough for second place behind the 92-62 Milwaukee Braves—and a *Sporting News* Major League Executive of the Year prize for Brown. After backsliding to 78-76 and fourth place in 1959, the Bucs were the 1960 NL pennant winners with a 95-59 record, finishing seven games ahead of the Braves. Their seven-game triumph over the favored New York Yankees—the team's first world championship since 1925—was as much a victory for Brown as for Murtaugh, World Series hero Bill Mazeroski, or any other Pirate. (Murtaugh was Brown's favored skipper. On several occasions, he temporarily left his post because of a heart ailment, but still managed the Bucs from 1957-64 and in 1967, 1970-71, and 1973-76; when not helming the team, Murtaugh toiled for Brown as an advisor-troubleshooter-super scout. In 1974, sportswriter Red Smith even quipped that Brown "suffers from the curious delusion that nobody except Danny Murtaugh can manage a team…")

Upon Brown's arrival in Pittsburgh, some of the pieces that shaped the 1960 champs already were in place.

Pitchers Vern Law, Bob Friend, and Elroy Face joined the club in 1950, 1951, and 1953. Shortstop Dick Groat had been with the team since 1952. Outfielder Bob Skinner arrived in 1954. Second sacker Bill Mazeroski, who signed with the Pirates in 1954, debuted in 1956. Most notably, on November 22, 1954, Rickey drafted a 20-year-old flychaser named Roberto Clemente from the Brooklyn Dodgers. But Brown worked out the trades that brought the team outfielder Bill Virdon (acquired from the St. Louis Cardinals on May 17, 1956); infielder Dick Schofield (St. Louis, June 15, 1958); third-baseman Don Hoak, catcher Smoky Burgess, and pitcher Harvey Haddix (Cincinnati Reds, January 31, 1959); catcher Hal Smith (Kansas City Athletics, December 9, 1959); out-fielder Gino Cimoli and pitcher Tom Cheney (St. Louis, December 21, 1959); and pitcher Wilmer "Vinegar Bend" Mizell (St. Louis, May 27, 1960).

Meanwhile, first basemen Dick Stuart, signed by the Bucs in 1951, joined the team in 1958. Fellow first sacker Rocky Nelson, an up-and-down big leaguer since 1949, was a December 1, 1958 Rule 5 draftee from the International League Toronto Maple Leafs. Brown was chided by his colleagues for his decision to draft the vet-eran. San Francisco Giants general manager Chub Feeney joked that Brown surely meant to draft *Ricky* Nelson, of *Ozzie and Harriet* fame. But *Rocky* Nelson was a valuable addition to the Bucs, hitting .300 in 200 at-bats for the 1960 club.

Not all of Brown's deals were steals. In order to obtain Mizell, along with utility infielder-outfielder Dick Gray, he gave up a pitcher to be named later and his AAA Columbus second baseman: Julian Javier, aptly described by the general manager as "one of the most brilliant pros-pects in the minor leagues." Javier later starred with the Cards. But Brown was more concerned with the present, with 1960. "I'm shooting everything for this year," he told the press.

In mid-September, as the Pirates inched toward the NL pennant, *New York Times* columnist John Drebinger wryly observed, "When Brown was tapped by Galbreath to direct the Bucs, most folks outside of baseball knew him chiefly as the son of the comedian, Joe E. Brown. Since Bing Crosby, the crooner, already was a stockholder, it was generally thought young Joe was added to produce more laughs." But then he admitted that Brown was a hardworking baseball professional, adding, "Before every game you could see him sitting behind the batting cage watching every pitch and swing." Later on, right after the World Series clincher, Brown was interviewed in the Pirates' jubilant clubhouse by broadcaster Bob Prince. "I think (the series) was just sheer guts against power," he declared, "and the guts came through."

During the rest of the decade, the Pirates fielded teams that finished as high as third place (in 1965, 1966 and, in the NL East, in 1969). One of his more controversial moves came in November, 1962, when he traded Dick Groat, the 1960 NL batting champion and Most Valuable Player as well as a Wilkinsburg, Pennsylvania native, to St. Louis. Groat, destined to be the Cards' starting short-stop on its 1964 World Series winner, was crushed—and remained angry at Brown for decades. (Actually, in December 1959, Brown considered trading Groat to the Kansas City Athletics for Roger Maris: a deal that would have drastically altered baseball history. "As soon as Danny [Murtaugh] and I closed the door [of their Miami Beach, Florida, hotel room]," the general manager admit-ted the following November, "we looked at each other and frowned—right away we knew we didn't like it." And so the trade was nixed.)

Under Brown, the Bucs' fortunes improved during the 1970s. They consistently remained in the thick of pen-nant races and were first-place finishers in the NL East in 1970-72, 1974-75, and 1979; they came in second place in 1976-78; and their worst campaign was a third-place finish in 1973. Most significantly, they were world champs again in 1971. Clemente and Mazeroski remained from the 1960 team; key additions made by Brown included Dave Cash, Al Oliver, Manny Sanguillen, Richie Hebner, Bob Robertson, Steve Blass, Nelson Briles, Dock Ellis, Dave Giusti, Bruce Kison, and, most prominently, Willie Stargell.

The Pirates' core players mostly were products of its farm system; Brown, like Rickey, believed that major league suc-cess was a direct result of employing a top-flight scouting staff and solid player-development program. Those in the know fully credited him for his team's accomplishments. Prior to the 1971 World Series, in which the Bucs beat the Baltimore Orioles in seven games, *New York Times* col-umnist Leonard Koppett described Brown as "extremely self-effacing (and) low-key" in a profession that otherwise "attracts and rewards flamboyance." Koppett added that Brown was a model of "the 'new-wave' career executives that flourished in baseball only after World War II." He observed, "Among baseball people, the Pirate organization is considered among the best for producing outstanding young players year after year," and he concluded, "The Pittsburgh Pirates are the creation of Joe L. Brown …"

Brown, to his credit, had a progressive view regarding minorities in baseball. He acknowledged that the Caribbean and Latin America were fertile sources of talent, and occasionally accompanied scout Howie Haak on his south-of-the-border excursions. In a September 1, 1971 game against the Philadelphia Phillies, his Pirates made history by fielding the first all-black starting nine. Brown downplayed the milestone by declaring, "Danny Murtaugh put out the best nine players." A decade earlier, in 1961, Brown hired 36-year-old African-American infielder Gene Baker, whom he has just unconditionally released, to manage the team's Class D Batavia, New York ball club. To Brown, this was no important thing. "(Baker) was most valuable to the Pirates organization in the past as a player, instructor and scout," he remarked. "He is a fine gentleman with outstanding baseball knowledge and experience. We're confident he'll do a fine job in the managerial field." Baker later was a player-coach on the Pirates' AAA Columbus Jets farm club and in 1963 followed Buck O'Neil as the second African-American to coach at the major league level.

Brown also was a beloved figure among his employees. When Kay Butler, a longtime Forbes Field hotdog vendor, died in 1979, he came to the funeral home to offer his condolences. By then, Brown had been retired from the Pirates for three years; he left the team after the 1976 season and was replaced by Harding Peterson, whom he had hired to operate the Bucs' farm system in 1967. But it was under Brown's stewardship that several key contributors to the 1979 championship came to Pittsburgh. Stargell and Sanguillen remained from 1971; others included Dave Parker (who arrived in 1973), Jim Rooker (1973), Kent Tekulve (1974), Bill Robinson (1975), Omar Moreno (1975), and John Candelaria (1975).

Brown settled in Newport Beach, California, but maintained his Pittsburgh ties by scouting for the ball club. He remained a valued member of baseball's inner circle. For example, in 1978, he helped devise a plan to realign the two major leagues by dividing each into three divisions. For years, he was an influential member of the Baseball Hall of Fame Veterans Committee. But his days in the Pirates front office had not ended. In May 1985, the team was mired in a headline-making drug scandal. Its on-field play was uninspired, attendance was declining, and the Galbreath family was rumored to be shopping the franchise. Old reliable Brown was called in to add some past-season glitter by becoming the team's acting general manager. He finished out the season, was replaced by Syd Thrift, and returned to California.

A wheelchair-bound Brown made his final public appearance on June 19, 2010 at Pittsburgh's PNC Park, during a ceremony commemorating the 50th anniversary of the Pirates' 1960 championship. At the time, the Bucs—who had compiled losing records for the past 17 seasons—were more like the team he inherited in 1955. But it was a day for celebration, with Brown earning a standing ovation from the crowd. "We beat a pretty good Yankee team with (Mickey) Mantle, (Roger) Maris, (Whitey) Ford, (Yogi) Berra (in 1960)," he told the *Pittsburgh Post-Gazette*. "The Pirates had not won in so long that nobody remembered what it was like. Pittsburgh is a football town. But we showed it was also a baseball town."

On this occasion, Brown was sought out by Dick Groat, who still resented being traded almost a half-century earlier. "We buried the hatchet," Groat reported. "We had a great conversation at the reunion. I said to myself, 'He's 91, and I'm 79. No use carrying this grudge till one of us dies'."

Brown indeed did pass away less than two months later, on August 15, in Albuquerque, New Mexico. He was suffering from an unnamed illness and recently had moved to an assisted living facility in Albuquerque near the home of daughter Cynthia. Information regarding Brown's funeral and burial were kept private by his family.

Upon his death, Bucs players added "JLB" patches to their uniform sleeves. Brown, in addition, was tributed in the Pittsburgh media. In his *Post-Gazette* blog, Bob Smizek dubbed him "one of the most important sports figures in Pittsburgh history." Steve Blass, the ex-Pirates hurler and current broadcaster, told the paper, "Yes, he built championship teams and made superb trades, but he also built a pipeline to supply that team. People don't understand how good that farm system was." Blass labeled Brown "the consummate GM" and added, "He was a baseball father to me…. He is living proof that not every champion wears a uniform."

Bob Friend, a starter on the 1960 world champs, noted, "He was one of the best baseball men of his time. Joe Brown was a winner…. His mind was so sharp when he was back with us in June. I think the ovation he received from the fans was tremendous. I think he was overwhelmed by it." Bill Virdon, another 1960 Bucs veteran, added that Brown was "sharp as a tack. He really knew his business. One of the best in the business. No doubt."

For information regarding the passing of Joe L. Brown, I would like to acknowledge the following: Clifton Parker, Bill Lee, Rod Nelson, Fred Worth, and especially Tim Wiles of the National Baseball Hall of Fame & Museum.

Sources

Books:

Joe E. Brown, as told to Ralph Hancock. *Laughter Is a Wonderful Thing.* (New York: A.S. Barnes, 1956).

Rob Edelman. *Great Baseball Films.* (New York: Citadel Press, 1994).

John Thorn and Pete Palmer, Michael Gershman, David Pietrusza, editors, *Total Baseball, Fifth Edition.* (New York: Viking, 1997).

Newspapers/Magazines:

Rob Biertempfel and Cohn, Bob. "Clement's season could be done after oblique injury." *Pittsburgh Tribune-Review*, September 4, 2010

Bob Cohn. "Joe L. Brown, who built Pirates championship teams, dead at 91." *Pittsburgh Tribune-Review,* August 17, 2010.

Arthur Daley. "Sports of *The Times*: The Mahatma Bows Out." *New York Times,* October 26, 1955.

John Drebinger. "Sports of *The Times*: A Strange Conglomeration." *New York Times,* September 15, 1960.

Joseph Durso. "3-Division Proposal for Major Leagues Facing Obstacles." *New York Times,* December 8, 1978.

Robert Dvorchak. "Joe L. Brown, architect of champion Pirates teams, dies." *Pittsburgh Post-Gazette,* August 16, 2010.

Dvorchak. "Obituary: Joe L. Brown/Pirates GM in team's glory days, Sept 1, 1918-Aug. 15, 2010." *Pittsburgh Post-Gazette,* August 17, 2010.

Dvorchak. "Pirates '60 Series champs celebrate again; Clemente's widow, Mazeroski greeted warmly by capacity crowd." *Pittsburgh Post-Gazette,* June 20, 2010

Rob Edelman. "Joe E. Brown: A Clown Prince of Baseball." *The National Pastime,* Number 27, 2007.

Richard Goldstein. "Joe L. Brown, Built Pirates' Championship Teams, Dies at 91." *New York Times,* August 18, 2010.

Leonard Koppett. "Sports of The Times: The Master Builders." *New York Times,* October 9, 1971.

William Nack. "Bring Back The Bucks," *Sports Illustrated,* October 23, 2000.

Red Smith. "A Man's Got a Right to Lose." *New York Times,* September 25, 1974.

Bob Smizik. "Blog Roll: Pittsburgh won't let go of 1960 Pirates." *Pittsburgh Post-Gazette,* August 18, 2010.

"Baker, Negro Infielder, To Manage in Minors." *New York Times,* June 20, 1961.

"BHHS Hall of Fame Member, Pirates General manager Joe L. Brown Dies at 91." *Beverly Hills Weekly,* September 2-8, 2010.

"Bragan Reported Out." *New York Times,* August 3, 1957.

"Bucs Drop Bragan; Murtaugh Is Pilot." *New York Times,* August 4, 1957.

"Career in Minors Spans 25 Years." *New York Times,* October 14, 1967.

"Milestones." *Time,* October 7, 1940.

"Murtaugh to Remain Pirate Pilot in '71." *New York Times,* November 13, 1970.

"New Orleans Pilot Quits." *New York Times,* September 15, 1954.

"Pirates, A's Planned 'Most Valuable' Trade." *New York Times*, November 18, 1960.

"Pirates Get Mizell." *New York Times*, May 28, 1960.

"Pirates of old: What a time it was under Joe L. Brown." *Pittsburgh Post-Gazette*, August 19, 2010.

"Pirates Rehire Brown." *New York Times*, November 21, 1956.

"Sports People: Straight Talk." *New York Times*, May 26, 1985.

Danny Murtaugh

by Andy Sturgill

SERIAL RETIREMENT HAS a long tradition in sports. Boxing has produced many serial retirees, aging fighters who swear each fight is their last until the promise of another big payday becomes too much to resist. In the 2000s, no NFL season was complete without the will-he-won't-he drama surrounding Brett Favre's retirement. But perhaps the king of sports retirements is Danny Murtaugh, who retired from baseball as a player in 1951 and then retired as manager of the Pittsburgh Pirates four times in a 13-year span in the 1960s and '70s.

Murtaugh was known for his wit and ability to give the media a good quote. As manager he often held court from a rocking chair in his office and offered up gems like "Why certainly I'd like to have a fellow who hits a home run every time at bat, who strikes out every opposing batter when he's pitching and who is always thinking about two innings ahead. The only trouble is to get him to put down his cup of beer, come down out of the stands, and do those things."[1]

Daniel Edward Murtaugh was born on October 8, 1917, at his parents' home in Chester, Pennsylvania, a city on the Delaware River halfway between Philadelphia and Wilmington, Delaware. He was the middle of five children—the four others were girls—born to Daniel and Nellie (McCarey) Murtaugh. Without the documentation that accompanies a hospital birth, Murtaugh was unsure of his actual birthdate. His family found definitive evidence of the birthdate, ironically enough, at his funeral. A man there remembered the day Murtaugh was born because it was the day that he himself had got married, and Danny's mother was unable to attend because she was having a baby. The man's anniversary?

October 8, 1917.[2] The Murtaughs lived in a working-class Irish neighborhood. Danny's father worked in the shipyards; Nellie took in laundry to make money and also baked pies that the children would sell around the neighborhood. In *The Whistling Irishman*, a biography of Murtaugh, his granddaughter Colleen Hroncich wrote that "modest" would be a generous description of the family's circumstances. She cited the Murtaugh children walking along railroad tracks in search of loose coal to bring home to heat the home, as well as the long-term presence of a large hole in the family dining room because the Murtaughs could not afford to fix it.[3]

As a youth, Murtaugh played baseball, basketball, and soccer, and even earned a football scholarship offer to attend Villanova University, which he had to decline because he could not afford textbooks or transportation to and from the nearby school.[4] Playing for Chester's team in American Legion ball, Murtaugh got well acquainted with another future major leaguer, Marcus Hook American Legion star Mickey Vernon, who went on to two batting championships and seven All-Star Games. The two established a friendship that endured until Murtaugh's death.

After leaving high school Murtaugh had no offers to continue his baseball career, so he went to work with his father at the shipyards for Sun Ship, and played baseball and basketball in a local semipro industrial league.[5] He followed in the footsteps of his father and grandfather by serving in the local volunteer fire company, and once carried a woman from a burning building only to realize that she had died in his arms.[6]

Murtaugh got a chance to play professional baseball in 1937, but to take his shot he had to give up his $35-a-week job at

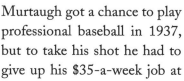

Sun Ship for a salary of $65 per month for the Cambridge (Maryland) Cardinals of the Class D Eastern Shore League. He played second base, third base, and shortstop and posted solid offensive numbers as he rose through the Cardinals' minor-league system between 1937 and 1940. Halfway through the 1941 season he earned a shot at the big leagues, but not with the Cardinals. In late June Murtaugh's hometown Philadelphia Phillies purchased his contract from the Cardinals, and he made his big-league debut on July 3 in a 4-1 loss to the Boston Braves. Murtaugh played in 85 games for the Phillies in 1941, hitting .219 with 11 RBIs. Though he played in the major leagues for only three months that season, his 18 stolen bases led the National League. The Phillies finished in last place with a woeful 43-111 won-lost record, the fourth of five consecutive seasons the team lost at least 103 games during one of the darkest eras for any team in major-league history.

Coming up as a second baseman, Murtaugh was described in the press as "peppery," "a spark," and a "flash."[7] He could run and throw, but felt that he wasn't adept enough at making the turn at second base, and asked Cincinnati second baseman Lonnie Frey for help after a game against the Reds. Frey obliged by working with Murtaugh on the field for nearly an hour after a game, and Murtaugh credited Frey with helping him stay in the majors for a decade as a second baseman.[8] In November after his rookie year, Murtaugh married his high-school sweetheart, Kate Clark.

Murtaugh began the 1942 season playing second base, but before long was moved to third base, then ended up back at the middle infield positions around the All-Star break. For the season he played 60 games at shortstop, 53 at third base, and 32 at second. His batting average increased to .241 and he had 13 stolen bases as the Phillies lost 109 games and finished last again. After the season Murtaugh returned to Sun Ship in Chester to aid in the US war effort.

In May 1943 the Murtaughs' first child, a son, Timothy, was born. On the field Murtaugh blossomed by hitting .273 and helping the Phillies out of the cellar for the only time between 1938 and 1945. In August he was inducted into the Army. His last game before going into the service was August 19, and the Phillies dubbed the game Danny Murtaugh Night at Shibe Park. Murtaugh reported to

Fort Meade, Maryland, where one of his first assignments was to play in a War Bond game in New York between an Army team and a mixed squad of the New York teams. Later he was granted a transfer to the Air Corps, but after a month it was discovered that he was colorblind, and he was disqualified from flying. He returned to the infantry and spent 1944 and '45 marching across Europe with the 97th Infantry in the 1st Army, a unit that saw significant battle action and earned three battle stars.[9] After the war ended, Murtaugh was assigned to the occupation forces in Japan. He was discharged from the Army 15 days before the start of spring training in 1946.[10]

Early in the season Murtaugh was sold back to the Cardinals, and spent the rest of the 1946 season at Triple-A Rochester. He was picked by the Boston Braves in the Rule 5 draft after the season, and spent most of the 1947 campaign at Triple-A Milwaukee. After the season Murtaugh was traded by the Braves to the Pittsburgh Pirates with outfielder Johnny Hopp for outfielder-pitcher Al Lyons, outfielder Jim Russell, and catcher Bill Salkeld. He spent 1948-51 with the Pirates, his seasons alternating between productive and weak. His first season 1948, was probably his most productive as a major leaguer; he hit .290 with 71 RBIs and 10 stolen bases as the Pirates vaulted from a last-place finish to fourth. Hobbled by injuries in 1949. Murtaugh batted a dismal .203. A nice bounce-back season in 1950 (.294) was interrupted on August 30 when he was hit in the head by a Sal Maglie fastball and was hospitalized for ten days with a skull fracture. Then, after hitting a meager .199 in 77 games as a 33-year-old in 1951, Murtaugh approached Pirates boss Branch Rickey and was offered a job as player-manager at the Pirates' Double-A farm team at New Orleans.[11]

Murtaugh managed the Pelicans for three seasons, then decided to be home with Kate and their two children in Pennsylvania. That desire was sidetracked when in 1955 he was named manager of the Triple-A Charleston (West Virginia) Senators, a financially ailing team that let him go in midseason to cut costs. Pirates general manager Joe Brown offered him the job as the manager at Williamsport of the Double-A Eastern League, but before he made it to Williamsport a spot opened on the Pirates' coaching staff, and Danny filled the role.[12]

In 1956 the Pirates posted a 66-88 record under manager Bobby Bragan. In 1957 the Bucs stood at 36-67 when general manager Brown fired Bragan and named the interim manager. Brown had wanted to give the job to first-base coach Clyde Sukeforth, but Sukeforth declined and recommended Murtaugh.[13] Danny led the Pirates to a 26-25 mark under his direction, and Brown removed the interim label before the end of the season.[14]

The Pirates followed up their strong finish in 1957 by finishing in second place in 1958 with an 84-70 record. He was an overwhelming choice for the Associated Press Manager of the Year award. (He received 149 points in the voting, while the runner-up got only six.)[15] But 1959 was disappointing; the Pirates fell to fourth place with a 78-76 mark. That led to a new team rule for 1960: no wives on the road. "Not that I don't approve of wives. I'd better, I've been married for 20 years," Murtaugh said. "But something ruined us on the road and I gotta find out."[16] He suggested that when wives travel with the team they want to go to shows, shopping, etc., which wears players out and distracts them from the task at hand. Whether or not the ukase was helpful, the 1960 Pirates sprinted out to a 12-3 start by May 1, and starting on May 30 were in first place each day for the rest of the season. (They won 12 more games on the road than they had in 1959.) The Pirates finished seven games ahead of second-place Milwaukee and won their first pennant since the 1927 team was swept by the Ruth-Gehrig Murderer's Row Yankees.

In the World Series, the Pirates again faced off with the Yankees, who were appearing in their tenth World Series since 1949. The Pirates won a thrilling Series in seven games on Bill Mazeroski's walk-off home run, and Murtaugh was praised for aligning his pitching staff so that Pirates ace Vern Law could start three games, including the decisive seventh game, while the Yankees' manager, Casey Stengel waited until Game Three before using his ace, Whitey Ford, allowing Ford only two starts. The Pirates won despite being badly outscored in the Series; the Yankees won three laughers in which they outscored the Pirates by 38-3. But the Pirates were able to scratch out wins in four hard-fought games to become world champions. Of his nerves during the deciding game, Murtaugh said, "I used four packs (of chewing tobacco) and don't remember spitting."[17] Afterward, Kate told Danny that she had never seen him so happy, to which he replied, "If you had been standing on one side of me and Bill Mazeroski on the other side, and somebody said I had to kiss one or the other, it wouldn't have been you."[18]

After their climactic Series victory, the 1961 Pirates stumbled to sixth place with a record under .500. Near the end of the season Murtaugh's oldest son, Tim, started college at Holy Cross. Between athletic and academic scholarships Tim was given nearly a full ride, but Danny, who years earlier had been unable to attend Villanova because of financial concerns, wrote to the school's president asking that his son's scholarships be awarded to another student, as he was fortunate enough to be able to pay for his son's education.[19]

During spring training in 1962 at Fort Myers, Florida, Murtaugh checked himself into the Lee County Hospital, claiming to be suffering the effects of the flu, but instead learned that he had a heart problem. After a few days of rest he was cleared to return to the team. The 1962 Pirates won 93 games (fourth place in the ten-team league), but the '63 and '64 teams fell badly to eighth and sixth, respectively. At the end of 1964 Murtaugh, only 46, walked away from managing the team, citing health concerns. (Few knew the extent and nature of his health issues, and he usually blamed his illnesses on the flu and

Managers Murtaugh and Stengel

stomach ailments.) He remained with the ballclub as a scout and adviser to GM Joe Brown.[20]

During Murtaugh's stay in the front office, which he referred to as the "golf tour of baseball," he was able to spend more time with Kate and their high-school-age daughter, Kathy. (Danny Jr. had joined Tim at Holy Cross.) The Pirates signed Tim in 1965, and he caught nine seasons in the organization, reaching the Triple-A level. He also managed for seven seasons.[21]

The Pirates muddled through the first half of the 1967 season under manager Harry Walker, who was fired after 84 games. Murtaugh agreed to manage the team the rest of the season, posting a 39-39 mark nearly identical to Walker's 42-42. Murtaugh admitted that he was not in the right frame of mind to manage and ended up serving more as a cheerleader on the bench than a real manager. Before the season ended the team announced that Murtaugh would not return as manager, and named him director of player acquisition and development, where he oversaw the farm system and scouting. After two seasons the Pirates sought a replacement for manager Larry Shepard, and Joe Brown and Murtaugh met deep into the night regarding potential candidates. Early the next morning Danny knocked on Brown's door and asked why he himself shouldn't be the manager, with Brown replying that the job was his any time as long as he had the permission of his doctor and his wife. Both consented and in Danny's return the Pirates closed down Forbes Field, moved into Three Rivers Stadium, and won the new National League East division before losing in the National League Championship Series to Cincinnati. Murtaugh was named Manager of the Year.[22]

Murtaugh and his star outfielder Roberto Clemente sought to assure all who asked that everything was fine with their relationship, which admittedly had had rough patches during Murtaugh's first tenure with the team. Murtaugh said, "Clemente is Clemente. He's the best player I've ever seen. I'm old enough and I think smart enough to get along with anybody on our ballclub—especially if he's a .350 hitter."[23]

On May 20, 1971, Murtaugh was admitted to Christ Hospital in Cincinnati with chest pains. After tests, doctors could find nothing wrong with him. He spent two weeks in hospitals in Cincinnati and Pittsburgh and was unsure if he would ever return to uniform. He finally did return to the dugout on June 6, ten pounds lighter.[24]

With and without Murtaugh, the 1971 Pirates ran roughshod over the National League, winning the East by seven games over St. Louis before dispatching the Giants in four games in the NLCS. They went on to beat Baltimore in seven games for their second world championship in 12 seasons, both under Murtaugh's direction. In a memorable game on September 1, a 10-7 victory over the Phillies, Murtaugh made history by writing out a lineup of Rennie Stennett, Gene Clines, Roberto Clemente, Willie Stargell, Manny Sanguillen, Dave Cash, Al Oliver, Jackie Hernandez, and Dock Ellis. For the first time in major-league history a team had a starting lineup of minority players. With the Pirates in the midst of a pennant race, the notion of a gimmick was easily brushed aside. Asked afterward if he realized the significance of the lineup, Murtaugh replied, "I knew we had nine Pirates."[25]

After finishing the 1971 season with his second World Series title, Murtaugh again moved into the front office, once again citing concerns over his health. (He did return to the field to manage the National League in the 1972 All-Star Game.)

Late in the 1973 season Joe Brown asked Murtaugh to take over as manager for a fourth time. After receiving the requisite doctoral and spousal permission, he returned to the dugout for the final 26 games of the 1973 season before winning back-to-back division titles in '74 and '75 and losing in the NLCS both years. Despite rumors that he would quit, Murtaugh returned for the 1976 season and led the Pirates to a second-place finish before announcing at season's end that he was stepping down—this time for good—because of his health and his desire to spend more time with his family, which now included grandchildren.

On November 30, 1976, Murtaugh went to a doctor's appointment and was told that everything looked good. But later that day he suffered a stroke at home. He died at Crozer Chester Hospital on December 2 at the age of 59. He was survived by his wife, Kate; his sons, Tim and Danny Jr.; his daughter, Kathy; and five grandchildren. His funeral drew many of his players, including Willie Stargell, Manny Sanguillen, and Al Oliver, as well as longtime GM Joe Brown and radio voice Bob Prince, former major leaguer Mickey Vernon, and Pittsburgh Steelers owner Art Rooney.[26]

Murtaugh's number 40 was retired by the Pirates in 1977. As of 2012 his 1,115 victories as a manager ranked him second on the team behind Fred Clarke.

Perhaps the most definitive words on why anyone would want to keep coming back to manage a ball club belong to Murtaugh himself, who said, "Managing a ballclub is like getting malaria. Once you're bitten by the bug, it's difficult to get it out of your bloodstream."[27]

Sources

Other than sources cited in the notes, the author also consulted:

Baseball Digest

Baseball-Reference.com

New York Times

The Sporting News

Sports Illustrated

Notes

1   *Sports Illustrated*, October 7, 1974.

2   Colleen Hroncich, *The Whistling Irishman: Danny Murtaugh Remembered* (Philadelphia: Sports Challenge Network Publishing, 2010), 1.

3   Hroncich, 2.

4   Hroncich, 5.

5   Hroncich, 6.

6   Hroncich, 7.

7   Hroncich, 19.

8   Hroncich, 22.

9   Hroncich, 41.

10   Hroncich, 43.

11   Hroncich, 62.

12   Hroncich, 82-83.

13   Harold Rosenthal, *Baseball's Best Managers* (New York: Thomas Nelson and Sons, 1961), 103.

14   Rosenthal, 104.

15   Hroncich, 98.

16   Rosenthal, 107.

17   Rick Cushing, *1960 Pittsburgh Pirates, Day by Day*. (Pittsburgh: Dorrance Publishing, 2010), 377.

18   Kal Wagenheim, *Clemente!* (Republished by E-Reads.com, original copyright 1973), 4.

19   Hroncich, 135.

20   Hroncich, 160-2.

21   Hroncich, 163.

22   Hroncich, 164-7.

23   Wagenheim, page number unavailable.

24   Hroncich, 176.

25   *Baseball Digest*, September 1995.

26   Hroncich, 233-4.

27   Cushing, 377.

Bill Burwell
By Gregory Wolf

AFTER HIS THIRD year in organized baseball, 22-year-old right-handed pitcher Bill Burwell was drafted into the United States Army in 1917 and was assigned to the recently formed 89th Infantry Division, the "Rolling W," and later deployed to Europe. During one of the last major offensives of the war, the Battle of Saint-Mihiel in northeastern France in September 1918, Burwell's unit was charged with attacking German machine-gun nests stationed along trenches. Volunteering for a dangerous assignment, Burwell was wounded when his pitching hand was struck by shrapnel. The second finger on his right hand was completely shattered and he lost the tip of the finger, all of which caused his fingers to have a slight curl.[1] "I thought the war was the end of me as a pitcher," Burwell later said.[2] After the war, he returned to the US and rejoined the Joplin (Missouri) Miners in the Class A Western League for the 1919 season. "When I started pitching again," Burwell said, "I discovered that I could throw a sinker." Burwell went on to have a 48-year career in Organized Baseball, pitched for the St. Louis Browns and Pittsburgh Pirates, won 239 games in the minor leagues, and was a longtime respected manager, coach, and scout.[3]

William Edwin Burwell was born on March 27, 1895, in the small town of Jarbalo, about 40 miles northwest of Kansas City in Leavenworth County, Kansas. His father, Joseph, originally from Virginia, and his mother, Ella, from Ohio, met in Kansas, married in 1885, and had three children, Frank, Ruth, and Bill, the youngest.[4] His family moved to Stranger township, also in Leavenworth County, and farmed wheat and grain. At the age of 17 in 1912, Burwell matriculated at the Kansas State Agriculture College (later known as Kansas State University), where he was introduced to baseball and

began to play sandlot and weekend ball. He quit college and in 1915 joined the Elgin (Illinois) Watch Makers in the inaugural season of the Class D Bi-State League. He pitched in 16 games until the league folded in early July, after which he returned to Kansas and played semipro baseball. The following spring he traveled to Topeka, about 40 miles from his hometown, and tried out for and made the Topeka Savages of the Class A Western League; and for the remainder of his life, save for his service during World War I, he was involved in baseball.

While with the Joplin Miners in 1919 (a 12-12 record in 224 innings pitched), Burwell drew the attention of the St. Louis Browns, whose scout Pat Monahan secured his purchase from the Miners and then signed him to a major-league contract for the 1920 season.[5] After an impressive spring training at the Browns' site in Taylor, Alabama, Burwell made the team as a relief pitcher. At 5-feet-11 and 175 pounds, Burwell was not an overpowering pitcher, but he had an excellent sinker and a deceptive curveball.[6] His pitching motion distinguished him from other pitchers of the era; he had a side-arm to submarine delivery that was sometimes compared to that of Carl Mays.[7] In his major-league debut, on May 1, he pitched a scoreless ninth inning at home against the Chicago White Sox and pitched primarily in relief all season, finishing 18 of the 33 games he pitched. In relief of 20-game winner Urban Shocker on May 12, Burwell pitched five scoreless innings for his first career win. He finished the season leading the league in relief appearances, with a 6-4 record and a respectable 3.65 ERA in 113 innings for the fourth-place Browns.

In 1921 Burwell continued his role as a relief pitcher and led the American League with 21

games finished. However, his pitches lacked the speed and movement to make him an effective major-league pitcher. He finished with a 2-4 record and his ERA ballooned to 5.12 in 84 innings. His career highlight may have been his first and only complete-game victory, on July 2, 1921, against the White Sox in one of the five games he started in his tenure with the Browns.[8] At the conclusion of the 1921 season, the Browns traded Burwell to the Columbus (Ohio) Senators of the American Association for pitcher Dave Danforth.[9] His move to the American Association, originally founded in 1902 as an independent league with teams located in the Midwest, proved to be a fortuitous one.

Over the course of the next ten years (1922-1931), Burwell established his reputation as "one of the greatest pitchers the American Association has seen,"[10] won 170 games, regularly ranked among the league's top ten in wins, innings pitched, and ERA, and in 1945 was named by sportswriters to the all-time American Association All-Star team.[11] After one season with Columbus, he was acquired by Indianapolis in 1923 in a trade for pitcher Harry Weaver and infielder Douglas Baird,[12] and Burwell responded with an 18-21 record in a league-leading and career-high 342 innings pitched for the seventh-place Indians. The following season, Indianapolis hired as manager former Detroit Tigers shortstop Donie Bush, who had managed the Washington Senators the season before. Bush and Burwell's career paths stayed connected for the next two decades while Bush played a major role in Burwell's development as a pitcher and also influenced his decision to enter coaching.

While Bush led the Indians to three consecutive second-place finishes from 1924 through 1926, rumors swirled annually about which major-league team would sign Burwell, who won 17, a league-leading 24, and 21 games respectively while pitching in the Indians' West Washington Street Park, considered the largest in the American Association. Despite his nicknames, Bad Bill or Wild Bill, Burwell was neither bad nor wild. He issued few walks and was considered one of the best-fielding pitchers in the league.[13] In the summer of 1925 the New York Giants pursued Burwell, but manager John McGraw ultimately purchased the contract of Burwell's younger teammate, Freddie Fitzsimmons, who finished with 217 wins in a 19-year major-league career.[14] At the conclu-

sion of the 1925 season, the Cincinnati Reds and manager Jack Hendricks, who had piloted the Columbus Senators and Burwell in 1923, attempted to purchase his contract from Indianapolis, but when the asking price soared over $30,000, negotiations ended.[15] Praising his pitching but also casting doubt on Burwell's future as a major leaguer, manager Bush, Burwell's staunchest supporter, commented, "Burwell is smart, has courage, and mixes them up. His fastball may not be good enough for the majors, but he's been a big winner in the American Association."[16] Finally, in 1928, Burwell made it back to the majors, albeit for a brief time, when the Pittsburgh Pirates, managed since 1927 by none other than Donie Bush, traded pitcher Erv Brame and outfielder Adam Comorosky to Indianapolis for Burwell. With his unorthodox delivery and mangled pitching hand, Burwell was often suspected of throwing a spitter, officially banned in the major leagues since 1920. Burwell lasted just one month and four appearances for the Pirates and was returned to Indianapolis for Erv Brame in early July. At 33, Burwell's chance had passed. He finished his major-league career with a 9-8 record in 70 games and a 4.37 ERA in 218 1/3 innings pitched.

Burwell returned to Indianapolis and helped lead the Indians to their first division title and to their first Junior World Series championship since 1917 by beating the Rochester Red Wings of the International League five games to one. Burwell pitched a complete-game victory in the series-clinching game, giving up 10 hits; he also scored a run in the 4-3 victory.[17] Noted for his durability and health, Burwell remained a regular starter for the Indians through the 1931 season, when he won 17 games and was named to the league All-Star team. After compiling 2,700 innings pitched in the previous ten years in the American Association and at the age of 37, Burwell began to slow down, though he still pitched more than 100 innings per year for the Indians over the next three seasons. With his wealth of knowledge and experience, Burwell served as a mentor and unofficial pitching coach for the young pitchers on the Indians' staff. "Bill Burwell ... gave me many pointers. I'll never forget how he worked with me. My personal opinion is that Burwell is one of the smartest pitchers in the game," said former teammate Oral Hildebrand coming off his All-Star season with the Cleveland Indians in 1933.[18]

Burwell's managerial career began in 1934 when he took the reins as player-manager of Indianapolis's newly formed farm club, the Fort Wayne Chiefs of the Class B Central League.[19] The financial situation of many teams in the lower minor leagues during the height of the Depression was unstable, sometimes leading to sudden and drastic movement for players and coaches. When the Central League folded after just one month, Burwell returned to the parent club as a pitcher and won eight games. In 1935 he was released from his contract to pitch and manage the independent Terre Haute Tots in the Class B Three-I League. He led the team to a 57-61 record and tutored the 20-year-old whiz Dizzy Trout, but the team was not fielded for the following season. Burwell joined his old friend Donie Bush in 1936 and served as his pitching coach for the Minneapolis Millers of the American Association, who had just begun their affiliation with the Boston Red Sox. The following season, 1937, must have tested Burwell's commitment to managing and baseball. He signed a contract to become the manager of another new team, the St. Joseph (Missouri) Saints of the Class A Western League, but the team folded before the start of the season.[20] Burwell then took over the Rock Island (Illinois) Islanders of the same league, and then they disbanded in midseason; at that point he returned to Minneapolis to serve as Bush's pitching coach again. At 42, Burwell also pitched, primarily in relief, and won four games.

Burwell led the Class D Crookston Pirates, an affiliate of the Minneapolis Millers, to the Northern League finals in 1938, and, at the age of 43, had a 1-3 pitching record. That was his last year pitching in Organized Baseball; he finished with a 239-206 minor-league record and 3,873 innings pitched in 601 games. In 1939 he reunited yet again with Donie Bush, who had been named manager of the Louisville Colonels, the Boston Red Sox' new affiliate in the American Association. And when Bush was forced to relinquish his position because of illness in May, Burwell was named manager,[21] guided the Colonels to the league championship, and then to the Junior World Series title when they defeated the Rochester Red Wings of the International League, four games to three. Burwell's reputation soared and he entertained coaching offers from major-league teams.[22] Even though Bush maintained that he would resume his managerial duties in 1940, Burwell decided to remain with the Colonels and signed a contract paying him $6,000 per year which made him one of the highest paid coaches in Organized Baseball.[23] Ultimately Bush stepped down and Burwell managed the Colonels for four more seasons, leading them to the Junior World Series again in 1940 and to the American Association finals in 1941.

Burwell was a patient manager who had the ability to coax maximum effort from his players. Big Jim Weaver, a former major-league pitcher who toiled for the Colonels as a 36-year old on what most thought was just an average Colonels team in 1940, remarked of Burwell, "He's not just the best manger, he's a Houdini without mirrors."[24] Players respected him for his honest approach and his fatherly concern for their welfare as players. "He'd talk about personal habits, our drinking, and things like that," said Johnny Pesky, who played for the Colonels and was the American Association MVP in 1941. "He told players they were only hurting themselves by not staying in their best physical shape."[25] Burwell was a quiet and selfless manager who genuinely wanted his players to succeed and gave them credit when they did. "Any success I've had the players gave to me," he said after the Colonels' surprising 1940 season."[26]

Burwell got his first taste of coaching in the big leagues when the Red Sox named him third-base coach in 1944, replacing Tom Daly. The Red Sox brass recognized Burwell's effect on player development, especially pitchers. "Burwell is a wonder at developing youngsters," said Herb Pennock, the former Yankees great who was the director of the Red Sox farm system at the time.[27] There was some speculation that if manager Joe Cronin, who at 38 was still draft-eligible for World War II, was drafted, then Burwell might succeed him.[28] Cronin was not drafted and Burwell resigned at the end of the season, ending his working relationship with the Red Sox.

Donie Bush and Indianapolis banker Frank McKinney had purchased the Indianapolis Indians before the 1945 season. Bush invited his longtime pitcher, coach, and confidante to skipper the team. Burwell accepted and responded by leading them to consecutive second-place finishes in 1945 and 1946. This led to speculation that he'd be offered the job of managing the Pittsburgh Pirates under their new ownership group led by Frank McKinney.[29] However, Billy Herman, the former All-Star second baseman and Burwell's good friend, was offered the job and he invited Burwell to join his staff, which he did for the 1947 season.[30]

From 1947 until he officially retired in 1962, Burwell served in the Pirates organization as major-league coach, minor-league manager, roving pitching instructor, and even for one game as their manager. When Herman resigned as manager before the last game of the 1947 season, Burwell was named interim manager, and won his one and only game, 7-0, over the Cincinnati Reds. Rumors swirled that Burwell would be named the new manager in the offseason;[31] however, the Pirates chose well-respected Billy Meyer, who had coached in the New York Yankees farm system since 1932, and Burwell was retained as a coach for the 1948 season. He was reassigned at the end of the season when ownership made wholesale changes to the entire Pirates system, including reducing the number of farm reams from 19 to 13.[32] He was named manager of the Davenport (Iowa) Pirates in the Class B Three-I League, where he developed two 19-year-old future All-Star pitchers, Vern Law and Bob Purkey. Law said Burwell "taught me how to utilize my legs and my body more so than my arm. He helped me hold runners on by developing a quick throw to first."[33] After beginning 1950 as a roving instructor, Burwell replaced Hugh Luby in midseason as manager of the New Orleans Pelicans in the Double-A Southern Association, where he continued tutoring Law and Purkey as well as future Pirates All-Star outfielder Frank Thomas.

Upon being named general manager of the Pirates after the 1950 campaign, Branch Rickey turned his attention to the Bucs' minor-league system and stressed player development. He promoted Burwell to "player overseer" of the entire farm system, which allowed Burwell to work with all of the Pirates minor-league teams and to scout the nation for talent.[34] With his reputation as a master teacher, Burwell participated in Pirates rookie camps, including the first fall rookie camp in major-league history, in 1951, as well as spring training.[35] At the age of 60 in 1955, Burwell was named manager of the Lincoln Chiefs in the Class A Western League, the last time he piloted a team. When Rickey resigned after the 1955 season, Burwell resumed his role as player overseer, scout, and managerial consultant under new general manager Joe L. Brown.

Burwell rejoined the parent club to start the 1958 season when Danny Murtaugh, in his first full season as manager of the Pirates, assembled his new coaching staff and named Burwell pitching coach, a position he held until his retirement in 1962. During Burwell's tenure with the Pirates, the pitching staff coalesced and served as one of the Pirates' strengths. In his first year as pitching coach, the Pirates enjoyed their best season since 1944 and Burwell's effect on the pitching staff deserved credit. Vern Law won 14, his career high to that point, and credited Burwell for his success via a change in pitching mechanics. Bob Friend won a career-high 22 games, which led the National League. Ronnie Kline responded with 13 wins, and the team ranked second in the National League in ERA at 3.56. "Bill picks out mistakes in a hurry, but he doesn't make a fuss about them—out loud," said Murtaugh. "One of his real assets is his patience with young pitchers. He doesn't try to make any radical change in their style . . . but you'll note that a kid breaking in who doesn't have a change-up starts working on one."[36]

In 1960 Burwell experienced the pinnacle of team success when the Pirates won the World Series. Despite giving up 55 runs to the Yankees in seven games, the pitching staff had pitched solidly all year. "Bill has done a tremendous job with the pitching staff, especially with the youngster boys," wrote *Pittsburgh Post-Gazette* sports editor Al Abrams.[37] Law won the Cy Young Award, Friend won 18 games, and the staff finished third in the league in ERA, only .09 of a run behind the league-leading Los Angeles Dodgers. Burwell's importance to the team couldn't be reduced to just his role as a pitching coach. Throughout his career as a manager and coach, batters as well as pitchers praised him for instilling confidence in their game. Roberto Clemente singled out Burwell and hitting instructor George Sisler as the reason for his success in 1960 and especially in 1961, when he won his first National League batting title, "They helped me all season by giving me encouragement. They kept telling me I could hit for high average."[38]

At the age of 67, the quiet, studious, and mild-mannered Burwell retired after the 1962 season during which the Pirates staff had led the National League in ERA. He settled with his wife, Virginia, with whom he had no children, in the Daytona, Florida, area where they had lived in the offseason for three decades. One year after

Virginia died in 1964, Burwell married Kappy Dudley, the widow of former Louisville Colonels president and general manager Bruce Dudley, with whom Burwell had stayed in touch since the early 1940s.

During his official retirement from baseball, Burwell continued to work closely with the Pirates staff and their pitching prospects in the minor leagues and also served as a scout. His passion for pitching never waned after retirement. He helped develop Bob Veale into an All-Star and spent the early part of the 1967, 1968, and 1969 seasons with the Gastonia Pirates of the Class A Western Carolinas League, where he assisted manager Don Leppert and then Frank Oceak with pitcher development.[39]

Not just a baseball player, manager, and coach, Burwell was a Renaissance man. He had an excellent tenor voice, enjoyed singing, and composed his own music. On June 11, 1973, Bill Burwell died of a heart attack at the age of 78. He was buried next to Virginia at the Daytona Memorial Park in Daytona Beach, Florida.

Sources

Statistics are from Baseball-Reference.com and Retrosheet.org.

David Cicotello and Angelo J. Louisa, eds., *Forbes Field. Essays and Memories of the Pirates Historic Ballpark, 1909-1971* (Jefferson, North Carolina: McFarland, 2007).

Rick Cushing. *1960 Pittsburgh Pirates Day by Day: A Special Season, An Extraordinary World Series.* (Pittsburgh: Dorrance Publishing Co., Inc., 2010).

David Finoli and Bill Ranier, eds., *The Pittsburgh Pirates Encyclopedia* (Champaign, Illinois: Sports Publishing, 2003).

Dick Groat. *The World Champion Pittsburgh Pirates.* (New York: Coward-McCann, 1961).

David Maraniss. *Clemente: The Pride and Passion of Baseball's Last Hero.* (New York: Simon & Schuster, 2006).

Richard Peterson, ed., *The Pirates Reader* (Pittsburgh: University of Pittsburgh Press, 2003).

Jim Reisler. *The Best Game Ever: Pirates vs. Yankees October 13, 1960.* (Philadelphia: Da Capo Press, 2007).

Notes

1 George L. Brickson, "Bullet Gives Burwell Power to Pitch Curve." *Ogden* (Utah) *Standard Examiner.* May 9, 1920, 27.

2 *The Sporting News,* June 30, 1973, 28.

3 All season and career records have been verified with Baseball Reference.com. See www.baseballreference.com.

4 www.Ancestry.com.

5 *The Sporting News,* January 30, 1952, 8.

6 *New Castle* (Pennsylvania) *News,* May 6, 1920, 12.

7 Ibid.

8 Single game box scores have been verified with Retrosheet. See www.retrosheet.com.

9 *The Sporting News,* January 5, 1939, 5.

10 *The Sporting News,* August 23, 1923, 03.

11 *The Sporting News,* April 21, 1945, 22.

12 *Pittsburgh Press,* June 5, 1928, 39.

13 "Bad Burwell is Slipping." *Milwaukee Journal,* December 9, 1930, 13.

14 *The Sporting News,* November 17, 1948, 10.

15 *The Sporting News,* December 24, 1925, 2, and December 31, 1925.

16 *Jeanette* (Pennsylvania) *News Dispatch,* June 26, 1926, 4.

17 *Charleston* (West Virginia) *Gazette,* October 7, 1928, 24.

18 *The Sporting News,* January 11, 1934, 3.

19 *The Sporting News,* April 5, 1934, 1.

20 *The Sporting News,* February 25, 1937, 3, and April 1, 1937, 5.

21 *The Sporting News,* July 6, 1939, 5.

22 *The Sporting News,* December 14, 1939, 2.

23 Ibid.

24 *The Sporting News,* October 17, 1940, 7.

25 *The Sporting News,* November 24, 1962, 3.

26 *The Sporting News,* October 17, 1960, 7.

27 *Milwaukee Journal,* July 13, 1943, 9.

28 *The Sporting News,* March 9, 1944, 4 and 6.

29 Chester L. Smith, "And Kennedy Due to Stay." *Pittsburgh Press,* August 5, 1946, 16.

30 *The Sporting News,* November 27, 1946, 16.

31 *The Sporting News,* September 24, 1947, 35.

32 "Bill Burwell out as Pirate Coach." *Pittsburgh Press,* October 2, 1948, 45.

33 Vern Law. "Vern Law Picks up Pointers Viewing other Top Hurlers." *Uniontown* (Pennsylvania) *Morning Herald,* July 6, 1962, 12. He may also have managed Davenport for at least a while in 1948, too.

34 Jack Hernon. "Bill Burwell Named Aid to Branch Rickey." *Pittsburgh Post-Gazette,* January 13, 1951, 10.

35 *The Sporting News*, October 31, 1951, 15.

36 Rick Cushing. *1960 Pittsburgh Pirates Day by Day: A Special Season, An Extraordinary World Series* (Pittsburgh: Dorrance Publishing, Co., Inc., 2010).

37 Bernhard Kahn, "Scholarly Bill Burwell Spurs Pirates Pitchers." *Daytona Beach Morning Journal*, August 30, 1958, 26.

38 David Maraniss, *Clemente. The Passion and Grace of Baseball's Last Hero* (New York: Simon & Schuster, 2006), 161.

39 *Gastonia* (North Carolina) *Gazette*, July 30, 1968, 6.

Lenny Levy

By Jack V. Morris

LENNY LEVY'S CAREER defies conventional logic. A washout in one year of minor-league D-level baseball (years later, *Baseball Digest* called him "hardly more than a semipro player"), he fashioned a professional career with the Pittsburgh Pirates that began in 1934 and ended in 1964 with only a break for World War II. He was a player, coach, and scout for the organization through the years. When Bill Mazeroski hit his historic Series-winning home run against the New York Yankees in 1960, the first person to shake his hand was Levy, who was the first-base coach that day.[1]

Indeed, Levy's connection with the Pirates went back even further if you take into account his time as a Pirates batboy and a ticket taker at Forbes Field. He may be the only connection bridging the 33-year gap between Pirates' World Series appearances in 1927 and 1960.

Leonard Howard Levy was born on June 11, 1913, in Pittsburgh, the third of five children born to Louis and Celia Levy. Louis was a produce wholesaler. Since the Levy family lived not far from the Pirates' Forbes Field, Lenny was often found at the park. He eventually was enlisted as a batboy for the Pirates. When he was old enough, he was given the job of being a ticket taker at Forbes. He held that job for six seasons. In the meantime, he developed into a fine athlete at Taylor-Allderdice High School. He starred not only in baseball but in basketball and football as well. In his senior season, he scored 274 points in basketball, an impressive total in the days of low-scoring basketball games. In 1932, he graduated from Taylor-Allderdice, where one of his classmates was character actor Edward Andrews.[2]

In 1935 Levy was still working as a ticket taker for the Pirates and was often invited to practice with the team. He was also playing semipro baseball in the Pittsburgh City League, where the year before he had hit .327 as a catcher. Pie Traynor, the Pirates' player-manager, liked what he saw and signed Levy to a contract. He went to spring training but rather than assign him to a minor-league team, Traynor kept him on the bench as a nonroster player. Levy was considered the Pirates' third-string catcher. He caught batting practice and generally helped Traynor in whatever duties needed to be done.[3]

In April 1936 the Pirates sent Levy to the spring-training camp of the Savannah Indians of the Class B South Atlantic League. Levy, a 5-foot-10½, 190-pounder who threw and batted right-handed, made the squad as a backup catcher. By June 5 he had played in 12 games but it was the last one that was the most fateful. In a game against the Columbus (Georgia) Red Birds, Levy was penciled into the lineup as the starting catcher. As the game wore on, some Savannah players became increasingly incensed at the umpires. Finally, Levy, teammate George Lunak, and manager Bobby LaMotte were thrown out of the game. This precipitated what was later described as a "near riot" after the game as Savannah fans spilled onto the field. Umpire Bob Burnett was knocked unconscious with a thrown soda bottle. The blow cracked his skull. His umpiring mate, W.C. "Mutt" Hammond, was also assaulted when a group of fans pinned him up against a fence, punching and kicking him.[4]

The president of the South Atlantic League, Eugene M. Wilder, fined Levy $10 for his role in the incident. He also suspended teammate Jack Colbern indefinitely and fined him $20 for "inciting the fans." Those were the only penalties given out. About a month later, National Association president W.G. Bramham upped the fine to Levy to $25. Two fans were sentenced in court to pay $100 fines or serve 30 days in jail.[5]

Shortly after the incident, with Levy batting only .115, he left Savannah and came back to Pittsburgh. Pirates backup catcher Al Todd had broken a finger so Levy was used to warm up pitchers as a nonroster player. In late July, when another Pirates farm team, the Portsmouth (Ohio) Pirates of the Class C Middle Atlantic League, needed a catcher, he was sent there to help out. He told the *Portsmouth Times* that Pirates owner William E. Benswanger had personally sent him to Portsmouth. He had a marginally better success in Portsmouth than in Savannah, playing in 20 games and batting .175.[6]

In 1937 Levy was invited to try out for the St. Joseph Saints of the Western League. But St. Joseph dropped out of the league before the season and transferred Levy to Rock Island, which had taken St. Joseph's place in the league. However, Levy didn't make the Rock Island team and again spent the season with the Pirates as a nonroster player.[7]

In 1938 Levy gave it one last try. The Jackson (Mississippi) Senators of the Class B Southeastern League signed him, but again he failed to make the squad. Again the Pirates gave Levy a uniform, and, though he wasn't under contract, he traveled with the team as a third-string catcher. On July 2 St. Louis Cardinals manager Frankie Frisch protested a game against the Pirates, contending that there were too many players in uniform on the Pirates bench. Not only was Levy on the bench but so were youngsters Johnny Mize and Andy Lipscomb, a West Point graduate who was a batting-practice pitcher. None was under contract to the Pirates. Mize, not to be confused with the Hall of Famer with the same name, later played a few seasons in the minors. Lipscomb, who was on a leave of absence from the US Army to be with the Pirates, was ordered back to the Army in September. He never played in Organized Baseball.[8]

From 1938 to 1942, Levy was loosely considered a coach for the Pirates. He traveled with the team and worked in the bullpen, warming up pitchers. He started as a coach under Traynor and then continued when Frankie Frisch took over the Pirates' helm in 1940. In 1942, he joined the Marines and was stationed in China for most of World War II.[9]

Levy rejoined the Pirates as a bullpen coach under manager Billy Herman in 1947. He would remain with the Pirates in one capacity or another for the next 17 years. Sportswriter Jonathan Mayo credited him with signing slugger Frank Thomas in 1947.[10]

In 1951 Levy transitioned to scout, assisting George Sisler with the operation of tryout camps in the Pittsburgh area. Sam Narron took his place as bullpen coach with the Pirates. It was also that year that the film *Angels in the Outfield* was shot at Forbes Field. Levy had a cameo in the film as an "arguing coach."[11]

Between seasons in the 1950s, Levy acted as a booking agent and player for a Pirates basketball team that toured the Pittsburgh area. By 1953 the team, which was now called the Major League All-Stars, was composed of not just Pirates but other Pittsburgh-area major leaguers.[12]

In 1954, Levy opened a Plymouth-DeSoto automobile dealership called Forbes Field Auto Sales located on Forbes Avenue very close to the ballpark. He operated the dealership until the 1980s. Many of the Pirates bought their cars from Levy through the years.[13]

On September 3, 1955, Levy married Estyre Rosenberg. For the 1957 season, the Pirates moved Levy back to coaching under Bobby Bragan. When Bragan was fired toward the end of the season, all the coaches, including Levy, were retained under interim manager Danny Murtaugh. Murtaugh was named the permanent manager for 1958 and increased Levy's duties by naming him the first-base coach.[14]

By the end of the 1958 season, the weight of owning the car dealership and being a full-time coach wore Levy down. On October 25 he resigned as a coach. The Pirates hired Jimmy Dykes to replace him, but four months later, the Pirates talked Levy into becoming a part-time coach. He didn't travel with the team and worked only home games. In May 1959 Dykes left the Pirates to manage the Detroit Tigers and Levy was moved back to first-base coach during home games. Frank Eck, an Associated Press sportswriter, wrote that Levy was "one of the most unusual coaches. He never makes road trips. His duties run from such chores as finding Manager Murtagh a fresh cut of plug to retrieving baseballs for the batting-practice pitcher."[15]

In reality, Levy was much more than that. He had a sharp eye for detail. Frank Thomas, who from 1953 through 1958 appeared in three All-Star games and was four times in the top 20 in voting for the National League Most Valuable Player award, credited Levy for much of his success. "Levy was a keen student of my form the last couple of years," said Thomas after he was traded to the Cincinnati Reds in 1959. "He could spot the little flaws that cropped up in a hurry." Levy, in fact, called himself a "handyman coach" and was quoted as saying that he was "mostly a batting-practice adviser."[16]

As a first-base coach, just as in his playing days, Levy was never averse to mixing it up with other teams whenever a dust-up started. On May 25, 1958, he was in the middle of a melee with the Giants. It was mild in comparison to a game on May 3, 1959, when he and St. Louis Cardinals pitcher Larry Jackson got into a "shoving match." Levy was credited with bloodying Cards manager Solly Hemus's chin in the resulting brawl.[17]

Levy coached first base through the 1960 season into the World Series. Thus he was in position to be the first to greet Mazeroski after his home run ended the 1960 World Series. He continued as first-base coach until after the 1964 season. At the end of that season, Murtaugh resigned for health reasons. In a clean sweep after finishing a disappointing seventh in the ten-team National League, the Pirates released all their coaches. The move effectively retired Levy from baseball.[18]

Levy continued to work at his dealership until he retired from the business in the 1980s. During his retirement, he was inducted into the Western Pennsylvania Jewish Sports Hall of Fame. Eventually, he and Estyre moved to California. On December 27, 1988, Estyre died in Riverside, California. In 1990 Levy was living in Rancho Mirage, California. On February 2, 1993, he died in nearby Palm Desert at the age of 79 of the effects of a stroke and heart problems. He was cremated. He left no survivors.[19]

Notes

1 Ritter Collet, "Never Aim At Fences" *Baseball Digest*, June 1959, 79-80.

2 Peter S. Horvitz and Joachim Horvitz, *The Big Book of Jewish Baseball: An Illustrated Encyclopedia and Anecdotal History* (New York: S.P.I, books, 2001), 106; *Christian Science Monitor*, June 27, 1935; *Pittsburgh Press*, September 16, 1972.

3 *Christian Science Monitor*, June 27, 1935; *Pittsburgh Post-Gazette*, February 5, 1993; *The Sporting News*, March 21, 1964; *Washington (Pennsylvania) Reporter*, November 12, 1958.

4 *Augusta (Georgia) Chronicle*, April 10 and June 10, 1936; *The Sporting News*, June 11, 1936.

5 *Augusta Chronicle*, April 10, June 10 and July 1, 1936; *The Sporting News*, June 11, 1936.

6 *Pittsburgh Post-Gazette*, April 3, 1936; *Portsmouth Times*, July 26 and 28, 1936.

7 *Augusta Chronicle*, March 12, 1937; *Pittsburgh Press*, March 20, 1937.

8 Peter S. Horvitz and Joachim Horvitz, op. cit., 106; *Pittsburgh Press*, July 3 and September 10, 1938.

9 *Pittsburgh Post-Gazette*, February 5, 1993; Jonathan Mayo, "Lenny Levy Left His Mark On the Pirates Without Ever Playing An Inning", *The Jewish Chronicle*, http://www.thejewishchronicle.net/view/full_story/3274984/article-Lenny-Levy-left-his-mark-on-the-Pirates-without-ever-playing-an-inning-?instance=column_5_page_right_column; 1964 Pittsburgh Pirates Media Guide, 5.

10 *Pittsburgh Post-Gazette*, May 20, 1948, February 5, 1993; Jonathan Mayo, op. cit. . Mayo also credits Levy with signing Dick Groat in 1952 and Bill Mazeroski in 1954.

11 *The Sporting News*, February 28, 1951; *New Castle (Pennsylvania) News*, February 20, 1951; *Pittsburgh Post-Gazette*, September 8, 1951.

12 *Charleroi (Pennsylvania) Mail*, December 12, 1952; *The Sporting News*, November 11, 1953; *Pittsburgh Post-Gazette*, December 12, 1952.

13 *The Sporting News*, February 10, 1954; Jonathan Mayo, op. cit.

14 1964 Pittsburgh Pirates Media Guide, 5; *The Sporting News*, January 9, 1957; *Syracuse Post-Standard*, August 4, 1957; *Morgantown (West Virginia) Post*, February 11, 1959.

15 *San Diego Union*, October 26, 1958; *Trenton (New Jersey) Times*, November 11, 1958; *Morgantown (West Virginia) Post*, February 11, 1959; *Joplin (Missouri) Globe*, December 16, 1960.

16 Ritter Collett, "Never Aim At Fences," *Baseball Digest*, June 1959, 79-80; Rick Cushing, *1960 Pittsburgh Pirates: Day by Day: A Special Season, an Extraordinary World Series* (Pittsburgh: Dorrance Publishing, 2010), 69.

17 *The Daily Herald*, Provo, Utah, May 26, 1958; *The Sporting News*, May 13, 1959; Vic Debs, *Missed It By That Much: Baseball Players Who Challenged the Record Book,* (Jefferson, North Carolina: McFarland & Company, 1998), 117.

18 *New Orleans Times-Picayune*, November 17, 1964.

19 Jonathan Mayo, op. cit.; "The 1960 World Champion Pirates—Today," *Baseball Digest*, October 1990, 30; *Pittsburgh Post-Gazette*, February 5, 1993; Lenny Levy Find-A-Grave website entry, http://www.findagrave.com/cgi-bin/fg.cgi?page=gr&GRid=55082721.

Sam Narron

By Skip Nipper

WHEN SUSIE FINNEY Narron, wife of Sam Narron, would say, "God picked Sam up and set him in baseball," Sam would respond, "I would have played for nothing."[1]

It did not hurt that Sam became a protégé of Branch Rickey, a "Rickey man."[2] Narron was signed by the St. Louis Cardinals during Rickey's tenure and spent parts of three seasons (1935, 1942, 1943) as a backup catcher on the team. After his playing career ended he became a coach, following Rickey to Brooklyn and then Pittsburgh, and was the Pirates' bullpen coach from 1951 to 1964.

The youngest of five children, Narron was born on August 25, 1913, in Middlesex, North Carolina, to Troy and Rachel Narron. His father was 50 when he married Rachel, and she was 25. When Sam was born, his father was 65 and his closest sibling was 7 years old. The children were expected to work on their 75-acre family farm alongside their parents. It was there that Sam learned what hard work meant, and how much family members depended on one another for support.

Sam never graduated from high school, but he would join baseball teams and play anywhere he could. "Every crossroads had a team," he told his son Samuel, who came to be known as "Rooster" and who insisted in an interview that his father's given name was Young Sammie Woody Narron although birth records do not show it.[3]

Working in the mills in Rocky Mount and playing semipro baseball, Narron wanted to play professional baseball so badly that in 1934, at 20, he hitchhiked to Greensboro, North Carolina, to attend a baseball tryout. He was noticed by St. Louis Cardinals scouts who encouraged him to attend the

Ray L. Doan All Star Baseball School in Hot Springs, Arkansas, but was told, "Be sure and bring your own uniform and equipment." The school was financed by Rogers Hornsby and the WPA (Works Progress Administration, one of President Franklin D. Roosevelt's New Deal initiatives), and instructors included Hornsby and Dizzy Dean.

A few years later, advertisements for the school listed Sam under the heading "A Few Players Who Made Good."[4]

After tryouts each day, Narron would check the big board near the locker room to see if his number was listed, which meant that a pro team was interested in signing him to a contract. After he hit a home run one day, the Cardinals signed him.[5] At first Narron was considered as a candidate for the Cardinals' team at Greensboro of the Class B Piedmont League,[6] but he was sent to Martinsville of the Class D Bi-State League (Virginia and North Carolina) as a third baseman. Playing in 78 games, Narron hit for a .365 average and tied for the team lead with ten home runs.

Narron returned to Doan's school in early 1935 to gain more baseball knowledge and take advantage of advance instruction. Soon after, during Cardinals spring training, general manager Branch Rickey told Narron he should switch to catching since he was not known for his speed. It was the best advice Narron ever got. "If you want to learn to be a catcher, you'll need to catch two hours in the morning and two hours in the afternoon," Rickey told the 5-foot-10, 185-pounder.[7]

For 1935 Narron was assigned to Class D Albany, Georgia, where he played in 93 games, slugged 16 home runs, and played the infield and outfield as well as catcher. His .349 batting average was good enough to lead the Georgia-Florida League as he outdistanced the runner-up by 11 points.[8]

At the end of the season Narron was called up to the St. Louis Cardinals, a jump from Class D to the major-league level. His first at-bat, on September 15, 1935, was as a pinch-hitter for Dizzy Dean against Carl Hubbell of the New York Giants, and Narron grounded out to Hubbell on the first pitch.[9] "I would have swung at it if he'd have thrown it to first base," Narron would say.

At spring training with the Cardinals at Bradenton, Florida, in 1936, manager Frankie Frisch told his young players to find an experienced, regular member of the team and do what that player did to get into shape. Leaning on a bat behind the batting cage later that afternoon, Frisch turned to see Sam Narron standing there, leaning on his bat.

"What are you doing, standing around here?" the manager yelled in front of his players. "Didn't I tell you to pick out some regular and do what he did?"

"Yes," answered Narron politely, "and I picked you."[10]

Narron underwent an emergency appendectomy a few days later.[11] He was kept in the Cardinals' camp, then was sent to Sacramento of the Pacific Coast League on April 20. Playing in only 57 games for the Solons in his weakened condition, Narron still was able to hone his catching skills in the bullpen for manager Bill Killefer under Rickey's direction.

Narron spent 1937 at Asheville in the Piedmont League, playing in 116 games and batting .328. At Rochester in 1938, he batted .311. He returned to play for the Red Wings again in 1939 and batted .302. He also continued learning the skills of catching and handling pitchers, which became his greatest assets.

Narron was demoted to the Texas League's Houston Buffaloes in 1940 and returned there in 1941. His batting average dipped below .300 in both seasons, but he caught in more games. Back at Rochester for the 1942 season, he shared catching duties with Sheriff Robinson and Ray Hayworth, then was called up to St. Louis as third-string catcher in June. He was with the team long enough to be voted a full $6,192.53 share of the victorious Cardinals' World Series winnings.

Branch Rickey left the Cardinals organization and became the president and general manager of the Brooklyn Dodgers, a move that figured into Narron's baseball future. He respected authority and was very loyal, and Rickey knew it.

Listed as the number four catcher on the 1943 Cardinals' preseason roster, Narron remained on the roster for the entire season, though he got into only ten games and spent most of his time in the bullpen as the Cardinals won 105 games and cruised to the pennant. He had one at-bat in the World Series against the New York Yankees, grounding out as a pinch-hitter in Game Four. The Yankees won the Series in five games.

Soon after the World Series the Cardinals sent Narron to Columbus of the International League. The Boston Red Sox offered the Cardinals $50,000 for him, but Branch Rickey wouldn't sell him, so Narron retired to his tobacco farm. After the season Columbus traded him to St. Paul, a Dodgers farm club, and Narron "unretired." He played in 90 games for the American Association club, mostly as a catcher. Despite a damaged finger, he knocked in 53 runs on a .253 average.

After playing in only two games for St. Paul at the beginning of the 1946 season, Narron was sold in May to Mobile, another Brooklyn farm club. Appearing in 39 games for the Southern Association club, he batted .261. In the winter of 1946-47 Narron was sold to Charleston of the South Atlantic League, where he was one of four catchers on the roster when spring training began in 1947. When the Cardinals released him, Narron simply went home.[12] Later in the season he signed with the Smithfield-Selma Leafs in the Class D Tobacco State League, where he batted .385 in 37 games. He began the 1948 season as player-manager, but was fired as manager in midseason. Narron stayed with the team and batted .317 in 49 games.

At the Winter Meetings in December, Narron ran into Branch Rickey's son, Branch, Jr., who asked him what he was doing there. "Looking for a job," Narron said. The younger Rickey said to come to spring training and he would certainly be able to find something.[13] Narron went to Brooklyn's spring-training camp in Vero Beach, Florida. Branch Rickey saw him there and asked what he was doing there. "Looking for a job," said Narron. "I don't have anything for you to do," Rickey said, but told him that as long as he was there he could warm up pitchers. As the team broke camp to head north, Rickey gave Narron the assignment that would lead to his future as a major-league coach: bullpen catcher.

In his bullpen role, Narron became known for getting a pitcher up to throw even before being signaled to do so by manager Burt Shotton. Lenny Yochim, a longtime scout, team executive, and adviser for the Pittsburgh Pirates, remembered that would "run" the pitchers, was the ball-keeper before games, and was counted on to catch during batting practice.[14] At one point during the season one of the catchers at Triple-A Montreal was hurt, and Rickey sent Narron to the team to fill in. The 35-year-old Narron played in one game, batted four times, and hit a home run. Then he returned to the Dodgers.

The Dodgers won the National League pennant with a 97-57 record, but lost to the New York Yankees in five games in the World Series. In a move at odds with later practice, the players voted Narron only a half-share of their losing World Series money.

Narron remained with the Dodgers for the 1950 season as the club finished second to the Philadelphia Phillies Whiz Kids. In November Walter O'Malley bought out Rickey's portion of the Dodgers ownership. Soon afterward Rickey became the general manager of the Pirates.[15] He took Narron with him as the chief of the bullpen. Narron stayed with the Pirates for 14 seasons. He was the bullpen coach for four Pirates managers, Bill Meyer, Fred Haney, Bobby Bragan, and Danny Murtaugh. Narron's experience was invaluable to each one, as he constantly offered advice on players and situations when asked (and oftentimes when not asked).

"Daddy always said, 'I wasn't the best, but I rubbed shoulders with the best,' Rooster remembers. "Daddy was a coach players would go to, and in return for how popular he was, guys like General Manager Joe Brown were good to my dad".[16]

Harry Walker replaced Danny Murtaugh as the Pirates' manager after the 1964 season and decided not to keep any of Murtaugh's coaches. Narron retired and went back to farming.[17] His major-league playing career consisted of 24 games and 28 at-bats. He hit .286 with one run batted in. He participated in one World Series as a player and two

as a coach, and coached in two All-Star Games. He was inducted into the Kinston (North Carolina) Professional Baseball Hall of Fame in 1988.

In the 1967 amateur draft, Sam's son Rooster was selected as a catcher by the New York Mets in the ninth round of the secondary phase. Thirty-five years later, in 2002, his grandson, also named Sam, was drafted in the 15th round as a pitcher by the Texas Rangers.

In later years, Narron suffered with Alzheimer's disease, and he died in Raleigh, North Carolina, on December 31, 1996, at the age of 83. He is buried in Antioch Baptist Cemetery in Johnson County, North Carolina.

Over the course of years since the mid-1930s, nine Narron family members have played or are playing Organized Baseball: Sam; his nephews Milt, Brandel, and John; his son Samuel ("Rooster"); his grandson Sam; and great-nephews Jerry and Johnny, and great-great nephew Connor. Jerry, a catcher like his great-uncle, has managed the Texas Rangers and Cincinnati Reds, and grandson Sam in 2012 was a pitching coach in the Washington Nationals organization.

Sources

Baseball Digest

Fourteenth Census of the United States: 1920 Population

Johnston County, North Carolina, General Index to Delayed Births

Pittsburgh Post-Gazette

The Sporting News

U.S. WWII Draft Cards

www.ancestry.com

www.baseball-almanac.com

www.baseball-reference.com

www.retrosheet.org

Notes

1   Interviews with Sam "Rooster" Narron on June 28, 2009, and August 15 and16, 2010, at Herschel Greer Stadium, Nashville, Tennessee. Quotations from his father are as attributed by his son unless otherwise noted.

2   Telephone interview with Lenny Yochim on September 27, 2012.

3   Interview with Sam "Rooster" Narron.

4   *The Sporting News*, February 9, 1936.

5 Bob Cairns, *Pen Men: Baseball's Greatest Bullpen Stories Told By the Men Who Brought the Game Relief* (New York: St. Martin's Press, 1992), 26.

6 *The Sporting News*, April 19, 1934.

7 Interview with Sam "Rooster" Narron.

8 *The Sporting News*, February 20, 1936.

9 *The Sporting News*, September 19, 1935.

10 *The Sporting News*, March 19, 1936.

11 Ibid.

12 Cairns, 30.

13 Ibid.

14 Interview with Lenny Yochim.

15 Lee Lowenfish. *Branch Rickey: Baseball's Ferocious Gentleman* (Lincoln and London: University of Nebraska Press, 2007), 51.

16 Ibid.

17 Telephone interviews with Larry D'Amato on July 22 and August 17, 2010.

Frank Oceak

By Gregory Wolf

AFTER HITTING HIS dramatic walk-off home run in the bottom of the ninth inning in Game Seven of the 1960 World Series, Bill Mazeroski excitedly circled first and then second base, waving his arms with his cap in his hand. As he reached third base he was greeted by Pirates third-base coach Frank Oceak, who gave him a slap on the back and ebulliently followed him to the melee of players, fans, and police at home plate. For Oceak, whose number 44 jersey can be seen clearly in historic footage of the hit, the 1960 World Series championship was the culmination of almost three decades primarily toiling as a player and manager in the lower minor leagues, Class B, C, and D, and a testament to his love of the game. "Frank Oceak was an extremely hard worker and patient," said Virgil Trucks, who had retired in 1959 and pitched batting practice for the Pirates in 1960. "He was one of the best coaches I ever worked with."[1]

Frank John Oceak was born to Frank and Ann Oceak on September 8, 1912, in the tiny coal-mining town of Pocahontas, Virginia, on the West Virginia border. In 1920, when he was 8 years old, Oceak and his parents, immigrants from the Abauj region in northeastern Hungary, left Appalachia and moved to Cliffside Park, New Jersey, across the Hudson River from New York City. In this urban setting, Oceak learned how to play baseball. After graduating from Cliffside Park High School in 1931 during the height of the Great Depression, Oceak followed his passion and embarked on a 40-year career in baseball.

Quick and agile, the 5-foot-9, 170-pound, right-handed Oceak had a 17-year minor-league career as a shortstop and later as a second baseman and third baseman. He never made it to the major leagues as a player. After a tryout, Oceak

signed in 1932 with the Cumberland (Maryland) Colts in the Class C Middle Atlantic League, a New York Yankees affiliate, but played in just seven games.[2] Much later he recalled: "I only stayed about five or six weeks. I was only 17½ [actually 19½] at the time and became so homesick that I went back home."[3] Like many minor-league teams during the Depression, Cumberland struggled financially, and disbanded at the end of the season. For 1933 Oceak was picked up by the Johnstown (Pennsylvania) Johnnies in the same league, nominally affiliated with the Yankees and managed by Leo Mackey, for whom Oceak played the previous season. He remained in the Yankees' organization for two more years and bounced around from Akron and Wheeling in the Middle Atlantic League to Norfolk in the Class B Piedmont League, batting typically in the .280s to .300 with little power. Oceak's one chance in Class A baseball was in 1934, when he started the season with the Binghamton (New York) Triplets in the New York-Pennsylvania League, but he batted just .236 in 16 games and was demoted. At Binghamton he was managed by Billy Meyer, who later piloted the Pittsburgh Pirates from 1948 to 1952. Even if Oceak had been a top prospect, it would have been difficult to dislodge Yankees stars Frank Crosetti from shortstop or Tony Lazzeri from second base. Oceak was released after the 1935 season.

Oceak's career shifted personally and professionally when he signed with the St. Louis Browns in 1936. He wound up back in Johnstown, where he played for two years, hitting .287 and .304. While in Johnstown he met his future wife, Mary Ann. Together they made the Johnstown area their permanent residence for most of the rest of their lives. Oceak's managing career began in 1938 when the Browns sent him to the Lafayette (Louisiana) White

Sox of the Class D Evangeline League as player-manager, a position he held for numerous teams for the next 12 years in an era when player-managers were common.[4] In 1939 Oceak led the Fayetteville (Arkansas) Angels to a 79-42 record and was called the best second baseman in the league.[5] He guided the Angels to the playoff finals and did the same with the Beaver Falls Browns in the Class D Pennsylvania State Association in 1940. He batted .310 in 1939 and .305 in 1940, part of a string of six straight seasons in which he batted over .300.

The low point of Oceak's career occurred at a Beaver Falls game on June 6, 1940, when he assaulted umpire Len Burgher. Team officials attempted to cover up the severity of the situation, including an apparently coerced statement from Burgher claiming he was the instigator. League President Elmer Daily fined Oceak $50 and suspended him for ten days and the umpire for 90 days for being the aggressor. Because of the seriousness of the situation and the threat to the integrity of baseball, Baseball Commissioner Kenesaw Mountain Landis intervened, rebuked Daily for his findings, overturned the umpire's suspension, and wrote, "Oceak was guilty of assault on Umpire Burgher."[6] Landis suspended Oceak for the entire 1941 season. (He gave four Beaver Falls team officials lesser suspensions.) The Browns cut their ties with Oceak and his future was in jeopardy. Years later, Oceak recalled: "[The year away from baseball] taught me a lesson never to blow my top. That year I worked in a steel mill and never thought I'd get back. I played semipro ball on Saturdays and Sundays."[7]

After a year away from baseball, Oceak began a 30-year relationship with the Pittsburgh Pirates (interrupted by one year with the Cincinnati Reds) when he was hired in 1942 as a player-manager for the Oil City Oilers, a Pirates farm team in the Pennsylvania State Association, and responded with a career-high .343 average in 111 games. Except for 1944 and 1945, when he served in the Navy Seabees (Construction Battalion) in the Pacific Theater during World War II, Oceak managed eight different Pirates farm teams from 1942 through 1957. He no longer played after 1947. His career batting average was .299 and he had 1,343 hits in 1,230 games.

Oceak reached the Triple-A level when he managed the Columbus Jets of the International League in 1957. In preparation for the task, he piloted the Poza Rica Oilers

in the Veracruz Winter League in Mexico for the 1956-57 season.[8] When Branch Rickey was named general manager of the Pirates in 1951, he invited Oceak and Danny Murtaugh, who had finished his playing career with the Pirates in 1951 and had been named skipper of the team's Double-A affiliate, the New Orleans Pelicans (Southern Association), to the Pirates' rookie camp in 1952 to work with emerging players.[9] In subsequent years, Oceak regularly worked with prospects and rookies at Pirates camps.

Murtaugh replaced Bobby Bragan as Pirates manager in August 1957. In 1958 he hired the "die-hard optimist"[10] Oceak as third-base coach. Oceak spent the next seven years in that job—including the magical 1960 season—until Murtaugh retired for health reasons in 1964. Oceak had definitely paid his dues: He managed 12 minor-league teams, ten of them in the Pirates organization, as well as Poza Rica in Mexico and Aguilas Cibaenas in the Dominican Winter League. Pirates sportswriter Les Biederman wrote of Oceak, "He made it up the hard way. . . . He drove the team bus, handed out meal money, even wrote publicity."[11] In an interview with the author, former Pirates pitcher Bob Friend said, "The players respected Oceak for all he'd done in baseball and recognized his loyalty to the Pirates and Danny Murtaugh. They had a close relationship."[12]

Oceak managed in the Pirates' farm system from 1966 through 1969. When Murtaugh came out of retirement to manage the Pirates again in 1970, he made Oceak his third-base coach again, underscoring their close relationship. Oceak coached another three years, including the 1971 World Series championship season, and retired after the 1972 season.

Throughout his career, Oceak developed a reputation as an astute observer of the game and as an attentive, patient instructor, especially for infielders. Having played shortstop, second base, and third base, Oceak stressed proper technique in fielding groundballs and executing double plays effectively. "He knew how to develop infielders from all of his years in the minors," backup catcher Bob Oldis said in an interview with the author.[13] He worked diligently with Bill Mazeroski and is often seen as one of Mazeroski's fielding mentors. Mazeroski won his first Gold Glove award in 1958 in Oceak's first year as third-base coach. "He'd always say, 'Catch the ball, then block it. Keep the ball in front of you!,' " remembered Bob Oldis.

During Oceak's two tours as third-base and infielders coach, the Pirates were typically considered among the best fielding teams in the National League. In his ten years with the Pirates, they were recognized as having the best double-play combination in baseball, led the National League in double plays in eight of the ten years, and ranked second and third in the other two. This can be traced to the fielding genius of Mazeroski, and to Oceak's development of other infielders, including shortstops Dick Schofield and Gold Glove winner Gene Alley and second baseman Dave Cash, who supplanted Mazeroski in 1971. Oceak even had the unenviable task of developing Dick "Dr. Strangeglove" Stuart as the Pirates' first baseman in 1958.[14] Oceak taught his players to recognize how infields and outfields play differently in various stadiums. On an offday after Game Two of the 1960 World Series, Oceak showed his outfielders how differently the ball caromed off the wall in Yankee Stadium and spun around the curve of the outfield than it did at Forbes Field.[15] "Oceak taught us to be aware of the game and the situation," catcher Hal Smith mentioned in an interview author and added, "Some players called him Suicide because he wanted us to be aware of the suicide squeeze."[16]

Oceak spent one season with the Cincinnati Reds in 1965 as first-base coach and infield instructor, charged with developing the fielding of third-year second baseman Pete Rose. "Frank wants me to cheat a little toward second," Rose said. "It's easier to make the play on your gloved-hand side than to the right. Maz cheats that way and if it's good enough for him, it's good enough for me."[17] Rose responded by leading the National League in putouts and was named to his first All-Star Team. Oceak lost his job when manager Dick Sisler was fired at the end of the 1965 season.

Despite his one season with the Reds, Oceak was a Pirate at heart and a trusted and respected instructor. The Pirates rehired him at the end of 1965 and from 1966 through 1969 he managed the Class A Clinton (Iowa) Pilots in 1966, the Double-A Macon (Georgia) Peaches in 1967, and the Class A Gastonia (North Carolina) Pirates in 1968 and 1969. At Gastonia he tutored future Pirates Milt May, Rennie Stennett, and Frank Taveras. His posted a career record of 1,310 wins and 1,383 losses in 21 seasons as a manager.

During the offseason, Oceak lived with his wife and two daughters in Johnstown, where he once owned a tavern, the Third Base Inn. In 1967 his wife died after a long illness. A year later he married Julia Patti of Johnstown, a widow whom he had known since the early 1940s.[18]

Oceak experienced the excitement of another World Series championship in 1971 when the Pirates were again overwhelming underdogs, this time to the Baltimore Orioles. The turning point in the Series may have come in Game Three after the Pirates lost the first two games in Baltimore. In the bottom of the seventh inning, clinging to a 2-1 lead against 20-game winner Mike Cuellar, the Pirates had Roberto Clemente on second base and Willie Stargell on first. Slugger Bob Robertson, who had crushed the San Francisco Giants in the National League Championship Series with a record-breaking four-home-run performance but was hitless so far in the World Series, was at bat. Playing for a run, manager Murtaugh gave Oceak the bunt sign to flash to Robertson, who had not had a sacrifice the entire season and only one in his career. Robertson either did not see the bunt sign or ignored it and didn't square to bunt; Clemente can be seen in historic footage attempting in vain to call time. But it didn't matter. Robertson belted a three-run homer and the Pirates went on to win the game, 5-1. Postgame discussion focused on this play and Oceak quipped sarcastically, "With all the decoys I gave Robertson, he must have missed the sign."[19] The Pirates ultimately won the World Series. Murtaugh and Oceak were the only team members remaining from the 1960 championship club.

Bill Virdon, who was named manager for 1972 after Murtaugh retired for the second time, retained Oceak as his third-base coach. "Bill and I had an understanding," Oceak said, "that when Maz retired, he would be offered the third-base coaching job. So when Bill told the club that this [1972] would be his last, I knew it would be mine."[20]After a disappointing and dramatic loss to the Reds in the NLCS, the Pirates reduced their coaching staff from five to four, citing economic reasons.[21] The 60-year old Oceak, hitting coach Joe Morgan, and pitching coach Don Osborn were dropped, and soon thereafter Oceak officially retired from baseball. He harbored no ill feelings toward Virdon or the Pirates and stayed close to the organization. In 1976 he briefly came out of retirement in midseason and served as first-base coach when coach Don Leppert was hospitalized.[22] In the early 1970s, Oceak's name popped up as a candidate for managerial vacancies, such as with Houston for the 1972 season;[23] however, he was never offered a managerial position in the major leagues.

Reflecting on his long career in the minors, Oceak recalled in an interview in 1958, "Billy Meyer [his former manager with Binghamton in 1934] told me that I'd never make it to the majors. I could make the double play, but I could not run. I wanted to be in baseball. Billy did me a great favor. He told me to try to become a manager."[24] The unpretentious Oceak persevered and ultimately spent 40 years in Organized Baseball. He was a players' coach who could relate to their concerns, frustrations, and anxieties as players, and had the ability to calm their nerves. "Players got along with Oceak very well," Bob Friend said. "He was a low-key kind of coach, but he would get on to players, too." Hal Smith recalled, "Oceak had a great personality and told jokes. He was a relaxed coach." Oceak died on March 19, 1983, in his longtime hometown, Johnstown, Pennsylvania. He was buried at St. Joseph Cemetery in Geistown, Pennsylvania, just a few minutes from his home.

Sources

Statistics are from Baseball-Reference.com and Retrosheet.org.

David Cicotello and Angelo J. Louisa, eds., *Forbes Field. Essays and Memories of the Pirates Historic Ballpark, 1909-1971* (Jefferson, North Carolina: McFarland, 2007).

Rick Cushing, *1960 Pittsburgh Pirates Day by Day: A Special Season, An Extraordinary World Series* (Pittsburgh: Dorrance Publishing Co., 2010).

David Finoli and Bill Ranier, eds., *The Pittsburgh Pirates Encyclopedia* (Champaign, Illinois: Sports Publishing, 2003).

Dick Groat, *The World Champion Pittsburgh Pirates* (New York: Coward-McCann, 1961).

David Maraniss, *Clemente: The Pride and Passion of Baseball's Last Hero* (New York: Simon and Schuster, 2006).

Richard Peterson, ed., *The Pirates Reader.* (Pittsburgh: University of Pittsburgh Press, 2003).

Jim Reisler, *The Best Game Ever: Pirates vs. Yankees October 13, 1960* (Philadelphia: Da Capo Press, 2007).

Notes

1 The author would like to express his gratitude to Virgil Trucks, who was interviewed on March 20, 2012.

2 *Cumberland* (Maryland) *Evening Times*, February 18, 1932, 10; J. Sutter Kegg, "Tapping the Kegg," *Cumberland Evening Times*, October 20, 1972, 10.

3 J. Sutter Kegg. "Tapping the Kegg," *Cumberland Evening Times*, October 16, 1960, 38.

4 *The Sporting News*, January 27, 1938, 6.

5 *The Sporting News*, July 13, 1939, 6.

6 *The Sporting News*, February 13, 1941, 2.

7 Frank Eck (Associated Press), "After 25 Years in the Minors, Frank Oceak Has His Day," *Oneonta* (New York) *Star*, April 29, 1958, 12.

8 *The Sporting News*, January 16, 1957, 23.

9 *The Sporting News*, February, 27, 1952, 18.

10 *The Sporting News*, August 14, 1957, 38.

11 Rick Cushing, *1960 Pittsburgh Pirates Day by Day: A Special Season, and Extraordinary World Series.* (Pittsburgh: Dorrance Publishing Co., 2010).

12 The author would like to express his gratitude to Bob Friend, who was interviewed on March 19, 2012.

13 The author would like to express his gratitude to Bob Oldis, who was interviewed on March 19, 2012.

14 *The Sporting News*, March 26, 1958, 15.

15 Bruce Markusen, "Cooperstown Confidential: The 1960 World Series," at The Hardball Times: http://www.hardballtimes.com/main/article/cooperstown-confidential-the-1960-world-series-part-2/

16 The author would like to express his gratitude to Hal Smith, who was interviewed on March 20, 2012.

17 Si Burick, "200 Grounders a Day. They Could Put Pete Rose in the All Star Game." *Baseball Digest,* July 1965, 80.

18 *The Sporting News*, July 28, 1968, 43.

19 *The Sporting News*, October 31, 1971, 6.

20 J. Sutter Kegg, 10.

21 *The Sporting News*, October 28, 1972, 12.

22 *The Sporting News*, August 14, 1976, 11.

23 *The Sporting News*, September 11, 1971, 28.

24 Frank Eck, 12.

Mickey Vernon

by Rich Westcott

IN THE 1940s and well into the 1950s, the premier first baseman in the American League was Mickey Vernon. On a daily basis, no other first sacker matched Vernon's considerable ability as both a hitter and fielder. With a bat in his hands, Vernon's classic left-handed stroke helped him win two batting titles, and he was regularly among the league leaders in a variety of offensive categories.

Vernon was such an accomplished hitter that Satchel Paige, the ageless wonder, once said: "If I was pitching and it was the ninth inning and we had a two-run lead with the bases loaded and Mickey Vernon was up, I'd walk him and pitch to the next man."

"I pitched him more carefully than anyone else," pitcher Allie Reynolds claimed. "He's not one of those powerful guys always looking down a pitcher's throat, but he's always ready. And he's always guarding the dish. You pitch him outside, and he hits to left. You pitch him inside, and he can put it out of the park."

Said pitcher Tom Ferrick: "Mickey was a very intelligent hitter with a good stroke. When Mickey went up to the plate, he knew who was pitching and how to handle the guy. He didn't just go up and swing indiscriminately. He was the kind of guy who always put the ball in play. That's why he got so many hits."

Mickey was equally adept with the glove. Smooth, elegant, and graceful, he played first base as though he were performing an outdoor ballet. Few balls were hit his way that didn't come to rest in his nearly flawless mitt. "He is the only man in baseball who could play first base in a tuxedo, appear perfectly comfortable, and never wrinkle his suit," claimed Jack Dunn, an executive with the Baltimore Orioles.

To that, Ferrick added: "He was not only an excellent hitter and defensive player, he could steal bases. Mickey played the game the way it should be played."

"I never patterned myself after anybody," Vernon himself said. "(Playing first base) just happened to come naturally."

Mickey was also durable. During his long career, he never missed much playing time because of injuries. His most serious injury came when he suffered a cracked rib when hit by a Tommy Byrne pitch in the last week of one season. Vernon is one of the few major leaguers who played in four decades, appearing from 1939 to 1960. He regularly played in 140 or more games a season, averaging 147 games per year between 1941 and 1955 and eight times performing in at least 150 games during an era of 154-game seasons.

As outstanding a player as he was, perhaps Vernon's greatest attribute was as one of baseball's finest gentlemen He was an upstanding citizen, a family man, kind, courteous, caring, unbiased, one who was neither loud, profane, nor mired in his own ego. "He was," said former New York sportswriter and baseball executive Arthur Richman, "one of the finest human beings I met in all my years in baseball. There was no one like Mickey Vernon. He shouldn't even have been in baseball. He should've been in the White House."

Added pitcher Mel Parnell, who played with Vernon on the Boston Red Sox: "I feel honored to have had him as a friend and a teammate. He is a wonderful individual who always commanded great respect in the clubhouse. I look back at him as being one of the best teammates I ever had." Once, Vernon was driving through the city of Chester, Pennsylvania, and he saw a group of boys playing baseball with broken bats and beat-up old baseballs. Mickey drove home, rounded up some bats and balls, and returned to the field, where he gave the equipment to the surprised but grateful youths.

When Philadelphia Phillies broadcaster Harry Kalas, then a 10-year-old boy, attended his first big-league game at Chicago's Comiskey Park, he got a special tour that boyhood dreams are made on. Vernon saw him sitting in the stands before the game began. "He reached over and picked me up and took me into the dugout," the Hall of Fame broadcaster recalled. "He gave me a ball and introduced me to some of the players. I was just in heaven. That started my love of the game of baseball."

Once, during an interview, former pitcher and Vernon roommate Walt Masterson asked this writer if "anybody had said anything bad about Mickey?" Of course not, he was told. Why would anyone do something like that? "Well, if anybody does," said Masterson, "you send him to me, and I'll have a few choice words for him."

Vernon played in all or parts of 20 big-league seasons. While most of his career was spent with the Washington Senators, Mickey also played with the Cleveland Indians, Red Sox, Milwaukee Braves, and Pittsburgh Pirates. Vernon's best years were with Washington, where he appeared in 14 seasons. With the Senators, he won batting championships in 1946, with a .353 average, and in 1953, with a .337 mark. He beat out Ted Williams for his first title, and then edged Al Rosen by one point for the second one. Mickey is one of 22 American Leaguers who have won two or more batting crowns.

During a career that included seven other times in which he hit .290 or above, Vernon slammed 2,495 hits while compiling a career batting average of .286. He drove in 1,311 runs and scored 1,196 while playing in 2,409 big league games. In 8,731 at-bats in the majors, Vernon hit 490 doubles, 120 triples, and 172 home runs. His career high for hits in one season was 207 in 1946. In that season he led both major leagues with 51 doubles.

Although first base is a position usually manned by home-run sluggers, Vernon's 172 homers were 101 less than the composite career average of the 17 major-league first basemen in the Hall of Fame. Vernon hit 15 or more homers in only four seasons. Nevertheless, Bob Feller

called Vernon "one of the toughest batters [I] ever faced." Mickey led the league in doubles three times (1946, 1953, and 1954), was second in total bases three times, and second in hits and triples twice each.

Mickey hit for the cycle on May 19, 1946, while facing the Chicago White Sox' Eddie Lopat at Comiskey Park. He hit two grand slams (on August 13, 1955 at Fenway Park off the Red Sox' Tom Hurd and on April 25, 1958 at Cleveland off the Detroit Tigers' Jim Bunning). He hit four inside-the-park home runs and two pinch-hit homers.

He was a member of seven All-Star teams (1946, 1948, 1953, 1954, 1955, 1956, and 1958) and twice among the top five in the Most Valuable Player voting (1946 and 1953). Vernon had a career fielding percentage of .990. As of 2008 he held the major-league career record for first baseman for most double plays (2,044), and American League career marks at his position for most games played (2,227), most chances (21,467), most assists (1,444), and most double plays (2,041). He also participated in two triple plays as a fielder, one on September 14, 1941, against Detroit, and one on May 22, 1953, against the New York Yankees.

James Barton Vernon was born on April 22, 1918, at his parents' home in Marcus Hook, a tiny borough that sits along the Delaware River in the southeastern part of Pennsylvania. He was the son of Clarence (known as Pinker) and Katherine, and had one sister, Edith, born seven years later. Pinker, a standout baseball player in local sandlot leagues, spent 43 years of his working career as a stillman and later as a jitney driver for Sun Oil Co. at its refinery in Marcus Hook. Katherine also worked briefly at Sun Oil before becoming a full-time housewife and mother.

By the time the boy was three years old, he had been given the nickname of Mickey. "There was a song called *Mickey*," he recalled. "I used to play it over and over on the Victrola. My aunt Helen (Konegan) started calling me Mickey, and the name stuck. Soon everybody was calling me that." Mickey attended Eddystone High School, where he was a basketball star. There was no baseball team at the school, so he played in youth leagues, including an American Legion team in nearby Chester. Although they had first met as opponents in a 12-year-old church basketball league, it was on that Legion team that Mickey became friendly with a Chester kid named Danny Murtaugh. The two became lifelong friends.

"In my first two years in Legion ball, I played right field because a bigger kid played first," Vernon said. "I finally played first base my last year of Legion ball. There were only three positions a left-hander could play—the outfield, first, and pitcher—and I wanted to play every day, so first base appealed to me."

As a teenager, Vernon hitchhiked to Philadelphia to see his favorite team, the Philadelphia Athletics, play at Shibe Park. In 1933, when he was in the 10th grade, he hitchhiked to Washington with three friends to see the Senators in the World Series. "I was crazy about baseball," Vernon said. "I've been crazy about baseball as long as I can remember."

Vernon was playing for Sun Oil in the Delaware Valley Industrial League when he accepted a baseball scholarship to Villanova University. At the time, Mickey also had a summer job at Sun Oil, walking a 3½-mile pipeline, looking for leaks. Mickey attended Villanova for one year, and played on the freshman team. After the season, he had an uneventful tryout with the Philadelphia Phillies. Then, at the urging of Villanova baseball coach George "Doc" Jacobs, who spent his summers as manager of the Easton (Maryland) Browns, a club in the Class D Eastern Shore League, Vernon worked out for the St. Louis Browns. The Browns signed him to his first contract, and in the spring of 1937, he headed to the minors.

Vernon hit .287 with 10 home runs in 83 games at Easton, which finished in second place. After the season, however, the Browns did not pick up his option, so he was signed by Washington super-scout Joe Cambria and became the property of the Senators. He spent spring training in 1938 with the Senators. "The thing I remember about that spring," he said, "was that the Senators had about 12 or 14 Cuban players in camp. Gil Torres, who later played for the Senators, got them together, and they had a strike over meal money. It lasted a couple of days. I think they got maybe another 50 cents."

Ultimately, Mickey was shipped to the Greenville (South Carolina) Spinners of the Class B South Atlantic League, where he hit .328 while playing in 132 games. The fol-lowing year, he began the season with the Springfield (Massachusetts) Nationals of the Single-A Eastern League. After hitting a league-leading .343 in 69 games, the 21-year-old Vernon was called up to Washington. He made his big-league debut on July 8, 1939. He entered the first game of that day's DH as a pinch runner in the ninth and scored a run. He started and went 1-for-5 in the second game with another run scored. He also helped turn the first of his 2,041 double plays. Vernon went on to hit .257 the rest of the season as the Senators' starting first baseman.

At the start of the 1940 season, Vernon was sent down to the Jersey City Giants of what was then the Double-A International League. Called "Jimmy" by local sportswriters, the youngster hit .283 in 154 games. At the end of the season, he was summoned again to Washington, where he played in five games. He never played in the minor leagues again.

The year 1941 was a big one in Vernon's life. On March 14, he married Elizabeth "Lib" Firth. He became the Senators' regular first baseman, and hit .299 in his first full season. He followed that with .271 and .268 averages in the next two years.

Shortly after the 1943 season ended, Vernon was inducted into the Navy. He spent the next two years as a sailor, serving some of the time in Honolulu and the South Pacific, where he was part of a traveling baseball team, made up mostly of major leaguers, that played before crowds of 10,000 to 12,000 troops. At one point, Mickey also ran softball and basketball leagues. One of the players especially attracted his attention. He was a 20-year-old sailor named Larry Doby. The two became close friends, and later Mickey helped Doby became the American League's first African American player. Vernon spent 1944 and 1945 in the service.

After his discharge, he returned home and began preparing for the start of the 1946 season. It was a special time in America, and baseball was no exception. All the big stars were back, and Americans, flocked to baseball parks in record numbers. In the American League, much of the attention focused on sluggers Ted Williams and Joe DiMaggio, both back from the war after each had missed three full seasons. No one figured on Mickey Vernon, the quiet, slender first baseman of the Washington Senators, whose fondest memory from 1941 was hitchhiking with a friend to the World Series in Brooklyn from his home in Marcus Hook, and then standing all night in line at Ebbets Field to get center-field bleacher tickets.

When the 1946 season began, Vernon had yet to hit .300 in three years as a big-league regular. Having just returned from two years in the war himself, he hadn't played at all in 1945—not even service ball. But Vernon took the lead in the batting race early in the season, withstood a late challenge by Williams, and held on to capture the crown with a .353 average, 11 points higher than the Boston slugger, who finished second.

"I don't know why I hit like that," Vernon recalled. "The balls were just falling in for me. I remember at the All-Star Game that year, Bob Feller was talking to people about going on a barnstorming trip after the season. He asked me if I'd like to go, and I said, 'Sure.' He told me if I was still leading the league at the end of the season, he'd give me a bonus."

Feller's tour featured a team of major leaguers playing the best players from the Negro Leagues on a 40-game, cross-country jaunt. The major-league team included Vernon, as well as Stan Musial, Sam Chapman, Phil Rizzuto, Ken Keltner, Johnny Sain, Spud Chandler, and Dutch Leonard. "We played every night," Vernon said. "Feller and Paige pitched the first three innings of every game. We played 11 doubleheaders. . . . We'd play Newark in the afternoon and Baltimore at night. Or New Haven in the afternoon and at Yankee Stadium at night."

After his great 1946 season, Vernon's average dropped significantly. He hit only .265 in 1947 and .242 the following year. Following the 1948 season he was traded to Cleveland along with pitcher Early Wynn for first baseman Eddie Robinson and pitchers Ed Klieman and Joe Haynes.

Although meeting Washington dignitaries was always one of the perks of playing with the normally downtrodden Senators, Vernon was still happy to leave Washington. "I was glad to get out of there," he remembered. "I knew I was going to a pretty good club (which had won the World Series in 1948). But after I was there a while, they got Luke Easter to play first, and I was traded back to the Senators. Again, I was glad to be traded, but not back to Washington."

Vernon's average had bounced up to .291 in 1949, his first season with the Indians. On June 14, 1950, with Easter taking over as the Indians' first baseman, Mickey went back to Washington, where he finished the season with a .281 batting average. He followed with .293 and .251 averages the next two years. During the 1952 season, Lib gave birth to the couple's only child, Gay Anne. Much later, Gay became a prominent news director and host of an award-winning interview show at a radio station in Boston, a position she had held for some 30 years as of 2008.

In 1953, Mickey was back in the chase for the American League batting crown. Again he led most of the season, but had to go down to the last day to edge Al Rosen for the title by just one point with a .337 average. Vernon also drove in 115 runs and scored 101, making it the only season in his career that he broke the century mark in either category.

"Rosen got hot and really came on strong," Vernon remembered of his race with the Cleveland Indians third baseman. "He had three hits the last day, and I had two. On his last at-bat, he was called out on a close play at first by Hank Soar. If he'd have gotten a hit there, he would have won the Triple Crown (Rosen led the AL with 43 home runs and 145 RBIs.)

"My guys didn't want me to come up in the last inning," added Vernon, who was due to bat fourth. "One guy got thrown out deliberately at second, and another guy let himself get picked off so I wouldn't have to bat." Vernon followed up his second batting title with .290 and .301 marks. In 1954, he hit a career-high 20 home runs.

After the 1955 season, the Senators again traded Vernon, this time to the Red Sox as part of a nine-player swap. Boston also received pitchers Bob Porterfield and Johnny Schmitz and outfielder Tom Umphlett, while the Senators got pitchers Dick Brodowski, Tony Clevenger, and Al Curtis, and outfielders Karl Olson and Neil Chrisley. With the trade, Vernon's very special days in Washington came to an end.

Throughout his career, other teams were always pursuing Vernon. On numerous occasions, it was the Yankees.

"When he was managing the Yankees, Bucky Harris once made a special trip during spring training from St. Petersburg to Orlando to get me," Vernon recalled. "Clark Griffith (the Senators owner) said, 'You're not going to get him.' Another time after I'd come back to Washington, I was walking out of the stadium, and Hank Greenberg, who was then the Indians' general manager, drove by. He said, 'I just made a good offer for you, and Griffith turned it down.'"

While he played in Washington, Vernon was only the third of three Senators first basemen who had covered the bag in a nearly unbroken string over four decades. Joe Judge manned the post from 1916 to 1930. Joe Kuhel was stationed at the initial sack from 1931 to 1937 and in the 1944-45 wartime years. Vernon made his debut late in 1939, and—except for 1940, when he was back in the minors, 1944-45 in the service, and 1949 and part of 1950 when he was with Cleveland—he occupied first for the Senators until 1955.

For much of the time, Mickey was not only one of the most popular players ever to pull on a Senators uniform; he was also the favorite of United States presidents, particularly Dwight Eisenhower. "One of my biggest thrills was on Opening Day one year [1954]," Vernon said. "I hit a home run in the 10th inning to beat Allie Reynolds and the New York Yankees. Right after I crossed home plate, some big guy—a Secret Service man, it turned out—came up and grabbed me by the arm and took me over to Eisenhower's box. Ike wanted to congratulate me for hitting the home run."

Mickey hit .310 and .241 in two seasons with Boston. In his first season, Vernon often batted fourth behind Ted Williams. "Pitchers would bear down on Ted, and have a tendency to let up on a fellow like me," Mickey said. "This was to my advantage."

During the 1956 season, Vernon got stuck in an 0-for-28 slump. But he also beat the Yankees, 6-4, with a two-run homer in the seventh inning, and bashed two doubles and a single in a 2-0 win over the Kansas City Athletics, and a two-run ninth inning homer to beat the Athletics, 3-2. He collected a home run, double, and single, and drove in four runs in a 9-3 win over the Tigers. The next day, he had five RBIs with a three-run homer and a single in an 8-6 victory over the Tigers. Over a 15-day stretch,

Mickey had 15 RBIs with five home runs, five doubles, and five singles. At the end of the season, Vernon had 15 home runs and 84 RBIs.

In the early part of 1957, Vernon's bat stayed hot. In one game, he collected four RBIs, three hits, and scored three runs in an 11-8 win over Detroit. His two-run homer in the eighth beat Baltimore, 5-4. Another two-run homer downed Kansas City, 3-2. And a two-pinch-hit home run with two outs in the bottom of the ninth beat the Yankees, 3-2.

Vernon's bat cooled off as the season progressed, and he wound up splitting first base duties with Norm Zauchin and Dick Gernert. Mickey wound up playing in just 102 games. After the season, Vernon asked Boston general manager Joe Cronin if he thought Mickey should retire and take a coaching job he was offered. Cronin's advice: "Don't quit. You can still hit."

That winter, however, Mickey was sold for $20,000 to the Indians. The Red Sox claimed that Vernon "couldn't get the bat around anymore."

In 1958, he hit .293 at Cleveland. The following spring, he was dealt to the Milwaukee Braves for pitcher Humberto Robinson. And Mickey's long career in the American League was over.

In a reserve role in 1959 for Milwaukee, Mickey hit .220. At the end of the season, he was released. Shortly afterward, his friend Danny Murtaugh, the manager of the Pittsburgh rates, asked Mickey to become one of his coaches. Mickey signed on as the team's first base coach. One of Vernon's other jobs was to work with first baseman Dick Stuart and try to make him a better fielder, an extremely difficult assignment given the error-prone Dr. Strangeglove's defensive shortcomings..

Late in the season, as the Pirates surged to the National League pennant, Vernon was activated as a player, appearing in nine games in September and collecting one hit in eight trips to the plate In the final at-bat of his career, Mickey grounded out in the 11th inning of a 4-3, 16-inning victory over the Cincinnati Reds.

Later, in one of the most riveting World Series in history, the Pirates met the Yankees. The Series went down to the final game with Bill Mazeroski's walk-off homer in the bottom of the ninth inning at Forbes Field giving the Pirates a 10-9 victory and the world championship. "As the first base coach when Mazeroski hit the home run, I was the first person to shake his hand," Vernon remembered. "When I saw the ball go out, I was just so charged up. That had to be one of my biggest thrills."

"But just playing baseball was a thrill," Vernon added. "I loved the game, and I'm very glad I played when I did and with the kinds of players I played with and against."

After one year with the Pirates, Vernon became the first manager of the expansion Washington Senators, after the original Senators had become the Minnesota Twins. With a rag-tag band made up mostly of tired veterans and untried youngsters, the Senators posted a 61-100 record in 1961, tying for ninth place with the Kansas City Athletics. The Senators had last place all to themselves in 1962, finishing the season with a 60-101 record. Midway through the following season, with the team holding a 14-26 mark, Vernon was discharged from his duties as manager. The following season, Mickey returned to Pittsburgh, once again as a coach under Murtaugh.

After spending the 1965 season as a batting coach with the St. Louis Cardinals, Vernon embarked on a stint as a minor-league manager. Over a six-year period, he piloted the Vancouver Mounties of the Pacific Coast League for three years, the Richmond Braves of the International League for two, and the Manchester Yankees of the Eastern League for one. His best seasons were second- and third-place finishes with Vancouver.

After his stint in Manchester in 1971, Vernon returned to coaching. Over the next 14 years, he served as a minor-league hitting instructor with the Kansas City Royals, Los Angeles Dodgers, and the Yankees, and as the major-league batting coach with the Dodgers, Montreal Expos, and Yankees. In his final years in baseball, Vernon served

as a scout with the Yankees, retiring in 1988 at the age of 70 after having spent 52 years in professional baseball.

Vernon is a member of another select group. He was pictured on baseball cards in four different decades. Mickey first appeared on a card in 1947 when his likeness joined the long and distinguished parade of Exhibit cards. With the exception of 1948, he was pictured either on Bowman or Topps cards every year from 1949 through 1963 and again in 1978.

Mickey and Lib lived for 52 years in Wallingford, Pennsylvania. Later, they resided near Media, Pennsylvania. Throughout those years, Vernon was a prominent member of the local community. He attended numerous events every year, a Little League was named after him, and a life-sized statue of him was placed in Marcus Hook. He also participated in numerous events for former major-league players that were held around the country.

"Mickey Vernon was the best first baseman in major-league baseball for most of the years of his long career," said Feller when the statue was dedicated. "You were a great hitter, and a credit to baseball," Musial added.

In his later years, Vernon was the recipient of numerous honors, including induction into the Pennsylvania, Philadelphia, and Delaware County Halls of Fame. He has also been on the ballot for the Baseball Hall of Fame, the last time being as recently as 2008. Following a stroke, Vernon passed away on September 24, 2008, at age 90.

Sources

Rich Westcott is the author of 19 books. All material above came from his book, *Mickey Vernon, The Gentleman First Baseman* (Philadelphia: Camino Books, 2005). Interviews for that book were conducted in person in 2003 and 2004.

Howie Haak

By Jim Sandoval and Rory Costello

CALLED THE "KING of the Caribbean" by baseball people and "Big Daddy" by players he was scouting, Howie Haak gained acclaim as the scout who threw open all of Latin America to major-league baseball. Living up to yet another nickname, "El Tiburón"—The Shark—Haak built upon the work Joe Cambria had done for the Washington Senators in Cuba. Known as a gravelly-voiced tobacco chewer, Haak spent many years scouting the Caribbean, plus Central and South America. He signed players that brought the Pittsburgh Pirates to prominence in the 1960s and 1970s. Perhaps his greatest find was his recommendation that the Pirates draft Roberto Clemente out of the Dodgers farm system.

Howard Frederick Haak (rhymes with cake) was born August 28, 1911 in Rochester, New York, son of Chester A. and Wanda (Ruddy) Haak. His grandfather, Fred Haak, was an immigrant from Germany. Howie's family included brothers named Chester Jr. and Robert. After attending local schools Madison Junior High and Rochester West High School, Haak enrolled at the University of Rochester, majoring in medicine and chemistry. While there he was a member of Psi Upsilon fraternity.

Haak served several stints in the military. The 1930 census of Hawaii listed him as a sailor stationed at Pearl Harbor. In 1994, Howie remembered, "I was getting bored at home. So I lied about my age and joined the Navy. My old man lied for me, too, 'cause he just wanted to get rid of me. He just couldn't take all the stuff that I used to do, like skip school and sing dirty words to the hymns in church, stuff like that."[1] A 1935 U.S. Marine muster roll showed him in the reserves as a platoon leader.

Several accounts claim Haak played minor-league baseball before joining the Rochester (a

St. Louis Cardinals farm club) team as a trainer/coach about 1939. In 1994, he said he'd blown out his arm and was working as traveling secretary for the Red Wings. A Howard Haack is listed as catching for the 1941 and 1942 clubs in the North Carolina State League. The authors believe this is our man. Ray Hathaway, who managed in the Pirates chain, remembered in 1999 how Howie—a big, solidly built man—would point with the crooked fingers he suffered as a receiver.[2]

World War II saw Haak serve as a Lieutenant Commander from 1942-46. He was at the pre-flight school at Chapel Hill, North Carolina. Upon his return from military service, he joined the Mobile club as a trainer. Mobile was a Dodgers farm team, and Branch Rickey offered Haak a position as a scout for the Brooklyn club. Rickey knew him from the St. Louis organization. One story says that while Rickey was running the Cardinals and Haak was with Rochester, they would converse about players. Rickey was much impressed with Haak's insights, including recommending a kid named Stan Musial as being ready for the big leagues (as well as Whitey Kurowski and Erv Dusak). Now that he had the opportunity, Rickey hired Haak.

Howie later said that he accompanied The Mahatma while Rickey observed Jackie Robinson in the minor leagues. (Haak also observed that a number of Latinos with at least some African heritage—he named Gil Torres and Tomás de la Cruz—made the majors before Jackie.[3])

Haak moved with Rickey to the Pittsburgh club in November 1950, serving as an area scout for the West Coast. He also served as a coach with the Hollywood Stars of the Pacific Coast League. In 1964, Howie began 20 years as a Special Assignment Scout, scouting Latin America and serving as a sort of cross-checker for the Pirates. Among other things, he helped prepare the Pirates' dossier on the Yankees ahead of the 1960 World Series.

His work in the Latin region had begun years before, however. One of the main reasons the Pirates ventured abroad was their low budget: they could sign the Latino prospects cheaply. In 1999, longtime Pirates general manager Joe L. Brown gave insight on Haak's operation. The son of the rubber-faced comic movie actor (*Some Like It Hot*) and the crusty, earthy, plug-chawing scout "worked together about as closely as a general manager and scout can work. We were friends and compatriots."[4] Often with Brown as company, twice a year Haak "would go down through the Caribbean, down into Central and into northern South America."[5] Over time Howie learned to speak rough but functional Spanish.

Haak was a pick-and-shovel man who practiced Branch Rickey's strategy of quality through quantity, assaying tons of raw ore through his time-honored tryout camps. "I'm a physical-ability man," he said in 1973. In later years, Howie would scoff at the academies various teams had set up in the Dominican. "These camps are all a bunch of baloney," he told author John Krich. "The other clubs are wasting their money."[6]

Among the lesser-known seams Haak worked were Nicaragua, Colombia, and the Virgin Islands. For such locations, "it all depended if there was someone there to see," said Brown. "He had bird dogs down there, people who covered the area for him and then would recommend people to him, and then he would hold tryout camps." Brown added, "Howie being Howie, he would know that people were there."[7]

In 1954 Haak married Crystal Tate, whom he had first spotted sitting in a box seat in Hollywood's Gilmore Field. They had four children. Crystal helped him type up the reports that were then organized in books. She still had them and a trove of memorabilia after her husband died.[8]

Haak was selected many times as the Scout of the Month by the Topps Company. In 1984, Haak was selected as the first recipient of the Scout of the Year award, voted on by his peers.

Plain-spoken, even blunt, Haak created a controversy in 1982 when he was quoted as saying the Pirates' atten-dance problems were because they were starting nine black players. He said the fans would not come out to see such a team. He later said he was just repeating what he had overheard people saying. Oddly, Haak had signed many of the players who comprised the Pirates lineup (for example, Omar Moreno). Some players, including Bill Madlock, were quoted as saying they had no problem with the statement. Though Hank Aaron also came to Howie's defense, Haak suffered quite a backlash from the incident before it blew over.

From 1984-88 Haak served as a scouting supervisor for the Pirates. Haak left the Pittsburgh organization after a disagreement with GM Syd Thrift. He moved on to the Houston organization where he worked as an area scout from 1989-91 and as an advance scout from 1992-93.

Howie's long list of signings includes the following:

United States: Gino Cimoli, Norm Sherry, Dick Stuart, Gabe Gabler, Clyde King, Gale Wade, Ken Lehman, Dale Berra, Rex Johnston, Steve Nicosia, Joe Gibbon, Larry Foss, Red Witt, John Candelaria, and Bob Veale.

Cuba: Lino Donoso, Román Mejías, Jose Martinez, Orlando McFarlane, Ed Bauta.

Dominican Republic: Julián Javier, Rafael Vásquez, Roberto Peña, Tony Peña, Gibson Alba, Frank Taveras, Alberto Lois, Nelson Norman, Cecilio Guante, Miguel Diloné, Jose DeLeón. The one he most regretted letting get away in his career was Juan Marichal, followed by the Alou brothers. The Giants also flourished in the region. The Astros also beat him out for César Cedeño.

Nicaragua: Albert Williams.

Panama: Manny Sanguillén, Omar Moreno, Rennie Stennett.

Puerto Rico: Ramón Hernández, Junior Ortiz, Orlando Merced.

Venezuela: Tony Armas.

Virgin Islands: Joe Christopher, Elmo Plaskett, Al McBean.

"Señor Howie" also did his best to help the young Latin Americans cope with homesickness and adjust to U.S. society. In his baseball novel *Prospect*, author Bill Littlefield speculated that some of the youths became like children to the scout. One of them was Alfredo Francisco Edmead, of whom Haak said late in his career that he always thought was the best prospect he ever signed. With the help of player Pablo Cruz, Haak signed Edmead when he was just 17 years old out of the Dominican Republic. On August 22, 1974, playing for the Salem, Virginia club, Edmead dove for a short fly ball, his head striking Pablo Cruz' knee. Rushed to the hospital, Edmead died of a massive skull fracture with brain injuries. Edmead was hitting .314 with seven home runs and 61 stolen bases at the time and was considered a definite major-league prospect.

After suffering his second stroke, Haak passed away at the Health Care and Rehabilitation Center in Palm Springs on February 22, 1999. His funeral was held at the St. Paul's of the Desert Episcopal Church in Palm Springs. Haak had told his wife to have his remains cremated and then thrown in the trash. The first part of that wish was carried out. He was survived by a son, Phillip, and two daughters, Betty and Marjorie, along with five grandchildren.

Said Joe L. Brown, "Nobody has driven more miles, nobody has stayed up longer, nobody has seen more games." Another Pirates GM, Harding "Pete" Peterson said, "Howie can see a kid three or four times and make

a decision about him. He does it better than anyone I've ever seen."[9] Haak himself said, "I get tired at times . . .[but] it's what I do. It's the only thing I know how to do. And the pay is too good not to do it."[10]

Sources

Tom Bird, "Howie Haak: Veteran Scout looks Back on Long Career." *Baseball Digest*, February 1994: 62-66.

Frank Deford, "Liege Lord of Latin Hopes." *Sports Illustrated*, December 24, 1973.

Dan Donovan, "Howie Haak Still Super Scout." *Pittsburgh Press*, March 11, 1979.

John Krich, *El Béisbol*. New York, NY: Prentice Hall, 1989.

Cleveland, Ohio, Society for American Baseball Research: *Baseball Research Journal #28*. 1999

www.ancestry.com

Census, Rochester County, New York, 1900-1930.

Obituaries from the Associated Press, *New York Times*, *Palm Springs Desert Sun*, *Philadelphia Inquirer*, *Pittsburgh Post-Gazette*, and *Rochester Democrat and Chronicle*.

Stars and Stripes, August 1948: 10.

The Sporting News: various issues

Notes

1 Tom Bird, "Howie Haak: Veteran Scout Looks Back on Long Career." *Baseball Digest*, February 1994: 62.

2 Rory Costello, *Baseball in the Virgin Islands*. New York, NY: self-published, 2000: 25. Quotes come from 1999 in-person interview, Rory Costello with Ray Hathaway, 1999, Asheville, North Carolina.

3 John Krich, *El Béisbol*. Chicago, Illinois: Ivan R. Dee, 1989: 157.

4 Costello, op. cit., loc. cit.. Quotes come from 1999 telephone interview, Rory Costello with Joe L. Brown, 1999.

5 Ibid., loc. cit.

6 Krich, op. cit.: 156.

7 Costello, op. cit., loc. cit.

8 Telephone interview, Rory Costello with Crystal Haak, 1999. Frank Deford's 1973 article noted that Howie had been married twice previously.

9 Bird, op. cit., 63-64.

10 Dan Donovan, "Howie Haak Still Super Scout." *Pittsburgh Press*, March 11, 1979.

Bob Prince

By James Forr

HALL OF FAME broadcaster Bob Prince was a man of paradox. He was often brash and loud, but tender and caring around the disabled children who meant so much to him; a carefree playboy who enjoyed a drink or two (or three), but a devoted family man who raised two children with his wife of 44 years; proud and sometimes arrogant, but gracious in his relations with players and younger broadcasters; occasionally hated, but ultimately loved by Pirate fans who invited him into their homes, offices, and cars every day of the baseball season for 28 years. Perhaps it is because of these paradoxes, this humanness, that Prince's name is still a magical one among fans in Pittsburgh and the entire Pennsylvania-Ohio-West Virginia tri-state area, almost two decades after his death.

Another paradox is that Prince, who would become a Pittsburgh institution, lived a rather nomadic existence during his youth. The son of Frederick and Guyla Prince, Robert F. Prince was born in Los Angeles on July 1, 1916. His father, a former West Point football standout, was a career military man whose job took him and his family all over the United States. The stereotypical army brat, Bob Prince attended, by his own estimation, 14 or 15 different schools before graduating from Schenley High School in Pittsburgh. A fine athlete, Prince lettered in swimming at the University of Pittsburgh. Although in his later days, Prince was known for his stick-figure physique, photographs of him in the mid-to-late 1930s reveal an athletic-looking young man with a well-developed upper body. Prince left Pittsburgh in 1937, to enroll at Stanford University (where he claimed to have intentionally flunked out), and finally ended up at the University of Oklahoma, where he was again part of the swimming team

and where he completed a bachelor's degree in business administration.

After an unsuccessful stint at Harvard Law School ("In those days, anybody could get in. It wasn't like it is now," Prince claimed), Prince turned his love of sports into a profession, winning an audition and become host of "Case of Sports" on WJAS Radio in Pittsburgh in 1941. Selling insurance during the day, then coming into the studio to host his show in the evening, Prince soon made a name for himself among Pittsburgh sports fans. He was opinionated, colorful, and a bit of a loudmouth—in some ways a forerunner of many of the bombastic radio sports talkers of today. On at least one occasion, the subject of a Prince harangue expressed his displeasure in no uncertain terms. On the air, Prince accused hometown boxer Billy Conn, who would nearly defeat Joe Louis for the heavyweight championship of the world in 1941, of ducking tough opponents. Several nights later, Conn encountered Prince at the Pittsburgh Arena, where he decided he would settle the disagreement by slamming Prince against a wall and threatening to beat him senseless. Ironically, the two men later became close friends.

Prince marketed himself brilliantly. He claimed his brash style in those early days stemmed simply from his desire to make a name for himself. He rarely hesitated to grab some gratuitous publicity, whether it was for a stunt in which someone drove a golf ball from a tee stuck in his mouth, or for forcing a frightened competitor off the track to win a celebrity stock car race. Throughout his broadcasting career, he was an inveterate joiner, building a network of personal connections and friendships through membership in organizations including the Pittsburgh Athletic Association, the Harvard-Yale-Princeton Club, the University Club, and four different country clubs. "Pure self-interest," Prince admitted. "That's how I made contacts, not through a resume or agent."

Following the 1947 baseball season, a job opened up in the Pittsburgh Pirates' broadcast booth when Jack Craddock resigned. Prince was acquainted with one of the Pirate owners, Tom Johnson, from his days at Harvard and that helped land him the job as the side-kick to beloved Pirate play-by-play man Rosey Rowswell. "Connections and associations," Prince said, "are important." At first, Rowswell—a sensitive, teetotaling man who wrote poetry—was suspicious of the brash, young Prince's intentions. During his first year in the Pirate booth, Rowswell marginalized Prince, limiting his on-air involvement to incidental activities like reading commercials during station breaks and serving as a glorified sound effects man (Prince would drop a tray filled with harness bells to mimic the sound of shattered glass in response to Rowswell's cry of "Open the window Aunt Minnie…here it comes!" when a Pirate player slugged a home run). "I had to convince Rosey that I wasn't out to upstage him," Prince remembered. "When he learned I was sincere, we worked well together."

Despite their different personalities off the air, Prince and Rowswell shared similar broadcasting styles. Both men saw themselves as entertainers, not just reporters. Each man coined his own set of memorable, folksy catch phrases. Rowswell's repertoire included his "Aunt Minnie" home run call and his mournful "Oh, my aching back!" when a Pirate rally fizzled. Prince had his own home run call, "You can kiss it goodbye!" A bang-bang play was "as close as the fuzz on a tick's ear", and the Pirates often missed a double play "by a gnat's eyelash." A sharp single through the hard-packed Forbes Field infield was an "alabaster blast." A Pirate player in slump merely needed the help of some "hidden vigorish." And if the Pirates were trailing in the late innings, Prince openly prayed for "a bloop and a blast" to get them back in the game. "Rosey taught me an important lesson," Prince said. "If you're losing 14-2 in the second inning, you've got to keep the people interested with funny stories, names, and reminiscences. You can't be worried about who hit .280 in 1943." Prince worked at Rowswell's side for seven seasons until

Rowswell's death in February 1955. At that point, Prince took over as the Pirates' number one broadcaster.

From the start, Prince enjoyed an unusual relationship with the Pirate players. Not merely a broadcaster, Prince became for many players a friend, confidante, and mentor. In return, the players accepted him as one of the guys. One of Prince's closest friends among the Pirate players was seven-time National League home run champion Ralph Kiner. In January 1951, Kiner and Prince formed Kiner Enterprises to handle the slugger's substantial outside business interests. At the time, Kiner endorsed 14 products, producing estimated annual income of $20,000 to $30,000. Kiner and Prince certainly had fun together, tooling around Pittsburgh in matching silver Jaguars and spending part of the winter months together at Kiner's home in Palm Springs, California. Financially, however, the partnership was something less than lucrative. Prince and Kiner purchased a restaurant and a UHF television station in Pittsburgh, both of which flopped. According to Kiner, "He was always getting me into one deal or another. Invariably, we lost our ass." (Indeed, Prince's record in business was marked by some spectacular failures. They included the loss of a significant amount of money to a man convicted of running an elaborate Ponzi scheme, an investment in an ill-fated professional team boxing league, and a disastrous financial plunge into Peruvian oil wells).

Prince's interest in the players went well beyond the financial, however. He seemed to genuinely care about them and like them. An example came after Game Seven of the 1971 World Series in Baltimore. Bucco pitcher Bruce Kison was scheduled to marry following the game. To ensure that Kison made it to the ceremony, Prince secured a private jet (in exchange for three World Series tickets) to shuttle the pitcher back to Pittsburgh immediately following the game. "The ballclub always wanted to take credit for that," Kison says, "but the truth of the matter is that [it was] Bob Prince. You don't see his kind in broadcasting anymore. A legend who will allow himself to come down to the players' level."

Relief pitcher Kent Tekulve, who was a rookie with the Bucs in 1974, said, "Prince was like a coach on the team, the way he led you through the p.r. aspects of being a big league ballplayer." Prince, who spoke Spanish, took many of the Pirates' black and Latin players under his wing, inviting them to his home and giving them advice on how to survive life as a major leaguer. One of those players was Roberto Clemente. Clemente's relationship with the media was strained, sometimes antagonistic. He was embarrassed by newspaper stories that, in his early days as a Pirate, quoted him in broken English, hurt that some members of the media accused him of exaggerating supposedly minor injuries, and angry that he didn't receive the respect and recognition that he believed he deserved. Over the years, Clemente and Prince became close. Prince was one of the few people, perhaps the only one, who regularly got away with referring to Clemente as "Bob" or "Bobby," an Americanization of his name that the proud Clemente despised. Following the 1971 season, Prince's 25th as a Pirate broadcaster, Clemente invited Prince to his native Puerto Rico. There, in a public ceremony, Clemente presented Prince with the silver bat he was awarded in 1961 for winning the first of his four National League batting titles—a bat Clemente once called the award that he treasured most, even more than his World Series rings.

Prince helped bridge the gap between player and fan by adorning players with weird, catchy, nicknames. When Clemente would bat in a clutch situation, for example, Prince would exhort fans with the cry of "Arriba!" which, when translated into English, means roughly "rise up" or "arise." Soon fans at Forbes Field began to yell "Arriba!" spontaneously as a display of support for the great right fielder. Other Prince-invented handles included "The Cobra" (Dave Parker), "The Dog" (Bob Skinner), and "The Deacon" (Vern Law). "These names just popped into my head. If a guy reminded me of an animal, I'd call him that," Prince said. Whenever Pirate slugger Willie Stargell would come to the plate in a crucial situation, Prince would crow, "Let's spread some chicken on the hill with Will." Stargell owned a fast food chicken restaurant in Pittsburgh's Hill district. The origin of Prince's own nickname, "The Gunner," is unclear. That appellation was the creation of Prince's longtime broadcast partner Jim Woods. Some say it was in honor of Prince's rapid-fire on-air delivery. However, another, slightly more sordid version of the story traces the name back to an alleged incident in which an angry, gun-toting husband accused Prince of flirting with the man's wife in a bar. (Woods, of course, also had a nickname: "The Possum").

Prince was a homer, an unabashed Pirate fan. After every Pirate win, regardless of the final score, he would croak in his raspy, cigarette-cured voice, "We had 'em *alllll* the way!" According for former Bucco shortstop Dick Groat, "One of the reasons he was so popular and so well-liked by everyone is that I don't remember him second-guessing the ballplayers or the manager." And Prince made no apologies for it. "Who do I broadcast for, the Pennsylvania Turnpike? If I did I'd tell you about the charm of the tollbooths. No, I broadcast for the Pittsburgh Pirates. I always call them 'Our Bucs.' They belong to every fan in Pittsburgh and I love them." *Sporting News* television critic Jack Craig panned Prince's work on NBC during the 1971 World Series as "glaringly biased." But Craig allowed that it was just Prince being Prince and that, "as a veteran announcer, and a wealthy one at that, Prince could not be expected to worry about any damage to his career resulting from a slanted one-shot performance in the World Series."

Prince believed that part of a broadcaster's job was to pull for the home team, make things interesting for the fans, and put people in the seats. This philosophy led to the birth of Pirate fans' erstwhile magic charm—the Green Weenie. During a 1966 game against Houston, Pirate trainer Danny Whelan screamed at Astros' pitcher Dave Giusti, "You're gonna walk him!" while waving a green rubber hot dog in the direction of the mound. Giusti, thus jinxed, indeed proceeded to walk the batter and eventually lose the game. Prince noticed this from the broadcast booth, and the next day he grilled Whelan about it on the air. And thereby the legend of the Green Weenie was born. Official Green Weenies, filled with little pebbles that would make noise when shaken, were sold at Forbes Field (known as "The House of Thrills" in Prince-speak). The Serta Mattress Company created a special mattress on which the Weenie could rest when not busy hexing opponents. Although Prince and the Pirate fans were unable to conjure up a pennant in 1966 (the Bucs finished third, three games behind Los Angeles) the Green Weenie did have its moments. In July, Prince implored Pirate fans to direct the power of the Weenie against Giants' pitcher Juan Marichal. Marichal won the game, but the next day slammed his hand in a car door, which caused him to miss two starts. During the seventh inning of a game against the Phillies, with the Pirates trailing 3-1, Prince's broadcast partner Don Hoak ("The Tiger" in his Pittsburgh playing days) urged Prince to use the Weenie. Prince declined, waiting until the eighth inning, at which time the Bucs responded with four runs to win 5-3. The lesson, according to Prince? "Never waste the power of the Green Weenie." In 1974, Prince would invent a similar talisman, encouraging female fans to waive their "babushkas" (handkerchiefs) to spark a rally.

When he chose to stay focused, Prince could deliver a very accurate, exciting play-by-play description. But he rambled-a lot. He would say hello to older fans listening at home who couldn't make it to the ballpark ("The shut-in lists are important," Prince argued. "When you mentioned the name of a fan in Delmont, [Pennsylvania], you made that person feel like a million dollars, especially if he or she was laid up in bed. He or she was recognized."). He told stories that had nothing to do with baseball. Seemingly no subject was off limits. He talked about the splendor of the trees in Schenley Park beyond the left field wall. He talked about his friends. He talked about college football. One fan recalls a broadcast in which "The Gunner" enlightened fans with an extended discourse about driving in fog.

Most Pirate fans seemed to like this kind of thing. Prince was funny, intelligent, and interesting-a genuine entertainer. But he also drove some people crazy. Now and then, a cry of "Shut up, Prince!" would emanate from the Forbes Field stands. Branch Rickey, general manager of the Pirates from 1950-1955, couldn't stand Prince. Rickey, a self-professed expert on almost everything, once wrote an epistle on baseball broadcasting in which he sniffed, "There should be very little horseplay in a broadcast. It is a business proposition. Every now and then an anecdote is quite proper…Broadcasters should have frequent conversations with club owners or secretaries…Scores of other games are interesting…The most important thing in all this world for a broadcaster is to have in mind constantly that 1,000 people have just turned on their radios and immediately start asking themselves 'Who is playing? What's the score?'" Rickey's broadcasting philosophy was anathema to Prince, who claimed to have never gone into a booth with anything more than a pencil, a scorecard, and his imagination. Rickey went so far as to criticize Prince in a memo to the Pirates' board of directors, claiming Prince detracted from the game with "editorial comment and comparison. He [also] has unfortunate stretches of

silence until anyone trying to get the game on the dial would think that there was no broadcast." Part of Rickey's angst probably stemmed from Prince's criticism (both on-air and off) of the trade of his friend Kiner to the Chicago Cubs in 1953. Prince groused that Rickey "got six jock straps for Kiner."

Chaos and tumult seemed to follow Prince wherever he went-not that he tried to discourage it. In 1957 in the Chase Hotel in St. Louis a thoroughly sober Prince, in response to a $20 wager from Pirate third baseman Gene Freese, leaped from a third floor window into the hotel pool. Mickey Bergstein, who broadcast Penn State University football games with Prince for nearly a decade, recalls Prince jumping to his feet after a particularly exciting touchdown, losing his balance, and nearly tumbling over a railing at the outside edge of the stadium. In July 1966, Prince was boarding a Pirates team flight to San Francisco when a flight attendant asked him to place the tape recorder he was carrying in a storage compartment. Prince declined, countering, "I handle this thing more carefully than a bomb." Prince was promptly removed from the plane and subjected to two hours of FBI and police questioning.

At times, Prince could be charmingly oblivious to what was happening around him. Broadcasting the 1960 World Series for NBC television, Prince missed one of the greatest moments in baseball history-Bill Mazeroski's Game Seven home run that gave Pirates their first championship in 35 years. In the top of the ninth inning, with the Pirates leading 9-7, Prince headed to the clubhouse to prepare for post-game interviews. When the Yankees tied it in the top of ninth, Prince was ordered back to the booth. He had just stepped off the Forbes Field elevator when he heard a roar and was told to head back down to the clubhouse. The roar was in response to Mazeroski's home run, but Prince had no clue what had happened. As the Pirate players thundered in, an NBC production assistant pulled Mazeroski aside and directed him toward Prince. The interview lasted mere seconds. "Well Maz, how does it feel to be a member of the world champions?" Prince asked. "Great," Mazeroski responded. To which Prince replied with finality, "Congratulations," as he shooed the World Series hero away. It wasn't until hours later, Prince claimed, that he learned from his wife how the game had ended. On another occasion, Prince nearly missed the kickoff of a Penn State-TCU football game he was scheduled to broadcast. Prince—whose multi-colored sport coats reflected a questionable fashion sense—had taken a little longer than expected at a shoemaker's shop, where he was being custom-fitted for a pair of purple and white cowboy boots with the image of the TCU horned frog mascot stitched into them. Prince once noted, "Maybe I could have been a lawyer and made a couple hundred thousand dollars a year, but I wouldn't have had half as much fun."

Beneath all the lunacy and bizarre antics, Prince was an exceedingly caring man who displayed his generosity in ways large and small. At the behest of wealthy heiress Patricia Hillman, Prince co-founded the Allegheny Valley School for Exceptional Children, dedicated to helping severely retarded kids. Regis Champ, the school's president and CEO, estimated that Prince raised $4 million for the school over the years. "He donated money he made from speaking engagements. No one knows that. He'd tell them to send the money directly to us," Champ said. Moreover, Prince volunteered countless hands-on hours with students at the school. According to Champ, "Every Christmas afternoon he is out here spending the day with children who cannot go home. And our kids feel his love-nothing more excites them than to hear Bob Prince is on our campus." Prince co-founded the Hutchinson Cancer Fund and the Fred Hutchinson Award, named for the Cincinnati Reds manager who died of cancer in 1964. Prince helped to convince Pittsburgh-based corporations U.S. Steel, Alcoa, and PPG to provide at no charge the raw materials used in the construction of the award. Prince, along with Commissioner William Eckert, presented the first Hutch Award to Mickey Mantle during spring training in 1966. In November 1970, Prince led a contingent of major league players to Vietnam, where they visited American GIs and tried to stay out of range of rock-throwing baboons on Hontre Island. ("One of those apes was a left-hander. He could really throw," Prince joked).

Despite Prince's popularity, he began to clash with his bosses in the late 1960s after KDKA Radio, owned by Westinghouse Broadcasting, purchased the rights to Pirate broadcasts from Atlantic Richfield. Trouble began for Prince shortly thereafter. In 1969, Prince's partner of 12 seasons, Jim Woods, left the Pirate broadcast-

ing team following a salary dispute with Westinghouse executives. Soon, Pirate general manager Joe L. Brown began to closely monitor Prince's broadcasts, even passing notes to Prince or telephoning the broadcast booth when Prince and partner Nellie King, a Pirate pitcher from 1954-57, drifted too far away from the action. Brown also told Prince after the 1974 season that he was dissatisfied with his performance and that he needed to "sell" the team better (Pirate attendance languished in the mid 70s, despite consistently competitive teams). As the Pirates were planning to move from Forbes Field to Three Rivers Stadium in 1970, Prince helped to design a spacious broadcast booth at the new park, but unfortunately that decision backfired. By the mid 1970s, Westinghouse executives were bringing guests and clients into the booth during games. Sometimes they would try to talk to Prince or ask for autographs during the broadcasts. On more than one occasion, they committed the cardinal sin of cheering the opposing team. During a game in 1975, when the Westinghouse guests became too raucous, Prince blurted over the air, "Ladies and gentlemen, we've got some idiots in the box rooting for Chicago." On October 30, 1975, Westinghouse Broadcasting shocked Pirate fans by announcing that Prince would not return for a 29th year behind the microphone. He and popular sidekick King were fired. At the time, no major league broadcaster had ever spent more years with one team than Bob Prince.

Pirate fans went berserk. One fan summed up the feeling around Pittsburgh quite nicely, "I can't believe they'd do that to someone who gave so much for 20 [sic] years… As far as I'm concerned he was the Pittsburgh Pirates." A KDKA switchboard operator received more than 600 calls between 5:30 pm and 11:30 pm the night the firing were announced. She estimated 95 percent of the callers were pro-Prince. Pirate broadcast sponsors were miffed as well. Jim Ficco, an executive for the ad agency that handled the account for Ford Motors, a Pirate sponsor, said, "The dealers are upset. I'm personally upset. We're reevaluating our position. We have $700,000 earmarked for radio and television for Pirate games. Prince is our man." The Pittsburgh Brewing Company, a sponsor since 1957 and a minority broadcast rights holder, denied initial reports that it had voted in favor of the dismissals. Brewery president Lou Slais explained, "We have a one-third vote and Westinghouse has two-thirds." (This didn't stop one downtown Pittsburgh restaurant from boycotting Iron City, Pittsburgh Brewing Company's most popular beer). *Pittsburgh Post Gazette* sports editor Al Abrams noted, "Utterly ridiculous is the charge that Prince and King did not help being people to the ballpark. They shilled so much for the club on the airwaves, I tuned them out at least 100 times."

Prince admitted that Brown (echoing beliefs expressed two decades earlier by Branch Rickey) wanted Prince to ramble less and stick closer to the action on the field. But, "I never dreamed that meant, 'If you don't, you're out.'" He pleaded to remain with the Pirates. "It's the first time I've ever begged for anything. I asked for another chance. I even offered to write out a resignation for ill health of they would let me come back for '76." But regional director of Westinghouse Broadcasting, Ed Wallis, would hear nothing of it. Wallis, who became the public bogeyman in the firings, initially ducked requests for comment on the firings. But later he responded, "Club management and station management met with him (Prince) at the beginning of this year and summarized specifically all of our previous concerns. It became clear last season that the issues in dispute could not be reconciled; therefore, the contracts were not renewed." He told a Rotary Club luncheon that he was looking for a play-by-play man who could provide "accurate, consistent, uninterrupted accounts of the baseball game." Prince contended, "The only person who doesn't want me back is Ed Wallis. It's that simple." The level of acrimony on both sides suggests that somewhere along the line the disagreements between Prince and King and the Westinghouse executives had crossed the line from professional to personal. King claims that Wallis laughed when he reminded the executive that he needed the job to support his family. "It was almost like dealing with someone from *The Godfather*," according to King. Indeed, one person at Westinghouse claimed that Prince simply had gotten "too big for his britches."

A Pittsburgh radio station hastily organized a parade to honor Prince and King. The day prior to the parade was Election Day, and turnout was the lowest it had been in the city 35 years. Pittsburghers might have been apathetic about their government, but not about Bob Prince. A crowd estimated at 10,000 lined the streets of downtown Pittsburgh in a display that was part demonstration, part farewell, and part revival meeting. Fans carried signs-one reading "Bring back royalty to Pittsburgh-Prince and

King." Women frantically waved their babushkas. Local politicians were there. Pirate players, current and former, lent their support. Ford Motors donated cars for the parade and affixed signs to the side of each vehicle reading, "The Pittsburgh District of Ford Dealers Support Bob Prince and Nellie King." Prince and King rode atop a fire truck, with Prince brandishing a Green Weenie. At the conclusion of the 90-minute parade, the dignitaries gathered at Point State Park to address the crowd. Allegheny County Commissioner William Hunt told the throng, "200 years ago, I don't think there were this many people on this spot defending Fort Duquesne." Willie Stargell spoke, likening the firing of Prince to "the U.S. Steel building falling down." Stargell was joined on the speakers' platform by teammates Dave Giusti, Bruce Kison, Jim Rooker, and Al Oliver. "It's overwhelming," Prince said. "Maybe these people will get Nellie back, but Wallis won't change his mind about me." Wallis would change his mind about neither of them.

In retrospect, Prince's dismissal was symbolic of the end of an era of Pirate baseball. Roberto Clemente was killed in a plane crash on New Year's Eve, 1972. Pitcher Bob Moose was killed in a car accident in October 1976. Danny Murtaugh, hired to manage the Pirates four times between 1957 and 1976, also would die following the '76 season. Bill Virdon, a popular player and manager, was fired in 1973. King says, "This (Pittsburgh) is not a transient area. There are second and third generations. Prince would talk about oldtimers—guys without big names—and people here would know who they were. He left…it was like a death. I know it sounds corny—but it was real. There was a love affair here." Although the Pirates would win a World Series in 1979, the next quarter century of Pirate baseball would be marked by sagging attendance, drug scandals, frustrations, and futility. Pittsburgh's love affair with the Pirates would never be quite the same.

Prince did not handle the firing well. His wife Betty recalled that "The Gunner" sunk into a depression. "It took the life out of him," she said. "He retreated to the bedroom for three days right after. He had the drapes drawn in the bedroom and kept the door closed." Years later he would admit, "If I would have been Westinghouse, I would have fired Bob Prince, too." But some who knew Prince say he never completely got over it. Upon his death, veteran Pittsburgh columnist Bob Smizik observed, "He seemed to be on a steady ever-so-slight decline ever since KDKA ripped out his heart."

Prince's replacements in Pittsburgh were Milo Hamilton, who had been recently fired by the Atlanta Braves, and Lanny Frattare, who had been doing play-by-play for the Pirates' AAA team in Charlestown, West Virginia. They were fine broadcasters in their own right-Hamilton later won the Ford C. Frick Award (1992), and in 2003 Frattare matched Prince by completing his 28th season as a Pirate broadcaster-but they were very different from Prince. Although Hamilton and Frattare were well prepared and technically accurate in their description of the game, they were thoroughly lacking in the zany unpredictability that marked Prince and, before him, Rosey Rowswell. Pittsburgh fans did not respond well. "It was like competing with a ghost," Hamilton recalled. "Everything was 'Prince did this, Prince did that.'" He accused Prince of working behind the scenes to sabotage him. "His situation cost me a friend," said Hamilton. "Prince was incredibly bitter [and] he directed that bitterness at me. Bob had bad-mouthed me in every bar in Pittsburgh, and he set the entire media against me." In the end, the Pittsburgh fans and media basically ran Hamilton out of town. "When I came back in '79 for the final year of my contract, I knew that was it. No way was I going to extend that kind of living hell."

Frattare, on the other hand, idolizes Prince to the extent that even after nearly three decades he refuses to refer to himself as "The Voice of the Pirates." Frattare insists, "I could do this for 40 years, and Bob would still be the shining example of Pirates broadcasting and be the only true voice of the Pittsburgh Pirates. I don't want, in any way, my longevity to detract from Bob." In 1974 and 1975, Prince invited Frattare to join him in the booth for a late-season game and broadcast an inning of play-by-play. Even after his firing, Prince remained generous to Frattare. "Despite the fact that I was one of the guys that replaced Bob and Nellie, Bob was extremely helpful to me. He sat me down on a regular basis and talked to me about things that he believed in, gave me theories, gave me rules to follow as a Pirates broadcaster." Frattare also admits that Hamilton "took most of the shots," in those years following Prince's ouster, which eased some of the pressure that he felt replacing a local legend.

It wasn't long before Prince was rescued from the scrap heap. Within weeks of his dismissal from Pittsburgh, Prince agreed to join Gene Elston in the Houston Astros' broadcast booth. Elston believes Prince, though grateful for the opportunity, viewed Houston as a remote outpost and his new job as a step down. "I heard that he made comments about going down to where there were Indians and people riding around in covered wagons and all that stuff. It was like he thought, 'What's Bob Prince doing down here?'" Elston, who had been behind the microphone for the Astros since their inception in 1962, doesn't think Prince showed him proper respect initially. "I felt like he was testing me. I remember in our first broadcast he said, 'I'll bet you don't know who the third baseman was for the Cubs when they had the infield of Tinker-to-Evers-to-Chance.' I knew it was Harry Steinfeldt, and he was taken aback by that. I think he was very upset that I knew the answer."

Despite that awkward beginning, Prince and Elston worked reasonably well together, but Prince's work habits left something to be desired. "He would never show up until right before the pre-game show started-sometimes later than that," Elston recalled. "He was always at the Astrodome Club having a drink or two. Never did I see him really drunk or anything, but he would always walk over to the booth with a drink in his hand. We had a lady working in the booth who would always prepare his scorecard for him, so he would just come in, sit down, and do the game. That was every day." Moreover, Elston says, Astros' fans couldn't adjust to Prince's irreverent, rambling style. "He was not accepted here. He got a lot of complaints. When he was doing play-by-play he would put his feet up on the desk and would spend more time talking to me than watching the game. I knew he was a better broadcaster than that." Prince admitted his heart wasn't in it in Houston. "I hated it. My wife couldn't come down for family reasons [so] I was there all by myself." Prince and the Astros parted ways after that one season. "I liked the guy. He was an icon, an excellent broadcaster, but I didn't see it [in 1976]," said Elston. "I really did enjoy working with him, but it's something that I would never want to do again."

During that '76 season the Astros' organization allowed Prince to accept an offer from ABC Sports to join Warner Wolf and Bob Uecker on the primary broadcast team for the inaugural season of Monday Night Baseball. It proved to be a poor fit. Prince, long accustomed to a starring role in Pittsburgh, was reduced to a being a ringmaster on ABC, suppressing his own personality to provide the flamboyant Wolf and comedic Uecker (of whom Betty Prince remarked, "My Bob always thought he was a buffoon") with an opportunity to shine. Those familiar with Prince from his Pittsburgh days could tell he wasn't comfortable. "When I heard him on TV, he wasn't the same Bob Prince," said friend and longtime Dodger announcer Vin Scully. "He wasn't the same guy I knew. They stripped him of his personality, of all the things that made him special. Here they had the best, most colorful baseball announcer in the country and they took the life out of him." Prince agreed. "I never got to be Bob Prince," he said. "I had too many people talking in my ear, 'Do this. Do that.' And all they wanted us to do was talk, talk, talk-didn't matter what we said as long as we kept babbling." Critics didn't like what they heard. Too much talk, too much manufactured hype. Ratings were poor. Prince became one of the fall guys, canned, along with Wolf, prior to the start of ABC's coverage of the 1976 postseason. The most memorable moment of Prince's brief tenure at ABC came on June 7, 1976 as "The Gunner" returned to Pittsburgh's Three Rivers Stadium for the telecast of the Pirates' Monday night game against the Cincinnati Reds. Before the game he signed autographs, shook hands, and received food and a "Babushka Power" T-shirt from fans. In the third inning, when the scoreboard flashed a welcome to Prince, Uecker, and Wolf, Pirate fans took the opportunity to say thanks, serenading Prince with a minute and a half standing ovation. Bruce Kison stepped off the mound and the game came to a halt. Prince bowed several times and waved a babushka. Then he cried, telling viewers, "I have to apologize to Warner and Ueck and turn over my mic." Wolf said, "I've never seen anything like it."

For the final decade of his life, Prince remained a highly visible jack-of-all-trades on the Pittsburgh scene. After the 1976 season, he made an unsuccessful bid for the broadcast rights to Pirate games. The National Hockey League's Pittsburgh Penguins hired him in a public relations role and to broadcast some games. He did play-by-play for Carnegie-Mellon University football, hosted a Saturday morning sports talk show on a small network of radio stations in Pennsylvania and Ohio, and returned as sports director at the radio station where he had gotten

his start 40 years earlier, WJAS. Prince also continued his charitable work and remained a popular master of ceremonies and after-dinner speaker. In 1981, Prince, along with Pittsburgh-area native Stan Musial, former Pittsburgh Steeler Andy Russell and others, briefly considered forming a consortium to purchase the financially troubled Pirates. In 1983, he broadcast a select number of Pirate games on a local cable outlet, Home Sports Entertainment. He was happy to be back doing play-by-play for his beloved Pirates but conceded, "I have to be honest-it's not like daily radio, like the good old days. But you go on, you hang in there."

In 1985, Prince, a smoker, was diagnosed with mouth cancer. In early April he underwent surgery to remove a tumor located between his tongue and jaw. But even while he was on the operating table, movements were afoot to bring "The Gunner" back to the Pirate radio booth full-time. It was Frattare's idea, and the Pirates, looking for anything that could spark a rebirth of interest in their dormant franchise, were amenable. On April 18, Prince dragged himself from his hospital bed to attend a press conference at Three Rivers Stadium, where it was announced that he had signed a three-year contract with the Pirates. Prince was overcome with emotion, tearfully declaring, "Other than my family, you've given me back the only other thing I love in the world." Prince looked and sounded terrible. Worn down from radiation treatments, his speech was slow and weak. He had lost weight and wore a bandage on his neck to cover a wound created by a tracheotomy. Writers openly speculated whether Prince physically would be up to the task of broadcasting baseball again. *Pittsburgh Post-Gazette* columnist Tom McMillan wrote, "He may not pull it off...but he is going to try." Prince said, "They must have some faith in the Lord and me. They gave me three years." But even as he spoke, Prince was dying.

The 1985 season was a horrible one for the Pirates, perhaps one of the lowest points in the organization's history. The team, filled with washed-up veterans and bad attitudes, lost 104 games. Current and former Pirates including Stargell, Dave Parker, Bill Madlock, and John Milner had their names sullied that summer during the Pittsburgh drug trials. Attendance dipped below 800,000 for the second straight year and, with the franchise for sale, the Bucs were widely thought to be on their way out of Pittsburgh. But for one surreal night, "the good old days" returned. On May 3, 1985, Bob Prince returned to the Pirate radio booth. Prince took the microphone for the top of the fourth inning, with the Pirates leading the Los Angeles Dodgers 3-2. With Prince calling the action for the first time in 10 years and fans waving their Green Weenies, the usually inept Bucs exploded for a nine-run inning. "It was like a 21-gun salute," said Frattare. At the end of the fourth, the crowd turned toward the booth and gave Prince a standing ovation, chanting "Gun-ner, Gun-ner." In the fifth inning, Prince urged Pirate first baseman Jason Thompson, "Jason, now just park one into the seats and we'll have a little of everything." Thompson drove the next pitch over the right field wall for a two-run homer. The Pirates won the game 16-2, the Dodgers' worst loss in a decade. Prince flashed his old sense of humor, remarking about Pirate pitcher Mike Bielecki, "He's so good-looking even I like him," and calling Los Angeles outfielder Mike Marshall a "big donkey." But the broadcast obviously was an ordeal for Prince. His voice wasn't clear and he struggled to keep pace with the action on the field as plays unfolded. He only made it through two of his three scheduled innings. King concedes, "It was kind of sad hearing him that night. If you heard Bob Prince when he was good, you knew this wasn't the same…but you could hear the uniqueness that made you remember, that was so different from anything else you ever heard."

Prince return to the booth lasted just two more games. He became ill while sitting through a long rain delay and on May 20 returned to the hospital, suffering from dehydration and pneumonia in both lungs. He was moved to intensive care two days later and physicians stopped his radiation treatments. He eventually lapsed into a coma and died June 10, 1985 at the age of 68. He was survived by his wife Betty; his son Robert Prince, Jr.; his daughter Nancy; his brother Frederick; and three grandchildren. The announcement of his death came prior to a Pirate home game against the Cardinals. Frattare was crushed. "I really didn't feel like doing the game," he says. "I've asked him for so much advice throughout the years. Now, I can't ask him." On the air Frattare asked Joe L. Brown, back for a second tenure as Pirates' general manager, about Prince's firing. Brown admitted, "No question [it was] a flat-out mistake." *Pittsburgh Press* columnist Gene Collier wrote, "Bob Prince is Pittsburgh baseball. Bob Prince is dead. Therefore…" Prior to the game, the Pirates put Prince's picture on the scoreboard and asked for a moment of silence. As Collier put it, "Suddenly, silence had degrees."

In the aftermath of Prince's death, KDKA again faced criticism from some quarters, this time not for firing Prince, but for bringing him back when he was gravely ill. KDKA general manager Rick Starr denied that he had re-hired Prince to boost his station's ratings. "I've heard those ideas and they are entirely wrong. We didn't bring him back because we knew he was terminally ill and felt we should give him one last moment in the sun, either. We brought him back because-to put it frankly-Pittsburgh doesn't like the Pirates and we stand a good chance of losing the team."

Nearly 800 people attended Prince's memorial service in suburban Pittsburgh. Among the mourners were team owners John and Dan Galbreath, Steelers' owner Art Rooney, most of the Pirates' front office, and many former players. Reverend Laird Stuart eulogized Prince as "no saint" but a man with "a heart as big as center field." Stuart told mourners about Prince teaching a lesson about David and Goliath to Sunday school classes. In Prince's version, David was an unheralded rookie pitcher and Goliath was a huge, fearsome slugger. "Heaven knows how many kids went through our church school and had that old story come to life, indelibly etched in their minds forever because of the way Bob told it," Stuart said.

The National Baseball Hall of Fame honored Prince with the Ford C. Frick Award in 1986, enshrining "The Gunner" in the Scribes and Mikemen's Wing of the Hall's Library. In Pittsburgh, Prince's impact is still felt, years after his death. In 1999, Prince was named posthumous winner of the "Pride of the Pirates" award, which recognizes members of the Pirate organization who demonstrate sportsmanship, dedication, and outstanding character during a lifetime of service. Pittsburgh's Catholic Youth Association presents a Bob Prince Award annually. On May 21, 2003, Bob Prince Talking Bobblehead Night attracted over 35,000 to PNC Park. For fans, Prince remains a link to a cherished past that is sacred in our memories and imaginations, a time when life seemed simpler, the city of Pittsburgh was thriving, and the Pirates were atop the baseball world.

Sources

Mickey Bergstein. *Penn State Sports Stories and More.* (Harrisburg, Pa., Seitz & Seitz, Inc., 1998)

Gene Elston telephone interview with author on February 12, 2004.

Bruce Markusen. *Roberto Clemente: The Great One* (Champaign IL: Sports Publishing, LLC, 2001)

New York Newsday (online edition), "Ex-Knicks Trainer Whelan Dies at 84," January 5, 2004.

New York Times April 3, 1966, p. 52.

Jim O'Brien. *We Had 'Em All the Way.* (Pittsburgh, James P. O'Brien Publishing, 1998)

Andrew O'Toole. *Branch Rickey in Pittsburgh.* (Jefferson, N. C., and London, McFarland & Company, Inc., 2000)

Pittsburgh Post-Gazette, October 31, 1975, 1, 4, 14; November 1, 1975, 6; November 4, 1975, 12; November 5, 1975, 1, 7; November 6, 1975, 13; June 8, 1976, 16; April 19, 1985, 29, 31; May 4, 1985, 19, 21; June 11, 1985, 1, 16, 28, 30; June 14, 1985, 13; April 6, 1999, D6.

Pittsburgh Press, October 31, 1975, A1, A8; June 11, 1985, A1, A6, C1, C2; June 17, 1985, D1, D4; June 17, 1985, D1, D2, D4.

Pittsburgh Tribune Review (online edition), "Frattare Matches Prince for Longevity," Jim Rodenbush, August 31, 2003.

Curt Smith. *Voices of the Game.* (South Bend, Ind., Diamond Communications, Inc., 1987)

The Sporting News, February 1, 1969, 14; October 24, 1970, 22; January 9, 1971, 44; October 30, 1971, 25; June 24, 1985, 53.

Sports Illustrated, September 13, 1965, 84; August 15, 1966, 44.

Time, August 12, 1966, 54.

The Wall Street Journal, May 1, 1968, 1, 23.

Washington Post, July 26, 1966, B2; June 13, 1975, D1; July 4, 1975, B1.

Jim Woods

By Curt Smith

FROM 1953 THROUGH 1956, Jim Woods was Mel Allen's and Red Barber's partner on New York Yankees radio/TV. One day, eying Woods' slight overbite and gray buzz cut, Enos Slaughter jibed, "I've seen better heads on a possum." In 1958 Jim moved to Pittsburgh, where announcer Bob Prince's wife called Woods' spouse "Mrs. Possum." In 1974-78 the Red Sox' Poss and Ned Martin bagged New England: Ned, wry and spry; Jim, booming like a barge. Who was better –Woods with Prince, or Martin? Did any trio top Jim, Mel, and Red? "It's no coincidence," said Allen. The common tie was Poss.

A 1960s Avis ad blared, "We're number two. We try harder." In a 31-year career, Woods was number two to Allen, Barber, Russ Hodges, Jack Buck, Monte Moore, Prince, and Martin: "baseball's peripatetic 'second' announcer' who has worked for a quarter of the clubs in the majors," wrote William Leggett. Being top gun seldom crossed Possum's mind. Drinking and betting at the flats and harness track did. "Having fun, Jim wanted *not* to try harder," Ned mused. He didn't have to, as 1960 attests.

From 1958 to 1969 you could walk down a street in Oil City and Wheeling and Titusville and hear perhaps baseball's all-time greatest booth. A fine play sparked Bob's "How sweet it is!" Woods used a line he later took to Boston. "There are a reported fifteen thousand people at the game. If that's true, then at least twelve thousand of them are disguised as empty seats."

Some thought Poss and Prince each a maniac. Both were maniacally riveting. Like Bogart and Bacall or Abbott and Costello, one still denotes the other.

The son of Army Colonel F.A. Prince, Bob was raised at six posts and 14 or 15 schools. Later the Army brat flunked out of four universities, got a B.A. at Oklahoma, and entered Harvard Law. In 1940 Prince, 24, read about a judge who frequented a burlesque house. One night papa saw Bob, with a stripper, in a newsreel on the jitterbug. "You're wasting my money," *pere* phoned from Alabama, yanking *fils* from school. "Here's $2,000. Go make a living." Prince had another aim.

Bob's unwritten memoir read *I Should Have Never Danced with the Stripper.* He should have never been scarred by a polo mallet, kicked in a rodeo, or jailed for vagrancy—but was. A pattern emerged, worthy of diffident respect. "Anything short of murder," he said, "I've been there"—like Woods, later naming Bob the Gunner after the husband of a woman Prince was talking to in a bar pulled a gun.

From Harvard, Prince moved to his grandmother's home in Zelienople, near Pittsburgh—"the only town where I could find a place to live." Upset, Dad phoned again: "Throw that bum out of the house." At 25 the vagabond finally settled on a career. "In the Army I'd played golf, polo, fenced. All I'd been trained to do was loaf. Broadcasting was the next easiest thing."

By day Prince sold insurance. At night he began "[Walter] Winchellizing" on radio. Once Woods charged that boxer Billy Conn ducked opponents. The next week Conn hit him in the gut. "I can't fight you," said Bob, the ex-college diver, "but I'll swim you." Conn later asked, "What would have happened if we'd fought in the pool?" Prince: "I'd have drowned you." Instead, he profited from a man immersed in God.

In 1948, Bucs mikeman Jack Craddock resigned to preach at revival meetings. The Gunner replaced him as lead Voice Rosey Rowswell's aide. "We were bad, and Rosey'd trip the light fantastic," said Bob, asking why. Rowswell: "Sponsors deserve fans, and fans deserve a show. Balls and strikes alone give 'em neither." In an inning, he might segue from U.S. Steel stock to poetry to a favorite song—what Prince called a "Rosey Ramble," learning well.

"Oh, by the way," Bob would footnote, "Clemente grounded out, Stuart flied out, and that's the inning." He was partisan: "Come on, we need a run." Unpredictable: Bob won a bet by waltzing from center field to home plate in stockings, pumps, neon jacket, bow tie, and Bermuda shorts. Controversial: "On purpose," Prince admitted. "I'd do anything to build my reputation."

Aging, Rosey often fell asleep as Bob re-created by ticker, Prince waking him in studio if the Bucs took the lead. At Forbes Field, he pointed to a base or position "to give Rosey some idea of the ball." From 1950 to 1957 the Pirates finished last or next to last. "Here's to the Rosey Ramble," Prince said after his mentor's death in 1955. Bob's riposte was "Gunner's Gallop"—anything but the game.

Woods's early life was as picaresque as Prince's: born 1916; Kansas City Blues mascot at 4; team batboy at 8; high school, local radio score reader; freshman dropout, University of Missouri.

Dad: "Son, I hate you leaving school."

Jim: "You won't when I get to Yankee Stadium."

In 1935 the ex-journalism major joined KGLO in Mason City, Iowa—*The Music Man*'s "River City." By 1939 he had replaced Ronald Reagan, dealing Big Ten football for Hollywood: Poss later crowing, "Nothing like topping a prez!" Reagan's voice soothed, like a compress. Woods's slapped you in the face. From 1942 to 1945, he rode the Navy War Bond circuit with actors Farley Granger, Dennis Day, and Victor Mature. By 1948, Poss succeeded Ernie Harwell at Triple-A Atlanta when the Georgian left for Brooklyn.

In 1949 Woods's Crackers became the first team to air an entire home year of television. Four years later a voice phoned topping even Jim's whiskied baritone. "Mel asks me to New York. I walk into his suite, and he's on the phone talking to Joe DiMaggio about Marilyn Monroe." Poss knew then he was in the bigs. In 1953 actor Joe E. Brown was to have succeeded DiMag on Yanks pre/post-game TV and air several innings. "Guess Brown should have stuck to film," Allen said. Replacing him, Woods stuck to ball.

One day Possum was at Toots Shor's restaurant bar, near Yanks and Dodgers owners Dan Topping and Walter O'Malley, respectively, when Brooklyn's boss began ripping his announcer. "I hate the son of a bitch," he said of Barber. Also gassed, Topping reciprocated: "I can't stand Mel." Amazed, Woods heard "the heads of baseball's biggest teams trashing sportscasting's then-biggest names." O'Malley raised his glass. "I'll trade you the SOB." Dan replied, "I'll give you Allen." Next day, "*sans* booze," they reneged.

The 1953 Yankees drew 1,537,811, down half a million since 1950. One cause was TV's growth, another Allen's sheen. Woods respected, but feared, Mel, especially his snapping fingers when something popped a cork. After Poss said Mickey Mantle "foul(ed) a ball on top," fingers snapped. "What'd I do?" Jim said. Allen: "On top of what?" Woods: "The roof." Mel: "Then say the roof and complete your sentence." Jim never forgot the tutorial. "I learned to take nothing for granted and not to fear dead air, surprising for a guy famed for talking."

Woods's first-year team won a fifth straight World Series. Stranger than fiction: The sole Yankee to play every pre-1956 Series against Brooklyn was born there. That August general manager George Weiss told shortstop Phil Rizzuto, "We've got a chance to get Slaughter. What do you think?" Scooter took cyanide, saying, "Boy, getting him would be a help." Enos replaced Rizzuto on the roster. Unemployed, Phil charmed sponsor Ballantine Beer, which told Weiss to put him in the booth. Odd man out, Woods was summoned to the GM's office. "Jim," George groped, "I have to do something I've never done—fire someone without cause."

Stunned—"It's a funny business. Things happen"— Woods joined the Giants and NBC's *Major League Baseball*. In 1957 he did NBC's first weekly baseball: a Brooklyn-Milwaukee exhibition. When the Giants moved to San Francisco, "I hoped to go, but they wanted someone local" to help Hodges. Instead, Poss joined Pittsburgh — his third team in as many years — "I needed a home, and here it was." Straightway he and Gunner seared sameness the way a laser cuts dead cells. "Everybody told me, 'Prince is out of control, you'll never get along,' but I decided to try him on for size."

From the start baseball's Ringling Brothers gilded 50,000-watt flagship KDKA with a pencil and scorecard. "That was it," said Bob. "We'd do play-by-play — or tap dance if the game stunk." On the last out Jim turned off his mike. "Enough of that! *Booze!*" The Bucs number two's *joie de vivre* also applied to number one.

By 1958 the Pirates led the major leagues in percentage of area radio/TV sets in use. It was easy to grasp why. Once what Woods called "the ugliest woman I ever saw" crashed the press box, barking "I want to see f___ing [Cubs Voice Jack] Brickhouse!"

A writer fingered Bob: "There, *that's* Brickhouse."

"Are you f___ing Brickhouse?" she bellowed. The network carried every word.

Convulsed, Woods watched her leave. "Gunner, if you think *that* one was ugly, look at the broad she's sitting with!" Bucs' G.M. Joe L. Brown phoned: "You can't call women *broads* on the air." Jim countered: "*Broad* is the only thing you *could.*"

Another game Prince spied "a broad" roaming an aisle. "Poss, check that one out in black!" he howled. You're on the air, Woods cautioned. "Geez," Bob replied, "when I think what I *coulda'* said!"

One rainy Friday NBC's Ken Coleman, in Pittsburgh for a Saturday game, heard Prince confess, " 'Poss, I wish they'd call the game so I could get home and watch that John Wayne Western.' So different than what I knew." Once Bob ribbed some Bucs about baseball being sedentary, making Gene Freese say, "Here's $20 you can't dive into this [hotel] pool." Later Woods recalled Prince clearing 12 feet of concrete from his third-floor room, asking "How'd your act check out now?" Gunner: "One way to find out," diving from the ledge.

Poss's play-by-play boasted similar *sangfroid.* "Clemente is on the move and runs it down, one-handed! A typical

Roberto catch!" he bayed. "Mr. Mays is out on a tremendous play! Usually he *makes* a tremendous play." Eddie Mathews, Woods noted, had said, "I hate your forkball pitcher" — Elroy Face. Don Hoak's "battle cry was, 'Boys, you've gotta keep driving' " — the 1960 Bucs driving to their first world title since 1925. "The Pirates clinch [the pennant]!" Poss growled on September 25 as Chicago beat second-place St. Louis. Prince and Allen telecast the World Series on NBC, though baseball banned local radio and TV — thus, Woods. Undeterred, he and Gunner later re-created Game Seven.

"The biggest ballgame ever played in the history of this city" packed 36,683 "into this old ball orchard," Poss began. The Yankees' lineup listed "glue-gloved" Clete Boyer; the Bucs', "the great Roberto," shortstop "Richard Morrow Groat," and "in a mild surprise, at first, Rocky Nelson," who stunned with a first-inning homer. Behind 4-0, Bill Skowron homered, Woods "never figuring out" why the pinstriped righty slugger was a left-footed kicker at Purdue. A sixth-inning four-spot gave the Bombers a 5-4 edge. "Yankee power has asserted itself, and you can feel the gloom."

In the top of the eighth, New York swelled its lead to 7-4. Leading off the bottom, Gino Cimoli singled. Bill Virdon then lanced a "high chopping ball down to [shortstop] Tony — hits him! The ball is down, and so is Kubek!" — the ball striking him in the larynx, said Woods. "Bob, your description of the Forbes Field infield ["alabaster plaster"] again comes into play!" As Kubek traveled to the hospital, Groat "hit a line drive, left field, base hit," Cimoli scoring: 7-5.

Each bullpen "had been the busiest place all day," said Possum. On cue, Jim Coates, his team nickname Crazy, replaced Bobby Shantz. Bob Skinner's bunt advanced the runners: "The tying run now in scoring position." Nelson popped to right. With two out, "It all rides now with Roberto Clemente," who topped "a high bounding ball to the right of Skowron! Over, and got it. *Nobody to throw to!* Coates did not come to cover! ... Maybe that's why they call him Crazy!" — Yanks, 7-6. Ex-pinstripe Hal Smith then worked a 2-2 count: "Long drive — deep left field!" Poss said. "Back goes Berra! It's gone, baby, and the Pirates lead, 9 to 7! *I don't believe it!*" The radio seemed to quiver.

Bobby Richardson and Long reached to start the ninth: the ballgame "riotous," said Prince, again voicing. Mantle singled: 9-8. Next, Berra smacked "a hot smash down to first, backhanded by Rocky Nelson. Steps on first. And Mantle slides back into first base, and the Yankees score the tying run! Holy Toledo! What a mishmash of a play!" At 3:36, Bill Mazeroski swung at Ralph Terry's last-of-the-inning slider. "There goes a long drive hit deep to left field!" said Gunner. "Going back is Yogi Berra! Going back! You can kiss it good-bye!" No smooch was ever lovelier.

"How did we do it, Possum? How did we do it?" Prince said finally, din all around. Woods didn't know—only that "I'm looking at the wildest thing since I was on Hollywood Boulevard the night World War II ended." How to top the topper? The Bucs spent the next decade trying.

"Controversial on purpose," Prince had defined his style. In 1966 Pirates Danny Whelan held a wiener painted green. "There," jibed Bob, "is a [TV] picture of a grown man pointing a green weenie at Lee May." May popped up. Trucks soon put the Weenie on their aerial. In Calcutta an Indian fakir played a pipe. The Weenie rose from his wicker basket. At Forbes, Prince once day said on-air, "Let's put the Green Weenie on [Don] Drysdale!" A roar commenced. Big D stood, sneering, umpire Ed Vargo finally ordering him to throw. Big D: "How can I pitch with these nuts going crazy and that skinny bastard up in the booth?" Vargo: "I don't know, but pitch." The batter tripled. Leaving, Don shook his fist. The Pirates then flew to San Francisco via Dallas, where Bob inadvertently mentioned the word "bomb" to a flight attendant, who told the captain, who called the FBI. Apprehended, Gunner was released after the Bucs plane had left, "finally getting to 'Frisco" after 30 hours without sleep, he said. Impressed, the Black Maxers—a small group of Pirates fixated by World War I flying gear—named Bob "official bombardier."

Would Prince ever settle down? "I am, or at least my wife thinks it's time I did."

Sports Illustrated described him as "shaped so distinctly in his mold that every listener feels he knows him"—like Woods. In 1968, a KDKA Westinghouse Company lawyer told them to sign "contracts so I can take them back to the office."

Bob: "Ready?"

Jim: "Whenever you are."

Each tore the paper. "There," Gunner said. "Take *those* back to your boss."

In the late 1960s, buying radio rights from Atlantic-Richfield Co., Westinghouse increasingly accused Poss and Prince of putting show-biz above seminar. In 1969 it spurned Woods's pay raise—"a pissing contest with the station," said Prince. "They and Poss were about $1,200 apart." For a decade, Jim had felt shortchanged. "So when an offer for more came from St. Louis, I jumped." In one sense, he regretted it. In another, he left in the nick of time.

Westinghouse began giving Gunner less promotion, less pre/post-game time, and more clients in the booth. "Some were bombed," Prince said. "You could hear 'em in Cleveland." He turned off a microphone, said, "Shut up," was called a "m_____-f_____," opened the mike, and said, "Westinghouse is making it impossible to do my job." At the same time, Woods said that St. Louis was making it impossible to do his.

"Great baseball city, my ass," Poss recalled. "The front office, [No. 1 Voice] Buck's ego, how you were afraid to smile." He left for Oakland, where the A's won the 1972 and '73 World Series. In November 1973 owner Charles O. Finley said that he liked homers more than Woods. "I was loyal," said Poss, "but Finley loved the Midwest style where you scream at a foul. He said, 'Jim, you're a great announcer when something happens, but when nothing is going on you're not.'"

Weiss, St. Louis, Finley: Woods pined for Pittsburgh. Instead, he signed with Boston in early 1974. That same morning, the phone rang. "I've thought this over," said Finley, "and I'd like you to come back."

"Charlie," Jim said, "I've obligated myself to the Red Sox for the next two years."

"S___," Charlie snapped, "everybody knows those contracts aren't worth the paper they're written on."

"I'm tied up! I'm not coming back," Woods said, arriving in Boston knowing that "Sox fans like it toned down. If I did a Prince I'd have been run out of town." Before long he *won* the town, noting "a couple of fans waving a Yankees banner—their parents must have raised some pretty foolish children." Ned Martin "reminded us that baseball is a game of wit and intelligence. Woods kept alive our sense of wonder," wrote novelist Robert B. Parker. "Between them they were perfect." He once was describing Pittsburgh.

Power can corrupt. Popularity can confuse. "Bob thought he had the sponsors and team behind him," said a Woods successor, Nellie King. In October 1975 Westinghouse sacked Prince, the Astros and ABC's 1976 *Monday Night Baseball* soon hiring him. That spring Bob told Woods, "I wouldn't say this to anyone else, but I'm worried," having never called a network series. Said Poss: "You can't *do* on ABC what you've done in Pittsburgh." Gunner bombed, retrieving baseball only in the '80s. "It's just cable TV, not as many homes. But you hang in there." Woods already had.

At Fenway Park, Poss found his next-to-Prince most pitch-perfect pal. A Philadelphian, Martin entered Duke University, joined the Marines, stormed Iwo Jima, then returned to Duke, a not-so-young man in a hurry, to major in English, read Wolfe and Hemingway, and—what? He tried advertising, publishing, and broadcasting, joining the Red Sox in 1961. Ned read poetry like Allen Ginsberg's, had politics like John Wayne's, and treated the Sox workforce like royalty. One moment he called Ted Williams "Big Guy." The next evoked Shakespeare: "Good night, sweet prince." His amalgam included a Woods-like disdain for radio jack, sham, and fools.

Ned and Poss completed each other's sentences, communing on-air by "a hand gesture, shrug, raised eyebrow," wrote the *Boston Globe*'s Bill Griffith. After a game "broadcasters, writers, and the coaching staff [gathered] during which Martin and Woods would be spellbinding with their baseball tales." Woods called Ned "Nedley." Martin ribbed Poss about his and Prince's booth as bar—"Did Budweiser sponsor you, or did you sponsor Budweiser?" Like Prince's, Martin's synergy with Poss wowed.

In 1975. Woods passed a final-day baton: "Now Ned Martin will steer our ship with all colors flying safely into port."

"What *are* our colors, Mr. [Fletcher] Christian?" Ned said, referencing *Mutiny on the Bounty*.

"Well, they ain't [Finley's] green and gold, I'll tell you," Poss said.

Martin: "Probably red, white, and blue."

Sports Illustrated termed them "the best day-in, day-out announcers covering the American League"—not unlike 1958-69's N.L. Poss/Prince. One moment Possum was gently manic: "[In] Baltimore … the Sox will play Brooksie-Baby and his merry mates." Another hailed Carlton Fisk conquering a broken wrist. "It is gone—his first home run of the year! And look at him jump and dance! He's the happiest guy in Massachusetts!" Jim froze anguish, too. In 1978 Bucky Dent's homer pivoted the Boston-New York A.L. playoff game. "It is gone!" Poss said. "Suddenly, the whole thing is turned around!"

Before long, so was Woods.

In Pittsburgh, Westinghouse had been clueless about what it had. Equally inept Sox flagship WMEX (later WITS) began a pregame-show, *during*-inning ad blitz, and home run inning to pay a record radio rights pact. "It demeaned the product," Ned said, "hurt the game." More cash demanded VIP schmoozing, which he and Poss loathed. In 1978 Mariner Communications bought the station, new head Joe Scallan pining to transform Red Sox Nation.

"I'm going to change listening habits," he informed Woods, incredulous. "What you don't know is that I could replace you and Ned with King Kong and Donald Duck and not lose one listener."

"Well, Joe," said Possum, "I don't know about King Kong, but I do believe that Donald is under contract [to Walt Disney-owned theme parks] in Anaheim and Orlando."

Like Westinghouse a decade earlier, WITS wanted company men, not a listener's good company. "Hit parties, ooze oil," Woods said. "I couldn't, nor would Ned," refusing to prostitute. In late 1978 the flagship fired each, creating "such an uproar," wrote the *Globe*, "that the fellow who fired them [Scallan] was soon gone as well."

Moving to USA Network's 1979-82 Thursday *Game of the Week*, Woods then retired, having keyed what Boston's Shaun L. Kelly called "a radio duo, unmatched, before or since, by anybody"—save Pittsburgh. Wrote the *Globe's* Bob Ryan: "You know what's sad? … The people who ruled over them and signed their paychecks had no idea how … special Martin and Woods were"—think Poss and Prince.

Too late, KDKA rehired Gunner in 1985. "Other than my family, you're giving me back the only thing I love." Prince had cancer surgery, did a game, and got lung dehydration and pneumonia. "It is a sad morning," Tom McMillan wrote June 11. "A piece of us is missing. Bob Prince is dead." Martin did 1979-92 Red Sox TV, was axed again, retired to Virginia, and had a heart attack in 2002.

Woods's last stop began on February 20, 1988, at 71, of cancer. He was survived by his wife, Audrey. "Leave it to Jim," said a friend. "He had to go to heaven to find a better friend than Ned or Prince." Not trying harder, baseball's ultimate number two became, in a Latin phrase, *primus inter pares*—first among equals. Forget dancing with a stripper. From 1958 to 1969, Prince danced with an Astaire.

Sources

Material, including quotes, is derived from Curt Smith's books *Voices of The Game, Voices of Summer, The Voice,* and *A Talk in the Park* (in order: Simon & Schuster 1992, Carroll & Graf 2005, The Lyons Press 2007, and Potomac Books 2011).

Forbes Field

By Curt Smith

Baseball links geography, and rivalry. In 1908 Philadelphia constructed the sport's first concrete and steel double-decked field—Shibe Park. Three hundred miles to the west the Phillies' main foe turned green. That fall Pirates owner Barney Dreyfuss began a search for an idyll that "will make people forget about Shibe," he told friend and business baron Andrew Carnegie.

Since 1892 the Bucs had inhabited 16,000-seat Exposition Park II. Dreyfuss wanted a larger park in Pittsburgh's future Oakland-Schenley section, three miles from the business district. "There was nothing there but a livery stable and a hot house, with a few cows grazing over the countryside," he said. "A ravine ran through the property [ultimately, right field]. The first thing necessary to make it suitable for baseball was to level off the entire field."

Critics panned downtown's snub. Oakland's Orchard! Dreyfuss's Folly! Barney smiled. His park would be expandable, accessible by trolley, and far from the smog of mills. Ultimately, the Pirates' hull conjured a soda fountain, stick dams, and unlocked homes. "You had the smell of grass, could park six blocks away, take a walk through the neighborhood," said Bucs 1948-75 announcer Bob Prince. "The House of Thrills it was, and in memory still is."

In 1909 the ravine was filled and building begun on the park named for John Forbes, a British general in the French and Indian War who bivouacked troops in Oakland, captured Fort Duquesne in a crucial battle, and renamed it Fort Pitt. "We shape our buildings," Churchill said. "Thereafter, they shape us." Racetrack architect Charles Leavitt shaped a vast lawn, irregular shape, and sun-baked infield where players despaired of safety and longevity.

Fans mill outside Forbes Field, the ballpark in Pittsburgh's Oakland neighborhood (1909 to 1971).

Forbes Field rose at the junction of Bigelow Boulevard, Joncaire Street, the Cathedral of Learning, and (General Henry) Bouquet Street, after a Swiss soldier who helped the British. Later, it was filled by an early-1900s melting pot—Slavs, Poles, Italians, Germans—who trooped through southwest Pennsylvania to the flatlands of the Middle West.

Thousands remained in Pittsburgh among hills and rivers that split the forest like aorta through the heart. The Roman Quintilian wrote, "It is feeling … that makes us eloquent." Forbes Field's feeling soon became that of pleasance and pioneer.

Men worked double shifts to open it on schedule. On June 30, 1909, a crowd of 30,388 swamped the 25,000-seat park. Thousands stood behind a rope barrier to watch the Cubs win, 3-2. Dreyfuss hymned I told you so. "The formal opening of Forbes Field … was an historic event," the 1910 *Reach Baseball Guide* wrote: "Words must fail to picture in the mind's eye adequately the splendors of the magnificent pile President Dreyfuss erected as a tribute to the national game, a beneficence to Pittsburgh and an enduring monument to himself. For architectural beauty, imposing size, solid construction, and public comfort and convenience, it has not its superior in the world."

Behind the plate, player and umpire clubhouses underlay the grandstand. Right field abutted Schenley Park. Two decks extended from beyond first base to the left-field line, left and center seats rimming a 12-foot wooden fence. Distances were pitcher-friendly—left to right, 360, 442, flagpole 462, and 376 feet—as Forbes' first year showed. The '09ers went 110-42, had a 2.07 earned-run average, and beat

Detroit in the World Series, Forbes luring "more [in three games] than the entire Series of '07 or '08," said future *Pittsburgh Press* writer Les Biederman. The yard presaged a franchise more atypical than most. Once two Pirates led off base, the day so dark Christy Mathewson had to approach the catcher to see his signs. A batter lined to right-center, lightning hitting the ball like a scene from *The Natural.* Red Murray leapt to make a barehand catch. DeMille could not have staged it better.

No one threw a no-hitter in Forbes' 4,728-game history. By contrast, unassisted triple plays seemed as common as a cold. In 1925 Pirates shortstop Glenn Wright caught Jim Bottomley's liner, stepped on second base to double Jimmy Cooney, and tagged Rogers Hornsby before the Rajah could retouch first. Wright encored as a Cub two years later. "For the unusual, go to Forbes," a saying went. "The impossible, go twice." In 1890 Exposition Park I had hosted baseball's first tripleheader. Thirty years later Forbes reprised its last three-for-the-price-of-one. "Three teams in each league got money from the Series pool, so the Bucs and Reds met to decide third place," Biederman said. Cincinnati won, 13-4 and 7-3. "The Bucs then lost a meaningless [6-0] third game. The age was a stickler for rules." In 1912 Chief Wilson hit a still-major-league record 36 triples. Some parks aid homers. Forbes spurred average, defense, and speed.

In 1925, Dreyfuss grooved a lollipop to lefties: Two pavilion decks shrank right field to 300 feet. Pitching countered in 1932: A 14½-foot in-play screen topped right field's 9½-foot concrete wall. Left waxed from 360 to 365. Center field and the flagpole waned to 435 and 457. The backstop was a big-league-high 100 feet from home plate. In 1923 the batting cage moved from behind it to left-center field: in play like the flagpole bottom and light tower cages in left-center, center, and right-center field.

Cars and trucks were repainted and sold under the left-field seats. Said 1921-27 Pirate Kiki Cuyler: "Size was just one thing that made Forbes special.

Exemple gratia: The Pirates were the first to use a tarpaulin (1906); put padding on the outfield wall (1930s); host a night All-Star and World Series game (1944 and 1971, respectively); wear knit uniforms (1970); and broadcast on radio (August 5, 1921, on America's first station, KDKA, Pittsburgh. Pirates 8, Phillies 5). Announcer Harold Arlin, 26, used a telephone as microphone, sat behind the screen, and chatted as though his audience were sitting around a pot-bellied stove.

Westinghouse-owned KDKA had debuted on Election Night 1920. "We were looking for programming," Arlin said, "so I went to Forbes and set up shop." Often the transmitter failed, or the crowd silenced him. "We didn't know whether we'd talk into a total vacuum or whether somebody would hear us."

Like a centerfold, TV leaves little to fantasy. Early radio left all. Fancy retail stores mounted sidewalk speakers. Streets filled with play-by-play, like shopping malls with Muzak. One day Arlin even pinch-spoke for the Sultan of Swat, Babe Ruth, scheduled to read a speech on KDKA.

"He was going on my show," Harold said. "I introduce him and this big, garrulous guy—he can't say a word."

"Babe Ruth froze?" a reporter said.

"Mute," he jabbed. "I read his script on air and now *I'm* Ruth as Babe tries to compose himself, smoking and leaning against the wall. You know something? We pull it off. I sign off and Babe hasn't made a sound."

Forbes' real sound of the 1920s was the uncorking of champagne.

Honus Wagner retired three years before KDKA debuted. Arlin's Bucs were still alight with stars. Pie Traynor batted .320 and was a 1920-37 palatine at third base. A writer mused: "So and so doubled down the left-field line, and Traynor threw him out." Ten times Max Carey led the NL in stolen bases. In 1925 Cuyler hit .357. By then, Forbes Field held 41,000 seats, Dreyfuss needing them that fall. The World Series ricocheted. Washington led three games to one; Pittsburgh won twice; then Walter Johnson yielded 15 hits in the fall classic final. "He might have survived even that," said Traynor, "if his [Senators] defense hadn't cracked." Roger Peckinpaugh's eighth-inning homer gave D.C. a 7-6 lead. Some recall the AL MVP's two late-inning errors, tying the score. Others remember Cuyler fouling off pitch after pitch, then doubling to right field to score the last two runs. Pittsburgh won, 9-7, its first title since 1909 and last till 1960. "It's been a long time coming," sang Crosby, Stills, Nash, and Young. Bill Mazeroski would be a long time gone.

About this time French Marshal Ferdinand Foch visited the Grand Canyon, noting, " What a marvelous place to drop one's mother-in-law." Forbes was a fine place to drop Cooperstown's sole brothers. Lloyd Waner—5-foot-8½-inch Little Poison—hit .355. Big Poison—brother Paul—led the league in average (.380), RBIs (131), and four other categories. The rightness of things inspired—Pittsburgh in the Series!—except its foil was as great a team as ever lived. The Yankees hit .307, clinched on Labor Day, and outhomered the Bucs, 158-54. Their Classic began on October 5. After a 10 a.m. workout, "Traynor and the Waner brothers and other Pirates went into the stands to look us over," said Yankees manager Miller Huggins. "I thought I'd give them something to see," telling practice pitcher Waite Hoyt to throw down the middle. Earle Combs and Bob Meusel tattooed Forbes' power alleys. Ruth and Gehrig bombed Schenley Park, presaging the Yankees' four-game sweep.

The *Pittsburgh Press* styled the 1930s Bucs "L. Waner, P. Waner, Vaughan [Arky's .385 leading the 1935 NL], and Traynor." In 1930-39 and 1942-46, Forbes also hosted the Pittsburgh Crawfords' and Homestead Grays' Josh Gibson—"The Black Babe Ruth"—who anchored a rare two-league doubleheader: Pirates-Phils and Negro East-West League Grays-Philadelphia Hilldales. On May 25, 1935, the real Ruth hit his last three homers—at Forbes. Said Guy Bush, yielding No. 714: "Leave it to Babe to [be first to] clear the [86-foot-high right-field] roof." Only 16 homers did, five by Willie Stargell. Staying inside the park: Chuck Klein's four homers in a 10-inning game, the Bucs taking Forbes' 1940 night debut, and traded-to-Boston P. Waner's hit number 3,000 off the Pirates' Rip Sewell.

In 1938, Pittsburgh finished two games behind the Cubs. "Dreyfuss had died in 1932," said Biederman. "His son-in-law, [president] Bill Benswanger, was sure they were going to make the Series. So he ordered a new deck of seats [Crow's Nest] built on the grandstand roof [also, a press box with baseball's first elevator]." A visitor could leave through an exit gate in right-center field. Nearby the Pirates erected a bronze and granite Dreyfuss statue. In 1943 it was joined by a wooden U.S. Marine, 32 feet high by 15 feet wide at his feet, standing at parade rest. "He was there to salute our World War II effort," said

Prince. "Maybe the most bizarre in-play object in baseball history."

Forbes soon added an *objet d'art:* a brick and ivied wall from right-center field to the left-field line. In left, a 27-foot-high hand-operated scoreboard listed balls, strikes, outs, scores, and pitching changes. Atop it lay speaker horns and a Western Union (later Longines) clock. Seats were blue (boxes), gray (reserved), and green or red (general admission). Beyond third base lay bleachers down the line. "This became the look," said 1955-76 general manager Joe Brown, "how we remember her—the scoreboard, brick, so beautiful." A pilgrim also recalled "dipsy-doodle" (curve) and "bases FOB" ("Full of Bucs") and "doozie marooney" (extra-baser). In 1936-55, announcer Rosey Rowswell ten times braved the second division, loving anything not germane to score.

When a Bucs drive neared the wall, Rowswell shouted, "Get upstairs, Aunt Minnie, and raise the window! Here she [the baseball] comes!" An aide then dropped a pane of glass: to a listener, it meant the window. "That's too bad," Rosey sobbed. "Aunt Minnie tripped over a garden hose! She never made it!"

Aunt Minnie debuted in 1938. A year later Rosey and a plump lass of that name hyped a KDKA-TV exhibit by entering Forbes in an Austin car. Few criticized baseball's Empress with No Clothes. Said Prince: "People knew she was fictitious, and didn't care."

Prince's arrival changed Rosey's tack. "Instead of glass—too messy—I had this big dumbwaiter's tray with bells and nuts and bolts—*anything* to make noise." On Rowswell's nod, Bob, standing, dropped it. "On radio, it sounded like an earthquake. And Rosey'd say, 'Poor Aunt Minnie. She didn't make it again.'"

Prince quickly picked up the nuts and bolts. "I had to have the tray ready again, just in case the *next* guy hit one out."

"You got a lot of practice," colleague Jim Woods once said.

"Who wouldn't," Bob said, "with Ralph Kiner around?"

In 1946 Pittsburgh bought slugger Hank Greenberg, moved pens from foul ground to left field, strung a fence to left-center, and shrank the line from 365 to 335. "The [30-foot] area between the new fence and scoreboard were called Greenberg's Gardens," said Kiner. "Balls landing there were homers." After one year Greenberg retired, his Gardens renamed Kiner's Korner.

Kiner had returned from war in 1946, later saying, "Home-run hitters drive Cadillacs." General manager Branch Rickey observed, "Ralph *was* our team," taking a *nonpareil* seven straight NL home run titles, including 1947's 51 and 1949's 54. The long ball didn't win a pennant, but kept the Pirates solvent: in 1948, placing fourth, Pittsburgh drew a record 1,517,021. "After my last up," Kiner laughed, "half the crowd would leave."

In 1952, he wafted 37 homers and requested a raise. Said Rickey, refusing:

"We could have finished last without you." Those Bucs were last in runs, doubles, triples, home runs, K's, walks, shutouts, ERA, and wins—42-112. "It was the most courageous team in the bigs," said reserve catcher Joe Garagiola. "We showed up for every game." The next year, Kiner joined the Cubs, and Forbes' inner fence came down. In 1955 Rickey dedicated an 18-foot, 18,000-pound statue of Wagner in Schenley Park. On May 28, 1956, before 31,221 at home, Dale Long homered in a major-league record eighth straight game. Long got a curtain call—a then-rarity. Even rarer: The '58ers finished second, Danny Murtaugh voted Manager of the Year.

In 1959 three new field- and dugout-level rows upped Forbes' capacity to 35,000. Dick Stuart became the first to clear left-center's 457 mark. Reliever Elroy Face won his 17th straight game. Said Brown: "We won't soon see that again." That was especially true of a year where western Pennsylvania, eastern Ohio, and West Virginia celebrated "Beat 'Em Bucs" and "The Bucs Are Going All the Way," an all-time Forbes attendance record of 1,705,828, and a surreal World Series. Wrote Biederman of 1960: "The Pirates were something special."

Pittsburgh won 23 games in its last at-bat. MVP shortstop Dick Groat hit a bigs-high .325. Vernon Law went 20-9, won the Cy Young award, and said of second baseman Bill Mazeroski, "When he pivoted [on a double play], the ball looked like it took a U-turn." First basemen Stuart and Rocky Nelson had 30 homers. In center field, Bill Virdon rivaled Willie Mays. In right, Roberto Clemente batted .314, drove in 94 runs, and threw out a league-best

19 runners. On September 25 Pittsburgh clinched its first pennant since 1927.

Ten days later the Series began at Forbes, its pews so near the players you could almost know what they were like. The Pirates took Games One, Four, and Five, 6-4, 3-2, and 5-2, respectively. The Yankees swaggered, winning 16-3, 10-0, and 12-0. Bobby Richardson set a Series mark for most RBIs in a game (six, Game Three) and Series (12). Whitey Ford threw two shutouts. The stripes outhit (.338-.256), outhomered (10-4), and outscored (55-27) the Bucs. Nova blur: diving stops by Don Hoak and Mazeroski; Mickey Mantle, batting righty, clearing the 436 right-center mark; Virdon's leaping catch off Yogi Berra, saving Game Four.

October 13 broke mild and bright for a Good God Almighty, one frantic play after another, top-this final. "We have been blessed again with summer weather," Mel Allen mused on NBC Television. Off-air he asked if Prince wanted a drink. "Don't worry," Bob passed. "I'm just as crazy sober." Game Seven left you feeling like a morning-after binge. Tide: Nelson, first inning. "There's a drive!" said Prince. "Deep into right field! Back she goes! You can kiss that one goodbye!"—Pirates, 2-0. Riptide: The Yankees rallied. Down, 4-2, Berra batted in the sixth. "There's a drive hit deep to right field!" Allen said, calling foul, then amending: "All the way for a home run!"—Yanks, 5-4.

In the eighth inning, behind, 7-4, Virdon slapped a one-on grounder to Tony Kubek. "A sure double play," said the shortstop, "except the ball hit something, came up, and hit me in the throat." Groat and Clemente singled: 7-6. Hal Smith's three-run "electrifying homer," read the *Press*, "turned Forbes Field into a bedlam"– 9-7, Pirates. New York tied the score in the top of the ninth. In the bottom, Ralph Terry threw a slider. The left-center field clock read 3:36 P.M. "There's a drive deep into left field!" said Allen, Berra retreating to the 406-foot sign. "Look out now! That ball is going ... going, gone! ... Mazeroski hits it over the left-field fence for a home run. And the Pirates win it, 10 to 9, and win the World Series!"

Maz's homer became a Baby Boomer touchstone. In Los Angeles, Bob Costas, 8, retired to his room. "I'm sitting there, eyes welling with tears as I take a vow of silence. My plan was not to speak until Opening Day of the '61 season." Reality soon intervened. "But I kept mute for 24 hours—protesting this cosmic curse." In suburban Pittsburgh, Larry Lucchino, 15, was walking home from school. "I was a Pirates fan, and had a radio. When Maz homered, I threw it toward the sky." Alight, the future president of the Orioles, Padres, and Red Sox raced home: "Really, I was walking on air."

For a long time a hangover shrouded bars, mail routes, and screened-in porches, where one radio after another ferried the Bucs. Five decades later, even a Yankees fan recalls the leaves and splashing hues and spooked-up days that cradled fancy. "We had 'em allll the way!" Prince cried upon a victory. 1960 has Pittsburgh, even now.

By default, Maz's shot sustained the 1960s. It is true that in 1966 Matty Alou won the batting title (.342), Prince coined a hex (the Green Weenie, a hot dog painted green, that locals bought at stores, shook at rivals, and hung on car antennas), and the Bucs barely missed a pennant. It is also true that the 1961-69 Pirates five times flunked the first division, relying on Clemente to grease their creaking gate. The Great One had 3,000 hits, five times led outfielders in assists, and won a dozen Gold Gloves and four batting titles. His MVP pinnacle was 1966's .317, 29 homers, and 119 RBIs. Clemente ran like Secretariat, hit like Ali vs. Frazier, and "treated baseball," wrote Roger Angell, "like a form of punishment on the field." Sadly, he also left Forbes for a very different kind of home.

In 1958 the Pirates sold The House of Thrills to the University of Pittsburgh for $2 million. The college wanted to expand graduate facilities. The Bucs wanted a new multisport stadium. "Amazingly, baseball didn't then grasp what it had—that intimate was better. It wanted something bigger, to accommodate football," said Costas.

Prince was personal. "Leaving Forbes Field, they took the players away from the fans. It was unique. So what if girders needed replacing? You could do it, add bleacher seats. They had a way—just not a will." It is likely that no baseball team ever suffered most by leaving one site for another.

Forbes Field closed on June 28, 1970, before 40,918, the Bucs' largest crowd since 1956, in a doubleheader vs. Chicago. "The Cubs won Forbes' first game [1909]," said Brown. "Now the Pirates returned the favor [winning, 3-2 and 4-1]." Mourners heisted soil, seats, and numbers from the scoreboard. Sterile and circular Three Rivers Stadium took two years to build, cost $55 million, and had Tartan turf, symmetrical distances, a large foul area, and an upper deck near the troposphere. A 10-foot inner fence ringed the outfield. Three levels of plastic chairs enclosed the park, including a huge upper deck. Sight lines favored the football Steelers, who soon ruled the city.

Three Rivers housed the Bucs through 2000—its zenith "being blown up [in February 2001]," said 1976-79 Voice Milo Hamilton—hard to reach, then leave after a game. In turn, it led the Pirates to almost leave Pittsburgh, no longer fitting in its emotional luggage. In 2001, baseball-

Bill Mazeroski at Forbes Field, where he hit the first ever walk-off home run to win a World Series' Game Seven.

only $228 million PNC Park opened downtown between the Fort Duquesne and Sixth Street (renamed Roberto Clemente) bridges by the Allegheny River. Designed by a Forbes II Task Force, PNC's brick, steel, terra-cotta-tiled plasters, masonry arches, corner pens, 16 light towers, and flat green roof evoked the Bucs' Oakland dinghy. Like Forbes, wall height and distance varied, the farthest seat a big-league smallest 88 feet from the field. "People never accepted Three Rivers," said Hamilton. "They loved this place since Day One — like Forbes."

Fire struck the original on July 17, 1971, wreckers soon crumpling it. Today home plate, in glass, anchors the University of Pittsburgh's Forbes Quadrangle, a large graduate-school classroom and office building. A plaque notes where Maz's homer cleared the fence. A lovely red brick path traces the left-field wall. Patches of the center field and right-center wall conjure the Waner brothers and the in-play batting cage. Arriba hovers at Mervix

Hall — once right field. You approach the plot on Roberto Clemente Drive.

Each October 13 hundreds flock there, like the devout to Lourdes. "We listen to Bob and Jim Woods re-create Game Seven," said Bucs once-pitcher and now Voice Steve Blass, "remember where we were, talk about why Forbes was special." Prince died in 1985, often returning to a place still pleasant, almost golden. "I'd come by myself, just look around, marvel at what we had." In Schenley Park, memory comes unbidden like a postcard from the past.

Sources

Material, including quotes, is derived from Curt Smith's books *Voices of The Game, Storied Stadiums, Voices of Summer, The Voice, Pull Up a Chair,* and *A Talk in the Park* (in order: Simon & Schuster 1992, Carroll & Graf 2001 and 2005, respectively, The Lyons Press 2007, and Potomac Books 2009 and 2011, respectively.)

1960 Pittsburgh Pirates Season Timeline

By Clifton Blue Parker

April 12—BUCS OPEN SEASON WITH ONE-RUN LOSS. On a fair afternoon in Milwaukee, 39,888 fans turned out at County Stadium to watch the Braves edge the Pirates, 4-3. Bob Friend started the game and pitched seven strong innings, but reliever Elroy Face lost the game in the bottom of the eighth on a home run by Joe Adcock that drove in Henry Aaron. Hal Smith had two doubles and Dick Stuart had three hits for the Bucs.

The Pirates' Opening Day lineup consisted of:

Bob Skinner	LF
Dick Groat	SS
Roberto Clemente	RF
Dick Stuart	1B
Don Hoak	3B
Gino Cimoli	CF
Bill Mazeroski	2B
Hal Smith	C
Bob Friend	P

April 13—No game played, an offday.

April 14—PIRATES RIP REDS, 13-0. Pirate bats blistered Cincinnati Reds pitchers and Vernon Law pitched a complete-game shutout before a home-opener crowd of 34,064 at Forbes Field. Roberto Clemente had a pair of doubles and five RBIs, and Bill Mazeroski had four RBIs and a home run over the left-field scoreboard. Seven of the Pirates' hits were for extra bases, and the team batted around in the fifth inning for six runs. Only one Red reached third base, as Law continued his mastery over Cincinnati—he had not lost to them since 1956.

April 15—No game played, an offday.

April 16—REDS BLAST BUCS—Cincinnati jumped all over rookie pitcher Jim Umbricht and pounded its way to an 11-3 win. Umbricht, 29, gave up six runs in 5 1/3 innings. The Bucs tallied a run in the first when leadoff hitter Don Hoak tripled and scored on a Dick Groat single.

April 17—PIRATES RALLY FOR TWIN-BILL SWEEP. Home runs by pinch-hitter Hal Smith and Bob Skinner drove in five runs in the ninth inning to win, 6-5, the second game of a doubleheader against Cincinnati. Bill Virdon had three hits, and lefty reliever Joe Gibbon pitched two shutout innings for the win. The Bucs won the first game, 5-0, behind the four-hit pitching of Bob Friend. In that game, Roberto Clemente socked a two-run homer in the first inning, his first of the season.

April 18—No game played, an offday.

April 19—PHILS EDGE PIRATES. Both teams scored all their runs in the third inning, but Philadelphia tallied one more to win, 4-3, on a three-hit complete game by Jim Owen. Starter Harvey Haddix didn't make it

The Pirates held spring training in Terry Park Ballfield in Fort Myers, Florida, from 1955 to 1968.

through the third, and all the Pirates' runs were scored on a three-run homer by Bob Skinner.

April 20—VERN LAW HURLS BUCS PAST PHILLIES. The Pirates pushed their record over the .500 mark (4-3) as they began a nine-game winning streak with a 4-2 victory over Philadelphia. Don Hoak smacked a two-run homer in the fifth inning after a single by Bill Mazeroski, and Bill Virdon scored a run in the seventh inning when he walked, stole second, moved to third on a wild pitch, and came home on Mazeroski's sacrifice fly. Vern Law notched his second strong start with a complete-game performance.

April 21—PIRATES GO DEEP, AGAIN AND AGAIN. The Bucs, who hit the fewest homers of any National League club the season before, broke out with three smashes in an 11-5 triumph over the Phillies. Bob Skinner, Hal Smith, and reliever Fred Green all homered as Pittsburgh rapped 15 hits. The Pirates knocked Phillies starter Curt Simmons out of the game in the first inning, and the home runs came off the Phillies' bullpen.

April 22—BOB FRIEND WINS SECOND GAME. The Bucs chased Juan Pizarro of Milwaukee in the first inning, then cracked a tie and put the defeat on Joey Jay in the third when he hit Don Hoak with a pitch and Hal Smith followed with a triple. The Bucs scored three more in the fourth, all with two out, on Roberto Clemente's two-run homer and Smith's double. Pittsburgh won, 6-2.

April 23—MISCUES LEAD TO PIRATES' WIN. Braves shortstop Johnny Logan's second error of the game led to Pittsburgh's winning run in a 5-4 victory over Milwaukee. The teams were deadlocked going into the Pirates' seventh when Don Hoak reached first on Logan's miscue. Dick Groat sacrificed, Bob Skinner drew an intentional walk, and Dick Stuart singled home Hoak with the deciding run.

April 24—PIRATES MOVE INTO FIRST. Reliever Elroy Face choked off a Milwaukee rally in the ninth inning and Pittsburgh pulled out a 7-3 victory, their fifth straight. Bob Skinner and Smoky Burgess homered, and Bill Mazeroski tripled and drove in three runs. Harvey Haddix got the win with 8 1/3 innings of solid pitching. The Pirates then headed off for a long road trip visiting all NL rivals. Their 8-3 record was their best start since 1938, when they lost the pennant to the Chicago Cubs in a late stretch drive. They would not return to Forbes Field until May 17.

April 25—No game played, an offday.

April 26—The game was rained out.

April 27—SKINNER LIFTS BUCS OVER PHILS. Bob Skinner banged out two hits and two RBIs as Pittsburgh prevailed over Philadelphia, 3-2, on the strong arm of Vern Law, who completed the game without help from the bullpen.

April 28—FRIEND BLANKS PHILADELPHIA. The Bucs won their seventh in a row as Bob Friend hurled a four-hit shutout over the Phillies. Dick Stuart banged out two hits, including a triple, and Roberto Clemente and Hal Smith also collected two hits.

APRIL 29—The game was rained out.

APRIL 30—PIRATES TOP REDS. First-place Pittsburgh erupted for ten runs in the second inning and went on to win the game, 12-7, with homers by Roberto Clemente and Bill Mazeroski. After a shaky start by Bennie Daniels, who gave up six runs but still won the game, Paul Giel and Roy Face came out of the bullpen to wrap up the game for the Pirates. Mazeroski had four hits. Pittsburgh finished April with an 11-3 record.

MAY 1—PITTSBURGH WINS NINTH IN A ROW. The Bucs crushed the Reds, 13-2, as Vern Law went the distance with offensive help from Roberto Clemente's grand slam and a three-run homer by Bill Mazeroski. The Bucs chased Cincinnati starter Don Newcombe in the fifth inning. Pittsburgh was up two games in the standings. The nine-game winning streak was the Pirates' longest of the season.

MAY 2—CARDINALS EDGE PIRATES. Former Pirate pitcher Ron Kline snapped Pittsburgh's nine-game winning streak as St. Louis won 4-3. The Cardinals prevailed when Elroy Face, who blew the lead in the seventh inning, gave up a bases-loaded walk to pinch-hitter Carl Sawatski in the ninth.

MAY 3—During this offday, general manager Joe L. Brown told the *Pittsburgh Post-Gazette* that the team's early success was due to better conditioning. "Some of our players were overweight last year," he said, referring to Bill Mazeroski and Bob Friend. "Those fellows worked hard in the offseason. Both lost weight."[1]

MAY 4—CUBS DOWN BUCS, 5-1. Dick Ellsworth, a 20-year-old bonus southpaw just up from the Houston farm club, scattered five hits and pitched the Cubs to a 5-1 win over Pittsburgh in Chicago.

MAY 5—CLEMENTE POWERS PIRATES TO WIN. Robert Clemente smacked a home run among three hits as Pittsburgh won over Chicago, 9-7. The Bucs erupted for seven runs in the last three innings, spoiling Lou Boudreau's managerial debut for the Cubs. Pinch-hitter Bill Virdon's two-out, two-run pinch triple in the ninth inning sealed the game for the Pirates.

MAY 6—GIANTS BEAT BUCS, 5-1. The three Willies—Mays, McCovey, and Kirkland—hit home runs and Sam Jones pitched a three-hitter to give San Francisco a 5-1 victory over visiting Pittsburgh. The Giants handed Vern Law his first defeat in five starts—the first time he did not pitch nine innings in 1960—and now trailed Pittsburgh by one game in the standings. Clemente (.364) stayed hot with a solo home run.

May 7—SAN FRANCISCO TIES PITTSBURGH FOR FIRST. A wild six-run seventh inning highlighted by Eddie Bressoud's inside-the-park three-run homer gave the Giants a 6-5 win over the Bucs and a tie in the standings. "A crowd of 33,065 watched a full afternoon of protests," wrote the Associated Press, noting several Pirate protests over umpiring calls that led to ejections for manager Danny Murtaugh and Dick Stuart, who was not even in the lineup.[2]

MAY 8—BUCS COMMIT SEVEN ERRORS IN LOSS. The Giants moved into first place as they won, 13-1, for a sweep of the series. The Pirates made seven errors — three by Dick Groat alone — and starter Joe Gibbon was chased in the first inning. The 13 runs allowed were the most the Pirates would give up during the season. (They twice matched the figure later.)

MAY 9—BUCS LOSE FOURTH IN A ROW. Los Angeles prevailed over Pittsburgh, 7-4, as Charley Neal hit a three-run homer off Roy Face in the bottom of the ninth inning. The Pirates had scored two runs in the eighth and ninth innings on home runs by Bill Mazeroski and Bob Skinner off Don Drysdale to tie it.

MAY 10—PITTSBURGH STOPS SKID. The Pirates won 3-2 over the Los Angeles Dodgers on home runs by Bill Mazeroski and Hal Smith. Vern Law pitched his fifth complete game in six starts to improve to 5-1. Pittsburgh was 14-9 and in second place.

MAY 11—PIRATES BEAT KOUFAX. Pittsburgh bested a still-developing Sandy Koufax, 6-3, chasing him in the eighth inning. Koufax had gotten the first two outs of the inning before Dick Stuart singled, Gene Baker walked, and Hal Smith stroked an RBI single to left. The Pirates added insurance runs in the ninth on a double by Bob Skinner and singles by Roberto Clemente and Smoky Burgess. They were 1½ games behind San Francisco.

MAY 12—An offday. The Pirates optioned Joe Christopher, Roman Mejias, and Red Witt to the minors. The move got the team down to the required 25-man roster.

MAY 13—BUCS SCORE EIGHT RUNS IN SEVENTH INNING. Pittsburgh topped host Milwaukee, 8-2, putting all eight runs on the board in the seventh thanks to homers by Bill Mazeroski and Dick Stuart and a double by Bob Skinner. Dick Groat went 6-for-6 and became the 20th major leaguer at that point to accomplish the feat. He had three doubles and two runs scored. Starter Bob Friend retired the final 17 batters and the Pirates did not make an error for the first time in seven games.

MAY 14—CLEMENTE TRIPLE POWERS PIRATES. Roberto Clemente's two-out, two-run triple to left-center in the 11th gave the Bucs a 6-4 victory over Milwaukee for the team's fourth win in a row. The Braves had come back from a 4-0 deficit with four homers off Vern Law. Roy Face pitched the last two innings, allowing only one hit, and earned the win.

MAY 15—BUCS SPLIT DOUBLEHEADER WITH BRAVES. The Pirates extended their win streak to five with a 6-4 triumph over Milwaukee in the first game, but then dropped the nightcap, 4-2. Harvey Haddix won the opener, thanks to Don Hoak and Dick Stuart, who each hit two-run homers, and to Bob Skinner, who led off the game with a clout. In the second game Bennie Daniels hurled seven innings for the win, allowing a three-run homer by Henry Aaron. Bob Skinner banged out a triple and double among three hits and scored both of the Pirates' runs.

MAY 16—No game played, an offday. Taking stock of the Pirates, Les Biederman of the *Pittsburgh Press* described them as the "best defensive team in the league, probably also the team with the most speed," while noting that the team needed more starting pitching depth behind Vern Law and Bob Friend.[3]

MAY 17—PIRATES MOVE WITHIN ONE GAME OF FIRST. Back at Forbes Field after a 10-7 road trip, the Pirates trounced Chicago, 11-6, in a 13-hit attack featuring three-hit performances by Don Hoak and Dick Stuart. Bob Friend went eight unspectacular innings and Roy Face closed. "Let's face it," Friend said, "I was lucky."[4] Clemente's 12-game hitting streak was snapped, but he stole two bases.

MAY 18—VERN LAW HURLS COMPLETE GAME. Pittsburgh bested St. Louis 4-2 as Vern Law scattered nine hits over nine innings and a red-hot Don Hoak and Bob Skinner pounded out two hits apiece. At 20-10, Pittsburgh moved into a tie for first place with San Francisco. "The Pirates seemed on the verge of collapse only two weeks ago," wrote Fred Down of United Press International.[5]

MAY 19—CLEMENTE'S FOUR HITS FUEL PIRATES. Roberto Clemente hiked his average to .372 with a four-hit game in Pittsburgh's 8-3 win over St. Louis. Joe Gibbon won the game with relief help from Fred Green. The Pirates' right fielder had two doubles and two singles. "They shout 'Arriba, arriba' when Roberto Clemente bats at Forbes Field, and perhaps no player better typifies the rise of the Pittsburgh Pirates," observed a sportswriter.[6]

MAY 20—BUCS WIN FOURTH IN A ROW. The sizzling Roberto Clemente again dominated the Bucs' offense as the Pirates won 5-4 over the second-place Giants in 12 innings at home. Clemente banged out three hits and drove in two runs. Don Hoak and Dick Groat each had two hits and two runs. Fred Green pitched the last three innings in relief and won the game after

Elroy Face blew the lead in the ninth inning when Willie McCovey homered.

MAY 21—GIANTS STOP WIN STREAK. San Francisco won 3-1, halting Pittsburgh's four-game win streak, on the strength of eight strong innings by Johnny Antonelli. Bob Friend allowed a two-run homer by Orlando Cepeda. The first-place Pirates' lead shrank to a half-game over the Giants.

MAY 22—17-HIT ATTACK DEFEATS GIANTS. Pittsburgh fell behind early, 4-0, but outlasted San Francisco, 8-7, in 11 innings. Roberto Clemente and Bob Skinner each had three hits; Dick Groat, Bill Virdon, Dick Stuart, and Bill Mazeroski had two apiece. Roy Face won the game with three innings of shutout relief work. "I think we've got the jump on them now," Face said of the Giants.[7]

MAY 23—KOUFAX BLANKS BUCS. Sandy Koufax gave up only one hit and struck out ten while walking six in Los Angeles' 1-0 victory over Pittsburgh. The lone Buc hit was a second-inning single by pitcher Bennie Daniels. It was the first time the Pirates were shut out in the season. After the game, Koufax mentioned to reporters that he had almost been a Pirate. Pittsburgh had given him a tryout in 1954 before he joined University of Cincinnati on a basketball scholarship. But the Pirates, led by Branch Rickey at the time, never made an offer.[8]

MAY 24—DODGER PITCHING AGAIN STYMIES PITTSBURGH. Johnny Podres of Los Angeles hurled his way to a 4-2 complete-game victory over the Pirates, scattering eight hits. Joe Gibbon took the loss; his three-base throwing error in the fifth inning led to two runs. Roberto Clemente pounded out a triple and double while Bill Mazeroski notched two hits.

MAY 25—DODGERS SWEEP SERIES. Los Angeles outfielder Frank Howard boomed a long home run (UPI said it went 560 feet) to back Don Drysdale's five-hitter as the Dodgers topped the Pirates, 5-1, sweeping the three-game series.[9] Howard's prodigious shot over the left-center wall was "about as high as the lights on the tower," Bucs outfielder Bill Virdon said, and some estimated that it was the longest ball ever hit at Forbes Field. After the game, Pirates manager Danny Murtaugh ordered extra batting practice for his cooled-off hitters.[10] Pittsburgh fell one game behind the Giants.

MAY 26—An offday, no game played.

MAY 27—The game against the Phillies was rained out.

MAY 28—BUCS SNAP LOSING STREAK. Pittsburgh won a 13-inning thriller against Philadelphia, 4-2. Starter Bob Friend was up 2-0 in the top of the ninth, but gave up four straight hits and the lead. In the last frame Bill Mazeroski singled and, with two out, stole second. Don Hoak then blasted a home run to win the game. In other news, Pittsburgh traded for starting pitcher Vinegar Bend Mizell. He was obtained from St. Louis with Dick Gray for Ed Bauta and prospect Julian Javier. Pittsburgh was hoping to add to its starting rotation depth.

MAY 29—PIRATES BACK IN FIRST PLACE. Vern Law, with relief help from Fred Green, won his seventh game of the year, an 8-5 triumph over the Phillies. The victory moved the Bucs back into a first-place tie with the Giants, who lost that day. Green shut the door on the Phillies in the seventh by striking out pinch-hitter B.G. Smith. Roberto Clemente's spectacular catch of pinch-hitter Pancho Herrera's sinking liner saved two runs in the inning.

MAY 30—CIMOLI LIFTS PITTSBURGH. Outfielder Gino Cimoli smacked three hits including a triple and had four RBIs to power Pittsburgh over Milwaukee, 8-3, at Forbes Field. Starter Harvey Haddix allowed three runs in the ninth after eight shutout innings, and the Pirate hitters knocked out Warren Spahn in the second inning. The second game of a scheduled Memorial Day doubleheader was postponed because of rain.

MAY 31—BUCS WIN FOURTH CONSECUTIVE GAME. Pittsburgh came out on top, 4-3, after 11 innings of play against Cincinnati. With runners on first and second and none out, Dick Groat, who had five hits in the game, beat out a bunt and then Roberto Clemente singled home pinch-runner Bill Virdon for the winning run. Vinegar Bend Mizell, in his first start with the Bucs, pitched eight innings and gave up three runs. Roy Face won the game in relief. Six Reds were ejected after arguing umpiring calls. Pittsburgh's 27-14 record led the league. The Bucs were 16-11 in May.

JUNE 1—FRIEND SHUTS OUT THE REDS. Bob Friend tossed a three-hit complete game for a 5-0 win over the Reds. He walked only one and struck out six; the hits he gave up were singles. It was his third shutout of the season. Hitters Dick Groat, Don Hoak, Bob Skinner, and Rocky Nelson had two hits apiece, and Clemente had a two-run double. It was the Bucs' fifth straight win and capped a 10-4 homestand.

JUNE 2—An offday, no game was played.

JUNE 3—LAW BLANKS PHILADELPHIA. Vern Law scattered eight hits as the Pirates beat the host Phillies, 3-0, thanks to a two-run single by Roberto Clemente. Meanwhile, Clemente was named Player of the Month for May (.336, 25 RBIs).

JUNE 4—Game postponed due to rain.

JUNE 5—PHILLIES DAMPEN BUC BATS. Gene Conley gave up ten hits to Pittsburgh but managed to keep runners from scoring as he outpitched Bob Friend, 2-0, in the first game of a doubleheader. In the second affair Jim Owens completed the game without help from the bullpen as the Phillies won again, 4-1. At 29-16, the Pirates remained one game ahead in first place.

JUNE 6—An offday, no game was played.

JUNE 7—CHICAGO TROUNCES PITTSBURGH. The Pirates committed four errors and were blasted, 13-2, by the Cubs at Wrigley Field. Starter Vern Law gave up five runs—only one earned—failing to last two innings, and reliever Bennie Daniels coughed up eight tallies. "That's the first bad game we played in a month," said manager Danny Murtaugh.[11]

JUNE 8—MIZELL BEATS CUBS. Bob Skinner and Dick Stuart homered in the Pirates' 5-3 victory over Chicago as Vinegar Bend Mizell won the game with relief help from Roy Face and Fred Green. It was Mizell's first victory with Pittsburgh. Smoky Burgess was 3-for-4 and Roberto Clemente made a defensive gem of a play in the right-field corner in the eighth inning.

JUNE 9—PITTSBURGH CRUSHES CHICAGO. Chicago pitchers were erratic on the mound, and Pirate hitters managed 11 runs on only eight hits—there were eight walks as well—in the 11-3 Pirate win over Chicago. Starter Bob Friend picked up the win. With the

Giants losing, the Pirates' lead in first place stretched to two games.

JUNE 10—CARDINALS OVERCOME PIRATES. Batters for host St. Louis knocked out 14 hits in defeating the Pirates, 9-6, behind Larry Jackson's pedestrian pitching performance. For the Bucs, starter Harvey Haddix was chased in the fifth inning. Don Hoak and Smoky Burgess homered.

JUNE 11—BUCS LOSE TO CARDINALS IN NINTH. St. Louis scored three runs in the bottom of the ninth to edge Pittsburgh, 7-6. Facing Roy Face, outfielder Bob Nieman clubbed a two-run double to win, though Fred Green took the loss. Bob Skinner, Dick Groat, and Bill Mazeroski had two hits while Dick Stuart homered for Pittsburgh.

JUNE 12—PIRATES SCORE 15, THEN LOSE NIGHTCAP. In the first game of a doubleheader, Pittsburgh blasted St. Louis, 15-3, in a 23-hit attack that marked their highest run total of the season. The Bucs routed Cards pitcher Ron Kline with a six-run first inning. Among the offensive fireworks: Dick Stuart's two homers, five hits and five RBIs, Dick Groat's four hits and three runs scored, Smoky Burgess's four hits, and Don Hoak's three-run homer. Leading the league in wins with nine now, Vern Law hurled a complete game, scattering 13 hits while giving up three runs. In the second game, the Pirates lost 5-2, as Vinegar Bend Mizell, facing his former teammates for the first time, allowed three runs and four hits over four innings.

JUNE 13—An offday, no game was played.

JUNE 14—PIRATES FACE DOWN SECOND-PLACE GIANTS. The Pirates opened a series in San Francisco with a 6-3 win over the Giants. In the second inning, they scored three runs, two of them coming on a Dick Groat single. Don Hoak went 3-for-3, Bob Friend pitched a complete game, and the Pirates were up two in the standings.

JUNE 15—BUCS CLOBBER SAN FRANCISCO. The Bucs crushed six Giants pitchers for 19 hits and a 14-6 victory to boost their lead to three games. Pirate hitters unleashed six doubles and a pair of triples to give Harvey Haddix the win while Billy O'Dell took the loss.

Still, the Bucs committed four errors. Dick Groat and Haddix each had four hits.

JUNE 16—PITTSBURGH SWEEPS SERIES. Pittsburgh completed a three-game sweep at San Francisco with a 10-7 win. Bob Skinner drove in five runs with three hits, including a grand slam in the fifth inning. Don Hoak and Dick Groat also had three hits and Vinegar Bend Mizell picked up the win despite the Giants scoring five runs in the bottom of the ninth. The Bucs now had a four-game lead over the Giants, who lost their fourth in a row.

JUNE 17—BUCS EDGE DODGERS. Pittsburgh won a pitchers' duel, 2-1, as Vern Law hurled a complete game and bested counterpart Stan Williams. Each team only had six hits. Bill Virdon hit a home run in the sixth inning to seal a fourth consecutive win for Pittsburgh.

JUNE 18—PIRATES RALLY TO WIN AGAIN. Pittsburgh staged arguably its greatest comeback of the regular season. With the Pirates down 3-0 in the ninth inning against the Dodgers, two outs and two strikes on Gino Cimoli, he started the rally when he got an infield single. Hal Smith homered to make it 3-2, Don Hoak singled and Bill Mazeroski walked. Smoky Burgess then lashed a single to tie the game. An RBI single by Smith in the tenth inning drove in Clemente with the winning run. After the game, Les Biederman of the *Pittsburgh Press* wrote, "If and when the Pirates clinch the pennant, then can look back on Saturday night's game in the Los Angeles Coliseum and say, 'This was the game that did it.'" It was their fifth straight win.[12]

JUNE 19—DODGERS STOP PIRATES. Despite getting a Dick Stuart grand slam and knocking Sandy Koufax out of the game in the fifth inning, the Pirates lost to the Dodgers, 8-6, snapping their five-game winning streak. Ed Roebuck and Stan Williams slammed the door in relief duties; Dick Groat had two hits. Bennie Daniels took the loss in relief.

JUNE 20—An offday, no game was played.

JUNE 21—VERN LAW WINS AGAIN. Vern Law went eight strong innings to lead the Bucs over the Cardinals, 3-2, at Forbes Field. In the fifth inning Bill Mazeroski singled (he was 3-for-3 with two runs scored), then was driven home by a Bill Virdon single. Dick Groat brought Virdon home with a single. Roy Face shut the door on the Dodgers in the ninth.

JUNE 22—BOB FRIEND TOSSES SHUTOUT. Pittsburgh beat the visiting Cardinals, 5-0, on the strong arm of Bob Friend, who hurled a complete game. Dick Groat banged out four hits, Roberto Clemente had a double and two RBIs, and Bill Virdon socked a triple.

JUNE 23—CARDINALS TOP BUCS. John Glenn and Julian Javier each drove in two unearned runs in the top of the seventh to put St. Louis ahead as the Cardinals won the game, 3-1. Pittsburgh managed only five hits, two of them by Bob Skinner, and Harvey Haddix took the loss after 6 2/3 innings pitched.

JUNE 24—MIZELL THROWS COMPLETE GAME. Vinegar Bend Mizell gave up seven hits in the Pirates' 4-1 win over Chicago at Forbes Field. Roberto Clemente had three hits and Mizell had two RBIs. In the sixth inning Bill Mazeroski singled home Gino Cimoli, and Mizell, after missing a squeeze bunt, on which Don Hoak was run down, dropped a hit behind first to drive in his second runner of the night. It was the third time Mizell beat the Cubs this season and his first complete game of the year for the Pirates.

JUNE 25—BUCS SQUEAK PAST CUBS. The Pirates rallied in the late innings to beat the Cubs, 7-6. Rocky Nelson hit a triple to right field, and Smoky Burgess drove him in for the go-ahead run. Virdon, Groat, and Hoak each had two hits.

JUNE 26—CUBS SWEEP BUCS IN DOUBLEHEADER. Pittsburgh lost 7-6 and 7-5 to Chicago in a doubleheader. In the first game, the Cubs' Mark Freeman tied the Pirates up in knots with an 8 2/3-inning performance despite a home run by Smoky Burgess in the ninth inning. In the second game, the Cubs scored two runs in the eighth inning on three singles off Vern Law.

JUNE 27—An offday, no game was played.

JUNE 28—BUCS AND GIANTS TIE. Pittsburgh and San Francisco tied 7-7 after nine innings of play in Pittsburgh. In a game that was delayed twice by rain, 30,000-plus saw the Pirates and Giants fight a back-and-forth battle for 3 hours and 19 minutes until, at 10 minutes before 1:00 A.M., the game was called due to curfew. Rocky Nelson drove in four of the Pirates' seven runs. Three came in on a home run in the bottom of the first. He tied the game in the fourth with a double that scored Dick Groat. It was Nelson's third round-tripper of the year. The stats counted.

JUNE 29—Game postponed due to rain. The Pirates were ahead of the Braves by 2½ games and the Giants by six games.

JUNE 30— BUCS, GIANTS SPLIT TWIN BILL. In game one, Bob Friend lost his second consecutive decision, 11-0, as Jack Sanford pitched a three-hit shutout for the Giants. Friend lasted only 3 1/3 innings, giving up six runs on seven hits, including a two-run homer by Willie Mays in the third. Paul Giel relieved Friend in a five-run Giants fourth inning. Giel had been acquired by the Pirates from the Giants the year before on waivers. In the next affair, a makeup game, Pirate first baseman Dick Stuart blasted three consecutive home runs and drove in seven runs, joining former Buc slugger Ralph Kiner as the second Pirate player to hit three home runs in a game at Forbes Field.

The Bucs closed June with a 15-11 record for the month.

JULY 1—PIRATES NIP DODGERS. In ten innings, the host Bucs prevailed over Los Angeles, 4-3, as Dick Stuart drove in Roberto Clemente on a single to right field in the last of the tenth. Vern Law pitched 9 2/3 innings, though the Dodgers rallied late, and Fred Green picked up the win in relief. Clemente had three hits, including a double.

JULY 2—STAN WILLIAMS STYMIES PIRATES. Los Angeles triumphed over Pittsburgh, 6-1, at Forbes Field as Stan Williams tossed a complete game. The Bucs' pitcher, Tom Cheney, in his Pirates debut, was lifted in the fourth inning. The Pirates managed only four hits, and their lone RBI came on a Dick Stuart single that scored Bob Skinner in the first inning.

JULY 3— DODGERS EDGE BUCS. Pittsburgh lost for the second day in a row, falling to Los Angeles, 6-2. Don Drysdale pitched a complete game for the Dodgers, striking out eight and walking one. The only extra-base hits by the Bucs were doubles by Bob Skinner and Bill

1960 World Series

By George Skornickel

Game One: Wednesday, October 5, 1960 at Forbes Field / Pittsburgh 6, New York 4

THE 1960 WORLD Series began at stately Forbes Field in Pittsburgh on October 5. Fans were urged by the newspapers, radio, and TV not to drive to the ballpark because of the expected large crowd for the first Series game in Pittsburgh in 35 years. The biggest deterrent to driving was that parking lots were charging $5 a car. The Yankees were favored by the oddsmakers at 13 to 10, but that didn't dampen the spirits of the Pirates fans.

Four former Pirates managers were present for the game: Bill McKechnie, who piloted the team in the 1925 World Series; Pie Traynor, who played in the 1925 and 1927 Series; Fred Haney, skipper from 1953-1955; and Bobby Bragan, Danny Murtaugh's predecessor.

The American League and the Yankees were also well represented. Yankees owners Dan Topping and Del Webb solved the hotel problem. They centered their base of operations in a private railroad car. Sitting next to the Yankees dugout were Will Harridge, retired president of the American League, Joe Cronin, his successor, and Mrs. Cronin. Warren Giles, president of the National League, was next to the Pirates dugout.

The oldest fan attending was 92-year-old Bertha Doak. She was a diehard Pirates fan who regularly attended four out of every five games played by the Bucs at Forbes Field.

Most of the Yankees swung at the ball during pregame batting practice to see if they could drive it out of the park. Meanwhile, Mickey Mantle practiced bunting. When questioned, he said, "I heard about the hard infield and wanted to see how far the ball would roll."[1]

Roger Maris spent 30 minutes playing caroms off the right-field wall as coach Ralph Houk hit line drives against it. "The ball takes some bad angles when it hits the corner and you have to watch out if it's right on the foul line, where that tin marker makes them bounce really funny," Maris commented. "I wish I had more time to work on it."[2]

The crowd was amused before the pregame festivities by Jack Heatherington of McKeesport, Pennsylvania, a member of the Pittsburgh Skydivers Club, who parachuted from a plane circling the field. A gust of wind caught his parachute and he landed on the roof of a warehouse across the street. Heatherington said he made the jump on a bet with a friend but denied that he had attempted to land inside the park.[3]

Bob Friend revealed before the game that Don Hoak had played for weeks despite an eight-inch cut on his foot suffered while getting out of a swimming pool in late August. Even though there was no anesthetic, Hoak insisted that a doctor stitch the injury. Often enduring extreme pain, Hoak continued to play for the rest of the season.

Finally the pregame ceremonies began. The University of Pittsburgh marching band entertained and then accompanied Pittsburgh-born Billy Eckstein as he sang the National Anthem.

Pirates manager Danny Murtaugh shakes hands with Yankee skipper Casey Stengel.

The governor of Pennsylvania, David L. Lawrence, tossed out the first ball. He flipped it into the hands of catcher Smoky Burgess over the heads of photographers.

When the game finally got under way, the Pirates proved that they were unafraid of the mighty Yankees, showing their opponents a little bit of everything. They executed double plays, and made the most of their eight hits.

Center fielder Bill Virdon was key both on offense and defense. After Roger Maris put the Yankees ahead, 1-0, with a home run in the top of the first inning, Virdon worked Yankees pitcher Art Ditmar for a leadoff walk in the bottom of the inning. Nervous at bat, Dick Groat scratched his foot in the batter's box, inadvertently giving the hit-and-run sign. Groat stepped out and rubbed his forehead to cancel the sign, but wasn't sure Virdon had seen it. Virdon hadn't. He broke for second as the pitch from Ditmar sailed past Groat. Yogi Berra made a perfect throw to second base, but neither Tony Kubek nor Bobby Richardson covered the base. Virdon ended up on third, and before the 23-minute inning was over, Ditmar was gone and the Pirates led 3-1.[4]

It was Virdon again in the fourth inning, this time on defense. Roger Maris opened the inning with a single and Mickey Mantle followed with a walk. Berra hit the ball to deep right-center field. Both Virdon and right fielder Roberto Clemente started after the ball. Virdon got there first and grabbed the ball when the two players were only inches apart, stopping the 400-plus-foot flight of the ball. Bill Skowron followed with an RBI single, but the rally had been stopped. After the game, Yankees manager Casey Stengel commented, "That stunt in center wrecked us."[5]

Twenty-game winner Vernon Law, the winning pitcher, ran into trouble in the eighth inning. After the first two Yankees batters, Hector Lopez and Maris, reached base, Pirates skipper Danny Murtaugh approached the mound and, after a short conference, waved his hands low and palms down — a signal that he wanted the little guy, Elroy Face. Face got Mantle on a called third strike and Berra on a fly ball, then struck out Skowron on four pitches.

There were more anxious moments for the Pirates and their fans. With the Pirates leading 6-2, Gil McDougald opened the ninth inning for the Yankees with a single.

Bobby Richardson hit into a force out, then Elston Howard, pinch-hitting for Ryne Duren, the fourth Yankee pitcher, hit a home run, his fourth in World Series competition, over the screen in right field to cut the Pirate lead in half. Then, after two strikes, Tony Kubek singled to center field. The tying run came to the plate in Hector Lopez. With two Pirates warming up in the bullpen, Lopez grounded to Bill Mazeroski, who started a routine double play that ended the game. Except for their two home runs, all the Yankees' hits had been singles.

After the game the questions began. The first was: Why had Casey Stengel started Art Ditmar instead of veteran World Series pitcher Whitey Ford? "How can you not pitch your best pitcher?" Mantle said. Bobby Richardson also couldn't understand Casey's move. "Ford was our best pitcher," he said, "and in any big game he would be the one to start." Stengel said he started Ditmar because Forbes Field was a small park and Ditmar threw a sinker; besides, he wanted to save Ford for Yankee Stadium. Stengel also said he felt Ditmar was the Yankees' steadiest pitcher during the season (Ditmar was 15-9, Ford was 12-9). Also, Ditmar had previously pitched 9 2/3 scoreless World Series innings.

Reporters also wanted to know why in the second inning, with Berra on second base, Casey had pinch-hit Dale Long for Clete Boyer. Boyer had commented, "I was never so shocked in my life." Stengel had allowed Boyer to take several steps toward the batter's box before whistling him back to the dugout.

"When Casey called me back, I thought he was going to talk to me — maybe tell me how he wanted me to swing," Boyer said. "But when he told me that Dale Long was going to hit for me, I was ready to crawl all the way home."[6]

Casey said he felt that since Long was a former National League player (and a former Pirate), he had a better chance with the Pirates pitchers. But Long flied out and when Bobby Richardson lined out to Skinner, the outfielder doubled off Berra, who had wandered too far off second base and was put out despite a head-first slide.

Bill Mazeroski's two-run home run in Game One is often forgotten in the excitement of what was to come in Game Seven. In the fourth inning, Hoak walked with one out. Yankee pitcher Jim Coates had a one-ball, two-strike count on Mazeroski when the 24-year-old second base-man lined a home run over the scoreboard just inside the left-field foul line, giving the Pirates a 5-2 lead.

Almost 50 years later, Mazeroski still relished the home run. Asked how he felt after hitting it, he answered with a twinkle in his eye, "I thought it was the greatest thing that had ever happened to me. It relaxed me for the rest of the Series."[7]

The next batter after Mazeroski, pitcher Vern Law, was hit on the left hand by a Coates pitch. Asked in 2009 if he felt the pitch was in response to Mazeroski's home run, Law merely smiled.[8]

After the game Danny Murtaugh said it was a typical Pirates victory. They executed three double plays, clustered their eight hits to make them more vital than the Yankees' 13, and the biggest hit of all was off the bat of Bill Mazeroski, their number eight hitter.

This Series was not to be another mismatch between the Yankees and the Pirates as it had been in 1927.

Game Two: Thursday, October 6, 1960 at Forbes Field / New York 16, Pittsburgh 3

After the first game, intermittent rain fell during the night and morning, but the sky cleared about 15 minutes before game time. Both teams had infield practice called off when the automatic tarpaulin was rolled out as rain began to fall again at 12:25 P.M.

The Pirates sold one-game tickets as well as four-game strips in order to give as many fans as possible a chance to see the Series. Television had made standing-room tickets less attractive to fans than they had been in pre-TV years. About 1,000 of 4,000 available standing-room tickets for Game Two were sold. (Many had also been unsold for the opener.) Seating for the press corps was another matter. The top-deck press box, which had been built for the 1938 World Series at a cost of $35,000 and which had never been used when the Cubs edged out the Pirates in the last days of the season, was filled with more than 600 writers.

Before the game Pirates manager Danny Murtaugh was forced to make some revisions to his lineup when Bob Skinner, who had been hurt sliding into third base during a rundown in Game One, reported to Forbes Field with a swollen left hand and a swollen thumb. Murtaugh had planned to use right-handed-hitting Dick Stuart at first base, but when Gino Cimoli, also a right-hander, went to left field for Skinner, Murtaugh inserted Rocky Nelson at first base to regain some left-handed hitting in the batting order.

This game was a right-handed battle between pitchers Bob Friend for Pittsburgh and Bob Turley for New York. The Yankees began the scoring with two runs in the third inning and one in the fourth.

The Yankees got two runs in the third inning on a single by Tony Kubek and a double by Gil McDougald. In the fourth, Friend struck out Bill Skowron and Elston Howard for the first two outs, but Bobby Richardson singled and moved to second on a passed ball by Pirates catcher Smoky Burgess. Turley helped his own cause with a single, scoring Richardson. New York held a 3-0 lead.

The Pirates were on the verge of knocking Turley out of the game in their half of the fourth inning. Gino Cimoli singled past a diving Skowron to open the inning. Burgess followed with another single. When Don Hoak doubled off the right-field wall, scoring Cimoli, the Pirates had

the tying runs in scoring position with nobody out. Yankees skipper Casey Stengel conferred with Turley on the mound, but kept him in the game.

Bill Mazeroski then hit a low line drive that was grabbed by Gil McDougald. Although Friend had struck out six in four innings and the Yankees agreed he had shown them better stuff than Vernon Law had in the opener, Murtaugh removed him for a pinch-hitter, Gene Baker, who popped up to Richardson on the grass, and Bill Virdon ended the inning with a groundball to Richardson. Having Baker hit for Friend was a logical decision on Murtaugh's part, but it turned into a bad break for the departed Pirates pitcher.

In the Yankees' fifth, Fred Green, Friend's replacement, walked McDougald with four successive wide pitches. Maris forced him at second. Then, with the count 2 and 2, Mickey Mantle stroked a line-drive home run into the right-center-field seats.

The Yankees were not finished. Elston Howard opened the sixth inning with a ball that bounced off the screen around the light tower in right-center field, eluding a leaping Virdon for a triple. Bobby Richardson then doubled to left to score Howard and finish off Green, who had given up three straight extra-base hits.

Clem Labine relieved Green. Richardson took third on a passed ball, but held there while Labine threw out Turley at first. Tony Kubek grounded to Groat, who fumbled the ball. By the time he recovered, Kubek was at first. McDougald's single scored Richardson, and Maris followed with a bases-loading walk. Mantle struck out, but Berra drove in Kubek and McDougald with a single to center field.

After Skowron singled to score Maris, Murtaugh brought in George Witt to face Elston Howard, up for the second time in the inning. Howard greeted the new pitcher with a single to center, scoring Berra, and Richardson got his second hit of the inning, a center-field single scoring Skowron. Finally, Bob Turley flied to center to end the inning.

Joe Gibbon came in to pitch in the seventh for the Pirates, but fared no better than his predecessors. After singles by Kubek and Joe DeMaestri, Mantle hit an enormous home run over the ivy-covered wall to right-center over the 436-foot sign. Mantle became the first right-handed

hitter to hit the ball over the wall in that area. It had, however been done by left-handers Dale Long, Duke Snider, and Stan Musial. The ball traveled an estimated 478 feet.

When Mantle came to bat in the ninth against Tom Cheney, batting left-handed, he received a big ovation. Cheney walked him on four pitches.

The Pirates, trailing 16-1, started some action in their half of the ninth inning when Joe Christopher was hit by a pitch. Singles by Nelson and Gino Cimoli loaded the bases with one out. Smoky Burgess drove a smash into right field that failed to clear the screen, dropping for a single. Nelson held, unsure whether Maris would catch the ball, and Burgess was trapped off first on the return throw to Richardson. But Richardson threw the ball wide past Skowron, allowing Nelson to score and Cimoli to go to third.

Stengel then brought in Bobby Shantz, who got Don Hoak on a tapper back to the mound to start a game-ending double play.

The 16-3 loss was the worst of the year for the Pirates. Their worst loss during the regular season had been a 13-1 defeat by the Giants in San Francisco on May 8. The Pirates left 13 runners on base, one short of the World Series record set by the Chicago Cubs in 1910 and equaled by the Milwaukee Braves in 1957.

Danny Murtaugh took the defeat philosophically. "I prefer getting beat by a large score as long as we have to lose," he said. "We don't have to worry about a mistake that might have cost us a 2-1 game. I got a chance to get all my young players in. Nobody got hurt, did they? Then we're okay."

The Yankees, unlike the Pirates, took their time leaving for New York. They boarded a Pennsylvania Railroad sleeper that departed at 11 P.M. The Pirates left earlier in the evening on a chartered United Air Lines plane.[9]

Game Three: Saturday, October 8, 1960 at Yankee Stadium / New York 10, Pittsburgh 0

After a one-day layoff the Series moved to Yankee Stadium, and the lopsided Yankee victory in Game Two raised the spirits of Yankees fans. There were approximately 3,500 fans in line when the Stadium gates opened. Three hundred had camped at the gate all night to purchase $2.10 bleacher seats.[10] The Yankees gave the fans their money's worth with a devastating 10-0 victory over the Pirates.

Dick Stuart, one of many Pirates who had never played in Yankee Stadium, was one of the first Pittsburgh players on the field for pregame practice. He measured off the number of steps between first base and the fence in foul territory. He reported that he could take 15 steps to his right for a foul ball.[11]

Pirates starter Vinegar Bend Mizell missed the players' bus from the Hotel Commodore and had to take a taxi to Yankee Stadium.

Finding that it was manager Danny Murtaugh's birthday, Yankees skipper Casey Stengel suggested to sportswriters that they buy him a new car. Reporters joked back that they would buy the car if Casey's bank would finance it.[12]

Pregame ceremonies began with the noted soprano Lucy Monroe singing the National Anthem, accompanied by the 69th Veterans Band, as a Marine color guard raised the flag. Recently retired Boston Red Sox great Ted Williams was given the honor of throwing out the first ball to Yankees catcher Elston Howard.

In the crowd of 70,001 were former President Herbert Hoover and Prime Minister Jawarhalal Nehru of India, who was attending the United Nations General Assembly. Nehru did not arrive until the sixth inning and missed all of the scoring.[13]

World Series records fell as the Yankees crushed the Pirates. New York second baseman Bobby Richardson became an unlikely slugger in the rout. In 1,499 major-league at-bats to that point, Richardson had hit only three home runs. He hit his only home run in the 1960 season on April 30, in Baltimore against Arnold Portocarrero. But on this World Series day he hit a grand slam and drove in six runs. (He had driven in only 26 runs during the regular season.) At first Richardson hadn't realized he had hit a home run. "I saw the left fielder move in while I was running to first base," he said after the game. "Then, after I had rounded first, I saw the umpire in left field twirling his arm above his head. That's the first time I realized the ball went out of the park. I'm not sure how I felt, but I said to myself, 'How about that?' and kept on running."[14]

Mickey Mantle also continued his assault, hitting his third home run of the Series, this one off Fred Green in the fourth inning. The home run put him within one of a tie with Babe Ruth for the World Series career record of 15 homers.

Bob Cerv, the third starting left fielder for the Yankees in three games, opened the game with a single to the left of shortstop Dick Groat. After Roger Maris drove Roberto Clemente to the wall, Mantle singled past pitcher Mizell into center field, moving Cerv to third. Moose Skowron drove in Cerv with a single to center field. After Mizell walked Gil McDougald on four pitches to load the bases, Murtaugh brought in Clem Labine. Labine got two strikes on Elston Howard, but the Yankees catcher tapped an outside pitch toward third base for a single, scoring Mantle. With the bases still full, Richardson was ordered to lay down a squeeze bunt, but fouled off the pitch. With the count 3 and 2, he homered into the lower left-field seats about 30 feet from the foul line. Kubek singled behind second to continue the rally. A Whitey Ford bunt forced Kubek at second, but Kubek's hard block by Kubek to Groat prevented a double play. Cerv hit his second single of the inning and Murtaugh brought in Green to relieve Labine. Maris fouled to catcher Hal Smith, and the 36-minute first inning was over.[15]

Yankees left-hander Whitey Ford kept the Pirates off-balance throughout most of the game. He ran through the Pirates batting order the first time without giving up a hit. In the fourth inning, he had a 3-and-1 count on Bill Virdon before the center fielder doubled off the right-field scoreboard.

Ford opened the Yankees' fourth with a single. Green retired the next two batters, but then Mantle sent his first pitch high into the upper deck in left-center field. Murtaugh called on George Witt to relieve Green. McDougald beat out a slow roller to Don Hoak, and Skowron singled to right. Elston Howard kept things going when his drive bounced off Hoak's shoe for a single, loading the bases. Richardson responded again by lining a single over short for the Yankees' final two runs. A wild pitch moved the runners to second and third, but after Kubek was walked intentionally, Ford grounded out to Bill Mazeroski. The Yankees now led by 10-0, and there was no more scoring in the game.

In the fifth Roger Maris walked with one out and was held up at third, when Mantle bounced the ball into the right-field stands for a double. Skowron grounded to Mazeroski and Maris was trapped off second. Skowron, meanwhile, had rounded first as Maris was ready to dash for home. Mazeroski, after bluffing both runners, threw home as Maris tried to score. Maris was out and was forced to leave the game after bruising his chest on his unsuccessful slide.[16]

Gino Cimoli received Ford's only walk, in the seventh inning after a one-out single by Dick Stuart, but Hal Smith hit a double-play ball to end the inning. Until Roberto Clemente singled in the ninth inning with two out, those were the Pirates' only baserunners. After Tony Kubek bobbled a grounder by Stuart, Ford guaranteed his shutout by striking out Cimoli.

Whitey Ford had superb control while tossing the first complete World Series game since 1958. He threw 111 pitches and had a three-ball count on a batter only three times. The Yankees left-hander said he did not become complacent even with a ten-run lead. "I kept bearing down," he said. "Whenever I have a big lead like that, I just pretend the score is 2-1 and keep bearing down."

For the first time since 1949, Yogi Berra was not in the starting lineup of a Yankees World Series game. He did, however, appear in his 57th consecutive Series game when he replaced Roger Maris in right field in the seventh. When a writer asked Casey Stengel if Yogi was unhappy, Stengel replied, "Why should he get mad? If your boss told you to take the day off, would you be mad?"[17]

"That was a heck of a birthday present," Danny Murtaugh remarked after the game. Earlier he had received two packs of chewing tobacco from his daughter to celebrate his 43rd birthday. Asked in the locker room after the game what he would like for his birthday, Murtaugh said, "To see my 44th birthday."[18] Murtaugh and his wife went to see the musical *My Fair Lady* that evening and most of the players dined with friends and relatives at Danny's Hideaway.

The Pirates had been blown out two games in a row, but Game Four would find Pirates ace Vernon Law on the mound. Law owned the lone Series win for Pittsburgh and had stopped the team's two longest losing streaks during the regular season.

It wasn't over yet.

Game Four: Sunday, October 9, 1960 at Yankee Stadium / Pittsburgh 3, New York 2

Yankee fans came to Game Four on the heels of two games that made them wonder how Pittsburgh had got into the World Series. Their hometown hitters had devastated Pirates pitching, and the Pirates' hitters had been blown away by Yankees pitching. Game Four would illustrate what the "real" Pirates were all about.

Yankees pitchers and hitters weren't the only ones treating their Pittsburgh guests inhospitably. During the pregame practice Bill Mazeroski's wife, Milene, came down to the railing to take a picture of her husband, but the Yankee Stadium guards wouldn't permit it.[19]

The weekend games in New York had brought a huge crowd of fans from Pittsburgh, including several busloads of steelworkers. At times the cheers for the Pirates were as noisy as the applause for the home-team Yankees.[20]

Back in the lineup for Game Four was Roger Maris, who suffered a bruised chest in his home-plate collision with Pirates catcher Hal Smith in the seventh inning of Game Three. Bob Skinner, who jammed his thumb sliding into third base in Game One, took batting practice for the first time since his injury. He had sponge rubber wrapped around the bat to absorb the shock where his injured thumb gripped, but found it still too painful to play. "I caught a line drive during practice and I thought my whole thumb was going to come off," Skinner said later. A suggestion to use Novocain to deaden the pain was rejected.[21]

To many, Game Four was arguably the finest game of the 1960 World Series. The Pirates trailed 1-0, after four innings, but seized the lead by scoring three runs in the top of the fifth off Ralph Terry, and used exceptional pitching and fielding to hold the lead and grab the win. Their 3-2 victory assured that for the sixth consecutive year it would take at least six games to declare the champions. It also meant the Series would go back to Pittsburgh for the conclusion.

Under the Yankee Stadium lights, which had been turned on to provide more light for the color TV cameras, the Pirates broke through against Ralph Terry. Starter Vernon Law supplied the key hit, a double after two outs. After relieving Law in the seventh, Elroy Face set down the eight Yankees he faced thanks to his amazing forkball and help in the field from Bill Virdon and Don Hoak.[22]

Before the Pirates' outburst in the fifth inning, Terry had experienced a rather easy outing. In the first three innings the only baserunner against him was Smoky Burgess, who walked in the second inning. Terry had an easy fourth, and was helped when Bill Skowron slammed a home run in the Yankees' half of the inning. But all this ended when the Pirates came to bat in the fifth. After 13 successive scoreless innings the Pirates magic returned.[23]

Gino Cimoli opened with a single that dropped in front of Roger Maris. Skowron went to his right for a half-speed roller by Burgess. He tried for a force play at second, but the ball was late and the Pirates had two men on. Don Hoak then tried to push a bunt over the heads of Richardson and Skowron, but he popped the ball up and Richardson caught it. When Skowron caught Bill Mazeroski's pop fly near the mound, it seemed as if Terry had pitched out of the jam. But Vernon Law, a .181 hitter during the season, lined Terry's first pitch to left. The ball bounced against the low barrier and Cimoli scored the tying run as Law went to second. With two strikes on him, Bill Virdon dropped a single in front of the charging Mantle, scoring Burgess and Law. Captain Dick Groat popped up to end the inning but the Pirates led, 3-1.[24]

The Pirates threatened again in the seventh inning. Hoak lined Terry's first pitch to center field for a single and Mazeroski sacrificed. Law then continued his hitting streak with a liner that bounced off third baseman Gil McDougald's glove into foul territory for a single that moved Hoak to third. Stengel called in southpaw Bobby Shantz to relieve Terry. Shantz struck out Virdon, then got Groat to ground into a force out, ending the threat.

Skowron led off the bottom of the seventh with a shot off the white foul pole for a ground-rule double. McDougald dropped a single in front of Clemente in right field, and Skowron went to third. Murtaugh went to the mound to confer with Law and decided to leave him in.[25] Richardson grounded to Mazeroski for a force-out and a possible

inning-ending double play, but Mazeroski's throw to first was late and Skowron scored. When John Blanchard, pinch-hitting for Shantz, drilled a single into right field, Murtaugh decided it was time for Face. Bob Cerv hit a drive to deep right-center field off Face, but Virdon caught up with the ball at the 407-foot marker. Face then finished off the inning by fielding Kubek's bouncer and throwing him out at first.

Yankees right-hander Jim Coates pitched for the Yankees in the eighth and threw a non-eventful 1-2-3 inning. Face retired the Yankees in order in the bottom of the inning. In the top of the ninth Mickey Mantle demonstrated that he could play center field as well as Virdon when he made a running one-handed catch of a drive by Hoak to deep right-center field.[26]

In the bottom of the ninth, Bob Oldis replaced Smoky Burgess as the Pirates' catcher. Skowron promptly hammered a long drive to right, but it curved foul. Then, on a 2-and-2 count, he lined the ball down the third-base line. Hoak shifted his glove to the right, made the stop, and threw to Stuart for the out. McDougald followed with a liner to Groat, and Long ended the game with a fly ball to Clemente.

After the game Mickey Mantle and Yogi Berra had nothing but praise for Roy Face. "They talk about his forkball and you get the wrong idea," Mantle said. "He's no junk pitcher. He's quick. His fastball is plenty fast enough." Yogi commented, "He has a funny, little jiggling motion as he lets go of the ball that confuses you a little. I suppose after a while you get used to it."[27]

Roy Face did not see the Pirates score their three runs in the fifth inning. Bob Oldis, who was in the bullpen then, commented, "We're not exactly superstitious. But we like to change things around when we aren't winning, like our seats. That's how come Face didn't see the inning. He had decided to sit with his back to the field."[28]

Mantle credited Bill Virdon with keeping the Pirates in the Series. "He's made two great catches that saved victories for them in the first and fourth games," Mickey said. "If it hadn't been for him, we probably would have the Series all wrapped up by now and been on our way home."[29] Virdon's response was, "I guess it's better to be lucky than good. I've been lucky in the outfield and today

I was lucky at the plate. Ralph Terry had two strikes on me and hung a curve up high and I hit it for a two-run single."[30]

After the game the Yankees complained that they had been hurt by the umpires on two decisions. Yogi Berra felt that he had beaten Don Hoak's throw to first for the double play that took Vernon Law out of a first-inning jam, and Ralph Terry thought his throw to second base for an attempted force out in the fifth inning beat Gino Cimoli to the bag.

Manager Casey Stengel would not support criticism of Bill Skowron because of his late throw to second that set up Pittsburgh's three-run inning. "If the play was as close as it looked, he had to try to get the man," said Casey. "Besides, we had our chances to score and there were some mistakes made by the pitchers that didn't help us."[31]

Through the first four games the Yankees had 56 hits, 32 runs, and 7 home runs. The Pirates had 32 hits, 12 runs, and one home run. But the Series was even at 2-2.

Game Five: Monday, October 10, 1960 at Yankee Stadium / Pittsburgh 5, New York 2

When the sportswriters questioned Yankees manager Casey Stengel about starting Art Ditmar in Game Five, at Yankee Stadium, his response was: "Well, I'll tell you. I spoke to the Baltimore writers and they've got the best pitching staff in the league and so I figure they know more about it than anybody else. They advised that I go with Ditmar." In typical Stengel style, he concluded his remark with a wink.[32]

Later Casey asked John Carmichael, a longtime friend and the sports editor of the *Chicago Daily News*, who he thought would be managing the Cubs in the coming season. "I don't know," Carmichael replied. "But the way you're going, they may even make you an offer."[33]

When reporters asked what the Pirates were paying him, Elroy Face replied, "That's between me and Joe Brown." Remembering he had left someone out, he quickly added, "And my wife."[34]

Face's spectacular Series performance may have been motivated by more than the money involved. Before the game he sent a program over to the Yankees clubhouse to be autographed. It came back without a single signature.[35]

In the Yankees' first inning, Bob Cerv beat out a slow roller to third base with two out, then went to second on Don Hoak's wild throw. Pirates pitcher Harvey Haddix walked Mickey Mantle intentionally, but struck out Bill Skowron to retire the side.

The Pirates' big inning was the second, which Dick Stuart started with a line single to left field. Gino Cimoli hit a slow bouncer to Bobby Richardson near second base. Richardson tagged Stuart, but had no chance for a double play. Smoky Burgess lined a double down the right-field line on the first pitch to him from Ditmar, and Cimoli went to third.

Don Hoak topped the ball to shortstop Kubek, who couldn't get to the ball quickly enough to keep Cimoli from scoring. Kubek threw to third to try to get Burgess, but the ball got away from McDougald. He was safe, and Hoak went to second. Bill Mazeroski hit a chopper that took an extremely high bounce and rolled into left field for a double. Burgess and Hoak scored. Luis Arroyo, a former Pirate, relieved Ditmar and promptly struck out Haddix and got Bill Virdon to foul out to McDougald. At the end of two innings the Pirates led 2-0.

Catcher Elson Howard opened the bottom of the second with a drive to the right-field wall for a double. Howard took third as Richardson grounded out, Mazeroski to Haddix, and scored when Kubek grounded to first baseman Stuart. Arroyo grounded to Groat for the third out.

The Pirates quickly disposed of Arroyo in the third. Groat doubled off the left-field fence, then scored on a single to left by Roberto Clemente. Stengel brought in Bill Stafford, who retired the next three batters.

In the bottom of the third, McDougald bounced to Haddix. Roger Maris then hit a 3-and-1 pitch into the third tier of the right-field stands for a home run, cutting the Pirates' lead to 4-2.

The Pirates' fourth had some strange plays, but the Yankees worked out of it. Leading off, Hoak got a hit on a ball that took a bounce just as Kubek was ready to field it. Mazeroski grounded to Kubek for the beginning of what seemed to be a double play, but Richardson threw past first and Mazeroski was safe. Stafford got Haddix to hit into a double play that ended the inning without any runs being scored.

The Pirates were guilty of two errant plays in the Yankees' fourth, but New York failed to capitalize. It began when Howard was safe at first on a high throw from Groat. The error was canceled out, however, when Mazeroski caught Richardson's liner and doubled Howard off first. Kubek struck out for what should have been the third out, but ended up on base when Burgess was charged with his third passed ball, a World Series record. Fortunately for Pittsburgh, Haddix struck out Stafford for the final out of the inning.

Haddix and Stafford were both in command through the sixth inning, but with two out in the Pirates' seventh, Haddix beat out a hit in back of first, and Bill Virdon doubled off first baseman Bill Skowron's glove. With men on second and third, Groat flied to Cerv in left field to end the threat.

In the Yankees' seventh, Hoak made what Pirates manager Danny Murtaugh later said was the most vital defensive play of the game when he grabbed a low liner off the bat of Bobby Richardson. What followed could have been disastrous for the Pirates if not for that play. That was because Kubek hit a single to center and Hector Lopez, batting for Stafford, hit to right for a single. Murtaugh brought in Elroy Face, got McDougald to hit into a force out. That brought up Maris, and after two fouls, Face got him with a forkball, ending the inning with no runs scored, and the score remained Pittsburgh 4, New York 2.

Ryne Duren, Stafford's replacement, got through the Pirates' eighth without any problems. Meanwhile, Face was looking at the Yankees power hitters. Bob Cerv flied out to Virdon in right-center, and, for the seventh time in the Series, Mantle walked—on four pitches. Moose Skowron excited the crowd with a foul "home run" to left, but eventually popped up to Groat near the third-base line. Yogi Berra, batting for Howard and appearing in his 66th World Series game, grounded to Mazeroski.

After the Yankee Stadium lights were turned on, the Pirates added an insurance run to their total in the ninth. Burgess singled to left to open the inning and went to second when Cerv bobbled the ball. Joe Christopher, running for Burgess, went to third on a Duren wild pitch off Berra's glove. Christopher scored when Duren just missed a ball hit by Hoak and it went into center field for a single. Duren got by Mazeroski, Face, and Virdon with no further scoring.

With Bob Oldis, the Pirates' best defensive catcher, as his batterymate, Face finished off the ninth. Groat threw out Richardson, then fielded Kubek's popup near first base for out number two. John Blanchard, hitting for Duren, sent Clemente to the warning track for the catch and the game was over. Face and the Pirates had done it again. They were up three games to two and heading back to Pittsburgh.

Questioned again after the game concerning his choice of Art Ditmar, Stengel this time responded, "After all, the fella is experienced and he was my top winner with 15 victories. He certainly had plenty of rest, too, didn't he?"[36]

Asked whether he would call the Yankees' position desperate, Casey replied, "You can call it that, if you like. I won't. But I can count, you know!"[37]

The Yankees manager also complained that the lights were turned on too late in the game. He said: "Both sides quit hittin' in the seventh and eighth and, when they got the lights on in the ninth, it was too late."[38]

On the Pirates' flight home, a stewardess on the chartered plane, in an attempt to be hospitable, offered a toast to the Pirates as the plane landed at the Pittsburgh airport. Perhaps not a baseball fan she declared: "Here's to the next world's champions, the Pittsburgh Steelers!"[39]

Game Six: Wednesday, October 12, 1960 at Forbes Field / New York 12, Pittsburgh 0

The Pirates came home leading the Series three games to two. If they won Game Six they would defeat the mighty New York Yankees and claim their first world championship since they defeated the Washington Senators in 1925. As the Series returned to Pittsburgh and Forbes Field for Game Six, the Pirates' regular fans, the ordinary people who formed the bulk of their supporters, predominated in the crowd. The fans began arriving early with lines for standing-room tickets stretching through Schenley Park across Panther Hollow Bridge and around the rear of Phipps Conservatory. The crowd eventually totaled 38,580. Benny Benack and his Iron City Six serenaded the fans with "The Bucs Are Goin' All The Way," the

Pirates' fight song, at the main entrance an hour before game time.

At his daily meeting with the writers in the Yankees dugout, manager Casey Stengel explained why Whitey Ford was his choice for starting pitcher: "If I'd have taken a vote of my fellers, you know what could have happened? Ford would have gotten all the votes but maybe six or eight and the reason he wouldn't have gotten those six or eight is because some of the pitchers would have voted for themselves."[40]

Continuing the double-talk that had made him famous, Casey continued, "Turley does better as a relief pitcher than Ford. I tried Ford in relief in a game up in Boston. The Red Sox had the bases full. Vic Wertz was coming to bat so I took out Turley and put in Ford. I figured Wertz would never hit one in the bleachers off'n Whitey. But Wertz did. So I knew that Ford doesn't do so good in relief as he does in starting. And I know that Turley pitched good in relief for me in the World Series against Milwaukee. That is how I picked Ford to be my starter for the sixth game."[41]

For his part, Ford said he hadn't known until 11 o'clock that he would be the starter. "I had an idea I was going," he said, "but I wasn't sure."[42] He was going to the mound on three days' rest after his 10-0 shutout of the Pirates in Game Three. Whitey was shaky in the first inning when Bill Virdon led off with a single. Dick Groat hit a double-play grounder to Richardson, but Roberto Clemente singled. That brought Bob Turley to life in the bullpen, but Ford fanned Dick Stuart for the third out.

The Yankees broke through in the second against Bob Friend. Yogi Berra walked with one out. Bill Skowron's single to right put Berra on third. When Elston Howard was hit on the finger by a pitch, the bases were loaded. Howard had to come out of the game with a broken finger and pitcher Eli Grba ran for him. The runners held on Bobby Richardson's short fly, but Ford lashed a single off Friend's glove, and Berra scored. Clete Boyer, back starting at third base, struck out on three pitches.

When he ran for Howard, Grba was the last of the two teams' 50 World Series-eligible players to get into action, and the only member of the Yankees pitching staff who had not been used on the mound. Even without Grba, the

Pirates and Yankees had set a record for the most different pitchers appearing in a World Series. Each used ten for a total of 20, surpassing the record of ten used in the Dodgers-Yankees World Series of 1953.

In the Pirates' second, Gino Cimoli was out on a high bounder to Boyer, but Hal Smith singled to left on a changeup. Boyer fielded Hoak's high chopper and Richardson stretched for the force at second base. Bill Mazeroski finished the inning by hitting a deep fly to Mickey Mantle.

Friend hit Kubek with a wide-breaking curveball to lead off the third inning, and that was the start of a five-run outburst by the Yankees. Roger Maris doubled off the right-field screen and Mantle lined a single past Friend into center, scoring Kubek and Maris. Yogi Berra singled, and that was it for Friend. Murtaugh brought in left-handed pitcher Tom Cheney, who couldn't stop the scoring. Bill Skowron drove in Mantle with a sacrifice fly, Johnny Blanchard singled, and Bobby Richardson drove in the two runners with a triple off the left-field scoreboard. The two RBIs were Richardson's 10th and 11th, a World Series record, and the Yankees led 6-0.

Friend had no excuses for his poor performance except that he could not control his breaking pitches. The one that fractured Elston Howard's right little finger in the second inning "moved at least a foot," he said.[43]

Vinegar Bend Mizell pitched a scoreless fourth and fifth for the Pirates, but Fred Green felt the sting of the Yankee bats in the sixth. Clete Boyer smashed a triple to right center and came in on Kubek's single to the same area. It was 7-0 Yankees. Roger Maris singled to right, and manager Murtaugh brought in Clem Labine. Mantle struck out, but Berra singled to right field, scoring Kubek.

In the Yankees' seventh Johnny Blanchard doubled off the top of the right-field screen. Richardson drove in his 12th run of the Series with a triple to the wall in right-center, and he scored when Ford beat out a bunt to third. Boyer bounced into a double play and Virdon made a tumbling catch of a Kubek low liner.

The Yankees' third consecutive two-run inning, the eighth, began with a Maris single to right, his third hit of the game. He was forced at second by Mantle, who advanced on Labine's wild pitch and scored on Berra's third hit, a single to center. Virdon was charged with an error when he threw past catcher Hal Smith, Berra going to second. Skowron grounded out, but Blanchard doubled off the right-field wall, scoring Berra. It was 12-0 in New York's favor. Neither team scored in the ninth.

The Bronx Bombers had deadlocked the Series on Whitey Ford's second shutout. And Ford had hung a second defeat on Bob Friend in his own Forbes Field.

The question now loomed—could the Yankees win the last big one? Precedent was on their side. In 1958, trailing Milwaukee three games to one, they had won three in a row. In 1956 they captured the seventh game from the Brooklyn Dodgers. In 1952 they won the last two of a seven-game set against the Dodgers. In 1951, they took three in a row from the Dodgers for the championship in six games.

For Whitey Ford, his victory in Game Six was his first in a World Series contest away from Yankee Stadium. He was now 6-1 at the Stadium and 1-3 away from home as a pitcher in the fall classic.

Danny Murtaugh was not pleased with Dick Stuart's batting and fielding. He said he would have Rocky Nelson on first base in the final game. Earlier, the Pirates manager had said, "Stuart will play at first base until he goofs off."[44] Stuart inflamed Murtaugh when he merely waved at a groundball single by Maris.

"This is a funny game," Yogi Berra said in the clubhouse. "We flatten them by scores of 16-3, 10-0, and 12-0 and still they're even with us in games. It just don't figure. Even if they beat us, we've got the much better club."[45]

The Yankees' 46-17 advantage in runs scored over the course of the first six games did not dishearten Danny Murtaugh. "The Series isn't decided on runs scored," he growled. "It's decided on games won."[46]

Commissioner Ford Frick more or less concurred: "In a Series, the only run that counts is the final winning one."[47]

Game Seven: Thursday, October 13, 1960 at Forbes Field / Pittsburgh 10, New York 9

Don Hoak felt that the 12-0 romp in Game Six would motivate the Pirates. "The sixth-game loss was the turning point for the team emotionally," Hoak insisted. "We had a short team meeting and everybody agreed we already had a great year. We could get beat 15 to nothing tomorrow, but still would have had a great season. We were more relaxed for the seventh game than any game in the Series."[48]

Manager Danny Murtaugh embellished a biblical quote prior to the start of the game when he stated to reporters, "Everybody else but Law will be in the bullpen, and if I may give you a twisted quote from the Bible, many are chosen, but I hope few will be called."[49]

A conservative crowd entered Forbes Field for Game Seven. Watching fans collect outside the ballpark, police Inspector Vincent Dixon commented, "Everybody's in a daze. They're confused. They took a beating and they know it."[50]

Hoping to arouse some pregame excitement, Benny Benack and his band once again played every song they could think of at the corner of Sennott and Bouquet Streets. But other than an occasional cheer of "Beat 'em, Bucs," the crowd was unresponsive. Marcy Lynn, the band's vocalist, was somewhat prophetic when she commented, "These people are so quiet. I think they are afraid to get excited. But we'll be here after the game and they'll be excited then."[51]

Leo Parker, a concessionaire, held the same optimism. "The spirit of the crowd is gone," he said, "But after the game—watch out. They'll go crazy."[52]

The Pittsburgh parking lot ordinance, enacted to protect World Series fans from sudden price increases, failed in its aim. In most of the lots prices, which had been dropped to $2, were back up to $5. Even so, most lots were full or nearly full.

A very legal-looking document appeared on the door of the office of Thomas E. Barrett, Allegheny County clerk of courts, in the County Courthouse on the morning of Game Seven. An official order, signed by Judge Samuel A. Weiss, authorized the clerk of courts to close at 12:30 P.M. Underneath the order was a supplementary document, not signed by Judge Weiss, stating: "Our other grandmother died. We have gone to bury her with the Yanks."[53]

For five innings it looked as if the Pirates' Vernon Law was headed for a record-tying third Series win. Two new faces in the starting lineup, Bob Skinner, starting in left field for the first time since Game One, and Rocky Nelson, replacing Dick Stuart at first base, combined for a 2-0 lead off Yankees pitcher Bob Turley in the first inning. Skinner walked and Nelson slammed a two-run homer over the screen in right field.

In the second inning it quickly became 4-0. Smoky Burgess rammed a pitch inside the first-base line and down into the right-field corner. Roger Maris's quick recovery held it to a single. Bill Stafford relieved Turley and walked Don Hoak on four straight pitches. Bill Mazeroski then bunted down the third-base line and beat Stafford's off-balance throw to fill the bases. Pirates pitcher Vernon Law hit a one-bouncer to Stafford for a home-to-first double play, but Virdon's long single to right-center field scored both Hoak and Mazeroski. The Pirates were working their magic.

Yankees pitcher Bobby Shantz took over for Stafford in the third inning and blanked the Pirates for five innings, facing only 15 batters. Meanwhile the Yankees did some scoring of their own. In the fifth Bill Skowron homered off Law, but "The Deacon" did not allow any further scoring. Earlier, Murtaugh had said, "All I want from Vern today is five good innings, if he can give me that, I'll have Face and Friend ready."[54]

Murtaugh kept his word after Bobby Richardson singled and Tony Kubek walked to start the sixth inning. Although his ankle was giving him a lot of trouble, Law felt that with the four-run lead he could win the game. But Murtaugh went out to the mound and told him, "You have a lot of years left in baseball and I don't want you to risk your arm because you have a bad ankle. Dizzy Dean did it and I don't want it to happen to you."[55] Danny asked if the ankle was bothering him, but Law shook his head no. However, Hoak said he felt the ankle was hindering Law, and that's when Murtaugh signaled for Elroy Face.

For the first time in the Series, the Pirates' magnificent relief pitcher didn't have it. He got Roger Maris out on a foul, but a skidding grounder by Mickey Mantle rolled past Dick Groat for a single. Yogi Berra then hit his 11th World Series home run high into the second deck in right field, erasing the Pirates' advantage and putting the Yankees ahead, 5-4.

In the eighth the Yankees added two more runs when, with two out, Berra walked, Skowron and Johnny Blanchard singled, and Clete Boyer doubled down the left-field line.

Bottom of the eighth, Game Seven, down 7-4. It was time for the Pirates to go to work.

Gino Cimoli, pinch-hitting for Face, singled to right-center field off Shantz. Then came what many call the break of the game. Bill Virdon slashed what appeared to be a routine double-play grounder at Tony Kubek. The ball came up hard and struck Kubek in the throat, knocking him to the ground, stunned. After Kubek had lain on the ground for several moments, Casey Stengel ordered him to the bench. Kubek protested, but was replaced by Joe DeMaestri.

When the game continued, Dick Groat singled home Cimoli with a shot to left. After Jim Coates relieved Bobby Shantz, Bob Skinner moved the tying runs up with a sacrifice. Both runners held as Nelson flied out, bringing Roberto Clemente to the plate. Clemente bounced a slow roller toward first. Another routine play except for one thing: No one covered first base. Clemente was safe and Virdon scored. It was 7-6, Yankees.

Up came catcher Hal Smith, in the game only because Smoky Burgess had gone out for a pinch-runner. With the count 2-2, Hal swung and smashed a home run over the left-field wall. He leaped and danced around the bases before being greeted by Clemente and Groat, who were also jumping with joy. With five runs scored, the Pirates had retaken then lead and held a 9-7 edge.

Casey Stengel, who had earlier gone to the mound to encourage Coates to bear down, went out again. This time he replaced him with Ralph Terry, who quickly ended the inning, getting Hoak on a fly ball to left. Only three outs stood between the Pirates and the world championship.

But the Yankees were not quite finished. Bob Friend came in to close the game down and they quickly jumped on him with singles by Bobby Richardson and pinch-hitter Dale Long. Murtaugh wasted no time bringing in Harvey Haddix. Haddix retired Maris on a popup, but Mantle singled to right, scoring Richardson. It was 9-8. Berra shot a one-bounce smash to first base. Rocky Nelson grabbed it spectacularly and stepped on first base for the second out. Instrad of running to second, Mantle dove back into first. Nelson tried to tag Mantle, but Mickey got back safely as pinch-runner Gil McDougald scored the tying run from third base. Skowron's grounder forced Mantle at second base for the third out.

Now it was the bottom of the ninth, score tied 9-9, with Bill Mazeroski at bat facing Ralph Terry as Art Ditmar warmed up in the Yankee bullpen and Dick Stuart waited in the on-deck circle to bat for Haddix.

This is how Bill Mazeroski described the at-bat: "Nobody told me what to do when I went up to hit in the ninth inning. The score was tied 9-9, and I knew the only important thing was for me to get on somehow.

"I let the first pitch go by. I was waiting for a high fast ball. The second pitch was a fast ball - much like the one I hit for a homer in the first game - and I knew I got good wood on it.

"A cold chill ran down my back a moment after I hit that ball in the ninth inning.

"For a second I didn't know quite what to do. But the message finally got to my legs and I set sail.

"I can't begin to describe how I felt when I saw the ball clear the wall. Time seemed to stand still for an instant.

"Then I ran.

"It was the biggest thrill I ever had. I was so happy I didn't even know what was going through my mind. I do remember when the ball disappeared over the wall. I grabbed my cap and started running. I never thought this would ever happen to me.

"That was some scene when I came into home plate. It looked like half of Forbes Field was there waiting for me. I didn't care though.

"The umpire (Bill Jackowski) cleared a path for me. I made doggone sure to touch home plate, though. I wouldn't miss that for the world.

"Getting back to the clubhouse was a real struggle, but I enjoyed every minute of the way. All I could see was a lot of faces in front of me. It reminded me of being downtown on New Year's Eve."[56]

The Pirates were World Champions!

There was a stunned silence in Forbes Field when the bat cracked against the ball and it began its flight toward the left-field wall.

Not even the calls of the vendors could be heard. They had all stopped to watch.

The silence lasted until the ball cleared the wall, then Forbes Field exploded.

It seemed as if all 36,683 present burst into cheers and screams. Paper billowed onto the field as confetti rained on the lower boxes.

Fans vaulted over the railings, mobbing the players at home plate.

Outside the park horns began blowing as people danced in the streets, hugging and kissing.

"Destiny's Darlings" had done it!

Notes

1 *Pittsburgh Post Gazette*, October 6, 1960.

2 Ibid.

3 Ibid.

4 Ibid.

5 Ibid.

6 Ibid.

7 Interview with Bill Mazeroski, 2009.

8 Interview with Vernon Law, 2009.

9 All information for Game Two was obtained from the *Pittsburgh Post Gazette* or the *Pittsburgh Press* editions of October 6, 1960.

10 *Pittsburgh Post-Gazette*, October 9, 1960.

11 Ibid.

12 Ibid.

13 *The Sporting News*, October 12, 1960.

14 *Pittsburgh Press,* October 9, 1960.

15 Ibid.

16 *Pittsburgh Post-Gazette*, October 9, 1960.

17 Ibid.

18 Ibid.

19 *Pittsburgh Post Gazette*, October 9, 1960.

20 Ibid.

21 Ibid.

22 *Pittsburgh Press*, October 9, 1960.

23 Ibid.

24 *Pittsburgh Post Gazette*, October 9, 1960.

25 Ibid.

26 *Pittsburgh Press*, October 9, 1960.

27 *Pittsburgh Post Gazette*, October 9, 1960.

28 Ibid.

29 *Pittsburgh Press*, October 9, 1960.

Ibid.

30 Ibid.

31 Ibid.

32 *Pittsburgh Post-Gazette*, October 11, 1960.

33 Ibid.

34 Interview with Elroy Face, June 18, 2009.

35 Ibid.

36 *Pittsburgh Press*, October 11, 1960.

37 Ibid.

38 Ibid.

39 Interview with Elroy Face, 2009.

40 *Pittsburgh Press*, October 13, 1960.

41 Ibid.

42 Ibid.

43 Ibid.

44 *Pittsburgh Post Gazette*, October 13, 1960.

45 Ibid.

46 Ibid.

47 Ibid.

48 *Pittsburgh Post Gazette*, October 14, 1960.

49 Ibid.

50 Ibid.

51 *Pittsburgh Press*, October 14, 1960.

52 Ibid.

53 Ibid.

54 Ibid.

55 Ibid.

56 Ibid.

The 1960 Pittsburgh Pirates, Local Sportswriters, and Coming to Believe in a Team of Destiny

by Jorge Iber

THE 1960 MAJOR-LEAGUE season has been referred to as the "Last Pure Season," for it was the final year in which each league played in the traditional eight-team format before the American League expanded to ten teams with the Los Angeles Angels and the "replacement" Washington Senators.[1] Entering the season it was 35 years since the Pittsburgh Pirates had won a World Series and 33 since they had won the pennant in 1927—the team that was swept by the Murderers Row Yankees. As *Pittsburgh Post-Gazette* sportswriter Robert Dvorchak noted in 2010, it had been so long since the Bucs had been in contention (though they did have a decent season in 1958—finishing 84-70, in second place, eight games out of first place) that "the city didn't know what a pennant race was like, nobody remembered it."[2]

More familiar to the fans of the Steel City was the bumbling and inept "Rickey Dinks" crew that struggled mightily during the 1950s, bottoming out with a ghastly 42-112 mark in 1952. One of the people who suffered through those extremely difficult years was a World War II veteran turned sports reporter for the *Post-Gazette* named John Lawrence "Jack" Hernon, Jr., who began working for the paper in 1949.[3] While Hernon witnessed some of the worst years in the Pirates' chronicle, he had also been a spectator to some of the glorious moments of the 1920s. Given the struggles he observed, it is not surprising that he wanted to share the excitement of the 1960 World Series with his

young son. In a warm and touching column at the start of the 1960 World Series, Hernon asked his boy's instructors at a local Catholic school for some indulgence, noting that:

In case Monsignor Thomas Henninger, out in St. Theresa's Parish, is reading this column, there was an absentee from the classroom yesterday. Thirty-three years ago my dad took me to a ball game on the same date, October 5. The Pirates then played in a World Series against the Yankees. That day my mom took me in, too, and bought the hotdogs and pop. Yesterday, my son's mom bought him the hotdogs.[4]

In a wonderful happenstance, three different generations of the Hernon family (Jack's father, John L. Hernon, had been a reporter for the Tri-State News Service during the 1920s) had been granted the privilege to witness their hometown Pirates in a World Series against the Yankees.[5] While there was certainly much excitement and joy at the events that bookended the family's tale, the intermittent lean campaigns made Jack leery of placing full faith on the success of the local nine. Hernon's reflections of the 1960 season, as demonstrated in his (and some of his colleagues') columns, reveal a level of trepidation that accompanied the desire to be an objective reporter of events but also support his hometown team and take part in the citywide enthusiasm as "his" squad, against seemingly long odds, became a "team of destiny."[6]

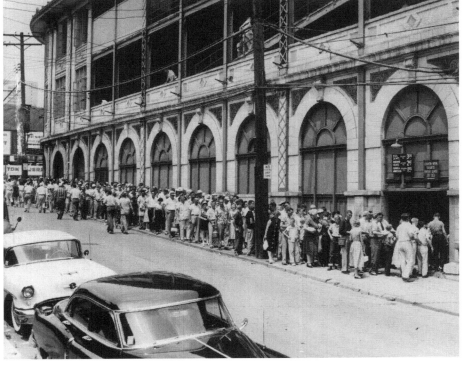

Starting in 1958, the Pirates drew more than 1 million fans each year to Forbes Field for five straight seasons.

After the dramatic upturn by the Pirates in 1958 (a 22-win improvement), it seemed that all was in place for a title run. "After many campaigns with little to cheer about, that season was an exhilarating one for long suffering Pirate fans," a writer asserted four decades later. "The Bucs had not been in a pennant race in September since World War II."[7] Among the many highlights that year were Dick Groat hitting .300; Bill Mazeroski belting 19 home runs and hitting .275; and Roberto Clemente playing outstanding defense and hitting .289. In addition, Bob Friend won 22 games, Vern Law chipped in 14 victories, and Elroy Face led the National League with 20 saves.[8] Unfortunately for the Pirates and their fans, things did not turn out as expected and the 1959 edition of the Bucs stumbled out of the gate, not reaching the .500 mark until the middle of May and being below breakeven as late as mid-July. In addition, as a perfect example of an having an off year, Friend went from winning 22 games to losing 19, and Clemente was out for six weeks with a sore elbow. The lowlight, undoubtedly, was Harvey Haddix's 12 innings of perfection and 13th-inning frustration on May 26 against Milwaukee. If anything could encapsulate a down year, it certainly would be the waste of such an outstanding and historic effort. Still, the team eventually rallied to move to within 3½ games of the lead by September 1. For a city that had waited so many years for a title, with the University of Pittsburgh Panthers football team enduring a similarly long dry spell, and the Steelers not yet amounting to much (for example, cutting Johnny Unitas in 1955 only to have him become a star with the Baltimore Colts), there was reason for both trepidation and sanguinity.[9]

The wide diversity of opinion concerning the Pirates' chances for 1960 were reflected in the local and national press. Fearless forecasters chimed in with guesstimates ranging from the *New York Daily News*' Dick Young and Rick Roberts of the *Pittsburgh Courier* arguing that the Pirates would win the pennant, to *Post-Gazette* sports editor Al Abrams prognosticating a second-place finish (though he did mention that the Pirates had the potential to be dark horses for the pennant), to Les Biederman of the *Pittsburgh Press* foreseeing the squad finishing in fourth place, and Bill Nunn of the *Pittsburgh Courier* anticipating a tumble into sixth place.

Jack Hernon concurred with his colleague Biederman and stated that Pittsburgh was "the iffiest" club in the circuit and that "maybe they can become contenders, but right now they don't appear in that capacity."[10] Indeed, Hernon joked in one of his spring-training columns that fans in Fort Myers (and, one would assume the writer himself) made fun of a local merchant, Chuck Ross of the Arcade Cigar Store, who in mid-March posted signs in his front window bearing the audacious proclamation: "Pirates, World Champions of 1960."[11] By the end of spring training Hernon summarized the outlook for the coming campaign by stating: "The league is strong … and the row will be a hard one. … the Pirates will … [be] scrambling for runs. The power isn't there to overcome anyone very often. Pitching will be the big thing. They don't appear as a serious threat, though."[12]

An early sign that 1960 might finally be "different" for the Pirates came early, and left most denizens of the city almost speechless. On Easter Sunday the Bucs swept a twin bill from the Cincinnati Reds, 5-0 and 6-5. The second game "proved a harbinger of the season" as Pittsburgh, shut out on five hits through eight innings, exploded for a six-run rally in the bottom of the ninth to win the game. As Hernon noted the next day, "rousing finishes have come to be expected in Forbes Field, but not anything like this one."[13]

By the close of April the Pirates sported a sparkling 11-3 record, and some of the local fourth estate started to take notice. Harry Keck of the *Sun-Telegraph* (recently merged with the *Post-Gazette*), for example, opined in early May that in "the language of the day, the Pirates are in orbit, man. … They're acting like the team they should have been in 1959. … It's a little too early for pennant talk, but we can dream, can't we?"[14] Still, Hernon generally stuck with his less optimistic views, writing on May 6 that while the Pirates, "are giving off the air they think they can win … so far, the pitching hasn't been pennant caliber."[15] He expounded upon his concerns about the club's hurlers by asserting later that month that players were disappointed with the lack of activity by general manager Joe Brown in pursuit of another starter. Hernon cited an unnamed Pirate who argued that "it looks like they waited too long. … Maybe it's too late now to get any help."[16] On May 27 he again harped in his column not only upon the weakness of the starting pitching, but also about the lack of pop coming off the bench, and the team's overall lack of power:

Perhaps you could say that the Pirates have the bench strength. But the strength there is defensive more than offensive. The glaring weakness showed itself in the Dodgers series particularly. Against lefthanded pitching the Bucs have no strong righthanded hitter sitting around. There is no one down there in the dugout who can come out and stroke the ball out of the premises against a southpaw hurler. ... So it might be that a good starting pitcher is not the only answer to the situation.[17]

Almost like manna from heaven, however, the pitching situation improved the very next day as Brown pulled off a trade for Vinegar Bend Mizell from the St. Louis Cardinals. Al Abrams crowed his approval, writing that "any time a ball club gets a seasoned starting pitcher ... it has to be a good trade," and declaring that "while no one was looking ... the major league sweepstakes passed the quarter-mile mark ... with the Pirates very much in contention."[18]

Hernon noted that some players were pleased, but he seemed to reserve judgment on the trade. Once again he spoke out about the lack of confidence that the 29-16 (on June 6) first-place Pirates had the right stuff to win the crown, at least as far as other National League managers were concerned. "The Pirates haven't seemed to convince anyone with their first place antics. Three managers in this league have come along now and spoken about the pennant race and none seems to believe the Pirates are going to win."[19] Hernon's tone did not deviate much during the remainder of June, as he continued to caution against the spreading wave of buoyancy in Pittsburgh. As late as the 28th, with the Pirates in first place with a record of 41-24 (three games in front of the Braves), he titled his column "Pirates Need Bounce to Get Back on Track." Again pitching was the issue as Hernon fretted about how the club would respond to "the shock of seeing the top pitchers, Vern Law and Bob Friend, take beatings from the last place Cubs." His trepidation may have infected other writers, for on the same day Harry Heck, who only a week earlier had been the first local sportswriter to use the word "destiny" in regard to this squad, argued that with the Giants and Dodgers coming into Forbes Field, "the lead built up by the Bucs could be dissipated in a hurry. They'll have to do a lot of bearing down to maintain it."[20]

Such apprehension is understandable when the hometown team has not won a title in more than three decades.

The Pirates had a sterling April and good months in May (16-11) and June (15-11), but July was their worst month of 1960 (though they did manage a winning record, 15-14). Not surprisingly, the columns of Hernon, Abrams, and Heck reflected concern that the long-hoped-for pennant was possibly slipping away from Danny Murtaugh's grasp. Some examples of the columns that (no doubt) churned Pirate fans' stomachs during that month were (by Heck), "20-Game Winners No Guarantee of Pennant" and "It's Earlier than You Think for Pirates in Pennant Race" (which included a recounting of the infamous 1938 collapse by the Bucs).[21] Al Abrams, though a bit more positively, reminded readers that the Pirates had not been in first place on July 4 since 1932, but also chimed in with concerns about the pitching staff, noting on July 6 that "we were beginning to wonder if Pirate pitching wasn't coming apart at the seams." On the 19th, in a column headlined "Pirates Falter Past Month," he wrote, "There's no getting away from the fact that the swash-buckling Buccos were slowed to a walk the past month."[22] Not surprisingly, Hernon also expressed pessimism. On July 6 he wrote that "right now the Pirates have gathered themselves together in one of those slumps that encompasses everything." A week later he argued that Law and Friend were overused in the two All-Star Games, on the 6th and 13th, and that this would be a detriment down the stretch. On the 20th he turned his attention to the Pirates' lack of hitting, noting that Clemente, batting in the fifth slot, had managed only two RBIs in the previous 12 games. Finally, Hernon finished the month noting that the Pirates had lost their league lead (but they bounced right back after one day) and adding:

Suddenly what seemed like a comfortable way of living for the Bucs turned into the advance season prediction of a dogfight; ... The Bucs started playing shaky baseball and the breaks they had been getting for such a long time turned the other way. Maybe the pressure of front running caught up with the Bucs. After all, it was something new for them to be out front and have the pack barking at their heels for so long.[23]

For long-suffering fans, the question to ask by the end of July was simple: Would 1960 be a repeat of the same old story for the Pirates (as in 1938?), or was this team different? Perhaps, given that the team still was 18 games above .500 on August 1 (57-39), all of these concerns were simply because of the lack of (both the team's and the writers') experience in a pennant run?

After all of the consternation apparent in July, August brought substantial relief for weary Buc fans: a 21-10 record. The change in attitude was also perceptible in Hernon's columns, particularly after the middle of the month. Columns early in August said that the Pirates had been quite fortunate to remain in the hunt for the pennant given their mediocre play during July. "The club has been rooting for the contenders to lose when they do, and that isn't the mark of a champion. … And it stands to reason … the Pirates aren't convinced they can beat the Dodgers." Still, by the 8th, after they had taken two games from the Giants, it was clear that the fan in Hernon was starting to feel a twinge of anticipation for the Pirates' chances: He proclaimed that "anyone who wants to win this National League pennant will have to come and get it now from the Pirates."[24] Over the next couple of weeks, as the Bucs continued to build momentum, the tone of Hernon's writing began to take on an air of inevitability (or destiny?). On the 10th, he gushed:

A final, and impressive, summation of the Pirates' chances was noted in a Hernon column on the 16th. He presented the faithful with statistical evidence of the likelihood of a pennant for the hometown nine (had he finally crossed a metaphorical bridge from reporter to fan?). The title says it all: ".512 Ball Will Give Pirates the Pennant: Cards Must Play .659, Braves .667, Dodgers .694—How Sweet it Is!"[25]

Just before that column the local business community had offered a sense of how significant an event a World Series would be for the city. "One of the nicest things about being overrun by this horde is that they will be drawing from their hips—their wallets." Still, just as with the sportswriters, the Chamber of Commerce types were still cautious (perhaps recalling 1938?), for "though merchants go to bed with visions of World Series dancing in their heads … (t)he policy is to keep one eye on the scoreboard, one eye on the cash register and wait and see."[26] Although there was still some fear that history might repeat, the team's record of 79-49 on September 1 gave it a 6½-game lead over the Cardinals and a seven-game bulge over the Braves). It now seemed that what had been previously deemed improbable, if not impossible, was becoming more and more likely.[27]

With the 1960 season coming down to the homestretch, Jack Hernon and his colleagues worked to remind folks in Pittsburgh how far a road they and the Pirates had traveled. The team had a 15-10 record in September and endured only two brief poor stretches, losing three of four between the 13th and 17th and three in a row to the Braves between the 23rd and 25th. In the midst of these ephemeral bumps in the pennant road, Al Abrams did his best to calm the waters and alleviate the spirits of anxious fans. On September 16 he wrote:

Feel better now? The question is directed at those Pirate fans who panicked when the club lost two in a row before knocking off the Dodgers yesterday afternoon. … (The) triumph should soothe the feverish brows of those customers who were wondering out loud Wednesday night whether the Bucs were ever going to win another game going down the stretch. I can't say I blame them. The near-yet-so-far pennant has them doing mental nip-ups even though the club was 5½ games in front. … Let's relax along with the players. Forget the booing, too. … Worry about how to get series tickets. That's what I'm doing.[28]

Hernon performed a similar civic duty as he sought to remind Pirate fans how far they had come from the days of the Rickey Dinks. On September 2 he generated for his readers a list of how many players had cycled through the team's clubhouse since the early 1950s, going through a laundry list of has-beens and assorted duds who served in various positions over the years. As a writer who had wasted many thousands of words and hundreds of columns covering the lean years, Hernon could now happily proclaim to his audience, "It's much better since times have changed, thank you."[29]

The glorious pennant-clinching day finally came on September 25, during the three-game sweep at the hands of the Braves, who by then had been reduced to the role of spoilers. No matter. The Pirates faithful went wild and delirious, though Hernon was more subdued and poignant. As an estimated 100,000 residents held up signs bragging of what the Pirates would do to the Yankees, Hernon's mind drifted back to some not-so-pleasant times. "One year this gent spent a summer in which a Pirate team won no more than two games in succession. … Those were the years when a baseball season lasted for what seemed like 254 games." By comparison, "Yes, (the 1960 season) was quite a nice trip with the Pirates. Thanks for the thrill and the experience, fellows."[30]

The columns by Abrams and Hernon concerning the World Series will, no doubt, be consulted in other articles in this collection and will not be discussed here. The principal focus here was these writers' recollections of the day-to-day ups and downs of the 1960 season leading up to this moment of destiny (what else can it be when a team is outscored 55-27 in a World Series yet still manages to win?) when the Pirates finally ended 3½ decades of waiting (a long time, obviously—though certainly just a tick of the clock by comparison for Cub fans). Unfortunately for the fans, it turned out that they had enjoyed a moment of destiny, not a decade. The triumph of 1960 passed quickly as the Pirates reverted to their more accustomed results (though not quite as bad as the Rickey Dink days) for the remainder of the 1960s. In 1961 they slid to sixth place with a record of 75-79. Similar mediocre seasons transpired over the remainder of the decade. Between 1961 and 1969, the Bucs had three 90-plus-win seasons (1962, 1965, and 1966), but achieved only one fourth-place and two third-place finishes respectively. It was not until the start of division play in 1969 (and the arrival of players who would form the core of the lineup known as the Lumber Company) that Pirate fans would once again savor the glory of pennant drives and a World Series title.

For Jack Hernon, 1960 proved to be the only opportunity to share a hot dog with his son at a hometown club's World Series game. Shortly before the start of spring training for the 1966 season, he was diagnosed with cancer. He continued to write for the *Post-Gazette* during his illness, but was limited to covering only home contests. He died on August 19, 1966, at the young age of 48. Al Abrams continued to write and serve as sports editor until 1974. His tenure at the paper (which began in 1926) allowed him another bird's-eye view of Pirate championships, including another World Series in 1971. He died on March 4, 1977 at the age of 73.[31]

Notes

1 The term "Last Pure Season" is taken from a video presentation by the *Pittsburgh Post-Gazette* commemorating the 50th anniversary of the 1960 Pirates and featuring sportswriter Robert

Dvorchak. It can be found here: http://old.post-gazette.com/60s-pirates/. Accessed on March 31, 2012.

2 Ibid.

3 Jack Hernon obituary, *Hartford Courant,* August 21, 1966.

4 Jack Hernon, "Roaming Around," *Pittsburgh Post-Gazette*, October 6, 1960. Almost all Hernon's comments cited in these notes were pubished in columns for the *Post-Gazette* that carried the standing headline "Roaming Around." They are cited here as "Hernon."

5 *Sporting News* obituary, October 27, 1954.

6 Robert Dvorchak, *Pittsburgh Post-Gazette*, "Pirates' 1960 Champs 'a team of destiny'". See: http://www.post-gazette.com/pg/10094/1047107-63.stm. Accessed on December 14, 2011.

7 Rick Cushing, *1960 Pittsburgh Pirates, Day by Day: A Special Season, an Extraordinary World Series* (Pittsburgh: Dorrance Publishing, Co., Inc., 2010), 35.

8 Ibid.

9 Ibid., 36-37.

10 Ibid., 82-83; Al Abrams, "Sidelights on Sports," *Pittsburgh Post-Gazette*, March 17, 1960. All of Abrams' comments cited here were published in columns in the *Post-Gazette* labeled "Sidelines on Sports." They are cited here as "Abrams."

11 Hernon, March 15, 1960.

12 Hernon, April 11, 1960.

13 Rick Cushing, op. cit., 88; Jack Hernon, "Bucs Bump Reds Twice, 5-0, 6-5,". *Pittsburgh Post-Gazette*, April 18, 1960.

14 Harry Keck, "Our Pirates in the Groove and Flying High in Orbit," *Pittsburgh Sun-Telegraph*, May 2, 1960.

15 Hernon, May 6, 1960.

16 Hernon, May 15, 1960.

17 Hernon, May 27, 1960.

18 Abrams, May 30 and May 31, 1960.

19 Hernon, May 15, 1960.

20 Harry Keck, "Pirates Beginning to Look Like 1960's Team of Destiny," *Pittsburgh Sun-Telegraph*, June 21, 1960; Keck, "Double Defeat by the Cubs Puts Pirates on Their Guard," *Pittsburgh Sun-Telegraph*, June 28, 1960; Hernon, June 28, 1960;

21 Harry Keck, "20 Game Winners No Guarantee of a Pennant," *Pittsburgh Sun-Telegraph*, July 2, 1960; Keck, "It's Earlier than You Think for Pirates in Pennant Race," *Pittsburgh Sun-Telegraph*, July 14, 1960.

22 Abrams, July 4, July 6, and July 19, 1960.

23 Hernon, July 6, July 13, July 20, and July 27, 1960.

24 Hernon, August 3, 1960; Hernon, "Pirates Sweep Giants, 4-1, 7-5," August 8, 1960.

25 Hernon, ".512 Ball Will Give Pirates the Pennant: Cards Must Play .659, Braves .667, Dodgers . 694—How Sweet it Is!," *Pittsburgh Post-Gazette,* August 16, 1960.

26 Carl Alpone, "Bucs in Series Will Give Us Boom Town," *Pittsburgh Post-Gazette,* August 14, 1960.

27 Rick Cushing, op. cit., 219.

28 Abrams, September 16, 1960.

29 Hernon, September 2, 1960.

30 Hernon, September 28, 1960. See also Cushing, op. cit., 240-241.

31 Jack Hernon obituary, *Hartford Courant,* August 21, 1966; Al Abrams obituary, *New York Times,* March 5, 1977.

What Upset?

By Jan Finkel

DID THE PIRATES really upset the Yankees? Should we phrase the question the other way around? Perhaps—just perhaps—a Yankee win would have been an upset. It's not as "clear" in retrospect as it seemed back then. Not to me, anyway.

Let's take a quick look at the most important individuals on each team, position by position, Yankees listed first.

Managers

Casey Stengel vs. Danny Murtaugh

Stengel had been through the wars with some horrendous teams in Brooklyn and Boston but had become accustomed to winning in New York. Murtaugh had been with the Pirates through the years in the wilderness and had helped his players grow into a tough, mature unit. The major difference between Murtaugh and Stengel may be that Murtaugh had his players' respect and support whereas Stengel may have been losing some of his authority. (The more I think about Stengel, I get the sense, intuition, or impression that the Yankees were planning to dump him and promote Ralph Houk no matter how the Series turned out. Maybe it's just me.)

Surprisingly EVEN, with no real edge either way, given the veneration accorded Stengel and the lack of recognition for Murtaugh, who belongs to an exclusive club of managers who won two World Series.

Starting Pitchers

Art Ditmar (15-9, 3.06), Whitey Ford (12-9, 3.08), Bob Turley (9-3, 3.27), Ralph Terry (10-8, 3.40), Jim Coates (13-3, 4.28) vs. Bob Friend (18-12, 3.00), Vernon Law (20-9, 3.08), Harvey Haddix (11-10, 3.97), Vinegar Bend Mizell (13-5, 3.12)

The Yankees worked almost by committee. Ditmar was the surprise ace and workhorse of the staff. Ford had an off-year and wasn't prospering under Stengel. Turley, though near the end of his career, was still effective. Terry was a year away from prominence but would achieve a certain kind of fame in Game Seven (and again in 1962). Coates' won-lost record is deceptive, to say the least, and he would play a pivotal role in Game Seven.

The Pirates operated on a pretty strict four-man rotation. Joe Gibbon, Jim Umbricht, and Tom Cheney started 20 games in spot roles, but Friend, Law, Haddix, and Mizell ran the show. Law won the Cy Young award, and Friend could have—they were that close. All but Haddix had ERAs (3.00 to 3.12) well under the team total figure.

Ditmar and Ford match up almost identically with Friend and Law in terms of ERA. Turley and Terry on the one hand and Haddix and Mizell on the other are close. Coates brings the Yankees down.

Probably a wash, possibly a very slight EDGE to the Pirates, who had two lefty starters to the Yankees' one.

Relief Pitchers

Bobby Shantz (2.79, 11 saves), Duke Maas (4.09, 4), Ryne Duren (4.96, 9), Johnny James (4.36, 2), Luis Arroyo (2.88, 7) vs. Elroy Face (2.90, 24), Fred Green (3.21, 3), and Clem Labine (1.48, 3).

Another operation-by-committee for the Yankees. Shantz was a smart, experienced veteran, the stereotypical stylish southpaw, who fielded his position brilliantly and didn't beat himself. Arroyo was moving up in the world, ready to do wonders for Ford in 1961. The others got some saves but gave up a lot in the process. Face was The Baron of the Bullpen. He may have been overworked, even with help from Green and Labine, but he was clearly The Man.

EDGE to the Pirates.

Catchers

Elston Howard and Yogi Berra vs. Smoky Burgess and Hal Smith

Howard hadn't come into his own (.245-6-39), as he would the next year, and Berra was still effective but a shadow of his former self. Burgess and Smith hit .294 and .295, respectively, and combined for 18 homers and 84 driven in. Burgess was a valuable pinch-hitter. Smith's become something of a forgotten man, but if he hadn't hit a three-run shot to put the Pirates ahead 9-7 in Game Seven, Mazeroski might not have had a chance for immortality.

Considerable EDGE to the Pirates.

First Basemen

Bill Skowron vs. Dick Stuart and Rocky Nelson

Skowron (.309-26-91) had one of the best years of a steady, solid career and had a decent glove. Neither Stuart nor Nelson was a Gold Glove candidate, but they combined for 30 home runs and 118 RBIs.

About EVEN, hard to say who has an edge.

Second Basemen

Bobby Richardson and Gil McDougald vs. Bill Mazeroski

Who could have imagined that the weak-hitting Richardson would have an epic Series? No one, that's who. McDougald was in his last year and had fallen off a bit, but his ability to play second, third, and short (though not in 1960) made him extraordinarily valuable, and Stengel knew it. Mazeroski was arguably the greatest defensive second baseman of all time and had some pop in his bat. People seem to forget that he also homered to help the Pirates win Game One.

Huge EDGE to the Pirates.

Shortstops

Tony Kubek vs. Dick Groat and Dick Schofield

Kubek was a good foot soldier having one of his better years with 14 homers and 62 driven in. Groat's .325 average led the NL in a poor hitting year (Pete Runnels topped the AL at .320), and won the Most Valuable Player award for the year. Schofield hit .333 with a .429 OBP filling in while Groat was hurt.

EDGE to the Pirates.

Third Basemen

Clete Boyer (and McDougald) vs. Don Hoak

Boyer usually hit for a low average with occasional power and was a magician with the glove. He'd have won a truckload of Gold Gloves if he hadn't been playing in the same league as Brooks Robinson. Hoak hit 16 homers to go with a .282 average and 79 driven in, played a sound third base—and was a battling team leader with a lot of

intangible qualities. He finished second in MVP voting behind Groat.

EDGE to the Pirates.

Left Fielders

Hector Lopez (and Berra) vs. Bob Skinner

Lopez had a decent year, with his .284 average good for second on the team, but left field was something of a committee for the Yanks in 1960. Berra filled in to keep his bat in the line-up and had the dubious pleasure of seeing Maz set off the fireworks up close. Skinner was a solid veteran whose 33 doubles led the team and were third in the NL; his career-high 86 RBIs were second on the team.

Fair-sized EDGE to the Pirates.

Center Fielders

Mickey Mantle vs. Bill Virdon

Mantle was Mantle, even in a down year one of the half-dozen premier players in the game. His .275 average was low for him, but he led the AL in home runs (40), runs (119, the only American Leaguer to score 100), total bases (294), and On-Base Plus Slugging (.957). His legs were bothering him, but he knew how to play center field. He was second in American League MVP voting behind Roger Maris. Virdon couldn't hit like Mantle (very few could), but he could lead off and execute the hit-and-run well, and was the best NL center fielder not named Mays, covering a lot of ground in spacious Forbes Field.

Solid EDGE to the Yankees but not as large as you might expect.

Right Fielders

Roger Maris vs. Roberto Clemente

What can you say? Maris led the AL in RBIs (112) and slugging (.581), and with Al Kaline playing center field was the league's best right fielder if not its best overall player, all while picking up the MVP award (albeit by one point over Mantle). Clemente had his first great year (.314-16-94), was the best right fielder in the game, and had an arm others can only dream of or pray for. The 1961 season would be a watershed for each of them.

This is EVEN. Any edge is slight and depends on what you're looking for.

Broadcasters

Mel Allen and Red Barber vs. Bob ("The Gunner") Prince and Jim ("The Possum") Woods

This is almost as difficult as right field. Allen, Barber, and Prince are rightly legends, and Woods was no slouch. Mel and The Redhead were wonderful, no question. Bob's sport coats made you grateful for radio, an important fact since anyone growing up in the Fifties in KDKA's vast range knew him as The Voice Under the Pillow. Betty and Bob Prince lived in the apartment above us, knew me from the crib, and were good family friends. You see where this is going, don't you?

EDGE to the Pirates.

How does it all shake out?

Managers: Even
Starting Pitchers: Even
Relief Pitchers: Pirates
Catchers: Pirates
Infielders: Pirates
Outfielders: Yankees
Broadcasters: Pirates (admittedly not my most objective judgment)

Suddenly the Yankees don't look invincible. Indeed, they look eminently beatable. In Mantle and Maris they had the two top players in the Series, and they give the Yankees the edge in the outfield. But that's it. The Pirates get the edge in the bullpen, behind the plate, and in the infield. Managers and starting pitchers are pretty even.

What upset?

1960 Pirates Platoon Starting Lineups with Platoon OPS
(OBP + Slug)

Against LH starters		Against RH starters	
1. Skinner, LF	.666	Virdon, CF	.795
2. Groat, SS	.895	Groat, SS	.706
3. Clemente, RF	1.044	Skinner, LF	.811
4. Stuart, 1B	.767	Stuart/Nelson, 1B	.814/.854
5. Cimoli, CF	.621	Clemente, RF	.716
6. Smith, C	.937	Burgess, C	.776
7. Hoak, 3B	.828	Hoak, 3B	.803
8. Mazeroski, 2B	.890	Mazeroski, 2B	.642
9. Pitchers	.408	Pitcher	.461

Created by Clem Comly from data extracted from www.retrosheet.org except platoon OPS for non-pitchers are from www.baseball-reference.com.

Game Seven Broadcast Yields Nostalgic Insights

By Stew Thornley

WHEN I FIRST saw the highlight film for the 1960 World Series, probably in the 1990s, I was struck by the simplicity of the production. Without the technological capabilities producers have now, those who put the film together didn't have access to the avant-garde features that add an artistic touch. And for whatever reason, earlier films didn't contain exclusive interviews with participants to add insight to the video. That's what I liked about them.

The last World Series highlight film I tried watching was from 2001. The incessant talking heads included Luis Gonzalez of the Arizona Diamondbacks explaining the shock he felt watching Yankee Scott Brosius's ninth-inning, game-tying homer sail into the stands in Game Five. Wow, that was great learning that Luis Gonzalez was shocked. The big moments of the Series weren't shown with the normal look that had appeared on the broadcast. They featured different angles and superimposed images. It sucked.

Unfortunately, even the 1960 highlight film didn't survive tampering. After Bill Virdon's bad-hop grounder hit Tony Kubek in the throat in the eighth inning of the final game, the ESPN version was interrupted by a talking head of Kubek some years later, describing the play. (Gee, it hurt, Tony? I'm glad we got this insight.) Apparently a producer at ESPN or elsewhere had the egotistical need to put his fingerprints on something that was already perfect. (At least this highlight film is still available without the tampering.)

At a young age, I became a Yankees fan, mainly as a way to annoy my dad, since this was still during the dynasty that made it more fashionable to hate the Yankees. As a Yankees fan, I read about this Series—in which the Yankees lost despite outscoring the Pirates 55-27 and all the wildness of the final game—but I don't think it bothered me, at least not much. Had I been a Yankees fan watching this Series as it happened, it would have been worse.

With this detached perspective, I can appreciate the quirks of the series and the seventh game. I've read about and participated in discussions of the play when

the Yankees tied Game Seven in the top of the ninth as Rocky Nelson missed Mickey Mantle coming back into first. Had Nelson made the tag before Gil McDougald reached home with the tying run, the Pirates would have won 9-8. The name of Hal Smith would be better known as the Pirate who hit the three-run homer in the eighth rather than as the actor who played town drunk Otis Campbell on *The Andy Griffith Show*. Bill Mazeroski, elected to the Hall of Fame for his defensive wizardry, might still be on the outside without the push he got from his game-winning homer after the Yankees tied the game. (In his article "For the Hall: Twelve Good Men" in the Winter 1985 SABR publication *The National Pastime*, Bob Carroll wrote, "Remembering Maz for his hitting is like remembering Dolly Parton for her elbows.")

The Nelson play unfolded this way: Trailing 9-8, the Yankees had McDougald on third and Mantle on first with one out when Yogi Berra hit a sharp grounder to Nelson, who stepped on first and then, surprised to see Mantle still in the vicinity, missed the Mick as he dived back into first. But the view on the highlight film doesn't provide a great look at what happened. The camera cuts from Berra hitting the ball to Nelson, after he had stepped on the base, lunging at Mantle.

While the highlight film, without the insertion of the talking head of Kubek, is great, an even bigger gem turned up a few years ago in the late Bing Crosby's basement. A part-owner of the Pirates, the singer and actor was too nervous to watch the Series, so he went to Paris. So he could watch later, Crosby hired a company to record the seventh game by kinescope. Crosby died in 1977. The reels from the kinescope were among the films found in his vault, a former wine cellar, more than 30 years later.

A number of other full-game broadcasts have become available in the last decade, including most of Don Larsen's perfect game and the next-to-last game of the 1967 season between the Twins and Red Sox. The fun of watching full-game broadcasts from 40 and 50 years ago includes noticing all the little things that are no longer present, nuances that don't survive the editing done for highlight films. The 1960 Game Seven film preserved by Crosby has many such gems.

The starting pitchers, Vernon Law for the Pirates and Bob Turley for the Yankees, warmed up from flat ground in front of their dugouts (Law in front of a group of men in suits, one with a saxophone, apparently the anthem performers). The starters didn't have a mound for warmups. The bullpens, where there were mounds, were down the lines in foul territory in the outfield.

The New York bullpen, down the left-field line, was tucked behind a section of seats that jutted out; the Pittsburgh bullpen wasn't protected by a grandstand, and a backstop was put up to protect relievers from batted balls as they warmed up. The bullpens are shown often, since there was frequent activity in them, as would be expected in a 10-9 game.

Even before the offenses got going, Yankees relievers were at work. Bill Stafford and Bobby Shantz were up in the New York bullpen in the top of the first, before Bob Turley even took the mound for the Yankees. In the final game of the season, it makes sense to have everyone ready, even before the starter gets in trouble. (This was evident in the final game of the 1965 World Series as well, as the Minnesota Twins had John Klippstein and Jim Merritt warming up as Jim Kaat started the game.) But in 1960, while Yankees manager Casey Stengel had pitchers warming up from the beginning, Pirates manager Danny Murtaugh did not.

The announcers, Bob Prince for the first half, and Mel Allen, who took over in the bottom of the fifth, did a good job of updating warmup activity, and the cameras showed the relievers getting loose (including Whitey Ford for the Yankees during the top of the seventh).

The routine of throwing the ball around the horn has changed over the decades (with the first baseman for some reason being left out of the mix for more than 25 years). The Pirates and Yankees let every infielder, including the catcher, handle the ball before returning it to the pitcher.

The game contained no replays. The only graphics were the names of the batters as they came to the plate. I recall these features (or lack of) during Minnesota Twins broadcasts in the 1960s. The postgame scoreboard show was worth sticking around for, mainly for the replays they showed. No instant replay back then; it took them a while to extract the highlights. The Twins broadcasts included

batting averages with the batters' names. I once took a tour of a television station during a Twins broadcast and saw a woman with a *Ready Reckoner* to update a player's average after each time at bat. Those old enough to remember life before calculators know what the *Ready Reckoner* was. (For the rest of you, it was a book published by *The Sporting News* with tables to determine percentages.)

Windups today are more compact. Law kicked and delivered with some motion, and Turley, after bringing his arms back behind his waist, brought his hands together only at the level of his chest, but Bobby Shantz had a full windup typical of pitchers at that time—arms flung behind the hips to start the motion, then brought together over the head. Bill Stafford, with the bases loaded in the second inning, used a similar windup but without bringing his arms behind him at the start of the windup. Roy Face went into a set position by first bringing his hands over his head, as did Shantz and Jim Coates, who relieved Shantz in the eighth. Recent pitchers I can think of with this kind of stretch are Rheal Cormier and Clayton Kershaw.

Another trait I remember well from the 1960s was players kneeling in the on-deck circle after swinging the bats a few times. In the second inning, Bill Virdon is shown kneeling on his left knee, his left arm extended and on top of his bat, which is vertical into the ground, with another bat at an angle into the top of his right leg. This is the on-deck stance I remember and imitated when I was on deck so I could look like a big leaguer, even though I rarely saw this particular style. We see more traditional poses in the following innings: Mickey Mantle kneeling on deck with top of bat tucked in up by his shoulder in the fourth; Mazeroski in bottom of the fourth kneeling with two bats across his upper leg; Dick Groat in the fifth kneeling with two bats with the knobs at the top of his bent leg, pushed into his belt; and Hal Smith kneeling before his big home run in the eighth, wearing his shin guards in case Roberto Clemente ended the inning (shin guards worn in the on-deck circle also being something that is rarely seen today). The batters often waved a couple of bats on the way to the plate, either tossing one or handing it to the batboy before stepping into the box.

There were no batting gloves then, and the batters often picked up dirt and rubbed it between their hands as they stepped in. While they sometimes rubbed dirt between pitches, they mostly stayed in the batter's box, reducing time between pitches. Pitchers and catchers rubbed up a new ball put into play, and congratulatory gestures were back pats and handshakes, not fist knocks and high fives.

Batters carried their caps with them, either folding them and stuffing them into their back pocket or putting the cap inside their helmets. (I recall players who wore the cap and helmet at the same time, normally fitting the cap inside the helmet, unlike the familiar manner used by Hank Aaron, who used both hands to place his helmet over his cap as he got up from the on-deck circle.) It looked as though most of the players used helmets rather than liners in the cap, and most appeared to leave their helmets on when they reached base. An exception was John Blanchard, who, after a single, is shown putting only his cap back on with first-base coach Ralph Houk appearing to put Blanchard's helmet on his head.

An umpire gesture used now to indicate a foul tip (brushing the left hand with the right hand) apparently was used only for balls fouled off on a check swing or bunt attempt. Plate umpire Bill Jackowski used this signal when Roger Maris checked his swing and fouled off a pitch in the first inning and again when Clete Boyer fouled a bunt attempt in the fifth.

The grandstand roofs had people on them, visible as the camera followed foul balls. Only a few were on the roof down the left-field line; more were on the roof on the right side, including newsreel photographers with movie cameras on tripods.

The center-field camera was used mostly when the bases were empty, and it was sometimes possible to see the catcher's signals and figure out the next pitch. The Yankees' John Blanchard used two fingers, easily seen, for a curveball. I wondered if he varied the signals with a runner on second, but the camera angles were usually different with runners on. In the bottom of the seventh the Pirates, trailing by one run, had pinch-runner Joe Christopher on first, and a behind-the-plate camera caught the batter on the left side of the picture, allowing the camera to also show Christopher taking his lead at first.

Plate umpires made their own judgments on checked swings, and it looked as though a batter could go a long way with the bat without it being called a swing. Both teams benefited by getting away with what would now

be called a swing. Tony Kubek didn't get rung up with a checked swing in the sixth and finally walked on a 3-and-2 pitch, prompting Danny Murtaugh to bring in Roy Face.

On a 1-and-2 pitch in the eighth, Hal Smith went far with a swing (not quite as far as Kubek had but far enough for what would now be called a swing). Still alive, Smith hit a three-run homer on the next pitch to give the Pirates a 9-7 lead.

The complete-game broadcast provides a great look at the strange play when the Yankees tied the game in the ninth, McDougald coming home on Berra's groundout to first. From this, it looks as though Mantle may not have been sure if Nelson had caught the ball on the fly, causing him to retreat. As first-base umpire Nestor Chylak signaled fair, Nelson backhanded the drive, stepped on the bag with his back to the plate as he got spun around, twirled to his left, and saw Mantle frozen two steps off the base. Mantle went to his knees and dived back into first, tumbling to his right on the home-plate side of the base. Nelson lunged after Mantle rather than staying with the tag at the base, allowing Mantle to avoid being tagged.

Play-by-play accounts tell almost everything that happens in a game, but they don't include non-events that are significant. The full-game broadcast does, including:

▸ Nelson strongly indicating his unhappiness about a strike call on a curve that made the count 2-and-1 instead of 3-and-0 in the first inning. On the next pitch, Nelson hit a two-run homer for the first runs of the game.

▸ Law hitting a drive long but foul in the fifth.

▸ Berra hitting a bouncer over first, barely foul down the right-field line in the sixth. On the next pitch he homered, Clemente never leaving his spot, causing Mel Allen to first call it foul and then have to change his call to a home run, which put the Yankees ahead 5-4. The highlight film, because of editing and splicing, shows Berra with a leap of joy as he approaches first, but this isn't seen in the full-game footage. (At least in the ninth, when Mazeroski homered, Allen didn't misidentify the pitcher as Art Ditmar, as Chuck Thompson did on the radio broadcast.)

▶ Shantz hitting a bouncer that chopped over third base and was just foul in the eighth. The Yankees had runners at second and third, and this grounder, if fair, would have given them a 9-4 lead.

This game was about the hitters, not the pitchers, so it's appropriate that Harvey Haddix, as the winning pitcher (by virtue of allowing two inherited runners to score), received far less notoriety than he did for being the losing pitcher in a game the year before—his near-perfect game broken up by Joe Adcock's blast.

After the game the Yankees left through the Pirates' dugout. Apparently there was no access to the locker rooms through the third-base dugout at Forbes Field. Though we couldn't see him during the game, Bob Prince was shown in the locker room interviewing players after the game, and he had a more hideous than usual sport coat on.

It was a great World Series, it was a great Game Seven, and the highlight film (without ESPN tinkering) and the complete-game broadcast are great, too.

By The Numbers

By Dan Fields

Pittsburgh Pirates in 1960

1st and 2nd

Order in which shortstop Dick Groat and third baseman Don Hoak finished in the voting for Most Valuable Player in the National League. Groat, whose 154 singles and .325 batting average both led the major leagues, was the first Pirate to win the MVP award since Paul Waner in 1927 (the last time the Pirates won the NL championship).

1.25

Walks and hits per inning pitched by the 1960 Pirates, lowest in the majors.

2

Wins by Pittsburgh pitchers in the 1960 All-Star games—the only time in the years (1959-62) with two All-Star Games that players representing the same team had both victories. Bob Friend, who started the July 11 game, threw three scoreless innings and got the win as the NL topped the AL, 5-3. Bill Mazeroski (the starting second baseman) and Bob Skinner (the starting left fielder) each drove in a run, Roy Face allowed no hits in 1 ²/₃ innings, and Vern Law was credited with a save for retiring the last two batters with two men on base. Law started the July 13 game and threw two scoreless innings as the NL won, 6-0. Other Pirates on the NL squad were catcher Smoky Burgess, right fielder Roberto Clemente, and Dick Groat.

3

Home runs in consecutive at-bats by first baseman Dick Stuart in the second game of a doubleheader against the San Francisco Giants on June 30. Stuart had four hits (he also had a single) and seven RBIs in the game, which the Pirates won, 11-6.

4.07

Ratio of strikeouts (183) to walks (45) by Bob Friend, tops in the majors. Friend was the first pitcher since fellow Pirate Babe Adams in 1920 to have a ratio of at least four strikeouts to walks in a season.

6

Hits (three doubles and three singles) in six at-bats by Dick Groat as the Pirates beat the Milwaukee Braves, 8-2, on May 13. Groat had a double and four singles against the Cincinnati Reds on May 31 as the Pirates won, 4-3.

9

Consecutive wins by the Pirates between April 20 and May 1—the longest winning streak by the team since 1945. The Pirates won 12 of their first 15 games.

12-5

Record by the 1960 Pirates in extra-inning games. The .706 winning percentage was best in the majors.

18

Complete games by Vern Law, tied for most in the majors with Lew Burdette and Warren Spahn, both of the Braves. Bob Friend pitched 16 complete games.

19

Assists by Roberto Clemente, most in the majors by an outfielder.

20

Wins by Vern Law against only nine losses. Law won the Cy Young Award, beating Ernie Broglio of the St. Louis Cardinals and Warren Spahn, each of whom won 21 games. Bob Friend won 18.

41

Age of pitcher Diomedes Olivo in his major-league debut on September 5. He is the oldest rookie in major-league history other than Satchel Paige.

61

Games finished by Roy Face, most in the majors. At the time, the only pitcher who had finished more games in a season was Jim Konstanty, who closed out 62 games for the Philadelphia Phillies in 1950. Face also had 24 saves, second in the majors.

95

Wins by the 1960 Pirates, who won the NL championship by seven games over the Braves. In 1959, the Pirates won only 78 games and finished in fourth place, nine games behind the Los Angeles Dodgers.

105

Home runs given up by the 1960 Pirates, fewest in the majors.

.276

Batting average of the 1960 Pirates, tops in the majors.

.335

On-base percentage (batting) of the 1960 Pirates, tops in the NL. The Pirates also led the league with an on-base percentage plus slugging average of .743.

386

Walks given up by the 1960 Pirates, fewest in the majors.

593

Runs given up by the 1960 Pirates, tied with the Dodgers for fewest in the majors.

734

Runs scored by the 1960 Pirates, most in the NL.

747

Strikeouts (batting) by the 1960 Pirates, fewest in the NL.

.989

Fielding percentage as a second baseman by Bill Mazeroski, tops in the majors. Mazeroski also led second baseman in putouts (413), assists (449), and double plays (127). He won his second of eight Gold Gloves in 1960, and Harvey Haddix won his third of three Gold Gloves that year.

.994

Fielding percentage as catcher by Smoky Burgess, best in the NL.

1,705,828

Attendance at Forbes Field in 1960, a Pirates single-season record that stood until 1988.

1960 World Series:

0.00

ERA of Whitey Ford of the New York Yankees in two complete-game shutouts (Games Three and Six).

0

Strikeouts by the Pirates and Yankees in Game Seven—the only game in World Series history with no strikeouts.

1 (and only)

Seven-game World Series to be decided by a walk-off home run, by Bill Mazeroski. (Joe Carter hit a home run to end the six-game 1993 World Series.)

2-0

Record of Vern Law (winner of Games One and Four), Whitey Ford (Games Three and Six), and Harvey Haddix (Games Five and Seven). The only other World Series in which three pitchers had 2-0 records was in 1926, when Pete Alexander and Jesse Haines of the Cardinals and Herb Pennock of the Yankees pulled off the feat.

3

Home runs by the Pirates in Game Seven, out of four total throughout the Series. The Yankees had 10 home runs during the Series.

3

Saves by Roy Face (in Games One, Four, and Five).

7

Past, present, or future MVPs in the Series. The Pirates had two—Dick Groat (1960) and Roberto Clemente (1966)—and the Yankees had five: Yogi Berra (1951, 1954, and 1955), Bobby Shantz (1952), Mickey Mantle (1956, 1957, and 1962), Roger Maris (1960 and 1961), and Elston Howard (1963).

12

RBIs by World Series MVP Bobby Richardson of the Yankees (still a World Series record), including six in Game Three. Mickey Mantle had 11 RBIs in the series. Richardson is the only player on a losing team to win the World Series MVP award.

24-17

Runs scored by the Pirates and Yankees, respectively, in the four games won by Pittsburgh (Games One, Four, Five, and Seven).

38-3

Runs scored by the Yankees and Pirates, respectively, in the three games won by New York (Games Two, Three, and Six).

.338

Batting average of the Yankees (91 hits). The Pirates had a batting average of .256 (60 hits).

7.11

ERA of Pittsburgh pitchers, more than double that of New York pitchers (3.54).

Around the Majors in 1960:

0

Hits allowed by Don Cardwell of the Chicago Cubs in a complete-game win over the Cardinals, 4-0, on May 15 (game two of a doubleheader). The no-hitter occurred in Cardwell's debut with the Cubs, after he was traded by the Phillies.

1

Game managed by Eddie Sawyer, who resigned after the Phillies lost 9-4 to the Reds on Opening Day. He quipped, "I am 49 years old and want to live to be 50." On August 3, the Cleveland Indians and Detroit Tigers traded managers; until the pair could change places, Jo-Jo White managed the Indians and Billy Hitchcock managed the Tigers for one game (both won).

1

Hit allowed by Juan Marichal of the Giants in his major-league debut on July 19. He struck out 12 batters in shutting out the Phillies, 2-0. Over his 16-year career, Marichal won 243 games, tossed 52 shutouts, and struck out 2,303 batters.

1st

Career home run by Billy Williams of the Cubs on October 1. He hit his 426th (and last) home run on August 8, 1976, as a designated hitter for the Oakland Athletics.

1st and 2nd

Order in which Yankees Roger Maris and Mickey Mantle finished in the voting for AL Most Valuable Player. Maris led the league in RBIs (112), slugging average (.581), and extra-base hits (64), and he had the top fielding percentage as a right fielder (.989). Mantle led the majors in runs (119) and the AL in home runs (40), on-base percentage plus slugging average (.957), and total bases (294).

2

Relief wins each by Ernie Broglio of the Cardinals on July 1 and Gerry Staley of the Chicago White Sox on August 7.

2

No-hitters caught by Del Crandall of the Braves on August 18 (with Lew Burdette pitching) and September 16 (with Warren Spahn getting his 20th win of the year). The opposing team in both games was the Phillies.

3

Passed balls by Gus Triandos of the Baltimore Orioles in the sixth inning against the White Sox on May 4. The catcher also allowed a passed ball in the third inning. On May 10, Joe Ginsberg of the Orioles allowed three passed balls in the second inning against the Kansas City Athletics and another in the fifth inning. The pitcher in both games was knuckleballer Hoyt Wilhelm.

3

Consecutive 1-0 losses by the Phillies on May 11, 12, and 13.

3

Triples by Willie Mays of the Giants in a September 15 games against the Phillies. Mays also hit two singles as the Giants won 8-6.

4

Pinch-hit home runs by George Crowe of the Cardinals in 1960. Crowe also hit four pinch-hit home runs in 1959. At the time of his retirement in 1961, he held the major-league record for most career pinch-hit home runs with 14.

4

Consecutive decades in which Ted Williams of the Boston Red Sox stole a base, after stealing second in a July 22 game against the Indians. He also stole two bases in 1939, 14 in the 1940s, and seven in the 1950s. The next player with steals in four consecutive decades was Rickey Henderson.

5

Runs driven in Ron Santo of the Cubs in a doubleheader sweep of the Pirates on June 26—his first day playing in the majors. In his 15-year career, Santo drove in 1,331 runs.

5

Extra-inning home runs by Charlie Maxwell of the Tigers in 1960, a single-season major-league record not matched until 2010 by Nelson Cruz of the Texas Rangers.

8

Runs scored by the Yankees in the first inning before a batter was retired, in a game against the Orioles on April 24. The Orioles had a grand slam in the eighth inning and another in the ninth but lost 15-9.

8

Hits in consecutive at-bats by Brooks Robinson of the Orioles on July 10 and 15 (the two games were separated by the All-Star games, in which he went 0-for-3). Robinson hit for the cycle on July 15.

9

Hits in 11 at-bats by Pete Runnels of the Red Sox in a doubleheader against the Tigers on August 30. The second baseman went 6-for-7 in the first game. Runnels led the AL in 1960 with a .320 batting average.

13

Relief wins each by Larry Sherry of the Dodgers and Gerry Staley of the White Sox in 1960.

14

Consecutive years in which Carl Furillo, Gil Hodges, and Duke Snider played together for the Dodgers, from 1947 through 1960.

15

Strikeouts by Camilo Pascual of the Washington Senators against the Red Sox on April 18, tying Walter Johnson's team record for most in a game.

15

Consecutive wins by the Yankees between September 16 and October 2 to close out the season.

16

Stolen bases by the Athletics in 1960. By comparison, Luis Aparicio of the White Sox had 51 steals and Maury Wills of the Dodgers had 50.

18

Wins by Jim Perry of the Indians. The hurler tied Chuck Estrada of the Orioles for most wins in the AL, even though Perry played for a losing team.

20+

Years between home runs hit by Ted Williams against Thornton Lee of the White Sox (September 17, 1939) and his son, Don Lee of the Senators (September 2, 1960).

22

Home runs by AL Rookie of the Year Ron Hansen of the Orioles.

23

Home runs by NL Rookie of the Year Frank Howard of the Dodgers.

26

Saves by Lindy McDaniel of the Cardinals, an NL record at the time.

28

Intentional walks received by Ernie Banks of the Cubs, most in the majors. Bill Mazeroski was second with 15.

32 ⅔

Consecutive innings pitched by Lew Burdette of the Braves without allowing a run, between August 10 and 27.

38

Consecutive scoreless innings by the Phillies between July 21 and 26.

40

Errors committed by Dodgers shortstop Maury Wills.

41

Home runs by Ernie Banks of the Cubs, most in the majors. It was his fourth consecutive season with more than 40 home runs.

136

Strikeouts by Pancho Herrera of the Phillies, then an NL record.

193

Home runs by the Yankees, an AL record at the time.

250

RBIs by Hank Aaron (126) and Eddie Mathews (124) of the Braves.

300

Career home runs by Eddie Mathews on April 17 and Mickey Mantle on July 4. Both players were only 28 years old.

.316

Batting average of Ted Williams in his last season, at age 41. He is one of the few players to hit .300 or higher in both his rookie and final seasons (minimum, five years); Williams had a .327 average in his first year, 1939.

500

Career home runs by Ted Williams on June 17. He became only the fourth player to hit that many, after Babe Ruth, Jimmie Foxx, and Mel Ott. Williams hit his 521st home run in his last career at-bat on September 28.

798

Consecutive games played at second base by Nellie Fox of the White Sox between August 7, 1956, and September 3, 1960. This is still the major-league record for second basemen.

.977

Fielding percentage as a third baseman by Brooks Robinson of the Orioles, who in 1960 won the first of 16 consecutive Gold Glove awards.

1.002

On-base percentage plus slugging average of Frank Robinson of the Reds, best in the majors.

2,000

Career walks by Ted Williams reached on August 20, joining Babe Ruth as only batters to accomplish this feat.

4,768

Attendance at Griffith Stadium in the last home game of the original AL Washington Senators, on October 2.

The Senators lost to the Orioles 2-1, as Pedro Ramos suffered his 18th loss, most in the AL that year. The Senators became the Minnesota Twins in 1961, and an expansion team (also named the Washington Senators) played one season at Griffith Stadium before moving to RFK Stadium in 1962.

42,269

Attendance at the first game at Candlestick Park, on April 12. Orlando Cepeda drove in three runs as the Giants beat the Cardinals, 3-1.

Sources

David Finoli and Bill Ranier. *The Pittsburgh Pirates Encyclopedia* (third edition). (Sports Publishing, 2003).

Society for American Baseball Research. *The SABR Baseball List and Record Book.* (New York: Scribner, 2007).

Burt Randolph Sugar (editor). *The Baseball Maniac's Almanac* (third edition). (New York: Skyhorse Publishing, 2012).

baseball-almanac.com

baseballlibrary.com/chronology

baseball-reference.com

retrosheet.org

thisgreatgame.com/1960.html

CONTRIBUTORS

Ron Antonucci lives in Greater Cleveland and has been a lifelong Indians fan. So he has had a few good years.

Thomas Ayers is a lifelong Blue Jays fan who was born and raised in Toronto. He has made several contributions to the SABR Biography Project whilst completing three university degrees.

Peter Bauck is a baseball enthusiast and notorious generalist who grew up in Billings, Montana. He now resides in Florida where he roots for the Tampa Bay (Devil) Rays alongside his wife, Lori.

Ron Briley has followed the Houston Astros since they were the Colt .45's in 1962, and he is concerned that the team may not win a World Series victory in his lifetime. Ron has taught history at Sandia Prep School in Albuquerque, New Mexico for 35 years. He is the author of five books and numerous academic articles on both baseball and film history.

Alan Cohen is a retired insurance underwriter who is spending his retirement doing baseball research. A native of Long Island, he continues to root for the Mets from his home in West Hartford, Connecticut, where he lives with his wife Frances and assorted pets. He did a presentation on "Baseball's Longest Day: May 31, 1964" at the 50th Anniversary of the New York Mets Conference in April, 2012, and is currently working on a history of the Hearst Sandlot Classic, a game that launched the careers of Dick Groat and Gino Cimoli.

Clem Comly is a 30-year SABR member and co-chair of its Statistical Analysis Committee. Clem is vice president and treasurer of Retrosheet and a volunteer from its beginnings. Clem is Retrosheet's Cy Young of play-by-play translation and computer input. If Clem never did another game, a new volunteer would have to code and enter each play from every game from 1932 through 1944 to beat Clem's record. In addition to creating the composite Pirate lineups, Clem was a fact checker for all of the bios in this book.

Warren Corbett is the author of *The Wizard of Waxahachie: Paul Richards and the End of Baseball As We Knew It* and has contributed articles to eight SABR books. He lives in Bethesda, Maryland.

Rory Costello became aware of the 1960 Pirates and their unique World Series accomplishment as a teenager. Later, after talking with and meeting Joe Christopher, he gained further personal appreciation for this team. Rory lives in Brooklyn, New York with his wife Noriko and four-year-old son Kai.

Rob Edelman teaches film history courses at the University at Albany. He is the author of *Great Baseball Films* and *Baseball on the Web*, and is co-author (with his wife, Audrey Kupferberg) of *Meet the Mertzes*, a double biography of *I Love Lucy's* Vivian Vance and fabled baseball fan William Frawley, and *Matthau: A Life*. He is a film commentator on WAMC (Northeast) Public Radio and a Contributing Editor of *Leonard Maltin's Movie Guide*. He is a frequent contributor to *Base Ball: A Journal of the Early Game* and has written for *Baseball and American Culture: Across the Diamond*; *Total Baseball*; *Baseball in the Classroom*; *Memories and Dreams*; and *NINE: A Journal of Baseball History and Culture*. His essay on early baseball films appears on the DVD *Reel Baseball: Baseball Films from the Silent Era, 1899-1926*, and he is an interviewee on the director's cut DVD of *The Natural*.

Greg Erion is retired from the railroad industry and currently teaches history part time at Skyline Community College in San Bruno, California. He has written several biographies for SABR's BioProject and is currently working on a book about the 1959 season. He and his wife Barbara live in South San Francisco, California.

Dan Even, 70, a 25-plus year member of SABR, retired journalist 28 years with AP in Iowa, Louisiana, Mississippi, and New Mexico as sports writer, statehouse correspondent and Chief of Bureau), Started as sports writer and sports editor at daily newspapers. Keeps hand in "the game" as an official scorer in AZ leagues and doing spring training games for AP. A 50-year friend of fellow Iowan Bob Oldis.

Charles Faber is a retired college professor and administrator, living in Lexington, KY. He has been a baseball fan since 1936, rooting for several teams, but always against the Yankees. A long-time SABR member, he has written 20 biographies for the BioProject and contributed to books edited by other SABR members. McFarland has published eight of his books so far, and number nine is due out in 2013. It has the working title *Major League Prodigies: Best Seasons by Players Under 21.*

Dan Fields is a manuscript editor at the *New England Journal of Medicine.* He loves baseball trivia, and he regularly attends Boston Red Sox and Pawtucket (R.I.) Red Sox games with his teenage son. Dan lives in Framingham, Massachusetts, and can be reached at dfields820@gmail.com.

A retired English professor, **Jan Finkel** has been a member of SABR since 1994. He has contributed several articles to various SABR projects, including the BioProject, where he serves as chief editor. He was born and grew up in Pittsburgh, where he saw much of what went on in Sweet 'Sixty. Jan and his wife Judy live on Deep Creek Lake in the westernmost part of Maryland.

David Fleitz is a SABR member and systems analyst who lives in Pleasant Ridge, Michigan. His eighth book, *Napoleon Lajoie: King of Ballplayers*, will be published in 2013 by McFarland and Company.

James Forr is a past winner of the McFarland-SABR Baseball Research Award, and co-author (with David Proctor) of *Pie Traynor: A Baseball Biography.* He lives in Scottsdale, Arizona.

Don Frank is Professor Emeritus at Portland State University. He has also contributed as a Professor at Texas Tech University, the University of Arizona, Harvard University, and the Georgia Institute of Technology. His current research focuses on professional association demographics and leadership in Major League Baseball. Growing up in St. Louis, he is an avid fan of the Cardinals as well as several other teams. A SABR member for nearly 20 years, Don feels privileged to be able to work with and to learn from the good people in SABR.

Gary Gillette is editor of the Society for American Baseball Research's annual *Emerald Guide to Baseball,* a member of Baseball Prospectus's advisory board, and co-chair of SABR's Ballparks Committee. Gillette has written, edited, or contributed to dozens of baseball books and Web sites, including ESPN.com. He was the editor of the *ESPN Baseball Encyclopedia,* executive editor of the *ESPN Pro Football Encyclopedia,* and a contributor to six editions of *Total Baseball.* His most recent trade book was

Big League Ballparks, a complete history of major-league parks (Metro Books, 2009). As a director of the Tiger Stadium Conservancy since 2007, Gillette fought to save the historic stadium and continues to fight to save the field at the corner of Michigan and Trumbull in Detroit. As president of the Friends of Historic Hamtramck Stadium, he is working to preserve one of the few remaining Negro League ballparks. Gillette lives in Detroit's historic Indian Village, two doors away from the house built for Chalmers Motors president Hugh Chalmers in 1910.

Joel Gross is an almost Atlanta native and long time SABR member who grew up a Yankee fan until Mickey Mantle retired and the Braves came to Atlanta. Now he is an avid Braves fan. He has seen Hank Aaron's 715th homerun in person and would love to better that one day as a top experience. As a youngster he won an autographed Atlanta Crackers baseball at Ponce de Leon Ballpark, which he proudly collected at home plate. His Pittsburgh connections are that he spent many years visiting Squirrel Hill and once even attended a wedding in Amberidge.

Tim Herlich has been a member of the Society for American Baseball Research since 1996. In August 2012, he appeared at the National Baseball Hall of Fame to commemorate the 50th Anniversary of Tom Cheney's single-game strikeout record. A native of Long Island, New York, Tim resides in Seattle, Washington. His favorite teams are the Seattle Mariners and Philadelphia Phillies.

Bob Hurte lives in the tiny hamlet of Stewartsville, NJ. Bob has been a member of SABR since 1998. He is a lifelong fan of the Pittsburgh Pirates, his father having "brainwashed" him at an early age. As an active member of BioProject, he has written over a dozen player bios, is a regular contributor to Seamheads, and written for *New Jersey Baseball Magazine.* He has been fortunate to meet and/or speak with many former players and one of his ultimate thrills was to interview Bill Mazeroski and write his bio for this book! He says, "Maz was the reason I wanted to play the game of baseball!"

Jorge Iber, PhD is a professor of History and Associate Dean of the College of Arts and Sciences at Texas Tech University and his research focuses on the role of Latinos/Latinas in US sports. His most recent co-authored work is entitled *Latinos in U.S. Sport: A History of Isolation, Cultural Identity and Acceptance* (Human Kinetics, 2011), and he will also have a new anthology (tentatively entitled *More Than Just Peloteros*) from Texas Tech University Press appearing in late 2013. He is currently working on a manuscript on the life and career of Mexican American pitching great, Mike Torrez. He and his wife Raquel are the proud parents of Matthew, a budding Pirates fan (thanks to the influence of his dad).

Michael H. Jaffe is a small animal veterinary surgeon. A lifelong NY Mets fan, his love of baseball came from his father Herb who was a sports writer for the *Newark Star-Ledger* and covered the Brooklyn Dodgers in the 1950's. He lives in Mesa, AZ with his wife Tracy; they have three children and four dogs.

Rodney Johnson is an expert on Arizona baseball and the Cactus League. His writings have appeared in many publications including the official 2010 MLB All-Star Game program. Rodney is the longtime president of Arizona's Flame Delhi SABR Chapter and served for five years on the SABR board. A graduate of Arizona State University, he lives with his family in Tempe, AZ.

Len Levin is a dyed-in-the-wool fan of the Boston Red Sox, but as one who appreciates baseball tradition, he has always liked the Pirates. He lives in Providence, Rhode Island, and was a newspaper editor for many years. Now retired, he enjoys editing for SABR-sponsored publications.

Mark Miller is a retired Recreation Department Director in Springfield, Ohio, where he lives with his wife Connie. A high school baseball coach for 22 years, he is currently President of the Springfield/Clark County Baseball Hall of Fame. His research, speaking, and writing are related to local baseball topics.

Jack Morris is a corporate librarian for an environmental engineering company. He lives in East Coventry, Pennsylvania with his wife and two daughters. His baseball biographies have appeared in the books, *The Team That Forever Changed Baseball and America* (1947 Brooklyn Dodgers) and *Bridging Two Dynasties* (1947 New York Yankees). He is not the Jack Morris of World Series fame but, every once in a while, wishes he was.

Skip Nipper is the author of *Baseball in Nashville* and shares his love of Nashville's famous ballpark, Sulphur Dell, through www.sulphurdell.com. A 1972 graduate of Memphis State University, Skip has been a sales representative for 40 years for New Era Cap Co., the official supplier of headwear to the major and minor leagues. He was a founder and president of the Grantland Rice-Fred Russell Nashville chapter, and currently serves as secretary for the Old Timers Baseball Association of Nashville.

Bill Nowlin remembers watching Bill Mazeroski hit the homer, watching from his home in Lexington, Massachusetts on a small black and white TV. He has been VP of SABR since 2004 and helped edit numerous BioProject team books for SABR. He is a co-founder of Rounder Records and author or editor of around 40 baseball books.

Clifton Blue Parker has written three books on baseball: *Bucketfoot Al: The Baseball Life of Al Simmons, Big and Little Poison: Paul and Lloyd Waner, Baseball Brothers*, and *Fouled Away: The Baseball Tragedy of Hack Wilson*. A magazine editor at the University of California, Davis, Parker is a former newspaper journalist, Congressional press secretary, and copywriter. He has a bachelor's degree in political science from The Pennsylvania State University, and attended graduate school in political science at the University of Pittsburgh and in journalism at the University of Florida. Parker spent his teen summers growing up in Pittsburgh on the baseball diamonds, sandlot and organized.

Paul Rogers is the co-author of four baseball books including *The Whiz Kids and the 1950 Pennant* (Temple Univ. Press 1996), with boyhood hero Robin Roberts, and most recently *Lucky Me: My 65 Years in Baseball* (SMU Press 2011), with Eddie Robinson. Paul is president of the Hall-Ruggles (Dallas-Fort Worth) Chapter of SABR, but his real job is as a law professor at Southern Methodist University, where he served as dean of the law school for nine long years. During the Seventh Game of the 1960 World Series, Paul, then 12, was traveling cross-country with his parents, listening to the game on the radio when they stopped at a restaurant for a late lunch/early dinner. Paul refused to budge and sat in the car to hear the climatic finish of the game while his mother brought a sandwich out to him.

Dick Rosen, an emeritus history professor first became enamored with baseball history when was eight years old. Even before he knew the names of his third grade classmates, he could recite the batting averages of the 1929 Philadelphia Athletics. He grew up with Connie Mack's A's and the 1950 Phillies but after a move to Western Pennsylvania, spent years of misery with the Pirates of the '50s; 1960 was very special to him. He has taught courses in baseball history, and, about six years ago, he began a lecture tour on the Athletics throughout the state for the Pennsylvania Humanities Council (PHC). This resulted in a WHYY-TV (PBS) production on the Philadelphia Athletics. He continues similar lectures today on behalf of the Philadelphia Athletics Historical Society. A SABR member since 2006, he is currently the co-chair of the SABR 43 conference to be held in Philadelphia in 2013.

Jim Sandoval was a history teacher, baseball writer, and associate scout for the Minnesota Twins who collects ballparks and baseball scout sightings. He was lead editor of *Can He Play? A Look At Baseball Scouts And Their Profession* and has contributed to SABR's NL and AL *Deadball Stars* books and *The Fenway Project* along with biographies for SABR's BioProject. A former small college baseball player, he realized he was more of a prospect writing baseball than playing it. He served with Rod Nelson as Co-Chairman of SABR's Scouts committee before his passing in late December 2012.

Joseph M. Schuster is the author of the novel *The Might Have Been* (Ballantine Books), a finalist for the CASEY Award for the best baseball book of 2012, and the nonfiction work, *One Season in the Sun* (Gemma Open Door), about ballplayers whose major-league careers lasted a few weeks or less. A member of the faculty at Webster University in St. Louis, he is married and the father of five.

George Skornickel has been a die-hard Pirates fan for over 50 years. A retired English teacher, he and his daughter collect memorabilia from the 1960 season. A member of the Forbes Field Chapter of SABR, he has written numerous articles and is the author of *Beat 'em Bucs: the 1960 Pittsburgh Pirates*. He lives with his wife Kathy and black Lab, "Maz."

Cary Smith is currently co-chair of SABR's Pictorial History Committee. He's been a member of SABR since 1998 and in 2004 was the individual trivia champion at the National Convention.

Curt Smith, raised a Yankees fan in Upstate New York, cried when Maz homered. Later, more mature, he adopted the Boston Red Sox. He is a former White House Speechwriter to George H.W. Bush; now teaches English at the University of Rochester; and is the author of 15 books. Some, like *Storied Stadiums* and *What Baseball Means to Me*, feature Forbes Field. Others, including *Voices of The Game* and *The Storytellers*, star Bucs Voices Bob Prince and Jim Woods.

Andy Sturgill is a college administrator and avid reader of books about baseball, football, and Presidents. A lifelong Phillies fan, he lives in suburban Philadelphia with his wife, Carrie.

Stew Thornley writes: I've been a SABR member since 1979 and was SABR vice president from 2002 to 2004. Work for the Minnesota Department of Health and, in spare time, write sports books, serve as official scorer for Minnesota Twins home games and as a datacaster for mlb.com, and am the backup official scorer for the Minnesota Timberwolves. Former class clown.

Alfonso Tusa is a writer who was born in Cumaná, Venezuela and now writes a lot about baseball from Los Teques, Venezuela. He's the author *Una Temporada Mágica* (A magical season), *El Látigo del Beisbol. Una biografía de Isaías Látigo Chávez.* (The Whip of Baseball. An Isaías Látigo Chávez biography), *Pensando en ti Venezuela. Una biografía de Dámaso Blanco.* (Thinking about you Venezuela. A Dámaso Blanco biography) and *Voces de Beisbol y Ecología (*Voices of Baseball and Ecology). He contributes in some websites, books and newspapers. He shares many moments with his little boy Miguelin.

Thomas E. Van Hyning grew up in Santurce, Puerto Rico, rooting for his beloved Santurce Crabbers (Cangrejeros) in Puerto Rico's Winter League (PRWL). His two books are a Crabbers' team history, plus a PRWL history. Tom's articles have appeared in *The National Pastime* and *Baseball Research Journal.* Tom is the Research Program Manager for Mississippi's Tourism Division since 1994, with a BBA from the University of Georgia and two Master's degrees.

Joseph Wancho lives in Westlake Ohio, and is a lifelong Cleveland Indians fan. Working at AT&T since 1994 as a Process/Development Manager, he has been a SABR member since 2005. He has made contributions to several BioProject book projects as well as the website. Currently, he serves as co-chairman of the Minor League Research Committee. He has edited a BioProject team book on the 1954 Cleveland Indians, which is being published by the University of Nebraska Press in 2014.

Rich Westcott is the author of 23 books, including *Mickey Vernon - The Gentleman First Baseman*. He has spent more than 40 years as a writer or editor with newspapers and magazines. He's written for publications throughout the country, and appeared in nine film documentaries on baseball. Considered the foremost authority on Phillies history, he was the founder, publisher, and editor of *Phillies Report*, and wrote the material for the historical exhibits at Citizens Bank Park. A native Philadelphian, Westcott has taught journalism at Temple and La Salle Universities. He's been inducted into three halls of fame, and is a recent president of the Philadelphia Sports Writers' Assn.

A lifelong Pirates fan, **Gregory H. Wolf** was born in Pittsburgh, but now resides in the Chicagoland area with his wife, Margaret, and daughter, Gabriela. A Professor of German and holder of the Dennis and Jean Bauman endowed chair of the Humanities at North Central College in Naperville, IL, he has published articles on baseball history at the The Hardball Times, regularly contributes to SABR projects, including the BioProject, and is currently editing a SABR book on the 1957 Milwaukee Braves.

Acknowledgements

Thanks first and foremost to Bree Main and Sally O'Leary of the Pittsburgh Pirates. Bree is the Publications Designer for the Pirates and Sally is the Liaison for Alumni Affairs, and historian for the team. We wish to thank them, and the Pittsburgh Pirates, for supplying almost all of the photographs for this book. The Pirates' support of SABR's non-profit mission is gratefully appreciated.

Thanks to Pat Kelly and John Horne of the National Baseball Hall of Fame for supplying additional photographs.

In addition to each and every contributor to this book, the editors would like to thank SABR Publications Director Cecilia Tan, designer Gilly Rosenthol (Rosenthol Design), and the staff and the Board of Directors of SABR for supporting the project.

Thanks also to: Curt Boster, Devon Guillery, Bob Sproule, and Tom Zocco.

SABR BioProject Books

In 2002, the Society for American Baseball Research launched an effort to write and publish biographies of every player, manager, and individual who has made a contribution to baseball. Over the past decade, the BioProject Committee has produced over 2,200 biographical articles. Many have been part of efforts to create theme- or team-oriented books, spearheaded by chapters or other committees of SABR.

DETROIT TIGERS 1984: What a Start! What a Finish!
The 1984 Detroit tigers roared out of the gate, winning their first nine games of the season and compiling an eye-popping 35–5 record after the campaign's first 40 games—still the best start ever for any team in major league history. This book brings together biographical profiles of every Tiger from that magical season, plus those of field management, top executives, the broadcasters—even venerable Tiger Stadium and the city itself.

Mark Pattison and David Raglin, editors
$19.95 paperback (ISBN 978-1-933599-44-1)
$9.99 ebook (ISBN 978-1-933599-45-8)
8.5" x 11" / 250 pages (Over 230,000 words!)

SWEET '60: The 1960 Pittsburgh Pirates
A portrait of the 1960 team which pulled off one of the biggest upsets of the last 60 years. When Bill Mazeroski's home run left the park to win in Game Seven of the World Series, beating the New York Yankees, David had toppled Goliath. It was a blow that awakened a generation, one that millions of people saw on television, one of TV's first iconic World Series moments.

Edited by Clifton Blue Parker and Bill Nowlin
$19.95 paperback (ISBN 978-1-933599-48-9)
$9.99 ebook (ISBN 978-1-933599-49-6)
8.5" x 11" / 340 pages, 75 photos

RED SOX BASEBALL IN THE DAYS OF IKE AND ELVIS: The Red Sox of the 1950s
Although the Red Sox spent most of the 1950s far out of contention, the team was filled fascinating players that captured the heart of their fanbase. In *Red Sox Baseball*, members of SABR present 46 biographies on players such as Ted Williams and Pumpsie Green as well as season-by-season recaps.

Edited by Mark Armour and Bill Nowlin
$19.95 paperback (ISBN 978-1-933599-24-3)
$9.99 ebook (ISBN 978-1-933599-34-2)
8.5" x 11" / 372 PAGES, over 100 photos

OPENING FENWAY PARK IN STYLE: The 1912 World Champion Boston Red Sox
Opening Fenway Park in Style details a season played 100 years ago, the first season played at Fenway Park by the World Series winning Boston Red Sox. Included are player and owner biographies and a variety of essays considering the role of the press and facets of baseball during that era.

Edited by Bill Nowlin
$19.95 paperback (ISBN 978-1-933599-35-9)
$9.99 ebook (ISBN 978-1-933599-36-6)
8.5" x 11" / 304 PAGES, over 200 photos

The SABR Digital Library

The Society for American Baseball Research, the top baseball research organization in the world, disseminates some of the best in baseball history, analysis, and biography through our publishing programs. The SABR Digital Library contains a mix of books old and new, and focuses on a tandem program of paperback and ebook publication, making these materials widely available both on digital devices and as traditional printed books.

MEMORIES OF A BALLPLAYER
by Bill Werber and C. Paul Rogers III
Bill Werber's claim to fame is unique: he was the last living person to have a direct connection to the 1927 Yankees, "Murderers' Row," a team hailed by many as the best of all time. Rich in anecdotes and humor, *Memories of a Ballplayer* is a clear-eyed memoir of the world of big-league baseball in the 1930s. Werber played with or against some of the most productive hitters of all time, including Babe Ruth, Ted Williams, Lou Gehrig, and Joe DiMaggio.

$14.95 paperback (ISNB 978-0-910137-84-3)
$6.99 ebook (ISBN 978-1-933599-47-2)
6" x 9 " / 250 pages

BATTING
by F. C. Lane
First published in 1925, *Batting* collects the wisdom and insights of over 250 hitters and baseball figures. Lane interviewed extensively and compiled tips and advice on everything from batting stances to beanballs. Legendary baseball figures such as Ty Cobb, Casey Stengel, Cy Young, Walter Johnson, Rogers Hornsby, and Babe Ruth reveal the secrets of such integral and interesting parts of the game as how to choose a bat, the ways to beat a slump, and how to outguess the pitcher.

$14.95 paperback (ISBN 978-0-910137-86-7)
$7.99 ebook (ISBN 978-1-933599-46-5)
5" x 7 " / 240 pages

NINETEENTH CENTURY STARS: 2012 EDITION
First published in 1989, *Nineteenth Century Stars* was SABR's initial attempt to capture the stories of baseball players from before 1900. With a collection of 136 fascinating biographies, SABR has re-released *Nineteenth Century Stars* for 2012 with revised statistics and new form. The 2012 version also includes a preface by John Thorn.

Edited by Robert L. Tiemann and Mark Rucker
$19.95 paperback (ISBN 978-1-933599-28-1)
$9.99 ebook (ISBN 978-1-933599-29-8)
6" x 9 " / 300 pages

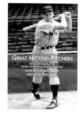

GREAT HITTING PITCHERS
Published in 1979, *Great Hitting Pitchers* was one of SABR's early publications. Edited by SABR founder Bob Davids, the book compiles stories and records about pitchers excelling in the batter's box. Now updated for 2012 by Mike Cook, *Great Hitting Pitchers* contain tables including data from 1979–2011 and corrections to reflect recent records.

Edited by L. Robert Davids
$9.95 paperback (ISBN 978-1-933599-30-4)
$5.99 ebook (ISBN 978-1-933599-31-1)
8.5" x 11" / 102 pages

SABR Members can purchase each book at a significant discount (often 50% off) and receive the ebook edtions free as a member benefit.

Each book is available in a trade paperback edition as well as ebooks suitable for reading on a home computer or Nook, Kindle, or iPad/tablet.

Join SABR today!

If you're interested in baseball—writing about it, reading about it, talking about it—there's a place for you in the Society for American Baseball Research.

SABR was formed in 1971 in Cooperstown, New York, with the mission of fostering the research and dissemination of the history and record of the game. Our members include everyone from academics to professional sportswriters to amateur historians and statisticians to students and casual fans who merely enjoy reading about baseball history and occasionally gathering with other members to talk baseball.

SABR members have a variety of interests, and this is reflected in the diversity of its research committees. There are more than two dozen groups devoted to the study of a specific area related to the game—from Baseball and the Arts to Statistical Analysis to the Deadball Era to Women in Baseball. In addition, many SABR members meet formally and informally in regional chapters throughout the year and hundreds come together for the annual national convention, the organization's premier event. These meetings often include panel discussions with former major league players and research presentations by members. Most of all, SABR members love talking baseball with like-minded friends. What unites them all is an interest in the game and joy in learning more about it.

Why join SABR? Here are some benefits of membership:

- Two issues annually of the *Baseball Research Journal*, which includes articles on history, biography, statistics, personalities, book reviews, and other aspects of the game.
- One issue annually of *The National Pastime*, which focuses on baseball in the region where that year's national convention is held (in 2013, it's Philadelphia)
- Regional chapter meetings, which can include guest speakers, presentations and trips to ballgames
- "This Week in SABR" e-newsletters every Friday, with the latest news in SABR and highlighting SABR research
- Online access to back issues of *The Sporting News* and other periodicals through *Paper of Record*
- Access to SABR's lending library and other research resources
- Online member directory to connect you with an international network of passionate baseball experts and fans
- Discount on registration for our annual conferences
- Access to SABR-L, an e-mail discussion list of baseball questions and answers that many feel is worth the cost of membership itself
- The opportunity to be part of a passionate international community of baseball fans

SABR membership is on a "rolling" calendar system; that means your membership lasts 365 days no matter when you sign up! Enjoy all the benefits of SABR membership by signing up today at SABR.org/join or by clipping out the form below and mailing it to: **SABR, 4455 E. Camelback Rd., Ste. D-140, Phoenix, AZ 85018.**

 -

SABR 2013 MEMBERSHIP FORM

2013 dues payable by check, money order, Visa, MasterCard or Discover Card;
online at: http://store.sabr.org; or by phone at (602) 343-6455

	Annual	3-year	Senior	3-yr Sr.	Under 30
US	❑ $65	❑ $175	❑ $45	❑ $129	❑ $45
Canada/Mexico	❑ $75	❑ $205	❑ $55	❑ $159	❑ $55
Overseas	❑ $84	❑ $232	❑ $64	❑ $186	❑ $55

Add a Family Member: $15 each family member at same address (list on back)
Senior: 65 or older before 12/31/2013
All dues amounts in US dollars or equivalent

Participate in Our Donor Program!

I'd like to desginate my gift to be used toward:
❑ General Fund ❑ Endowment Fund ❑ Research Resources ❑ _____
❑ I want to maximize the impact of my gift; do not send any donor premiums
❑ I would like this gift to remain anonymous.
Note: Any donation not designated will be placed in the General Fund.
SABR is a 501(c)(3) not-for-profit organization & donations are tax-deductible to the extent allowed by law.

NAME _____

ADDRESS _____

CITY _____ STATE _____ ZIP _____

HOME PHONE _____ BIRTHDAY _____
E-MAIL: _____
(Your e-mail address on file ensures you will receive the most recent SABR news.)

Dues $ _____
Donation $ _____
Amount Enclosed $ _____

Do you work for a matching grant corporation? Call (602) 343-6455 for details.
❑ check/money order enclosed   ❑ VISA, Master Card, Discover Card

CARD # _____

EXP DATE _____ SIGNATURE _____

Mail to: SABR, 4455 E. Camelback Rd., Ste. D-140, Phoenix, AZ 85018

Printed in Great Britain
by Amazon.co.uk, Ltd.,
Marston Gate.